The UNIX Dictionary
of Commands, Terms,
and Acronyms

Other McGraw-Hill Titles of Interest

UNIX Security: A Practical Introduction by *Arnold*

UNIX System V Release 4: The Complete Reference by *Coffin*

UNIX: A Database Approach, Featuring System V Release 4 by *Das*

C++ by Example: Object-Oriented Analysis, Design & Programming by *Dorfman*

C++ Memory Management by *Dorfman/Neuberger*

Portable C++ by *Giencke*

The UNIX Audit: Using UNIX to Audit UNIX by *Grottola*

Open Computing UNIX Unbound by *Hahn*

The UNIX Companion: A Handbook for Everyone by *Hahn*

The C Primer by *Hancock*

Safer C: Developing Software for High-Integrity and Safety-Critical Systems by *Hatton*

C+ C++: Programming with Objects in C and C++ by *Holub*

Enough Rope to Shoot Yourself in the Foot: Rules for C and C++ Programming by *Holub*

UNIX Power Toolkit by *Leininger*

Introducing UNIX System V by *Morgan/McGilton*

UNIX Made Easy: The Basics and Beyond—2nd Edition by *Muster*

Unix for Application Developers by *Parrette*

The Elements of C Programming Style by *Ranade*

C++ Primer for C Programmers by *Ranade/Zamir*

The J. Ranade UNIX Primer by *Ranade/Zamir*

C++ and the OOP Paradigm by *Rao*

Open Computing Guide to UnixWare by *Reiss*

UNIX System V Release 4: An Introduction—2nd Edition by *Rosen*

C: The Complete Reference—3rd Edition by *Schildt*

C++ From the Ground Up by *Schildt*

C++ Nuts and Bolts: For Experienced Programmers by *Schildt*

Concepts of Object-Oriented Programming by *Smith*

C++ Applications Guide by *Smith*

Practical C++ by *Terribile*

Portable User Interface Programming in C++ by *Watson*

C++ Power Paradigms by *Watson*

The UNIX Dictionary of Commands, Terms, and Acronyms

John Levine, Margaret Levine Young, Chris Negus, and Larry Schumer

McGraw-Hill

New York San Francisco Washington, D.C. Auckland Bogotá
Caracas Lisbon London Madrid Mexico City Milan
Montreal New Delhi San Juan Singapore
Sydney Tokyo Toronto

McGraw-Hill

A Division of The McGraw-Hill Companies

©1996 by **The McGraw-Hill Companies, Inc.**
Published by The McGraw-Hill Companies

pbk 1 2 3 4 5 6 7 8 9 FGR/FGR 9 0 0 9 8 7 6
hc   1 2 3 4 5 6 7 8 9 FGR/FGR 9 0 0 9 8 7 6

Library of Congress Cataloging-in-Publication Data
0-07-037644-1 (pbk.)
0-07-037643-3 (hc.)

Acquisitions editor: Jennifer Holt DiGiovanna
Editorial team: Marianne Krcma, Book Editor
            David M. McCandless, Associate Managing Editor
            Lori Flaherty, Executive Editor

EL1

To Annette, Shawn, and Austin, who taught me the value of love and laughter.
—Chris Negus

To Elaine, for her love, life, and music.
—Larry Schumer

"The only thing harder than reading a dictionary is writing a dictionary!"

Acknowledgments

Chris and Larry would like to thank the following people:

Wendy Gooditis and Greg Patterson for their invaluable help in preparing definitions.

Margo at Waterside Productions for helping us get started on this project.

Jennifer DiGiovanna and David McCandless at McGraw-Hill for helping us get through this project.

Introduction

Ever since UNIX was created, its proponents have struggled to define what it is.

AT&T, where UNIX was invented, originally owned the UNIX source code and tried to define UNIX through the System V Interface definition (SVID). Other companies, such as Sun Microsystems, first threw their weight behind the Berkeley Software Distribution (BSD) version of UNIX, making networking and other BSD features defacto UNIX standards. From System V and BSD, dozens of computer vendors created their own derivative UNIX systems, often with different names (Solaris, UnixWare, etc.) and proprietary features.

The various UNIX "religious" factions battled to mold UNIX. They formed consortiums, and created definitions and standards. Lately, all the major UNIX vendors have come together to define a single UNIX system, finally realizing that while they were battling over the shape of their cookie jar, Microsoft had taken most of the cookies. But even this effort to put UNIX in a cage seems too little and too late as free, public domain UNIX-like systems, such as Linux, have set their own course and are on the verge of becoming viable for commercial use.

Despite all efforts, UNIX continues to defy definition.

Yet even in chaos, UNIX is still the world's most powerful computer operating system. The infrastructure of the Internet is built mostly on UNIX systems. UNIX is found in almost every major computer center, bringing together PCs, minicomputers, and mainframes. In chaos, UNIX thrives.

So, in the spirit of chaos, we bring you this UNIX dictionary. This book takes no sides in the UNIX wars. We present definitions from BSD UNIX, UNIX System V, Linux, and any other source we could find. Thousands of them.

To put the dictionary together, we used a unique combination of talents. BSD portions started from contributions by John R. Levine and Margaret Levine Young. Larry Schumer added the UNIX System V perspective, as did I. Friends and co-workers from many years of working with UNIX were called in.

Many C programming definitions were contributed by Wendy Gooditis, who managed C documentation for AT&T for several years. (Those at AT&T will remember her as Wendy Negus.) Greg Patterson, from Novell, contributed network management expertise.

All in all, we've tried to cover UNIX in a way that supports most any UNIX system you might be using. If we've missed a term, let us know by dropping an email to cnl@xmission.com. If you don't like the way UNIX is defined, go ahead and try to create your own UNIX-like system. Maybe we'll add definitions for it to the next edition of this dictionary.

Chris Negus, December 1995

Symbols

& (ampersand)
1. Special character used to run an entire shell command-line in the background.
2. In the C language, an address operator that assigns the address of a variable to another variable.

* (asterisk)
1. Special character (sometimes called a *wild card*) used by the shell and other UNIX interfaces to represent any combination of characters. *See also* ?.
2. In the C language, the multiplication operator used to multiply the numbers on the right and left of the character.
3. In the C language, a prefix operator that performs indirection through a pointer.

*= (asterisk equals) In the C language, a compound operator (multiply and equals) in which two operands may represent any arithmetic type.

@ (at sign)
1. Character used in some UNIX shells to delete the entire line.
2. Character used to separate a user's name from a computer's name in addresses for e-mail or other TCP/IP services. For example, cnl@xmission.com could be used to send mail to user cnl at a computer named xmission.com.

**** (backslash) Character used to escape another character. For example, in the shell, * prevents the shell from interpreting the asterisk as a wildcard. *See also* *.

**`** (back quote) Character used to indicate that the output of a command be taken as the input to another command. For example ls `cat file1` feeds the data from file1 to the ls command.

[ ] (brackets) In the shell, characters used to match any characters enclosed within them.

^ (caret) Special character used to represent the beginning of a line in a search string or in the vi editor.

: (colon) In the C language, a character used to represent a conditional expression.

- (dash)
1. In the C language, the subtraction operator used to subtract the number on the right from the number on the left.
2. Character preceding an option on the command line.
3. Character used with several UNIX commands to indicate that the standard input, rather than a filename, be used to input data.
4. Character used in many UNIX con-

figuration files to indicate that a field will be left blank.

-= (dash equals) In the C language, a compound assignment operator (subtract and equals) in which two operands may represent any arithmetic type.

$ (dollar sign)
1. Special character used in a search string or in the vi editor to indicate the end of a line.
2. Special character used in the shell to indicate that the following string represents an environment variable. For example, $HOME represents the user's home directory.

= (equal sign) Character used to store the value of the right operand into the value of the left operand.

! (exclamation point)
1. Character used in many UNIX utilities to escape to the shell.
2. Character used in UUCP-style addressing to separate the computer name from the user name. It is also used to separate multiple computer names the transmission needs to hop across. This is sometime referred to as *bang-style addressing.*

< (left arrow)
1. In the shell, a character that takes the contents of a file as input to a command.
2. In the C language, an operator that tests if the number on the left is less than the number on the right.

<= (left arrow equals) In the C language, an operator that tests if the number on the left is less than or equal to the number on the right.

<< (left arrow left arrow) In the C language, a binary operator that indicates that the value be shifted to the left.

% (percent) Character used in the shell, along with a job number, to identify a job running in the background.

. (period)
1. Character (sometimes called a *dot*) used to indicate the current directory. For example, to run a command called prog in the current directory, type ./prog.
2. Character used at the beginning of a file if you don't want the file to appear in a default ls listing. For example, the .profile file is in most home directories, but it doesn't show up when you type ls.
3. Character used to separate the four parts of an IP address for example, *123.45.67.89.*
4. In the vi editor, a character that repeats the previous action.

.. (period period) Characters (sometimes called *dot dot*) used to indicate the parent directory. For example, to move from the current directory to its parent, you could type cd .. from the current directory.

... (ellipses) Characters (sometimes called *dot dot dot*) used on UNIX manual pages to indicate that an option may be repeated.

| (pipe) Character used in the shell to pipe the output from one command to the input of another command.

+ (plus sign) In the C language, addition operator used to add the numbers on the right of the character to the numbers on the left of the character.

(pound sign)
1. Character used in many UNIX files indicating that anything that follows on the line is a comment and therefore should not be processed.
2. In some shells, a character used to erase the previous character typed at the command line.

? (question mark)
1. In the shell, a character used to represent any other single character. For

example, ls ?? lists any files with two-character names.

2. Character used in many applications to request help text.

3. Character used in the vi editor to request a backwards search for a string.

" (quotes) In a shell, a character used to surround text that is to be interpreted literally and not as special characters. Text may include white space.

> (right arrow)

1. In the shell, a character that directs the output of a command to a file or device.

2. In the C language, an operator that tests if the number on the left is greater than the number on the right.

>= (right arrow equals) In the C language, an operator that tests if the number on the left is greater than or equal to the number on the right.

>> (right arrow left arrow) In the C language, a binary operator that indicates that the value be shifted to the right.

; (semicolon) Character used to separate multiple commands on a single command line. Each semicolon-separated command is executed, from left to right, with each one finishing before the next one begins.

/ (slash)

1. In the UNIX file system, a character used to separate directories in a pathname.

2. In the C language, a division operator used to divide the number on the left by the number on the right.

3. In WWW Internet names, a character that separates protocol identifiers from the name of the computer on which the resource is located, for example, *http://www.cnl.com.*

.a File extension for files containing Ada source code.

A1 Department of Defense (DoD) level of certification or security level. A1 is a designator of system trustworthiness issued by the National Computer Security Center (NCSC). Levels currently include A1, B3, B2, B1, C2, C1, and D; division A systems provide the most security, D systems provide the least.

a64l Function that is used to maintain numbers stored in base-64 ASCII characters. The function defines a notation for long integers up to six characters.

abbrev *See* abbreviation word.

abbrev-mode Command in the emacs text editor that enters or exits word abbreviation mode.

abort
1. To terminate a program abruptly.
2. The name of the C library function that aborts a program.
3. Command in the Epsilon text editor that aborts the currently executing command. *See also* library.
4. A C library function that closes all open files and then causes a signal to be sent to the calling process. *See also* exit, kill, signal.

abort-recursive-edit Command in the emacs text editor that stops recursive editing and returns to the most recently-interrupted global-search-and-replace operation. This command is usually bound to the keystroke Ctrl-].

abs The integer absolute value function in the C library. For example, abs(-12) is 12.

absolute address An address that is permanently assigned to a storage location by the machine designator. Also, a pattern of characters that identifies a unique storage location without further modification. Synonymous with *machine address*.

absolute pathname A pathname that specifies how to find a file by starting at the root directory and working down the directory tree. Absolute pathnames start with a slash character. *See also* pathname.

absolute permissions File permissions given to the chmod command as a set of specific permission bits to set, regardless of what the previous permissions were. The bits may be given as a three-digit octal number or using the mnemonic letters *r*, *w*, and *x* for read, write, and execute permissions. *See also* permission.

absolute starting address The starting memory address of a program or data set.

absolute symbol In an object file, a symbol defined as a specific numeric value that does not change when its file is relocated by the linker. *See also* symbol, relocate, linker.

accelerator A shortcut method of executing a particular function without the use of a mouse.

accent grave A reverse accent or reverse quote. In the shell, the character used to enclose a command whose result is substituted into the command line. For example, rm `cat badfiles` removes the files listed in the file badfiles.

accept
1. In the System V print spooler, the command that tells the spooling system to allow users to queue requests for a printer. Compare this to enable, which tells the spooling system actually to print spooled files on a printer. *See also* enable, lp, lpstat, lpadmin, lpsched.
2. In Sockets network programming, the function in a server program that awaits a connection from a client. *See also* spooler, enable, socket, poll, bind, connect, listen, select, netconfig.

acceptance testing The process of testing a system to determine if it meets its specifications and, hence, will be accepted by the buyer.

access Library routine that validates whether the real user and group ID of the process are allowed to open, read, or write a particular file. In general, accessing refers to using a file or other resource. *See also* system call, user ID, group ID, process.

access mode *See* access permission.

access permission The ability to read from, write to, or execute a file. In UNIX, these permissions are set for the owner, group, and other.

access protection The protection of a file's read, write, execute, and delete privileges.

access time The time that is required to access and retrieve data from a storage device. This time is composed of the following values: (1) Cylinder seek time, the time that it takes for the disk read heads to move to the disk cylinder. (2) Track latency, the time that it takes until the track index mark passes under the read head so that the head can begin to read data. (3) The data transfer rate from the disk surface to the communications channel connected to the computer system.

account A name representing a UNIX user and associated privileges.

accountability The security property that enables activities on a system to be traced to specific individuals who can be held responsible for their actions.

accounting
1. (process accounting) Keeping records about the usage of CPU time and other resources by processes started by each particular user.
2. (disk accounting) Keeping records about the amount of disk space used by each particular user.

acct
1. Library routine that enables or disables the process accounting system and identifies the log file to use. Also, the general name used for the System V accounting system commands.
2. Accounting software as a set of tools. *See also* acctcom, acctcms, acctcon, acctmerg, acctprc, acctsh, acct, utmp.
3. File format for files produced by calling the acct library routine. The

file format is defined in the <sys/acct.h> header file. *See also* acctcom, acct.

acctcms Command that reads files produced from processing accounting records and writes summary information to standard output. The files are in the format described by acct file format. *See also* acctcom, acct, acctcon, acctmerg, acccprc, acctsh, fwtmp, runacct.

acctcom Command that searches and prints information from process accounting files. Each record represents the execution of one process. The options for this command enable the user to select statistics or specific information about the runtime of each process. *See also* ps, acct, acctcms, acctcon, acctmerg, runacct, acct.

acctcon Commands that create System V connect time accounting files. *See also* wtmp.

acctmerg Command that reads standard input from accounting process files and merges, adds, and summarizes information from those files. *See also* acctcom, acct, acct.

acctprc Command that reads standard input from process accounting files and examines and summarizes accounting information on user and machine statistics, such as CPU time and memory size. *See also* acctcom, acct, acctcon, acctmerg.

acctsh Set of shell scripts used by the System V accounting system to create, maintain, and process accounting data.

acos Library routine used for the floating- point arc cosine function. *See also* libm.

acosh Library routine used for the hyperbolic floating-point arc cosine function. *See also* libm.

action
1. Segment of code to be run when a given event occurs.
2. In the yacc and lex programming tools, the C code to be executed when a lexical or grammatical rule is matched. *See also* yacc, lex.

active grab Action performed by the X Window System XtGrabPointer function, telling the X server to grab an item and not let go until the grab is specifically released with the function XtUngrabPointer.

active window In the X Window System, the window that is currently receiving keystrokes and mouse events. *See also* X, event.

ada
1. Programming language developed by the U.S. Department of Defense and required for many DoD contracts.
2. Add-on package for the emacs text editor, which implements a major mode for editing programs in the Ada programming language.

ada-mode Command in the emacs text editor that enables Ada mode, which is designed for editing programs in the Ada programming language.

adapter Hardware unit, usually a printed circuit card, that connects a device such as a disk drive to the computer.

adapter cards *See* adapter.

adaptive Lempel-Ziv-Welch coding Method of compressing the contents of a file, used by the compress utility, which encodes frequently occurring strings of characters in the file to be compressed by single tokens in the compressed file. *See also* token, compression.

adb Command used as an interactive general-purpose debugger to examine files and provide a controlled environment for program execution.

adbgen Command that generates an adb script. *See also* adb.

addbib Command for creating or extending a bibliographic database.

addch Library routine (curses) that places a character in a screen window. *See also* curses.

add_drv Command that is used to inform the system about newly installed drivers. *See also* devlinks, disks, drvconfig, modinfo, ports.

adder Basic digital logic unit; it sums two numbers that are represented in digital code and produces a result.

addition sign Plus sign (+), used to signify addition in most programming languages, including C, C++, and awk.

address
1. Location of a file, file system, network, or machine. The address can be specified by a name, a concatenation of hierarchal directory names or a numerical or alphanumerical pathname. *See also* pathname.
2. Network name to which electronic mail is sent. An electronic-mail address consists of a local address (often the user name), an at-sign (@), and a host name (often the name of the user's computer).
3. In a computer's main memory, the numeric value that identifies a particular memory location.

address mask Bit mask used to select bits from an Internet address for subnet addressing. The mask consists of 32 bits. It selects the network portion of the Internet address and one or more bits of the local portion.

addseverity Library routine that builds a list of severity levels for an application to be used with a formatting facility called fmtmsg. Severity refers to an integer value indicating the seriousness of a specified condition. *See also* fmtmsg.

addstr Library routine (curses) that places a string of characters in a screen window. *See also* curses, string.

adduser Command used to add, modify, and delete user accounts.

adjmsg Device-driver library routine that trims bytes from the head or tail of a message.

adjtime Library routine (BSD) that adjusts the rate at which the system clock ticks to account for drift, or to synchronize with other clocks on a network.

admin
1. Command that creates and sets parameters on SCCS files. *See also* SCCS.
2. An ASCII file that defines default installation actions by assigning values to specified installation parameters.
3. Abbreviation for administer or system administration.

admind Daemon used by system administration tools to perform distributed administration operations.

administer To control and maintain a UNIX system by issuing administrative commands and executing system programs to maintain its existing status or upgrade it. *See also* system administration.

administrative commands Set of UNIX commands that ensure that the operating system continues to run and provide service and access to users.

administrative logins Special UNIX login accounts for doing system administration. The root login has full control of all system files and commands.

Other logins have special permission for managing specific tasks, such as uucp (UUCP network administration), lp (printer administration), and smtp (e-mail administration).

administrative space Set of hosts, managed by the same organization, in which all users share a common set of user IDs (UIDs) and group IDs (GIDs).

admintool Command used for performing system administration tasks in a distributed environment. *See also* NIS, admind.

adm login Administrative login that owns many of the process-accounting administrative commands and files. This user can manage accounting facilities without having full root privileges.

Advanced Research Projects Agency Former name for DARPA, the Defense Advanced Research Projects Administration. This government agency funded much computer research, particularly in computer networking, leading to the ARPAnet and eventually the Internet. *See also* ARPA, DARPA, ARPAnet, Internet.

advertised-undo Command in the emacs text editor that undoes (or reverses) the last editing operation. This command is usually bound to the keystroke Ctrl-X U.

advertising Term used with distributed file system products (such as the UNIX Remote File Sharing) to describe how a computer makes its files and directories available to other computers.

advisory message System message that provides information, but doesn't necessarily indicate an error condition.

AFS Andrew File System, a system from Carnegie-Mellon University that allows files to be shared among multiple com-puters on a network. Unlike most other file networking packages, AFS copies whole files at a time from one computer to another, rather than fetching pieces one at a time as programs request them. *See also* NFS, RFS.

Aho, Alfred Coauthor of the awk utility and author of egrep.

aint Library routine that computes the floating-point greatest integer function. *See also* libm, floating_point.

aiocancel (Asynchronous I/O Cancel) Library routine that cancels a previously started asynchronous I/O call. *See also* asynchronous.

aio_error Library routine that retrieves the error status of an asynchronous I/O operation.

aio_fsync Library routine that queues an asynchronous fsync or fdatasync request for all currently queued I/O operations. *See also* fcntl, fsync, aio_error, aio_return.

aioread (Asynchronous I/O Read) Library routine that starts an asynchronous read I/O call. *See also* asynchronous.

aio_return Library routine that retrieves the return status of an asynchronous I/O operation.

aio_suspend Library routine that waits until at least one of previously started asynchronous I/O operations has completed.

aiowait (Asynchronous I/O Wait) Library routine that waits for a previously started asynchronous read I/O call to complete. *See also* asynchronous.

aiowrite (Asynchronous I/O Write) Library routine that starts an asynchronous write I/O call. *See also* asynchronous.

AIX (Advanced Interactive Executive) IBM's primary implementation of

UNIX. AIX 1 is for the RT PC workstations, AIX 2 is for the PS/2 PCS, and AIX 3 is for the RS/6000 workstations and IBM mainframes.

alarm Library routine that signals a process after a given number of seconds. The sleep call and sleep command use alarm. *See also* process, signal, sleep.

alias
1. Refers to a shorthand name assigned to a command. For example, a user can assign the alias *dir* to the command ls -al. (Korn and C shells only.)
2. Command that displays all defined aliases, or defines an alias. (Korn and C shells only.)
3. Name that is used as an abbreviation for an electronic mail address.

aliasadm Command used to modify and manipulate the Network Information Service (NIS+) aliases map.

aliases File, usually kept in /etc or /usr/lib that contains the list of valid mail addresses, or aliases, and the actual addresses they correspond to.

alias lists List of usernames and addresses that are referenced by a single alias or name used for multi-user or group mailings. *See also* aliases.

allexport Korn shell mode that automatically exports shell variables whenever they are modified or defined. Specified with the set command. (Korn shell only.)

alloca Library routine that allocates extra space for a function, which is automatically freed when the routine returns. Present in PWB libraries and in GCC, not part of Standard C. *See also* C, GCC, PWB.

allocate
1. To obtain storage, disk, or other resource for the use of a program.

2. Command that manages the ownership of devices and ensures that only one user has access to a device at one time.

allocation Amount of storage, disk, or other resource allocated for the use of a program.

allocation error Failure that occurs when the system cannot assign enough resources for the requested function. For example, an allocation error occurs when the hard disk is full or memory buffers are not available.

allocb Device-driver library routine that allocates a STREAMS message block.

.allow Suffix added to files that contain a list of users who can use a particular feature. For example, at.allow and cron.allow contain lists of users that can use at and cron, respectively.

alpha
1. First level of testing when a product is released from development. It usually implies testing by knowledgeable users, without planning to use the results of the program for anything important. *Compare to* beta.
2. Alpha AXP is a line of high-performance RISC chips, introduced in 1993, used by Digital Equipment in their workstations. *See also* RISC, architecture.

alphabet Letters of a language arranged in an order specified by the using the language.

alphanumeric character Single character from the alphabet set A to Z or numeric set 0 to 9. The character can be either upper- or lowercase.

alphasort Library routine (BSD) used in connection with the scandir routine to produce an alphabetical list of the files in a directory. *See also* scandir.

ALRM Name of signal number 14 which can be sent to a running process (short for alarm clock) to indicate that a given amount of wall-clock time has elapsed.

alt Refers to a type of "alternate" USENET newsgroup not included in the official USENET hierarchy of newsgroups. Many USENET sites do not receive alt newsgroups. The names of newsgroups of this type begin with alt. *See also* USENET, newsgroup.

alternate media Media onto which migrated data blocks are stored, usually tapes or front-end disks accessible through a station.

Alt key Key used as a shift key. In conjunction with other keys on the keyboard, the Alt key is used in Motif, Open Look, and other windowing systems to choose commands from menus. In emacs, the Alt key can be used as the meta key. In System V/386, the Alt key is used in conjunction with function keys to switch from one virtual terminal to another. *See also* virtual_terminal.

Altos Line of multi-user UNIX systems based on Intel processors, primarily used in commercial applications.

alt-prefix Command in the Epsilon text editor that treats the next keystroke as if the Meta key had been pressed. This is the same as the emacs ESC-prefix function. It is usually assigned to the Esc key.

ambiguous file reference Reference to a file that is not one specific file. The file reference may include many files with the same set of characters in the filename along with special symbols such as a the asterisk (*). *See also* special symbols.

Amdahl Manufacturer of mainframe computers. Models of Amdahl computers running UNIX can support hundreds of simultaneous users.

am I Special arguments to the who command that cause it to report the user name of the user issuing the command. *See also* who am I.

ampersand
1. The character &, usually meaning and.
2. In any of the UNIX shells, a symbol that means to execute the preceding command asynchronously. That is, the shell doesn't wait for the command to complete, but instead returns immediately for another command. For example, the wait command can be used to wait for a command that started with an ampersand.
3. In shell scripts, two ampersands (&&) separating a pair of commands means to execute the following command if the preceding command failed.
4. In the C and C++ programming languages, a single ampersand is the bitwise AND operator.
5. In the C and C++ programming languages, a pair of ampersands is the "logical AND" operator, meaning to evaluate the expression to the right of the ampersands only if the expression to the left produced a nonzero value. *See also* shell, wait.

analyze To separate something into basic parts to determine a better understanding of the whole.

analyzer *See* lexical analyzer.

and *See* ampersand.

angle bracket
1. Either of the characters < (left angle bracket) or > (right angle bracket). Also known as less-than and greater-than characters.
2. In the shell, a left angle bracket means to take the input for a command from the file named after the left angle bracket.
3. In the shell, a pair of left angle

brackets introduces a "here document," a section of text included inline which is used as the input to a command. (Bourne and Korn shells only.)

4. In the shell, a right angle bracket means to place the output of a command in the file named after the right angle bracket, replacing any previous contents of the file.

5. In the shell, a pair of right angle brackets means to append the output of a command to the file named after the right angle brackets, adding the output after any existing contents of the file.

6. In the C and C++ languages the operators to compare two numbers or pointers to determine if one is numerically less than or greater than the other. *See also* >.

anint Library routine used for the floating point nearest integer function. *See also* libm, floating_point.

anon Option to the NFS share command for mapping remote users.

anonymous ftp Method of distributing files using the ftp file transfer program and the Internet. It is anonymous because many systems allow any user to log in for file transfer using the conventional username *anonymous* without having an individual account on the system. *See also* Internet.

ANSI American National Standards Institute, the organization charged with promulgating national standards in the United States.

ANSI C Dialect of the C language, adopted in 1989 as an ANSI standard, ANSI x3.159-1989, and subsequently by the ISO as ISO 9899:1990. Most current C compilers conform to ANSI C. *See also* ANSI C, ISO.

anytopnm In the PBM package, the program that attempts to convert an arbitrary file to one of the PBM formats by guessing the format of the file. *See also* PBM.

AOS A UNIX-like operating system that runs on older Data General computers.

a.out
1. Default name of the output object file created by the assembler **as** and linker ld is a.out.
2. Informal name for the format of object files created by the the assembler or link editor. *See also* cc, as, ld, COFF.

apgen Short for application generator, a program that writes application programs.

Apollo Computer One of the first manufacturers of workstations, now part of Hewlett-Packard.

apostrophe Forward single-quote character. In the shell, strings surrounded by apostrophes are taken literally without expansion of wildcards or shell variables. In the C and C++ languages, single characters used as constants are enclosed in apostrophes. *See also* ', quote.

app Motif term that refers to the context of an event. The app of a Motif window manager (mwm) window is the client application that is contained within the border and title.

append
1. To add data to the end of a file.
2. Function in the emacs LISP programming language for concatenating items into a list.

appendix Collection of supplementary material, usually at the end of a book.

append-next-kill Command in the Epsilon text editor that causes the next kill command to append its information to the kill buffer.

Apple Computer Manufacturer of personal computers. Apple's version of

UNIX, which runs on its Macintosh computer, is called A/UX.

AppleTalk Medium-speed network designed by Apple Computer, used primarily with Macintosh computers. *See also* network.

application Program designed to do work of interest to end-users, like a word processing program, database program, spreadsheet program, or communication program. Contrast applications with utilities and systems software, which are designed to perform housekeeping tasks within the computer system. Application software can be single-purpose, like an order-entry system, or multipurpose, like a database or spreadsheet program that can be customized for a variety of uses. *See also* software.

application compatibility Refers to tests run on applications to ensure that they run on different, usually the latest, versions of an operating system.

application-defaults file File that contains a set of default resource specifications that are used in the absence of user-defined resource specifications.

application gateway *See* gateway.

application instance name Name specified for a particular X client variable during the creation of the X client.

application layer
1. Topmost layer in TCP/IP architecture to provide application services on TCP/IP internetworks.
2. Topmost layer in the OSI reference model. It provides communication services used by applications such as electronic mail and file transfer.

application mode In certain terminals, a mode in which the function keys on the terminal send character sequences to be interpreted by an application program being run rather than by the

system. *See also* terminal.

application packaging Format in which application software is stored on the installation medium. UNIX applications are usually packaged in pkgadd, tar, custom, and cpio formats.

application programming Programming that is intended to run in UNIX user space to provide particular application services.

application programming interface (API) Set of programming functions that provides a cohesive interface to a set of services. An API may provide services to write programs for a particular GUI, network protocol, or database.

application software Programs that perform specific tasks for a user on a computer system. These applications run on top of the operating system. *See also* applications.

applications software installation Act of and instructions for installing and configuring a single application or suite of applications on top of an operating system. *See also* package.

apply
1. Command that applies a user-specified command to its arguments, passing the arguments to the command a fixed number at a time. For example, apply -2 cmp a1 b1 a2 b2 a3 b3 compares pairs of files. *See also* xargs.
2. Part of the eighth-edition research UNIX and public domain versions in wide use elsewhere.

apropos Shell command to look up a keyword in the online manual pages. Also a command in the emacs text editor that lists the commands about a topic. *See also* man page.

ar
1. Command for maintaining files in an archive file. The ar command is

frequently used to create or maintain libraries of object code. A version of ar is also available from the Free Software Foundation as part of binutils, q.v. *See also* library object.
2. The archive file format that the ar command uses to combine several files into one.

arbitron Program run at many USENET sites each month that collects statistical information on the popularity of newsgroups and e-mails the result to a common collection point for analysis. Also, the collected results of that analysis. Originally, a commercial service that determined the listenership of radio stations.

arc Library routine that displays an arc of a circle on the output device. *See also* plot, library.

arch Command that returns a string identifying the architecture of the local computer. Typical results are i386, sparc, or u3b. *See also* architecture.

archie Internet facility that allows users to search a database listing files and directories available for anonymous FTP. *See also* anonymous FTP, Internet.

architecture Refers to the design of a computer as seen by the programmer or systems engineer. Two computers are said to have the same architecture if they can run the same binary programs, even if their physical design is entirely different.

archive
1. File containing other files, sometimes in compressed form. The most commonly used archiving program is ar, followed by zoo and zip.
2. Tape containing backup or archival copies of disk files. The most commonly used tape archiving programs are cpio, tar, and pax. *See also* tar, bar, zip, cpio, pax, ar, zoo.

archiver Program that creates or processes file or tape archives.

archives File format device header.

aref (Array-indexing function) Function in the emacs LISP programming language that returns individual characters from within strings.

arepdaemon Daemon that implements the autoreply feature of elm, sending mechanically generated replies to incoming mail. *See also* daemon, autoreply, Elm.

argc and argv Numeric values representing the options on a command line of a C program. The argc value represents the argument count, while argv is an array of character pointers that point to each argument itself.

ARG_MAX Tunable parameter, representing the highest number of characters that can be passed to an exec system call in the argument and environment strings.

ARGSUSED Keyword used in comments in C source code, indicating that lint should refrain from reporting unused arguments to a function.

argument
1. Information provided on the command line after the command. For example, in the command line cp letter1 letter2, *cp* is the command, *letter1* is the first argument, and *letter2* is the second argument. Commands use information provided by arguments to determine what action to take. For example, arguments to the cp command specify which file to copy and the filename to use for the new copy. *See also* command line.
2. Command in the Epsilon text editor that sets the argument for the next command.
3. In C or C++ programs, the parameters to a function. *See also* command line.

argument keyword Name of a dummy argument. These names are used in the subprogram definition and also may be used when the subprogram is invoked to associate dummy arguments with actual arguments that can appear in any order.

argv In the C shell, a predefined shell variable that contains a list of the command-line arguments. In C or C++ programs, a list of the command-line arguments, passed to the main procedure in the program.

arithmetic Mathematics of integers, including addition, subtraction, multiplication, division, and other operations.

arithmetic expression Group of numbers, operators, and parentheses. *See also* eval, let.

arithmetic operator Programming language operator that performs an arithmetic operation, such as addition, subtraction, multiplication, or division.

ARP (Address Resolution Protocol) Data-link layer protocol used with TCP/IP to dynamically map a computer's Internet Protocol (IP) address with its Media Access Control (MAC) address.

arp Program that displays and modifies the Internet-to-Ethernet address translation tables used by the address resolution protocol ARP.

ARPA *See* Advanced Research Projects Agency.

ARPAnet Packet-switched, resource-sharing, long-haul network developed in the early 1970s by the Advanced Research Projects Agency. This network initially linked government, industrial, and academic installations around the world. It served primarily as an experimental research and development network. ARPAnet was decommissioned in June 1990. *See also* Advanced Research Projects Agency, Internet.

array
1. Arrangement of elements (numbers or character strings) in one or more dimensions.
2. In a programming language such as C or C++, a group of data stored under one name, with individual items referenced by a number known as a subscript.
3. In the awk language, a similar group of data, except that the subscripts may be an y number or string. Also known as an associative array. Also, a group of disks used together as a single logical storage volume.

array assignment Numeric or alphanumeric values assigned to the elements of an array. *See also* set, array.

arrow Character symbol used to specify the direction of output.

arrow widget In a windowing system such as Motif, a screen element that displays an arrow. *See also* widget.

article In USENET, a news item, usually stored in an individual file and transmitted from one system to another as a unit. *See also* USENET.

as Assembler program on most UNIX systems. It reads an assembly language source file and creates an object file. *See also* assembler.

as386.sed In System V/386, a sed script that semi-automatically translates assembler programs using Intel's syntax into the syntax used by **as**. *See also* sed, assembler.

AS/400 Line of minicomputers produced by IBM, descended from the System/38. This line doesn't run UNIX, but can be networked with UNIX systems.

asa
1. Command that processes Fortran output files and translates Fortran carriage control characters into the

spacing codes used by printers. *See also* Fortran.

2. American Standards Association, the former name for ANSI. *See also* ANSI.

ascftime Library routine that takes a time and date as binary values and translates them to a formatted ASCII string in a user-specified format.

ASCII (American Standard Code for Information Interchange)

1. Defines the codes most computers use for storing letters, numbers, punctuation, and control codes. Almost all UNIX computers use ASCII (except for some mainframes, which use a code called *EBCDIC*). ASCII represents each character with a one-byte code.

2. Option used on the command line with the dd command. It specifies that the information be converted from EBCDIC to ASCII. *See also* EBCDIC.

3. Sorting sequence used by default with the ls command. ASCII sorting sorts capital letters before lowercase letters, so files beginning with A, B, C, would be sorted before those beginning with a, b, and c.

asctime Library routine that takes a time and date as binary values and translates them to a formatted ASCII string in a standard format.

aset Command used to activate the Automated Security Enhancement Tool (ASET).

ASET (Automated Security Enhancement Tool) Set of administrative utilities that can improve system security by allowing the system administrators to check the permissions settings and contents of system files.

asetenv File containing environment variables for the Automated Security Enhancement Tool (ASET).

asetmasters Files used by the Automated Security Enhancement Tool

(ASET). These files include tune.low, tune.med, tune.high, uid_aliases, cklist.low, cklist.med, and cklist.high. These files are provided by default to accommodate most environments.

aset.restore Command that restores system files that are affected by the Automated Security Enhancement Tool (ASET) to their pre-SET content. When ASET is executed , it saves and archives original system files. The aset.restore command reinstates these files.

asin Library routine used for the arc-sine function.

asinh Library routine used for the hyperbolic arc-sine function.

asm Assembly language source file extension. Also, a keyword used with the cc and cb commands.

assembler Computer program that creates an object language program from a symbolic language program. The assembler substitutes machine operation codes for symbolic operation codes and substitutes absolute addresses for symbolic instructions.

assembly language Low-level programming language where, generally speaking, each statement in the language corresponds to a single instruction for the underlying machine. Assembler is usually the lowest level language used on a UNIX system. The assembler program, usually called *as*, translates an assembler language program into the binary that can be executed directly on the computer. *See also* as.

ASSERT Device-driver function used to verify code that is compiled with the DEBUG option.

assert In the C language, a standard macro used to place assertions into a program.

assertion In a programming language, a predicate or condition that is always supposed to be true when a program reaches a particular point. If at that point the assertion is not satisfied, the program is in error.

assign To associate some value, such as 2, with some variable, such as i, so that whenever you subsequently refer to i, you are in reality accessing 2.

assignment operator Programming language operator that assigns a value to a variable. In many languages, including C and C++, the operator is =.

association Permits an entity to be referenced by different names in a scoping unit or by the same or different names in different scoping units. Several kinds of association exist, including pointer association, argument association, host association, use association, and storage association.

assurance Measure of confidence that the security features and architecture of a B1 rated system fulfill security policies.

asterisk
1. The * character. *See also* wildcard.
2. In the shell, a wildcard that matches any filename or substring of a file name.
3. In C and C++, the unary indirection operator, which obtains the contents of a variable to which a pointer points.
4. In many programming languages including C and C++, the multiplication operator.

asy In many UNIX systems, the Device-driver for a port used for asynchronous communication. *See also* device driver.

async (asynchronous communication). Command-line option used with the stty command for setting terminal settings for asynchronous communication.

async_daemon Library routine that starts the NFS asynchronous I/O daemon, a program that makes NFS requests for the benefit of client programs. *See also* NFS daemon.

asynchronous
1. Technique that allows a program to continue execution after starting an I/O operator, but before the operation completes. Most UNIX I/O is not asynchronous.
2. Communication technique in which each character is transmitted with the necessary information to allow the receiver to determine the timing for the character. Most terminals running at 19,200 bps or less use asynchronous communication. *See also* I/O synchronous.

asynchronous communication Refers to the transmission of one character at a time across a link such as a telephone line. Asynchronous terminal devices are used for this type of communication.

asynchronous event Event that does not occur regularly or synchronously with another event.

asynchronous terminal Inexpensive terminal type designed to support asynchronous communication. *See also* asynchronous communication.

at Command that schedules other commands to be run at a later time. The command line for **at** includes the date and time for the command execution to start. The commands to be executed are read from the standard input. *See also* cron.

atan Library routine used for the arc tangent function that takes one argument.

AT&T (American Telephone and Telegraph Corporation) The company that created, developed, and originally owned the UNIX System.

AT&T UNIX System V The standard version of the UNIX operating system originally developed by AT&T. In release 4 of this product (SVR4.0), AT&T brought together the major versions of UNIX (System V, BSD, and XENIX) into one product. That product is now owned by Novell and sold under the name UnixWare.

atan2 Library routine used for the arc tangent function that takes two arguments.

atanh Library routine used for the hyperbolic arc tangent function.

atexit Library routine that calls and registers a program termination routine.

athd On systems running on PC-compatible hardware, the kernel driver for disk drives using the original PC AT controller, or a controller such as IDE or ESDI, which is compatible with that controller. *See also* IDE, ESDI.

atime Command-line option used with the find command that specifies files by last access time. *See also* find.

atktopbm In the PBMPLUS library, the command that converts images from Andrew Toolkit format to PBM format.

atof Library routine that converts an ASCII string representing a floating-point number into a binary representation of that number.

atoi Library routine that converts an ASCII string representing an integer number into a binary representation of that number.

atol Library routine that converts an ASCII string representing a long integer number into a binary representation of that number.

atom In a list- or string-processing language, a string or item treated as an indivisible unit. Also called a token. *See also* token.

atq Command that displays jobs that have been scheduled to run by the at command.

at queue List of jobs scheduled to run using the at command for some time in the future.

atrm Command to delete a job from the at queue.

at-sign
1. The character @.
2. The default line-kill character on UNIX systems, almost invariably changed to something else by users or administrators.
3. The character used to separate a user name from a domain name when specifying addresses in many Internet utilities. For example, joe@saturn.com could be used to send e-mail to the user named joe at the Internet address saturn.com.

attach A kernel device-specific initialization entry point. Attach is called once for each instance of the device on the system.

attroff Library routine (curses) that turns off special attributes such as blink, underline, or color, for text to be drawn. *See also* curses.

attron Library routine (curses) that turns on special attributes, such as blink, underline, or color, for text to be drawn. *See also* curses.

attrset Library routine (curses) that sets special attributes, such as blink, underline, or color, for an entire window.

Audio Tool Program running under Open Windows that allows the user to record and play audio files.

audio_bytes_to_secs Library routine that determines the approximate number of seconds that a recorded sound represents, given the number of bytes in the recording.

audio_c2d Library routine that converts 8-bit PCM values used by sound interfaces to floating point numbers.

audio_c2u Library routine that converts 8-bit m-law values used by SPARC sound interfaces to unsigned integers.

audio_cmp_hdr Library routine that compares the encoding type, precision, and sample rate of the headers to two recorded sounds.

audio_convert Library routine that converts between floating-point and integer PCM sound data.

audio_d2c Library routine that converts floating point numbers to 8 bit PCM values used by sound interfaces.

audio_d2l Library routine that converts floating-point numbers to 32-bit PCM values used by sound interfaces.

audio_d2s Library routine that converts floating-point numbers to 16-bit PCM values used by sound interfaces.

audio_decode_filehdr Library routine that decodes the header of an audio file into a more convenient format.

audio_device Set of library routines that control the audio I/O equipment present on many Sun workstations.

audio_enc_to_str Library routine that produces an ASCII text string describing the format of an encoded sound file.

audio file File containing encoded audio data, consisting of a header describing the details of the encoding, followed by the data representing the sounds.

audio_filehdr Group of library routines that handle the headers of audio files.

audio_hdr C programming language structure that describes the header of an audio file.

audio_isaudiofile Library routine that checks whether a particular file is actually an audio file.

audio_l2d Library routine that converts 32-bit PCM values used by sound interfaces to floating point numbers.

audio_l2u Library routine that converts 32-bit m-law values used by SPARC sound interfaces to unsigned integers.

audioplay Command that copies specified audio files or standard output to the audio device.

audio_read_filehdr Library routine that reads and validates the header of an audio file.

audiorecord Command that copies audio data from the audio device to a specified audio file.

audio_rewrite_filesize Library routine that changes the size of the file as stored in the file header.

audio_s2d Library routine that converts 16-bit PCM values used by sound interfaces to floating point numbers.

audio_s2u Library routine that converts 16-bit m-law values used by SPARC sound interfaces to unsigned integers.

audio_secs_to_bytes Library routine that determines the approximate number of bytes in the recording, given the number of seconds that a recorded sound represents.

audio_str_to_secs Library routine that converts an ASCII string representing minutes and seconds into a floating point number of seconds.

audiotool Program running under Open Windows that allows the user to record and play audio files.

audio_u2c Library routine that converts unsigned integers to 8-bit m-law values used by SPARC sound interfaces.

audio_u2l Library routine that converts

unsigned integers to 32-bit m-law values used by SPARC sound interfaces.

audio_u2s Library routine that converts unsigned integers to 16-bit m-law values used by SPARC sound interfaces.

audio_write_filehdr Library routine that creates and writes the header of an audio file, and optionally also writes file data.

audit
1. Daemon that is a general administrator's interface to maintaining the audit trail.
2. Library routine that adds entries to the audit trail. In Ultrix, the pseudo-device to which audit trail entries are written.

audit_args Library routine that adds a message to the audit trail.

audit_log Files that are the depository for audit records stored locally or an audit server.

auditing Refers to selectively auditing records, so that events related to security can be traced to the responsible user.

auditon Library routine that enables audit trail entries.

auditsvc Library routine that identifies the file to use for audit trail entries.

audit_text Library routine that adds a detailed message to the audit trail.

audit trail Log of security-related events used to track access to a system.

Auspex Manufacturer of high-performance UNIX-based NFS file servers.

authdes_create Library routine that creates an authorization item using DES encryption. *See also* RPC, DES.

authdes_getucred Library routine that extracts user ID and group ID infor-

mation from a DES credential. *See also* RPC.

auth_destroy Library routine that destroys an authorization item. *See also* RPC.

authenticate To verify the identity of a user, device, or other entity in a computer system.

authentication
1. Process of authenticating a user, device, or other entity in a computer system.
2. Verification of the identity of the user or device requesting or providing services.

authnone_create Library routine that creates an authorization item using no authentication information.

authorization file File that contains host and user information verified by the system before user privileges are granted on a remote system.

authunix_create Library routine that creates an authorization item using the UNIX user and group IDs.

auto
1. Statement used in the bc desk calculator to declare variables that are local to a function definition.
2. In the C and C++ languages, the keyword to create an automatic local variable that exists for the duration of a routine's execution.

autobaud Feature of a communication protocol (usually associated with modems) that automatically selects the line speed for a particular communication session. Usually the highest possible speed is tried first, then progressively lower ones until a working line speed is found.

auto-fill-mode Command in the emacs text editor that enables or disables automatic line filling. In Epsilon, this command is sometimes bound to the keystroke Ctrl-Alt-Q.

autoload
1. Command in some versions of the Bourne shell that defines functions only when they are used. A similar command is found in the Korn shell. It is equivalent to the command typeset -fu.
2. Command in the emacs text editor that tells emacs the names of files that contain the code for additional commands and functions.

autologin Facility that allows a user log into an account on a remote host without going through a login procedure. The user logging in does not have to enter a login name or password because the system verifies the information automatically. *See also* rlogin.

automagically Refers to something that happens automatically, by a process that is too complex to explain, or not germane to the current discussion. Something that happens by itself, as if by magic.

automated testing Technology that runs programs and automatically checks whether the outputs produced in response to given inputs are correct.

automatic line filling Mode in the emacs text editor in which characters are entered on the current line until it reaches a preset length, when a newline character is inserted after the last word that fits entirely on the line.

auto-mode-alist Variable in the emacs text editor that contains a list of source files used to implement emac's major and minor modes.

automount Command that installs autofs mount points and associates an automount map with each mount point. *See also* autofs, automount map.

automountd RPC server that answers file-system mount and unmount requests from the autofs filesystem.

automounter Optional NFS feature that automatically mounts remote directories as subdirectories of a local directory, as the subdirectory names are referenced from programs. The names of the remote directories are stored by NIS. The automounter is often used in a cluster of workstations to provide cluster-wide automatic mounting. *See also* NFS, NIS.

autonomous system Internet terminology for a collection of gateways (routers) that fall under one administrative entity and use a common Interior Gateway Protocol (IGP).

autopush Command that is used to configure the list of modules to be automatically pushed onto the stream when a device is opened.

autoreply Program that automatically sends replies to a user's incoming mail messages. Often used when the user is on vacation or otherwise won't be able to respond to mail.

auto-save-default Variable in the emacs text editor that controls whether emacs automatically saves versions of all buffers by default.

auto-save file File in which the emacs text editor automatically saves the contents of a buffer. The filename of an auto-save file is the same as the buffer's name, with hashmarks (#) added to the beginning and end. For example, the auto-save file for the letter1 buffer is named #letter1#.

auto-save-interval Variable in the emacs text editor that controls how often buffers are automatically saved, measured in the number of keystrokes. If the value of the variable is zero, buffers are not automatic ally saved.

auto-save mode In the emacs text editor, a minor mode in which buffers are saved automatically to their associated files at regular intervals.

auto-save-visited-file-name Variable in the emacs text editor that controls the filename used when auto-saving a buffer.

A/UX Version of UNIX for the Apple Macintosh.

awk Pattern-matching program which is widely used on UNIX systems. The awk program (or related programs such as nawk and gawk) searches the input for patterns. When a pattern is located, awk performs a procedure. An awk program consists of a list of patterns and procedures.

AXP Line of high-performance RISC chips, introduced in 1993, used by Digital Equipment Corporation (DEC) in their workstations.

B

B2 Designator of computer system trustworthiness issued by the National Computer Security Center (NCSC). B2 is an example of a class within the four divisions of the DoD Trusted Computer System Evaluation Criteria (TCSEC). These divisions and classes represent a hierarchical structure for levels of computer security. The divisions and classes currently include A1, B3, B2, B1, C2, C1, and D; division A systems provide the most security; D systems provide the least.

background
1. UNIX can run many programs at the same time, of which many can be run in the background. Programs running in the background operate with no user interaction. An ampersand at the end of the command line specifies that a command should be run in the background. *See also* foreground, process, job control.
2. Keyword used in a user's .Xdefaults file to configure the emacs text editor. It controls the color used for the background of the emacs window, and is equivalent to the emacs -bg command-line option.

background execution To execute a process or procedure in the background, so work can continue at the current shell as the background process runs. *See also* background process.

background job Job that is run in the background. *See also* background process.

background process Process that is executed in the background with no user interaction. Also known as a *detached process,* it is initiated by issuing a command line that ends in an ampersand (&).

backq Library routine that gets a pointer to the queue behind the current queue.

back quote *See* `.

backslash Shell symbol (\) used as an escape character. The character following the backslash is interpreted literally, not as a special character to the shell.

back-to-indentation Command in the emacs text editor that moves the cursor back to the first non-blank character on the current line. This command is usually bound to the keystroke Meta-M.

backup
1. Copy of one or more files, usually on a removable medium, that you can restore to the computer if the originals

becomes damaged or destroyed.
2. Command used for backing up files.

backup-by-copying Variable in the emacs text editor that controls how backup files are stored.

back-up file Copy of a file, typically stored on magnetic tape or other removable media.

backup methods Refers to different techniques used for backing up files. Backup options available with the UNIX backup command include incfile (only files that have changes since previous full backup), ffile (all files and directories in a mounted file system), fdisk (all information needed to recover an entire disk), and fimage (full image, byte-for-byte, of a file system).

backup register File containing descriptions of what files should be backed up during a backup operation.

backward Toward the beginning of the file. For example, moving the cursor backward in a screen editor means moving it to the left or upward on the screen.

backward-char (also called backward-character) Command in the emacs text editor that moves the cursor backward (leftward) one character. This command is usually bound to the keystroke Ctrl-B.

backward-delete-character (Or backward-delete-char) Command in the emacs text editor that deletes the character immediately to the left of the cursor. This command is usually bound to the keystroke DEL.

backward-kill-level Command in the Epsilon text editor that kills the last bracketed expression, that is, text enclosed in (), {}, or [] pairs.

backward-kill-paragraph Command in the emacs text editor that kills the paragraph immediately before the cursor.

backward-kill-sentence Command in the emacs text editor that kills the sentence immediately before the cursor. This command is usually bound to the keystroke Ctrl-X DEL.

backward-kill-sexp Command in the emacs text editor, used in LISP mode to kill the S-expression immediately before the cursor.

backward-kill-word Command in the emacs text editor that kills the word immediately before the cursor. This command is usually bound to the keystroke Meta-Del.

backward-level Command in the Epsilon text editor that moves the cursor backward to beginning of a bracketed expression, that is, text enclosed in (), {}, or [] pairs.

backward-list Command in the emacs text editor in LISP mode to move the cursor backward by one list. This command is usually bound to the keystroke Meta-Ctrl-P.

backward-page Command in the emacs text editor that moves the cursor backward one page, that is, one screen. This command is usually bound to the keystroke Ctrl-X [.

backward-paragraph Command in the emacs text editor that moves the cursor backward one paragraph. (emacs considers paragraphs to be separated by one or more blank lines.) This command is usually bound to the keystroke Meta-[.

backward-sentence Command in the emacs text editor that moves the cursor backward one sentence. This command is usually bound to the keystroke Meta-A.

backward-sexp Command in the emacs

text editor, used in LISP mode to move the cursor backward by one S-expression. This command is usually bound to the keystroke Meta-Ctrl-B.

backward-text-line Command in the emacs text editor, used in nroff mode to move the cursor to the next text line, skipping lines that contain only mark-up commands. This command is usually bound to the keystroke Meta-P.

backward-up-list Command in the emacs text editor in LISP mode to move the cursor backward and up one parenthesis level. This command is usually bound to the keystroke Meta-Ctrl-U.

backward-word Command in the emacs text editor that moves the cursor backward one word. This command is usually bound to the keystroke Meta-B.

bang Slang term for the exclamation point (!). The address style used with UUCP is sometimes referred to as *bang-style network addressing* (for example, computer!user).

banner
1. Headline spanning a page.
2. Command that makes headers or banners with large letters on the standard output.

base address Base address is loaded into a register and used as a starting point from which instructions form addresses. The operating system assigns the absolute starting address to a program.

basename
1. Command that deletes any prefix ending with the slash (/) symbol and prints the result on the standard output. *See also* dirname
2. Library routine that returns the last element of a pathname.

base system device drivers Those de-vice-drivers that are delivered and in-stalled as part of the UNIX system. These included drivers for hard disks, floppy drives, serial ports, and tape devices.

bash (Bourne Again Shell) Shell program available from the Free Software Foundation. bash is a POSIX-compatible shell, with full Bourne shell syntax as well as some C shell commands. *See also* shell.

Basic Networking Utilities package *See* BNU.

batch
1. Method of grouping job requests for a single run of a program or command.
2. Command that puts a job into the background for execution when system load levels are low.

batch job File of commands that may be executed in batch mode. Also, group of commands that produces a specific result/output that the user requires.

batch mode Mode of processing in which all commands to be executed by the operating system and, optionally, data to be used as input to the commands, are placed in a file and submitted to the system for execution.

batch networking To send programs to remote computers from workstations with a remote-job submittal program.

batch processing File that contains a program that is submitted from a host computer to a remote, where it then executes.

batch request File that contains a shell script to be processed by the cron dae-mon.

baud Unit of speed in data transmission: one bit per second for binary signals.

baud rate The rate of data transmission over a line by modem or terminal, measured in baud units. Baud rates range from 110 to more than 19,200 baud.

bc Command that acts as an interactive preprocessor for a language that resembles C. It provides unlimited precision arithmetics. It is automatically called by the UNIX desk calculator program dc. *See also* dc.

bcanput Device-driver routine used to test for flow control in a particular band of priority.

bcanputnext Device-driver routine that searches a stream of data for a queue containing a service routine, then tests the queue to find if a message in the priority band can be enqueued.

BCC: Field in an electronic-mail message indicating who should receive blind copies of the message.

bcheckrc System-initialization procedure that checks the root file system. If errors are encountered with the file system, this command tries to repair it. It also mounts the /stand, /proc, and /var file systems (if they exist).

bcmp Kernel function that compares two byte arrays. *See also* array.

bcopy Library routine that copies data between address locations in the kernel.

bd
1. STREAMS module that processes the byte streams generated by Sun Microsystem SunButtom, buttonbox, and SunDial dialboxes.
2. Command-line option used with the emacs text editor to control the color used for the border around the emacs window.

bdconfig Command that configures the bd buttons and dials stream. *See also* autopush, bd.

bdiff Command used to differentiate files too large for the diff command. *See also* diff.

beautifier Command that makes programming source code neater and easier to read. The cb command is used to beautify C program code.

beep Default warning sound produced by the computer when an illegal action for the application is requested from the keyboard. For example, pressing the Esc key while you are in command mode in vi causes a beep.

beginning-of-buffer Command in the emacs text editor that moves the cursor to the beginning of the buffer. This command is usually bound to the keystroke Meta-<.

beginning-of-defun Command in the emacs text editor, used in C mode to move the cursor to the beginning of the current C function definition. This command is usually bound to the keystroke Meta-Ctrl-A.

beginning-of-fortran-subprogram Command in the emacs text editor, used in Fortran mode to move the cursor to the beginning of the current subprogram. This command is usually bound to the keystroke Meta-Ctrl-A.

beginning-of-line Command in the emacs text editor that moves the cursor to the beginning of the current line. This command is usually bound to the keystroke Ctrl-A.

beginning-of-line metacharacter In regular expressions, the character that represents the beginning of the line. This character can be used to match only strings that occur at the beginning of a line.

beginning-of-tape Beginning-of-tape (BOT) reflective marker. *See also* end-of-tape.

beginning-of-window Command in the Epsilon text editor that moves the cursor to the upper-left corner of the window.

bell Warning sound issued by the computer for a specified reason. Bell notification in a user environment can be turned on and off by UNIX users.

Bell Laboratories New Jersey research subsidiary of AT&T that developed the UNIX operating system. *See also* Berkeley Software Development.

benchmark Standard by which something can be measured or judged. In the UNIX operating system the speed and efficiency of operating system operations can be measured and reported in the form of *benchmarks*.

benchmark code Automated tests used to test benchmarks. *See also* benchmark.

benchmarking Act of judging and measuring the speed or efficiency of UNIX operating system operations.

Berkeley Software Distribution (BSD) Version of the UNIX operating system developed at the University of California at Berkeley (UCB). The BSD term used to describe different versions of the Berkeley UNIX software.

Berkeley Systems Distribution Development group in the department of computer science at the University of California at Berkeley, California that developed Berkeley UNIX.

Berkeley yacc Tool for generating language parsers developed by Berkeley Software Development at the University of California at Berkeley. It literally stands for "yet another compiler-compiler." Yacc converts a context-free grammar into a set of tables that drive a LR parsing automaton. *See also* LR.

bessel Suite of mathematical functions, known as *Bessel functions*, used for mathematical calculations. Bessel functions include j0, j1, jn, y0, y1, and yn.

bfs
1. (boot file system) A special UNIX file system type, containing stand-alone boot programs (including unix) as well as other files needed to boot the operating system.
2. Command used to edit large files. It was designed originally to read large files that were too big for the ed editor to handle. The name stands for "big file scanner."

bg Command that runs a process in the background. This command is available only under job-control shells. Also, command-line option used with the emacs text editor to control the color for the background of the emacs window.

bgets Library routine that reads the stream into the buffer to the next delimiter. *See also* gets.

bgnice Korn shell mode that automatically runs background jobs at low priority. It is specified with the set command. (Korn shell only.)

bibtex-mode Command in the emacs text editor that enables bibtex mode, which is designed for editing LaTeX bibliography files.

bidirectional transfer Ability of a communications protocol to transfer files in both directions across a connection, regardless of which end initiated the connection.

biff Command that gives notice of incoming mail messages. Notification status can be turned on or off with this command. *See also* mail.

binarsys File containing information that notes whether or not a remote system can accept mail messages that contain binary contents. The file is located in /etc/mail/binarsys.

binary
1. Characterized by or composed of two different parts; based on the number two or the binary numeration system.
2. Adjective that describes code or data that exists in machine language form. See also binary data.

binary data The base unit for data storage in memory; also called a bit from the contraction of *binary digit*. *See also* bit.

binary file A file created by compilers such as the C language compiler. A binary program is a sequence of instructions as they appear in memory when a program starts executing.

binary license The common UNIX term for a license that covers the machine-specific code actually read by the computer and not the source code.

bind Library routine that binds a specified name to a socket. *See also* socket.

BIND An acronym used to describe the TCP/IP daemon called named, which provides domain-name system service. The acronym stands for *Berkeley Internet Name Domain* service.

Binder Program running under Open Windows that allows the user to change the appearance of icons, or which programs each icon runs.

binding
1. Specifies the way in which one component in a resource is related to another component.
2. In the emacs text editor, the assignment of a command to a keystroke.

bin directory In UNIX operating systems, a directory where commands, scripts, and tools (commands) are stored. The public bin directory is /bin

(which is also linked to /usr/bin). Often, users have their own bin directories in their home directories to store their own commands ($HOME/bin).

bin login Special administrative user login that owns many of the commands stored in the system bin directory (/bin or /usr/bin).

bind-to-key Command in the Epsilon text editor that binds a named command to a key. Compare it to the emacs commands define-key, global-set-key, and local-set-key.

binutils Utilities for dealing with compiled programs, available from the Free Software Foundation. The binutils includes ar, demangle, ld, nm, objdump, ranlib, size, strip, and gprof.

biod Command used to start the asynchronous block I/O daemons.

biodone A kernel function that notifies about blocked processes waiting for the I/O to complete.

bioerror Device-driver library routine used within a buffer header for manipulating error fields.

biowait Library routine that suspends processes pending completion of an I/O block.

bisynchronous communication A type of synchronous communication in which a group of characters is sent at one time and a timing mechanism separates the characters at the receiving end. *See also* asynchronous communication.

bit The smallest piece of information a computer can handle. A bit represents either a one or zero.

bit bucket Place where discarded data goes. The equivalent in UNIX, where unwanted output is usually directed, is /dev/null.

bit-level verification Way of verifying that two items, such as data files or executables, are exactly the same. Each bit in the two items is compared.

bitmap Two-dimensional array of bits, where each bit represents one pixel value of either on or off.

bitmapIcon Keyword used in a user's .Xdefaults file to configure the emacs text editor. It controls whether the icon that represents emacs looks like a tiny kitchen sink, or whether the regular icon is used. It is equivalent to the emacs -i command-line option.

bit-mapped display Display monitor used for graphics; also called a *dot-addressable display*.

BITNET (Because It's Time Network) Low-cost academic network.

bitwise AND Operator that combines two values one bit at a time using a logical AND. For each bit in each byte of the two input values, the resulting bit is 1 only if both of the input bits are 1. For example, the bitwise AND of 15 and 24 is 8. The binary representations of 15 and 24 are 00001111 and 00011000, so the result is 00001000, which contains a 1 in only the positions in which both input values contain 1.

bitwise exclusive OR Operator that combines two values one bit at a time using a logical exclusive OR. For each bit in each byte of the two values, the resulting bit is 1 if either of the input bits are 1. For example, the bitwise OR of 15 and 24 is 31. The binary representations of 15 and 24 are 00001111 and 00011000, so the result is 00011111, which contains a 1 in the positions in which either input value contains 1.

bitwise inversion Unary operator that reverses the sense of each bit in a byte, converting each 0 into a 1 and each 1 into a 0. For example, the bitwise inversion of 15 is 240. The binary representation of 15 is 00001111, which when inverted becomes 11110000, or 240.

bitwise left shift Operator that rotates the bits in a byte one (or more) places to the left. For example, if the value 4 is rotated two places to the left, the resulting value is 16. The binary representation of 4 is 00000100, which when rotated two places to the left becomes 00010000, or 16.

bitwise operator Programming language operator that performs a bitwise operation, such as bitwise left or right shift, bitwise inversion, bitwise AND, or bitwise OR.

bitwise OR Operator that combines two values, one bit at a time using a logical OR. For each bit in each byte of the two values, the resulting bit is 1 if either of the input bits are 1. For example, the bitwise OR of 15 and 24 is 31. The binary representations of 15 and 24 are 00001111 and 00011000, so the result is 00011111, which contains a 1 in the positions in which either input value contains 1.

bitwise right shift Operator that rotates the bits in a byte one (or more) places to the right. For example, if the value 4 is rotated two places to the right, the resulting value is 1. The binary representation of 4 is 00000100, which when rotated two places to the right becomes 00000001, or 1.

bkexcept Command that lets an administrator change or display an exception list for files that are excluded when a backup is done.

bkhistory Command that reports on completed backup operations.

bkoper Command that lets an administrator service requests for media insertion during backup procedures.

bkreg Command used by administrators to modify or view the contents of a backup register.

bkstatus Command used to show the status of backup operations as they are in progress. Status is reported as either active, pending, waiting, or suspended.

blackbox
1. Add-on package for the emacs text editor that implements a major mode for playing the game "blackbox."
2. A piece of code or hardware item that takes input and produces output, but keeps everything that goes on in between a mystery.

blackbox-mode Command in the blackbox add-on package to the emacs text editor that plays the game "blackbox."

black hole Networking term referring to a location where packets go in, but are not routed forward to their destination.

blank character Either a Space or a Tab character; also called *white space*.

blinking attribute Attribute of a character or graphical terminal that causes the text or graphical item to blink off and on.

blink-matching-paren Variable in the emacs text editor that controls whether emacs blinks the matching open parenthesis when a close parenthesis is typed.

blink-matching-paren-distance Variable in the emacs text editor that controls the maximum number of characters that emacs searches for the matching open parenthesis when a close parenthesis is typed.

block Section of a disk or tape that is written at one time. Typically, it is 1,024 bytes long.

block allocation bitmap Bitmap that controls block allocation across an entire file system.

block device Disk or tape drive. A block device stores information in blocks of characters. It is represented by a block special file.

blocked
1. Refers to the delivery of a signal that can be blocked.
2. Signal that is pending but blocked remains pending until the signal is unblocked.

block number Disk or tape blocks are numbered so the UNIX operating system can track the data on the device. The block number is an integer.

block size Size of a block or section of disk or tape space. This is often 1,024 bytes long, but can be shorter or longer.

BNU (Basic Networking Utilities) Software utility package that includes uucp, uuto, uupick, uux, and other UUCP utilities and protocols. This package is used for serial communications over modems and direct lines.

bobp Function in the emacs LISP programming language that returns *t* if the cursor is at the beginning of the buffer, and nil otherwise.

body lines In the outline mode of the emacs text editor, lines of text that are not designated as headers.

bold Heavier version of a typeface. Sometimes used to show emphasis.

bolp Function in the emacs LISP programming language that returns *t* if the cursor is at the beginning of a line, and nil otherwise.

Boolean Boolean value: either true or false.

Boolean value Logical value, that may be true or false. In the shell, true is represented by a zero, while false is represented by any other value. In C, true is represented by one and false by zero. In LISP, true is represented by the *t* value, while false is represented by nil.

boot
1. Short for *bootstrapping procedure,* the process of loading and executing a standalone program. In particular, *boot* usually refers to starting the program that starts the operating system. 2. Command that is used to loading and executing a standalone program. 3. Options used in /stand/boot that change how a system boots.

bootp TCP/IP feature that allows a server system to provide information needed to start up TCP/IP on a client system. Information can include the local network's netmask, DNS server, and broadcast.

bootparamd Command that provides information from a bootparams database to diskless clients at boot time. It is used with the Network Information Service (NIS). *See also* NIS.

bootparams database Database that contains a list of client entries that diskless clients use for booting or starting a standalone program. The diskless clients issue requests to a server running the bootparamd program to retrieve this information.

bootpd Command that implements an Internet bootstrap protocol. *See also* bootp.

bootserver Computer that offers the files and information needed to allow a client system, such as a diskless workstation, to boot.

bootstrapping *See* boot.

border Motif, or other windowing system, term that refers to the context of an event. The border of a Motif window manager (mwm) window is the area that surrounds the application and contains resize handles.

borderColor Keyword used in a user's .Xdefaults file to configure the emacs text editor. It controls the color used for the border around the emacs window and is equivalent to the emacs -bd command-line option.

borderWidth Keyword used in a user's .Xdefaults file to configure the emacs text editor. It controls the width of the emacs window's outside border and is equivalent to the emacs -b command-line option.

bound Refers to a command in the emacs text editor that is assigned to a keystroke. When the keystroke is pressed, the command is performed.

Bourne Again Shell *See* bash.

Bourne shell Standard UNIX System V command processor, developed by Steve Bourne at AT&T Bell Laboratories. The command that represents the Bourne shell is /bin/sh. *See also* shell, sh.

Bourne, Steven Author of the Bourne shell.

box Library routine (curses) used to create a border.

bp_mapin Library routine that is used to allocate virtual-address space to a page list maintained by the buffer header during a paged-I/O request.

bp_mapout Library routine that is used to deallocate virtual-address space to a page list maintained by the buffer header during a paged-I/O request.

bpp Driver that provides a general-purpose bidirectional interface to parallel devices. The programmable driver controls relationships between output and input devices with various handshake signals.

bps Bits per second (ANSI standard term is *b/i*), which is a measure of the rate of data transmission. *See also* baud rate.

braces *See* {,}.

bracket *See* [,], {, }, <, >.

bracketed expression String enclosed within parentheses, square brackets, or curly brackets.

branch
1. In a UNIX hierarchal directory structure, a branch connects files and directories. The UNIX file system is often described as an upside-down tree with the root at the top and user directories at the bottom.
2. In UNIX SCCS (UNIX Source Control System) a branch occurs when a delta is made to a file which is not included in subsequent deltas to the file.

brc Obsolete command used for file-sharing administrative tasks.

break Command that exits from a loop in a shell program. Also, a statement used in the bc desk calculator to indicate the end of a while or for statement.

Break key Key available on some keyboards that interrupts activity of the current program.

breakpoint Point in a program at which execution can be suspended to permit examination and manipulation of data.

breakpointing Method of debugging in which an instruction is placed in a program that will cause it to stop or to perform some other useful debugging function (such as checking the value of a variable) at a specified point.

break statement Shell programming statement indicating that the script should exit from the current for, while, until, or select loop.

breaksw In the C shell, a command that continues processing in a shell script after the next endsw command.

brelse Device-driver library routine that returns a specified buffer to the system's buffer-free list.

browse To search around a file system, database, or other collection of information.

browser Software program for searching computers for information. A browser may be used to search a database, a file system, or the Internet.

BSD UNIX *See* Berkeley Software Distribution.

buffer Place where information is stored temporarily on a computer. Data stored in buffers in physical memory can be more quickly accessed by applications that are using the data.

buffer pool Area of computer memory or a particular storage device in which space is allocated to use as buffers.

bug Fault or an error in a computer program or computer system. Debugging is the processing of identifying and removing bugs.

built-in commands Shell commands that are built into the shell, rather than being stored and accessible from the file system. The cd and pwd commands are built into most UNIX shells.

bus The hardware that connects the basic hardware units of a computer together. A bus architecture defines how the CPU, the memory and the peripheral devices are connected together.

bus mouse Mouse that is connected to a computer's bus, rather than to a standard serial port.

bye Command used during an ftp session to exit from ftp.

byte Eight-bit unit of information. A byte typically represents a single character.

C General-purpose, medium-level programming language used for writing both application and system programs. It was invented by Dennis Ritchie of Bell Laboratories in 1972. Most UNIX programs are written in the C programming language. All UNIX operating system versions contain C compilers. *See also* compilers, language.

C- Notation used to describe the combination of the Ctrl or Control key with another key. For example, C-d is short for Ctrl-d, that is, holding down the Ctrl key while pressing the D key.

C++ High-level programming language developed by AT&T Bell Laboratories. Based on its predecessor, the C programming language, C++ is a nonprocedural object-oriented programming language in which program elements are conceptualized as objects that can pass messages to each other. Each object contains its own code and is internally self-reliant. The objects are built into a hierarchy of layers.

c++filt Command used to demangle names in ASCII text that are encoded by the C++ compiler.

C2 Level of computer security in the Trusted Computer Systems Evaluation Criteria (TCSEC) standard published by the National Computer Security Center (NCSC). C2 is the most common level adhered to by most computer vendors.

C2 auditing Part of the C2 security standard that requires that audit events be logged to monitor for intrusions on the system.

cable Wiring used to connect the ports of a computer to other computers or peripherals.

cache manager Client daemon that controls the size and access of cache memory. Cache is pronounced *"cash"*. *See also* cache memory.

cache memory Special, fast section of random-access memory (RAM) set aside to store the most frequently accessed information. *See also* RAM, cache memory.

CAD (computer-aided design) The use of a computer and computer-aided design applications to design and illustrate a wide range of physical objects, including architecture and machinery.

cal
1. Utility that prints a calendar for the current month or the month specified on the command line. Alternatively, cal can print a 12-month calendar for any year.
2. Add-on package for the emacs text

editor that implements a function to print calendars.

3. Command in the cal add-on package to the emacs text editor that generates a calendar.

calc Desk calculator available from the Free Software Foundation. It runs as part of GNU Emacs, and is an extensible, advanced desk calculator and mathematical tool.

calctool Calculator program running under Open Windows that displays an on-screen calculator.

Caldera Company that produces the Caldera Network Desktop.

Caldera Network Desktop UNIX client and server operating system, consisting of an easy graphical interface, built on the Linux operating system. Unlike other desktop operating system running on PCS, Caldera allows peer-to-peer, as well as client/server, communications.

calendar

1. Text file consisting of a list of appointments or other events, one per line, with the date at the beginning of each line.

2. Utility that reads the calendar file and displays all lines that contain the current date.

Calendar Manager Program running under Open Windows that displays a calendar and allows the user to set up appointments.

call In programming, a statement that directs the flow of program control to a function, routine or set of procedures.

callback Characteristic of a computer that enables it to return a call from another computer. Callback is often used to increase security in a system where many users can dial in.

CALLBACK option Option in the /etc/uucp/Permission file that requires the local computer to call back the remote computer before any file transfer can take place. It is used with Basic Networking Utilities (uucp, uux, etc.).

call-last-kbd-macro Command in the emacs text editor that executes the last macro defined. This command is usually bound to the keystroke Ctrl-X E.

calloc Library routine that allocates memory space for an array of elements of a particular size.

callout Command used to print the call-out table. *See also* callout table.

callout table Table in the UNIX kernel that stores information about kernel functions that must be invoked at set times.

call terminal *See* ct.

call UNIX computer *See* cu.

can Type of USENET newsgroup distribution in which articles are distributed only within Canada (with exceptions).

Canaday, Rudd One of the developers of the UNIX file system, with Dennis Ritchie and Ken Thompson.

cancel

1. In the UNIX System V print spooler, the program that cancels a previous request to print a file.

2. In general, to remove a previously made program request. *See also* lprm can_change_colors.

canonical input Terminal setting in which erase and kill characters are processed. This setting is controlled by the icanon option of the stty command.

canput Device-driver library routine that tests for room in a message queue. It searches through a stream until it finds a queue containing a service routine where a message can be enqueued or until it reaches the stream end.

canputnext Device-driver library routine that tests for room in the next module's message queue. This routine is atomic and similar to invoking the canput function.

capitalize-region Command in the emacs text editor that capitalizes the first letter of all words in the currently-marked region. The remaining letters in each word are then converted to lowercase.

capitalize-word Command in the emacs text editor that capitalizes the first letter of the current word (or the previous word, if the argument is negative). The remaining letters in the current word are converted to lowercase. This command is usually bound to the keystroke Meta-C.

captoinfo Command that converts a termcap description into a terminfo description. This command looks into a specified file for a termcap description, then an equivalent terminfo description is written to standard output.

car LISP function that returns the first item in a list.

card Electronic circuit board designed to fit into a slot on a computer's motherboard. The card may contain memory, hard-coded instruction sets, device-driver code for peripherals, or other circuitry.

caret (^) Symbol on a standard keyboard. The caret is used visually to indicate a control character for such as ^G (Control-G). The caret is also used for cursor positioning and editing statements in the vi editor.

c-argdecl-indent Variable in the emacs text editor, used in C mode to control how far to indent the type declarations of C function arguments.

carriage return Action that returns the cursor to the beginning of the line. Most often, a carriage return is accompanied by a line feed (a new line) so that the cursor is returned to the beginning of the *next* line. A carriage return is entered into a file by pressing the keyboard's Enter or Return key.

Cartesian coordinate system Method of defining two-dimensional space by horizontal x coordinates and vertical y coordinates. This method was created by the seventeenth-century French mathematician Rene Descartes. A computer mouse uses this system to locate a pointer and specific coordinates for applications such as X Windows on a monitor screen.

cartridge tape A plastic, removable medium containing readable and writeable magnetic tape for storing and transferring digitized information.

case Command that allows conditional processing in a shell script. In the Bourne and Korn shells, the case command begins the condition code. In the C shell, the switch command begins the conditional code, and the case command identifies what command(s) to run in a particular case.

case folding Ignoring the case of letters during a search. That is, a search for "Cat" would find "CAT," "cat," "Cat," and "cAT."

case-fold-search Variable in the emacs text editor that controls whether emacs distinguishes between upper- and lowercase when searching.

case-indirect Command in the Epsilon text editor that performs the reverse-case binding of the invoking key. This command is usually bound to the keystroke Ctrl-X E. case-replace Variable in the emacs text editor that controls whether emacs preserves the case when replacing text.

case sensitive search Search in which the program or script attempts to match the exact pattern of upper- or lowercase letters in the specified search string.

case sensitivity Sensitivity to capitalization of letters. This controls whether a distinction is made between uppercase and lowercase letters.

cat (concatenate) Program that sends the entire contents of one or more files to stdout (usually the screen). For paging through files on the screen, the commands more and pg are commonly used instead.

catalog Collection of entries provided in a logical order.

catclose Library routine that closes the specified message catalog.

catenet Network in which hosts are connected to networks with varying characteristics. The networks are interconnected by gateways. The Internet is a catenet.

catgets Library routine that reads a program message from a specified message catalog.

cathode ray tube *See* CRT.

catman Command that creates the pre-formatted versions of an online manual from nroff input files. *See also* cat, nroff.

catopen Library routine that opens a specified message catalog and returns a message catalog descriptor. The NLSPATH variable is often used to provide the location of the message catalogs.

caught signal Signal is described as "caught" if the delivery of the signal to a process causes a signal-handler procedure to be invoked.

c-auto-newline Variable in the emacs text editor, used in C mode to control whether emacs automatically inserts newline characters before and after curly braces ({) and after semicolons and colons.

cb (C program beautifier) Utility that formats C source code using standard C structure and indentation. This makes the source code more readable without changing how it functions.

C-block Data buffer that holds the data in a C-list structure.

cb_ops Data structure specific to SPARC architecture. It contains all entry points for drivers that support both character and block entry points.

c-brace-imaginary-offset Variable in the emacs text editor, used in C mode to control how far open curly braces ({) are indented when they follow other text on the same line.

c-brace-offset Variable in the emacs text editor, used in C mode to control how far to indent lines that begin with open curly braces ({).

cbreak One of a group of library routines called curs_inopts. These routines are used to control curses terminal input options. This group of routines includes cbreak, nocbreak, echo, noecho, halfdelay, intrflush, keypad, meta, nodelay, notimeout, raw, noraw, noqiflush, qiflush, timeout, wtimeout, and typeahead

cbreak mode Option used with the stty command to enable and disable canonical input. This handles Erase and Kill processing. The cbreak option is synonymous with the icanon option.

cbrt Library routine that returns the cube root of the indicated number.

cbs (conversion buffer size) Option used on the command line with the dd command. It sets the size in bytes of the conversion buffer used while copying. *See also* dd.

CBT Abbreviation for computer-based training, the use of computer-aided instructions to train users for specific computer environments and applications.

CC Field in an e-mail message indicating who should receive copies of the message.

cc (C compiler) Program that compiles one or more files of C source code, assembler source code, or preprocessed C source code and creates an object file. It is an ANSI C compiler.

CCA emacs Version of the emacs text editor distributed by CCA.

c-comment Command in the emacs text editor that enables a minor mode, which is designed for formatting comments in programs in the C programming language. *See also* C mode.

c-continued-brace-offset Variable in the emacs text editor, used in C mode to control how far to indent lines that begin statement blocks, including if and while blocks.

c-continued-statement-offset Variable in the emacs text editor, used in C mode to control how far to indent the continuation lines of multiline statements.

cd Built-in shell command that changes the current directory to the directory specified on the command line. If no directory is specified, the current directory changes to the user's home directory.

CDB (command descriptor block) Information structure that contains the command that is sent to a target controller by a device-driver function.

cdc Command used to change the comment for a delta in a SCCS file.

cddevsuppl Command used to get or set device numbers (major and minor) relating to a CD-ROM device.

cddrec Command used to read the directory record relating to a CD-ROM file or directory.

CDE (Common Desktop Environment) UNIX system standard, proposed by COSE, that is designed to standardize the graphical user interfaces used on UNIX systems.

cdevsw (character device switch table) Table in the UNIX system kernel that contains an entry for each character device on the system. The table directs system call requests to the appropriate driver interfaces.

cdio.h Header file containing symbolic constant and macro definitions for CDROM control operations.

cdmntsuppl Command used to set and get administrative CD-ROM attributes. Attributes may include permissions, user and group IDs, and ownership.

CDPATH Shell variable that contains the list of directories search by the cd command (Bourne and Korn shells only).

cdpath Shell variable that contains the list of directories search by the cd, popd, and pushd commands (C shell only).

cdptrec Command used to read a path table record for a CD-ROM.

cdr LISP function that returns all but the first item in a list.

CD-ROM Computer disk using the same physical medium as a music CD, but containing data. *See also* disk.

cdsuf Command used to read information from the system-use fields in the system-use areas of a CD-ROM.

cdtoc (table of contents file) ASCII file residing in the top-level directory of a file system that describes the contents of a CD-ROM or other software distribution media.

cdvd Command used to read the primary volume descriptor from a CD-ROM.

cdxar Command used to read the extended attribute record for a CD-ROM.

cdxon Command-line option used with the stty command for setting the method of flow control.

ceil Library routine that returns the smallest integer not less than the indicated number.

cell Code that identifies the coordinates of a single location. In Network Information Service plus (NIS+) table, a single entry in a specified column. In a spreadsheet application, a cell is a location on a worksheet that is identified by the row and column. *See also* cell address, cell formula.

cell address Code that identifies the location of an entry or set of coordinates in a table or worksheet used to contain data.

cell definition Actual contents of a cell in a spreadsheet application displayed on the screen or in hard-copy.

cell format Syntax of the values and labels displayed in a Network information service, or in a spreadsheet application. *See also* cell.

cell formula Code that defines the function that produces the value for a specified cell. *See also* cell, cell address.

center-line Command in the emacs text editor that centers the current line horizontally. This command is usually bound to the keystroke Meta-S.

center-paragraph Command in the emacs text editor that centers the current paragraph horizontally.

center-region Command in the emacs text editor that centers the current region horizontally.

center-window Command in the Epsilon text editor that centers the current window vertically, by moving the text so that center is in the vertical center.

central processing unit Primary computational unit in a computer containing internal storage, processing and control circuitry, often abbreviated *CPU*. The CPU runs applications.

CERT/CC Computer Emergency Response Team Coordination Center, an organization run by Carnegie-Mellon University to deal with computer security problems. CERT gathers and disseminates information, then works with computer vendors to fix the problems.

cfgetospeed One of a group of library routines called *termios*. These routines are used to describe a terminal interface for asynchronous communications ports control. This group of routines includes tcgetattr, tcsetattr, tcsendbreak, tcdrain, tcflush, tcflow, cfgetispeed, cfsetispeed, cfsetospeed, tcgetpgrp, tcsetpgrp, and tcgetsid.

C. Files Work files created in spool directories by file transfers (uucp) or remote command executions (uux). The syntax for these files is C.sysnxxxx, where *sys* is the name of the remote computer, *n* represents the job's priority, and *xxxx* is the four-digit job sequence number.

c-fill Add-on package for the emacs text editor that implements a minor mode for formatting multi-line C comments.

cflow
1. Utility that reads C, lex, yacc, assembler, or object files and creates a

flowchart of external function calls.
2. Command used to analyze one or more C, yacc, lex, assembler, or object files and create a graph of the external function references.

cfsadmin Command that is used to administer cache file systems. The command functions include cache creation, deletion of cache file systems, listing of cache contents and statistics and resource parameter adjustment.

cfsetispeed One of a group of library routines called *termios*. These routines are used to describe a terminal interface for asynchronous communications ports control. This group of routines includes tcgetattr, tcsetattr, tcsendbreak, tcdrain, tcflush, tcflow, cfgetospeed, cfgetispeed, cfsetospeed, tcgetpgrp, tcsetpgrp, and tcgetsid.

cfsetospeed One of a group of library routines called *termios*. These routines are used to describe a terminal interface for asynchronous communications ports control. This group of routines includes tcgetattr, tcsetattr, tcsendbreak, tcdrain, tcflush, tcflow, cfgetospeed, cfgetispeed, cfsetispeed, tcgetpgrp, tcsetpgrp, and tcgetsid.

cftime Library routine used to convert the date and time into a string.

CGA (color graphics adapter) Outdated, low resolution, graphics adapter used to drive a computer's monitor.

change-modified Command in the Epsilon text editor that changes the modified status of the buffer.

change-name Command in the Epsilon text editor that changes the name of a command, function, or variable.

channel Path along which signals can be sent. Also, that part of a communication system that connects the message source with the message sink.

channel access In a network, the method used to gain access to the data communication channel that links computers. Three-channel access methodologies are local area network, token-ring Network, and polling.

char C programming language variable that can hold a single character.

character Datum that represents a single printable symbol. A character is usually, but not limited to, 8 or 16 bits. *See also* ASCII, character sets.

character-based program Program that relies on a built-in character set and block graphics rather than a windowing interface. Character-based applications take command-line input.

character device Device that provides a character-stream-oriented I/O interface or an unstructured raw interface. Devices that are not character devices are usually block devices. *See also* block devices.

character-device interface Conventions established for accessing character-oriented devices within the kernel. These conventions include a set procedures parameters that can be called to do I/O operations and parameters that must be passed in each call.

character-device table Table within the kernel that contains the device-driver routines that support the character-device interface for each device.

character set Group of letters and symbols comprising a complete set of characters.

character string Group of letters and numbers.

chargefee One of a group of commands, called *acctsh*, used for system accounting. This group of commands includes chargefee, ckpacct, dodisk, lastlogin, monacct, nulladm, prctmp, prdaily, prtacct, runacct, shutacct, startup, and turnacct.

char-to-string Function in the emacs LISP programming language that converts a character to a string.

chat To communicate in real-time with another user, usually by typing messages that appear on the remote user's screen.

chat script Series of requests and responses that allows a networking connection to be set up. For example, a chat script may send a phone number to the modem, wait for a login prompt, send a user name, wait for a password prompt, and then send a password.

chdir
1. In the C shell, another name for the cd command.
2. Library routine that causes a specified directory to become the current working directory.

check To examine the status of various attributes and operations of software or hardware.

check bits Bits held in a segment of data that are used to verify that the data are not damaged.

check box Iconic box that is marked to select the associated entry.

checkeq Command (BSD) used to check that .EQ and .EN delimiters are correctly matched in the specified file.

checklist File located in the /etc directory, that contains a listing of default file systems used by the fsck command to check file systems if none are given specifically.

checkmm Command used to check that troff Memorandum Macros (mm) have been used correctly in a troff document file.

checknews Command used to check if the user has unread news. Often, checknews is run in a startup file (such as .profile or .login) to alert the user that new news is available.

checknr Command used to check a list of nroff or troff input files for certain kinds of errors involving unknown commands or mismatched opening and closing delimiters. See also nroff, troff.

checksum Number computed arithmetically from a group of characters. The checksum is used to determine if the group of characters has changed. For example, when transmitting a file, a checksum may also be transmitted; when the receiving system recomputes the checksum and compares it to the original checksum, it can confirm that the file was received correctly. *See also* file transfer.

checkworld FMLI command that causes all posted objects with a reread descriptor of TRUE, to be reread.

Cherry, Lorinda Author of wwb (the Writer's Workbench), coauthor of the eqn utility, and coauthor of the bc and dc utilities.

chgrp Command used to change the group ID of specified files to a different, specified group ID.

child directory In a hierarchal directory structure, a directory of files that exists below or underneath a parent directory. The child directory name is listed after the parent directory name in a pathname. Also called a *subdirectory*.

child process Process that is a direct descendent of another process as a result of being created by the fork system call.

chistory Add-on package for the emacs text editor that implements a function for editing and repeating commands.

chkey Command that prompts for a password and encrypts it.

chkshlib Command used with C language programs to check for shared libraries.

chmod
1. Command that changes the access mode of one or more files or directories. This command can specify which users can read, write, or execute the file(s).
2. Library routine used to set the access permission portion of a specified file mode.

chown
1. Command used to change the ownership of one or more files or directories to a different user.
2. Library routine that sets the owner ID and group ID of a specified file or referenced by an open file descriptor to a specified owner and group different than the previous owner.

chpoll Device-driver library routine used by non-STREAMS character device-drivers that want to support polling.

chroot
1. Command that changes the root directory for a command.
2. Library routine that causes a directory to become the root directory.

chrtbl Command that creates character type and numeric layout files for single-byte locales.

chsh Command used to change the login shell field of your password file. The command takes a specified login name and shell for arguments.

chsize Library routine (XENIX) used to change the size of a file.

c-indent-level Variable in the emacs text editor, used in C mode to control how far statements are indented.

CISC Acronym for Complex Instruction Set Computer, type of CPU (central processing unit) chip, pronounced "sisk." Compare to RISC.

ckbinarsys Command used to check if a particular remote system can accept mail messages that contain binary data.

ckdate Command that prompts the user for a date. It also validates the user response and date.

ckgid Command that prompts the user for a group ID and validates the response.

ckint Command that prompts the user for a response and returns an integer value based upon the user's response.

ckitem Command that builds a menu and then prompts the user to choose from the menu of items.

ckkeywd Command that prompts the user for a response and returns a validated keyword.

ckpacct One of a group of commands, called *acctsh*, used for system accounting. This group of commands includes chargefee, ckpacct, dodisk, lastlogin, monacct, nulladm, prctmp, prdaily, prtacct, runacct, shutacct, startup, and turnacct.

ckpath Command that prompts the user, and verifies and returns a pathname.

ckrange Command that prompts a user for an integer between a specified range and determines whether this response is valid.

ckroot Command that sets the mount options for the root file system. This command is run automatically from the /etc/inittab file during system startup.

ckstr Command that prompts the user for a response and returns a string upon the user's response.

cktime Command that prompts the user for a response and returns the time of day upon the user's response.

ckuid Command that prompts the user for a response and validates a user ID upon the user's response.

ckyorn Command that prompts the user for a yes or no response and validates that response.

cl (Common LISP)
1. Version of the LISP programming language.
2. Add-on package for the emacs text editor that implements functions and macros for use in writing emacs LISP programs compatible with Common LISP.

c-label-offset Variable in the emacs text editor, used in C mode to control how far C labels are indented.

clari *See* ClariNet.

ClariNet Type of newsgroup, not formally part of USENET, that consists of information from commercial news services and other sources. The names of newsgroups of this type begin with *clari*.

class Pool of Internet Protocol (IP) addresses that define the logical size of a network connected to the Internet. Common classes are A, B, and C.

Class A network Logical Network connected to the Internet that can contain up to 16,581,375 host computers. Very few organizations are assigned a Class A address.

Class B network Logical Network connected to the Internet that can contain up to 65,025 host computers. As with Class A networks, very few Class B network addresses are assigned.

Class C network Logical Network connected to the Internet that can contain up to 254 host computers. Class C is the most commonly assigned network class.

class, scheduler *See* scheduler class.

cleanup After the processing of a program is complete, to return the system to the state it was in before the program started. This can include removing temporary files and releasing memory so it can be used by other processes.

clear
1. Command used to clear a terminal screen.
2. One of a group of library routines, called *curs_clear*, used to clear various parts of a curses window. This group of routines includes erase, werase, clear, wclear, clrtobot, wclrtobot, clrtoeol, and wclrtoeol.

clearerr Library routine used to reset the error indicator and EOF indicator to zero on the named stream.

clearok One of a group of library routines, called *curs_outopts*, used to control curses terminal output. This group of routines includes clearok, idlok, idcok immedok, leaveok, setscrreg, wsetscrreg, scrollok, nl, and nonl.

clear-rectangle Command in the emacs text editor that deletes the currently marked rectangle (the rectangular regions between the mark and the cursor).

clear-tags Command in the Epsilon text editor that deletes all tags in the current tag file. *See also* select-tag-file, tag-files.

C library Collection of functions and routines that can be compiled into a C programming application to provide a set of features. *See also* C.

click Action and sound of depressing a button on a computer mouse.

click-and-drag Action of clicking or selecting by pressing the button on a mouse and moving an icon or string of text from one position to another on a terminal screen.

clicking Depressing the button on a mouse while the mouse pointer is positioned on a screen object. For example, "clicking on an icon" means moving the mouse until the cursor is on the icon, then pressing and releasing the mouse button. If not otherwise specified, the leftmost mouse button is used. *See also* mouse.

click-to-type Method used by GUIs to control which window is active. With click-to-type, when the user moves the mouse pointer to a different window, the window doesn't become active until the user clicks in it.

client
1. Physical machine or workstation.
2. Process that contacts another host or server to request service. The client contains both procedures and specifications so that two machines can talk to one another over a network. The code is also called the client-side program in client-server application programming. *See also* client-server communication, server.

client caching Refers to a client computer storing information in local cache memory so it can be used in the near future. Client caching improves performance by storing data locally that might otherwise have had to be retrieved from the server system.

clients Set of workstations connected on a Network to a server with a distributed file system service.

client-server architecture
1. In systems other than the X Window System, client-server architecture refers to a system that enables one program (the client) to use a shared resource on a central machine (the server). The shared resource may be a database, an application, a file system, or some other computing resource.
2. In the X Window System, a computing framework that enables a program (the client) to run on a remote machine while the program that displays its results (the server) runs on a local machine. *See also* client, server, X Window System.

client/server model *See* client-server architecture.

clipboard Buffer that contains information selected and saved by the user. Most GUI programs (and some other programs) provide a mechanism for copying information to and from the clipboard. Because many applications can read it, the clipboard serves as a method for moving information from one application to another.

clipboard selection In the X11 version of the X Window System, the xclipboard utility stores the currently selected object(s) on the clipboard. The contents of the clipboard is the *clipboard selection,* as opposed to the *primary selection.*

C-list Linked-list data structure used by the system in supporting terminal I/O.

clnt_call Library routine from the group called *rpc_clnt_calls.* These routines allow procedure calls to be made on other machines across the Network by C language programs. This group of routines includes clnt_freeres, clnt_geterr, clnt_perrno, clnt_perror, clnt_sperrno, clnt_sperror, rpc_broadcast, rpc_broadcast_exp, and rpc_call.

clnt_control Library routine from the group called *rpc_clnt_create.* These routines allow procedure calls to be made on other machines across the Network by C language programs.

This group of routines includes clnt_create, clnt_destroy, clnt_dg_create, clnt_pcreateerror, clnt_raw_create, clnt_spcreateerror, clnt_tli_create, clnt_tp_create, and clnt_vc_create.

clnt_create Library routine from the group called *rpc_clnt_create*. These routines allow procedure calls to be made on other machines across the Network by C language programs. This group of routines includes clnt_control, clnt_destroy, clnt_dg_create, clnt_pcreateerror, clnt_raw_create, clnt_spcreateerror, clnt_tli_create, clnt_tp_create, and clnt_vc_create.

clnt_destroy Library routine from the group called *rpc_clnt_create*. These routines allow procedure calls to be made on other machines across the Network by C language programs. This group of routines includes clnt_control, clnt_create, clnt_dg_create, clnt_pcreateerror, clnt_raw_create, clnt_spcreateerror, clnt_tli_create, clnt_tp_create, and clnt_vc_create.

clnt_dg_create Library routine from the group called *rpc_clnt_create*. These routines allow procedure calls to be made on other machines, across the Network by C language programs. This group of routines includes clnt_control, clnt_create, clnt_destroy, clnt_pcreateerror, clnt_raw_create, clnt_spcreateerror, clnt_tli_create, clnt_tp_create, and clnt_vc_create.

clnt_freeres Library routine from the group called rpc_clnt_calls. These routines allow procedure calls to be made on other machines across the Network by C language programs. This group of routines includes clnt_call, clnt_geterr, clnt_perrno, clnt_perror, clnt_sperrno, clnt_sperror, rpc_broadcast, rpc_broadcast_exp, and rpc_call.

clnt_geterr Library routine from the group called *rpc_clnt_calls*. These routines allow procedure calls to be made on other machines across the Network by C language programs. This group of routines includes clnt_call, clnt_freeres, clnt_perrno, clnt_perror, clnt_sperrno, clnt_sperror, rpc_broadcast, rpc_broadcast_exp, and rpc_call.

clnt_pcreateerror Library routine from the group called *rpc_clnt_create*. These routines allow procedure calls to be made on other machines across the Network by C language programs. This group of routines includes clnt_control, clnt_create, clnt_destroy, clnt_dg_create, clnt_raw_create, clnt_spcreateerror, clnt_tli_create, clnt_tp_create, and clnt_vc_create.

clnt_perror Library routine from the group called *rpc_clnt_calls*. These routines allow procedure calls to be made on other machines across the Network by C language programs. This group of routines includes clnt_call, clnt_freeres, clnt_geterr, clnt_sperrno, clnt_sperror, rpc_broadcast, rpc_broadcast_exp, and rpc_call.

clnt_raw_create Library routine from the group called *rpc_clnt_create*. These routines allow procedure calls to be made on other machines across the Network by C language programs. This group of routines includes clnt_control, clnt_create, clnt_destroy, clnt_dg_create, clnt_pcreateerror, clnt_spcreateerror, clnt_tli_create, clnt_tp_create, and clnt_vc_create.

clnt_spcreateerror Library routine from the group called *rpc_clnt_create*. These routines allow procedure calls to be made on other machines across the Network by C language programs. This group of routines includes clnt_control, clnt_create, clnt_destroy, clnt_dg_create, clnt_pcreateerror, clnt_raw_create, clnt_tli_create, clnt_tp_create, and clnt_vc_create.

clnt_sperrno Library routine from the group called *rpc_clnt_calls*. These routines allow procedure calls to be made on other machines across the Network by C language programs. This group of routines includes clnt_call, clnt_freeres, clnt_geterr, clnt_perror, clnt_sperror, rpc_broadcast, rpc_broadcast_exp, and rpc_call.

clnt_sperror Library routine from the group called rpc_clnt_calls. These routines allow *procedure* calls to be made on other machines across the Network by C language programs. This group of routines includes clnt_call, clnt_freeres, clnt_geterr, clnt_perror, clnt_sperrno, rpc_broadcast, rpc_broadcast_exp, and rpc_call.

clnt_tli_create Library routine from the group called *rpc_clnt_create*. These routines allow procedure calls to be made on other machines across the Network by C language programs. This group of routines includes clnt_control, clnt_create, clnt_destroy, clnt_dg_create, clnt_pcreateerror, clnt_raw_create, clnt_spcreateerror, cln_tp_create, and clnt_vc_create.

clnt_tp_create Library routine from the group called *rpc_clnt_create*. These routines allow procedure calls to be made on other machines across the Network by C language programs. This group of routines includes clnt_control, clnt_create, clnt_destroy, clnt_dg_create, clnt_pcreateerror, clnt_raw_create, clnt_spcreateerror, clnt_tli_create, and clnt_vc_create.

clnt_vc_create Library routine from the group called *rpc_clnt_create*. These routines allow procedure calls to be made on other machines across the Network by C language programs. This group of routines includes clnt_control, clnt_create, clnt_destroy,

clnt_dg_create, clnt_pcreateerror, clnt_raw_create, clnt_spcreateerror, clnt_tli_create, and clnt_tp_create.

clocal Command-line option used with the stty command for enabling or disabling modem control. This option is used for terminals that connect to a computer via serial lines.

Clock Program running under Open Windows that displays a clock on-screen. It also lets you set and change alarms.

clock Library routine that returns the amount of CPU time used since the first call to the clock function. The time reported is the sum of the user and system times of the calling process and the terminated child processes. The time value returned is measured in microseconds.

clock_settime Set of Library routines used for high-resolution clock operations. These routines include clock_gettime and clock_getres. *See also* ctime, time.

clone STREAMS software driver that finds and opens an unused device on another STREAMS driver.

close
1. Library routine that closes the file descriptor indicates by fildes (an open file descriptor). All the file descriptors associated with an open file descriptor are closed with close and the open file descriptor, fildes, is freed.
2. Device-driver library routine that is called by STREAMS drivers through the cb_ops table entry for a device. The close routine ends the connection between the user and the device and prepares the device so that it is ready to open again.

close angle bracket
1. Symbol (>) used to delineate the closing of a header file name that is to be listed in an #include preprocessor

directive in a program source file.
2. In the shell, symbol used to direct output of a command to a particular file or device.

close curly brace Symbol (}) used to indicate the close of a C function definition.

closedir Library routine used for directory operations.

closelog Library routine used for controlling the system log.

close parenthesis *See* ")".

close square bracket *See*].

clrbuf Device-driver library routine used to erase the contents of a buffer. This function zeroes a buffer and sets the b_resid member of the buf structure to zero. *See also* buf.

clri Command that clears inodes by writing zeroes on the inode on a specified stored file system.

clrtobot Library routine (curses) used to clear the screen below the cursor.

clrtoeol Library routine (curses) used to clear the line to the right of the cursor.

cluster Logical grouping of contiguous physical pages of memory.

.clustertoc The cluster table of contents file. The .clustertoc file is an ASCII file that describes a hierarchal view of a software product. A .clustertoc file is required for a base UNIX operating system product.

cm_args Device-driver function used to input and output arguments into configuration management routines.

cmacexp Add-on package for the emacs text editor that implements a function for expanding.

cmdtool Program running under Open

Windows that opens a new UNIX command window.

cmn_err Device-driver library routine that displays a specified message on the console and/or stores it in the putbuf array. *See also* putbuf.

c-mode
1. Add-on package for the emacs text editor that implements a major mode for editing source code in the C programming language.
2. Command in the emacs text editor that enables Cmode, which is designed for editing programs in the C programming language. *See also* C mode.

CMOS Type of computer memory in a personal computer that maintains its contents, even after the computer is shut down. This memory holds the general hardware setup of the computer.

cmp Utility that compares two files and reports on the differences. *See also* comm, diff.

CMU Abbreviation for Carnegie-Mellon University.

code
1. Symbolic representation of information. For example, ASCII codes represent letters of the alphabet and other characters using patterns of seven bits.
2. Text of a program. For example, source code is the text of a program in its original (source) programming language.

code fragment Small sample of program code, often used as an example in books.

code review Practice used among computer software engineers to check each other's programming code for accuracy and consistency.

cof2elf Utility that converts one or more

files from COFF format to ELF format. *See also* COFF, ELF.

COFF (Common Object File Format) Old file format used for C object files. Executable and Linking Format (ELF) is the newer object file format. *See also* ELF.

Coherent Publisher of a UNIX version.

col Post-processor filter for the output of tbl or nroff text formatting that allows the output to appear in legible form on the screen.

cold start Initial phase of a bootstrap procedure. The term is derived from the assumption that the software knows nothing about the state of a machine that has just been turned on.

colltbl Command that reads locale specifications for collation order from a specified filename, then creates a shared library composed of four functions: strxfrm, wsxfrm, strcoll, and wscoll.

colon Character often used in UNIX configuration files to separate fields in an entry. In the vi editor, it is used in command mode to escape to an **ex** mode prompt.

colormap
1. Set of colors available in a graphical user interface.
2. In the X Window System Xlib library, a structure that maps color pixel values to RGB values.

COLUMNS Shell variable that contains the number of columns that can be displayed across the screen (Korn shell only). This variable is picked up by various application, including the vi editor.

columns Command-line option used with the stty command for setting the window size.

com (Commercial) Top-level domain name in the Internet. Hosts that fall under this domain are considered to be business (i.e., commercial) types of installations.

comb Command used to combine deltas to reconstruct an SCCS file.

comm Utility that compares two files, reporting on the lines that the files have in common. *See also* diff, cmp, uniq.

command Word typed on the command line that either specifies that the UNIX shell should take an action, or that it should run a program. Internal commands are commands that are processed by the UNIX shell itself, like cd and pwd. External commands are programs stored in files on disk. Different UNIX shells may have different internal commands, as well as different ways of interpreting commands. *See also* internal command, external command, program.

command-apropos Command in the emacs text editor that lists information about commands that pertain to a specified concept. This command is usually bound to the keystroke Ctrl-H A.

command-driven Type of software user interface. Command-driven programs allow the user to enter commands. Command-driven software is hard to learn because the user must type the correct commands, but it is usually flexible because the user's choices aren't limited by menus. *Contrast with* menu-driven.

command history Feature of the Korn shell and C shell that allows you to recall previously issued commands without typing in the entire command name. Once the command is recalled, it can be modified and entered.

command interpreter *See* shell.

command line Refers to the line where

you type in commands to be run by the shell interpreter.

command mode One of two operating modes in the ed or vi text editors. The other operating mode is input mode. In command mode, whatever you type is interpreted as a command. *See also* ed, vi.

command name abbreviation *See* alias.

command prompt One or more characters that indicate where you should type commands for the command interpreter.

command separator Character that separates one command from the next on the command line. The command separator is usually a semicolon. The command after the semi-colon doesn't start until after the first command is completed.

command substitution State in which the UNIX shell takes the output from a command as input to the command line. This is done by surrounding the command, and any options, with single quotes ('). For example, cat 'ls d*' displays the output of all files that begin with *d* in the current directory.

Command Tool Program running under Open Windows that opens a new UNIX command window.

comma-separated list List of items, frequently filenames or path names, separated by commas. Comma-separated lists can be used as arguments or options to some commands.

comment character Character that introduces a comment. All text after a comment character, or enclosed within comment characters, is ignored by the program reading the text. For example, in the C programming language, comments are introduced by the command characters /* and end with */. In shell scripts, the comment character is

a pound sign (#), and all text on a line following this character is ignored.

comment indentation style Method used by the emacs text editor when automatically indenting comment lines in a C, LISP, Fortran, or other program. The style is set using the fortran-comment-indent-style and comment-multi-line commands. *See also* indent-for-comment.

comment-start Variable in the emacs text editor, used in Fortran mode to contain the string that is inserted at the beginning of comments that appear at the end of Fortran statements.

communication To exchange information between computing entities.

communication domain Abstraction used to organize the properties of a group of computers that need to exchange information.

communication network Set of protocols or rules for manipulating names, addresses, and other intrinsic properties such as the ability to communicate access rights. This design makes it possible to write applications that are independent of the communication domains supported by a particular system.

comp Type of USENET newsgroup that discusses topics of interest to both computer professionals and hobbyists, including topics in computer science and information on hardware and software systems. The names of newsgroups of this type begin with *comp.*

Compaq Computer Corporation One of the world's largest manufacturers of personal computers.

compare-w Add-on package for the emacs text editor that implements a function for comparing.

compare-windows Command in the compare-w add-on to the emacs text editor that compares the contents to two buffers and displays the first difference it finds.

comparison operator Programming language operator that compares two values to determine if they are equal, if one is larger or smaller, or if a filename matches a filename pattern.

compilation-error-regexp Variable used in the emacs text editor when compiling programs written using the editor. The variable contains a regular expression that matches the error messages of many compilers.

compile To translate a high-level language into a form that can be understood and executed by a particular computer system.

compile-command Variable used in the emacs text editor when compiling programs written using the editor. The variable contains the shell command that compiles a program; its default value is make -k.

compiler Command that converts high-level program code into a form that can be used by the intended computing system. The C language compiler is the cc command. *See also* cc.

completion Feature of an interactive program in which the user types partial information and the program completes it automatically. For example, the C shell provides filename completion.

completion-auto-help Variable in the emacs text editor that controls whether emacs provides online help if completion is ambiguous.

completion-ignore-case Variable in the emacs text editor that controls whether emacs ignores case when doing completion.

completion-ignored-extensions Variable in the emacs text editor that contains a list of filename extensions that are ignored when emacs does completion on filenames.

compound statement In the C programming language, a series of declarations followed by a sequence of statements, enclosed in brackets. Typically, a compound statement processes all declarations, then executes the statements.

compress Utility that shrinks a file using adaptive Lempel-Ziv coding. *See also* uncompress, zcat.

compression Method for shrinking files so they use less space on disk or so that they can be transported more efficiently on networks or removable storage medium. File-compression programs include compress and pack. To uncompress a compressed file, use uncompress, unpack, or zcat. *See also* compress, pack, uncompress, unpack, zcat.

compver ASCII file used to specify previous versions of the associated package that are upward compatible.

concat Function in the emacs LISP programming language that concatenates strings.

concatenate To gather a series together, one after the other. The cat command can take a list of files and direct them, one after the other, to the standard output.

concentrator In computer networking, a device that provides power and a common interface for a group of Network devices. The devices may include bridges, routers, and Network servers.

concurrent processes Processes actively running on a computer at a given point in time.

cond Function in the emacs LISP programming language that contains pairs of conditions and statement blocks. If a condition is true (or t), the following statement block is executed.

condition Set of variables that enables threads to automatically block until a condition is satisfied. Condition variables may be used to synchronize threads among processes if they are allocated in memory that is writeable and shared by the cooperating processes. The set of condition variables includes cond_init, cond_destroy, cond_wait, cond_timedwait, cond_signal, and cond_broadcast.

conditional compilation To eliminate or pass through source text during preprocessing, based on a particular condition.

conditional expressions Set of programming statements that operate differently in different conditions.

condvar Set of condition variable routines designed to be used with mutual exclusion locks (mutexes). Condition variable routines signal the conditions of device states, data structures, and reference counts while keeping other threads from changing the condition. The set of condition variable routines includes cv_init, cv_destroy, cv_wait, cv_signal, cv_broadcast, cv_wait_sig, and cv_timedwait.

config File used with TCP/IP to configure Internet networking services. The file is located in the /etc/inet directory.

config file File used with UNIX serial communications that contains a list of parameters that can be set globally. For example, you can change the default parity and stop bits used by the system in this file.

configuration Process of setting, tuning and adjusting the operating system on a specific machine to accommodate a particular set of machines, group of users, or repeated requests for service.

configuration file File that contains parameters for a system configuration program. In UNIX, the /etc/config directory contains configuration files that describe license information.

configuration procedure Procedure followed by a system administrator for setting up a UNIX system. This procedure might include setting up hardware, software, and networks.

configure
1. To adjust or tune hardware or software for a particular environment. To set the adjustable parameters of a machine or set variable values in an application or operating environment for a user or network of users.
2. Command located in /etc/confnet.d/inet that is used for configuring communications boards and associated information for TCP/IP. Among other things, the configure command can be used to set netmask and broadcast information for the network.

connect Library routine that initiates a connection on a socket.

connection errors Refers to problems encountered during the process of establishing a connection between two communication entities.

connection establishment Phase of connection-oriented data communications in which two communication endpoints agree to communicate, as well as agree on the way in which they will communicate.

connection release Final phase of connection-oriented data communications in which the connection is ended between two communication endpoints and any necessary clean-up is done.

connectionless sockets Sockets that communicate by broadcasting information, rather than establishing a connection with the peer communication entity. *See also* connectionless mode.

connectionless mode Style of data communications in which each unit of data is sent individually, without being transported over an established connection. To achieve this, each unit of data must carry its own address information.

connection mode Style of data communications in which a connection is negotiated and established between two communication entities before data units are sent. Data units are then passed over that connection.

connection-oriented transports Communications protocols, operating roughly at the OSI transport layer, that establish a connection before exchanging data. X.25 is a connection-oriented protocol.

connect request Request passed to the user-request routine of a communication-protocol module as a result of a process making a connect system call on a socket. The result of this request is to establish a connection between a local and remote socket.

connld STREAMS-based module that provides connections between server and client processes.

cons Function in the emacs LISP programming language that creates a new list.

console System console device accessible through the /dev/console special device file.

console monitor Terminal attached to the console port on a computer. In UNIX, system messages are typically directed to the console monitor.

console terminal window Xterm or graphical window dedicated to receiving and displaying system and error messages to the user's screen. The terminal user interfaces (Open Windows, Motif, and X Window System) all have the ability to display a console window for system information.

constant Item in programming that retains the same value through execution of a program.

constant expression Expression that is made up only of constants and, therefore, doesn't change during the execution of a program.

Constraint Class of widgets used in programming Motif applications. Constraint widgets inherit resources and behavior from Composite and Core widget classes, and maintain that data for each child process.

continue Command that skips to the end of a loop in a shell program.

continue signal Signal that is delivered to a stopped or sleeping process, and causes that process to resume execution.

continue statement Program statement that contains a continue signal. The signal causes a process to resume execution. *See also* continue signal.

control character Set of nonprinting characters that provide special functions in UNIX. In ASCII, control characters are between octal 000 and 037. When written, control characters are often displayed as a caret sign and a letter (for example, ^D). To send a control character to UNIX, you typically hold the Ctrl key on the keyboard and press the associated letter.

Control key (Ctrl) Key on the keyboard labeled Control or Ctrl. The Control key is used as a shift key; that is, it is held down while another key is pressed. *See also* keyboard.

Control-key sequence Set of keystrokes that includes pressing the Control (or Ctrl) key.

controller Computer hardware device that provides an interface for other devices to connect to the computer. A hard-disk controller allows one or more hard disks to connect to the computer.

controller interface Means of connecting to a particular type of hardware controller. For example, a SCSI controller allows you to connect SCSI hard disks, tape drives, and other equipment.

controller lock To prevent further access to a controller until a specific event occurs, releasing the lock.

controlling terminal The terminal device associated with a particular session. Signals can be sent from the controlling terminal to processes running under that terminal to modify the behavior of those processes.

control request Request passed to the user-request routine of a communication-protocol module as a result of a process making an ioctl system call on a socket.

conv
1. Option used on the command line with the dd command. It specifies that the input be converted as indicated by keywords on the command line, for example, from EBCDIC to ASCII. *See also* dd.
2. Group of library routines used to translate characters from upper- to lowercase or to ASCII characters. This set includes toupper, _toupper, _tolower.

conversion set What iconv uses when converting files. *See also* iconv.

convert Command used to convert a file from a UNIX System V Release 1.0 archive file format to whatever the current archive format is. Using the convert command with the -x option, you can convert from a XENIX system archive file.

convert-mocklisp-buffer Command in the mlconvert add-on package to the emacs text editor. The command converts Gosling emacs mocklisp code to emacs LISP code.

cooked Command-line option used with the stty command for disabling raw mode.

cooked mode Refers to terminal settings in which the eot, erase, intr, kill, quit, and switch characters are handled and postprocessing is performed. *Compare to* raw mode.

coproc Group of coprocessing functions that provide a flexible means of interaction between FMLI and an independent process. This set of functions includes cocreate, cosend, cochck, coreceive, and codestroy.

coprocessor Computer chip designed to provide additional functionality to the computer's central processing unit (CPU). For example, the Intel 80386 CPU computer could be enhanced by adding a 80387 chip as a math coprocessor.

Copy In a graphical user interface, a menu item that copies the selected object from the current application and stores it on the clipboard. *See also* clipboard.

copyb Device-driver library routine that allocates a new message block. It copies it from a specified block.

copy files To make an exact replica of a file to a new name or a new directory.

copyin Device-driver library routine that copies data from a user-program source address to a device-driver.

copyleft Name sometimes used to refer to the copyright for GNU General Public License software from the Free Software Foundation.

copylist Library routine that copies a list of items from a file into freshly allocated memory, replacing newlines with null characters.

copymsg Device-driver library routine that is used to form a new message by allocating new message blocks and copying the contents from a specified message.

copyout Device-driver library routine that copies data from driver buffers to user data space.

copy-rectangle Command in the Epsilon text editor that copies the currently marked rectangle to a kill.

copy-region-as-kill Command in the emacs text editor that copies the currently marked region to a kill buffer. This command is usually bound to the keystroke Meta-W. In Epsilon, this command is called *copy-region*.

copyreq Structure used in a STREAMS M_COPYIN message block. The structure contains the ioctl command from ioc_cmd, full credentials, the ioctl id, the address to copy the data to or from, the number of bytes to copy, and private state information.

copyresp Structure used in a STREAMS M_IOCDATA message block. The structure contains the ioctl command from ioc_cmd, full credentials, the ioctl id, the status of the request (success or failure), and private state information from cq_private.

copyright ASCII file that contains a copyright notice for a package. This file is displayed on the terminal at installation time.

copyright messages Text messages displayed on a terminal that identify the legal owner of software, hardware, and documentation products.

copysign One of a set of math library functions used to return absolute values. The copysign function, which is expressed by copysign(x,y), returns x with y's sign bit.

copy-to-file Command in the Epsilon text editor that copies the current buffer contents to a file. *See also* write-file.

core Old-fashioned term for memory. In the 1960s and 1970s, most memory consisted of tiny, metal toruses (cores), strung in arrays. *See also* memory, RAM.

coreceive Command used with FMLI processes to read input from the coprocess identified by a process id. The output of coreceive is all the lines that were read, excluding the expect_string line.

core dump Refers to an operating system's attempt to save the contents of memory during a system panic.

core file File that is created by the system when certain signals are delivered to a process. The file contains information such as the state of the process at the time the signal occurred, the contents of the process's virtual address space, and the user structure. *See also* core dump, core.

core map Data structure used by the BSD UNIX kernel to manage main memory. The core map contains one entry for each cluster of main memory.

COSE Common Open System Environment, a set of standard interfaces intended to be useable on a wide variety of UNIX and UNIX-like systems. Members of COSE include major UNIX system vendors.

cosend FMLI command used to send strings of information to the coprocess. It sends the information via a pipe, then waits for a response from the coprocess.

count Option used on the command line with the dd command. To specify the number of input.

count-lines Command in the Epsilon text editor that displays the number of lines in the buffer.

count-text-lines Command in the emacs text editor, used in nroff mode to count the text lines in the currently marked region, excluding lines that contain only mark-up commands. This command is usually bound to the keystroke Meta-?.

cp Command that copies one or more files, either to new files with new names or to new files in a different directory. *See also* mv.

cperf Program that generates minimally perfect hash functions for sets of keywords. It is available from the Free Software Foundation.

cpi Abbreviation for characters per inch, the command-line option used with the lp command that sets character spacing across the line.

cpio
1. Utility that copies file archives to or from tape or disk, or to another location.
2. Command-line option used with the find command. It specifies that files found should be copied to a device. (It is used in SVR3 only.)

cpp C language pre-processor that is invoked in the first pass of any C compilation. *See also* cc.

cproto Command that comes with Linux that reads C source files and generates function prototypes for all the functions.

CPU *See* central processing unit.

cr
1. Command-line option used with the stty command, now outmoded. The op-

tion provides a way to slow down the output of carriage returns to very slow terminals.
2. Command-line option used with the emacs text editor to control the color used for the text cursor in the emacs window.

cr1 Command that implements the cr1 identification and authentication protocol. This command operates within the framework of the Identification and Authentication Facility (IAF).

cram CMOS RAM interface driver, a driver that provides an interface to the 64-byte battery-backed-up RAM. This memory area holds diagnostics and configuration information.

crash
1. Unexpected operating system failure.
2. Command used to examine the system memory image of a system by formatting and printing control structures, tables, and other information. Typically, this command is used in a postmortem fashion, to examine memory after a system or application has crashed.

crash dumps File containing a system memory image. This file can be examined using the crash or kdb commands.

cread Command-line option used with the stty command for enabling or disabling the receiver. This option is used for terminals that connect to a computer via serial lines.

creat Library routine that creates a new file or rewrites an existing one specified by a specific pathname.

create Command used in the shl program. This command creates a new layer. *See also* layer.

create-prefix-command Command in the Epsilon text editor that defines a new prefix key.

create-variable Command in the Epsilon text editor that defines a new EEL variable.

creatiadb Command used to create security tables. This command is often started automatically from the /etc/inittab file when the system is first started.

creatsem Inter-Process communications library routine that defines a binary semaphore and returns a unique semaphore number. The semaphor number is used by waitsem and sigsem calls to set parameters.

credentials In Remote Procedure Calls, this describes what client processes send to identify themselves to the RPC server. Credentials include the person's name, address, and birthdate, among other information. This is used in secure RPC.

cron Clock daemon that starts a process to execute commands at specified dates and times. Instructions for the cron daemon are stored in the crontab file. *See also* at, crontab.

cron file Option file used by the cron command. Located in /etc/default/cron, you can set options that effect cron logging activities. For example, options let you allow cron to log its activities, backup its log file to /var/cron/olog, set the number of last lines to keep in the log file, and set the maximum size of the log file before it is backed up.

CRONLOG Option used in the /etc/default/cron log file to set whether logging is enabled or disabled for cron.

crontab Command used to create crontab files. With this command, you can create, edit, remove, or list the contents of crontab files.

crontab file File consisting of a list of commands, one per line, with the date and time each command should be executed. The cron daemon reads the crontab file and executes the specified commands and the indicated times. Each user can have his or her own crontab file.

CRT (cathode ray tube) Vacuum tube used as a display screen for a terminal. CRT is often used to refer to a dumb, character-based terminal.

crt Option used with the mailx command to set that messages containing more than the number of lines specified be piped through a command such as pg.

crtplot Command (BSD) used to do graphical plotting on CRTs.

crypt
1. C library function for password encryption based on a one-way encryption algorithm with variations. Used with the setkey and encrypt functions, the crypt function provides encryption.
2. Along with setkey and encrypt, crypt is a front-end routine that invokes the encryption functions: des_crypt, des_setkey, and de_encrypt.

CRYPTKEY Environment variable used by the crypt utility as the password when encrypting files. *See also* crypt.

cs Command-line option used with the stty command for setting the character size as it appears on the screen.

cscope Program that finds code fragments in C, lex, or yacc source files. It is interactive and allows the user to search for functions, variables, and other items.

cscope.files File that contains the filenames of the source files to be analyzed by the cscope utility.

cset Group of wide character functions including cset, csetlen, csetcol, and wcsetno that are used to get information on a specified Extended UNIX Code set.

csh (C shell) Program and command interpreter with a syntax similar to the C language. It provides some convenient features not available in the standard UNIX or Bourne shell including filename completion, command aliasing, history substitution, job control, and some built-in commands.

C Shell UNIX program written to interpret and execute user commands. The C shell is both an interface for the user and a program that is written using the symbols and syntax of the C programming language. Its prompt is usually %. Its program name is csh. *See also* shell, csh.

.cshrc C shell file that contains aliases and variables that are set to customize the user environment. The file is usually configured by the user and stored in a home directory. It is executed each time the C shell is started. It is not used by the Bourne or Korn shells.

csplit Utility that splits one or more files into sections, separating the files based on information on the command line. *See also* split.

cstopb Command-line option used with the stty command for controlling the number of stop bits (one or two) per character. This option is used for terminals that connect to a computer via serial lines.

ct Command that dials the telephone number of a modem attached to a terminal and spawns a login process to that terminal. It is often used so that the host computer, rather than the user, pays for the telephone call. *See also* login.

ctab Command-line option used with the stty command for setting the ctab control character.

ctags Command used with ex or vi to create a tags file from a specified C, Pascal, Fortran, Yacc or Lex source.

The tags file gives the locations of specified objects such as functions and typedefs in a group of files. Using ex or vi and the tags file, these objects can be found quickly.

ctermid I/O function that generates the pathname of the controlling terminal for the current process and stores it in a string.

ctime
1. Command-line option used with the find command. It specifies files by the date they were last changed. *See also* find.
2. One of a group of library routines including ctime_r, localtime, locatimne_r, gmtime, gmtime_r, asctime, asctime_r, tzet, and tzsetwall that are called and used to convert date and time information into a string. *See also* time, timezone.

ctl-arrow Variable in the emacs text editor that controls how emacs displays control characters.

ctl-x-map Keymap in the emacs text editor for handling commands that are bound to multikey keystrokes. *See also* esc-map.

ctrace Utility that reads a C source file and creates a debugged version.

Ctrl key *See* Control key.

ctrl-prefix Command in the Epsilon text editor that treats the next keystroke as if the Ctrl (or Control) key had been pressed.

ctsxon Command-line option used with the stty command for setting the method of flow control.

ctype Group of C library routines or macros used for testing and handling characters. The macros include the following: isdigit, isxdigit, islower, isupper, isalnum, isspace, iscntrl, ispunct, isprint, isgraph, and isascii.

Each ctype macro tests for a specific condition of a set of characters.

cu Program that calls another computer or terminal, either over a direct line or by using a modem. The cu command is only available on UUCP networks.

CUI Acronym for character-based user Interface, a programming interface that displays only text (i.e., characters) to the user. GUI is the other kind of computer user interface, which can use text plus graphical elements, such as icons and windows.

current directory *See* current working directory.

current_field Curses library routine that identifies the current field on a curses screen.

current_item Curses library routine that identifies the current location of the cursor on a curses screen.

current job Job most recently started or stopped. The jobs command indicates the current job with a plus sign (+). *See also* job.

current working directory Directory from which relative pathnames are interpreted for a process. The current working directory for a process is set with the chdir system call. *See also* chdir, working directory.

curs_addch Group of library routines used to add a ch character and attributes to a curses window and advance cursor. This set of functions includes addch, waddch, mvaddch, mvwaddch, echochar, and wechochar. *See also* curses.

curs_addchstr Group of library routines that are used to add a string of characters and attributes to a curses window. This set of library routines includes addchstr, waddchstr, mvaddchstr, mvwaddchstr, and mvwaddchnstr. *See also* curses.

curs_addstr Group of library routines that are used to add a string of characters to a curses window and advance the cursor. This set of library routines includes addstr, waddstr, waddnstr, mvwaddstr, and mvwaddnstr. *See also* curses.

curs_addwch Group of library routines that are used to add a wchar_t character and attributes to a curses window and advance the cursor. This set of library routines includes addwch, waddch, mvwaddwch, echowchar, and wechowchar. *See also* curses.

curs_addwchstr Group of library routines that are used to add a wchar_t character and attributes to a curses window. This set of library routines includes addwchstr, waddchstr, mvwaddwchstr, mvwaddwchstr, and mvwaddwchnstr. *See also* curses.

curs_addwstr Group of library routines that are used to add a wchar_t character to a curses window and advance the cursor. This set of library routines includes addwstr, waddwstr, mvaddwstr, mvwaddwstr, and mvwaddnstr. See also curses.

curs_alecompat Group of functions added to the ALE library that are used for moving the cursor. This set of functions includes movenextch, wmovenextch, moveprevch, wmoveprevch, adjcurspos, and wadjcurspos. See also curses.

curs_attr Group of library routines that are used to manipulate the current attributes of a specified window. Attributes are a property of the character that is written into the window. This group of routines includes attroff, wattroff, attron, wattron, attrset, wattrset, standend, wstandend, standout, and wstandout. *See also* curses.

curs_beep Group of library routines, including beep and flash, that are used to signal a terminal user. The beep routine sounds an alarm on the terminal, and the flash routine flashes the screen. *See also* curses.

curs_bkgd Group of library routines that are used to manipulate the background of a specified window. This group of routines includes bkgd, bkjgdset, wbkgdset, and wbkgd. *See also* curses.

curs_border Group of library routines that are used to create borders and horizontal and vertical lines in a specified curses window. This group of routines includes border, wborder, box, whline, and wvline. *See also* curses.

curs_clear Group of library routines that are used to clear all or part of a curses window. This group of routines includes erase, werase, clear, wclear, clrtobot, wclrtobot, clrtoeol, and wclrtoeol. *See also* curses.

curs_color Group of library routines that are used to manipulate colors and color pairs on a alphanumeric terminal. This group of routines includes start_color, init_pair, inint_color, has_colors, can_change_color, color-content, and pair_content. *See also* curses.

curs_delch Group of library routines that are used to delete the character under the cursor in a curses window. This group of routines includes delch, wdelch, and mvwdelch. *See also* curses.

curs_deleteln Group of library routines that are used to delete and insert lines in a curses window. This group of routines includes deleteln, wdeleteln, insdelln, winsdelln, insertln, and winsertln. *See also* curses.

curses CRT screen-handling and optimization package. The curses package is a library of routines that allows over-all screen, window and pad manipulation, output to windows and pads, terminfo access, environment query, color manipulation, and independent terminal control.

curses.h Curses header file. This file contains symbolic constant and macro definitions for using curses. It also contains other header files such as <stdio.h> and <uncntrl.h>. Header files are listed in an #include preprocessor directive in each program source file that uses the symbolic constants and macros.

curses library Library of routines that enables the user to use the UNIX curses package, a terminal control and interface package. Curses routines are used to create character-based applications, as opposed to the X Window System which allows you to create graphical applications.

curs_getch Group of library routines that are used to push back characters from a curses terminal keyboard. This group of routines includes getch, mvgetch, mvwgetch, and ungetch. *See also* curses.

curs_getwstr Group of library routines that are used to get wchar_t characters from a curses terminal keyboard. This group of routines includes getwstr, getnwstr, wgetwstr, wgetnwstr, mvgetwstr, mvgetnwstr, mvwgetwstr, and mvwgetnwstr. *See also* curses.

curs_getstr Group of library routines that are used to get characters from a curses terminal keyboard. This group of routines includes getstr, wgetstr, mvgetstr, mvwgetstr, and wgetnstr. *See also* curses

curs_getwch Group of library routines that are used to push back wchar_t characters from a curses terminal keyboard. This group of routines includes getwch, wgetwch, mvgetwch, mvwgetwch, and ungetwch. *See also* curses.

curs_getyx Group of library routines that are used to get curses cursor and window coordinates. This group of routines includes getyx, getparyx, getbegyx, and getmaxyx. *See also* curses.

curs_inch Group of library routines that are used to get a character from a curses window. This group of routines includes inch, winch, mvinch, and mvwinch. *See also* curses.

curs_inchstr Group of library routines that are used to get a string of characters and attributes from a curses window. This group of routines includes inchstr, winchstr, mvinchstr, mvwinchnstr, and mvwinchnstr. *See also* curses.

curs_initscr Group of library routines that are used to initialize and manipulate a curses screen. This group of routines includes initscr, newterm, endwin, isendwin, set_term, and delscreen. *See also* curses.

curs_inopts Group of library routines that are used to control curses terminal input. This group of routines includes cbreak, nocbreak, echo, noecho, halfdelay, intrflush, keypad, meta, nodelay, notimeout, raw, noraw, noqiflush, qiflush, timeout, wtimeout. and typeahead. *See also* curses.

curs_insch Group of library routines that are used to insert a character before the character under the cursor in a curses window. This group of routines includes insch, winshc, mvinsch, and mvwinsch. *See also* curses.

curs_insstr Group of library routines that are used to insert a string before the character under the cursor in a curses window. This group of routines includes insstr, insnstr, winsstr, winsnstr, mvinsnstr, mvwinsstr, and mvwinsnstr. *See also* curses.

curs_instr Group of library routines that are used to get a string of characters from a curses window. This group of routines includes instr, innstr, winstr, winnstr, mvinstr, mvinnstr, mvwinstr, and mvwinnstr. *See also* curses.

curs_inswich Group of library routines that are used to insert a wchar_t character before the character under the cursor in a curses window. This group of routines includes inswich, winswch, mvinswch, and mvwinswch. *See also* curses.

curs_inswstr Group of library routines that are used to insert a wchar_t string before the character under the cursor in a curses window. This group of routines includes inswstr, insnwstr, winswstr, winsnwstr, mvinswstr, mvinsnwstr, mvwinswstr, and mvwinsnwstr. *See also* curses.

curs_inwchstr Group of library routines that are used to get a string of wchar_t characters and attributes from a curses window. This group of routines includes inwchstr, inwchnstr, winwchstr, winwchnstr, mvinwchstr, mvinwchnstr, mvwinwchnstr, and mvwinwchnstr. *See also* curses.

curs_inwich Group of library routines that are used to get a wchar_t character and its attributes from a curses window. This group of routines includes inwch, winwch, mvinwch, and mvwinwch. *See also* curses.

curs_inwstr Group of library routines that are used to get a string of wchar_t characters from a curses window. This group of routines includes inwstr, innwstr, winwstr, winnwstr, mvinwstr, mvinnwstr, mvwinwstr, and mvwinnwstr. *See also* curses.

curs_kernel Group of low level curses routines used inside of library routines to access curses functionality. This group of routines includes def_prog_mode, def_shell_mode, reset_prog_mode, reset_shell_mode, resetty, savetty, getsyx, setsyx, ripoffline, curs_set, and napms. *See also* curses.

curs_move Group of library routines used to move a curses window cursor. This group of routines includes the move and mvove routines. *See also* curses.

cursor Screen indicator that shows where the user is working. The cursor's shape depends on the program in use. It may be a blinking underscore, a box, an arrow, a little hourglass, a little pencil, or another shape. Some programs provide two cursors: the insertion point, where text appears when typed, and the mouse pointer, where mouse clicks take effect. *See also* mouse, pointer.

cursorColor Keyword used in a user's .Xdefaults file to configure the emacs text editor. It controls the color used for the text cursor in the emacs window, and is equivalent to the emacs-cr command-line option.

cursor movement key Key on the keyboard usually used for moving the cursor. Most keyboards have keys marked with arrows pointing up, down, left, and right, that move the cursor one increment in these directions, as well as Home, End, Page Up, and Page Down keys. Some programs, especially text editors, use other key combinations for moving the cursor. For example, in emacs, pressing Ctrl-F moves the cursor forward (right) one letter. *See also* arrow key.

curs_outopts Group of library routines that are used for curses terminal output option control. This group of routines includes clearok, idlok, idcok, immedok, leaveok, setsccreg,

wsetscrreg, scrollok, nl, and nonl. *See also* curses.

curs_pad Group of library routines that are used to create and display curses pads. This group of routines includes newpad, subpad, prefresh, pnoutrefresh, pechochar, and pechowchar. *See also* curses.

curs_printw Group of library routines that are used to print formatted output in curses windows. This group of routines includes printw, wprintw, mvprintw, mvwprintw, and vwprintw. *See also* curses, printf.

curs_refresh Group of library routines that are used to refresh curses windows and lines. This group of routines includes refresh, wrefresh, wnoutrefresh, doupdate, redrawwin, and wredrawln. *See also* curses.

curs_scanw Group of library routines that are used to convert formatted input from a curses window. This group of routines includes scanw, wscanw, mvscanw, mvwscanw, and vwscanw. *See also* curses.

curs_scr_dump Group of library routines that are used to read or write a curses screen from or to a file. This group of routines includes scr_dump, scr_restore, scr_init, and scr_set. *See also* curses.

curs_scroll Group of library routines that are used to scroll a curses window. This group of routines includes scroll, scrl, and wscrl. *See also* curses.

curs_slk Group of library routines that are used to manipulate soft function-key labels common on many terminals. This group of routines includes slk_init, slk_set, slk_refresh, slk_noutrefresh, slk_label, slk_clear, slk_restore, slk_touch, slk_attron, slk_attrset, and slk_attroff. *See also* curses.

curs_termattrs Group of library routines that are used to query a curses environment. This group of routines includes baudrate, erasechar, has_ic, has_il, killchar, longname, termattrs, and termname. *See also* curses.

curs_termcap Group of library routines that emulate the curses interface to the termcap library. These routines are a conversion aid for programs that use the termcap library. This group of routines includes tgetent, tgetflag, tgetnum, tgetstr, tgoto, and tputs. *See also* curses, termcap.

curs_terminfo Group of low-level routines used by programs that deal directly with the terminfo database to handle terminal capabilities such as function keys. This group of routines includes setupterm, setterm, set_curterm, del_curterm, restartterm, tparm, tputs, putp, vidputs, vidattr, mvcur, tigetflag, tigetnum, and tigetstr. *See also* curses, terminfo.

curs_touch Group of curses refresh-control routines that return information on a curses window. This group of routines includes curs_touch, touchwin, touchline, untouchwin, wtouchln, is_linetouched, and is_wintouched. *See also* curses.

curs_util Group of miscellaneous utility routines for curses. This group of routines includes unctrl, keyname, filter, use_env, putwin, getwin, delay_output, and flushinp. *See also* curses.

curs_window Group of library routines that are used to create curses windows. This group of routines includes newwin, delwin, mvwin, subwin, derwin, mvderwin, dupwin, wsyncup, syncok, wcursyncup, and wsyncdown. *See also* curses.

cuserid Library routine that generates a character-string representation of the name under which the owner of the current process is logged in.

custom Command used to install SCO UNIX or XENIX software packages.

cut
1. In a GUI, to delete the selected object from the current application and store it on the clipboard. *See also* clipboard
2. Utility that selects one or more columns from a text file containing information in a columnar format. Usually columns are separated by tab characters. *See also* join, paste, newform.

cut buffer In X Windows, a buffer for storing information cut (deleted) from an application. There are eight cut buffers, used for moving information from one application to another.

cvs Set of software release and revision-control utilities available from the Free Software Foundation.

cvtomflib Command used to convert XENIX OMF libraries to Executable and Linking Format (ELF) libraries. This command can be used with application packages having only OMF libraries that you want to run in an environment that supports ELF.

cxref Utility that reads one or more C source files and creates a cross-reference table of all symbols in the C code. *See also* cc.

cylinder Tracks of a disk that are accessible from one position of the disk-reading head assembly. *See also* cylinder group

cylinder group Collection of cylinders on a disk drive that are grouped together for the purpose of localizing information. For a file system, inodes and data blocks are allocated on a cylinder-group basis.

D

D. (data) Files In UUCP, files created when command-line options request that a source file is to be copied to the spool directory. The syntax for these files is D.systmxxxxyyy, where *systm* is the first five characters of the name of the remote computer, *xxxx* is the four-digit uucp job sequence number, and *yyy* is a three-digit job sequence number that is used if there are multiple data files (D.) needed for a work file (C.).

daemon Process (pronounced "demon") that runs in the background, performing a housekeeping task. For example, most UNIX systems have a printer daemon that listens for printing requests, then either prints the file or hands it to another process for printing. Many daemon processes on a UNIX system handle requests for networking services, such as login, routing, or connection serving. *See also* process.

dalign Command line option used with the cc C compiler. It specifies that the compiler should use double load/store instructions to speed up the resulting program. It is used only in Solaris 2.0.

DARPA (Defense Advanced Research Projects Agency) *See* ARPA.

DARPA protocols *See* TCP/IP.

dash *See* -.

DAT (Acronym for digital audio tape) Tape technology where the information is recorded as a digital signal instead of analog signal. It is used for backing up computers, as well as audio applications.

data Any information input to or output from a computer.

data blocks In STREAMS, the packets that carry data between STREAMS modules and drivers. This is opposed to STREAMS message blocks, which carry instructions for STREAMS components to interpret.

data_ahead Library routine (curses) from the group called form_data. These routines are used to tell if a forms field has off-screen data. *See also* data_behind.

datab Device-driver data block structure used to describe a STREAMS message.

database Any related set of data stored and processed by a computer.

data_behind Library routine (curses) from the group called *form_data*. These routines are used to tell if a forms field has off-screen data. *See also* data_ahead.

data encryption Refers to the special coding of data so unauthorized users cannot read or make use of it. The same algorithm used to encode the data is required to decode the data.

Data Encryption Standard Standard encryption technique specified by the NIST (National Institute of Standards & Technology) for encoding data intended for transmission on a public network. The standard uses a binary number as the encryption key, which provides 72 quadrillion combinations.

Data General Computer manufacturer founded by Edson de Castro in 1968. Their UNIX-based computers use the 88000 family of CPU chips from Motorola.

Data Link Layer Second layer of the OSI reference model for computer networking. This layer standardizes the services that provide data transmission between two communications nodes. These services may be actually provided by a variety of protocols, such as Ethernet or Token Ring communications protocols.

Data Link Provider Interface UNIX standard that, if adhered to, allows a variety of data link layer protocols to be used under standard higher-level networking protocols (such as TCP/IP or UUCP). By adhering to this standard, a networking board vendor can create standardized UNIX drivers.

data model Text that describes how the information, operators, and rules in a database are organized.

datamsg Device-driver library routine used to test whether a message is a data message.

data structure In the C programming language, a sequence of named members. Each structure member may be of a different object type. A structure is identified by the struct key-word.

data type Specific definition for a type of data. For example, numeric, boolean (true/false), alphanumeric are data types in most programming languages.

data validation Process of checking data so it meets specified criteria.

date Command that displays the current date and time, or that sets the system time.

DBM Data-base manager application that is supplied with BSD UNIX.

dbm Group of library routines (BSD) used as database subroutines. This group includes dbminit, dbmclose, fetch, store, delete, firstkey, and nextkey.

dbm_clearerr Library routine (BSD) from the group called *ndbm*. This group of routines is used as database subroutines. *See also* dbm_close, dbm_delete, dbm_error, dbm_fetch, dbm_firstkey, dbm_nextkey, dbm_open, dbm_store.

dbm_close Library routine (BSD) from the group called *ndbm*. This group of routines is used as database subroutines. *See also* dbm_clearerr, dbm_delete, dbm_error, dbm_fetch, dbm_firstkey, dbm_nextkey, dbm_open, dbm_store.

dbmclose Library routine (BSD) from the group called *dbm*. This group of routines is used as database subroutines. *See also* dbminit, fetch, store, delete, firstkey, nextkey.

dbm_delete Library routine (BSD) from the group called *ndbm*. This group of routines is used as database subroutines. *See also* dbm_clearerr, dbm_close, dbm_error, dbm_fetch, dbm_firstkey, dbm_nextkey, dbm_open, dbm_store.

dbm_error Library routine (BSD) from the group called *ndbm*. This group of routines is used as database subroutines. *See also* dbm_clearerr, dbm_close, dbm_delete, dbm_fetch, dbm_firstkey, dbm_nextkey, dbm_open, dbm_store.

dbm_fetch Library routine (BSD) from the group called *ndbm*. This group of routines is used as database subroutines. *See also* dbm_clearerr, dbm_close, dbm_delete, dbm_error, dbm_firstkey, dbm_nextkey, dbm_open, dbm_store.

dbm_firstkey Library routine (BSD) from the group called *ndbm*. This group of routines is used as database subroutines. *See also* dbm_clearerr, dbm_close, dbm_delete, dbm_error, dbm_fetch, dbm_nextkey, dbm_open, dbm_store.

dbm.h Header file (BSD) previously used with data-base subroutines. This file has been replaced by the ndbm.h header file.

dbminit Library routine (BSD) from the group called *dbm*. This group of routines is used as database subroutines. *See also* dbmclose, fetch, store, delete, firstkey, nextkey.

dbm_nextkey Library routine (BSD) from the group called *ndbm*. This group of routines is used as database subroutines. *See also* dbm_clearerr, dbm_close, dbm_delete, dbm_error, dbm_fetch, dbm_firstkey, dbm_open, dbm_store.

dbm_open Library routine (BSD) from the group called *ndbm*. This group of routines is used as database subroutines. *See also* dbm_clearerr, dbm_close, dbm_delete, dbm_error, dbm_fetch, dbm_firstkey, dbm_nextkey, dbm_store.

dbm_store Library routine (BSD) from the group called *ndbm*. This group of routines is used as database subroutines. *See also* dbm_clearerr,

dbm_close, dbm_delete, dbm_error, dbm_fetch, dbm_firstkey, dbm_nextkey, dbm_open.

dbx Source code debugger provided with Solaris 2.0. dbx can be used to debug C, C++, Fortran, and Pascal source code.

.dbxinit File containing commands for the dbx source code debugger.

dc Utility that performs arbitrary-precision integer arithmetic. This utility is not usually run directly, but is invoked by bc. *See also* bc.

DCE (data circuit-terminating equipment) Communications hardware device that takes data from a DTE (data terminal equipment) device and modifies the data so it can be sent to the intended recipient. A modem is an example of a DCE device, while the computer is a DTE device.

dclshar Program available from the Free Software Foundation that makes a shar-type COM file for VAX/VMS systems, for transferring file system hierarchies.

dcopy Command used to copy a file system to optimize access time.

dd Utility that copies information from one file or device to another. The dd command can also reformat the information while copying, including converting between ASCII and EBCDIC, changing capitalization, and changing block sizes. *See also* cp.

DDI/DKI Device driver interface/driver-kernel interface, programming interfaces used to write portable device-drivers.

DEAD Environment variable that lets you redefine where dead letters are sent. By default, dead letters are put into the dead.letter file in the user's home directory.

Dead letter Mail message the user has begun composing, but has discarded by hitting the break key twice in the mail or mailx program.

deadlock Error situation where two processes are waiting for a response from each other before continuing (also called deadly embrace).

deadly embrace *See* deadlock.

DEBUG Name of a signal which can be sent to a running process. This signal is used for debugging purposes (Korn shell only).

debugger Program used in debugging other programs. The UNIX system comes with many different tools for debugging, such as the kernel debugger (kdb), the symbolic debugger (sdb), and the crash utility.

debugger, kernel *See* kdb.

debugger, symbolic *See* sdb.

DEC *See* Digital Equipment Corporation.

Decimal Base-ten numbering system, which is the one used in daily life. *Compare with* octal and hexadecimal.

decimal_to_double Library routine (BSD) from the group called *decimal_to_floating*. This group of routines is used to convert records to floating-point values. *See also* d e c i m a l _ t o _ s i n g l e , decimal_to_extended.

decimal_to_extended Library routine (BSD) from the group called decimal_to_floating. This group of routines is used to convert records to floating-point values. *See also* decimal_to_single, decimal_to_double.

decimal_to_floating Group of library routines (BSD) used to convert records to floating-point values. This group includes decimal_to_single, d e c i m a l _ t o _ d o u b l e , a n d

decimal_to_extended

decimal_to_single Library routine (BSD) from the group called *decimal_to_floating*. This group of routines is used to convert records to floating-point values. *See also* d e c i m a l _ t o _ d o u b l e , decimal_to_extended.

declaration Programming statement that defines a specific part of the program, such as a variable name.

DECnet Networking architecture produced by Digital Equipment Corporation. DECnet is built into Digital's VMS operating system.

decode Process of taking a coded signal or file and creating the original, uncoded signal or file. *See also* encode.

decrement To gradually decrease the value of a number.

decrypting The opposite of encrypting. To take a file that has been encrypted (typically for security purposes) and returning it to its original form so it can be used. Decryption usually requires that the user have access to the program (or a related program) that encrypted the file, as well as the password used during the encryption process.

dedicated line Communications line used exclusively for communications between two nodes. This differs from a LAN, in which all computers broadcast information on the same wires.

default
1. The action that occurs if no other instruction is given.
2. In the C shell, a command that specifies the default case within a switch statement.

defconst Function in the emacs LISP programming language that defines a new constant value, including providing text to be included in the emacs online help.

define Statement used in the bc desk calculator to indicate the beginning of a function definition.

define-key Command in the emacs text editor that binds a command to a key.

define-mail-alias Command in the emacs text editor that defines an abbreviation for a user name or mailing list to use when addressing electronic mail.

defs Command-line option used with the ld command that causes an undefined symbol to cause a fatal error.

defun Function in the emacs LISP programming language that defines a new function. In LISP, defun is a function definition.

defvar Function in the emacs LISP programming language that defines a new variable, including providing text to be included in the emacs online help.

dejagnu Software-testing framework available from the Free Software Foundation.

delay Device-driver library routine used to delay the execution of a process for a specified number of clock ticks.

delay_output Library routine (curses) from the group called *curs_util*. This group of routines is used as curses utility routines. *See also* unctrl, keyname, filter, use_env, putwin, getwin, draino, flushinp.

delch Library routine (curses) from the group called *curs_delch*. This group of routines is used to delete the character under the cursor in a curses window. *See also* wdelch, mvdelch, mvwdelch.

delete
1. To remove one or more characters, files, or other data.

2. Command used in the shl program to delete a layer. *See also* layer.
3. Library routine (BSD) from the group called *dbm*. This group of routines is used as database subroutines. *See also* dbminit, dbmclose, fetch, store, firstkey, and nextkey.

delete-auto-save-files Variable in the emacs text editor that controls whether automatically saved backup files are deleted when the buffer is saved using a **save** command.

delete-blank-lines Command in the Epsilon text editor that deletes blank lines immediately above or below the cursor.

delete-char Command in the emacs text editor that deletes the character immediately after the cursor. This command is usually bound to the keystroke Ctrl-D.

delete-horizontal-space Command in the Epsilon text editor that deletes whitespace on either side of the cursor.

delete-indentation Command in the emacs text editor that joins the current line to the previous one, deleting the newline character between them. This command is usually bound to the keystroke Meta-^.

delete-line Command in the emacs text editor that deletes the rest of the current line, including the newline at the end. This command is usually bound to the keystroke Meta--Ctrl-K (that is, Meta-dash Ctrl-K).

deleteln Library routine (curses) from the group curs_deleteln. This group of routines is used to delete and insert lines in a curses window. *See also* wdeleteln, insdelln, winsdelln, insertln, winsertln.

delete-name Command in the Epsilon text editor that deletes a function, variable, or other named object.

delete-other-windows Command in the emacs text editor that deletes all but the current window. This command is usually bound to the keystroke Ctrl-X 1.

delete-rectangle Command in the emacs text editor that delete all characters in the currently-marked rectangle. *See also* kill-rectangle.

delete-window Command in the emacs text editor that deletes the current window. This command is usually bound to the keystroke Ctrl-X 0.

delete-windows-on Command in the emacs text editor that deletes all windows that contain information from the specified buffer.

delimit To append a special character at the beginning and end of a string; to enclose. For example, if a string is delimited by quotes, a quote character is appended at the beginning and end of the string.

delimiter Character used to separate characters or sets of characters from each other. For example, in a comma-delimited database, each field is separated from the next by a comma.

delsysadm Command used to delete a task or menu from the sysadm interface.

delta Command used to make a change to an SCCS file.

deluser Command used to remove a user's login from a system.

delwin Library routine (curses) from the group called *curs_window*. These routines are used to create curses windows. *See also* curs_window: newwin, mvwin, subwin, derwin, mvderwin, dupwin, wsyncup, syncok, wcursyncup, wsyncdown.

demangle Utility program for dealing with compiled programs, available from the Free Software Foundation as part of binutils.

density Refers to the concentration of data on a physical medium. For example, high-density floppy disks can hold 1.44MB of data, while low-density floppies can hold only half as much (720KB).

depend File (ASCII) that contains information about software dependencies for a particular package.

depth
1. Location of a file in the directory tree, measured by the length of the file's absolute pathname. The depth is the number of directories in the pathname.
2. Command-line option used with the find command. It specifies that find should navigate the directory tree by starting at the bottom and working up. *See also* find.

dequeue To remove packets of data that are waiting on a queue to be processed.

deroff Utility that reads an input text file that contains nroff or troff requests and macros, and creates a file without the requests and macros. *See also* nroff, troff.

DES *See* Data Encryption Standard.

describe-bindings Command in the emacs text editor that displays information about the key bindings in effect in the current buffer. This command is usually bound to the keystroke Ctrl-H B.

describe-command Command in the Epsilon text editor that displays information about a specified named command. *See also* describe-bindings, describe-key.

describe-copying Command in the emacs text editor that displays the General

Public License for emacs. This command is usually bound to the keystroke Ctrl-H Ctrl-C.

describe-distribution Command in the emacs text editor that displays information about ordering emacs from the Free Software Foundation. This command is usually bound to the keystroke Ctrl-H Ctrl-D.

describe-function Command in the emacs text editor that displays information about emacs functions. This command is usually bound to the keystroke Ctrl-H Ctrl-F.

describe-key Command in the emacs text editor that displays information about what command is bound to a specified key and what the command does. This command is usually bound to the keystroke Ctrl-H Ctrl-K.

describe-key-briefly Command in the emacs text editor that displays information about what command is bound to a specified key. This command is usually bound to the keystroke Ctrl-H C.

describe-mode Command in the emacs text editor that displays information about the current mode. This command is usually bound to the keystroke Ctrl-H M.

describe-no-warranty Command in the emacs text editor that displays information about the warranty that applies to emacs. This command is usually bound to the keystroke Ctrl-H Ctrl-W.

describe-syntax Command in the emacs text editor that displays information about the syntax table for this buffer. This command is usually bound to Ctrl-H S.

describe-variable Command in the emacs text editor that displays information about a variable. This command is usually bound to Ctrl-H V.

descriptor Word, such as an index entry, used to retrieve data in an information retrieval system.

des_crypt Library function for encrypting passwords. The basis of this function is a one-way hashing encryption algorithm.

desk calculator Program for doing simple calculations. In UNIX, the dc command provides desk calculator functions.

DeskSet Set of programs that run under Open Windows. The programs include File Manager, Text Editor, Mail Tool, and Command Tool.

desktop Graphical user interface used with standard UNIX System V Release 4.2 systems. This interface is based on the X Window System, Motif look-and-feel, and a set of windowing applications for administering and using the UNIX system.

Desktop Intro Program that provides an introduction to the Open Windows environment.

desktop publishing Application program for typesetting and preparing books, newsletters, and other printed matter. The most common UNIX desktop publishing programs are Interleaf and FrameMaker. *See also* word processing.

DESQview/X Program by Quarterdeck that allows DOS-based PCS to run the X Window System.

destination Resulting location for copying, printing, or other type of data delivery. In networking, the destination may be a host name and location in the file system to which a delivery is made.

/dev Directory under the root directory containing device-specific files.

devattr Command used to display the values of a device's attributes.

development tools Software routines and commands used by developers to more easily write programs for specific operating systems or environments.

devflag Name of the man page for the prefixdevflag variable, which contains a bitmask of flags used to specify a device-driver's characteristics.

devfree Command used to release devices from exclusive use.

device Any component, section, or peripheral of a computer system. Devices are always hardware, and often require their own, specific software called a *device driver. See also* device-driver.

device alias Alternate name for a hardware device. A device alias is usually a name that is more intuitive than the device name assigned by the UNIX system. *See also* device name.

device, block *See* block device.

device, character *See* character device.

device database File containing tags and definitions for the system's hardware devices. Applications such as sysadm and the UNIX Desktop require that devices be defined in a device database. *See also* device.tab.

device driver Software used to provide an entry point from the UNIX system to a specific hardware device. Device-drivers are built into the UNIX system kernel for those devices that are connected to the computer. *See also* device.

device files Files that allow access to a physical device. Device files are stored in the /dev directory.

device-independent color Color definitions that apply to any type of device.

Contrast with color definitions for specific screens and printers.

device name Name used in the UNIX file system to identify a particular hardware device. For example, most UNIX systems use *lp0* to identify the first parallel port.

device nodes File in the UNIX file system that provides access to a hardware device. A device is designated by a c (character device) or b (block device) in a long listing of the file (ls -l command).

device numbers Major and minor numbers associated with a device file that determine what physical device the device file accesses.

Devices file In UUCP, the file located in the /etc/uucp directory that defines the ports and devices used for UUCP communications on the local system. This file defines such devices as modems and LAN devices.

device.tab File located in /etc/device.tab that describes hardware devices available on the UNIX system. Besides defining the devices name and type, it might include information on how the medium associated with the device is formatted or erased.

devnm Command (used most commonly by the brc command) that identifies the device file associated with the mounted file system where the specified name resides.

/dev/null Special device used when output is to be thrown away. Output redirected to /dev/null is discarded.

devreserv Command used to reserve devices for exclusive use. To free the device, use devfree. *See also* devfree.

df Utility that displays the number of free disk blocks and inodes of all mounted file systems.

dfmounts Command used to display information about mounted resources.

dfshares Command used to list available resources from remote or local systems. This command is used to list resources for Network File System (NFS) as well as other distributed-file-system products.

dfstab File containing commands for sharing resources across a network. This file is located in the directory /etc/dfs/dfstab. Using dfstab, an administrator can centrally administer all the file systems that are shared from the local system to all other systems on the network.

Dhrystone Benchmark program for testing a general set of instructions. Dhrystones per second are the number of times a program can be executed per second.

diagnostics Messages or error codes returned by commands, intended to help the user determine what problems might have occurred with the application. Many UNIX man pages have a diagnostics section that lists the errors that might occur with the component and describes how to correct the problem, if appropriate.

dial Library routine that establishes an outgoing terminal line connection. The dial routine relies on the connection server to establish the connection. *See also* cs.

Dialcodes file Administrative file used with UUCP. In the Dialcodes file, you can set up abbreviations for telephone numbers that can be called into entries to contact remote systems (Systems file) or modems (Dialers file). The Dialcodes file is located in /etc/uucp/Dialcodes.

dialect Particular "flavor" of a programming language. Programming code compiled on different dialects of the same languages might not compile correctly.

Dialers file Administrative file used with UUCP. The Dialers file contains entries identifying different types of devices connected to your computer, including chat scripts needed to complete connections with those devices. In particular, this file has entries for different types of modems and direct connections.

dialog box Pop-up box in a graphical environment, giving instructions to the user.

dial terminal *See* ct.

dial UNIX computer *See* cu.

diff Utility that reads two files and reports on the differences. *See also* cmp.

diff3 Utility that reads three files and reports on the differences among them. *See also* diff.

diffmk Utility that reads two files and creates a new file containing troff change mark requests showing the differences.

difftime Library routine that returns the difference between two specified calendar times.

digest USENET group and mailing list activity whereby a group of articles are put together as a single unit. This method provides a more efficient way of transmitting information, while making it easier to follow a particular topic.

Digital Equipment Corporation (DEC) Computer hardware and software producer. Some of the earliest versions of the UNIX system ran on DEC VAX processors. DEC created the first computer to run UNIX (PDP-11).

digit-argument Command in the emacs text editor that specifies how many times to run either a command or the last defined macro. This command is usually bound to the keystroke Meta-*number*, where *number* is the number of times to run the command or macro. *See also* call-last-kbd-macro.

dingbats Set of fonts that provide special characters such as snowflakes, check-marks, boxes, airplanes, and a hand holding a pencil.

dip Software package that runs on Linux, providing dial-up services for SLIP protocols.

dir
1. Command implemented on some UNIX systems to display a DOS-like listing of a directory. The output contains each file name (truncated to eight characters), the number of characters in the file, and the date and time the file was last modified.
2. Section-4 UNIX manual page that describes the structure of a directory for different file system types.

dircmp Utility that compares the contents of two directories. *See also* diff, cmp.

direct access storage devices Devices, such as memory and hard disks, that allow direct access to data storage locations.

DirectColor Colormap used by X Windows to define the colors used on the screen.

direct memory access *See* DMA.

directory
1. Name associated with a collection of files. A directory is equivalent to a file folder in a GUI environment. Directories can also contain other directories.
2. Group of library routines used for directory operations. This group of routines includes opendir, readdir, readdir_r, telldir, seekdir, rewinddir, and closedir.

directory permission Permissions assigned to a directory that determine what the owner, group, or others can do with the directory. As with regular files, directories can be protected with standard read, write, and execute permission. The most common directory permission is 755, which allows anyone to change to the directory, execute, and read files, but only allows the directory's owner to create or modify files. *See also* chmod.

directory stack Stack of directories maintained by the C shell. The user adds directories to the stack using the pushd command and removes them using the popd command. The dirs command lists the directories on the stack.

dired Buffer in the emacs text editor that contains a directory listing to be edited, or the directory editing mode. Also a command in the Epsilon text editor that edit the contents of a directory.

dired mode Directory-editing mode in Epsilon, in which files in a directory can be renamed, moved, printed, or deleted.

dirent File format containing file-system-independent directory information.

dirname
1. Utility that converts a path-name into a directory name by discarding the filename. This utility is usually used with command substitution. *See also* basename.
2. Library routine that returns all but the last level of a specified path name.

dirs In the C shell, a command that lists the directories in the directory stack, showing the current working directory first. *See also* pushd, popd.

dis (disassembler) Utility that reads an object file and creates an assembler source file. *See also* assembler.

disable Command used to disable the specified printer. A printer can continue to accept and queue print jobs for later, so the print jobs will print when the printer is enabled again.

disassemble Command in the emacs text editor that enables a function for disassembling programs written in the emacs LISP programming language. *See also* C mode.

disassembler Program that reads an object file and creates an assembler source file.

discard Command-line option used with the stty command for setting the discard control character.

discipline Set of rules that a module follows to handle the interactions between processes. For example, line disciplines handle the flow of communications on a serial connection between the user process and the network.

discriminated unions Unions used with RPC and XDR that are more like Pascal variant records than typical C unions.

disk Device for storing information magnetically or optically. There are many types of disks, including fixed disks (or hard disks) on which data is stored magnetically on hard metal platters; diskettes (or floppy disks) on which data is stored magnetically on flexible plastic; and CD-ROMs, on which data is stored optically. Unlike memory, the information stored on a disk is saved when the computer is powered off. *See also* diskette, fixed disk.

diskadd Command used for initial set-up of new hard disk. Because diskadd is an interactive command, it prompts for information needed to set up the disk.

diskcfg Command used to configure system files for Portable Device Interface

(PDI) drivers. This command is often used in conjunction with the pdiconfig command, which gathers and delivers the configuration information needed by diskcfg.

diskette Removable plastic disk, also called a floppy disk, on which data is stored magnetically. The disk is enclosed in a protective sleeve or box. Diskettes come in several sizes, measured by their diameters; the most widely used sizes are 5-¼ inches and 3-½ inches. *See also* disk.

disksetup Command used to perform the low-level activities required to install the primary drive or additional drives. For example, it can identify a particular device as the one from which the system is booted.

diskusg Command used to generate disk accounting data. *See also* bfsdiskusg, sfsdiskusg, ufsdiskusg, vxdiskusg.

dispadmin Command used for process scheduler administration. It can list the scheduler classes configured for the system or change parameters associated with scheduler classes.

dispatcher *See* scheduler.

dispgid Command used to display a list of valid group names on the systems.

DISPLAY Environment variable used to identify the display used by X Window System applications. Because the X Window system is a networked graphical facility, the display may be the local display or any X Window System display terminal accessible on the network.

display Device that displays information from the computer to the user. Also called a *monitor* or *screen*. The most widely used type of display is the CRT, which looks like a TV. Other types of displays include LCD and plasma displays. Displays may use only one color (monochrome) or may provide full-color output. The quality of a display is also determined by its resolution.

display adapter Device inside a computer that connects it to a display. Display adapters, which are usually single printed circuit-boards, differ in resolution, speed, and ability to display color. *See also* display.

DISPLAYH variable FMLI variable that evaluates the height of the available frame display. This height is measured in total lines in the frame, minus the message line, command line, and screen-function-key label line.

displaypkg Command used to display all packages installed with the installpkg command.

Display PostScript Version of PostScript used to display PostScript language data on a computer's display. The NeXT computer uses Display Post-Script.

display-time Command in the time add-on package to the emacs text editor that displays the current time on the mode line.

display-time-day-and-date Variable in the emacs text editor that controls whether the display-time command also displays the day and date on the mode line.

DISPLAYW FMLI variable that evaluates the width of the available frame display.

dispuid Command used to display a list of all valid user names on the system.

dissass Add-on package for the emacs text editor that implements a function for disassembling emacs LIST code.

dissociate Add-on package for the emacs text editor that implements a function to scramble text at random.

dissociated-press Command in the dissociate add-on package to the emacs text editor that scrambles text in buffers at random.

distributed computing environment Method of connecting computers on a network that allows the computers to share essential services. For examples, different computers in a distributed computing environment might handle file sharing services, application services, and client services.

distributed file systems Method of connecting files and directories from one computer on a network to the file system of another computer. In UNIX, the Network File System facility is the most popular way of distributing file systems. NetWare performs essentially the same services.

distribution category Type of distribution used by USENET newsgroups. The distribution category determines how widely articles in the newsgroup are distributed. The most commonly used categories are world, can, eunet, na, and usa. There are also distributions for states, cities, regions such as the San Francisco Bay area, and individual organizations.

div Library routine used to compute the quotient and remainder of the specified numbers. *See also* ldiv.

dlclose Library routine used to close a shared object. *See also* dlopen.

dld Dynamic link editor available from the Free Software Foundation.

dlerror Library routine used to get diagnostic information.

dlopen Library routine used to open a shared object. *See also* dlclose.

dlsym Library routine used to obtain the address of a shared object symbol.

DMA (Direct Memory Access) Refers to the ability to transfer data to and from system memory without going through the CPU. This method of accessing memory can significantly increase CPU performance.

DMAABLEBUF parameter Obsolete, tunable parameter that defined the number of DMA pages to reserve.

DMA allocation routines Set of programming routines that let programmers interface with DMS controllers and work with the operating system to manage DMA transfers.

dma_buf Device driver structure for the DMA buffer descriptor.

dma_cb Device driver structure for the DMA command block.

dma_disable Device-driver library routine used to disable recognition of hardware requests on a DMA channel.

dma_enable Device-driver library routine used to enable recognition of hardware requests on a DMA channel.

DMAEXCL Tunable parameter used to restrict a four-channel DMA controller to only use one channel at a time. This feature prevents simultaneous transfers on separate channels.

dma_free_buf Device-driver library routine used to free a previously allocated DMA buffer descriptor.

dma_free_cb Device-driver library routine used to free a previously allocated DMA command block.

dma_get_best_mode Device-driver library routine used to determine best transfer mode for a DMA command.

dma_get_buf Device-driver library routine used to allocate a DMA buffer descriptor.

dma_get_cb Device-driver library routine used to allocate a DMA command

block.

dma_pageio Device-driver library routine that breaks up I/O requests into more manageable units.

dma_prog Device-driver library routine used to program a DMA operation for a subsequent hardware request.

dma_stop Device-driver library routine used to stop and release software-initiated a DMA operation on a channel.

dma_swsetup Device-driver library routine used to program a DMA operation for a subsequent software request.

dma_swstart Device-driver library routine used to initiate a DMA operation via software request.

DMD 5620 Terminal Bitmapped display terminal produced by AT&T. The terminal was an early means of providing graphical terminal features, such as multiple windows and icons, in UNIX.

dname Command used with the obsolete Remote File Sharing (RFS) distributed-file-system facility for reporting and changing the RFS domain name.

dn_comp One of a group of library routines used for making, sending, and interpreting packets among clients and Internet domain name servers. *See also* resolver, res_mkquery, res_send, res_init, dn_expand.

dn_expand One of group of library routines used for making, sending, and interpreting packets among clients and Internet domain-name servers. *See also* resolver, res_mkquery, res_send, res_init, dn_comp.

DNS *See* Domain Name System.

do Keyword in the Bourne and Korn shell, used in the do-for, do-while, do-until, and do-select statements. Also a keyword in the C programming language, used in do-while loops.

doconfig Library routine used to execute a configuration script.

doctor Add-on package for the emacs text editor that implements an Eliza-like game, which emulates a Rogerian psychiatrist.

doctor mode In the emacs text editor, a major mode for playing an Eliza-like game in which emacs emulates a Rogerian psychiatrist.

document Any related group of information, usually processed in a word processing or desktop publishing program.

documentation files Files containing documentation, either to be printed or displayed online.

Documenter's Workbench UNIX system software package, containing tools for text formatting. Besides text formatters, such as nroff, troff, and mm, it also includes tools for preprocessing tables (tbl), equations (eqn), drawings (pic), and graphs (grap).

document formatting Process of creating headers, footers, paragraph styles, and other elements that give a document a specific format.

DoD Department of Defense of the United States, funder of many computing projects, including the ARPAnet (precursor to the Internet).

dodisk Library routine from the group called *acctsh*. This group of commands is used for system accounting. *See also* chargefee, ckpacct, lastlogin, monacct, nulladm, prctmp, prdaily, prtacct, runacct, shutacct, startup, and turnacct.

dollar sign *See* $.

domain Hierarchical structure for organizing and uniquely identifying computers in a network. The Internet uses domain-naming structure to ensure that every node on the network has its own way of being identified. Domains contain one or more subdomains, separated by periods. For example, chris.homeboy.com identifies a computer named chris, within the subdomain homeboy, within the top-level domain com.

domainname Command used to get or set the name of the current, secure NIS domain.

Domain Name Service (DNS) Common misuse of the abbreviation DNS, which actually stands for Domain Name System. *See also* Domain Name System.

Domain Name System (DNS) Method of multipart host names used by the Internet. DNS allows host names to be made up of several parts, separated by dots. This service also allows names and network addresses to be centrally located for a group of computers. This method eliminates the need of administrators to keep complete lists of computer names and addresses on every computer on a local network.

DOOM Graphical 3-D game that runs on many different operating systems, including the UNIX clone Linux. In DOOM, you traverse a space colony filled with monsters, as you look for lost space marines.

done Keyword in the Bourne and Korn shells that identifies the end of a for, select, until, or while statement.

dos Group of commands used to access and manipulate DOS files. This group of commands includes doscat, doscp, dosdir, dosformat, dosmkdir, dosls, dosrm, dosrmdir.

DOS Acronym for disk operating system, an operating system patterned in some ways after UNIX that runs on PCS. Also called PC-DOS (the version marketed by IBM) or MS-DOS (the version marketed by Microsoft). *See also* operating system.

doscat Command used to copy one or more DOS files to the standard output in UNIX. It is part of a group called *dos*. This group of commands are used to access and manipulate DOS files from a UNIX system. *See also* doscp, dosdir, dosformat, dosmkdir, dosls, dosrm, dosrmdir.

doscp Command used to copy one or more DOS files in UNIX. It is part of a group called *dos*. This group of commands are used to access and manipulate DOS files from a UNIX system. *See also* doscat, dosdir, dosformat, dosmkdir, dosls, dosrm, dosrmdir.

dosdir Command used to list the names of files and directories in a UNIX file system as though they were on a DOS file system. It is part of a group called *dos*. This group of commands are used to access and manipulate DOS files from a UNIX system. *See also* doscat, doscp, dosformat, dosmkdir, dosls, dosrm, dosrmdir.

dosformat Command used to format a DOS floppy from UNIX. It is part of a group called *dos*. This group of commands are used to access and manipulate DOS files from a UNIX system. *See also* doscat, doscp, dosdir, dosmkdir, dosls, dosrm, dosrmdir.

DOS Merge Software package that simulates a DOS environment on a UNIX system. DOS Merge allows running DOS applications simultaneously with UNIX applications.

dosls Command used to list DOS directories and files in a style consistent with the UNIX system. It is part of a group called *dos*. This group of commands are used to access and manipulate DOS files from a UNIX system. *See also* doscat, doscp, dosdir, dosformat, dosmkdir, dosrm, dosrmdir.

dosmkdir Command used to make a directory in UNIX using the same syn-

tax you would use with the DOS mkdir command. It is part of a group called *dos*. This group of commands are used to access and manipulate DOS files from a UNIX system. *See also* doscat, doscp, dosdir, dosformat, dosls, dosrm, dosrmdir.

dosrm Command used to remove a DOS file. It is part of a group called *dos*. This group of commands are used to access and manipulate DOS files from a UNIX system. *See also* doscat, doscp, dosdir, dosformat, dosmkdir, dosls, dosrmdir.

dosrmdir Command used to remove a DOS directory from UNIX. It is part of a group called *dos*. This group of commands are used to access and manipulate DOS files from a UNIX system. *See also* doscat, doscp, dosdir, dosformat, dosmkdir, dosls, dosrm.

dot (.)
1. Way of specifying the current directory. For example, to copy a file to the current directory you can enter cp file . where *file* is the name of the file you want to copy.
2. Character used to separate elements, such as the elements of an Internet domain name.

dot dot (..) Way of specifying the parent directory for the current directory. For example, to move a file up one directory, you can enter mv file .. where *file* is the name of the file you want to move.

dot file *See* hidden file.

dot-matrix printer Printer that presses a ribbon against paper using a grid (or matrix) of tiny pins, each of which makes a dot on the page. Dot-matrix printers are one type of impact printer. *See also* printer.

double-clicking Depressing and releasing the mouse button twice in rapid succession. Unless otherwise indicated, the leftmost mouse button is used. *See also* mouse.

double-density Type of floppy disk that holds twice as much data as a single-density type.

double-dot *See* dot dot.

double quote *See* quote.

double_to_decimal Library routine (BSD) from the group called *floating_to_decimal*. This group of routines is used to convert floating-point values to decimal records. *See also* s i n g l e _t o _d e c i m a l, extended_to_decimal.

doupdate Library routine (curses) from the group called *curs_refresh*. This group of routines is used to refresh curses windows and lines. *See also* refresh, wrefresh, wnoutrefresh, redrawwin, wredrawln.

do-while statement Programming statement that allows an operation to continue while a particular circumstance is still true.

down Term indicating that a computer is not operating.

downcase-region Command in the emacs text editor that converts all letters in the currently-marked region to lowercase. This command is usually bound to the keystroke Ctrl-X Ctrl-L.

downcase-word Command in the emacs text editor that converts all letters in the current word (or the previous word, if the argument is negative) to lowercase. This command is usually bound to the keystroke Meta-L.

down-line Command in the Epsilon text editor that moves the cursor to the next line. This is the same as the emacs next-line command.

down-list Command in the emacs text editor in LISP mode to move the cursor forward and down by one parenthesis level. This command is usually bound to the keystroke Meta-Ctrl-D.

download
1. To transfer a file from one computer to another, usually from a larger (more powerful) computer to a smaller (less powerful) one. *Compare with* upload, file transfer.
2. Command used to download host-resident PostScript Type 1 fonts.

downstream In STREAMS, the direction that messages travel from the Stream head (i.e. the device accessible to the application) to the driver. This is also referred to as the write-side of the STREAMS driver.

downtime Period of time that a computer system or network is inoperable (down).

downward compatible Refers to when a software or hardware feature created for a particular version of an operating system or compatible program that will work with an earlier version of the system or program. Compare to upward compatible.

dpost Utility post-processor that reads a text file formatted with troff requests and macros and creates a PostScript program that prints the text. *See also* troff.

drag-and-drop (also called dragging) In graphical user interfaces, the process of positioning the mouse cursor over an object (such as an icon for a file), pressing and holding the left mouse button, dragging the object to a new location, and releasing the mouse button.

dragging *See* drag-and-drop.

draino Library routine (curses) from the group called curs_util. This group of routines is used as curses utility routines. *See also* unctrl, keyname, filter, use_env, putwin, getwin, delay_output, flushinp.

drand48 One of a group of library routine used to generate uniformly distributed pseudo-random numbers. *See also* erand48, lrand48, nrand48, mrand48, jrand48, srand48 seed48, lcong48.

drawing area In a graphics application, the area within a window in which graphics can be created.

drawing direction In the emacs text editor in picture mode, direction in which the picture-motion command draws a line.

driver *See* device driver.

Driver-Kernel Interface *See* DDI/DKI.

drv_getparm Device-driver library routine used to retrieve kernel state information.

drv_hztousec Device-driver library routine that is used to convert clock ticks to microseconds.

drv_priv Device-driver library routine used to determine whether credentials are privileged.

drv_setparm Device-driver library routine used to set kernel state information.

drv_usectohz Device-driver library routine used to convert microseconds to clock ticks.

drv_usecwait Device-driver library routine used to wait for specified interval.

DSP Abbreviation for driver software package, method of creating and installing software packages for UNIX device-drivers. DSPs are used in conjunction with the UNIX packaging tools idcheck, idinstall, idbuild, and idtune.

DSTFLAG Tunable parameter that sets

the daylight-savings-time flag for XE-NIX applications.

dsusp Command-line option used with the stty command for setting the dsusp control character.

dtimeout Device-driver library routine used to execute a function on a specified processor after a specified length of time.

DTP Abbreviation for desktop publishing.

dtrxoff Command-line option used with the stty command for setting the method of flow control.

du Command used to display how storage space is used on the disk. It stands for *disk usage*. The du command lists how many blocks are used by each directory.

dumb terminal Refers to a terminal that has no processing power of its own. Such terminals simply receive and transmit characters and display them on the screen. *See also* terminal.

dump
1. Command used to dump selected parts of an object file.
2. File that contains keywords recognized by the timeout code.
3. To take the contents of memory and place it in a file that can be evaluated for problems.

dungeon Text-based adventure game, based on old adventure games. In dungeon, you make your way through the world of dungeons and dragons using typed commands.

dup Library routine used to duplicate an open file descriptor.

dup2 Library routine used to duplicate an open file descriptor.

dupb Device-driver library routine used to duplicate a message block.

dup_field Library routine (curses) from the group called *form_field_new*. This group of routines is used to create and destroy forms fields. *See also* new_field, link_field, free_field.

dupmsg Device-driver library routine used to duplicate a message.

dupwin Library routine (curses) from the group called *curs_window*. These routines are used to create curses windows. *See also* curs_window: newwin, delwin, mvwin, subwin, derwin, mvderwin, wsyncup, syncok, wcursyncup, wsyncdown.

DVI Format used for files that are created by TeX document processing tools.

dynamic addressing Method of network addressing used by RPC whereby the listener daemon asks the particular transport provider to select a transport address at the time the listener starts listening for a service.

dynamically loadable modules (DLMs) Operating system feature that lets you add device-drivers or other kernel modules to a running UNIX system. You don't have to rebuild the kernel or reboot the system for the modules to take effect.

dynamic dependency Refers to shared objects that would be loaded if a file were executed.

dynamic_field_info Library routine from the group called *form_field_info*. This group of routines is used to get forms field characteristics. *See also* field_info, dynamic_field_info.

dynamic linking Method of mapping the entire contents of a shared object into a virtual address space of the process at run time. This shared object is then available to other processes so the object, such as a shared library, only needs to be copied into memory once

on the computer.

dynamic rerouting Method of routing network messages that allows the route to be determined dynamically. If a network connection fails, dynamic rerouting allows messages to detour around the failure.

E

EBCDIC Acronym for the Extended Binary-Coded Decimal Interchange Code designed for representing data. This eight-bit code, developed and used mainly by IBM, allows 256 possible character combinations. ASCII is the other standard code for representing character sets. *See also* ASCII.

ebcdic Option used on the command line with the dd command. It specifies that the information be converted from ASCII to EBCDIC. *See also* dd.

EBUSY error code Value that is returned if an attempt to access a device fails. The reason might be that an attempt was made to mount a device that was already mounted, to unmount a device that is in use, or to enable accounting when accounting is currently enabled.

ecc Error-correction checking program available from the Free Software Foundation. The ecc command uses Reed-Solomon error correction.

echistory Add-on package for the emacs text editor that implements a major mode for editing and repeating commands.

echo
1. Command used to display characters on a screen.
2. Library routine (curses) from the group called *curs_inopts*. This group of routines is used for curses terminal input option control. *See also* cbreak, nocbreak, noecho, halfdelay, intrflush, keypad, meta, nodelay, notimeout, raw, noraw, noqiflush, qiflush, timeout, wtimeout, typeahead.

echoctl Command-line option used with the stty command for selecting how control characters typed at the keyboard are echoed back to the terminal. This option is used for terminals that connect to a computer via serial lines.

echoe Command-line option used with the stty command for selecting how the erase character (usually # or Ctrl-H) typed at the keyboard is echoed back to the terminal. This option is used for terminals that connect to a computer via serial lines.

echok Command-line option used with the stty command for selecting how the kill character (usually @ or Ctrl-U) typed at the keyboard are echoed back to the terminal (NL after KILL). This option is used for terminals that connect to a computer via serial lines.

echoke Command-line option used with the stty command for selecting how the kill character typed at the keyboard is echoed back to the terminal (BS-SP-BS erase entire line). This option is used for terminals that connect to a computer via serial lines.

echo-keystrokes Variable in the emacs text editor that controls whether emacs displays prefixes for unfinished commands in the minibuffer. That is, when the user enters a multikey keystroke (such as Ctrl-X Ctrl-C), this variable controls whether the first keystroke (Ctrl-X) is displayed in the minibuffer until the user enters the second keystroke (Ctrl-C).

echonl Command-line option used with the stty command for selecting whether newlines (ASCII character code 10) typed at the keyboard are echoed back to the terminal. This option is used for terminals that connect to a computer via serial lines.

echoprt Command-line option used with the stty command for selecting how erase characters typed at the keyboard are echoed back to the terminal. This option is used for terminals that connect to a computer via serial lines.

econvert One of a group of library routine (BSD) used for output conversion. *See also* fconvert, gconvert, seconvert, sfconvert, sgconvert.

ecvt One of a group of library routines used to convert floating-point numbers to strings. *See also* ecvtl, fcvt, fcvtl, gcvt, gcvtl.

ecvtl One of a group of library routines used to convert floating-point numbers to strings. *See also* ecvt, fcvt, fcvtl, gcvt, gcvtl.

ed Command used to edit text. The ed text editor is the standard line editor for UNIX. Because terminals are more sophisticated today, and support features that allow full-screen editors to be used, vi and emacs have all but replaced ed as the standard text editor.

edata Represents the address of the first address above the initialized data region in a program.

edit Command name for a text editor that is a variant of the ex editor.

edit-abbrevs Command in the emacs text editor that allows the user to modify word abbreviations.

Edit button Button available on most graphical user interfaces that pulls down a menu for text manipulation or file manipulation, depending on the type of window. Text functions can include cut, paste, delete, and undo. File editing functions can include copy, move, delete, select all, and rename.

edit-options Command in the options add-on package to the emacs text editor that sets emacs variables.

editor Program designed for editing text files. For example, ed and vi are editor programs.

edit-picture Command in the emacs text editor used to enter picture mode.

edit-tab-stops Command in the emacs text editor that allows the user to set the tab stops. It displays a tab-stops buffer.

edquota Command used to edit user quotas for ufs file system. Quotas limit the amount of disk space that a particular user may use in a selected file system.

edsysadm Command used to edit the sysadm interface.

edt-emulation-on Command in the edt add-on package to the emacs text editor. The command enables emulation of the VAX/VMS EDT editor.

edu (Educational) Top-level domain name in the Internet domain name hierarchy. The edu domain contains educational institutions, such as colleges and universities.

edvtoc Command used to edit a VTOC (volume table of contents).

ef Command-line option used with the test command in the Korn shell. This option determines if two filenames refer (via links) to the same file contents.

EFAULT error code Value that is returned to a system call where a bad address was encountered while accessing the hardware.

effective group ID Group ID that is in effect during a particular operation. Using SET-GID bits, a utility can run with group permissions that are different than those assigned to the user running the utility.

effective user ID User ID that is in effect during a particular operation. Using SET-UID bits, a utility can run with user permissions that are different than those assigned to the user running the utility.

EFT Data Types Types of data (expanded fundamental types) that can exist in standard UNIX System V file systems to extend the available file system attributes.

EGA (enhanced graphics adapter) Medium-resolution (640x350) video standard for IBM-compatible PCS that predates the VGA (video graphics array) video standard.

egrep Command used to search a file for a specified pattern. *See also* grep.

eign File containing words to be ignored by the ptx command when creating a permuted index.

EINVAL error code Error-return value indicating that an invalid argument was entered.

EISA (extended industry standard architecture) 32-bit bus standard based on the standard AT bus architecture. It was developed by supporters of the AT bus after IBM's 32 bit Micro Channel architecture became available.

ek Command-line option used with the stty command for resetting the erase and kill characters to # and @, respectively.

.el File extension for files containing emacs LISP source code.

.elc File extension for files containing byte-compiled emacs LISP source code.

electric-command-history Command in the echistory add-on package to the emacs text editor that allows the user to edit and repeat emacs commands.

electric nroff mode In the emacs text editor, a minor mode for editing files to be formatted using nroff or a related text formatter. This mode allows the user to insert pairs of formatting codes quickly.

electric-nroff-mode Command in the emacs text editor, used in nroff mode to enter electric nroff mode.

electric-nroff-newline Command in the emacs text editor, used in electric nroff mode to automatically enter the nroff macro that completes the pair started on the current line. For example, if the user entered a macro to begin italics, this command would automatically enter the matching macro to end italics. This command is usually bound to the keystroke Ctrl-J.

electronic mail *See* e-mail.

electronic publishing Process of producing documents intended to be distributed and read online. Often these documents will contain links, allowing users to jump from one point in a document to a related subject in another document.

ELF Acronym for executable and linking format, standard file format for executable files in UNIX System V. It replaces the former COFF standard.

elf Object file access library.

ELF file File in the ELF format. *See also* ELF.

elf32_fsize Library routine returns the size of an object file. *See also* elf_fsize.

elf32_getehdr Library routine from the group called *elf_getehdr*. This group of routines is used to retrieve class-dependent object file header. *See also* elf32_newehdr.

elf32_getphdr Library routine from the group called *elf_getphdr*. This group of routines is used to retrieve a class-dependent program header table. See also elf32_newphdr.

elf32_getshdr Library routine used to retrieve class-dependent section header. See also elf_getshdr

elf32_newehdr Library routine from the group called *elf_getehdr*. This group of routines is used to retrieve class-dependent object file headers. *See also* elf32_getehdr.

elf32_newphdr Library routine from the group called *elf_getphdr*. This group of routines is used to retrieve a class-dependent program header table. See also elf32_getphdr.

elf32_xlatetof Library routine from the group called *elf_xlate*. This group of routines is used for class-dependent data translation operations. See also elf32_xlatetom.

elf32_xlatetom Library routine from the group called *elf_xlate*. This group of routines is used for class-dependent data translation operations. See also elf32_xlatetof.

elf_begin One of a series of library routines used together to process ELF object files. *See also* elf_next, elf_rand, elf_end.

elf_cntl Library routine used to control an ELF file descriptor.

elf_end One of a series of library routines used together to process ELF object files. *See also* elf_begin, elf_next, elf_rand.

elf_errmsg Library routine from the group called *elf_error*. This group of routines is used for ELF file error-handling. *See also* elf_errno.

elf_errno Library routine from the group called *elf_error*. This group of routines is used for ELF file error-handling. *See also* elf_errmsg.

elf_error Group of library routines used for ELF file error-handling. This group of routines include elf_errmsg and elf_errno.

elf_fill Library routine used to set the file byte for ELF files.

elf_flag Group of library routines used to manipulate flags on ELF files. This group of routines includes elf_flagdata, elf_flagehdr, elf_flagelf, elf_flagphdr, elf_flagscn, elf_flagshdr.

elf_flagdata Library routine from the group called *elf_flag*. This group of routines is used to manipulate flags on ELF files. *See also* elf_flagehdr, elf_flagelf, elf_flagphdr, elf_flagscn, elf_flagshdr.

elf_flagehdr Library routine from the group called *elf_flag*. This group of routines is used to manipulate flags on ELF files. *See also* elf_flagdata, elf_flagelf, elf_flagphdr, elf_flagscn, elf_flagshdr.

elf_flagelf Library routine from the group called *elf_flag*. This group of routines is used to manipulate flags on ELF files. *See also* elf_flagdata, elf_flagehdr, elf_flagphdr, elf_flagscn, elf_flagshdr.

elf_flagphdr Library routine from the group called *elf_flag*. This group of routines is used to manipulate flags on ELF files. *See also* elf_flagdata, elf_flagehdr, elf_flagelf, elf_flagscn, elf_flagshdr.

elf_flagscn Library routine from the group called *elf_flag*. This group of routines is used to manipulate flags on ELF files. *See also* elf_flagdata, elf_flagehdr, elf_flagelf, elf_flagphdr, elf_flagshdr.

elf_flagshdr Library routine from the group called *elf_flag*. This group of routines is used to manipulate flags on ELF files. *See also* elf_flagdata, elf_flagehdr, elf_flagelf, elf_flagphdr, elf_flagscn.

elf_fsize Name of the section 3 man page describing the elf32_fsize library routine. *See also* elf32_fsize.

elf_getarhdr Library routine used to retrieve archive member header.

elf_getarsym Library routine used to retrieve archive symbol table.

elf_getbase Library routine used to get the base offset for an object file.

elf_getdata One of a group of library routines used to get section data. *See also* elf_newdata, elf_rawdata.

elf_getehdr Group of library routines used to retrieve class-dependent object file header. This group of routines includes elf32_getehdr and elf32_newehdr.

elf_getident Library routine used to retrieve file identification data.

elf_getphdr Group of library routines used to retrieve a class-dependent program header table. This group of routines includes the routines elf32_getphdr, and elf32_newphdr.

elf_getscn One of a group of library rou-
tines used to get section information. *See also* elf_ndxscn, elf_newscn, elf_nextscn.

elf_getshdr Name of the man page describing the elf32_getshdr library routine. *See also* elf32_getshrd.

elf_hash Library routine used to compute the hash value.

elf_kind Library routine used to determine the file type.

elf_ndxscn One of a group of library routines used to get section information. *See also* elf_getscn, elf_newscn, elf_nextscn.

elf_newdata One of a group of library routines used to get section data. *See also* elf_getdata, elf_rawdata.

elf_newscn One of a group of library routines used to get section information. *See also* elf_getscn, elf_ndxscn, elf_nextscn.

elf_next One of a series of library routines used together to process ELF object files. *See also* elf_begin, elf_rand, elf_end.

elf_nextscn One of a group of library routines used to get section information. *See also* elf_getscn, elf_ndxscn, elf_newscn.

elf_rand One of a series of library routines used together to process ELF object files. *See also* elf_begin, elf_next, elf_end.

elf_rawdata One of a group of library routines used to get section data. *See also* elf_getdata, elf_newdata.

elf_rawfile Library routine used to retrieve uninterpreted file contents.

elf_strptr Library routine used to make a string pointer.

elf_update Library routine used to update an ELF descriptor.

elf_version Library routine used to coordinate ELF library and application versions.

elf_xlate Group of library routines used for class-dependent data translation. This group of routines contains elf32_xlatetof and elf32_xlatetom.

ellipsis *See* ...

ellipsis notation Three-dot notation (...) used to indicate that a function or command is followed by an unknown number of arguments.

elm Command used to start the Elm screen-oriented mail reader.

elmalias Command used to display and expand address aliases for the Elm mail reader.

else statement Part of the if conditional branch statement in many programming languages.

elvis Text editor available from the Free Software Foundation; a clone of ex and vi.

emacs Command used to start the emacs text editor. The emacs editor is a screen-oriented editor that contains many extensions for specialized editing functions.

emacs.background Keyword used in a user's .Xdefaults file to configure the emacs text editor. It controls the color used for the background of the emacs window, and is equivalent to the emacs -bg command-line option.

emacs.bitmapIcon Keyword used in a user's .Xdefaults file to configure the emacs text editor. It controls whether the icon that represents emacs looks like a tiny kitchen sink, or whether the regular icon is used. It is equivalent to the emacs -I command-line option.

emacs.borderColor Keyword used in a user's .Xdefaults file to configure the emacs text editor. It controls the color used for the border around the emacs window and is equivalent to the emacs -bd command-line option.

emacs.borderWidth Keyword used in a user's .Xdefaults file to configure the emacs text editor. It controls the width of the emacs window's outside border and is equivalent to the emacs -b command-line option.

emacsbug Add-on package for the emacs text editor, which implements a function to send bug reports about emacs to the Free Software Foundation via electronic mail.

emacs.cursorColor Keyword used in a user's .Xdefaults file to configure the emacs text editor. It controls the color used for the text cursor in the emacs window and is equivalent to the emacs -cr command-line option.

emacs.font Keyword used in a user's .Xdefaults file to configure the emacs text editor. It controls the font used for text in the emacs window and is equivalent to the emacs -font command-line option.

emacs.foreground Keyword used in a user's .Xdefaults file to configure the emacs text editor. It controls the color used for text in the emacs window, and is equivalent to the emacs -fg command-line option.

emacs.geometry Keyword used in a user's .Xdefaults file to configure the emacs text editor. It controls the size of the emacs window and is equivalent to the emacs -geometry command-line option.

emacs.internalBorder Keyword used in a user's .Xdefaults file to configure the emacs text editor. It controls the width of the emacs window's inside border and is equivalent to the emacs -ib command-line option.

emacs LISP Variant of the LISP programming language used for configuring the emacs text editor.

emacs LISP mode In the emacs text editor, major mode designed for editing programs in the emacs LISP programming language.

emacs-lisp-mode Command in the emacs text editor that enables emacs LISP mode, which is designed for writing programs in the emacs LISP programming language. *See also* C mode.

emacs.pointerColor Keyword used in a user's .Xdefaults file to configure the emacs text editor. It controls the color used for the mouse pointer in the emacs window and is equivalent to the emacs -ms command-line option.

emacs.reverseVidoe Keyword used in a user's .Xdefaults file to configure the emacs text editor. It controls whether reverse video is used in the emacs window and is equivalent to the emacs -r command-line option.

emacs.title Keyword used in a user's .Xdefaults file to configure the emacs text editor. It contains the text that appears in the title bar of the emacs window and is equivalent to the emacs -wn command-line option.

emacs-version Command in the emacs text editor that displays the version of emacs which is running.

e-mail Electronic messages sent using a computer network rather than on paper. E-mail can be sent within a hard-wired network of computers, or to remote systems via phone lines. Also called email or electronic mail.

emergency boot floppy Floppy disk, usually created just after the UNIX system is installed, that contains a bootable UNIX operating system. Theoretically, if the computer's hard disk should become inaccessible, you could use the emergency boot floppy to reboot the system and correct the problem.

emoticon One of a group of characters used to express emotions in a newsgroup article or e-mail message. Emoticons are used to express sarcasm, happiness, sadness, and other emotions that are otherwise difficult to express in typed words.

empty string Text value that contains no characters, only the C string-ending character (the ASCII code 0).

EMT Name of signal number 7, which can be sent to a running process (short for EMT instruction).

emulate Refers to when software or hardware that acts as though it were some other type of software or hardware. For example, the DOS Merge application emulates a DOS environment within UNIX, wile a Terminal window emulates a VT100 terminal.

enable Command used to enable a printer. Once a printer is enabled, UNIX will send any queued print jobs to that printer.

enableok Device-driver library routine used to allow a queue to be serviced.

Encapsulated PostScript File format for PostScript language files where a preview header is included in TIFF, Windows Metafile, or Macintosh PICT format. Encapsulated PostScript files often have an EPS suffix.

encode Process of taking a signal or file and coding it so that it can only be read by proper decoding. *See also* decode.

encrypt Function used to encrypt a file so that a password is required to read the file. The encrypt function has access to the hashing function.

encryption Process of coding a signal or file in such a way that it can be read only if the proper encryption algorithm is used to in the decoding.

encryption keys Passwords created with the chkey command to protect user files. The encrypted key is kept in the publickey database.

end The first address above the uninitialized data region in a program.

end of input Character that indicates the end of a set of data (usually the Ctrl-D character). Also called *EOD*.

endgrent One of a group of library routines used to get group file entry. *See also* getgrent, getgrgid, getgrnam, setgrent, fgetgrent.

endhostent One of a group of library routines used to obtain entry to a network host. *See also* gethostent, gethostbyaddr, gethostbyname, sethostent.

endif In the C shell, the command that ends an if statement.

end-kbd-macro Command in the emacs text editor that ends the definition of a keyboard macro. This command is usually bound to the keystroke Ctrl-X). *See also* start-kbd-macro, last-kbd-macro, name-kbd-macro.

endnetent One of a group of library routines used to get network entry. *See also* getnetent, getnetbyaddr, getnetbyname, setnetent.

endnetgrent One of a group of library routines used to get network group entry. *See also* getnetgrent, setnetgrent, innetgr.

end-of-buffer Command in the emacs text editor that moves the cursor to the end of the buffer. This command is usually bound to the keystroke Meta->.

end-of-defun Command in the emacs text editor used in C mode to move the cursor to the end of the current function definition. This command is usually bound to the keystroke Meta-Ctrl-E.

end-of-fortran-subprogram Command in the emacs text editor, used in Fortran mode to move the cursor to the end of the current subprogram. This command is usually bound to the keystroke Meta-Ctrl-E.

end-of-line Command in the emacs text editor that moves the cursor to the end of the current line. It's usually bound to the keystroke Ctrl-E.

end-of-line metacharacter In regular expressions, the character that represents the end of the line. This character can be used to match only strings that occur at the end of a line. In the emacs text editor, it is the dollar sign ($).

end-of-window Command in the Epsilon text editor that moves the cursor to the last character in the current window.

endpoint In data communications, the place where information is ultimately received. Both the sender and receiver are considered endpoints in communications.

endprotoent One of a group of library routines used to get protocol entry. *See also* getprotoent, getprotobynumber, getprotobyname, setprotoent.

endpwent One of a group of library routines used to manipulate password file entry. *See also* getpwent, getpwuid, getpwnam, setpwent, fgetpwent.

endrpcent One of a group of library routines used to get rpc server entry. *See also* getrpcent, getrpcbyname, getrpcbynumber, setrpcent.

endservent One of a group of library routines used to get service entry. *See also* getservent, getservbyport, getservbyname, setservent.

end-user Person, or in some cases the application, that is the final recipient of a particular computing service.

endusershell One of a group of library routine (BSD) used to obtain legal user shells. *See also* getusershell, setusershell.

endwin Library routine from the group called *curs_initscr*. This group of routines is used for curses screen initialization and manipulation. *See also* initscr, newterm, isendwin, set_term, delscreen.

enlarge-window Command in the emacs text editor that enlarges the current window by one line. This command is usually bound to the keystroke sequence Ctrl-X^.

enlarge-window-horizontally Command in the emacs text editor that enlarges the current window by one column. This command is usually bound to the keystroke Ctrl-X.

ENOMEM error code Value that is returned if there is not enough memory, or enough of the right kind of memory, to complete an operation. This condition can occur during an exec, brk, or sbrk function.

Enter key Key that is usually pressed to actually send information that has been typed into a computer terminal. Also known as the Return key.

entity Item that can be treated as a separate unit. For example, in databases an entity is a record. In computer-aided design, an entity might be a drawn element or shape.

enumeration (enum) Unique data type, consisting of a set of constants (called enumerators). Enumerators consist of a set of constants and an optional tag.

ENV Variable used by the K shell (ksh) to identify where to find the environment file that is read each time the shell is started.

env Command used to display the contents of the current environment. The output is a listing of shell environment variables and their current values.

environ Standard set of environment variables to the shell that are described in the environ man page in UNIX System V. Variables contain information about the current configuration: the type of terminal being used, the language version of the system, the home directory, the network path, and so on.

environment variable Variable in the user's shell environment that can be assigned a value. Environment variables set the user's path, home directory, terminal type, and other information specific to the current user configuration.

envp Argument to the exec system call that consists of an array of character pointers to null-terminated strings.

eobp Function in the emacs LISP programming language that returns t if the cursor is at the end of the buffer and nil otherwise.

EOD Marker at the end of data, signaling that the end of the data has been reached. Usually used with tape commands.

EOF Marker at the end of a file, signaling that the end of the file has been reached.

EOL Marker at the end of a line, signaling that the end of the line has been reached.

eol2 Command-line option used with the stty command for setting the eol2 control character.

eolp Function in the emacs LISP programming language that returns *t* if the cursor is at the end of a line and nil otherwise.

EOT Marker that signals the end of a transmission of data.

Epoch Extended version of the emacs text editor that works with the X Windows System.

epsilon Command used to start the Epsilon text editor.

Epsilon debugger Debugging program that comes with the Epsilon text editor, used for debugging EEL programs.

eq Command-line option used with the test command in the Korn shell. This option determines whether one number equals another.

eqn Command (BSD) used as an equation preprocessor for troff. *See also* troff.

eqnchar Name of the man page that describes special character definitions for eqn.

equal In the LISP programming language, an operator that returns a true value if two string values are equal, and a false value otherwise.

equal sign *See* =.

erand48 One of a group of library routines used to generate uniformly distributed pseudo-random numbers. *See also* drand48, lrand48, nrand48, mrand48, jrand48, srand48, seed48, lcong48.

erase Library routine from the group called *curs_clear*. This group of routines is used to clear all or part of a curses window. *See also* werase, clear, wclear, clrtobot, wclrtobot, clrtoeol,

wclrtoeol.

erasechar Library routine from the group called *curs_termattrs*. This group of routines is used to query the curses environment. *See also* baudrate, has_ic, has_il, killchar, longname, termattrs, termname.

erf One of a group of library routines used for error function and complementary error function. *See also* erfc.

erfc One of a group of library routines used for error function and complementary error function. *See also* erf.

ERR Name of a signal which can be sent to a running process (short for *error*). Korn shell only.

errexit Korn shell mode that exits if a command returns a nonzero (unsuccessful) exit status. It is specified with the set command (Korn shell only).

errno Externally declared variable that indicates the reason for a system call failure. To determine the value of errno, programmers must include the errno.h header file in their programs.

error handling UNIX system call feature whereby, after a system call failure, the value of errno is set to a particular value that allows the programmer to deal with the condition.

esac Keyword in the Bourne and Korn shells that identifies the end of a case statement. (*esac* is *case* spelled backwards.)

esballoc Device-driver library routine used to allocate a message block using an externally-supplied buffer.

esbbcall Device-driver library routine used to call a function when an externally supplied buffer can be allocated.

Esc key *See* Escape key.

escape To protect a character on the command line using quoting characters. For example, since an asterisk has a special meaning when creating a regular expression, the string * designates an asterisk.

escape character Character used to allow some other character be interpreted as itself, rather than interpreting it as a special character to the shell. The backslash (\) and quote ("") characters can be used as escape characters. *See also* escape.

Escape key Key labeled Escape or Esc. Its meaning depends on the program in which it is used. The vi editor uses it to switch from input mode to command mode. The emacs editor uses it as its Meta key. *See also* Meta key.

escape sequences Special means of representing characters that are not in the source character set. The escape sequence usually consists of a backslash and a single letter. For example, \n represents a new line, \v represents a vertical tab, and \b represents a backspace.

esc-map Keymap in the emacs text editor for handling commands that are bound to multi-key keystrokes. *See also* ctl-x-map.

ESC-prefix Function in the global-map keymap of the emacs text editor. The function is called when the Esc or Escape key is pressed, and waits for the next keystroke to determine which command to run.

ET_AGE_INTERVAL Tunable parameter specifying the elapsed-time aging interval. ET_AGE_INTERVAL represents the greatest number of seconds that a process which is not swapped out can continue without scheduling an aging event.

etags Add-on package to the emacs text editor for finding function definitions in any source code file in the current directory. Also the program in the etags package that begins the etags facility.

/etc Directory containing many of the configuration files used by the UNIX system. For example, the password file (passwd) and TCP/IP address file (hosts) are both contained in the /etc directory.

etext Address of the first address above the program text in a program.

ether_aton Library function that converts an Ethernet number, represented by an ASCII string in the standard Ethernet representation, back to a 48-bit Ethernet number.

Ethernet Popular LAN product, originally developed by Xerox Corporation in the late 1970s. Ethernet was later standardized through the IEEE 802.3 standard. In Ethernet, messages are broadcast onto the network using the CSMA/CD access method. This allows many nodes to communicate on the network at once, while minimizing the number of collisions that occur. The first Ethernet standard allowed baseband transmission of 10 million b/s.

ether_ntoa Library function that converts a standard 48-bit Ethernet number to its ASCII representation. The number is represented by eight hexadecimal digits, each between the numbers 0 and ff.

ether_ntohost Library function that maps an Ethernet number to its associated hostname, represented by a string of characters plus a null character.

ethers
1. Library routine used for Ethernet address-mapping operations.
2. File containing the Ethernet address to hostname database. The file contains information on all of the known 48-bit addresses of hosts on the Internet.

ETI (extended terminal interface) Set of screen-management library subroutines. ETI is built on curses and promotes faster development of text and menu-based applications. Special functions let the programmer manipulate help messages and error messages.

etoimajor Device-driver library routine used to convert external to internal major device number.

EUC (extended UNIX code) Scheme for configuring up to four code sets concurrently in an 8-bit byte stream. EUC's main intent is to support the many types of ideograms needed to do I/O in many Asian languages. The first of the four code sets is always the 7-bit U.S. ASCII set.

EUNet European *Usenet* network, a group of mostly UNIX systems within Europe that exchange mail, news, and other networked information. EUNet newsgroup articles are distributed only to European sites within EUNet (with exceptions).

even parity Type of parity checking where the number of ones in each transmission must be an even number. If the number is not even, this indicates an error in transmission.

eval Command used in shell scripts to force variable expansion before the command is executed.

eval-defun Command in the emacs text editor used in emacs LISP mode to evaluate the function definition around or after the cursor. This command is usually bound to the keystroke Meta-Ctrl-X.

eval-expression Command in the emacs text editor used in emacs LISP mode to evaluate a one-line LISP expression entered in the minibuffer and display the result in the minibuffer. This command is usually bound to the keystroke Meta-Meta.

evenp Command-line option used with the stty command for controlling parity and character-size terminal settings. This option is used for terminals that connect to a computer via serial lines.

event Action that an administrator or programmer might want to track in the running system or within an application. For example, UNIX audit events represent actions that might affect the security of the system. The types of events an administrator might audit include changing user or group information, init states, date and time, and other security-related information.

event handler Part of a device-driver that is called to handle external hardware or software events, such as a failure of the hardware that cannot be determined by the UNIX kernel.

evgainit Command used to initialize an extended VGA keyboard and display driver.

ex Command used to start the ex text editor. The ex text editor is the underlying line editor used by the vi visual editor. You can use ex editor commands from vi by entering a colon (:) and typing ex.

Exabyte 8mm helical-scan tape device.

exchange-point-and-mark Command in the emacs text editor that swaps the locations of the cursor and the mark. This command is usually bound to the keystroke Ctrl-X Ctrl-X.

exclamation point *See* !.

exclusive access Reservation type in PDI drivers that temporarily restricts access of a device to a particular process. There are three types of exclusive access: read exclusive, write exclusive, and exclusive access.

exclusive lock Action performed by the lockf library function, using symbolic constants, to lock a region for exclusive use. Lock constants include F_ULOCK, F_LOCK, F_TLOCK, and F_TEST.

exclusive OR Operator that combines two logical values. The result is true if exactly one (not both) of the two input values is true. Also called *XOR*.

EXE Extension added to file-names in DOS to indicate that the file is an executable. Often, UNIX systems with graphical user interfaces will recognize DOS executables and let you run them in DOS emulation.

exec Group of library routines used to execute files. This group includes execl, execv, execle, execve, execlp, and execvp.

execl Library routine from the group called exec. This group of routines is used for executing files. This routine executes a file with a list of arguments. *See also* execv, execle, execve, execlp, execvp.

execle Library routine from the group called *exec*. This group of routines is used for executing files. This routine is synonymous eith execl. *See also* execl, execv, execve, execlp, execvp.

execlp Library routine from the group called *exec*. This group of routines is used for executing files. This routine is like execl, but allows you to automatically search multiple directories. *See also* execl, execv, execle, execve, execvp.

Executable and Linking Format *See* ELF.

executable file File that can executed, such as a program file.

executables Files in the UNIX file system that can be run as programs. Typically, executables will have the execute permission bits turned on.

executable script File that contains a shell script and has execute permission.

execute To run a file as a program.

execute permission Attribute of a file that allows it to be run as a program. Execute permissions are represented by the third, sixth, and ninth bits in the nine-bit permissions set for each file. Those bits represent the owner, group, and other permission as it relates to running the file as a program.

execute (X.) file In UUCP networks, a prefix attached to execute files in the UUCP spool directories. Execute files are those that contain commands to run by the remote execution daemon. The commands are typically sent from a remote computer for execution on the local computer.

execution time Time that elapses from when a process starts to when it exits. The timex command prints execution time, which consists of elapsed time, user time, and system time.

execv Library routine from the group called *exec*. This group of routines is used for executing files. *See also* execl, execle, execve, execlp, execvp.

execve Library routine from the group called *exec*. This group of routines is used for executing files. *See also* execl, execv, execle, execlp, execvp.

execvp Library routine from the group called *exec*. This group of routines is used for executing files. *See also* execl, execv, execle, execve, execlp.

EXINIT Shell environment variable that contains a string of ex commands used by ex and vi at startup.

exit
1. Library routine used to terminate a process.
2. Built-in shell command that causes

the current shell to exit. Exiting from the login shell causes the login session to be terminated.

exit code Code that is returned to reflect the state of a process when it completes. *See also* exit status.

exit-level Command in the Epsilon text editor that exits from a recursive edit and resumes a query-replace command. If the user is not in a recursive edit, it exits from the program.

exit-recursive-edit Command in the emacs text editor that exits from a recursive edit and resumes a query-replace command. This command is usually bound to the keystroke Meta-Ctrl-C. *See also* exit-level.

exit status Status of a process when it completes. An exit status is typically 0 (successful) if the process ends normally. Other exit statuses can reflect that the process failed because of invalid parameters or because it did not complete its entire task.

exp Library routine from the group called *cplxexp*. This group of routines is used for exponential, logarithm, power, and square root functions. *See also* log, pow, sqrt.

Expand Button available on the graphical debugger window for viewing more details about what a particular symbol points to. Expand lets you easily dereference a pointer.

expedited data At the OSI transport level, expedited data is typically information that is urgent. For those transport providers that support expedited data, expedited data will be processed before any normal data waiting to be processed.

expired password Password that has remained unchanged for too long to suit the system administrator. When a password expires, the user must use the passwd command to define a new one.

explicit-shell-file-name Variable in the emacs text editor that contains the name of the shell program to run in shell mode, usually $ESHELL.

exponential Mathematical expression, indicating the operation of raising a number to a power. In UNIX, an exponential part of a number is represented by e or E.

export Command in the Bourne and Korn shells that "exports" a shell variable and its value for use by other processes associated with the shell.

expr Command used to evaluate arguments as an expression.

expression String of characters that represents a pattern. For example, a regular expression is a string of characters that can be used to search for a particular location in a file.

exstr Command that reads a C source file and creates a file of the strings it contains. It is used to extract the strings from a C program so that they can stored separately, the first step in internationalizing a program. *See also* string, C source code.

extcompose Command used to compose a reference to data existing outside of a mail message so it can be included in a mail message.

Extended backup and restore Set of utilities for creating backup copies of UNIX files. Backups can be done on a file, file system, partition, or whole disk basis.

Extended Inode Operations Map Structure that keeps track of inodes that have operations pending for too long to keep them on the intent log. During a file system check (fsck utility), this map is used to identify inodes that have operations pending after the system crashes.

extended_to_decimal Library routine (BSD) from the group referred to as *floating_to_decimal*. This group of routines is used to convert floating-point values to decimal records. *See also* single_to_decimal, double_to_decimal.

extensible Property of being extended. Often used to describe operating systems that can easily be enlarged.

extension Suffix used on a file, following a period. For example, the letter *Z* is used as an extension on files processed by the compress command.

extern Storage class identifier that provides a declared object with static storage duration.

external command Command that is not built-into the operating system or shell. For example, echo is a shell built-in command while cat is an external command.

External Data Representation *See* XDR.

external storage Storage device that exists outside of the central processing unit. For example, disk and tape devices provide external storage.

F

fabs Command that returns the absolute value of x.

FACE Menu-based interface for managing files, running programs, and doing UNIX administration. It is an archaic interface developed by AT&T.

face Command used to start the FACE interface.

factor Command used to return the prime numbers of a positive number under 10*EXP14. If used without a value it waits for a value, prints out the prime numbers, and waits for another value. It exits when given a zero or any nonnumerical character.

false Command that returns a value of false when executed used in shell scripts with other commands.

FAQ Acronym for frequently asked questions, a list of questions and answers pertaining to a topic of an online information group. They are commonly used with USENET newsgroups to keep new users from asking repetitive questions.

fast Command-line option used with the cc C compiler that specifies fast compilation. It is used with Solaris 2.0.

fastboot Shell script that will invoke reboot with the proper arguments and reboot without checking the disks.

fasthalt Shell script that will invoke halt with the proper arguments, without checking the disks.

fattach Programming function used to attach a STREAMS-based file descriptor to an object in the file system.

fault Negative reaction, sometimes called an error in a process.

fax Refers to facsimile transmission and reception via telephone lines. A fax machine can send and receive faxes, which are low-resolution images. By using a fax/modem, a computer can act as a fax machine. Group 3 fax transmission and reception programs are available from the Free Software Foundation.

fax viewer Program that displays a faxed image on the screen. It is used in conjunction with a fax/modem, which receives the faxed image.

fc Command in the Korn shell that displays or allows the user to edit commands in the command history.

FCC Field in an electronic-mail message indicating the name of the file to which a copy of the message should be appended.

FCEDIT Shell variable that contains the name of the editor used by the fc command (Korn shell only).

fchmod Function call that changes the access permissions of a file whose name is referenced by a file descriptor.

fchown Function call that changes the owner and group of a file specified by a path or file descriptor to the file. If the user or group is specified as -1 the respective ID will not be changed.

fclose Library call used to close a file, causing unwritten data to be written out to the named stream and then the stream to be closed.

fcntl Function call that provides for control over open files. On success, fcntl returns a value depending on the options.

fcntl.h Header file that defines the requests and arguments used by the fcntl and open functions.

fcol descriptor Curses library parameter used to identify the location of a form column.

fconvert Library routine (BSD) used to convert a string of digits and return a pointer to a buffer. *See also* econvert.

fcvt Library routine used to convert a floating-point number into a string where the correct digit is rounded for printf %f output of the number of digits specified.

fd
1. Character specific devices, used to refer to files accessible through file descriptors. By convention, these devices are contained in the /dev/fd directory, and are named 0, 1, 2, and so on.
2. Generic device name assigned to floppy disk drives. For example /dev/rdsk/fd0 provides access to the first floppy disk drive.

FD_CLR Macro used with the select library call that removes fd, a file descriptor, from fdset, a file descriptor set.

FDDI Abbreviation for fiber distributed data interface, a physical network using fiber-optic media that run at 100 Mbits per second.

FDDI protocol FDDI protocol that specifies a high-speed token-passing ring LAN using fiber-optic media. This protocol includes a physical layer, MAC sublayer, and station management (SMT) specifications. It was created to fill the need for a high-bandwidth, local-to-medium-area network. It is most similar to IEEE 802.5.

fdetach Library routine used to detach a name from a STREAM-based file descriptor. The user making the call must be the owner of the file or a user with appropriate permissions.

fdisk Command used to create or modify partitions in the hard disk partition table, and set the active partition. This command can be found in UNIX, DOS, and other operating systems.

fdopen Library routine that associates a stream with a file descriptor.

FD_SET Macro used with the select library function to include a particular file descriptor in a file descriptor set.

feed
1. To direct input into a function.
2. The input that is directed into a function.

feof Library routine that reads a named input stream. When an EOF has been detected, it returns a value of nonzero.

ferror Library routine for stream-status inquiry for file errors.

fetch Library routine (BSD) used to access data stored under a key from a database.

ff Command used to list file-names and statistics for a file system.

fflush Library routine used to flush all files open for writing to a stream if the stream is a null pointer.

ffs Library routine that finds the first bit set in the argument passed to it and returns the index of that bit.

fg Shell command that brings a process in the background to the foreground. This command is available only under job control shells.

fgetc Library routine used to get the next character or word from the named input stream as an unsigned char converted to an integer.

fgetgrent Library routine that returns a pointer to the next group structure in the stream. Information in the stream matches the format of the /etc/group file.

fgetpwent Library routine that returns a pointer to the next passwd structure in the stream. Information in the stream matches the format of the /etc/passwd file.

fgets Library routine that reads a character from a stream into an array pointed to by s.

fgrep Command used to search a file for a character string. It differs from grep and egrep commands because it searches for a string instead of searching for a pattern that matches an expression.

fi Keyword in the Bourne and Korn shells that identifies the end of an if statement.

field Defined area on a screen that displays and/or lets you modify an item of information. This term is also used to describe one of the parameters of a command, delimited string in a line, or entries in a structure.

field_arg Library routine (curses) that returns a pointer to the field arguments associated with a field in a curses application.

field_back Library routine (curses) that returns the background attribute of a field. It returns a default value if the field is Null.

field_buffer Library routine (curses) that returns the value of field buffer buf.

field_count Library routine (curses) that returns the number of fields connected to form.

field_fore Library routine (curses) that returns the foreground attribute of field.

field_index Library routine (curses) that returns the index in the field pointer array of field.

field_info Library routine (curses) that returns the size, position, and other named field characteristics, as defined in the original call to the new_field, to the locations pointed to by the arguments rows, cols, frow, fcol, nrow, and nbuf.

field_init Library routine (curses) that returns a pointer to the function, if any, associated with the function form_hook.

field item help message Field-item help message appears whenever a user requests help from within an FMLI form. Each field on a form has a help message defined in the item help file.

field_just Library routine (curses) that returns the type of justification assigned to field.

fieldmsg descriptor Descriptor used by the message command that displays a message on the message line and stdout for each field in an FMLI form.

field_opts Library routine (curses) that returns the options set for the field.

field_opts_off Library routine that turns off the named options. No other options are changed.

field_opts_on Library routine (curses) that turns on the named options. No other options are changed.

field_pad Library routine (curses) that returns the pad character of field. If field is Null, it returns default values.

field_status Library routine (curses) that returns the status of field.

field_term Library routine (curses) that returns a pointer to the function, if any.

fieldtype Refers to curses routines that are used to create new field types for validating fields.

field_type Library routine (curses) that returns a pointer to a field of a particular type. Null is returned if no field type is assigned.

field_userptr Library routine (curses) that returns the user pointer of field.

FIFO STREAMS first-in first-out, algorithm used in queues, which states that the first item into the queue will be the first that is processed.

fifo Permanent pipe, existing in a UNIX file system. It is used to exchange information between connected processes. *See also* FIFO.

FIFOBLKSIZE General UNIX file system parameter used to specify the FIFO block size.

fignore In the C shell, a predefined shell variable that contains a list of filename suffixes to ignore during filename completion.

file
1. Command used to determine a file type.
2. Collection of data with a beginning and end that is given a name and stored in memory or a storage device. Files are organized in groups under a directory, which keeps a list of the names of the files and their address in the storage device. Files are given attributes for security reasons. *See also* file permissions.

file access permissions File attributes that determine how a file may be used by the owner, group, and others. Permissions are qualified by read, write, and execute attributes that are mapped to each file. These attributes can be viewed with the ls -l command or modified using the chmod command or library calls.

file and device input/output Data read from or written to a file or device used for storage or data transfer.

file and record locking Process of locking a record or file when in use so a third party can't modify the data while the current user or process is using it.

file archive
1. Act of storing files in a compact, organized way.
2. Organized unit of data kept on a storage device that stores files for security and future use.

filec In the C shell, a predefined shell variable that controls whether filename completion is enabled.

filecabinet FACE feature that lets a user access and manage files and directories. *See also* FACE.

file creation mode mask Value that defines the permissions initially assigned to a file or directory. *See also* umask.

file descriptor Pointer to a file used by UNIX commands or programming functions to reference a file for use in functions.

file descriptor passing Act of passing a file descriptor from one process or function to another to hand the reference of the file to the next function for use in accessing the file.

filehdr File header for the common object file format (COFF). *See also* COFF.

file inquiry operator Shell language operator that determines whether the argument is a file or directory, whether the file or directory exists, and, if so, its owner, and its permissions.

File Manager Program running under Open Windows that allows the user to copy, rename, delete, and move files and directories. Most UNIX graphical user interfaces include a file manager.

file manipulation Act of modifying a file. Manipulation can include editing, deleting, moving, or renaming the file, or changing attributes such as ownership, group, read, write, or execute permissions.

filemgr Program that is run to start the file manager under Open Windows. This allows the user to copy, rename, delete, and move files and directories.

file mode Permissions of a file. *See also* file permission.

filename Name given to a file that helps the user associate the data with a name. Different UNIX file system types allow different maximum filename sizes.

filename completion Feature of the C shell that allows the user to type the first part of a filename, then press the Esc key to fill in the rest of the filename automatically. If more than one filename begins with the letters typed, the user can press Ctrl-D (or some other EOF key) to display other possible command completions.

filename metacharacter Special character that can be used in a filename. Also known as a *wildcard* character. For example, the asterisk is a filename metacharacter that represents any string of characters.

filename pattern Filename or pathname that contains one or more characters called *wildcards*; for example, /usr/john/chap*.ms.

fileno Command that returns the integer file descriptor associated with the named stream.

file operations Operations performed on a file, such as read, write, truncate, delete, create, and move.

file permission Permissions given to files for UNIX are separated into three categories: owner, group and other. The permissions for each of these groups include read, write, and execute permissions. Permissions are set or changed using the chmod command.

file sharing Process in which files can be shared between multiple users or systems. Files are shared between computers in UNIX using the Network File System (NFS). *See also* NFS.

file system Set of files stored on a disk or on one partition or slice of a disk. Each file system is assigned a type, which defines attributes such as maximum length of filenames, how data are stored on disk, and what attributes are maintained by its files.

file system hardening Act of securing the data on a file system that reduces the risk of damage from system crashes.

File System Switch (FSS) UNIX System V internal architecture that allows file systems of different types to reside on the same operating system.

file system types Types of file systems include UNIX local file systems such as VXFS, UFS, BFS, and S5, or DOS file system and remote file systems such as NFS and NUCFS.

file system utilities Utilities used to create and administer file systems such as mount and fsck.

file transfer Action of moving a file from one place to another. The other location can be a different file system or storage medium or another system in the networking environment.

fileutils Set of utilities distributed by the Free Software Foundation, including programs that set the attributes of files, move files, delete files, and set the date and time for a file.

fill character Character used to place space between strings of characters. Besides a space character, a tab or other character may be used.

fill column Maximum number of characters to allow on a line in emacs. Used in fill mode.

fill-individual-paragraphs Command in the emacs text editor that reformats the lines in indented paragraphs, deleting and moving spaces and newline characters as needed to fill each line except the last to its full length, while retaining the indentation.

fill mode Minor mode in the emacs text editor in which wordwrap is performed automatically.

fill-paragraph Command in the emacs text editor that reformats the lines in the current paragraph, deleting and moving newline characters as needed to fill each line except the last to its full length. This command is usually bound to the keystroke Meta-Q.

fill-region Command in the emacs text editor that reformats the currently marked region, deleting and moving newline characters as needed to fill each line except the last to its full length. Paragraphs are separated by blank lines. This command is usually bound to the keystroke Meta-G.

filter Library routine (curses) that is called before initscr or newterm to makes curses think that there is a one-line screen.

find Command used to find files. It recursively descends the directory hierarchy for each pathname in the pth-name-list seeking files that match a boolean expression given by the parameters.

find-alternate-file Command in the emacs text editor that replaces the current buffer with another file, used when the wrong file was opened. This command is usually bound to the keystroke Ctrl-X Ctrl-V.

find-delimiter Command in the Epsilon text editor that displays the left parenthesis, square bracket, or curly bracket that matches the right parenthesis, square bracket, or curly bracket immediately before the cursor. This command is very useful for checking that parentheses and brackets match.

find-file Command in the emacs text editor that reads a file, either from an existing buffer or from disk. This command is usually bound to the keystroke Ctrl-X Ctrl-F.

find-file-other-window Command in the emacs text editor that reads a file into another window, either from an existing buffer or from disk. This command is usually bound to the keystroke Ctrl-X 4 F.

find-file-run-dired Variable in the emacs text editor that controls whether emacs runs dired when visiting directories rather than files.

find-tag Command in the emacs text editor, used with the etags facility to find a C function definition in a source code file. The file that contains the function definition is displayed in the current window, and the cursor is positioned at the beginning of the function definition. This command is usually bound to the keystroke Meta-. (that is, Meta-period).

find-tag-other-window Command in the emacs text editor, used with the etags facility to find a C function definition in a source code file. The file that contains the definition is displayed in the other window within emacs. This command is usually bound to the keystroke Ctrl-X 4 . (that is, Ctrl-X 4 Period).

finger Command to display information about local and remote users logged in including login name, full name, terminal name, idle time, login time, and location if known.

fingerd Process that implements the server side of the Name/Finger protocol, and provides remote user information to the finger command.

finite Library routine that returns true if the argument dsrc is neither infinity nor NaN; otherwise, it returns false (0).

firmware Nonvolatile random access memory (NVRAM), that permanently holds a few special programs required to control the computer hardware.

firmware mode Mode in which firmware can be modified while UNIX is not booted. Firmware mode is accessible in init state 5. This mode is not available on all UNIX systems.

firstkey Library routine (curses) in dbm that will return the first key in the data base.

fixed In the emacs text editor, the default value of the fortran-comment-indent-style variable in Fortran mode. This value causes emacs to indent comments to column seven.

fixed disk Type of storage medium that is not removable, such as a hard disk.

fixperm Command included in the UNIX System V Application Compatibility Package, used by an administrator to configure a XENIX system upon installation. It is also used to correct or initialize XENIX file permissions and ownership.

fixshlib Command run for a SCO UNIX System V/386 Release 3.2 application that is not installed using the custom command so that it will have references to the libnsl library. SCO applications installed with the custom command will automatically have references to libnsl changed to reference a SCO UNIX System V/386 Release 3.2-compatible libnsl.

fixterm TAM transition library routine used with the curses library.

flag Variable used in programming to signify an event or the lack of one.

flame Term popularized by online newsgroup participants to describe ranting and raving at someone in news or mail messages. To reduce flaming in reasonable newsgroups, whole flaming groups have been created.

flash Library routine (curses) used by curs_beep to flash characters on the screen or, if that is not possible, sound the audible signal.

flavor Slang term to describe the type or version of a computer product. For example, the two most common flavors of UNIX are UNIX System V and BSD.

FLCKREC General file system parameter that controls the number of record-locking structures used by the system.

flex-address Arbitrary sequence of octets, of length greater than zero, represented by a netbuf structure.

float Add-on package for the emacs text editor that implements functions for floating-point arithmetic. Also, a command in the float add-on package to the emacs text editor that enables functions for floating-point arithmetic.

floating-point constants Floating-point number that retains a constant value throughout the life of a program.

floating-point notation Means of expressing numbers with many places (i.e., 19400000 or .000106) in a more compact way. The number is presented as digits and an exponent.

floating-point operation Operation that manipulates numbers expressed in floating-point notation.

floatingpoint File that defines constants, types, variables, and functions that are used to implement standard floating-point operations according to ANSI/IEEE Std 754-1985.

floatingpoint.h Header file used to define floating-point variables.

floating_to_decimal Function used to convert a floating-point number into a decimal records.

flock Category of standard I/O locking synchronization routines that include flockfile, funlockfile, and ftrylock.

flockfile Library routine that grants thread ownership of a file and suspends that thread until ownership is granted.

floor Library routine that returns the largest integer not greater than x.

floppy disk Removable disk, also called a *diskette*. A floppy disk stores information on a plastic disk, enclosed in a protective sleeve or box. The data is arranged in concentric circles called *tracks*. Though original floppy disks were flexible, modern floppy disk are more rigid.

floptical disk New type of media that uses both the optical and magnetic properties to get more capacity on a smaller, removable disk.

flow control Term used to describe the control of input or output between a server and client on the network or between applications or processes. Flow control prevents the receiver from being fed more information than it can handle.

flush To clean an object of any data that it previously held, such as a buffer or queue. The result usually sets the buffer to all zeroes.

flushband Library routine used to flush messages associated with the priority band specified.

flush handling Ability of STREAMS modules and drivers to handle M_FLUSH messages.

flushinp TAM transition library routine used with the curses library.

flusho Command-line option used with the stty command for controlling whether output is flushed. This option is used for terminals that connect to a computer via telephone lines.

flushq Library routine that frees messages on a queue by calling the freemsg routine for each message.

fmlcut Function that cuts out columns from a table, or fields from each line of a file.

fmlexpr Function that evaluates its arguments as expressions. After evaluation, the results are written on the standard output.

fmlgrep Command that searches a file for a pattern and prints all lines that contain that pattern.

FMLI Abbreviation for forms menu language interface, a programming interface used to create character-based applications.

fmli Command that invokes the Forms and Menu Language Interpreter and opens the frame(s) specified by the file argument.

fmod Library routine that returns the floating-point remainder of the division of x by y.

fmt Utility that reads a text file and creates a file in which test lines are filled to a width of 72 characters. In contrast, nroff and troff commands also perform other formatting. The fmt utility fills and joins lines to produce output lines of the number of characters specified by the -w option

fmtmsg
1. Utility that sends an error message to standard error (stderr). It is used in shell scripts to display error messages.
2. Based on a message's clarification component, this command displays a formatted message on stderr or system console.

Fn Variable used by the ftw function to reference a user-defined function.

fnonstd Command-line option used with the cc C compiler. It specifies that the resulting object code use SIGFPE signals for floating-point overflows and for dividing by zero.

fold Command that reads a text file and produces text output with line-ending characters added to break the lines of the input file at a specified width. This command does not perform true wordwrap, because it breaks lines at the exact length specified, even if the break occurs in the middle of a word.

folder Term used to describe a window in a X Window System session that represents a directory in a local or mounted file system.

follow Command-line option used with the find command. It specifies that find follow symbolic links when searching for files. *See also* find.

font Character set unique by its design and used for graphical interfaces, text applications, and printing.

fopen Library routine that opens a file named by filename and associates it with a stream.

for Statement used in C, the bc desk calculator, and many other places to specify repeated processing. Also, a command in the Bourne and Korn shells that performs one or more commands repeatedly for each item in a list. Frequently the list consists of the arguments on the command line when the shell script is run. It is a programming statement used most commonly to step through a fixed-length data structure such as an array.

foreach In the C shell, a statement that executes a list of commands once for each word in a wordlist.

foreground Information shown on the front of a screen, usually covering other information. Also, a way of referring to a process that runs until it is completed without letting you continue work at the current shell.

foreground execution Term used to describe a process being executed from a terminal with no other operations using stdin or stdout, as compared to background execution, which does not take control of the terminal.

foreground job Program that is running, accepting input from the keyboard, and displaying output on the screen. UNIX can run several programs at once, with one in the foreground and the others in the background.

fork UNIX system call that causes the creation of a new process that is an exact copy of the parent process.

Form and Menu Language Interface *See* FMLI.

format Command used to format floppy disks.

Form_Choice Built-in variable in the Form and Menu language that evaluates to the last choice made from a choices menu.

form_cursor Set of library functions that includes set_form_cursor, which position forms window cursor.

form_driver Command processor of the forms subsystem that checks to determine whether the character *c* is a forms request or data. If it is a forms request, then the form driver executes the request and returns the result. If it is data, then it enters the data into the current position of the current field.

formfeed Character that marks the end of a page. In ASCII, it is stored as character code 12.

form feed Term that describes the action of a printer feeding one blank form. This can be done from the printer or specified by the printer process on the computer that is accessing it.

form_field Set of library routines that connect fields to a form.

form_field_attributes Set of library functions that format the general display attributes of forms.

form_field_buffer Set of library functions that set and get form field attributes.

form_field_info Set of library functions that get forms field characteristics.

form_field_just Set of library functions that format the general appearance of forms.

form_field_new Set of library functions that create and destroy forms fields.

form_field_opts Set of library functions that are forms field option routines.

form_fields Library routine that returns a pointer to the field pointer array connected to form.

form_fieldtype Set of forms library field-type routines.

form_field_userptr Set of library functions that associate application data with forms.

form_field_validation Set of library functions used for forms field data-type validation.

form_hook Set of library functions that assign application-specific routines for invocation by forms.

form_init Forms library routine that returns a pointer to the initialization function, if it exists.

form_new Set of library routines, including new_form and free_form, that create and destroy forms.

form_new_page Set of library routines, including set_new_page and new_page, that handles forms pagination.

form_opts Library routine that returns the options set for form.

form_opts_off Library routine under form_opts that turns off the named options only.

form_opts_on Library routine under form_opts that turns on the named options, while no other options are changed.

form_page Library routine that returns the current page number of a form.

form_post Library routine that includes the functions post_form and unpost_form, used to write or erase forms from associated subwindows.

forms Character-based forms package that gives an application programmer a terminal-independent method of creating and customizing forms for user interaction.

form_sub Library routine that returns the pointer to the subwindow associated with form.

form_term Library routine that returns a pointer to a function if one exists.

form_userptr Library routine that returns a pointer to the user pointer of form, which points to pertinent data that is stored.

form_win Library routine that returns a pointer to the window associated with form.

Fortran Programming language developed in the 1960s for use by scientists and engineers. The name stands for *formula translator.*

fortran Add-on package for the emacs text editor that implements a major mode for editing programs in the Fortran programming language.

fortran-column-ruler Command in the emacs text editor used in Fortran mode to display a two-line "ruler" above the current line. This command is usually bound to the keystroke Ctrl-C Ctrl-R.

Fortran comment indentation style Method used by the emacs text editor in Fortran mode when automatically indenting comment lines in a Fortran program.

fortran-comment-indent-style Variable used in the emacs text editor, used in Fortran mode to control how comment lines are indented.

fortran-comment-line-column Variable used in the emacs text editor, used in Fortran mode to control how far to indent comment lines.

fortran-comment-region Variable used in the emacs text editor, used in Fortran mode to contain the string that is inserted by the fortran-comment-region command.

fortran-continuation-char Variable used in the emacs text editor, used in Fortran mode to contain the character that is placed in column six of continuation lines.

fortran-continuation-indent Variable used in the emacs text editor, used in Fortran mode to control how far continuation lines are indented.

fortran-do-indent Variable used in the emacs text editor, used in Fortran mode to control how far statements within Fortran do statements are indented.

fortran-if-indent Variable used in the emacs text editor, used in Fortran mode to control how far statements within Fortran if statements are indented.

fortran-indent-subprogram Command in the emacs text editor used in Fortran mode to indent the subprogram surrounding the cursor, using the specified indentation rules. This command is usually bound to the keystroke Meta-Ctrl-Q.

fortran-line-number-indent Variable used in the emacs text editor, used in Fortran mode to control how far line numbers are indented.

fortran-minimum-statement-indent Variable used in the emacs text editor, used in Fortran mode to control how far statements are indented.

fortran-mode Command in the emacs text editor that enables FORTAN mode, which is designed for editing programs in the Fortran programming language.

Fortran mode In the emacs text editor, a major mode designed for editing programs in the Fortran programming language.

fortran-next-statement Command in the emacs text editor, used in Fortran mode to move the cursor forward one Fortran statement. This command is usually bound to the keystroke Ctrl-C Ctrl-N.

fortran-previous-statement Command in the emacs text editor, used in Fortran mode to move the cursor backward one Fortran statement. This command is usually bound to the keystroke Ctrl-C Ctrl-P.

fortran-split-line Command in the emacs text editor used in Fortran mode to split the current line at the cursor position, indenting the new second line and inserting a continuation character. This command is usually bound to the keystroke Meta-Ctrl-J.

fortran-window-create Command in the emacs text editor used in Fortran mode to set the width of the current window to 72 characters, which is the maximum length of Fortran source code lines. This command is usually bound to the keystroke Ctrl-C Ctrl-W.

forward-char Command in the emacs text editor that moves the cursor forward (to the right) one character. This command is usually bound to the keystroke Ctrl-F.

forward-level Command in the Epsilon text editor that moves the cursor immediately after the next bracketed expression. In other words, it moves the cursor to a string enclosed in parentheses, square brackets, or curly brackets.

forward-list Command in the emacs text editor in LISP mode to move the cursor forward by one list. This command is usually bound to the keystroke Meta-Ctrl-N.

forward-page Command in the emacs text editor that moves the cursor forward (downward) one screen. This command is usually bound to the keystroke Ctrl-X-].

forward-paragraph Command in the emacs text editor that moves the cursor forward (downward) to the beginning of the next paragraph. This command is usually bound to the keystroke Meta-].

forward-sentence Command in the emacs text editor that moves the cursor forward (downward) to the end of the current sentence. This command is usually bound to the keystroke Meta-E.

forward-sexp Command in the emacs text editor, used in LISP mode to move the cursor forward by one S-expression. This command is usually bound to the keystroke Meta-Ctrl-F.

forward-text-line Command in the emacs text editor, used in nroff mode to move the cursor to the next line, skipping lines that contain only formatting codes. This command is usually bound to the keystroke Meta-N.

forward-word Command in the emacs text editor that moves the cursor forward (downward) past the next word. This command is usually bound to the keystroke Meta-F.

FPATH Shell variable that contains a list of directories to search for function definitions (Korn shell only).

fpathconf Library routine that returns the current value of a configurable limit or option associated with a file or directory.

fp_class Library routine under ieee_functions that classifies arguments as zero, subnormal, normal, infinity, or quiet.

FPE Name of signal number 8, which can be sent to a running process. It is short for *floating-point exception.*

fpgetmask IEEE floating-point environment-control function call that returns the current exception masks.

fpgetround IEEE floating-point environment-control function call that returns the current rounding mode.

fpgetsticky IEEE floating-point environment-control function call that returns the current exception sticky flags.

fp.h Header file that contains variables and many library functions used for variable conversion, floating-point operations, and other functions.

fprintf Library routine that converts, formats, and outputs its args under the control of the character string format to the stream indicated by a file pointer.

fpsetmask IEEE floating-point environment-control function that sets the exception masks and returns the previous setting.

fpsetround IEEE floating-point environment-control function that sets the rounding mode and returns the previous rounding mode.

fpsetsticky IEEE floating-point environment-control function that sets the exception sticky flags and returns the previous setting.

fputc Library routine, similar to putc, that writes a character as an unsigned character to the output stream at the position where the file pointer is point-

ing and advances the file pointer appropriately.

fputs Library routine similar to puts, which writes a string to the standard output stream without adding a newline character.

fragments Subdivision of a block, in a ufs file system, equal to or smaller than the standard block size. Fragments are used to avoid potential waste with small files.

frame Data unit containing a stream of bits that flows across Ethernet, Token Ring, or some other networking transmission medium as one unit. It is used to describe data link layer (OSI level 2) data units.

Framed Access Command Environment *See* FACE.

FrameMaker Desktop publishing application used to do page layout as well as text editing. It is one of the more popular desktop publishers available with the UNIX operating systems.

fread Library routine that reads binary data into an array.

free
1. Library routine similar to malloc which makes space available that was previously allocated by malloc.
2. Term that generically means to make available for use as a resource by the same or other processes.

freeb Device-driver library function call used to deallocate a message block.

free_field Library routine under form_field_new that frees the space allocated for the field specified.

free_fieldtype Library routine under form_fieldtype that frees the space allocated for the field type specified.

free_form Library routine under form_new that disconnects the form from its allocated field pointer array and deallocates the space for the form.

free_item Library routine used to free the storage allocated for the item. Once an item is freed, the user can no longer connect it to a menu.

freemsg Library routine used to free all message blocks, data blocks, and data buffers associated with a message.

freerbuf Library routine used to free a raw buffer header previously allocated by the getrbuff function.

free_rtn STREAMS driver's message free routine structure needed for messages allocated by esballoc.

Free Software Foundation Organization committed to the ideal of freely sharing software. It is associated with the GNU (which stands for GNU is not UNIX) general public license, which protects an author's rights to his or her software without restricting the distribution of the software or its source code.

freeware Application program that is given away without cost. Although freeware is usually distributed freely, its developers usually retain some rights to their work.

freezestr Device-driver function used to set the interrupt priority level and freeze the state of the stream containing the queue specified.

freopen Library routine used to change a file from unbuffered, or line buffered, to block buffered.

FRESCO Object-oriented interface to X, developed by the X Consortium.

frexp Library routine that returns the mantissa of a double value and stores the exponent indirectly in the location pointed to by an argument, expr.

From Field in an electronic mail message indicating who sent the message.

fromsmtp Command that reads an RFC822 message from its standard input, does some conversion of the message to make it acceptable to the UNIX System mail, and then pipes the results to rmail.

frow descriptor Descriptor used in the move_field function call and several other function calls to specify the field row in the forms subwindow.

fs
1. UnixWare X font server.
2. Format of the specified file system. For example, fs(4bfs) is the format of the bfs file system. There is a format specified for bfs, cdfs, s5, sfs, vxfs, and ufs.

fsba Command that determines the disk space required to store the data from one file system to a new file system with the specified logical block size.

fscanf Library routine that reads from the stream at the position indicated in the arguments.

fsck Administrative command that checks and interactively repairs any inconsistencies found in selected file systems. Some corrective actions will result in some loss of data.

fsdb File system debugger that allows for the manual repair of file systems after a crash.

fseek Library call used to set the position of the next input or output operation on a stream.

fsetpos Command that repositions the next input or output operation in a stream according to the value pointed to by pos.

fsingle Command-line option used with the cc C compiler. It specifies that all float expressions should be evaluated as single-precision.

fsirand Command that installs random inode generation numbers on all the inodes of the device specified.

fspec File format specification for text files used to maintain files with non-standard tabs.

fstat Library routine that obtains information about an open file identified by its file descriptor.

fstyp
1. Command that allows a user to determine the type of an unmounted file system using heuristic programs.
2. Command line option used with the find command. Specifies which file system to search.

FSTypes *See* file system types.

fstypes File, residing in the /etc/dfs directory, that contains listings of distributed file system utilities packages.

fsync Library routine that synchronizes a file's in-memory state with the copy of the file on the physical medium.

ftell Library routine that returns the offset of the current byte relative to the beginning of the file associated with the named stream.

ftime XENIX command used to get time and date.

ftok Library routine that returns a key based on a specified path and id. That key is usable in subsequent msgget, semget, and shmget system calls.

ftp Internet utility that is the user interface to the ARPAnet standard File Transfer Protocol (ftp). It transfers files to and from a remote network site.

ftpd Command is the DARPA Internet file transfer protocol server process that listens at the port specified and is invoked to handle any incoming ftp service requests.

ftruncate Library routine that sets a file to a specified length, where the file must be open for writing.

ftrylockfile Command that is similar to flockfile in that it grants thread ownership of a file and returns a value for success or failure.

ftw Library routine that recursively descends the directory hierarchy rooted in path.

full backup Procedure in which all the data on the hard disk, on in a specific area of the hard disk is copied to another medium (typically cartridge tape).

full duplex Physical channel that has two ends, each serving as both transmitter and receiver. Each interface can both transmit and receive at the same time.

full-height drive Computer hardware device, such as a hard disk or floppy disk drive, that fills an entire bay on a computer.

full pathname *See* pathname.

fumount Command used with NFS that unadvertises a local file resource and disconnects remote access to the resource.

funcall Function in emacs LISP that evaluates a list as a function. The list must consist of a symbol (the function name) and a group of expressions (the function arguments).

function Alias that is built in to the Korn shell. It is equivalent to the command typeset -f.

function call Call made to a function in a program that consists of the name of the function and any necessary arguments.

function declaration Declaration of a function in a file, usually towards the beginning, that includes the name of the function and the arguments specified by type.

function definition Definition of a function that includes all of the code and argument declaration and any comments that will keep the programmer up-to-date.

function keys Keys on the keyboard labeled F1, F2, etc. The meanings of these keys depend on the program being run or any special mapping the user might have done to the function keys.

fundamental-mode Command in the Epsilon text editor that turns off any special key bindings, such as those made by entering C mode or dired mode.

fusage Command that reports disk access information. When it is used without options, fusage reports block I/O transfers to and from locally mounted file systems.

fuser Command that outputs the process IDs of the processes that are using the files or remote resources specified as arguments.

fuzzy logic Programming logic that allows for results that do not have distinct true/false types of answers. The results may fall within a range of values.

fwrite Library routine that writes to the named output stream at a specified number of items of data from the array pointed to.

fwtmp
1. Command that reads from the standard input and writes to the standard output, converting binary records of the type found in /var/adm/wtmp to formatted ASCII records.
2. Command used with UNIX process accounting software that reads from the standard input and writes to the standard output, converting binary records into ASCII formatted records.

G

g++
1. Command used with arguments to compile a C++ program using the C++ compiler distributed by the Free Software Foundation.
2. The C++ compiler distributed by the Free Software Foundation.

gadget Object in a graphical user interface that can be selected, such as an item in a pull-down menu. It can have a submenu attached to itself that is displayed when the gadget is activated.

gadget widget *See* gadget, widget.

gamma Library routine that returns the result of the logarithmic gamma function for a double value passed to it as a parameter.

garbage Corrupted data that is output from a command, contained in a file, or appears on your screen.

gated Command used to start the TCP/IP gateway routing daemon which handles multiple routing protocols.

gateway Network device used to link systems using different protocols. The gateway translates between incompatible protocols, allowing small networks to integrate into a larger heterogeneous network. (Sometimes the term *gateway* is incorrectly used to refer to a device that simply routes information between like networks.)

gawk Command similar to the awk command, used for pattern scanning and processing.

gcc GNU C compiler used to compile code for UNIX systems. This compiler is free and available to anyone who wants it.

gcd Library routine that is used to find the greatest common denominator between two variables.

gconvert Library routine used to convert a numerical value to a string with a sign and exponent, making it ready for printing.

gcore "Get core image," a command that displays the contents of memory used by one running process.

gcvt Library routine used to convert a numerical value to a string with a sign and exponent, making it ready for printing.

gdb debugger Debugger command used with GNU software. Like other debuggers, gdb lets you examine running programs to detect error conditions.

gdb mode In the emacs text editor, a major mode for using the gdb debugger.

gdb-mode Command in the emacs text editor that enables gdb mode, which is designed for debugging programs using the gdb debugger. *See also* C mode.

ge Command-line option used with the test command in the Korn shell. This option determines whether one number is greater than or equal to another.

gencat Command that merges a message text source file or files into a formatted message database file. The database file catfile will be created if it does not already exist.

gencc Interactive command designed to aid in the creation of a front-end to the cc command.

GEnie Online subscription service provided by General Electric Information Services. It provides e-mail, forums, and file archives to its subscribers.

geometry
1. Keyword used in a .Xdefaults file to configure the emacs text editor. It controls the size of the emacs window.
2. Command-line option used with the emacs text editor to control the size of the emacs window.
3. Standard command-line option used with X Window System applications to indicate the size of the window when the X application starts up.

get Command used with an SCCS database that generates an ASCII text file from each named SCCS file according to the specifications given by arguments included with the command.

getacl Command that displays the owner, group, and Access Control List for each argument that is a regular file, special file, or named pipe.

getc Library routine that returns the next character in a stream and converts it into an integer. It will also move the character pointer in the stream ahead one character if the pointer is defined.

getch Library routine that returns a character from the terminal specified. If getch is in no-delay mode, it will return ERR if there is no character already in the buffer. If it is in half-delay mode, it will wait for input.

getchar Library routine that operates the same as getc, except that it takes the next character input from standard input instead of from a stream.

getconf Command that writes the value of the variable specified by the arguments to standard output.

getcontext Library routine used to initialize a structure to a user level context of the calling thread. *See also* setcontext, makecontext.

getcwd Library routine used to return the pointer to the current directory pathname.

getdate Library routine used to convert a user-defined date or time string into a structure that is defined in the time.h header file.

getdents Library routine that takes a file descriptor to read file directory entries and put them in a file-system independent format.

getdev Command that generates a list of devices defined in the Device Database, based on given criteria.

getdgrp Command that generates a list of device groups that contain devices matching the given criteria.

getdtablesize Library routine that returns the current maximum size of a processes descriptor table.

geteblk Device-driver library routine used to get a free buffer from the buffer cache, if one is available. Otherwise, geteblk sleeps until one is available.

getegid Library routine that returns the group ID for the calling process.

getemajor Device-driver library routine that gets the external major number of the device number given as an argument.

geteminor Device-driver library routine that gets the external minor number of the device number given as an argument.

getenv Library routine used to return the value of the variable specified as an argument. If none is specified, then a null pointer is returned.

geterror Device-driver library routine used to return the error number in the error field of the buffer header.

geteuid Library routine that returns the effective user ID for the calling process.

getfilename Command that prompts the user for the name of an input file in the specified format and then copies that file to the filename given as the second argument.

getfrm Command that returns the current frame ID number for an FMLI frame.

getgid Library routine that returns the real group ID of the calling process.

getgrent Library routine that returns a structure made up of a line of the /etc/group file.

getgrgid Library routine that returns a pointer to a structure (consisting of a line from the /etc/group file) that matches the GID passed to the call as an argument.

getgrnam Library routine that returns a pointer to the structure (a line in the /etc/group file) that matches the group name passed to the call as an argument.

getgroups Library routine that gets the current supplemental group access list of the calling process and stores the results in the array of group IDs specified.

gethostbyaddr Library routine that returns a pointer to an object in a structure containing the broken-out fields from /etc/hosts, based on its address.

gethostbyname Library routine that returns a pointer to an object in a structure containing the broken-out fields from /etc/hosts, based on its name.

gethostent Library routine that returns a pointer to an object in a structure containing the broken-out fields from /etc/hosts. It returns the first structure the first time called and then the next structure the next time called, and so on.

gethostid Library routine that returns the 32-bit identifier for the current host, which should be unique across all hosts.

gethostname Library routine that returns the standard host name for the current processor.

getid Command used to get identification information from system MIB variables from a local or remote SNMP entity.

getitems FMLI function that returns a list of currently marked menu items.

getitimer Library routine that stores the value of a timer specified into a specified structure.

getlogin Library routine used by processes to get the login name as specified in the /var/adm/utmp file.

getmajor Device-driver library routine used to extract the internal major number from a given device number.

getmany Command used to retrieve classes of objects from an SNMP entity.

getminor Device-driver library routine used to extract the internal minor number from a given device number.

getmntent Library routine used to make successive calls for mount table entries in the /etc/mnttab file.

getmsg Library routine that, after retrieving the contents of a message located at the Stream head-read queue from a STREAMS buffer, places the message contents into one or more buffers specified by a user.

getnetbyaddr Library routine used to search /etc/networks based on a network address, and return a pointer to a structure representing a particular type of network.

getnetbyname Library routine used to search /etc/networks based on a network name, and return a pointer to a structure representing a particular type of network.

getnetconfig Library routine used to search /etc/netconfig for network configuration information.

getnetent Library routine used to search /etc/networks for the next available network entry in the file.

getnetgrent Library routine used to search /etc/netgroup and return the next member of a network group. If getnetgrent reaches the end of the file, it will restart at the beginning.

getnetname Library routine used to install the unique, operating-system-independent netname of the caller in a fixed-length array.

getnetpath Library routine that searches the /etc/netconfig file, sometimes called the *network configuration database*, for the next valid entry that matches the NETPATH environmental variable

and returns a pointer to it.

getnext Command used to retrieve the next object after the one specified as an argument from an SNMP entity on a local or remote system.

getnextpg Device-driver library routine used to get the pointer to the next page in the buffer header's page list and return it as the result.

getone Command used to get the object specified as a parameter from a local or remote SNMP entity.

getopt
1. Command that is used to break up options in command lines for easy parsing by shell procedures and to check for legal options.
2. Library routine used to return the next option letter in the argument that matches a letter in the string passed to it.

getoptcvt Command used to convert a shell script in the file specified to be used by getopts, and write the results to standard output.

getopts Command used by shell procedures to parse positional parameters and check for valid options.

getpagesize Library routine that returns the size of the system page in bytes.

getpass Library routine that reads up to a newline or EOF from a terminal device file (/dev/tty) while turning off echoing so that output is not displayed on standard output.

getpeername Library routine that returns the name of the peer system connected to a specified socket.

getpgrp Library routine that returns the process group ID of the process making the call.

getpid Library routine that returns the process ID of the calling process.

getpmsg Library routine used to put into a user specified buffer, the contents of a message at the place pointed to in a Stream head-read queue from a STREAMS buffer. It also provides better control over the priority of the messages that are received.

getppid Library routine that returns the parent process ID of the process making the call.

getpriority Library routine used to find out the scheduling priority of the process, process group, or user as indicated in the parameters.

getprotobyname Library routine used to search /etc/protocols and return a pointer to a structure for each protocol name specified as an argument.

getprotobynumber Library routine used to search /etc/protocols and return a pointer to a structure file for a protocol number specified as an argument.

getprotoent Library routine used to search /etc/protocols and return a pointer to the next protocol structure in the file.

getpublickey Library routine that returns the public key for the network specified from the public-key database.

getpw Library routine that searches the /etc/passwd file for a UID that matches the one specified as an argument in the call. It then copies that line into an array pointed to as another argument.

getpwent Library routine used to search /etc/passwd and return a pointer to a structure representing each line in the file.

getpwnam Library routine used to search /etc/passwd and return a pointer, based on a login name, to a structure created by lines in the file for each login name specified.

getpwuid Library routine used to search /etc/passwd and return a pointer to a structure, based on a user ID number, created by lines in the file for a matching UID specified as arguments.

getq Device-driver library routine used to return the next message available in the queue, as specified by an argument.

getrbuf Device-driver library routine that allocates space in memory for a buffer header.

getrlimit Library routine that lists the limits of consumption of system resources by processes and child processes created by the system.

getroute Command used to extract routing information from a local or remote SNMP entity.

getrpcbyname Library routine used to search /etc/rpc and return a pointer to a structure for names matching those specified in an argument.

getrpcbynumber Library routine used to search /etc/rpc and return a pointer to a structure for numbers matching the number specified in an argument.

getrpcent Library routine used to search /etc/rpc and return a pointer to a structure representing the next line in the file, starting with the first line.

getrpcport Library routine used to search /etc/rpc and return a pointer to a structure for ports matching those specified in an argument.

getrusage Library routine that returns information about the resources utilized by the process specified and/or its terminated child processes.

gets Library routine used to read a string from a stream, normally standard input, until a newline or EOF is read in.

getservbyname Library routine used to search /etc/services and return a pointer to a structure, for a specified protocol name, representing the services associated with the specified protocol name.

getservbyport Library routine used to search /etc/services and return a pointer to a structure, for a specified port number, representing the service associated with the specified port number.

getservent Library routine used to search /etc/services and return a pointer to a structure representing the next line in the file starting with the first line.

getsid Library routine used to return the session ID for the process whose ID is specified as an argument in the call.

getsockname Library routine that returns the socket name for the number specified as an argument.

getsockopt Library routine used to get options that are associated with a socket.

getspent Library routine used to search /etc/shadow and return a pointer to a structure representing the next line in the file, starting with the first line.

getspnam Library routine used to search /etc/shadow and return a pointer to a structure for a specified name, representing a line in the file.

getstr Library routine that retrieves a string of characters from the keyboard until a newline or carriage return is encountered. It places the string in the area pointed to by the character pointer specified as an argument.

getsubopt Library routine that parses suboptions, separated by commas, initially parsed by getopt.

gettable Program used with TCP/IP to obtain the DoD Internet host table

from a hostname server.

gettxt
1. Command that retrieves a text string from a message file in the /usr/lib/locale/locale/LC_MESSAGES directory. *See also* gencat.
2. Library routine that retrieves a text string from a message file specified as an argument in the call.

getty Command used for backward compatibility with previous UNIX releases for the applications that still call getty directly. The getty command is used to listen for and respond to login requests from terminal devices.

gettydefs File located in /etc that contains terminal definitions, such as line speed and parity.

getuid Library routine that returns the real user ID for the process making the call.

getusershell Library routine that returns a pointer to a legal user shell defined in /etc/shells by the system administrator.

getut Group of library functions that access utmp file entries.

getutent Routine that returns the next entry in a utmp file specified in the arguments.

getutid Library routine that returns data forward from the current position in a utmp file specified by the arguments, until it finds a match for the ID specified or reaches the end of the file.

getutline Library routine that searches from the current position in a utmp file for an entry of either type LOGIN_PROCESS or USER_PROCESS where the ut_line string matches the one specified as an argument, or until the end of the file is reached.

getutx Group of library functions that access the entries in a utmpx file.

getvfsent Library routine used to search /etc/vfstab and return a pointer to a structure of successive lines in the file, starting with the first line.

getvol Command that verifies that the specified device is accessible and that a volume of the appropriate medium has been inserted. This command is interactive.

getw Library routine that returns the next word in a stream, where the stream pointer is specified as an argument.

getwd Library routine that fills the area pointed to by a character pointer with the absolute pathname of the current working directory and returns the result.

getyx Library routine (curses) macro used by curs_getyx to position the cursor in the window according to the integer values of x and y.

ghostscript Freeware command used to view PostScript files in UNIX.

GID Abbreviation for group ID, the ID number of the group to which a file or directory belongs. *See also* group.

GIF Acronym for graphics interchange format, a format used to store a graphics file. GIF is a popular format for images used on the Internet's World Wide Web.

gigabyte Measurement used to measure data. It is equivalent to one billion bytes, where each bytes is equivalent to a character.

glob C shell command that performs expansions of filenames and other word lists. It is used mainly in shell scripts.

global
1. In the emacs text editor, word abbreviation that works in all major modes. *See also* word abbreviation mode.
2. Refers to something visible to all objects in a specific scope of reference.

global-map Keymap in the emacs text editor for handling default key bindings. *See also* ctl-x-map.

global-set-key Command in the emacs text editor that binds a command to a key globally, that is, in the global keymap in use for all types of buffers.

global symbols Symbols that are visible or known to a defined world.

global variables Variables used in programming that are visible to all functions in the program.

gmatch Library routine used to match a string with a pattern, where both are specified as arguments.

gmon.out File containing call-graph profile data about a C program. The gmon.out file is created when the program is compiled. *See also* gprof, cc.

gmon.sum File containing the summary of call-graph profile data from several C programs. It is created by the gprof utility. *See also* gprof.

gmtime Library routine that returns a pointer to the tm structure.

gnu *See* GNU Project.

GNU emacs Version of the emacs text editor available from the Free Software Foundation. The program is usually named either emacs or gmacs.

GNU General Public License Text that accompanies GNU software, defining the terms and conditions by which a user can copy, distribute, or modify GNU software.

GNU Project Project of the Free Software Foundation to reimplement the entire UNIX system in freely redistributed form. The acronym stands for GNU's not UNIX.

gnUSENET Set of USENET newsgroups associated with the Internet mailing lists of the GNU Project of the Free Software Foundation. The names of newsgroups of this type begin with gnu. *See also* UseNet.

gopher Internet utility used to find files that relate to a specific subject.

Gosling emacs Version of the emacs text editor distributed by Unipress. Also called Unipress emacs.

goto
1. C shell command that resumes execution of a shell script at the specified label.
2. Programming language command that is shunned by many programmers, especially proponents of goto-less programming.

goto-beginning Command in the Epsilon text editor that moves the cursor to the beginning of the buffer. This command is bound to the keystroke Meta-<. *See also* beginning-of-buffer.

goto-char Command in the emacs text editor that moves the cursor to the specified character in the file, that is, to the nth character, after prompting for n.

goto-end Command in the Epsilon text editor that moves the cursor to the end of the buffer. This command is usually bound to the keystroke Meta->. *See also* end-of-buffer.

goto-line Command in the emacs text editor that moves the cursor to the specified line of the file, that is, to the nth line after prompting for n.

goto-tag Command in the Epsilon text editor that moves the cursor to the specified tagged function.

gov Top-level Internet domain that con-

tains host computers related to the U.S. government (with the exception of military computers, which are contained in the mil domain).

GPGSLO Parameter used by the memory swapper to determine the minimum level of free memory before it will swap out the smallest processes.

gprof Command that displays a call-graph profile of a C program. It is available in Solaris 2.0 or from the Free Software Foundation as part of binutils.

grace period Period of time between when the system administrator gives the shutdown command and when the system actually changes state. The default grace period is 60 seconds.

grantpt Library routine that changes the ownership and mode of the slave pseudo-terminal device associated with its master pseudo-terminal controller.

graphic file format Codes used to represent a graphical image in a file. Various graphical formats are available, including GIF, TIFF, and bmp.

graphic toolkits *See* GUI toolkit.

graphical user interface *See* GUI.

graphics adapter Video board that drives the images that appear on a graphical terminal. It can present text as well as images.

graphics mode State of operation of a piece of hardware or software where images are represented in a graphical way by using pixels on an individual basis. *Compare with* text mode.

GrayScale Colormap used by X Windows to define the colors used on the screen.

greater-than sign
1. Mathematical symbol, where the value on the left is greater than the value on the right.

2. Symbol used for redirection. It indicates that the output of a command is to be redirected to the file to the right of the symbol.

grep Command used to search files for a pattern that matches the expression given.

group
1. Term used to associate several users on a system. All members of a particular group are bound by the group permission of a file or directory.
2. File, located in /etc, that describes the groups defined on the system.

groupadd Command that creates a new group definition on the system by adding the appropriate entry to the /etc/group file.

groupdel Command that deletes a group definition from the system.

group ID Identification number associated with a group on a system.

groupmod Command that modifies the definition of the specified group by changing the appropriate entry in the /etc/group file.

groups Command that displays the name of the group to which the user belongs.

groupware Term used to describe software designed to be used by a group of people on one system or one network.

grpck Command (BSD) that checks to ensure that the group file (/etc/group by default) does not contain any errors.

gs 16-bit register in the CPU used to store data.

gsignal Library routine that raises a software signal identified by its argument.

gt Command-line option used with the test command in the Korn shell. This option determines whether one number is greater than another.

GUI Acronym for graphical user interface, an interface created graphically that allows interaction between the user and the application using a mouse to manipulate windows and icons on a screen.

GUI builder *See* GUI toolkit.

GUI toolkit Set of tools used to build a graphical user interface for an application.

gunzip GNU command used to uncompress a file that was compressed with the gzip command.

guru Refers to an expert in a specific field. "The person with the answers."

gzip GNU command used to compress a file. Use the gunzip command to uncompress a file compressed with gzip.

H

.h Extension used at the end of a header file. *See also* header file.

hacker
1. Computer expert.
2. A computer expert who tries to break security, gain access to a machine, steal data, or just be mischievous.

hacking What a hacker does: steal data, break through security, gain access to unauthorized places, or cause havoc on someone else system or tampering with licensed software.

half-bright attribute Attribute for the display where the character is only half of the normal brightness.

half-duplex Physical channel used in networking where each channel serves as both transmitter and receiver, but only one interface can transmit at a time.

half-height drive Hard drive that takes up only half the size opening where it's installed.

halt
1. Command that writes out any information pending to the disks and then stops the processor. *See also* shutdown, reboot.
2. Routine used to shut down the driver when the system is shut down.

handle Pointer or other "grip" on an object allowing the process to have access to use that object for its needs.

hang When a process stops processing, but still appears as active in the process table. The kill command or a reboot is usually needed to get rid of a hung process.

hanoi Add-on package for the emacs text editor that implements the game "Towers of Hanoi." Also, the command in the hanoi add-on package to the emacs text editor that plays the game.

hard-coding Refers to using the actual name of a value in a program instead of using a variable.

hard disk Storage medium capable of storing very large amounts of data. It uses multiple oxide-coated platters, made out of glass or metal.

hard disk, SCSI *See* SCSI hard disk.

hard link File descriptor, treated as a file in the directory table, which points to the same address as the original file to which it was linked at creation. Hard links allow more than one access point to data located in the file system. Hard links differ from soft links in that hard links point to the address rather than the filename.

hard mount Remote file system that is mounted to a client through NFS, where the client continually retransmits to the server to ensure the connection is there, even if the server crashes.

hardpaths In the C shell, a predefined shell variable that controls how the dirs command displays symbolic links.

hardware Physical components of a computer system, including the system unit, terminal, keyboard, screen, modem, printer, mouse, trackball, disk drive, and other devices. *Contrast with* software, firmware.

hardware emulation module Module placed downstream from the ldterm module to understand and acknowledge the ioctls that may be sent to the process at the Stream head and to mediate the passage of control information downstream.

HASCOLORS Built-in variable in the FORMS tool used to test for color support.

has_colors Routine that returns a boolean value; True if the terminal supports colors, False if the terminal doesn't.

hash To make something fit by finding the quickest and easiest cuts.

hashcheck Library routine under spell that reads a compressed spelling list and recreates the nine-digit hash codes for all the words in the list. The codes are written to standard output.

hash function Function used to find a position in a hash table. It optimizes the possibility of finding an empty position for new records as well as quick access to existing records.

hashmake Library routine under spell that reads a list of words from standard input and writes the corresponding nine-digit hash codes to standard output.

hashstat In the C shell, a command that displays information about the hash table.

hash table Table used to store objects for data storage and retrieval. A hash function is used to access the position of an object in the file.

has_ic Library routine under curs_termattrs that returns true if the terminal has insert- and delete-character capabilities.

has_il Library routine under curs_termattrs that returns true if the terminal has insert- or delete-character capabilities, or can simulate them using scrolling regions.

HA_VER Command used for a 80386-based computer to determine the Driver Interface Version supported by the driver.

Hayes-compatible Term used to describe hardware (usually modems) or software that is compatible with modems produced by Hayes Microcomputer. All UNIX systems support Hayes-compatible modems.

HCORLIM Resource-limit parameter that equals the maximum value of SCORLIM.

HCPULIM Resource-limit parameter that equals the maximum value of SCPULIM.

hcreate Library routine that allocates sufficient space for a hash table, and must be called before hsearch is used.

hd Command that displays the contents of files in hexadecimal, decimal, and character formats.

HDATLIM Resource-limit parameter that equals the maximum value of SDATLIM.

hdestroy Library routine, used with hsearch, which destroys a hash search table and may be followed by another call to hcreate.

head Command that displays the first few lines of a text file.

header descriptor Descriptor that defines information to be permanently displayed at the top of a text frame for a character user interface program.

header files Files used in programming that define variables and functions. Header files can be reused by programs, providing for reusability in programming.

heading First line in a document that gives the title of what is presented.

help
1. FMLI command used to evaluate the current help descriptor if one has been defined for the current frame in a form.
2. Command used to find information to explain a message from another command, or explain the use of an SCCS command. Zero or more arguments may be specified.

help buffer Buffer in the emacs text editor created by the help-or-help command. The buffer displays online help.

help-command Command in the emacs text editor that displays on-line help. This command is usually bound to the keystroke Ctrl-H.

help-for-help Command in the emacs text editor that displays online help in the Help window. This command is usually bound to the keystroke Ctrl-H Ctrl-H.

help messages Messages added to an application that help the user understand how to use the application.

Help window Buffer in the emacs text editor created by the help-or-help command. The buffer displays online help.

help-with-tutorial Command in the emacs text editor that displays the emacs tutorial. This command is usually bound to the keystroke Ctrl-H T.

HEPnet
1. Collections of networks interconnecting high-energy and nuclear physics research sites.
2. Type of USENET newsgroup that discusses high-energy and nuclear physics. The names of newsgroups of this type begin with *hepnet*.

heterogeneous network Network where multiple operating systems exist and communicate using the same protocol, such as TCP/IP or IPX/SPX.

Hewlett-Packard Major manufacturer of computers that support UNIX.

hex See hexadecimal.

hexadecimal Base 16 numbering system. In hexadecimal (or *hex*), the number 10 represents the decimal number 16. Compare with decimal, octal.

hexadecimal escape Escape sequence provided by the compiler for characters not contained in a source character set.

HFNOLIM Resource limit parameter equal to the maximum value of SPNOLIM. *See also* SPNOLIM.

HFSZLIM Resource limit parameter equal to the maximum value of SFSZLIM. *See also* SFSZLIM.

hidden file File whose name begins with a period. These files do not appear on regular ls directory listings. The ls -a command produces a directory listing that includes hidden files. Also called *dot files*.

hidden text In the outline mode of the emacs text editor, lines of text that are not currently visible.

hide-body Command in the emacs text editor used in outline mode to hide (not display) all lines of text except header lines.

hide-entry Command in the emacs text editor used in outline mode to hide (not display) all the body text under the header on which the cursor is located.

hide-leaves Command in the emacs text editor used in outline mode to hide (not display) all body text lines.

hide-subtree Command in the emacs text editor used in outline mode to hide (not display) all the subheaders and body text under the header on which the cursor is located.

hierarchical mounts Refers to mounting each resource on the subdirectory of another resource.

hierarchy Means of organizing information that begins at a single point and branches downward. The UNIX file system structure and the Internet domain-naming structure are organized in a hierarchy.

high-density Term that refers to the format for 1.2MB, 5.25-inch or 1.44MB, 3.5-inch floppy disks.

highlight_bar Descriptor that defines the color of the menu selector bar for a character user interface.

highlight_bar_text Descriptor that defines the menu selector bar text for a character user interface.

highlighting Method of distinguishing an element of a user interface by using any one of the cursor location mechanisms, such as inverting the colors of the selection, or drawing a solid or dashed box around the elements of the selection.

High Sierra Standard used in creating CD-ROMs

hip Command-line option used with the stty command for controlling whether the telephone line is disconnected (hung up) after the user logs off. This option is used for terminals that connect to a computer via telephone lines.

hi-res Term that refers to a high-resolution monitor or mode of operation.

histchars In the C shell, a predefined shell variable that contains two characters, the history-substitution character (usually !) and the quick-substitution character (usually ^).

HISTFILE Shell variable that contains the name of the file in which to store the shell command history. This variable usually refers to a file named .sh_history (Korn shell only).

history Recorded account of past actions and states of being.

history list File containing a list of the most recently typed commands (C shell only). The file is named .history and is stored in the user's home directory.

history modifier In the C shell, strings that modify previously typed commands to issue a new command.

history substitution In the C shell, using the list of previously typed commands to issue a command.

history-substitution character In the C shell, the special character that accesses the history list. This character is usually the exclamation point (!).

HISTSIZE Shell variable that contains the number of commands to be stored in the command history list. The default number is 128 (Korn shell only).

hold Command-line option used with the lp command that notifies the user before printing the job.

HOME Environment variable used as a reference to each user's home directory. It is set by default at the beginning of each user's session.

home directory Term used to describe the directory given to each user for use in storing data.

Honey DanBer UUCP Early, major revision of UUCP. It was developed at AT&T Bell Laboratories by Peter Honeyman, David A. Norwitz, and Brian E. Redman. The product name was derived from the names of the developers.

hooks Object used in protocols for passing authentication information from the host to the server.

Horton, Mark Developer of curses and terminfo and contributor to the development of USENET.

host Refers to a system in network environment to which one connects for a service, such as printing or a terminal connection (through telnet or some other method).

Host adapter Device used as a SCSI bus that acts as the interface for SCSI peripherals.

Host adapter release number Release number for a particular host adapter from a particular vendor.

Host adapter version number Version number of a specific host adapter that uniquely identifies it from other host adapters of the same type from the same manufacturer.

host name Name of a host system on the Internet. The most common system of naming hosts is the domain name system. Each host name must be unique. A list of host names can be kept on the local system in the /etc/hosts file or accessed from a DNS server on the Internet.

host number Number that uniquely identifies a host on the Internet. Host numbers are in the form 123.45.67.89.

host2netname Library function that converts a domain-specific host name to an operating-system-independent net name.

hostid Command that displays the identifier of the current host in hexadecimal.

hostname Command that prints the name of the current host.

host-resident font Fonts that reside on the host and are transmitted to the printer as needed for particular print requests.

hosts Host name database or file that contains a list of host systems. Usually located in /etc.

hosts.equiv File that contains a list of trusted host names. Users with the same user name on the local and remote systems may rcp without supplying a passwd. This is similar to a .rhosts file.

HP9000 Computer system manufactured by Hewlett-Packard used primarily as an HP/UNIX server.

HP/UX Hewlett-Packard's proprietary UNIX operating system.

HRTIME Timer and schedule parameter used to define the size of the itimes array, which is used for keeping track of the alarm requests for the clocks measuring user-process virtual time and a process's virtual time.

HRVTIME Timer and schedule parameter used to define the size of the hrtimes array, which is used for keeping track of sleep and alarm requests for the standard real-time clock.

hsearch Hash-table search routine that returns a pointer into a hash table indicating the location at which an entry can be found.

HSTKLIM Resource limit parameter that is equal to the maximum value of SSTKLIM.

htable Command that converts a host table in the format specified by RFC952 to the format used by the network library routines. The three files that are created by running htable are hosts, networks, and gateways.

HTML *See* hypertext markup language.

htonl Library function call used to convert 32-bit quantities from host byte order to network byte order.

htons Library function call used to convert 16-bit quantities from host byte order to network byte order.

hub Central point on a star network that provides connection between each device in the network.

Huffman coding Method of compressing data for minimum redundancy coding, used by the pack command on a byte-by-byte basis. *See also* compression.

hung *See* hang.

hunt sequence Sequence used and maintained by sttydefs.

HUP
1. Name of signal number 1, which can be sent to a running process (short for *hang up*).
2. Command-line option used with the stty command. This option is used for terminals that connect to a computer via telephone lines.

hupcl Option for the stty command that hangs up or doesn't hang up connection on the last close. *See also* hup.

HVMMLIM Resource limit parameter that is the maximum value of SVMMLIM.

hypertext Type of text used in online documentation and other applications. You can click on a highlighted, hypertext term with a mouse and automatically jump to a reference linked to the term.

hypertext markup language (HTML) Document markup language (a subset of SGML) used to creating World Wide Web home pages.

hypertext transfer protocol (http) Protocol that allows a World Wide Web browser to connect to a Web page. This protocol supports the connection of hypertext links across the Internet.

hyphen Character used before a command option.

hypot Euclidean distance function that returns the sqrt(x*x+y*y).

I

i286 Trademark of the Intel Corporation, used for a processor chip in the 8086 family.

i286emul Command available on some UNIX systems to emulate an i286 processor in UNIX.

i386 Trademark of the Intel Corporation used for a processor chip in the 8086 family.

iasy Name of a device-driver that controls the terminal ports (/dev/tty) on some UNIX systems.

ib Command-line option used with the emacs text editor to control the width of the emacs window's inside border.

ibase Keyword used with the bc desk calculator program. It specifies the base for numbers that are input.

ibm Option used on the command line with the dd command. It specifies that the information be converted from ASCII to EBCDIC with IBM conventions. *See also* dd.

ibs Option used on the command line with the dd command to specify the input block size in bytes. *See also* dd.

icanon Command-line option used with the stty command for enabling or disabling canonical input, that is, whether erase and kill characters are pro-

cessed. This option is used for terminals that connect to a computer via serial lines.

ICCCM Abbreviation for inter-client communication conventions manual, a specification that sets policy for application inter-operability.

ICL Company headquartered in England that produces a version of UNIX for their own line of computers.

ICMP Abbreviation for internet control message protocol, a protocol used to communicate error messages and other conditions that need attention, and is considered part of the IP layer.

icon Graphical representation of a file, directory, or application in a folder in a UNIX graphical user interface.

iconedit Command running under Open Windows that allows the user to create or modify the appearance of icons.

Icon Editor Program running under Open Windows or some other UNIX graphical user interface that allows the user to create or modify the appearance of icons.

iconize To minimize a window into an icon in an X Window System environment.

ICON mode In the emacs text editor, a major mode for editing programs in the ICON programming language.

iconv
1. Command that converts characters or sequences of characters in a file from one code set to another and writes the results to standard output.
2. Library routine that converts characters or a sequence of characters from one code set to another and places them in an array.

icrnl Command-line option used with the stty command for selecting whether carriage-return characters (ASCII character code 13) in the input are converted to newline characters (ASCII character code 10). This option is used for terminals that connect to a computer via serial lines.

ics Device dual-port memory queue.

ID Term used to describe a number that identifies a particular object, such as a group ID or a device driver ID number.

id Command that returns the group and user IDs for the current user. If a user is specified, it returns the user and group ID information for that user.

idadmin Command that displays and updates entries in the system ID mapping database.

idbuild Command that builds a new UNIX System kernel using the current system configuration in /etc/conf.

idcheck Command that returns selected information about the system configuration.

idconfig Command that takes as its input a collection of files specifying the configuration of the next UNIX System to be built and generates a collection of output files for use by idmkunix.

#ident Directive used in programming, which must be followed by a normal string literal.

identifiers Variable name associated with a programming structure such as an integer, string, or array.

idinstall Command that is called by a driver software package (DSP) install script to add, delete, update, or get device-driver configuration data.

idle Refers to a resource that is not busy or in use.

idload Command used on Remote File Sharing server machines to build translation tables for user and group IDs from the /etc/passwd and /etc/group files.

idlok Curses library routine that, when called, is either enabled or disabled for a specified window. If enabled, curses will consider using the hardware insert/delete line feature for terminals if they are so equipped. If disabled, curses will not use this option.

idmkinit Command that constructs /etc/inittab from configuration data.

idmknod Command that creates device nodes (in the /dev directory) based on the configuration defined for the current UNIX system. It also deletes nodes that are no longer valid.

idmkunix Command that creates a bootable UNIX system kernel from software and configuration information.

idspace Command that investigates free space in / (root), /usr, and /tmp file systems to see whether sufficient disk blocks and inodes exist to build a new UNIX system kernel.

IDT Abbreviation for *interrupt descriptor table*.

idt Option under the crash command that prints the interrupt descriptor table.

idtune Command that attempts to set the value of a specified tunable parameter.

ieee Type of USENET newsgroup that discusses the IEEE (the Institute of Electrical and Electronics Engineers). The names of newsgroups of this type begin with *ieee*.

ieee_functions Library routines (BSD) used for IEEE arithmetic.

ieee_handler Library routine (BSD) used for IEEE exception-trap handling.

iexten Command-line option used with the stty command for enabling or disabling extended functions for input data. This option is used for terminals that connect to a computer via serial lines.

if
1. Keyword in a shell script that signals the beginning of conditional processing. In the Bourne and Korn shells, an if statement can contain the then and elif keywords and must end with the fi keyword. In the C shell, an if statement can contain the then and else keywords and must end with the endif keyword.
2. Option used on the command line with the dd command. It specifies the name of the input file to be copied.
3. Statement used in C, the bc desk calculator, and other languages to specify conditional processing.
4. Function in the emacs LISP programming language that executes a statement block if a condition is true (or t) and another statement block otherwise.

ifconfig Command used to assign an address to a network interface or to configure network interface parameters. It is used with TCP/IP.

#ifdef Conditional compilation statement used to determine if an identifier is currently defined by a #define state-

ment. It returns a boolean value of true if it is defined or false if has not been defined yet.

#ifndef Conditional compilation statement used to determine if an identifier is not currently defined by a #define statement. It returns a boolean value of true if it is not yet been defined or false if has been defined already.

IFS Abbreviation for internal field separators, a shell variable that contains a list of the internal field separators, usually a space, tab, and newline characters (Bourne and Korn shells only).

ignbrk Command-line option used with the stty command for selecting whether break characters in the input are ignored. This option is used for terminals that connect to a computer via serial lines.

igncr Command-line option used with the stty command for selecting whether carriage-return characters (ASCII character code 13) in the input are ignored. This option is used for terminals that connect to a computer via serial lines.

ignoreeof Korn shell mode that ignores EOF characters from the keyboard. It is specified with the set command (Korn shell only). In the C shell, a predefined shell variable that controls whether typing the EOF character (usually Ctrl-D) logs the user off.

ignpar Command-line option used with the stty command for selecting whether parity errors in the input are ignored. This option is used for terminals that connect to a computer via serial lines.

I-list List used under an option of ncheck that contains a list of files that ncheck can use for its report.

ILL Name of signal number 4 (short for illegal instruction). It can be sent to a running process.

ilogb Second parameter of the scalbn library function.

imake Facility used by the Makefile and make commands.

imaxbel Command-line option used with the stty command for selecting whether a BEL character (ASCII character code 7) is output when an input line is too long. This option is used for terminals that connect to a computer via serial lines.

immediate Command-line option used with the lp command that assigns a high priority to a print job.

IMO Abbreviation for in my opinion, used in e-mail and newsgroups.

impact printer Type of printer where the character on the paper is formed by the impact of a head on the paper. A daisywheel printer is a type of impact printer.

importing Refers to taking a variable from an existing environment and bringing it into the current working environment.

in Keyword that occurs in the case statement in Bourne and Korn shell scripts. The command identifies the end of the case statement.

inactive descriptor Descriptor used in the character user interface that defines an item as inactive when a menu is displayed.

inactive_border descriptor Descriptor used in a character user interface that defines the color of the frame border when the frame is noncurrent.

inactive_title_bar descriptor Descriptor used in a character user interface that defines the color of the title background when the title the frame is not the currently active frame.

inactive_title_text descriptor Descriptor

used in a character user interface which defines the color of the title text when the title the frame is not the currently active frame.

inb Device-driver library routine that provides a C language interface and is used to read a byte from an 8-bit I/O port.

inbox Place to store incoming data from outside sources. In some UNIX versions, a UUCP inbox stores messages sent to the system using uucp.

inch Library routine used to return the character at the current position in the specified window.

#include Conditional compilation statement used to specify the .h files to include in compilation. These files contain functions that are used in the program with the #include statement.

includedemo Command-line option used with the openwin command that allows the Open Windows demonstration programs to be run.

include files Type of file that contains a library of functions and is compiled with a program. An #include statement is added to the beginning of the program file.

incoming events Term used to refer to input that occurs sporadically from an input device that is being monitored by a process. The input typically triggers the process for some other action.

incomplete types Array type of unknown size.

increment To increase a number by a set value.

incremental backup Backup that only stores information that was not included in the previous full backup.

indented text mode Major mode in the emacs text editor in which each tab stop defines how subsequent lines are indented.

indented-text-mode Command in the emacs text editor that enters indented text mode in which each tab stop defines how subsequent lines are indented.

indent-for-comment Command in the emacs text editor used in nroff mode to insert an nroff comment marker at the cursor location. This command is usually bound to the keystroke Meta-; or Ctrl-X ;.

indent-new-comment-line Command in the emacs text editor used to continue a comment on another line. This command is used in C mode, Fortran mode, LISP mode, or other modes for writing source code and automatically inserts the comment characters appropriate to the language. This command is usually bound to the keystroke Meta-J.

indent-previous Command in the Epsilon text editor that indents the current line based on the indentation of the previous line.

indent-region Command in the emacs text editor that indents the currently-marked region to match the indentation of its first line. This command is usually bound to the keystroke Meta-Ctrl-\.

indent-rigidly Command in the Epsilon text editor that moves all the lines in currently marked region to the left or right by a fixed amount by adding or deleting spaces at the beginning of the line.

indent-tabs-mode Variable in the emacs text editor that controls whether tabs and spaces are used for indenting.

indent-under Command in the Epsilon text editor that indents the current line to match the next text (that is, text to the right of the cursor position) on the previous line. *See also* indent-previous.

index Library routine that returns a pointer to the first or last occurrence of a character in a string.

indexed Refers to being ordered according to some logical order with a unique ID attached to each object in the group.

indicator FMLI function that displays application-specific alarms and/or the working indicator.

indxbib Command that creates an inverted index to a bibliographic database. The database consists of bibliographic references or other kinds of information separated by blank lines.

inet Term used to define the Internet protocol family.

inet_addr Library routine that converts a character string consisting of numbers expressed in the Internet standard "." (dot) notation into numbers suitable for use as an Internet address.

inetd Internet-services daemon that is started at boot time and listens for connections on the Internet addresses for the services requested by remote computers.

inetd.conf File located in the /etc/inetd.conf directory that describes the TCP/IP services available from the local UNIX system. For example, this file will indicate if remote computers can use ftp, telnet, login, or other services from this local computer.

Inet/DDN Type of newsgroup that is circulated among sites on or gatewayed from the Internet. These newsgroups parallel those of the USENET and have names of the same form as regular USENET groups.

inet_lnaof Library routine that takes a host address and breaks it apart to return the local network address part.

inet_makeaddr Library routine that takes an Internet network number and a local network number to make an Internet address.

inet_netof Library routine that takes a host address and breaks it apart to return the network number part.

inet_network Library routine that converts a character string consisting of numbers expressed in the Internet standard "." (dot) notation into numbers suitable for use as an Internet network number.

inet_ntoa Library routine that converts an Internet network number into a character string consisting of numbers expressed in the Internet standard "." (dot) notation.

inet utilities Group of functions that perform manipulation of Internet addresses and include the following: inet_addr, inet_network, inet_makeaddr, inet_lnaof, inet_netof, and inet_ntoa.

infinity Mathematical range used by library functions for positive and negative infinity. In mathematical terms, infinity means forever in a positive or negative direction on the number scale.

info
1. Command in the emacs text editor that starts the info documentation reader. This command is usually bound to the keystroke Ctrl-H I.
2. Device-driver man page entry that describes the STREAMS driver and module information.

infocmp Command used to compare a binary terminfo entry with other terminfo entries or print out terminfo descriptions.

Informix Popular database software available on many UNIX systems.

Ingres Distributed information software available on many UNIX systems.

Init Configuration file for the Installable driver/tunable parameters that contains information to construct inittab entries for modules in /etc/inittab.

init
1. Command used to change states or restart commands run in the current state.
2. Device-driver entry-point routine used to initialize drivers and the devices they control, usually at boot time.
3. Library routine used to initialize and register a host bus adapter.
4. General-process spawner whose primary purpose is to create processes from information stored in the /etc/inittab file when UNIX starts up. The system is in one of eight possible run levels at any time, and init is called to change levels.

init descriptor Used in character user interface programming, the init descriptor defines whether or not the emenu frame will be opened.

init_color Library routine used to change the definition of a color based on the values for the three RGB components and the number of the color to be changed.

init.d Directory in a file system that contains initialization scripts for many of the networking features such as nfs and snmp. These scripts, if linked to run directories, can be used to start or stop a feature from running.

initdefault Entry in the /etc/inittab file that defines the state that the system will come up in.

initgroups Library routine used to initialize the supplemental group access list of the calling process by reading the group file to get the group membership for the user specified in the function call.

initialization Process of putting an object in an initial state. The value is usually defined by a default value or configuration.

initialization file In FMLI, application-level file that defines global features used by the application.

initialization string String variable used to initialize a device such as a terminal or printer.

initialize To put an object into an initial state so that it has a predictable starting value.

init_pair Library routine that changes a color-pair's definition.

initprivs Command that sets the system privilege information.

init state *See* system state.

initscr Library routine (curses) that determines the terminal type and initializes the curses data structures.

initstate Library routine used to initialize a state array.

inittab File, located in /etc, used to control the process dispatching that is used by init.

inkjet printer Type of printer based on a technology that uses a printhead to shoot a fine jet of ink on the paper. Print quality is usually very good and the printers are reasonably priced.

inlcr Command-line option used with the stty command for selecting whether newline characters (ASCII character code 10) in the input are converted to carriage returns (ASCII character code 13). This option is used for terminals that connect to a computer via serial lines.

inl Device-driver function that is used to read a 32-bit word from a 32-bit port using the I/O address space.

innetgr Library routine used to find out whether a specified network group contains a machine, user, or domain specified also in the arguments of the function call.

inode Structure representing a file, directory, or other item in a UNIX file system. It contains information about the item, such as its ownership and permission. It also points to the location of the item's data on the storage medium.

inpck Command-line option used with the stty command for enabling or disabling parity checking of the input. This option is used for terminals that connect to a computer via serial lines.

input Data that is received by a process.

input block Block of input from a device or file system consisting of a number of bytes. This is specifically referenced by the dd command, which can specify the size of input blocks to be transferred from one place to another.

input mode Mode or time in which a process or application is accepting data.

input/output (I/O)
1. Term used to reference retrieving and transferring data.
2. Device that can send or receive data.

input/output polling Act of validating whether data is being sent or received by some object.

input redirection Act of retrieving data and sending it to another process or storage site.

insch Library routine used to insert characters in a curses window before the character under the cursor.

insert Function in the emacs LISP programming language that inserts text at the cursor position.

insert-binding Command in the Epsilon text editor that creates a bind-to-key command to reestablish a key's current binding.

insert-default-directory Variable in the emacs text editor that controls whether emacs displays the current default directory in the minibuffer when prompting for a filename.

insert-file Command in the emacs text editor that inserts the specified file before the current cursor location. This command is usually bound to the keystroke Ctrl-X I.

insert-kbd-macro Command in the emacs text editor that inserts the LISP mode that represents a macro into a buffer.

insert-last-keyboard-macro Command in the emacs text editor that inserts a macro into a file.

insertln Library routine that inserts a blank line above the current line and the bottom line is lost.

insert-macro Command in the Epsilon text editor that creates a define-macro-command to define a macro again later.

insert mode
1. In the vi text editor, a mode in which characters typed are entered into the file being edited. Compare this to command mode, in which characters typed are interpreted as commands.
2. In emacs and other text editors, mode in which characters are inserted at the cursor position. Compare to overwrite mode or typeover mode, in which characters typed replace existing characters.

insq Device-driver library routine used to insert a message into a queue.

insque Library routine that inserts an element into a queue that is built from a doubly linked list.

install Command used within makefiles to copy new versions of files into a destination directory, and then create the destination directory itself.

installable driver Refers to device-drivers that can be installed and configured in the UNIX system.

installation Process of installing or setting up and configuring a system. This process can involve software, hardware, or both.

installation scripts Scripts used during the installation of a package to configure the system properly before and after the package is installed in the system.

installf Command used to add a file to the software installation database.

installpkg Command used to install packages on a UNIX system.

instance Refers to a variable with a value at a specific time.

int Short for interrupt, the name of signal number 2. It can be sent to a running process.

integer Numeric value that is whole and not a fraction or imaginary number.

integral constants Identifier with a fixed value that can be a decimal, hexidecimal, or octal number either unsigned, long, or both, used in C programming.

integral types Variable type used in C programming that consists of an integer, but can be of several types, such as signed, long, or short.

integration testing Testing that follows the development of a project and tests multiple independently developed segments in an integrated environment to see that they perform together without errors. This phase of testing usually comes after unit testing and before system testing.

interactive Refers to an application or utility that allows the user to participate by choosing options or entering data through prompts or menus from the application.

interface Refers to the style by which one object communicates with another. This is predefined to allow for clear communication. Human interfaces, such as graphical user interfaces and character interfaces, define how a user interacts with a computer.

interface builder Tool used to build interfaces to be used in applications that allow user interaction. An interface builder allows the programmer to use prebuilt interfaces to save time in programming.

interface modifications Modifications to an existing interface to customize that interface for a specific purpose.

internalBorder Keyword used in a user's .Xdefaults file to configure the emacs text editor for an X Window System environment. It controls the width of the emacs window's inside border and is equivalent to the emacs -ib command-line option.

internal device number Number that is given to a device, used to address various data structures. It includes major and minor components.

internationalization Enabling the messages and text of a product for use with other languages. This includes the configuration of foreign keyboards, and allows the product to handle other sorting schemes, foreign date formats, currencies, and other language-specific data.

internationalized Product that has gone through the process of internationalization.

Internaut Someone who navigates the Internet with skill. *See also* Internet.

Internet Global computer network that links federal, educational, research, and defense-related facilities.

Internet Point to Point Protocol *See* PPP.

Internet Protocol *See* IP.

Internet Relay Chat Facility over which Internet users can converse in real-time.

Internet Utilities Utilities used on the Internet to provide better communication and a means of gathering and sending data. Some of the Internet utilities that are included with TCP/IP include ftp, telnet, rlogin, rsh, and rcp. Other utilities available for the Internet include Mosaic, Netscape, and archie.

internetwork Combination of several networks linked by routers, bridges, and gateways.

interprocess communication Communication between two or more processes. The processes may be running on the same machine or on different machines connected by a network.

interrupt Signal sent from a device or process that informs the operating system of an occurrence. Interrupts can have different priorities and other information used by the kernel to make decisions on what action to follow.

interrupt descriptor
1. Descriptor designated for an action.
2. Descriptor in an FMLI application that is used to interrupt the application.

interrupt-driven socket I/O (SIGIO) Notifies a process when a socket or file descriptor has data waiting to be read.

Interrupt routine Routine associated with an interrupt that is executed when that interrupt is encountered.

interrupt-shell-subjob Command in the emacs text editor that terminates the current job being run as a sub-job. This command is usually bound to the keystroke Ctrl-C Ctrl-C.

interrupt signal handling Way in which an FMLI executable is interrupted from a user.

intr Command-line option used with the stty command for setting the intr control character.

intrflush Library routine that, when set to true, allows all output to the tty driver queue to be flushed when an interrupt key is pressed on the keyboard.

intro
1. Introduction to the section 1 man pages. The intro includes an introduction of the user, programming, and administrative commands and application programs.
2. Introduction to the section 2 man pages. It covers system calls, error numbers, privileges, lightweight processes and threads.
3. Introduction to the section-2D man pages That includes a description of driver entry-point routines.
4. Introduction to the section-2I man pages that includes an introduction of PDI driver entry point routines.
5. Introduction to the section-3 man pages. It includes an introduction of functions and libraries.
6. Introduction to the section-3D man pages that includes an introduction of kernel entry routines.
7. Introduction to the section-3I man

pages. It includes an introduction of PDI Driver Utility Routines.
8. Introduction to the section-3L man pages. It includes an introduction of the data link provider interface.
9. Introduction to the section-4 man pages that covers the file formats.
10. Introduction to the section-4D man pages. It includes a description of kernel data structures.
11. Introduction to the section-4I man pages. It includes an introduction to PDI data structures.
12. Introduction to the section-4L man pages. It includes an introduction of data link interface quality-of-services measurements.
13. Introduction to the section-5 man pages containing miscellaneous subjects not already covered.
14. Introduction to the section-5D man pages. It includes an introduction of kernel #defines.
15. Introduction to the section-7 man pages that includes an introduction of special files.
16. Introduction to the section-7D man pages. It includes an introduction of data link provider interface data structures.
17. Introduction to the section-7T man pages. It includes an introduction of transport provider interface data structures.

introductory frame In FMLI, a message frame displayed at the beginning and end of an application.

int-to-string Function in the emacs LISP programming language that converts an integer to a string.

inum Command-line option used with the find command. It specifies the inode number that files should have. *See also* find.

I-number Inode number associated with a file or directory.

invalidmsg descriptor Message used to display an appropriate error message in a conditional statement for an FMLI application.

inverse-add-global-abbrev Command in the emacs text editor that types a global abbreviation and its definition. This command is usually bound to the keystroke Ctrl-X - (Ctrl-X Dash).

inverse-add-local-abbrev Command in the emacs text editor that types a local abbreviation and its definition. This command is usually bound to the keystroke Ctrl-X Ctrl-H.

inverse-video Display method used to distinguish text by switching the background and foreground colors.

inw Device-driver library routine used to read a 16-bit word from a 16-bit I/O port.

I/O Information going into or coming out of a program or other device. *See also* input/output.

I/O addresses Addresses given to input or output devices that are in memory. They can be accessed from the I/O device or the internal operating system for use in the exchange of data.

IOA Input/output accelerator that uses a SDLI (synchronous data link interface) for synchronous data communication.

I/O requests Request issued to an I/O device for accessing data that is handled by kernel routines.

iocblk structure M_IOCTL structure used to describe a user's ioctl request.

ioctl (input/output control routine)
1. Library routine that performs control functions on STREAMS and devices.
2. Library routine used to control a character device.

I/O multiplexing Ability to multiplex I/O requests among multiple files or sockets.

I/O redirection Refers to using information from a source other than the keyboard as the input to a program or directing the output of a program to a location other than the screen. *See also* redirection, stdin, stdout.

IOT Name of signal number 6 (short for IOT instruction). It can be sent to a running process.

iovec Device-driver data structure used for I/O storage for uio structures.

IP
1. Abbreviation for Internet Protocol, an internetwork datagram delivery protocol used by higher-level protocols such as TCP or UDP.
2. Internetworking datagram delivery protocol.

IPC Abbreviation for interprocess communication, a set of software facilities that enable independent processes to share information through semaphores, shared memory, or messages.

ipcrm Command that removes a message queue semaphore set or shared memory identifiers.

ipcs Command used to report information about interprocess communication facilities.

IPL Abbreviation for interrupt priority level, the priority level for a specific interrupt used by device controllers.

IP network Network that uses the IP and that usually connects with the Internet. *See also* Internet.

IPX Abbreviation for internetwork packet exchange, a connectionless network layer protocol used to perform addressing and routing function in the internetwork. It is popular with NetWare networks.

IPX/SPX Abbreviation for internetwork packet exchange/sequenced packet exchange, a set of protocols used together or separately by Novell for its NetWare networks.

isalnum Library routine that checks to see if the character-coded value passed to it is an alphanumeric character. It returns true if it is, otherwise it returns false.

isalpha Library routine that checks to see if the character-coded value passed to it is an alphabetical character. It returns true if it is, otherwise it returns false.

isascii Library routine that checks to see if the character-coded value passed to it is an ASCII character. It returns true if it is, otherwise it returns false.

isastream Library routine used to determine whether the file descriptor passed to it as an argument represents a STREAMS file.

isatty Library routine that determines whether a specified file descriptor is associated with a terminal device.

iscntrl Library routine that checks to see if the character-coded value passed to it is a control character defined by the character set. It returns true if it is, otherwise it returns false.

isdigit Library routine that checks to see if the character-coded value passed to it is a decimal-digit character. It returns true if it is, otherwise it returns false.

ISDN Abbreviation for integrated services digital network, a set of standards initiated by CCITT to have standard interconnectivity for a variety of services world-wide. It includes interconnectivity of telephones, terminal, computers, video, voice mail, and many other services. These services are available for both businesses and individuals.

isearch-backward Command in the emacs text editor that searches backward through the buffer for a string as the user types it. This command is usually bound to the keystroke Ctrl-R.

isearch-backward-regexp Command in the emacs text editor that searches backward through the buffer for a regular expression as the user types it.

isearch-forward Command in the emacs text editor that searches forward through the buffer for a string as the user types it. This command is usually bound to the keystroke Ctrl-S.

isearch-forward-regexp Command in the emacs text editor that searches forward through the buffer for a regular expression as the user types it.

iseek Command-line option for the dd command that specifies the number of blocks to seek from the start of the input file. *See also* dd.

isencrypt Library routine that takes a specified pointer to an array of characters and the number or characters in the array and determines whether or not it is encrypted.

isgraph Library routine that checks to see if the character-coded value passed to it is a printing character or a space character. It returns true if it is, otherwise it returns false.

isig Command-line option used with the stty command for enabling or disabling processing of intr, quit, and switch characters. This option is used for terminals that connect to a computer via serial lines.

islower Library routine that checks to see if the character-coded value passed to it is a lowercase ASCII character. It returns true if it is, otherwise it returns false.

ismpx Command that reports whether standard input is connected to a multi-plexed xt channel and whether it's running under layers or not.

isnan Library routine that returns true (1) if the argument passed to it is not a number, otherwise it returns false (0).

isnand Library routine that returns true (1) if the argument passed to it is not a number, otherwise it returns false (0).

isnanf Library routine, implemented as a macro, that returns true (1) if the argument passed to it is not a num-ber, otherwise it returns false (0).

isochronous Refers to an equal time in-terval.

isochronous communication Variation of asynchronous communication where two devices that want to communicate do it by transmitting or receiving clock signals from each other so that they have an equivalent time interval.

ispeed Command-line option used with the stty command for setting the termi-nal input baud rate. This option is used for terminals that connect to a computer via serial lines.

ispell Command for interactively check-ing the spelling of a document.

isprint Library routine that checks to see if the character-coded value passed to it is a printing character, including the space character. It returns true if it is, otherwise it returns false.

ispunct Library routine that checks to see if the character-coded value passed to it is a printing character but not a space or an alphanumeric character. It returns true if it is, otherwise it re-turns false.

isspace Library routine that checks to see if the character-coded value passed

to it is a whitespace character, includ-ing space, tab, carriage-return, new-line, vertical-tab, or formfeed. It re-turns true if it is one of these, other-wise it returns false.

issue File, located in /etc, used to identi-fy a system. Its contents are printed to the terminal at the login prompt.

istrip Command-line option used with the stty command for selecting whether input characters are stripped to seven bits, dropping the high-order bit. This option is used for terminals that con-nect to a computer via serial lines.

isupper Library routine that checks to see if the character-coded value passed to it is an uppercase ASCII character. It returns true if it is, otherwise it re-turns false.

isxoff Command-line option used with the stty command for setting the meth-od of flow control.

item Object such as a line in a menu that is used to represent information or an action in a character interface.

item_count Library routine that returns the number of items of a specified menu.

item_description Library routine that returns a pointer to the description of a specified item.

item help file Help message that is linked to an item that provides help, on request, to a user who is interested in that item and its purpose.

item_index Library routine that returns the index to a specified item in a menu if the item is in an item pointer array.

item_init Library routine that is called when a menu is posted or just after the current item changes to return the pointer to the item initialization rou-tine.

itemmsg FMLI descriptor used to display a message on the message line when it is navigated to. The information stored in this descriptor is the message that is displayed.

item_name Library routine that returns a pointer to the name of the specified item.

item_opts Library routine that returns the current options for the specified item.

itimeout Device-driver library routine that executes a specified function when the specified time increment has expired.

item_opts_off Library routine that turns off the specified options for an item specified in the function call.

item_opts_on Library routine that turns on the specified options for an item specified in the function call.

item_term Library routine that is called when a menu is unposted or just before the current item changes to return the pointer to the item termination function.

item_userptr Library routine that returns the user pointer for the specified item.

item_value Library routine that returns the value of a specified item. This value is the select value, a binary value that is true if the item has been selected and false if it hasn't.

item_visible Library routine that returns a value of true if the specified value is visible and false if it isn't.

itoemajor Device-driver library routine that converts an internal major number specified in the arguments to an external major number.

itom Library routine that is used to initialize pointers to an integer array and allocates the memory for use in arithmetic operations.

iuclc Command-line option used with the stty command for selecting whether uppercase characters in the input are converted to lowercase characters. This option is used for terminals that connect to a computer via serial lines.

ixany Command-line option used with the stty command for selecting whether the XON character or any character in the input can restart output. This option is used for terminals that connect to a computer via serial lines.

ixoff Command-line option used with the stty command for controlling how Start and Stop characters are used in flow control. This option is used for terminals that connect to a computer via serial lines.

ixon Command-line option used with the stty command for enabling or disabling Start/Stop output control. This option is used for terminals that connect to a computer via serial lines.

J

j0 Library routine that returns the Bessel function of x of the first kind of order of zero.

j1 Library routine that returns the Bessel function of x of the first kind of order of one.

jn Library routine which returns the Bessel function of x of the first order of n.

job control Feature provided by the BSD UNIX operating system that breaks a login session into smaller units called *jobs*. Each job consists of one or more cooperating processes.

job number Number that batch gives to a submitted job. This number is different from the process number that the system generates.

job Program started from the shell that can start, stop, and move between the foreground and background. Running a program starts one or more jobs.

jobs Command that lists all jobs, including those that are running, stopped, in the foreground, and in the background.

join Command that performs a relational join on two text files.

Joy, William Developer of the vi text editor, the C shell, and many BSD enhancements.

jrand48 Library routine that returns the signed long integers uniformly distributed over the interval (-2EXP31 to 2EXP31).

jsh Job control version of the Bourne shell.

jterm Command that resets a layer of the windowing terminal after a program changes the terminal attributes of the layer. *See also* layer.

jwin Command that displays the size of the current window. *See also* layer.

K

k12 Type of USENET newsgroup that discusses topics concerning the education of school children from kindergarten through the 12th grade. The names of newsgroups of this type begin with *k12*.

KB Abbreviation for *kilobyte*. One kilobyte equals 1024 bytes.

kbd
1. Option used on the command line with the dbx source code debugger. It specifies that the program put the keyboard in up-down translation mode.
2. Kernel debugger used to set breakpoints, display kernel stack traces and other structures, and modify the contents of memory, I/O, and registers.

kdbcomp Command used to compile tables for use with the iconv utility and with the kdb STREAMS module.

kdbload Command used to load or link kdb tables into the kdb STREAMS module.

kbd-macro-query Command in the emacs text editor that inserts a prompt for information from the keyboard into a macro definition. This command is usually bound to the keystroke Ctrl-X Q.

keeptmp Command-line option used with the cc C compiler (Solaris 2.0). It specifies that cc should not delete its temporary files.

kept-new-versions Variable in the emacs text editor that controls the number of new backup versions that are stored.

kept-old-versions Variable in the emacs text editor that controls the number of old backup versions that are stored.

kerberos Secure authorization scheme.

kermit Terminal-emulator application used to connect to a remote system using a protocol and running over a network or modem connection.

kernel Heart of the UNIX system which provides services to applications and the shell. These services include controlling the hardware, schedules, and priorities; being the arbitrator between requests for services from the processes; and managing the memory, disk storage, and permissions.

kernel debugger *See* kdb.

kernel I/O Part of the kernel made up of device-drivers that manages the device hardware and retrieves and sends information to and from the kernel.

kernel memory allocator Abbreviated *kmalloc*, a command used by the kernel or a device-driver to allocate memory from the kernel memory pool.

Kernel Memory Allocator buffers Often referred to as KMA buffers, these buffers are allocated by drivers from a common pool of memory used by all parts of the kernel.

kernel-mode scheduler parameter table Table used to manage sleeping, time-sharing lightweight processes (LWPs).

kernel parameters Parameters used by the kernel to deliver available resources and set boundaries on how the system is used. These parameters define how system resources, such as memory, are allocated.

Kernighan, Brian Coauthor of the C programming language and the awk utility.

key
1. Button on a keyboard.
2. Field in a database table that uniquely identifies each record in the table.

key binding In the Motif environment, the key that is significant in a menu, which causes an action when selected from the menu.

keyboard
1. Hardware device, used like a typewriter, to input information into a computer.
2. Device that manages the keyboard part of a system console.

keyboard layout Arrangement of a keyboard, usually associated with a language, such as U.S. ASCII that is specified in the environment variables on a UNIX system. The keyboard layouts differ in the position of characters and the addition of foreign characters not included in the English language.

keyboard-quit Command in the emacs text editor that aborts a command. This command is usually bound to the keystroke Ctrl-G. *See also* abort.

keycode Code or numerical value associated with a keystroke on a keyboard.

key_decryptsession Keyserver interface routine used to decrypt a DES key given a server netname, the public key of the server, and the secret key associated with the effective UID of the calling process.

key_encryptsession Keyserver interface routine used to encrypt a DES key given a server netname, the public key of the server and the secret key associated with the effective UID of the calling process.

key_gendes Library routine used to get a secure conversation key from the keyserver.

keylogin Command that decrypts an encrypted message after prompting the user for a password. *See also* encryption.

keylogout Command that prevents access to the secret key for decrypting or encrypting messages. *See also* encryption.

keymap Set of key bindings in the emacs text editor. The basic key bindings are stored in a keymap called global-map. *See also* key binding.

keypad Library routine that is used to enable or disable a variable for curs_inopts. If enabled, it allows users to press a function key so wgetch will return a single value. If disabled, curses does not treat the function keys specifically.

keys *See* encryption keys.

keyserv Server daemon used to store the encryption keys for the users logged into the system.

key_setsecret Library routine used by the calling process to set the key for its effective UID.

keystrokes One or more keys that are pressed to give a command or perform an operation. For example, the EOF command in the shell is usually assigned to the keystroke Ctrl-D (that is, hold down the Ctrl key while typing D). *See also* Ctrl, Meta, Alt.

keyword
1. Korn shell mode that controls how variable definitions are handled on the command line. It is specified with the set command (Korn shell only).
2. Words used in commands for a special purpose.

kill
1. Command that sends a kill signal to a process specified in the arguments. It is most often used to stop a running process.
2. Library routine that sends a signal to a process or group of processes specified by a PID included in the call.
3. To stop a process from running.

killall Command used by the /etc/sbin/shutdown command that kills all of the active processes not directly related to the shutdown process.

kill-all-abbrevs Command in the emacs text editor that disables the use of abbreviations for this editing session.

killchar Library function call used with curses that returns the user's current line kill character.

kill-comment Command in the emacs text editor that deletes a comment on the current line. It is used in C mode, Fortran mode, LISP mode, or other modes for writing source code, and locates a comment based on the presence of comment characters appropriate to the language.

kill-emacs Command in the saveconf add-on package to the emacs text editor that enables the user to restart the program with the same buffers open and windows visible.

kill-level Command in the Epsilon text editor that kills a bracketed expression, deleting it from the current buffer and storing it in a kill buffer.

kill-line Command in the emacs text editor that kills the text from the current cursor position to the end of line, deleting it from the current buffer and storing it in a kill buffer. This command is usually bound to the keystroke Ctrl-K.

kill-paragraph Command in the emacs text editor that kills the text from the current cursor position to the end of paragraph, deleting it from the current buffer and storing it in a kill buffer.

killpg Library routine used to send sig to a process group.

kill-rectangle Command in the emacs text editor that kills the rectangular area between the cursor location and the mark, deleting it from the current buffer and storing it in a kill buffer.

kill-region Command in the emacs text editor that kills (or whomps) the currently marked region, deleting it from the current buffer and storing it in a kill buffer. This command is usually bound to the keystroke Ctrl-W.

kill-ring-max Variable in the emacs text editor that controls the number of kill buffers to keep. The default is usually 30.

kill-sentence Command in the emacs text editor that kills the text from the cursor to the end of the current sentence, deleting it from the current buffer and storing it in a kill buffer. This command is usually bound to the keystroke Meta-K.

kill-sexp Command in the emacs text editor, used in LISP mode to kill the S-expression following the cursor. This command is usually bound to the keystroke Meta-Ctrl-K.

kill-shell-input Command in the emacs text editor that deletes the current line.

kill-some-buffers Command in the emacs text editor that prompts the user for each open buffer, asking which should be closed.

kill-window Command in the Epsilon text editor that deletes the current window without deleting its associated buffer.

kill-word Command in the emacs text editor that kills the word immediately after the cursor, deleting it from the current buffer and storing it in a kill buffer. This command is usually bound to the keystroke Meta-D.

kilobit Term describing a unit of 1024 bits.

kilobits per second (Kbps) Speed of data transfer, measured by the number of 1,024-bit units transferred each second.

kilobyte (KB) Measurement of data that signifies 1,024 bytes of data.

kitchen-sink icon Bit-mapped icon used for the emacs text editor, resembling a tiny kitchen sink. This refers to emac's plethora of features and commands.

kludge Computer slang meaning to put together or fix computer software or hardware in a makeshift fashion. A derogatory way of describing inelegant computing.

KMA (Kernel Memory Allocator) Refers to the buffers that devices allocate for use from a common memory pool.

kmem Set of ioctl commands that read or write to kernel memory based on specification given.

kmem_alloc Device-driver library routine used to allocate a specified number of bytes of kernel memory and return a pointer to the allocated memory.

kmem_free Device-driver library routine used to return allocated kernel memory that was previously allocated using kmem_alloc.

kmem_zalloc Device-driver library routine used to allocate a specified number of bytes of kernel memory, clears the memory by filling it with zeros, and returns a pointer to the allocated memory.

Korn, David Author of the Korn shell.

Korn shell *See* shell and ksh.

Korn shell mode Mode that controls how the Korn shell handles shell variables, runs jobs, and edits commands. Korn shell modes are specified using the set command (Korn shell only).

ksh Standard/restricted programming and command-language interpreter used to execute commands and read from a terminal or a file.

kvtoppid Device-driver library routine used to return the physical page ID for a virtual address specified in the arguments.

L

.l File extension for files containing LISP source code.

l3tol Library routine that converts a list of three-byte integers packed into a character string pointed to by cp into a list of long integers pointed to by lp.

l64a Library routine that returns a pointer to the corresponding base-64 representation when given an argument that's a long integer.

labelit Command used to provide labels for unmounted disk file systems or for file systems being copied to tape.

label widget Widget used to display a non-editable string.

LAN *See* local area network.

landscape
1. Paper orientation when printing. Landscape orientation prints lines parallel to the long edge of the paper.
2. Command line option used with the dpost utility, specifying that the PostScript output print in landscape orientation.

LANG Shell Environment Variable that contains information used by language-dependent programs (Bourne and Korn shells only).

langinfo Header file containing constants used to identify items of langinfo data.

language Term used to describe a program or set of rules used to create software.

language mode Major mode used in the emacs text editor for writing source code in a given language. Emacs supports C, LISP, and Fortran modes.

laptop Computer small enough to fit on the user's lap.

laser printer Type of printer that uses laser technology to put the image of a page on paper.

last Command that indicates the last user or login on the system.

lastcomm Command that shows, in reverse order, the last commands executed on the system.

last-kbd-macro Command in the Epsilon text editor that executes the last keyboard macro defined.

lastlogin Command run by runacct that shows the last date on which each user logged in.

latency, disk Time it takes for the selected sector to rotate to the correct position for data to be read.

latency, software Time between requesting data and the actual transfer of the data.

LaTeX Macro package used with TeX. Its intent is to simplify the markup needed for TeX documents.

LaTeX mode In the emacs text editor, a major mode designed for formatting text files for LaTeX.

LaTeX-mode Command in the emacs text editor that enables LaTeX mode, which is designed for editing text files formatted for LaTeX.

layered architecture Way of constructing programs where one or more levels of routines lie between the computing hardware and the application. Activities are separated according to their type of task. Computer networking is an example of layered architecture.

layers Command for creating multiple windows on an AT&T DMD or similar terminal.

lc Command used to list the contents of a directory. The default output is columnar. *See also* ls.

lcase
1. Command-line option used with the stty command for selecting whether to convert automatically between upper- and lowercase (also spelled LCASE).
2. Option used on the command line with the dd command. It specifies that all text be converted to lowercase. *See also* dd.

LCD (liquid crystal display) Type of display that employs liquid crystals, often used in digital watches and read-outs on electronic equipment.

LCK. Abbreviation for lock file, used by many programs to indicate that a particular file is locked.

LC_MESSAGES Environment variable that points to a directory containing a message file. *See also* gencat, gettxt.

lcong48 One of a family of functions that generate pseudorandom numbers using a linear congruential algorithm and 48-bit integer arithmetic. This function should be called before either drand48, lrand48, or mrand48 is called.

ld Command for link-editing object files.

ldd Command that displays a list of dynamic dependencies.

ldexp **Library** routine to manipulate parts of floating-point numbers.

LD_LIBRARY_PATH Environment variable used to specify the library search directories for the dynamic linker at run time. *See also* ld.

LD_RUN_PATH Environment variable that contains a list of directories for the dynamic linker to check at run time. *See also* ld.

ldterm STREAMS module that provides most of the terminal interface.

le Command-line option used with the test command in the Korn shell. This option determines whether one number is less than or equal to another.

leaveok Library routine for controlling curses terminal-output options.

LED (light emitting diode) Display technology once used for digital watches and readouts, now replaced by LCDs. *See also* LCD.

left-margin Variable in the emacs text editor that controls the left margin in fundamental and text modes. If this is greater than zero, all lines are indented.

Lempel-Ziv coding Method of compressing the contents of a file.

length Command-line option used with the lp command that sets page length. It is used in the bc desk calculator to calculate the number of digits in a number.

Lesk, Mike Author of the UUCP system, the tbl preprocessor, ms macros, and the lex utility.

less Command used in Linux. Similar to the more command in other versions of UNIX.

less-than sign Relational operator used to compare two values.

let
1. Command used in the Korn shell that assigns the results of an arithmetic expression to a variable.
2. Function in the emacs LISP programming language that defines a variable or statement block.

lex Command that generates programs for simple lexical tasks.

lfind Library routine that performs a linear search.

lgamma Library routine that provides the log gamma function.

libc Library containing C programming functions.

library Collection of routines that can be linked into a program when it's compiled.

life
1. Add-on package for the emacs text editor that implements a major mode that plays the "Game of Life."
2. Command in the life add-on package to the emacs text editor that enters life mode, in which emacs plays the "Game of Life."

life mode In the emacs text editor, a major mode that plays the "Game of Life."

limit In the C shell, a command that displays or sets limits on resources used by the current process.

limits Header file (limits.h) for implementation-specific constants.

line Command that reads one line; usually used in shell files to read from a user's terminal.

line discipline Rules governing communications between a computer and a terminal.

line discipline module Module that handles the rules for communications between a computer and a terminal. *See also* ldterm.

line-edit mode In the Korn shell, the mode in which the user can modify and reissue previous commands.

line editor Editor, such as ed, that operates on one line at a time. *See also* ed.

line feed Character sent to a device, such as a terminal or printer, that advance the cursor to the next line.

LINES Shell variable that contains the number of lines that can be displayed on the screen (Korn shell only).

line printer Type of printer that prints a full line at a time.

line printer services *See* LP print service.

LINENO Built-in shell variable that contains the current line number of the script or function currently being executed (Bourne and Korn shells only).

line terminator Character that signals that the end-of-line has been reached.

link
1. Command to link files and directories. The link command performs no error checking and can only be used by the root user. *See also* ln.
2. Library routine that creates links to a file.
3. To create an executable by bringing together different pieces of object code.

linkb Device-driver library routine used to concatenate two message blocks.

linkblk Device-driver library routine used as a STREAMS multiplexor link structure.

link count Number of hard links that exist to a particular UNIX file.

link_field Library routine (curses) used to duplicate a field at the specified location.

link_fieldtype Library routine (curses) that returns a pointer to the field type built from two specified types.

links Command-line option used with the find command. Specifies the number of links files should have. *See also* find.

lint Command used to check for problems in a C program.

LINTED Keyword used in comments in C source code, indicating that lint warnings should be enabled.

LINTLIBRARY Keyword used in comments in C source code, indicating that lint should ignore unused arguments to functions and unused variables in extern declarations.

Linux UNIX clone distributed free on the Internet.

LISP Acronym for the List-oriented programming language, designed for use in artificial intelligence applications. Many variants of LISP exist, including Gosling LISP, emacs LISP, Common LISP, and mocklisp. It is an add-on package to the emacs text editor that implements additional major modes, minor modes, commands, and functions.

.lisp File extension for files containing LISP source code.

lisp-complete-symbol Command in the emacs text editor used in emacs LISP mode to perform completion based on the symbol preceding the cursor. This allows the user to type the beginning of a symbol and have emacs complete it. This command is usually bound to the keystroke Meta-Tab.

LISP interaction mode In the emacs text editor, a major mode designed for editing and evaluating programs in the LISP programming language.

lisp-interaction-mode Command in the emacs text editor that enables LISP mode, which is designed for writing and testing programs in the LISP programming language. *See also* C mode.

LISP mode In the emacs text editor, a major mode designed for editing programs in the LISP programming language.

lisp-mode Add-on package for the emacs text editor that implements major modes for LISP, emacs LISP, and LISP interaction. Also, a command in the emacs text editor that enables LISP mode.

lisp-send-defun Command in the emacs text editor used in LISP mode to send a function definition to an external LISP interpreter.

list-abbrevs Command in the emacs text editor that displays a list of word abbreviations.

list-all Command in the Epsilon text editor that describe the program's state in text form, in a new buffer named list-all. Also, an Epsilon buffer created by the list-all command.

list-buffers Command in the emacs text editor that displays a list of all open buffers. This command is usually bound to the keystroke Ctrl-X Ctrl-B.

list-changes Command in the Epsilon text editor that finds the differences between two list-all files, which is useful when updating to a new version of Epsilon.

listdgrp Command used to list the members of a device group.

listen
1. Command used to "listen" for service requests on a network. When requests arrive they are accepted and the appropriate server is invoked.
2. Networking library routine that listens for connections on a socket.

list-options Command in the options add-on package to the emacs text editor that lists the values of emacs variables.

listserv Mailing list software developed to automate the maintenance of mailing lists. For example, it can allow a user to subscribe to a mailing list without administrative intervention.

list-tags Command in the emacs text editor, used with the etags facility to list all the tags in the tag table.

listusers Command used to list login information for users.

list widget Widget used for managing row-column geometry.

literal Something written into a program that doesn't change, such as the text for a message.

LK Password status displayed by the passwd command, indicating that the user's password is locked.

ln Command used to link files and directories. *See also* link.

lnext Command-line option used with the stty command for setting the lnext control character.

lo Device used to return (loopback) all packets received instead of invoking a hardware device.

load-buffer Command in the Epsilon text editor that interprets a buffer as a command file.

load-bytes Command in the Epsilon text editor that loads a file containing compiled EEL commands and variables.

load-changes Command in the Epsilon text editor that loads the changes from the list-changes command into Epsilon, which is useful when updating to a new version of Epsilon.

loader Software that loads program code into memory to be run. A *bootstrap loader* loads the initial operating system code, preparing the computer to start running.

load-file Command in the emacs text editor that loads a macro file.

load-library Command in the emacs text editor that loads a private LISP library into emacs.

load-path Variable in the emacs text editor that contains a list of directories to search when loading LISP packages.

LOADPFK Variable used to direct FMLI to download alternative keystrokes into a terminal's function keys.

load testing Testing of a device or system under varying load conditions.

loblk Command-line option used with the stty command for controlling whether layer output is blocked. This option is used for terminals that connect to a computer via serial lines.

local abbreviation In the emacs text editor, a word abbreviation that works only in the current major mode. *See also* word abbreviation mode.

local area network (LAN) Type of network used to connect computers and other devices that are relatively near each other (usually in the same building). Most UNIX systems support Ethernet and Token Ring LANs.

local dictionary Text file containing words that should not be considered misspelled by the spell command. This file usually contains names and other valid words that are used by a particular writer or group of writers.

locale Term used to refer to the language, related characteristics, and settings for a computer system.

localeconv Library routine used for getting the correct numeric formatting information.

localhost address IP address of the local host.

local mount Refers to logically connecting several disk drives on the same machine so that they appear as one file system.

local network Network that is local to the immediate environment, as opposed to a wide-area network that may connect systems over wide geographic areas.

local-set-key Command in the emacs text editor that binds a command to a key locally, that is, in the temporary keymap in use for the current buffer.

localtime Library routine used to convert the time to a string.

LOCK Device-driver library routine that acquires a basic lock as specified by lockp.

lock Library routine (XENIX) used to lock a process in primary memory.

LOCK_ALLOC Device-driver library routine that allocates and initializes a basic lock.

lockd (network lock daemon) Command that processes lock requests sent by either the kernel (locally) or another lock daemon (remotely).

LOCK_DEALLOC Device-driver library routine that deallocates a basic lock.

See also LOCK_ALLOC.

lockf Library routine used to lock sections of a file.

lock file *See* LCK.

locking
1. Securing a file against changes by other processes while one process controls the file.
2. Library routine (XENIX) that locks or unlocks a region of a file for reading or writing.

lock manager User-level daemon used by Network File System (NFS) to implement a network lock.

Lock Screen Program running under Open Windows that displays a pattern on the screen and prevents keyboard input until a password is entered.

log10 Library routine used to get the base-ten logarithm of a number.

log
1. Library routine that performs the logarithm function.
2. STREAMS device driver that provides an interface for console logging and for the processes of STREAMS error logging and event tracing.

logb Library routine used to manipulate parts of floating-point numbers.

log files Files that keep records of system activities, often used for statistical purposes.

logger Command used to add a string to a log file for later review.

logging in Process by which the user identifies himself or herself to the UNIX system and provide a valid password. Each user has a unique log-in ID, user ID, or user name. At the end of a work session, the user logs out. *See also* login ID.

logging off Process of ending a session with a computer and disconnecting from the connecting line.

logical AND Operator that combines two logical values. The result is true if both of the two input values are true.

logical exclusive OR Operator that combines two logical values. The result is true if exactly one (not both) of the two input values is true. Also called *XOR*.

logical negation Unary operator that changes a true value to false and a false value to true.

logical operator Programming-language operator that performs a logical (boolean) operation, such as AND, OR, or NOT.

logical OR Operator that combines two logical values. The result is true if one or both of the two input values is true.

logical value Value that can be either true or false. A true value is usually represented by a zero and a false value by a one.

logical XOR Exclusive OR operator that combines two logical values. The result is true if exactly one (not both) of the two input values is true.

log in *See* logging in.

login
1. Process of starting a computer session by identifying yourself through your login ID (user name) and password.
2. Command that prompts the user to enter a user name and password.
3. File used by the login command to control login options.

login directory Directory you're immediately placed in when you log in, also called the home directory.

login ID *See* user name.

loginlog File located in /var/admin, used to log unsuccessful login attempts when a user attempts to log in more than the number of times set by LOGFAILURES.

login name *See* user name.

logins Command that displays information about user logins, such as login name, user ID number, group name and group ID number.

logname Command that displays the login name of the user.

LOGNAME Environment variable whose value is the user's log in name.

logout
1. In the C shell, a command that terminates the shell. This is equivalent to using the exit command.
2. To end a session with the computer system.

.logout Shell script that is executed when the user logs out (C shell only).

longjmp Library routine (BSD) used in low-level subroutines of programs when errors and interrupts are encountered.

longname Library routine (curses) that returns a pointer to the location that contains the description of the current terminal.

look Command (BSD) used to locate words in the system dictionary or lines in a sorted list.

lookbib Command (BSD) used to find references in a bibliographic database.

looking-at Command in the emacs text editor that accepts a regular expression and determines whether the text following the cursor matches it.

loopback transport Networking module that loops information intended for the local system back to the local system without going out on the network.

lorder Command used to search object or library archive files for ordering relation.

lower multiplexor Part of a multiplexing driver that is nearest the hardware interface.

lowercase To use lowercase (a, b, c) instead of uppercase (A, B, C) letters. UNIX is case-sensitive and typically uses lowercase letters for commands.

lowercase-word Command in the Epsilon text editor that converts the current word to lowercase. *See also* downcase-word.

lp
1. Command used to send print requests to a print queue.
2. Device-driver for parallel ports.

LP print service Printing system that controls print requests and print queues.

lpadmin Command used to configure the LP print service.

lpc Command (BSD) used to control one or more printers.

lpfilter Command used to administer (add, change, delete, list) LP print-service filters.

lpforms Command used to administer LP print-service forms.

lpi Abbreviation for lines per inch, a command-line option used with the lp command that sets line spacing vertically.

lpmove Command used to move queued lp requests between lp destinations.

lpq Command (BSD) used to display the print requests queued to print.

lpr Command (BSD) used to send print request to the printer.

lpr-buffer Command in the emacs text editor that prints the current buffer without page numbers or headings. *See also* print-buffer.

lprm Command (BSD) used to remove print requests from a print queue.

lprof Command used to display how a program executes, line-by-line. It provides a way to check how often portions of code execute.

lpr-region Command in the emacs text editor that prints the currently marked region, without page numbers or headings. *See also* print-region.

lpr-switches Variable in the emacs text editor that controls how emacs prints text. It contains options to be passed to the lpr or lp command.

lpsched Command used to start the LP print service. *See also* lpshut.

lpshut Command used to shut down the LP print service. *See also* lpsched.

lpstat Command used to check the status of the LP print service. The information includes printer availability and jobs queued.

lpsystem Command used to define parameters for the LP print service for use with remote systems, as when used over a network with TCP/IP.

lptest Command (BSD) used to send a "ripple test" pattern to a printer. Normal output goes to standard output. To use a printer test pattern, redirect output to the printer.

lpusers Command used to set the maximum queue-priority level that a user can assign to a print request.

lrand48 One of a family of functions that generate pseudorandom numbers using a linear congruential algorithm and 48-bit integer arithmetic.

ls Command used to list the contents of a directory.

lsearch Library routine that performs a linear search.

lseek Library routine used to move a read/write file pointer.

.lsp File extension for files containing LISP source code.

lstat Library routine used to get information about a file. *See also* stat.

lt Command-line option used with the test command in the Korn shell. This option determines whether one number is less than another.

ltol3 Library routine that converts a list of long integers packed into a character string pointed to by lp into a list of three-byte integers pointed to by cp.

lynx Command used to browse the Internet. It provides a text-based interface for browsing Web pages (without letting you view graphics or listen to audio).

M

M- Notation used to describe the combination of the Meta key with another key. For example, M-d is short for Meta-d. On keyboards with an Alt key, this is performed by holding down the Alt key while pressing the D key. On other keyboard, this is performed by pressing the Esc or Escape key followed by the D key.

m4 Command that servers as a macro processor to the C compiler.

Mach Type of UNIX developed at Carnegie-Mellon University, used in the NeXT operating system.

mach Command (BSD) that displays the type of processor for the system on which the command is run.

macro Series of keystrokes or commands that have been recorded for later playback.

macro expansion When a macro is replaced with the keystrokes or commands for which it was defined.

macro packages Group of macros designed to perform a set of functions. For example, macro packages (such as mm and me) for the troff text formatter provide macros that simplify the process of producing memos and other standard documents.

macroprocessor Program that replaces the macro with its defined keys and commands.

madd Library routine (BSD) used for multiple-precision integer arithmetic. The third argument is assigned the sum of the first two arguments.

magic File (in /etc/magic) containing "magic numbers," which are use by the file command to determine what type of file is being accessed. If the file command finds a matching magic number in the file it is checking, it reports the file's type based on the associated name in /etc/magic.

magnetic disk *See* hard disk.

magneto-optical Technology that uses a laser to heat a disk (similar to a CD-ROM disk) and then uses a magnetic field to store bits of data. Magneto-optical disk can be erased, where CD-ROM disks cannot.

magneto-optical disk Disk that uses magneto-optical technology.

mail Command used to send and receive mail from other users. *See also* mailx.

mail buffer Buffer for sending and receiving electronic mail while using the emacs text editor. Also called the *mail* buffer.

mailalias Command that lists the e-mail addresses that are assigned to one or more aliases. *See also* e-mail.

mail-archive-file-name Variable in the emacs text editor that contains the filename in which emacs stores outgoing electronic mail messages. If the value is nil, outgoing messages aren't saved.

mail-bcc Command in the emacs text editor that moves the cursor to the Bcc field in the mail buffer. This command is usually bound to the keystroke Ctrl-C Ctrl-F Ctrl-B.

mailbox Place where incoming mail messages are stored. Mailboxes are usually located in the /usr/mail directory.

mail-cc Command in the emacs text editor that moves the cursor to the Cc field in the mail buffer. This command is usually bound to the keystroke Ctrl-C Ctrl-F Ctrl-C.

MAILCHECK Shell variable that contains the frequency (in seconds) with which the user's incoming mail file should be checked (Bourne and Korn shells only).

mailcnfg File used for configuration information for the mail and rmail commands.

mail-default-reply-to Variable in the emacs text editor that controls whether emacs automatically inserts a name in the Reply-to field of outgoing electronic mail messages.

mailer Program used to transfer mail messages to their destinations. The mailer for many UNIX systems is /etc/mail/mailsurr.

.mailfile File in which the notify command stores incoming mail messages.

mailing list List of addresses to which mail can be sent. Mailing lists are lists of users who want to share information on a particular subject. Participants in a mailing list can contribute articles on the subject to others on the list.

maillock Library routine that creates a lock file for a user's mail box.

mail notification Automatic notification when new electronic mail messages arrive for the user. The notification is in the form of an on-screen message. The notify command turns automatic notification on and off.

mail-other-window Command in the emacs text editor that opens a mail buffer in the other window. This command is usually bound to the keystroke Ctrl-X 4 M.

MAILPATH Shell variable that contains a colon separated list of files (Bourne and Korn shells only). Each listed file is checked for new mail, the frequency of which is defined by the MAILCHECK variable.

mail_pipe Command invoked by the mail command when a user's mail is to be piped as input to another command.

mailq Command (BSD) used to display the contents of a mail queue.

.mailrc File containing configuration and alias information used by the mailx program. *See also* mailx.

mail-self-blind Variable in the emacs text editor that controls whether emacs automatically inserts the user's name to receive blind copies of outgoing electronic mail.

mail-send Command in the emacs text editor that sends the mail message in the mail buffer and leaves the cursor in the mail buffer. This command is usually bound to the keystroke Ctrl-C Ctrl-S.

mail-send-and-exit Command in the emacs text editor that sends the mail message in the mail buffer and closes the buffer. This command is usually bound to the keystroke Ctrl-C Ctrl-C.

mail-signature Command in the emacs text editor that inserts the contents of the user's signature file at the cursor location. This command is usually bound to the keystroke Ctrl-C Ctrl-W.

mailstats Command (BSD) that displays the statistics collected by the sendmail program.

mail-subject Command in the emacs text editor that moves the cursor to the subject field in the mail buffer. This command is usually bound to the keystroke Ctrl-C Ctrl-F Ctrl-S.

mailsurr Configuration file used to control routing of mail. It is contained in the /etc/mail directory.

mail-to Command in the emacs text editor that moves the cursor to the To: field in the mail buffer. This command is usually bound to the keystroke Ctrl-C Ctrl-F Ctrl-T.

mailtool Program running under Open Windows that allows the user to read and send electronic mail.

mail-use-rfc822 Variable in the emacs text editor that controls whether emacs uses the full RFC822 parser on mail addresses.

mailx Command used to send and receive mail from other users. *See also* mail.

mainframe connectivity Ability of a program, computer, or network to connect to a mainframe computer.

main function Starting point for most programming languages. Other functions can be used along with the main function to construct the entire program.

major Library routine that returns the major number component from a specified device.

major device number Number that identifies a type of device installed on your system. For example, all terminal devices may have the same major number, but each one (/dev/tty00, /dev/tty01, etc.) would each have a different minor device number. *See also* minor device number.

major mode In the emacs text editor, an operational mode that determines which features are active. Each buffer can be in one major mode at a time. The most commonly used major mode is fundamental mode.

major number *See* major device number.

make Command used to create, maintain, and regenerate one or more programs.

make-backup-files Variable in the emacs text editor that controls whether emacs saves a copy of a file when it saves a modified version for the first time.

makecontext Library routines used to implement user-level context switching.

makedbm Command used to create a Network Information Service (NIS) dbm file.

makedepend Command used with the X Window System to create dependencies in make files.

makedev Library routine that returns a formatted device number. Can be used to create a device number for the mknode routine.

makedevice Device-driver library routine used to create a device number from a major and minor device number.

makefile File used with the make command. It contains the commands that are used by the make command.

makekey Command used for creating an encryption key. It is provided with the set of encryption utilities supplied only in the United States.

make-local-variable Function in the emacs LISP programming language that defines a new variable that is local to the current mode.

malloc Library routine used to allocate memory.

mallopt Obsolete library routine provided for source compatibility only.

man Command used to display UNIX manual pages.

mandatory locking Feature that, when implemented, prevents a user from accessing a file or record until the lock is released.

Mandelbrot, Benoit Coined the term *fractal* to describe a class of shapes that, while irregular, appears as a pattern. Mandelbrot was one of the pioneers in the area of chaos theory.

Mandelbrot program Program that produces fractals. *See also* fractals.

man Macros Macro definitions used with nroff and troff for formatting manual pages.

man page Abbreviation for manual page, a document that describes a particular component (command, library routine, file format, device, etc.) of UNIX. On-line man pages are displayed with the man command.

MANPATH Shell environment variable that defines the location of the UNIX online manual pages displayed by the man command. *See also* man.

manual Technical book, often accompanying computer hardware or software.

manual-entry Command in the emacs text editor that displays UNIX online manual pages in an emacs buffer.

mapchan
1. Command used to map tty devices, intended for users of non-English applications.
2. File used for configuring the mapping of input and output information.

mapfiles Files that contain information distributed by an NIS server to its clients. *See also* maps.

mapkey Command used to configure the mapping of function keys to a virtual terminal.

maplocale Command (XENIX) that converts System V Release 4 locale information to another format.

maps
1. Collections of information used by the automount command to locate the NFS file server, exported file system, and mount options for an NFS resource that is automatically mounted.
2. Collections of basic UNIX files used by NIS servers to distribute information that is pertinent to an entire NIS domain. NIS maps can include information on login accounts, group accounts, host names, and network services supported.

mapstr Command used to configure the mapping of function keys to a virtual terminal.

mark Location in an emacs buffer used for marking a region to be operated on. The set-mark-command command, usually bound to the Ctrl-@ or Ctrl-Spacebar keystrokes, locates the mark at the current cursor location. The user moves the cursor so that the region to be operated on is between the mark and the cursor. Also, the function in the emacs LISP programming language that returns the character position of the mark. *See also* marked region.

mark-c-function Command in the emacs text editor used in C mode to move the cursor to the beginning of the current C function definition. It also locates the mark at the end of the C function, so that the currently marked region is the entire current function. This command is usually bound to the keystroke Meta-Ctrl-H.

mark-defun Command in the emacs text editor used in C mode to move the cursor to the beginning of the current C function definition and the mark to the end of the function, so that the C function becomes the currently marked region. This command is usually bound to the keystroke Meta- Ctrl-H.

markdirs Korn shell mode that adds a slash (/) to end of directory names in ls listings. It is specified with the set command (Korn shell only).

marked region Contiguous text that has been marked for operation in the emacs text editor. The mark is at one end of the marked region and the cursor is at the other.

mark-fortran-subprogram Command in the emacs text editor used in Fortran mode to move the cursor to the beginning of the current Fortran subprogram. It also locates the mark at the end of the subprogram, so that the currently marked region is the entire current subprogram. This command is usually bound to the keystroke Meta-Ctrl-H.

markp Command-line option used with the stty command for controlling parity terminal settings.

mark-page Command in the emacs text editor that marks the current page as the currently marked region by moving the mark to the beginning and the cursor to the end of the page. This command is usually bound to the keystroke Ctrl-X Ctrl-P.

mark-paragraph Command in the emacs text editor that marks the current paragraph as the marked region. This command is usually bound to the keystroke Meta-H.

mark ring List of the last 16 locations of the mark in the emacs text editor. *See also* set-mark.

mark-sexp Command in the emacs text editor used in LISP mode to locate the mark at the end of the current S- expression. It also moves the cursor to the beginning of the current S-expression, so that the currently marked region is the current S-expression. This command is usually bound to the keystroke Meta-Ctrl-@.

mark-whole-buffer Command in the emacs text editor that marks the entire contents of the current buffer as the marked region. This command is usually bound to the keystroke Ctrl-X H.

master name server Name server used in TCP/IP to provide Domain Name System (DNS) service to a group of host systems. There can be both primary and secondary master servers providing DNS, so name service can continue even if the primary name server goes down.

master server Computer used to contain the definitive NIS records that are distributed to NIS clients. Slave servers contain copies of these records, so NIS services can continue even if the master server is down.

match-beginning Function in the emacs text editor that returns the beginning of a matched expression saved by the looking-at command. It accepts a character position to specify how may characters from the beginning of the expression to return.

match character *See* metacharacter.

match-end Function in the emacs text editor that returns the end of a matched expression saved by the looking-at command. It accepts a character position to specify how may characters from the end of the expression to return.

math Header file containing math functions and constants.

matherr Library routine for error handling, used by math libraries.

max
1. In the emacs LISP programming language, a function that returns the larger of two values.
2. Device-driver library routine that returns the larger of two integers.

MAXDUPREQS NFS tunable parameter that sets, on the server side, the maximum cached items in the duplicate request cache.

maximize In a graphical user interface, to cause a window to go to its maximum size, usually to occupy the entire screen area.

maybe-break-line Command in the Epsilon text editor that inserts a newline if the cursor position is to the right of the the fill column. *See also* auto-fill-mode.

MB Abbreviation for *megabyte.* One megabyte equals 1,048,576 bytes.

mbchar Group of library routines used for multibyte character handling.

mblen Library routine used for multibyte character handling. It determines the number of bytes in the multibyte character.

mbox Default name for a user's mailbox file for mail messages that have been read, but not deleted. The mbox is created and maintained in the user's home directory ($HOME/mbox) *See also* e-mail.

M_BREAK STREAMS control message, used to generate a line break.

mbstowcs Library routine used to convert a sequence of multibyte characters into a sequence of wide character codes.

mbstring Group of library routines used for multibyte string functions.

mbtowc Library routine used for multibyte character handling. It determines the number of bytes in the multibyte character.

MCA Abbreviation for Micro Channel Architecture, the bus design used in IBM's PS/2 computers.

McIlroy, Doug Author of the spell and diff utilities and developer of the concept of pipes and filters.

mcmp Library routine (BSD) used for multiple-precision integer arithmetic.

mconnect Command (BSD) used to connect to an SMTP mail server socket.

M_COPYIN STREAMS control message used to copy data from a user to a STREAMS message. This is a high-priority message, used during transparent ioctl processing.

M_COPYOUT STREAMS control message used to copy data to a user from a STREAMS message. This is a high-priority message, used during transparent ioctl processing.

mcs Command used to modify the comment section of an ELF object file.

M_CTL STREAMS control message indicating a user ioctl request.

mctl Library routine (BSD) used for memory management.

M_DATA STREAMS data message.

M_DELAY STREAMS control message that generates a real-time delay.

mdevice.d Directory containing files that designate device numbers for UNIX device-drivers. The location of the directory is /etc/conf/mdevice.d.

mdiv Library routine (BSD) used for multiple-precision integer arithmetic.

me Macro definitions used with nroff and troff for formatting technical papers.

media Term used to refer to the physical material on which data is stored by a computer, for example, tape, disks, and paper. The singular form of the word is *medium*.

meg Short way of referring to one megabyte.

megabyte *See* MB.

mem Device representing the core memory of a system.

memalign Library routine used for memory allocation. It allocates memory on a specific alignment boundary.

memccpy Library routine used to copy memory data between two specified areas.

memchr Library routine used for memory operations.

memcmp Library routine used to compare two arguments and determine if one is lexicographically greater than the other.

memcntl Library routine used for memory-management control of an area of memory.

memcpy Library routine used to copy memory data between two areas.

memo field Field in a file or record used for miscellaneous information.

memory Group of library routines used for memory operations.

memory management Refers to control of how various parts of memory are used.

memory-mapped files *See* map files.

memset Library routine that sets a specified area of memory to a specified value.

menu
1. Command used to generate full screen menus and forms for displaying information and accepting user input.
2. A list from which you can select a function or a file. You can select items using either a mouse or a keyboard, depending on the interface.

menu_attributes Library routine used to control menu display attributes.

menu_back Library routine used to control menu display attributes.

menu_cursor Library routine (curses) used to correctly position a menu cursor.

menu-driven Type of software user interface that displays menus from which the user can choose. Menu-driven software is easy to learn because choices are always presented, but frequently inflexible and cumbersome to use. *See also* menu.

menu_driver Library routine (curses) used as a command processor for the menus subsystem.

menu_fore Library routine used to control menu-display attributes.

menu_format Library routine (curses) used to determine and set a menu's maximum number of rows and columns.

menu_grey Library routine used to control menu display attributes.

menu_hook Group of library routines (curses) used to assign routines to applications for automatic invocation by menus.

menu_init Library routine (curses) that points to the menu-initialization routine when the menu is posted.

menu_item_current Library routine (curses) used to determine and set the cursor position.

menu_item_name Library routine (curses) used to get a menu's item description and name.

menu_item_new Library routine (curses) used to destroy and create menu items.

menu_item_opts Group of library routines (curses) used for menu item option routines.

menu_items Group of library routines (curses) used for connecting and disconnecting items to and from menus.

menu_item_userptr Library routine (curses) used to associate menu items with application data.

menu_item_value Library routine (curses) used for determining and setting values of menu items.

menu_item_visible Library routine (curses) used for determining whether a menu item is visible.

menu_mark Library routine (curses) used to distinguish menu items.

menu_new Library routine (curses) used to create new menus.

menu_opts Library routine (curses) used to return the current menu options.

menu_opts_off Library routine (curses) used to turn off the specified menu option.

menu_opts_on Library routine (curses) used to turn on the specified menu options.

menu_pad Library routine (curses) that returns the pad character of a menu. Pad characters fill the space between item names and descriptions.

menu_pattern Library routine (curses) used to determine and set the buffer for menus pattern matching.

menu_post *See* post_menu, unpost_menu.

menus Library routine (curses) used to create character-based menus.

menu_sub Library routine (curses) that returns a pointer to a menu's subwindow.

menu_term Library routine (curses) used to assign routines to applications for automatic invocation by menus.

menu_userptr Library routine (curses) used to associate application data with menus.

menu_win Library routine (curses) used to associate subwindows and menu windows.

Merge Software available on many PC versions of UNIX that allow users to emulate a DOS environment and run DOS applications.

M_ERROR STREAMS control message that notifies the process that there is a fatal error on the Stream.

mesg Command used to permit or deny messages being sent to a user's terminal.

message
1. Command used to write arguments to a FMLI message line.
2. Unit of data used to relate information from one entity to another. There are mail messages, error messages, STREAMS messages, and so on.

message block Part of a STREAMS message. It contains STREAMS control information and points to zero or more data blocks.

message database File containing messages created by gencat and accesses by gettxt. *See also* gencat, gettxt.

message line Area on the screen, in a GUI or menu interface, where the application sends error messages or informational messages to the user.

message of the day Message stored in /etc/motd that is displayed each time a user logs in. (It is run from the /etc/profile script.)

message queue In STREAMS, a place where messages are held for processing before they are passed to the next STREAMS module or driver.

message queue parameters Set of tunable parameters used to limit the size of messages, queues, and number of outstanding messages for interprocess communications.

messages Device-driver header file containing STREAMS message types (usually, /usr/include/sys/stream.h).

meta Library routine (curses) used to control terminal input options.

metacharacter Refers to keys that have special meaning to the shell, such as the backslash (\), quote mark ("), and ampersand (&).

Metafont Language for font and logo design.

meta key Key specified by some programs to be used in conjunction with other keys. On PC keyboards, the meta key is often the Alt key. On dumb-terminal keyboards, the Meta key is often the Esc key.

mf Command used for processing Metafont files.

M_FLUSH STREAMS control message indicating that the queues should be flushed.

mfree Library routine (BSD) used for

multiple-precision integer arithmetic.

mft Command that translates Metafont code to code that can be printed using the TeX document-formatting tools.

M_HANGUP STREAMS control message indicating that a device has been disconnected.

mh-e Add-on package for the emacs editor that implements functions for running the MH electronic-mail system.

mh-rmail Command in the mh-e add-on package to the emacs text editor, for reading electronic mail.

mh-smail Command in the mh-e add-on package to the emacs text editor, for sending electronic mail.

microcomputer Computer whose architecture centers around a single CPU chip.

mil Top-level domain name of the Internet host system, appearing at the end of Internet addresses designated as military hosts.

mim Add-on package for the emacs text editor, which implements a major mode for editing programs in the MIM programming language.

mim-mode Command in the emacs text editor that enables MIM mode, which is designed for editing programs in the MIM programming language.

min Library routine (BSD) used for multiple-precision integer arithmetic.

mincore Library routine used to determine memory pages' residency.

minibuffer Bottom line of the the emacs text-editor screen, below the mode line. This line displays commands as they are entered, along with other information.

minimize In a graphical user interface, to reduce a window to an icon.

Minix UNIX-like environment written by Andrew Tannebaum to demonstrate computer-science operating system concepts. Minix was, in some ways, a precursor to Linux.

minor Library routine that returns the minor number component from a specified device.

minor device number Number reflecting an instance of a device in UNIX. While a major number represents the type of device, each minor number identifies a particular device. A listing of the /dev directory (ls -l /dev) shows the major and minor numbers associated with each device. *See also* major device number.

minor mode In the emacs text editor, an operational mode that determines whether specific features are available. *See also* major mode.

M_IOCACK STREAMS high-priority control message indicating that an ioctl request has completed successfully.

M_IOCDATA STREAMS control message that returns the status and data of a completed M_COPYIN or M_COPYOUT request during transparent ioctl processing.

M_IOCNAK STREAMS high-priority control message indicating that an ioctl request has failed.

M_IOCTL STREAMS control message indicating a user ioctl request.

misc One of the top-level newsgroups available on USENET. It includes topics that cover for-sale items, investments, legal issues, and writing.

MIT Abbreviation for the Massachusetts Institute of Technology, a prestigious school where, among other things, the X Window System was developed.

mkdir

1. Command used for creating directories.
2. Library routine used for creating directories.

mkdirp Library routine used to create a directory in a path.

mkfifo
1. Command used to create a FIFO special file.
2. Library routine used to create a new FIFO.

mkfs Command used to create new file systems.

mkmsgs Command that converts a list of text strings into a message file. *See also* exstr, srchtxt.

mknod
1. Command used to create a special file.
2. Library routine used to create a directory, special, or ordinary file.

mkstemp Library routine (BSD) used to create a unique filename.

mktemp Library routine used to create a unique filename.

mktime Library routine used to convert a tm structure to a calendar time.

.ml File extension for files containing LISP source code.

ml Option used on the command line with the deroff utility. It specifies that text that appears on macro lines, as well as mm macro lists, be deleted. *See also* deroff.

mlconvert Add-on package for the emacs text editor that implements a function to convert Gosling emacs mocklisp code to emacs LISP.

mlock Library routine used to lock pages in memory.

mlockall Library routine used to lock a memory address space.

mm Macro definitions used with nroff and troff for formatting articles, theses, and books.

mmap
1. Library routine used to map pages of memory.
2. Library routine used for virtual mapping of memory-mapped devices.

MMU Abbreviation for memory management unit, part of a computer chip used to map virtual memory addresses into the physical memory.

mnttab File containing the mounted file system table, located in the /etc directory.

mocklisp Version of the LISP programming language used in the Gosling emacs text editor for programming editor commands and customizing the editor.

mode line Bottom line of a buffer on the emacs text editor screen. This line displays the name of the buffer, the mode it is in, and other information about the buffer.

mode-line-inverse-video Variable in the emacs text editor that controls whether mode lines are displayed in inverse-video.

modem Device that allows a computer to send signals over standard telephone lines.

moderated newsgroup USENET newsgroup where all messages must pass through a moderator who determines what messages get posted.

moderator Person who reviews submissions to a USENET newsgroup. The moderator is responsible for avoiding repetitive messages, incoherent messages, and messages that do not relate to the topic of the newsgroup.

modf Library routine used to manipulate parts of floating-point numbers.

modified status Status that indicates whether a buffer has been modified since it was opened. emacs and other text editors use the modified status to warn the user about unsaved buffers when exiting from the program.

modifier Option to a command that overrides the way the command works by default.

Modula-2
1. Programming language developed by Nicklaus Wirth, who also developed Pascal.
2. Add-on package for the emacs text editor that implements a major mode for editing programs in the Modula-2 programming language.

modula-2-mode Command in the emacs text editor that enables Modula-2 mode, which is designed for editing programs in the Modula-2 programming language.

module In STREAMS, a special type of programming code that is pushed between the stream head and the device-driver to implement a particular driver feature. For example, a STREAMS module might add line disciplines or higher-level protocols to an existing networking driver.

module_info Information structure for STREAMS drivers and modules.

monacct Command used with system accounting that produces summary files in the /var/adm/acct/fiscal directory and restarts the summary files in the /var/adm/acct/sum directory.

monitor
1. Library routine used to prepare execution-profile information.
2. Another name for the screen and keyboard that provides access to your computer.

monitoring To follow the processing of a particular feature. UNIX includes tools for monitoring system performance, printing, and networking.

monochrome Type of monitor that uses two colors, one for the background, such as black, and one for the foreground, such as white.

mon.out File containing profile information about an object file. This file is created by the monitor function.

montbl Command used to create a monetary database.

more Command used to page through a text file one screen at a time.

Morris, Robert Coauthor of the bc and dc utilities.

motd *See* message of the day.

Motif Graphical user interface (GUI) developed by the Open Software Foundation (OSF). It runs on any system that supports X Window System.

Motorola Manufacturer of semiconductor devices and other electronic equipment, known for its 68000 family of microprocessors.

mount
1. Command used to mount or unmount remote resources and file systems.
2. Library routine used to mount file systems.
3. Process of connecting a directory structure to the local file system. That directory structure may exist on a separate partition, hard disk, CD-ROM, or another computer connected over the network (in the case of NFS).

mountall Command used to mount all the file systems listed in the file system table.

mountd Command used to service NFS mount requests.

mounting directories Refers to logically attaching a directory of one file system to a directory in another file system. This method allows the files in one file system to be used as though they were in subdirectories of the other file system. Mounts can be local (on the same machine) or remote (on a different machine).

mountpoint Directory where a directory structure is connected into the local file system.

mouse
1. Device, usually rolled around the surface of a desk, used for selecting object from a graphical user interface, such as menu items and windows.
2. Device-driver for use with a mouse. Usually supports bus, serial, and PS/2 type mice.

mouseadmin Command used for changing the mouse type being used with a system and performing other administration tasks.

mouse-map Keymap in the emacs text editor for storing command bindings to mouse buttons.

mout Library routine (BSD) used for multiple-precision integer arithmetic.

move Library routine (curses) used to move the window cursor.

move_field Library routine (curses) used to connect a disconnected field to a location in the forms subwindow.

mp Group of library routines (BSD) used for multiple-precision integer arithmetic.

M_PCPROTO High-priority STREAMS protocol-control message.

M_PCSIG High-priority STREAMS message that sends signals to processes.

mprotect Library routine used to set access protection of memory mapping.

M_PROTO STREAMS protocol control message.

mrand48 Library routine used to generate pseudorandom numbers. The mrand48 routine returns a signed long integer over the range of -231 to 231.

M_READ STREAMS high-priority control message indicating that a read request occurred when no data is available in the stream head-read queue.

MS
1. Abbreviation for Microsoft. For example, MS Windows is Microsoft Windows, and MS-DOS is a series of versions of DOS marketed by Microsoft.
2. Command-line option used with the emacs text editor to control the color used for the mouse pointer in the emacs window.

ms Macro definitions used with nroff and troff for formatting articles, theses, and books.

MS-DOS Primitive operating system (as compared to UNIX) from Microsoft that runs only on personal computers.

M_SETOPTS STREAMS control message used to set options on the Stream head.

msgb Device-driver header file containing the STREAMS message block structure.

msgctl Library routine that provides various message control operations.

msgdsize Device-driver library routine that returns the number of data bytes in a message.

msgget Library routine used to get a message queue.

msglist *See* mailx.

msgop Pair of library routines used for message operations.

msgpullup Device-driver library routine used to concatenate bytes in a message.

msgrcv Library routine used to read a message from a message queue.

msgsnd Library routine used to send a message to a specified message queue.

MSGVERB Shell environment variable used by the fmtmsg utility to display error messages from shell scripts. *See also* fmtmsg.

M_SIG STREAMS control message that sends a signal to a process.

msqrt Library routine (BSD) used for multiple precision integer arithmetic.

M_START STREAMS high-priority control message, indicating that the Stream is ready to restart output.

M_STARTI STREAMS high-priority control message, indicating that the Stream is ready to restart input.

M_STOP STREAMS high-priority message, indicating that input should stop.

M_STOPI STREAMS high-priority message, indicating that input should stop immediately.

msub Library routine (BSD) used for multiple-precision integer arithmetic. The third argument is assigned the difference between the first two arguments.

msync Library routine used to synchronize memory and physical storage.

mt Command used to control tape devices. It is portable across systems from various vendors.

mtime Command-line option used with the find command that specifies files by date last modified. *See also* find.

mtox Library routine (BSD) used for multiple-precision integer arithmetic.

mtune.d Directory of files containing tunable parameter definitions for the UNIX system, located in /etc/conf.

MUD Acronym for multi-user dungeon, a popular multi-user fantasy game loosely based on the "Dungeons and Dragons series" of games.

mult Library routine (BSD) used for multiple-precision integer arithmetic. The third argument is assigned the product of the first two arguments.

multiple redirection Input or output redirection that redirects standard error and standard output to different targets.

multiplexing Communications technique where two or more signals are sent over one line.

multiplexor Device for sending several channels of information over one line.

multiplexor driver Device-driver that allows multiplexing.

multiprocessing Refers to running simultaneous tasks, possibly from the same process, on a computer with two or more processing units (CPUs).

multiprocessor Type of operating system that makes use of two or more processors in a single computer.

multitasking Refers to running multiple simultaneous processes on a single computer.

multithreaded Program designed to run on a multiprocessor computer.

multithreading Refers to running multiple tasks from within one program.

Multi-user dungeon See MUD.

multi-user state When a computer is able to accept more than one user at a time. In single-user states, only one user can be logged in.

munlock Library routine used to unlock pages in memory.

munlockall Library routine used to un-

lock a memory address space.

munmap Library routine used to unmap pages of memory.

mv Command used to rename files and directories and to move files and directories from one place to another place.

mvaddch Library routine (curses) to place the specified character into a window at the current cursor position and then advance the window cursor position.

mvaddstr Library routine (curses) used to add a string of characters to a curses window and advance the cursor.

mvcur Library routine (curses) used as an interface to the terminfo database.

mvdelch Library routine (curses) used to delete the character immediately under the cursor.

mvdir Command used to move a directory within a file system.

mvgetch Library routine (curses) used to push back characters from a curses terminal keyboard.

mvgetstr Library routine (curses) used to get character strings from a curses terminal keyboard.

mvinch Library routine (curses) used to get a character along with its attributes from a curses window.

mvinsch Library routine (curses) used to insert a character before the character under the cursor.

mvprintw Library routine (curses) used in a curses window to display formatted output.

mvscanw Library routine used in a curses window to convert formatted input.

mvwaddch Library routine (curses) used to place the specified character into a window at the current cursor position and then advance the window cursor position.

mvwaddstr Library routine used to add a string of characters to a curses window and advance the cursor.

mvwdelch Library routine (curses) used to delete the character immediately under the cursor.

mvwgetch Library routine used to push back characters from a curses terminal keyboard.

mvwgetstr Library routine used to get character strings from a curses terminal keyboard.

mvwin Library routine used to create a curses window.

mvwinch Library routine used to get a character along with its attributes from a curses window.

mvwinsch Library routine (curses) used to insert a character before the character under the cursor.

mvwprintw Library routine used in a curses window to display formatted output.

mvwscanw Library routine used in a curses window to convert formatted input.

mwm Command that starts the Motif window manager.

.mwmrc File that contains the resources that define the characteristics of a Motif window-manager session. It is usually located in the user's home directory.

M-x Abbreviation for Meta-x, a commonly-used keystroke in the emacs text editor. Pressing the Meta key followed by an *x* tells emacs to accept a command name and run it.

na Type of USENET newsgroup distribution, in which articles are distributed only within North America (with exceptions).

name Command-line option used with the find command that specifies files by filename. Wildcards can be used in the filename. *See also* find.

named Command used to start the Internet domain name server.

named-command Command in the Epsilon text editor that invokes the specified command or macro by name.

named pipe Pipe that exists as a node in the files system. Named pipes are created with the mknod command. When you type ls -l, a named pipe is listed with a *p* as its first character in the permissions field. A named pipe is also called a *FIFO* (first in, first out).

named stream Stream that is attached to a file system node. When a stream is attached to the file system using the fattach library routine, it is given attributes, such as permissions, user ID, and group ID.

namefiles File used by the mail subsystem to determine the alias files that are configured for the local system. By default, namefiles contain the names of the alias files /etc/mail/names and /etc/mail/lists. The location of namefiles is /etc/mail/namefiles.

name-kbd-macro Command in the Epsilon text editor that names the last keyboard macro defined.

name-last-kbd-macro Command in the emacs text editor that names the last keyboard macro defined.

names File used by the mail subsystem to hold aliases used by mail. *See also* namefiles.

name-to-address mapping Networking activity, whereby a node on the network is assigned an address (usually numeric) based on an assigned name (usually human-readable). For example, a computer may be named uranus and its address may be mapped to an IP address of 148.52.77.99.

nap Library routine (XENIX) used to suspend an executing process for a short period of time.

narrow-to-region Command in the Epsilon editor that temporarily restricts editing to the currently marked region.

National Science Foundation Founder of NFSNET, a network to connect supercomputing centers. These supercomputers provide the backbone for the Internet.

NAUTOUP Tunable parameter used to specify the number of seconds between automatic file-system updates. Updates are done for both buffer cache and file-system pages.

navigation Term used to describe moving around a program or network.

nawk Command used to scan files for a pattern and then process the text. This was the latest version of awk as of UNIX System V Release 4. The name was changed to *awk* in UNIX System V Release 4.2 (UnixWare).

NBLK1024 Obsolete tunable parameter, used to assign the number of 1024-byte blocks of memory to be used by Streams modules and drivers to hold messages. There were also parameters for other size memory blocks (NBLK512, NBLK256, etc.).

NBUF Tunable parameter that defines the number of buffer headers dynamically allocated by the system when a buffer header is needed.

NCALL Tunable parameter that defines the number of call-out table entries to allocate.

ncheck Command used to generate a list of pathnames versus inode numbers.

NCR Manufacturer of accounting equipment, especially for the banking and retail markets. NCR is now owned by AT&T, and produces much of AT&T's computer and networking equipment. UNIX is used on most of this equipment

ndbm Group of library routine (BSD) used for manipulating databases.

ne Command-line option used with the test command in the Korn shell. This option determines whether one number is not equal to another.

neighbor system Computer system you can reach directly, either over a direct connection or a modem. In other words, there is no need to go through a router or to hop across multiple systems to establish a connection.

neqn Command (BSD) used as a preprocessor for nroff for processing equations.

nerd Person who spends too much time at the computer. Someone who needs to "get a life."

net Abbreviation for networking organization, a type (or zone) of Internet host system appearing at the end of Internet address names of hosts that are used to maintain the network.

netconfig File located in /etc, used to store network information.

netdir Group of library routines used for name-to-address translation for generic transports.

netdir_free Library routine used for name-to-address translation for generic transports.

netdir_getbyaddr Library routine used for name-to-address translation for generic transports.

netdir_getbyname Library routine used for name-to-address translation for generic transports.

netdir_options Library routine used for name-to-address translation for generic transports.

netdir_perror Library routine used for name-to-address translation for generic transports.

netdir_sperror Library routine used for name-to-address translation for generic transports.

netiquette Term used to describe the accepted behavior when using the Internet.

netmasks File containing the network masks that are used to implement IP subnetting. *See also* network mask.

netname2host Library routine used for secure remote-procedure calls.

netname2user Library routine used for secure remote-procedure calls.

net number *See* Internet number.

NETPATH Environment variable that defines the transports available on a system and the order in which they are used.

.netrc File containing data used for ftp file transfers.

Netscape Graphical Internet browser. UNIX versions of Netscape runs on the X Windows System, allowing you to use a mouse and keyboard to display text, graphics, and audio as you traverse the Internet.

netstat Command used to display network status information.

NetWare *See* Novell NetWare.

NetWare UNIX client *See* NUC.

network In computing, the hardware and software that allows computers to communicate. In the OSI model, a network includes everything that occurs between applications from different computers that communicate together.

network addressing Numbers and/or strings of letters that represent each node on a network that can be reached by other nodes. Each network must be unique within a particular network name space.

Network File System *See* NFS.

Network Information System *See* NIS.

networking hardware Hardware used for networking computers, such as Ethernet cards, cables, bridges, routers, etc.

networking protocol Set of rules followed by peer processes that allow them to exchange data in a meaningful way.

network listener Process that runs continuously on a UNIX system, awaiting requests from an outside source, such as a dumb terminal or network. Once a request is received, the listener hands off the request to the appropriate process (such as a login daemon) to handle the request.

network management Task of managing multiple computer systems attached to a network. Network management can include monitoring performance, centrally administering domains, and implementing security policies.

network mask Number that is used to determine what part of an IP address represents the network and what part represents the host. This feature lets a network administrator divide a network number into several subnets.

Network News Transfer Protocol *See* NNTP.

network number Number that uniquely identifies a network, or a subnetwork, on the Internet. In IP addresses, the network number is, by default, the first four-bits (Class A), first eight-bits (Class B), or first 12 bits (Class C) of the 16-bit IP address. An administrator can change which part of the address is the network number by changing the netmask. *See also* network mask.

network packet Unit of information that is transmitted across a network. In TCP/IP, a packet contains both data and addressing information.

network security Procedures implemented on a network to prevent unauthorized access and use of the computer systems on that network. UNIX network security can range from simple password protection to firewalls that block access to particular features on the system.

network selection Process by which the system selects which network to communicate on. It usually this refers to a system with multiple network types, deciding on the network based on the type of address used in the communication.

networks File containing a list of networks that make up the DARPA Internet. This file is located in /etc/networks.

network services Refers to communication services offered by a server system. For example, network services available with TCP/IP include ftp and telnet.

newaliases Command (BSD) used to reconstruct the mail aliases database.

newer Command-line option used with the find command. It specifies files that have been modified more recently than a given file. *See also* find.

new_field Library routine (curses) used to create a new field within a form.

new_fieldtype Library routine (curses) used to create a new field type.

newform Command used to reformat the contents of a text file.

new_form Library routine (curses) used to create a new form.

newgrp Command used to change the effective group of the current user.

new_item Library routine (curses) used to create a menu item.

newkey Command used for creating a new key in the publickey database.

newline Character that defines the end of a line of text, stored in ASCII as character code 10.

newmail Command (BSD) used to notify a user of new, incoming mail.

new_menu Library routine (curses) used to create a new menu.

newpad Library routine (curses) used to create a new pad.

new_page Library routine (curses) used for forms pagination.

news Command used to display the contents of the files located in the /var/news directory.

newsgroup Forum for discussing a topic through electronic messages. There are hundreds of newsgroups on USENET.

newterm Library routine (curses) used for screen initialization.

newvt Command used to open a new virtual terminal.

newwin Library routine (curses) used to create a new window.

nextafter Library routine used to manipulate part of a floating-point number.

next-error Command in the Epsilon text editor that finds the filename and line number of the next error message in the process buffer.

nextkey Library routine (BSD) that is one of the dbm database subroutines.

next-line Command in the emacs text editor that moves the cursor down one line. This command is usually bound to the keystroke Ctrl-N.

NeXT machine Obsolete UNIX workstation manufactured by NeXT, Inc., and running the NeXTstep graphical user interface.

next-page Command in the Epsilon text editor that displays the next window of text. *See also* scroll-up.

next-screen-context-lines Variable in the emacs text editor that controls how many lines emacs scrolls at a time.

NeXTstep GUI that originally ran only on NeXT machines. It has since been ported to other platforms, such as PCS.

next-token Function in the emacs LISP language that processes the next token from the input.

next-video Command in the Epsilon text editor that changes the number of lines or columns displayed on the screen, cycling through Epsilon's video modes.

next-window Command in the Epsilon text editor that move the cursor to the next window. *See also* other-window.

NFS Abbreviation for Network File System, a distributed file system facility developed by Sun Microsystems that allows UNIX administrators to connect remote file systems to the local file system tree. It supports most UNIX semantics, including file and directory ownership, groups, and permissions.

nfs Directory containing many of the daemons used by NFS. The full path is /usr/lib/nfs.

nfsd Command used to start the NFS daemon.

NFS lock manager User-level daemon used by NFS to support advisory and mandatory file and record locking. The daemon is called *lockd*.

NFSNET Network to connect supercomputing centers, established by the National Science Foundation (NSF). The NSFNET carries traffic related to research and education, and is connected to the Internet.

NFS resource File or directory that has been made available with NFS to other computers that, with proper per-missions, can mount that file or directory.

NFS_RETRIES Tunable parameter that defines the number of times NFS can retry a soft mount before failing the NFS operation.

nfsstat Command used to display statistics for the Network File System.

ngeteblk Device-driver library routine used to retrieve an empty buffer of the indicated size.

NHBUF Tunable parameter that specifies the how big the hash table is that is used to locate a buffer.

nice
1. Command used to run a command at a lower CPU priority.
2. Library routine used to alter the priority of a time-sharing process.
3. Library routine (BSD) used to change a process's priority.

nil Zero. In the emacs text editor, when used as the value of the comment-start variable in Fortran mode, disallows comments that appear on the same line as a Fortran statement. In the emacs text editor, when used as the value of the fortran-comment-indent-style variable in Fortran mode, it allows comments to be entered anywhere on a line that begins with *c* in column one.

NIS Abbreviation for Network Information System, a networking service that lets a UNIX administrator share basic UNIX system information among a group of computers. Information can include the contents of password files, group, host, and networks.

nl Command used to number the lines in a text file.

nlist
1. Command used to display NetWare users, servers, and volumes.

2. Library routine used to retrieve entries from a name list.

nl_langinfo Library routine that returns a pointer to information relating to a language or cultural area, as defined in the program's locale.

nlsadmin Command used for administration of the network listener service.

nlsgetcall Library routine used to pass a client's data via the listener.

nlsprovider Library routine used to retrieve the name of a transport provider.

nlsrequest Library routine used to format and send a listener service-request message.

nl_types Header file containing native-language data types.

nm Command used to display an object file's name list.

NNTP Abbreviation for NetNews Transfer Protocol, a networking protocol used to transfer articles among USENET sites.

nobanner Command-line option used with the lp command that suppresses printing the default banner page.

nobeep In the C shell, a predefined shell variable that controls whether the terminal beeps when the C shell cannot do file completion (because more than one filename matches what the user has typed).

nocbreak Library routine (curses) used to control terminal input options.

noclobber Korn shell mode that prevents files from being deleted by redirection. It is specified with the set command (Korn shell only). In the C shell, a predefined shell variable that controls whether output redirection can delete existing files (C shell only).

node Addressable item connected to a network. It can be a computer, router, or other item on a network.

nodefs Command-line option used with the ld command that causes an undefined symbol not to cause a fatal error.

nodelay Library routine (curses) used to control terminal input options.

node name Name that identifies a node on a network. In a UNIX system, the node name is displayed using the uname -n command.

noecho Library routine (curses) used to control terminal input options.

noenable Device-driver library routine used to prevent a queue from being scheduled.

noerror Option used on the command-line with the dd command. It specifies that dd continue processing when up to five errors occur. *See also* dd.

noexec Korn shell mode that reads commands without executing them. It is specified with the set command (Korn shell only).

nofilebreak Command-line option used with the lp command that suppresses sending formfeed characters between files.

noflush Command-line option used with the stty command for enabling or disabling output flushing after the intr, quit, or switch characters. This option is used for terminals that connect to a computer via telephone lines.

noglob Korn shell mode that ignores wildcards and metacharacters in filenames. It is specified with the set command (Korn shell only). In the C shell, a predefined shell variable that controls how wildcard characters are used in filenames.

nogroup Command-line option used with the find command. It specifies files that belong to a group that is not in /etc/group. *See also* find.

nohup Command used to run a command so that the command is not canceled when a hangup or quit occurs. In other words, you can log off and the command continues running.

nohup.out File containing the output of a command run using the nohup command.

nolog Korn shell mode that omits function definitions from the command history file. It is specified with the set command (Korn shell only).

nonl Library routine (curses) used to control terminal output options.

nonomatch In the C shell, a predefined shell variable that controls how wildcard characters are used in filenames.

noraw Library routine (curses) used to control terminal output options.

NOREAD Option used in the UUCP Permissions file that indicates exceptions to those directories that can be read by a remote system as defined by a READ option.

normal-character Command in the Epsilon text editor that inserts the invoking key into the buffer.

NOT Unary operator that changes a true value to false and a false value to true.

notify
1. Command that notifies the user when electronic-mail messages arrive.
2. In the C shell, a predefined shell variable that controls whether the shell notifies the user as soon as background jobs are completed.
3. In the C shell, command that causes the shell to notify the user immediately when a background job finishes

executing.

nounset Korn shell mode that causes as error if an unset variable is used in a substitution. It is specified with the set command (Korn shell only).

nouser Command-line option used with the find command. It specifies files that belong to a user who is not in /etc/passwd. *See also* find.

Novell NetWare Popular network operating system that provides file services, printing services, and other network services to DOS, Windows, UNIX, Mac, and other client systems. NetWare is developed and distributed by Novell, Inc.

NOWRITE Option, used in the UUCP Permissions file, that indicates exceptions to those directories that can be read by a remote system as defined by a WRITE option.

NP Password status displayed by the passwd command, indicating that no password is defined for the user.

NPBUF Tunable parameter that indicates the total number of physical input/output buffers to allocate. One input/output buffer is used for each physical read and write.

NPROC Tunable parameter that sets the boundary on the highest number of processes allowed to simultaneously run on the system.

NQUEUE Tunable parameter that sets the number of STREAMS queues configured on the system. This parameter is not supported in post-SVR4.2 systems because queues are dynamically allocated.

nrand48 Library routine used to generate pseudorandom numbers. The nrand48 routine returns a non-negative long integer over the range of 0 to 231.

nroff Command (BSD) used to format documents to be displayed on a screen or printed. *See also* troff.

nroff macro Codes added to nroff documents that give instructions to the nroff formatter. Macros do things like identify headings, spaces, font changes, and page breaks. Each macro begins with a period (.) and is followed by one or two letters, then zero or more arguments.

nroff mode In the emacs text editor, major mode designed for formatting text files for nroff and related text formatters.

NSF *See* National Science Foundation.

nslookup Command used to query DARPA Internet domain name servers.

nsquery Command used to query the name server on systems that support Remote File Sharing (RFS). RFS is a UNIX distributed-file-system facility, like NFS, that is no longer supported.

NSTREAM Tunable parameter that sets the number of Stream head structures to be configured. This parameter is not supported in post-SVR4.2 systems because structures are dynamically allocated.

NSTREVENT Tunable parameter that sets the number of Stream event cells to be configured. This parameter is not supported in post-SVR4.2 systems because cells are dynamically allocated.

NT Relatively new multitasking operating system by Microsoft. It is said to be an important component in the original Denver Airport baggage handling system.

ntohl Library routine used to convert between network byte order and host byte order.

ntohs Library routine used to convert between network byte order and host byte order.

NUC Abbreviation for NetWare UNIX client, a UNIX facility that provides connectivity between a UNIX client and a NetWare server. Most of the features center around the file system, but, other features include printing, application sharing, and NVT services over IPX/SPX protocols.

NUCLOGINS Tunable parameter used with NetWare connectivity to define the maximum number of NetWare logins for each UNIX user.

NUCNWMPOPENS Tunable parameter used with NetWare connectivity to define the maximum number of NetWare management-portal opens.

NUCUSERS Tunable parameter used with NetWare connectivity to define the maximum number of UNIX users using NetWare.

null Device (/dev/null) used for discarding data.

nulladm Command used in shell accounting. It creates a file with 664 permissions where the owner and group are adm.

number-nine kill Command used to terminate a process that has proved hard to terminate. The command consists of the kill command with the -9 option. *See also* kill.

NUMREGPT Tunable parameter that specifies the number of pseudo-terminals available on the system. One pseudo-terminal is used for each shell session from a remote login, xterm window, or other shell interface.

NUMSCOPT Tunable parameter that defines the number of SCO-compatible pseudo terminals available on the system.

nuucp login Special login account used with the UUCP networking facility. Usually, uucp will initiate a file transfer by logging in as the nuucp user and communicating with the uucico process.

NVRAM Acronym for non-volatile random access memory, part of the physical memory on a computer that holds information, even after the computer is turned off. Instructions needed to first start a computer are held in NVRAM.

NVT Abbreviation for NetWare virtual terminal, a service that allows remote login from client systems to NetWare servers.

nw Command-line option used with the emacs text editor to control whether emacs starts in a new window or in the existing terminal window.

oawk Old version of the awk command. Both awk and nawk contain more recent versions of awk.

obase Keyword used with the bc desk calculator program. It specifies the based for numbers displayed by bc.

objdump Utility program for dealing with compiled programs, available from the Free Software Foundation as part of binutils.

object Identifiable programming entity that can be manipulated and reused by an application program.

object code Executable code produced by a compiler, such as the C compilation system compiler.

object file File containing object code. UNIX System V supports three main types of object files: relocatable files, executable files, and shared object files. A relocatable file contains code and data that can link with other object file to make an executable. An executable file contains a program that can execute on its own. A shared object file can be linked in two ways: the link editor links it to other object file to create another object file or the dynamic linker creates a process image by linking it to other executable files or shared objects.

object-oriented Programming style, implemented in such languages as C++, that groups common data structures together in objects, allowing those objects to be shared among different pieces of code. When other programs reuse the object, they can also inherit the behavior of the object along with the data.

obs Abbreviation for output block size, an option used on the command line with the dd command. It specifies the output block size in bytes. *See also* dd.

OCR Abbreviation for optical character recognition, software that converts graphic images into text by identifying the characters in the image.

ocrnl Command-line option used with the stty command for selecting whether carriage returns (ASCII character code 13) in the output are converted to newlines (ASCII character code 10). This option is used for terminals that connect to a computer via serial lines.

octal Numbering system in base 8 that includes the digits 0 through 7.

od Command that dumps files in a variety of formats (short for octal dump).

oddp Command-line option used with the stty command for controlling parity terminal settings.

ODI Abbreviation for open data-link interface, an interface created by Novell,

Inc. for writing device-drivers that provide interfaces to communications equipment. Some UNIX systems, such as UnixWare, support ODI drivers.

OEM Abbreviation for original equipment manufacturer, the manufacturer of computer (or other) components or equipment. OEMs often buy components from other OEMs, build a finished product, and sell to either retailers or end-users.

of Option used on the command line with the dd command. It specifies the name of the output file. *See also* dd.

ofdel Command-line option used with the stty command for selecting whether NULL (ASCII character code 0) or DEL (ASCII character code 127) is the fill character. This option is used for terminals that connect to a computer via serial lines.

offsetof Library routine (macro) that is the offset of a specified structure member.

ofill Command-line option used with the stty command to delay output using either timing or fill characters. This option is used for terminals that connect to a computer via serial lines.

OK Commonly used label for buttons in GUI-based applications. The OK button allows the user to accept the settings in a dialog box and continue. Also, a command-line option used with the find command. It specifies the command(s) that find should execute each time it finds a file, and that find should prompt the user before executing the command(s). *See also* button.

olcuc Command-line option used with the stty command for selecting whether lowercase characters in the output are converted to uppercase. This option is used for terminals that connect to a computer via serial lines.

OLDPWD Shell environment variable that contains the previous current working directory (Bourne and Korn shells only).

olwm Command used to start the OPEN LOOK window manager. Today, the Motif window manager (mwm command) is most often used.

OMF Libraries in which XENIX objects are stored. In UNIX System, OMF libraries can be converted to ELF objects using the cvtomflib command. *See also* cvtomflib.

O_NDELAY Flag that may be set on a Streams device-driver that may affect subsequent reads and writes on the device.

one's complement *See* bitwise inversion.

one-window Command in the Epsilon text editor that displays only the current window.

on_exit Library routine used to register a function that is called when an application terminates normally. Normal termination may come from the exit system call or the program's main function.

onintr In the C shell, a command used in shell scripts to handle interrupt signals. It is similar to the trap command used in the Bourne and Korn shells.

onlcr Command-line option used with the stty command for selecting whether newlines (ASCII character code 10) in the output are converted to carriage returns (ASCII character code 13). This option is used for terminals that connect to a computer via serial lines.

online In a multiprocessor system, a term describing a processor that is connected and ready to dispatch processes and do normal system functions. The psradm command is used to bring a processor online.

on-line device Device such as a printer or terminal that is connected to a computer and ready to use. A device may be connected to a computer but not be online.

online help Help documentation that can be accessed electronically through a computer.

online service Computer service that can be used remotely, usually by dialing in, for an hourly fee. Some services provide a specific set of information: Lexis, for example, provides legal information, and Nexis provides news. Others provide general information: CompuServe, Delphi, AOL, and Prodigy provide a wide range of information, including weather, airline flights, and support for many software programs. Others, like MCI Mail, provide electronic mail.

onlret Command-line option used with the stty command for selecting whether to insert a carriage return (ASCII character code 13) after each newline (ASCII character code 10) in the output. This option is used for terminals that connect to a computer via serial lines.

onocr Command-line option used with the stty command for selecting whether a carriage return (ASCII character code 13) is inserted at the beginning of each line. This option is used for terminals that connect to a computer via serial lines.

OOP *See* object-oriented.

open
1. Library routine used to open a file for reading or writing. It opens a file descriptor for the specified file and sets the file status flags.
2. Device-driver routine used to gain access to a device.

open angle bracket *See* <.

open bracket *See* [, {, and <.

open curly brace *See* open bracket.

opendir Library routine used to open the specified directory and associate a directory stream with it. The opendir routine returns a pointer to be used to identify the directory stream in subsequent operations.

open-dribble-file Command in the emacs text editor to help in reporting bugs. The command saves every keystroke in a file.

open-line Command in the Epsilon text editor that inserts a newline character after the cursor position.

openlog Library routine used to initialize the system log file.

OPEN LOOK Graphical user interface based on X and developed by AT&T. The Open Windows windowing system is based on OPEN LOOK. OPEN LOOK has largely been supplanted by OSF/Motif.

OPEN LOOK Intrinsics Toolkit (OLIT) Set of programming functions used to build graphical applications that conform to OPEN LOOK specifications.

open-rectangle Command in the emacs text editor that inserts a blank rectangular region into the buffer, with its upper-left corner at the mark position. The cursor determines the lower-right corner of the inserted rectangle.

opensem Library routine used to open a specified semaphore and return the unique semaphore identification number.

open quote *See* '.

open square bracket *See* [.

open system Used to describe computing interfaces that are made public so they may be implemented by a wide variety of computers. Each vendor that implements an open system interface may have underlying code that is proprietary.

Open Systems Interconnection Reference Model (OSI-RM) Seven-layer model developed by the International Standards Organization (ISO) and CCITT that provides a framework for computer networking. This framework can be implemented using a variety of protocols. The seven layers, from the bottom up, are: physical, data link, network, transport, session, presentation, and application. Often, real-world networking products will implement several layers at once. For example, in UNIX, an Ethernet product may handle the physical and data link layers, built-in Streams drivers may implement network and transport layers, and the applications may handle session, presentation, and application layer features.

open-termscript Command in the emacs text editor to help in reporting bugs. The command saves every keystroke and every character displayed on the screen in a file.

openwin Command that runs Open Windows, a windowing system based on OPEN LOOK (Solaris only). The openwin command is available only with Solaris. *See also* Solaris.

OPENWIN Shell environment variable that contains the directory Open Window programs.

Open Windows Windowing system based on OPEN LOOK, available only with Solaris. *See also* Solaris.

OPENWINHOME Shell environment variable that contains the directory in which the Open Windows programs are stored.

operand Part of a computer instruction that refers to either an address, a symbol, or a number.

operating mode *See* system state.

operating system Software that controls how the computer's resources are used. The operating system is the first software loaded when a computer is booted. It usually manages the computer's CPU, provides an interface to the file system, and manages interfaces to hardware devices. Applications are usually designed for and loaded onto specific operating systems, although sometimes an application can be run in an emulation mode.

operating system release number Number that identifies the release of an operating system. For example, the last version of UNIX produced by UNIX System Laboratories was UNIX System V Release 4.2. Earlier releases of UNIX included 3.2 and 4.0.

operator Symbol or character that indicates what operation should take place. For example, the pipe symbol (¦) is often used to indicate the or operation.

opost Command-line option used with the stty command for selecting whether to postprocess all output. This option is used for terminals that connect to a computer via serial lines.

optarg Tag designating an argument that follows an option in a command. For example, a command might allow an -f option that must be followed by a filename to use as input, such as -f file1. The name *file1* would represent the optarg.

optimization Process of creating more efficient programs through the careful selection of programming elements, such as instructions, and algorithms.

optimizer Software that automatically analyzes a program's code and makes changes to the instructions and other elements so the program runs more efficiently.

OPTIND Shell environment variable that tracks the index of the most recent option argument that has been handled by the getopts command.

option Part of a command that modifies the command's behavior. Most options for UNIX commands consist of a single letter preceded by a hyphen.

OR Operator that combines two logical values. The result is true if one or both of the two input values is true.

Oracle Corporation Software developer known for its relational database program called Oracle.

ordered delivery Communications method employed by most connection-oriented networks, whereby data are delivered in the order in which they need to be used. Compare this with packet-switching networks, in which packets might be received in any order, then are reassembled at the destination.

orderly release Data communication concept that lets two communications entities close a connection without losing information. Orderly release is only supported in connection-oriented networking protocols.

ordinary file UNIX file that contains text or data. Compare this to special files, such as devices, FIFOs, Semaphores, or shared memory files.

org Top-level domain name used on the Internet to contain domains and hosts from other organizations. Other organizations include those that don't fit into standard categories, such as government (gov), education (edu), commercial (com), military (mil), or network operations (net). User groups are among the organizations under the org domain.

OS *See* operating system.

Osanna, Joseph Author of the troff utility.

oseek Option used on the command line with the dd command. It specifies the number of blocks to seek from the start of the output file. *See also* dd.

OSF Abbreviation for Open Software Foundation, an organization, backed primarily by IBM, dedicated to producing an open operating environment. OSF is responsible for, among other things, Motif and DCE standards.

OSF/Motif *See* Motif.

OSI-RM *See* Open Systems Interconnection.

ospeed Command-line option used with the stty command for setting the terminal output baud rate. This option is used for terminals that connect to a computer via serial lines.

OSPF Networking protocol used to determine the most efficient route to get messages to a destination. OSPF (open shorter path first) is used on the Internet to do load balancing, routing to the least expensive routes, and routing over multiple paths.

ot Command-line option used with the test command in the Korn shell. This option determines whether one file is older than another.

OTHERQ Device-driver library routine used to get a pointer to the partner queues of a Streams queue.

other-window Command in the emacs text editor that moves the cursor to the other window. This command is usually bound to the keystroke Ctrl-X O.

outb Device-driver library routine used to write a byte to an 8-bit I/O port.

out-of-band data Information sent between two communications entities on a channel that is independent of normal data transmission. Out-of-band data allows priority messages to be sent without waiting for normal data to be processed.

outl Device-driver library routine used to provide a C language interface to the machine instruction that writes a 32-bit long word to a 32-bit I/O port using the I/O address space, instead of the memory address space.

outline Add-on package for the emacs text editor that implements outline mode.

outline mode In the emacs text editor, a major mode that shows the text in a buffer in outline form. Headings are designated by asterisks at the beginning of the line. The outline-mode command switches to outline mode.

outline-mode Command in the emacs text editor that enters outline mode. This mode is supported by the outline add-on package to emacs.

outline-regexp Variable in the emacs text editor that controls which lines are considered to be headings in outline mode.

output Results from computer processing. The output may be directed to the screen or to another device, such as a printer.

output redirection Refers to changing the destination for a processes output. For example, most UNIX commands send their output to standard out (usually the screen). This can be redirected to a file or other device by using the greater-than sign (>).

outw Device-driver library routine used to provide a C language interface to the machine instruction that writes a 16-bit short word to a 16-bit I/O port using the I/O address space, instead of the memory address space.

overlay Library routine used to overlay the source window on top of the destination window. The windows are not required to be the same size; only text where the two windows overlap is copied. The overlay routine is nondestructive (blanks are not copied).

overwrite Library routine used to overwrite the source window on top of the destination window. The windows are not required to be the same size; only text where the two windows overlap is copied.

overwrite mode In emacs and other text editors, a minor mode in which characters are typed destructively. That is, each character typed replaces the characters at the cursor position. Compare to insert mode.

overwrite-mode Command in the emacs text editor that enables or disables overwrite mode.

owner User's name representing the owner of a file, directory, or process. The owner is usually the only user (besides root) than can change or delete a file, directory, or process.

ownership Designation of the user who has complete control of a file or directory. A file or directory's owner can change any of the attributes to that file or directory.

P

P1003 POSIX standard 1003 from the Institute of Electrical and Electronics Engineers (IEEE) that defines many aspects of open UNIX systems. UNIX System V, Linux, and many other UNIX-like computer systems are made to conform to the P1003 standard.

p2open Library routine used to fork and execute a shell running the specified command line.

pack Command used to store the specified files in a compressed form. A .z is appended on a pack file when it has been compressed.

package
1. Separately installable program or group of programs.
2. Add-on to the emacs text editor that implements additional major modes, minor modes, commands, or functions.

packed file File that has been compressed using the pack command.

packet Unit of information that is sent on a network. Each packet contains the address of the recipient as well as any data.

packet encapsulation Address, error detection, and protocol information that encloses any data that are sent. Once the packet reaches its destination, the encapsulation information is inter-preted and stripped off.

packet-switched network Type of network that transmits information in packets. In a packet-switched network, each packet of information is transmitted individually, then reassembled with other packets to form the logical communication. TCP/IP, which is a packet-switched network, is the most prominent protocol used on the Internet.

page-delimiter Variable in the emacs text editor that controls the page-break character.

PAGER Shell environment variable that defines how the man command displays its output. *See also* man.

pagesize Command used to print the size of a page of memory in bytes.

PAGES_NODISKMA Tunable parameter that sets the number of pages not available to be locked down by kernel memory allocation.

pages per minute Method of determining the output of printers (abbreviated *ppm*). Printers are measured by the number of printed pages they can produce per minute.

PAGES_UNLOCK Tunable parameter that sets the number of pages not available to be locked down by the user.

paging Technique for managing memory. With paging, active programs can be transferred between main storage, such as RAM, and secondary storage, such as the paging area on a hard disk.

panel_above Library routine (curses) used to handle panels-deck traversal primitives. The panel_above routine returns a pointer to the panel just above the specified panel.

panel_below Library routine (curses) used to handle panels-deck traversal primitives. The panel_below routine returns a pointer to the panel just below the specified panel.

panel_move Library routine (curses) used to move a panels window on the virtual screen.

panel_new Library routine (curses) used to create new panels. *See also* del_panel.

panels Character-based panels library. A program using these routines must be compiled with the -lpanel and -lcurses options specified on the cc command line.

panel_show Group of library routines (curses) used to manipulate panels decks.

panel_top Group of library routines (curses) used to manipulate panels decks.

panel_update Library routine (curses) used for panels virtual screen refreshing.

panel_userptr Group of library routines (curses) used to associate application data with a panels panel.

panel_window Library routine (curses) from the group called panel_window. This group of routines is used to get or set the current window of a panels panel. The panel_window routine returns a pointer to the window of the specified panel. *See also* replace_panel.

panic When an error occurs from which the operating system cannot recover. During a panic, a PANIC message appears on the system console.

paragraph In the vi text editor, a group of characters ending with a blank line or paragraph macro. In the emacs text editor, text that ends with a blank line, or with a line that starts with whitespace.

paragraph-separate Variable in the emacs text editor that controls how emacs considers paragraphs to be delimited.

parallel make When the make command is run with a -p option, requesting that more than one target be built at a time.

parallel port Outlet on a PC that is used to attach peripheral hardware. Typically, a parallel port is connected to a printer.

parallel processing Computer architecture consisting of multiple, simultaneously operating processors.

parameter Value assigned to a variable within a program. For example, parameters can be filenames, ranges of values, or other data.

parameter tuning *See* tunable parameters.

parenb Command-line option used with the stty command for enabling or disabling parity checking. This option is used for terminals that connect to a computer via serial lines.

parent directory Directory that contains the current working directory. The current working directory is a subdirectory of the parent directory.

parenthesis level Level of nesting within parentheses, used in LISP and other list-oriented languages.

parent process ID Identifying number of the process that is the parent of another process.

parext Command-line option used with the stty command for enabling or disabling the use of extended parity checking. This option is used for terminals that connect to a computer via serial lines.

parity checking Error-checking procedure used within or between computers. When parity is checked, the number of ones in the group of bits being transmitted must always be the same (either odd or even).

parmrk Command-line option used with the stty command for selecting whether parity errors in the input are marked. This option is used for terminals that connect to a computer via serial lines.

parodd Command-line option used with the stty command for selecting odd or even parity. This option is used for terminals that connect to a computer via serial lines.

parse Process of breaking down statements into smaller chunks that can be acted upon by a program.

parser Program that analyzes the syntax of a set of information and interprets its components.

partition Logical section of memory or a hard disk that acts as if it is a physically separate section.

partsize Command used to print the size of the active UNIX System partition for the raw-device disk drive. The size value returned is in megabytes.

Parts-per-million Unit of time used to illustrate frequency of error.

Pascal High-level computer language designed by Niklaus Wirth between 1967 and 1971. Use of Pascal was made popular by Borland International's release of Turbo Pascal.

pass-through interface SCSI Interface that allows the programmer to access the SCSI-bus subsystem directly using the driver's pass-through interface. *See also* SCSI.

passwd Command used to change the password or get a list of the current password attributes for the user's log-in name. Privileged users may run passwd to perform these functions for any user, and to set the password attributes for any user.

passwd file ASCII file in /etc/passwd that contains basic information about each user's account.

password Word or code used to allow a user to log in to a system. For security purposes, a user cannot log in without the proper password.

password aging Method used by system administrators to ensure that users change their passwords at regular intervals.

password status Status of a user's password, as displayed by the passwd command. Statuses are NP (no password defined), PS (password defined), and LK (locked).

paste Command used to merge the same lines of several files or subsequent lines of one file.

patch Command used to read a path or source file containing one of the three forms of listings produced by the diff utility and apply those differences to a file.

patched software Refers to software that has been changed by a patch or update to the original program.

PATH Environment variable that holds the user's path. *See also* path.

path
1. Route that leads to a given file. For example, the full path for the passwd file is /etc/passwd.
2. In a network, the route to a given computer or node.

pathconf Library routine used to obtain configurable pathname variables.

pathconv Command used to search FMLI criteria for a specified filename.

pathfind Library routine used to search for a specified file in specified directories.

path, full Complete name showing the route and name for a file, beginning from the root directory.

pathname *See* path.

path prefix Part of the path that shows the directories leading to the file.

path, relative *See* relative pathname.

pathrouter Command used with the UnixWare mailer to enable a host to perform smart routing.

paths file File that serves as the routing database for the pathrouter command.

pattern String of characters, typically used to match other characters. In the shell command line, a pattern may include metacharacters. For example, in the command ls ab*, any files in the current directory that match the pattern *ab* followed by any other characters would be displayed.

pause Library routine used to suspend the calling process until it receives a signal of any type.

pbind Command used to bind a process to a processor.

PC Computer that is compatible with IBM personal computers. PCS were originally designed to be used by one user at a time. However, with improved CPUs and operating systems like UNIX that include multiuser and multitasking features, it is possible for many users to access a PC simultaneously.

pcat Command used to concatenate packed files. The pcat command cannot be used as a filter. The specified files are unpacked and written to the standard output.

PC-DOS Version of MS-DOS sold by IBM. The basic functionality of PC-DOS is the same as MS-DOS, although IBM usually adds some additional features to its version.

pcinfo data structure Data structure containing process class information, such as class *id*, class name, and class information.

pckt Refers to a STREAMS module that may be used with a pseudo-terminal to packetize certain messages.

PCL Abbreviation for Printer Control Language, a printer language made popular by Hewlett-Packard and its LaserJet printers.

PCL printer Printer that accepts input in PCL format. *See also* PCL.

pclose Library routine used to close a stream opened by popen. The pclose routine waits for the associated process to terminate and returns the exit status of the command.

pcmsg Device-driver library routine used to test the type of message to determine if it is a priority control message (also known as a high-priority message).

pcparms data structure Process-management data structure used by the pc getparms and pc setparms commands to set scheduler parameters for regular and lightweight processes. The structure contains the process (or lightweight process) class, as well as any class-specific information.

PDP-7 Computer made in the 1960s by Digital Equipment Corporation that was used at AT&T Bell Laboratories to develop the first prototypes of the UNIX system.

PDP-11 Computer from Digital Equipment Corporation on which the second wave of UNIX system development occurred. The C programming language, pipes, and redirection were among the UNIX features developed on the PDP-11.

peer-to-peer communications Networking entities that connect with each other on equal terms. In peer-to-peer, each computer can act as both client and server. The design of UNIX provides peer-to-peer services.

pendin Command-line option used with the stty command for selecting whether pending input is retyped at the next read or input character. This option is used for terminals that connect to a computer via serial lines.

Pentium CPU chip designed by Intel as a successor to the 80486 chip.

percent sign *See* %.

perfmeter Program running under Open Windows that displays error messages or system messages.

performance monitoring Refers to using software programs to measure how efficiently the computer system is running. Performance monitoring might check CPU usage, memory activities, system calls made, and time spent processing applications in user space, to name a few.

period *See* .

peripheral Device that allows a computer to communicate with the user or with other computers. The keyboard, screen, mouse, printer, and modem are all peripherals.

perl UNIX utility for reading and working with text file. Perl is similar to shell programming and includes many features that are similar to those in the awk utility. Today, perl is often used to process requests to HTTP Web pages on the Internet.

perm Command-line option used with the find command that specifies files by permissions. *See also* find.

permission flag Bit that indicates what permissions a user has for accessing a file or directory. *See also* permissions.

permissions Set of rules governing user access to files and directories.

Permissions file File used with UUCP to define what permissions outside users and hosts have to the local UNIX system. By default, remote users can only send mail and write files to the uucppublic directory structure. Using the Permissions file, remote users can be allowed to remotely execute programs and write to other parts of the file system.

permuted index Special index found in UNIX reference manuals. It's created by sorting a table of contents line into three columns. It's used by locating a desired topic in the middle column and finding the related manual page in the right column. The left column contains the remainder of the text from the middle column.

perror Library routine used to produce a message on the standard error output describing the last error encountered during a call to a system or library function.

persistent link Similar to a Streams multiplexor link, except that to hold the links together, a process is not needed. After a process closes the last file descriptor open on the stream and exits, the multiplexor protocol stack stays connected.

pexbind Command used to change the exclusive binding of processes. The user of the command must be a privileged user.

pg Command used as a filter that allows the examination of files one screenful at a time.

phalloc Device-driver library routine used to allocate and initialize a pollhead structure for use by non-STREAMS character drivers that wish to support polling.

phfree Device-driver library routine used to free the pollhead structure specified.

physical layer First layer in the seven-layer Open Systems Interconnection (OSI) Reference Model. This layer defines specifications for physical transmission of data between adjacent data link nodes.

physiock Device-driver library routine that is called by the character-interface ioctl, read, and write routines of block drivers to help perform unbuffered I/O while maintaining the buffer header as the interface structure.

physmap Device-driver library routine used to allocate a virtual address mapping for a given range of physical addresses.

physmap_free Device-driver library routine used to release a mapping allocated by a previous call to physmap.

phystoppid Device-driver library routine used to return the physical page ID corresponding to the physical address.

PIC Acronym for programmable interrupt controller, an interface on most Intel-based systems in which hardware device interrupts are routed. Once interrupts go through PICs, they are directed to the processor.

pic Command used to process simple graphics commands that can be included in nroff and troff documents. The pic command interprets macros for drawing lines, circles, and squares, and positions them on the page.

picture-backward-column Command in the emacs text editor used in picture mode to move the cursor backward one character. This command is usually bound to the keystroke Ctrl-B.

picture-clear-column Command in the emacs text editor used in picture mode to replace the character at the cursor position with a space. This command is usually bound to the keystroke Ctrl-D.

picture-clear-line Command in the emacs text editor used in picture mode to delete the text on the current line. This command is usually bound to the keystroke Ctrl-K.

picture-clear-rectangle-to-register Command in the emacs text editor used in picture mode to make a copy of the currently marked rectangle for later retrieval. This command is usually bound to the keystroke Ctrl-C Ctrl-W.

picture-duplicate-line Command in the emacs text editor used in picture mode to copy the current line onto the next line of the buffer. This command is usually bound to the keystroke Ctrl-J.

picture-forward-column Command in the emacs text editor used in picture mode to move the cursor to the right one character. This command is usually bound to the keystroke Ctrl-F.

picture mode In the emacs text editor, a major mode for editing line drawings.

The edit-picture command enters picture mode.

picture-mode-exit Command in the emacs text editor used in picture mode to exit from picture mode and return to the previous mode. This command is usually bound to the keystroke Ctrl-C Ctrl-C.

picture-motion Command in the emacs text editor used in picture mode to move the cursor forward in the default drawing direction. This command is usually bound to the keystroke Ctrl-C Ctrl-F.

picture-motion-reverse Command in the emacs text editor used in picture mode to move the cursor backward, in the reverse of the default drawing direction. This command is usually bound to the keystroke Ctrl-C Ctrl-B.

picture-move-down Command in the emacs text editor used in picture mode to move the cursor down one line. This command is usually bound to the keystroke Ctrl-N.

picture-movement-down Command in the emacs text editor used in picture mode to set the default drawing direction to downward. This command is usually bound to the keystroke Ctrl-C . (that is, Ctrl-C period).

picture-movement-left Command in the emacs text editor used in picture mode to set the default drawing direction to leftward. This command is usually bound to the keystroke Ctrl-C<.

picture-movement-ne Command in the emacs text editor used in picture mode to set the default drawing direction to northeast, that is, upward and to the right. This command is usually bound to the keystroke Ctrl-C' (that is, Ctrl-C apostrophe).

picture-movement-nw Command in the emacs text editor used in picture mode

to set the default drawing direction to northwest, that is, upward and to the left. This command is usually bound to the keystroke Ctrl-C" (that is, Ctrl-C open-quote).

picture-movement-right Command in the emacs text editor used in picture mode to set the default drawing direction to rightward. This command is usually bound to the keystroke Ctrl-C>.

picture-movement-se Command in the emacs text editor used in picture mode to set the default drawing direction to southeast, that is, downward and to the right. This command is usually bound to the keystroke Ctrl-C\.

picture-movement-sw Command in the emacs text editor used in picture mode to set the default drawing direction to southwest, that is, downward and to the left. This command is usually bound to the keystroke Ctrl-C/.

picture-movement-up Command in the emacs text editor used in picture mode to set the default drawing direction to upward. This command is usually bound to the keystroke Ctrl-C^.

picture-move-up Command in the emacs text editor used in picture mode to move the cursor up one line. This command is usually bound to the keystroke Ctrl-P.

picture-open-line Command in the emacs text editor used in picture mode to insert a blank line at the cursor position. This command is usually bound to the keystroke Ctrl-O.

picture-yank-rectangle Command in the emacs text editor used in picture mode to insert a rectangle of text that was previously saved in a register. The rectangle is inserted at the cursor location. This command is usually bound to the keystroke Ctrl-C Ctrl-X.

pine Screen-oriented interface to the UNIX mail system. Pine is good for first-time mail users because it includes extensive online help.

pinfo Command used to display information about the processors named in the command line by their processor IDs. If no processors are specified, information is displayed about all processors in the system.

ping Command that utilizes the ICMP protocol's ECHO_REQUEST datagram to elicit an ICMP ECHO_RESPONSE from the specified host or network gateway. If the host responds, ping prints that the host is alive on the standard output and exits. Otherwise, after a specified number of seconds, it writes *no answer from host.*

pinned window In the OPEN LOOK GUI, a pop-up window that is set to stay open even after its function completes. To pin a window, the user clicks on the pushpin in the upper left corner of the window using the mouse.

PIOMAP Tunable parameter that sets the map entry array. This array is used by the programmed I/O breakup routine to work with large data blocks at interrupt level by breaking them up into smaller pieces. This parameter is no longer used in SVR4.2 systems.

PIOMAXSZ Tunable parameter that sets the maximum number of pages that programmed I/O can use at one time. This parameter is no longer used in SVR4.2 systems.

PIOSEGSZ Tunable parameter defines the number of "clicks" of virtual address space that can be used by programmed I/O. This parameter is no longer used in SVR4.2 systems.

pipe
1. Library routine used to create an I/O mechanism called a *pipe* and return descriptors of two STREAMS files, both of which are opened for reading and writing.
2. Special shell character (|) that allows the output of one command to be used as input to the next command. For example, ls | more pipes the output of ls (a list of files) to the more command, which lets you page through the listing. Named pipes are represented by nodes in the file system.

pipemod module Streams module that can be pushed onto a pipe to allow bit switching to take place. This module can handle any type of data flushing. Only M_FLUSH messages are consumed by this module. All others are passed to the next module.

pixel Abbreviation for picture element, an individual dot or group of dots that make up a video screen. In monochrome screens, a pixel is one dot. In color screens, a pixel is usually three dots.

pixmap Screen area that is defined as a bitmap (collection of dots) that is stored within a program. In the Xt (X Window System Toolkit) Intrinsics library, pixmap is defined as a data type.

pkgadd Command used to transfer the contents of a software package or set from the distribution medium or directory to install it onto the system.

pkgask Command that allows an administrator to store answers to an interactive package (one with a request script) or a set of packages.

pkgchk Command used to check the accuracy of installed files or display information about package files. The command checks the integrity of directory structures and the files.

pkginfo
1. Command used to display information about software packages or sets that are installed on the system or

that reside on a particular device or directory.

2. Refers to an ASCII file that describes the characteristics of the package along with information that helps control the flow of installation. It is created by the software developer.

pkgmap Refers to an ASCII file that provides a listing of the package contents. It is automatically generated by the pkgmk command using the information in the prototype file.

pkgmk Command used to produce an installable package to be used as input to the pkgadd command. The package contents will be in directory structure format.

pkgparam Command used to display package parameter values. The pkgparam command looks for the values in the pkginfo file, a specified device, and a specified file.

pkgproto Command used to scan the indicated paths and generate a prototype file that may be used as input to the pkgmk command.

pkgrm Command used to remove a previously installed or partially installed package or set from the system.

pkgtrans Command used to translate an installable package from one format to another. It translates a file system format to a datastream, a datastream to a file system format, or a file system format to another file system format.

.pl File extension for files containing Prolog source code.

plain-tex-mode Command in the tex-mode add-on package to the emacs text editor that enables TeX mode, which is designed for editing text files formatted for TeX.

.plan Optional file in a user's home directory that can contain plans. A user's plan information can be displayed using the finger command.

plock Library routine that allows the calling process to lock into memory or unlock its text segment (text lock), its data segment (data lock), or both its text and data segments (process lock). Locked segments are immune to all routine swapping.

plot Command used to read plotting instructions from the standard input and produces plotting instructions suitable for a particular terminal on the standard output.

pluck-tag Command in the Epsilon text editor that moves the cursor to the definition of the function that the cursor points to.

plus sign *See* +.

pmadm Command for the lower level of the Service Access Facility hierarchy, that is, for service administration. It can add or remove a service, enable or disable a service, add or delete authentication scheme and user ID information, install or replace a per-service configuration script, or print requested service information.

pmmsg In the UNIX Service Access Facility, the structure that defines the format of messages from the port monitor to the service access controller. The structure contains the type of message, the current state of the port monitor, the maximum message class the port monitor understands, the port monitor's tag, and the size of the optional data area.

_pmtab file Administrative file associated with each port monitor in the Service Access Facility. This file defines such things as the port monitor's tag name, the user it runs under, and the daemon command that responds to the service request.

pnch File format consisting of a concatenation of card images. Each card record includes a control byte, followed by data bytes. The control byte identifies the number of data bytes. The number of data bytes must be between 0 and 80.

pnoutrefresh Library routine (curses) used to refresh the specified pad. Parameters are needed to indicate what part of the pad and screen are involved.

point Mouse technique where you move the mouse pointer over the desired object on the screen.

point and click Mouse technique where you move the mouse pointer over the desired object on the screen and click the left mouse button.

pointer
1. Onscreen indicator that moves as you move a pointing device, such as a mouse.
2. In programming, a variable (memory location) that references data.

pointerColor Keyword used in a user's .Xdefaults file to configure the emacs text editor. It controls the color used for the mouse pointer in the emacs window, and is equivalent to the emacs -ms command-line option.

pointing device Device such as a mouse, used to move a cursor (pointer) around the screen. *See also* pointer.

point-max Function in the emacs LISP programming language that returns the maximum position for the buffer (usually the number of characters in the buffer).

point-min Function in the emacs LISP programming language that returns the minimum position for the buffer (usually 1).

Point-to-Point Protocol *See* PPP.

policy independence Characteristic of X Windows in which windows can look and act any way the software developers choose.

poll Library routine that provides a mechanism for multiplexing I/O over a set of file descriptors that reference open files. The poll routine identifies those files with which a user can send or receive messages, or on which certain events have occurred.

pollfd structure Data structure used by the poll library routine to identify each open file descriptor. Elements of the pollfd structure includes the file descriptor, requested events, and returned events.

Poll file UUCP file used to define which computers are polled by the local system and when those remote systems are polled.

polling Checking a computing entity on a regular basis. For example, a remote computer can be polled for pending file transfers or to regularly synchronize time between two computers.

pollwakeup Device-driver library routine used to provide non-STREAMS character drivers with a way to notify processes polling for the occurrence of an event.

p_online Library routine used to bring the specified processor online or take it offline.

popd In the C shell, a command that pops a directory from the directory stack.

popen Library routine used to create a pipe between the calling program and the command to be executed.

pop-up window In a graphical user interface, a window that appears to display a warning or to request a particular piece of information.

port Connector that lets you plug peripheral devices into a computer. Most computers come with serial ports and parallel ports.

portability Ability of computer software to be adapted, or *ported*, to another computer system environment. The UNIX operating system itself is said to be portable because it can be adapted to run on a wide variety of computer hardware.

porting Act of adapting computer software to run in an environment other than the particular one it was designed for.

port monitor Type of process in the UNIX Service Access Facility that constantly checks for incoming service requests. A port monitor might monitor serial devices to check for incoming login requests or monitor LAN devices for a variety of service requests.

port number In TCP/IP, a number that is mapped to a particular service. Port numbers are defined in the TCP/IP file /etc/services.

portrait
1. Paper orientation when printing. Portrait orientation prints lines parallel to the short edge of the paper (the most common orientation).
2. Command line option used with the dpost utility, specifying that the PostScript output print in portrait orientation.

pos_form_cursor Library routine (curses) used to move the form window cursor to the location required by the form driver to resume form processing. This may be needed after the application calls a curses library I/O routine.

positional argument Information typed on the shell command line to control how the command is executed. The first word on the command line is $0, the name of the command itself. The next word(s) are assigned to positional arguments $1, $2, etc. These arguments can be referred to within programs and shell scripts.

POSIX 1003 *See* P1003.

POSIX Portable Operating System Interface for UNIX, a standard developed by IEEE that defines a standard set of interfaces between the operating system and application programs. Most UNIX systems are POSIX-compliant.

pos_menu_cursor Library routine (curses) from the group called menu_cursor. This group of routines is used to correctly position a menus cursor.

post
1. To place an article in a USENET newsgroup.
2. In FMLI, displaying a frame from a frame definition file and making that frame the current frame.

postdaisy Command used to start a filter that translates Diablo 630 daisywheel files into PostScript and writes the results on the standard output.

postdmd Command used to translate DMD bitmap files or files written in the Ninth Edition bitfile format into PostScript and write the results on the standard output.

post_form Library routine (curses) used to write the specified form into its associated subwindow. The application programmer must use curses library routines to display the form on the physical screen or call update panels if the panels library is being used.

postio Command used to provide a serial interface for PostScript printers. The postio command sends files to the PostScript printer attached to line.

postmd Command used as a filter that reads a series of floating-point numbers from files, translates them into a PostScript grayscale image, and writes the results on the standard output. In a typical application, the numbers might be the elements of a large matrix, written in row major order, while the printed image could help locate patterns in the matrix.

post_menu Library routine (curses) used to write a menu to the subwindow. The application programmer must use curses library routines to display the menu on the physical screen or call update panels if the panels library is being used.

post office protocol Electronic mail protocol (abbreviated POP) that lets an administrator set up mail to be gathered and disseminated from a central location.

postplot Command used as a filter to translate graphics files (BSD) into PostScript and writes the results on the standard output.

postprint Command used to provide a filter that translates text files into PostScript and writes the results on the standard output.

post-processor Software that processes data after the main processing has been completed.

postreverse Command used as a filter that reverses the page order in files that conform to Adobe's Version 1.0 or Version 2.0 file structuring conventions, and writes the results on the standard output.

PostScript Page description language created by Adobe Systems that is commonly used by software and hardware. For example, software such as word processors can use PostScript to define the output going to the printer. A PostScript printer then interprets the output and prints the page.

PostScript printer Printer that accepts input in the form of PostScript language. *See also* PostScript.

posttek Command used as a filter that translates tektronix 4014 graphics files into PostScript and writes the results on the standard output.

pound sign *See* #.

pow
1. Library routine (BSD) used to used to perform arithmetic on integers of arbitrary length.
2. C++ library routine providing power mathematical functions.

powerdown Process of shutting down a computer system.

powerup Process of turn on (booting) a computer system.

PPID Built-in shell variable that contains the process number of the parent of the current shell (Bourne and Korn shells only).

PPP Point-to-Point Protocol, the TCP/IP protocol used to connect two Internet nodes over serial lines. Common means of providing full Internet services to a computer over telephone lines.

pptophys Device-driver library routine used to convert a pointer to a page to the page's physical address.

pr Command used to format and print the contents of a file. The named files are printed on standard output. The pr command processes supplementary codeset characters in files, and recognizes supplementary codeset characters in the character or string arguments given to certain options.

#pragma C directive that controls the instantiation of particular template entities.

prctmp Process accounting command used to print the session record file. Typically, this file is located in /var/adm/acct/nite/ctmp. The acctcon command creates this file.

prdaily Process accounting command, started by the runacct command, to produce a report of a day's accounting data.

preempt When a process takes priority over a process that is ahead of it in the queue.

prefix Device-driver command used to enable driver entry points to be identified by configuration software. It decreases the possibility of global symbol collisions in the kernel.

preprocessing Processing data before it runs through the main processing procedure. For example, the pic preprocessor interprets graphics in a troff document before the rest of a document is processed by the troff process.

presentation layer Sixth layer in the seven-layer Open Systems Interconnection (OSI) Reference Model. This layer defines specifications for data representations that are available to the seventh layer (application layer).

previous-line Command in the emacs text editor that moves the cursor up to the previous line. This command is usually bound to the keystroke Ctrl-P.

previous-page Command in the Epsilon text editor that displays the previous screen of text. *See also* scroll-down.

previous-window Command in the Epsilon text editor that moves the cursor to the previous window.

prf File containing operating-system profiler data. The special file /dev/prf provides access to activity information in the operating system. The profiler commands load the measurement facility with text addresses to be monitored. Reading the file returns these addresses and a set of counters indicative of activity between adjacent text addresses.

prfdc Profiler command used to perform the data collection function of the profiler by copying the current value of all the text address counters to a file where the data can be analyzed. This command will store the counters into a file every specified period and will turn off at the specified time.

prfld Command used to initialize the recording mechanism in the UNIX operating system. It generates a table containing the starting address of each system subroutine as extracted from the system namelist and the modules in /etc/conf/mod.d.

PRFMAX Tunable parameter that sets the number of kernel symbols that have been allocated space to be used by the kernel profiler.

prfpr Profiler command used to format the data collected by prfdc or prfsnap. Each text address is converted to the nearest text symbol and is printed if the percent activity for that range is greater than the specified cutoff.

prfsnap Profiler command used to perform the data collection function of the profiler by copying the current value of all the text address counters to a file where the data can be analyzed. The prfsnap command collects data at the time of invocation only, appending the counter values to file.

prfstat Profiler command used to enable or disable the sampling mechanism. Profiler overhead is less than 4% as calculated for 3000 text addresses. The prfstat command will also reveal the number of text addresses being measured.

primary prompt string Shell prompt used when the shell is waiting for the next command. In the Bourne and Korn shells, it is stored in the PS1 shell variable. In the C shell, it is stored in the prompt predefined variable.

primary selection In the X11 version of X Windows, the selection (selected object or objects) shared by all the applications running on one X server.

primary source window Window that is displayed with the graphical UNIX debugger to display the current source line when the current process halts.

print
1. To send information to a printer to be recorded on paper.
2. To send information to the screen to be displayed.
3. To send information to another device to be stored or recorded.
4. Command in the Korn shell that displays its argument on the screen. It is similar to the echo command.
5. Command line option used with the find command. It specifies that find should display the pathname of files it finds. *See also* find.

print-buffer Command in the emacs text editor that prints the current buffer with page numbers and headings.

printenv Command used to obtain the current environment, modify it according to its arguments, then execute the command with the modified environment. The printenv command replaces env if the Application Compatibility Package is installed.

printer Hardware device used for printing the output from a computer. *See also* PostScript printer.

printer class Means of defining a group of printers whereby print jobs directed to that class can be handled by the first printer in the class that is available.

printer queue List of print jobs waiting to be printed on a printer. *See also* lp, lpstat.

printer server Computer on a network dedicated to printing. Users on the network print by sending their jobs to a printer on the print server.

printf
1. Command used to convert, format, and print specified input as dictated by the format given.
2. Library routine used to convert, format, and output its arguments under control of the given formatting character string. The printf routine places output on the standard output stream.

printing Process of sending output to a printer.

printmail Command that formats mail messages into a form that is readable for printing.

print-region Command in the emacs text editor that prints the currently marked region with page numbers and headings.

Print Tool Program running under Open Windows that allows the user to print files, check the print queue, select printers, or cancel print jobs.

printtool Program running under Open Windows that allows the user to print files, check the print queue, select printers, or cancel print jobs.

printw Library routine (curses) used to print formatted output to a specified curses window.

priocntl
1. Command used to display or set scheduling and working-set aging parameters of the specified process(es). It can also be used to display the current configuration information for the system's process scheduler or execute a

command with specified scheduling parameters.
2. Library routine used to provide control over the scheduling and working-set aging aspects of active processes.

priocntlset Library routine used to change the scheduling properties of running processes. It has the same functions as the priocntl system call, but a more general way of specifying the set of processes whose scheduling properties are to be changed.

priority In Streams, a system of determining the order in which information is passed between Streams modules and drivers. Streams message-queuing priority is done by assigning messages to classes. Priority classes include ordinary messages, priority band messages, and high-priority messages. *See also* process priority.

priority band data Priority class of information that is delivered by Streams modules and drivers. Priority band messages are urgent data messages that are sent through the queue ahead of regular data, but after high-priority messages.

private data structures Streams data type that lets programmers reference their own private data structures.

privileged Korn shell mode that starts the shell as a privileged user. Specified with the set command.

privileged user User with specific privileges to perform a certain task. For example, one user might have appropriate privileges to add a new user to a system, while another user might have appropriate privileges to configure networking on the system.

proc File system that provides access to the state of each active process and lightweight process in the system.

process Instance of a program that is currently being executed. Because UNIX is a multitasking system, it is possible to have the same program running as different processes by different users at the same time. Likewise, a particular application program may be managing several different processes concurrently.

process address space Area of memory in which an instance of a running process is stored.

process buffer In the Epsilon text editor, a buffer in which a shell process is running. To create a process buffer, use the start-process command.

process execution time Amount of time from when a process starts to when it completes. Process execution time can be measured in real time or CPU time (the amount of processor time the process consumes).

process group Every running process is a member of a process group, which is related to a process ID of a group leader. Process groups allow any of the processes in the group to be killed or otherwise signalled as a group. For example, if you run several processes in the background from a shell, all those processes are in the same group. By exiting from the shell, all the related processes will be exited as well.

process group ID Process ID of the group leader of a process.

process group leader Process that does not have a group leader above it. When you list process information for such a process (using the ps command), its process ID and process group ID are the same.

process ID Number representing a running process (abbreviated *PID*). Using the kill command with a process ID, you can signal that process to exit, reread configuration files, flush cached data, or close active connections.

processor *See* CPU.

processor ID In a multiprocessor computer, the identification tag associated with a particular processor chip.

processor_bind Library routine used to bind a process, a light weight process (LWP), or a set of LWPs to a specific processor.

processor_info Library routine used to obtain information about a single specified processor in the system.

process priority Value assigned to a running process that determines its access to CPU time as it relates to other running processes. Process priority can be changed with the nice command.

process scheduler *See* scheduler.

proc_ref Device-driver library routine used to direct a non-STREAMS character driver to obtain a reference to the process in whose context it is running.

procset data structure Process-management data structure that defines scheduler parameters for a set of processes or lightweight processes.

proc_signal Device-driver library routine used to post a signal to the specified process. This will interrupt any process blocked in SV_WAIT_SIG or SLEEP_LOCK_SIG at the time the signal is posted, causing those functions to return prematurely, in most cases.

proc_unref Device-driver library routine used to release a reference to a specified process.

prof
1. Command used to interpret a profile file produced by running an executable file that has either been instrumented for profiling or has been linked with an object that was built for profiling.
2. Method of running a profile within a function. The user can introduce a mark that is treated the same as a function entry point. Execution of the mark adds to a counter for that mark, and program-counter time spent is accounted to the immediately preceding mark or to the function if there are no preceding marks within the active function.

profil Library routine used to provide CPU-use statistics by profiling the amount of CPU time expended by a program. The profil command generates the statistics by creating an execution histogram for a current process.

profile Files used in setting up an environment at login time. The system administrator uses /etc/profile to perform services for the entire user community. Each user can have his or her own file (called .profile) to set environment variables and terminal modes.

profiler Group of commands used to facilitate an activity study of the UNIX operating system. *See also* prfld, prfstat, prfdc, prfsnap, prfpr.

profilers *See* lprof, prof.

PROFOPTS Shell environment variable that controls program profiling.

progn Function in the emacs LISP programming language that returns the value of the last statement in the block of statements it contains.

program Set of computer instructions that tell the computer what to do. A program can be a single file or a set of files. For example, both the cat command and a complete word processing package can be referred to as programs.

program-keys Command in the Epsilon text editor that changes the low-level keymapping.

Programmer's Guide Manual available with most UNIX systems, providing a tutorial approach to learning programming, unlike programmer's reference manuals, which include manual pages that describe UNIX features on a component basis.

programming Process of writing of the individual instructions that create a program.

programming language Specific set of rules and instructions that are used for programming. Examples of programming languages include C, C++, COBOL, and Pascal.

.project File in the user's home directory that can be set up to include information on any projects the user is working on. This file can be read by the finger command as a handy way of determining a person's work assignments along with his or her user name.

.prolog File extension for files containing Prolog source code.

Prolog mode In the emacs text editor, a major mode for editing programs in the Prolog programming language.

prolog-mode Command in the emacs text editor that enables Prolog mode, which is designed for editing programs in the Prolog programming language.

Prolog programming language Add-on package for the emacs text editor that implements a major mode for editing programs in the Prolog programming language.

prompt Designation that appears on the screen, telling the user that the shell is ready to accept a command. The default shell prompt is a dollar sign ($). The default root user prompt is a pound sign (#).

protocol In computer networking, a series of rules through which communication can occur. Two communications entities must use the same protocol in order to exchange information. A protocol can define how data units are structured and assembled, how requests are made, and how error-checking and recovery are done.

protocols File called /etc/protocols that contains information regarding the known protocols used in the DARPA Internet.

prototype ASCII file used to specify package information. Each entry in the file describes a single deliverable object. An object may be a data file, a directory, a source file, an executable object, etc. This file is generated by the package developer.

prototypes *See* function prototypes.

prs Command used to display part or all of an SCCS file in a user-supplied format.

prt Command (BSD) used to display the delta and commentary history of an SCCS file.

prtacct Process accounting command used to format and print total accounting files.

prtvtoc Command used to display the contents of the VTOC (volume table of contents). The information displayed for each valid slice includes slice number, slice tag, slice flag/permissions, slice start sector, and slice size.

prune Command-line option used with the find command. *See also* find.

ps Command used to print information about active processes and lightweight processes (LWPs).

PS1 Shell variable that contains the primary prompt string (the shell prompt used when the shell is waiting for the next command) in the Bourne and Korn shells only.

PS2 Shell variable that contains the secondary prompt string (the shell prompt used in multiline commands) in the Bourne and Korn shells only.

PS3 Shell variable that contains the prompt string used by the select command (Korn shell only).

PS4 Shell variable that contains the prompt string used for execution trace (Bourne and Korn shells only).

PseudoColor Most common colormap used by X Windows to define the colors used on the screen.

pseudo-driver Device-driver that is not associated with a physical hardware device. Examples are multiplexor drivers or log drivers.

pseudo-terminal Device that represents a terminal interface to a process without being associated with a physical terminal. So, for a Streams pseudo-terminal, there is no hardware driver downstream of the pseudo-terminal.

psignal Library routine (BSD) used to produce a short message on the standard error file describing the indicated signal.

psradm Command used to bring a processor online in a computer running a multiprocessor UNIX system.

ptem STREAMS module that, when used in conjunction with a line discipline and pseudo-terminal driver, emulates a terminal.

ptob Device-driver library routine used to convert size in pages to size in bytes.

ptrace Library routine used to allow a parent process to control the execution of a child process.

ptsname Library routine that returns the name of the slave pseudo-terminal device associated with a master pseudo-terminal device.

pty Pseudo-terminal subsystem that provides terminal interfaces to processes without being associated with physical terminals.

public directory Directory that can be read from and/or written to by users from another computer. In UUCP, the public directory (PUBDIR) is /var/spool/uucppublic and its associated subdirectories. Often, UNIX systems set up as ftp sites will have a /pub directory with files that are accessible to users logging in under anonymous ftp.

public-key
1. Refers to a pair of library routines (getpublickey, and getsecretkey) used to retrieve public or secret keys.
2. File (/etc/publickey) that is the public-key database used for secure RPC.

public network Computer network that is managed or controlled by a public organization, such as the government. For example, the Internet, BITNET and CSNET are all public networks.

punctuation Character other than a letter or number.

push In Streams, to place a module on a Streams protocol stack.

pushd In the C shell, a command that changes the current working directory and adds the directory name to the directory stack. When given with no argument, it pops a directory from the stack, makes the current working directory, and pushes the previous working directory onto the directory stack. This is a quick way to switch between two directories.

pushpin In OPEN LOOK, a feature that lets you keep a pop-up window from disappearing after you have entered the requested information. An icon of a pushpin appears in the upper left corner of a pinned window.

put Device-driver library routine used to call the put procedure for the queue specified, passing it pointers to a message queue and the message block.

putbq Device-driver library routine used to puts a message back at the head of a queue.

putc Library routine used to put a character on a stream.

putchar Library routine used to put a character on a stream.

putctl Device-driver library routine used to send a control message to a queue.

putctl1 Device-driver library routine used to send a control message with a one-byte parameter to a queue.

putdev Command used to add a new device to the device database (DDB), modify an existing device's attributes, or remove a device entry from the DDB.

putdgrp Command used to modify the device group table. It can modify the table by creating a new device group or by removing a device group. It can also change group definitions by adding or removing a device from the group definition.

putenv Library routine used to change or add value to environment.

putmsg Library routine used to create a message from user-specified buffer(s) and send the message to a STREAMS file.

putnextctl Device-driver library routine used to send a control message to a specified queue.

putnextctl1 Device-driver library routine used to send a control message with a one-byte parameter to a queue.

putnext Device-driver library routine used to pass a message to the put routine of the next queue in the stream.

putpwent Library routine that is the inverse of getpwent. Given a pointer to a password structure created by getpwent (or getpwuid or getpwnam), putpwent writes a line on the specified stream, which matches the format of /etc/passwd.

putq Device-driver library routine used to put messages on a queue after the put routine has finished processing the message.

puts Library routine used to write the specified string, followed by a newline character, to the standard output stream.

putspent Library routine that is the inverse of getspent. Given a pointer to a structure created by the getspent routine (or the getspnam routine), the putspent routine writes a line on the specified stream, which matches the format of /etc/shadow.

pututline Library routine used to access the utmp file entry. It writes out the supplied utmp structure into the utmp file. It uses getutid to search forward for the proper place if it finds that it is not already at the proper place.

putw Library routine used to write the specified word (that is, integer) to the output stream (where the file pointer, if defined, is pointing). The size of a word is the size of an integer and varies from machine to machine.

pwck Command used to scan the password file and note any inconsistencies. The checks include validation of the number of fields, login name, user ID, group ID, and whether the login directory and the program-to-use-as-shell exist.

pwconv Command used to create and update the /etc/shadow file with information from the /etc/passwd file.

PWD Shell environment variable that contains the name of the current working directory.

pwd Command used to display the path name of the working (current) directory. *See also* working directory.

PWR Name of signal number 19 which can be sent to a running process, used to restart after a power failure.

Pyramid Computer manufacturer specializing in mid-sized UNIX-based computers.

qenable Device-driver library routine that puts a specified queue on the linked list of those whose service routines are ready to be called by the STREAMS scheduler.

QIC-80 Popular small tape format used for backing up data.

qinit Device-driver structure that contains pointers to processing procedures and default values for a queue.

qprocsoff Device-driver library routine that disables the put and service routines of the driver or module whose read queue is specified.

qprocson Device-driver library routine that enables the put and service routines of the driver or module whose read queue is specified.

qreply Device-driver library routine that sends a message in the opposite direction from that of the stream.

qsize Device-driver library routine that evaluates a queue and returns the number of messages it contains.

qsort Library routine that implements the quicker-sort algorithm, which sorts a table of data in place. The contents of the table are sorted in ascending order according to the user-supplied comparison function.

qt Name formerly used to identify UNIX quarter-inch cartridge tape drivers.

quad dotted notation Refers to the four-part Internet Protocol (IP) address in which the parts are separated by dots (periods).

query-replace Command in the emacs text editor that replaces each instance of a specified string, prompting the user regarding each replacement. This command is usually bound to the keystroke Meta-%.

query-replace-regexp Command in the emacs text editor that replaces each instance of a specified regular expression, prompting the user regarding each replacement.

question mark *See* ?.

queue Description of the STREAMS queue structure. An instance of a STREAMS driver or module consists of two queue structures, one for upstream (read-side) processing and one for downstream (write-side) processing.

quick-save Boolean variable used with the nn USENET news reader. When quick-save is on, nn automatically places all saved files into the default location (default-save-file) without prompting the user for a location.

quick substitution In the C shell, modifying the last command typed in order to issue a new command.

quick-substitution character In the C shell, the special character that modifies the last command typed to produce a new command. This character is usually the caret (^).

quiet
1. Option to the debug command in which no output is generated.
2. Option to the lpadmin that terminates an alert on an active printer.

quiet NaN C Programming language data type. NaN stands for "not a number." NaNs hold diagnostic information. Quiet NaNs go through operations without raising invalid operation exceptions when they are used as operands in floating-point operations. The result of these operations is the same quiet NaN.

quit
1. Command used in the shl program. This command exits from the shl program and terminates all layers.
2. Command-line option used with the stty command for setting the quit control character.
3. Name of signal number 3, which can be sent to a running process.
4. Command used in many interactive applications, such as ftp, to exit the application.

quot Command that displays the number of blocks (1,024 bytes) in the named filesystem currently owned by each user.

quota Command that displays users' disk usage and limits. Only a privileged user may use the optional username argument to view the limits of other users.

quotacheck Command that examines each file system, builds a table of current disk usage, and compares this table against that stored in the disk quota file for the file system.

quotaoff Command that announces to the system that file systems specified should have any disk quotas turned off.

quotaon Command that announces to the system that disk quotas should be enabled on one or more file systems.

quote
1. To surround a character or string of characters with quoting characters with an accent grave (`) to tell the shell that the information in quotes should be run as a command and its output used as input to the current command. For example, ls `cat file1` displays a listing of all of the files contained in file1.
2. In the shell, the backslash (\) can be used instead of quoting a single character. For example, to include an asterisk in an argument without the shell interpreting it as a wildcard character, the characters * can be used.
3. To enclose a string in special quoting characters, so that the special meanings of characters in the string are ignored. In the shell, single (') or double (") quotes can be used as quoting characters. For example, to include an asterisk in an argument without it being interpreted as a wildcard character, you could enclose the argument in quotes as follows: "chap*" or 'chap*'.

quoted-insert Command in the Epsilon text editor that interprets the next character literally and enters it into the buffer. This is useful for including control characters, meta characters, or graphics characters in a buffer.

quoting modifier Variable modifier used in the C shell that quotes the value of a variable. The two quoting modifiers are :q and :x.

R

r Korn shell command used to execute the previous command.

radio box In wksh, a set of graphical buttons that have the appearance and similar function of a set of buttons on a radio. Because in a radio box only one button can be selected at a time, when a button is selected, the previous button is cleared.

raise Library routine used to send a specified signal to the executing program.

RAM Random Access Memory, memory chips on which data can be written and read by the central processing unit.

ramd Prefix used on RAM disk driver routines, including ramdopen, ramdclose, ramdsize, ramdstrategy, and ramdprint.

rand Library routine that uses a multiplicative congruential random number generator with period 2**32 to return successive pseudo-random numbers in the range from 0 to (2**31)-1.

random
1. Command that generates a random number on the standard output, and returns the number as its exit value. By default, this number is either a zero or a one.

2. Library routine that uses a nonlinear additive-feedback random number generator employing a default table of 31 long integers to return successive pseudorandom numbers in the range from 0 to (2**31)-1. The period of this random number generator is very large, approximately 16*((2**31)-1).

Random Access Memory *See* RAM.

ranlib Utility program for dealing with compiled programs, available from the Free Software Foundation as part of binutils.

RARP Reverse address resolution protocol, a protocol used with the TCP/IP protocol suite to do reverse-address resolution. RARP maps a known, 48-bit Ethernet address to 32-bit IP addresses. This is the opposite of the function performed by the ARP protocol.

rarpd Command that acts as a DARPA reverse-address resolution protocol server. It starts a daemon that responds to RARP requests.

raster image Graphical means of representing a picture as a matrix of dots.

raw Library routine used to place the terminal into raw mode. Raw mode is similar to cbreak mode, in that characters typed are immediately passed through to the user program. The differences are that in raw mode, the interrupt, quit, suspend, and flow control characters are all passed through uninterpreted, instead of generating a signal.

raw device Type of device that reads and writes data one character at a time. Also called a *character device*. *Compare to* block device.

raw disk slices Unformatted areas of a hard disk where data can be written asynchronously.

raw mode Terminal setting in which the eot, erase, intr, kill, quit, and switch characters are ignored and no postprocessing is performed. *Compare to* cooked mode.

raw sockets Sockets that provide direct access to the communications protocols. Raw sockets are intended for programmers who want to get to nonstandard features of a protocol.

rc initialization scripts Shell scripts contained in the /etc subdirectories rc.d, rc0.d, rc2.d, rc3.d, and init.d. These scripts are run when the system goes up or down to a particular run level. When the system goes down to a level, the scripts associated with that level are executed with the stop option. When the system goes up to a level, scripts are run with the start option.

rc0 Command that is executed at each system state change that needs to have the system in an inactive state. It is responsible for those actions that bring the system to a quiescent state, traditionally called *shutdown*.

rc1 Command that is executed, via an entry in /etc/inittab when the system enters run level 1. Run level 1 is a single-user state, used on occasion by system administrators to do maintenance on the system before it is made

available to all users.

rc2 Command that is executed via an entry in /etc/inittab and is responsible for those initializations that bring the system to a ready-to-use state, traditionally state 2, called the *multi-user state*.

rc6 Command that is executed when the system executes init state 6. This command runs the commands needed to shutdown and restart the system.

rcache Performance metric that represents the fraction of logical reads found in the system buffers.

rcibrg Command-line option used with the stty command for setting how the terminal's clock is set.

rcmd Library routine used by a privileged user to execute a command on a remote machine using an authentication scheme based on reserved port numbers.

rcp Command that performs remote file copies between networked computers. This command is used with TCP/IP.

rcrset Command-line option used with the stty command for setting how the terminal's clock is set.

RCS Revision control system, a utility for doing software version control.

rctset Command-line option used with the stty command for setting how the terminal's clock is set.

RD Device-driver library routine used to accept a queue pointer as an argument and return a pointer to the read queue of the same module or driver.

rdate Networking command used to notify a system that the system date has changed.

rdchk Library routine that checks to see if a process will block if it attempts to read the file designated.

rdist Command used for remote file distribution. The rdist command can place identical files on remote computers while maintaining the permissions associated with the files.

read
1. Command that obtains the next line (up to a newline) from the standard input and parses it into fields, assigning each field value to the shell variables that are listed as parameters.
2. Library routine that attempts to read specified bytes from a file into a buffer.
3. Device-driver library routine called during the read system call. The read routine is responsible for transferring data from the device to the user data area.

readdir Library routine used to return pointers to the next active directory entry and position the directory stream (dirp) at the next entry.

readfile Command that reads a file and copies it to the standard output. No translation of NEWLINE is done. It keeps track of the longest line it reads, and if there is a subsequent call to longline, the length of that line, including the NEWLINE character, is returned.

readlink Library routine used to read the value of a symbolic link.

read lock To set a file or device so that data cannot be read from it until the lock is removed.

README File containing information the user needs to know about a particular operating system, software package, or directory of information. For example, a README file might describe how to compile the programs in a directory, then how to use the resulting applications. README files are usually in plain text, so a user moving around a file system can simply display the contents of the file on the screen.

readmsg Command used to extract selected messages from a mail file. The readmsg command can be used within the elm mail reader.

readnews Command used to read USENET news. The readnews interface is relatively simple, compared to readers such as rn and trn.

readonly Command in the Bourne and Korn shells that makes one or more shell variables read-only, so that new values cannot be assigned to them.

read-only Characteristic of a file system, floppy disk, or other device where only reads of the data can be performed. Writes are prohibited.

read-only buffer Buffer in the emacs text editor containing text to be viewed but not modified.

READ option Parameter set in the UUCP Permissions file to identify directories from which files can be read by remote systems.

read permission File permission that allows the associated owner, group, or other user to view or copy the contents of the file. Read permissions are set in the first, fourth, and seventh bit of the nine-bit permission field (rwxrwxrwx).

read queue In STREAMS, the lower queue in the pair of queues associated with each STREAMS module or driver. The other queue is called the *write queue*.

readv Library routine that performs the same action as read, but places the input data into the iovcnt buffers specified by the members of the iov array.

real group ID Group ID assigned to the user when the user first logged in. This differs from the effective group

ID, which can reflect the group ID that is currently in effect.

realloc Library routine that changes the size of the specified block and returns a pointer to the (possibly moved) block. The contents will be unchanged up to the lesser of the new and old sizes.

real user ID User ID assigned to the user when the user first logged in. This differs from the effective user ID, which can reflect the user ID that is currently in effect.

real-time
1. Refers to a computing activity that is designed to respond to a user or application as requests occur.
2. When an application is run without interruption, so the system can respond to the application's request without delay. Compare this to time-sharing, where many processes may be serviced on a rotating basis.

realpath Library routine that returns the real filename. It resolves all links, symbolic links, and references to "." and ".." in the specified filename.

reboot
1. Command that restarts the kernel. The kernel is loaded into memory by the PROM monitor, which transfers control to it.
2. Library routine that reboots the system. It is invoked automatically in the event of unrecoverable system failures.
3. Term used to describe the process of restarting a computer.

reboot system state Initialization state 6, where the system is shutdown and the computer is rebooted. You can change to the reboot system state using the init 6 command.

rec Type of USENET newsgroup that discusses the arts, hobbies, and recreational activities. The names of newsgroups of this type begin with *rec*.

receive To accept data from another entity.

recenter Command in the emacs text editor that redisplays the text on the screen, scrolling as needed so that the current line is in the center. This command is usually bound to the keystroke Ctrl-L. *See also* redisplay.

re_comp Library routine that compiles a string into an internal form suitable for pattern matching.

recompile To compile a program again, usually after making corrections or enhancements to the program.

record Structure of data that contains a set of fields.

record locking Feature that prevents more than one process from changing a record at the same time.

recover To return to a stable condition after an error condition.

recover-context Command in the saveconf add-on package to the emacs text editor that enables the user to restart the program with the same buffers open and windows visible.

rectangle mode Mode of operation of the Epsilon text editor in which kill operations use a rectangular block of text.

rectangle-mode Command in the Epsilon text editor that enters rectangle mode and makes the currently marked region the rectangular area between the cursor and the mark.

recursive edit In the emacs text editor, putting a global-search-and-replace operation on hold while performing another editing operation. After a query-replace command, the keystroke Ctrl-R begins recursive editing.

recursive-edit Command in the emacs text editor that stops a global-search-and-replace operation and enters recursive editing. During recursive editing, the user can make any changes to the buffer. To return to the global-search-and-replace operation, the user presses Meta-Ctrl-C.

recv Library routine used to receive messages from another socket. The recv routine may be used only on a connected socket.

recvfrom Library routine used to receive messages from another socket. The recvfrom routine may be used to receive data on a socket whether it is in a connected state or not.

recvmsg Library routine used to receive messages from another socket. The recvmsg routine may be used to receive data on a socket whether it is in a connected state or not.

red Command that is a restricted version of the text editor ed. It will only allow editing of files in the current directory. It prohibits executing shell commands via the ! shell command.

redirection Process of directing either input or output to a location other than the default location. For example, most UNIX commands take their input from standard in and their output from standard out. With redirection you can, for example, direct input from and output to a file.

redisplay Command in the Epsilon text editor that redisplays the text on the screen. *See also* recenter.

redo Command in the Epsilon text editor that re-executes the last edit or cursor movement. This command reverses the effect of the last undo command.

redo-changes Command in the Epsilon text editor that re-executes the last edit.

re_exec Library routine used as a regular expression handler. It checks the argument string against the last string passed to re_comp.

refer Command that is a preprocessor for nroff or troff, which finds and formats references.

refresh Library routine (curses) used to get any output on the terminal. It copies the named window to the physical terminal screen, using the specified standard screen as the default window.

regcmp
1. Command that compiles the regular expressions in a specified file and places the output in file.
2. Library routine that compiles a regular expression (consisting of the concatenated arguments) and returns a pointer to the compiled form.

regex
1. Command that takes a string from standard input, and a list of pattern/template pairs, and compares the string against each pattern until there is a match.
2. Library routine that executes a compiled pattern against the subject string.

regexp Refers to a header file, regexp.h, defining general-purpose regular expression-matching routines to be used in programs that perform regular expression-matching.

regexpr Group of library routines used to compile regular expressions and match the compiled expressions against lines. The regular expressions compiled are in the form used by ed. *See also* compile, step, advance.

regex-replace Command in the Epsilon text editor that replaces each instance of a specified regular expression. *See also* replace-regexp.

regex-search Command in the Epsilon text editor that searches for a regular expression starting at the cursor position and moving forward through the buffer. *See also* isearch-forward-regexp.

region In the emacs text editor, a string of text that has been marked for editing. A region can be marked using the set-mark command or by the mark-paragraph, mark-page, or mark-whole-buffer commands. Once a region is marked, it can be killed, searched, sorted, etc.

register Temporary storage space used in the emacs text editor in picture mode. Rectangles of text can be stored in registers for later retrieval. *See also* picture-clear-rectangle-to-register.

regression testing Type of software testing designed to ensure that a new piece of software doesn't interfere with any existing software.

regular expression String of characters used for such things as finding the string of characters within a file.

regular file *See* text file.

rehash In the C shell, update the hash table of commands and their locations. This command should be used whenever new commands are stored in directories listed in the PATH variable.

reinit Command used to change the values of descriptors defined in the initialization file that was named when FMLI was invoked and/or used to define additional descriptors.

reject Command that prevents queuing of print requests for the named destinations. A destination can be either a printer or a class of printers.

relational version Calls a programmer-defined function when a program needs to compare two values.

relative In the emacs text editor, when used as the value of the fortran-comment-indent-style variable in Fortran mode, indents comment lines to the right of column seven. The indentation is controlled by the variable fortran-minimum-statement-indent.

relative pathname Route to a file relative to the current directory. For example, the relative path to the /etc/inet directory from the /etc/conf.d directory is ./conf.d.

relcom Type of USENET newsgroup consisting of postings in Russian, using the KOI-8 8-bit representation of the Cyrillic alphabet, and mostly circulated in Russia. The names of newsgroups of this type begin with *relcom*.

relocatable object files Files that contains references to symbols that are not linked with their definitions.

relogin Command that changes the terminal line field of a user's utmp entry to the name of the windowing terminal layer attached to standard input.

remainder Library routine that returns the floating-point remainder of the division of x by y. More precisely, it returns the value $r = x - yn$, where n is the integer nearest the exact value x/y. Whenever $|n - x/y| = \frac{1}{2}$, then n is even.

remote Generally, any computer system or device that is located externally to a computer and accessed via a network, for example, a printer available for your use but attached to another computer on your network is a remote printer.

remote file copy Feature that lets you copy the contents of a file to another computer on a network. The rcp and ftp commands are used to do remote file copy in TCP/IP networks.

Remote File Sharing (RFS) Distributed file system software, built into the UNIX System V Release 3 operating system. RFS allowed UNIX systems to share files, directories, and devices transparently across a network, by connecting remote directories to the local file system tree. Because Network File System (NFS) has become the standard distributed file system software for UNIX systems, RFS is no longer developed or supported.

remote host Computer on a network that is not the local computer. The word *remote* doesn't imply that the remote host is any great distance from the computer you are working on.

remote login Ability to connect to another computer by logging in over a network.

remote mount To connect part of a remote file system (whether it is a directory, file, or device) to the local file system tree. By doing so, it allows the local system to access the remote resources as though they existed on the local system.

remote printer Printer attached to another computer on your network.

Remote Procedure Call *See* RPC.

remote resources Computing entities on remote hosts that may be accessible from your local computer. A remote resource may include files, directories, devices, objects, records, or other items available from another computer.

remote.unknown File used with UUCP to define how the UNIX system behaves when a communication request arrives from a computer it doesn't know about.

remove Library routine that causes the specified file or empty directory to be no longer accessible by that name. A subsequent attempt to open that file using that name will fail, unless the file is created anew.

removef Command that informs the system that the user or software intends to remove a pathname. Output from removef is the list of input pathnames that may be safely removed (no other packages have a dependency on them).

removepkg Command that removes the specified UNIX system software package, or a user-selected package if no argument is specified.

remque Library routine that manipulates queues built from doubly linked lists to remove an entry from a queue.

rename
1. Command used to change the name of a file.
2. Library routine used to change the name of a file.
3. Process of assigning a new name to a file.

rename-buffer Command in the emacs text editor that changes the name of the current buffer.

rendering To make an image from geometric forms, colors, and shades to create a life-like picture.

renice Command that requests that the system scheduling priorities of one or more running processes be changed. By default, the applicable processes are specified by their process IDs.

repeat In the C shell, a command that executes another command a specified number of times.

repeater Communications equipment that rebroadcasts a signal on a communications line. A repeater does not change the communications signal, but simply repeats a potentially weakened signal so it can be transmitted over a greater distance.

repeat-matching-complex-command Command in the chistory add-on package to the emacs text editor that allows the user to edit and repeat an emacs command.

repinsb Device-driver library routine used to provide a C language interface to the machine instructions that read a string of bytes from an 8-bit I/O port using the I/O address space, instead of the memory address space.

repinsd Device-driver library routine used to provide a C language interface to the machine instructions that read a string of 32-bit words from a 32-bit I/O port using the I/O address space, instead of the memory address space.

repinsw Device-driver library routine used to provide a C language interface to the machine instructions that read a string of 16-bit short words from a 16-bit I/O port using the I/O address space, instead of the memory address space.

replace-regexp Command in the emacs text editor that replaces each instance of a specified regular expression.

replace-string Command in the Epsilon text editor that replaces each instance of a specified string. *See also* query-replace.

REPLY Built-in shell variable that contains the default reply message used by the select and read commands (Bourne and Korn shells only).

Reply-to Field in an electronic-mail message indicating the electronic-mail address to which replies should be sent.

report-emacs-bug Command in the emacsbug add-on package to the emacs text editor that generates an electronic-mail message to the Free Software Foundation reporting a bug in emacs.

reportscheme Command that provides authentication-scheme information to networking applications. The authentication service is added to SAF port monitors to enforce authentication when a networking service is re-quested.

repoutsb Device-driver library routine used to provide a C language interface to the machine instructions that write a string of bytes to an 8-bit I/O port using the I/O address space, instead of the memory address space.

repoutsd Device-driver library routine used to provide a C language interface to the machine instructions that write a string of 32-bit long words to a 32-bit I/O port using the I/O address space, instead of the memory address space.

repoutsw Device-driver library routine used to provide a C language interface to the machine instructions that write a string of 16-bit short words to a 16-bit I/O port using the I/O address space, instead of the memory address space.

repquota Command that prints a summary of the disk usage and quotas for the specified file systems. For each user, the current number of files and amount of space (in kilobytes) is printed, along with any quotas created with edquota.

reprint Command-line option used with the stty command for setting the re-print control character.

require-final-newline Variable in the emacs text editor that controls whether emacs automatically adds a newline to the end of a file when saving the file, if the final newline is missing.

Request for Comment (RFC) Form in which standards for the Internet (such as protocols) are defined. For example, RFC 819 describes Internet domain-naming conventions, and RFC 821 describes the Simple Mail Transfer Protocol (SMTP).

re-search-backward Command in the emacs text editor that searches backward through the buffer, starting at the cursor position, for a specified regular expression.

re-search-forward Command in the emacs text editor that searches forward through the buffer, starting at the cursor position, for a specified regular expression.

reserved name Name of a file or device that is reserved for use by the operating system or some other program.

reset
1. To return a program or operating system to an initialization state.
2. FMLI command that causes the value descriptor of the current field to be re-evaluated, restoring the default value of the field if the current value is different.

reset button Physical button on a computer that, when pressed, causes the system to reboot without turning off the computer.

Reset Input Program running under Open Windows that allows input from the keyboard.

resetterm Library routine used to reset a terminal.

resetty Library routine used to save and restore the state of the terminal modes. It restores the state to what it was at the last call to **savetty**.

res_init Library routine used to read the initialization file to get the default domain name and the Internet address of the initial hosts running the name server.

resize To change the size, and possibly the shape, of a graphical element. Often, the term is used to identify a feature that lets you resize a window on the screen.

res_mkquery Library routine that makes a standard query message and places it in the specified buffer. The res_mkquery routine returns the size of the query or -1 if the query is larger than the specified buffer length.

resolution Measure of sharpness of a displayed or printed character. For example, the resolution for a standard VGA display is 640x480. With high resolution video cards, resolution can be increased to 1280x1024, or higher.

resolv.conf Refers to the resolver configuration file, resolv.conf, which contains information that is read by the resolver routines the first time they are invoked in a process. In particular, it is used by TCP/IP to identify domain-name system servers on the network that the local system should use to resolve Internet host names into IP addresses. Once this file is configured, the local computer doesn't have to keep a list of all hosts with which it wants to communicate.

resolver Group of library routines used as resolver routines. This group includes res_mkquery, res_send, res_init, dn_comp, and dn_expand.

resource In Motif, an item that defines graphical elements on the screen, such as background colors or window border sizes.

resource file In Motif, a file that contains resource descriptions that define graphical elements. Each user has a resource file called .Xdefaults in their home directory. System-wide resources are defined in the app-defaults/Mwm file.

res_send Library routine used to send a query to name servers and return an answer. It will call res_init if RES_INIT is not set, send the query to the local name server, and handle timeouts and retries.

restore Command used to restore files to their original directories. The restores are done from backup copies that were made of the original files and directories.

restricted shell Version of the Bourne or Korn shell that does not allow the user to change directory, modify the value of the PATH variable, run programs that are not in directories in the PATH variable, or redirect output. The restricted version of the Bourne shell is called rsh. The restricted version of the Korn shell is called rksh.

resume Command-line option used with the lp command that resumes a print job that was held. This command, used in the shl program, returns to the specified layer.

RET In FMLI, a variable that represents the last executable run. If the exec fails, the RET variable is set to the return code plus 1,000.

return value Number or string that is sent to a controlling entity after a command or function completes. For example, when a command exits with an error the return value might be set to a negative one to identify an error.

Return key Key on the keyboard, interchangeable with the Enter key. In all UNIX shells, pressing Return indicates that the user has typed a command to be executed. In most text editors, pressing Return begins a new line. *See also* Enter key.

reverse-incremental-search Command in the Epsilon text editor that searches incrementally backward through the buffer, starting at the cursor position, for the specified text. *See also* isearch-backward.

reverse-regex-search Command in the Epsilon text editor that searches backward through the buffer, starting at the cursor position, for the specified regular expression.

reverse-string-search Command in the Epsilon text editor that searches backward through the buffer, starting at the cursor position, for the specified text.

reverseVideo Keyword used in a user's .Xdefaults file to configure the emacs text editor. It controls whether reverse video is used in the emacs window, and is equivalent to the emacs -r command-line option.

reverse video attribute When a graphical element is set to its opposite color. For example, a black background with white text might change to a white background with black text.

revert-buffer Command in the emacs text editor that restores the current buffer to the text it contained the last time it was saved.

revision control system *See* SCCS.

rewind Library routine used to reposition a file pointer in a stream.

rewinddir Library routine used to reset the position of the named directory stream to the beginning of the directory. It also causes the directory stream to refer to the current state of the corresponding directory, as a call to opendir would.

rexec Library routine that returns a stream to a remote command. It looks up the named host using the gethostbyname routine, returning -1 if the host does not exist.

rexecd Command used as a server that provides remote execution facilities with authentication based on user names and encrypted passwords.

rfadmin Administrative command for managing RFS facilities.

RFC *See* Request for Comment.

rfmaster RFS file used to define hosts in an RFS domain.

rfpasswd RFS command used to change host passwords.

RFS *See* Remote File Sharing.

RFS resources Files, directories, and devices that are made available for sharing in an RFS network.

RFS system state Original name for UNIX system state 3. State 3 has now come to refer to a more general networking start-up state.

rfstart Command that starts up RFS on a host computer.

rfstop Command that shuts down RFS on a host computer.

RGB Colors (red, green, and blue) used for displaying images in a video system. White is produced by combining all three colors. Other colors are produced by varying the levels of red, green, and blue.

RGB database Database that holds definitions of screen colors used by X Windows.

.rhosts File in a user's home directory that lists remote computers. A user from a remote computer with the same name as the local user can log in or copy files from the local system without a password. The remote user will have the same permissions as the local user.

richtext Command used to view a richtext document.

richtext document File based on a simple markup language that contains markup to allow the document to be presented as more than just text. For example, rich text might contain markup to do bold, italic, or underlining. The advantage of rich text is that it can be sent in mail or other facilities that only support ASCII text, yet it can be viewed with other characteristics.

rindex Library routine used to operate on NULL-terminated strings. It does not check for overflow of any receiving string. The rindex routine returns a pointer to the first (last) occurrence of the named character in the named string, or a NULL pointer.

rint Library routine used to return the nearest integer value to its floating-point argument x as a double-precision floating-point number.

ripinfo Command that displays router driver statistics.

ripquery Command that lists all routes known by an RIP gateway. The ripquery command can be used to debug problems with a RIP gateway.

RISC Acronym for reduced instruction set computing, an architecture of a CPU where only a limited number of instructions can be performed. As a rule, RISC chips out-perform CISC (complex instruction set computing) chips. *See also* CISC.

RISC machine Computer based on a RISC CPU.

Ritchie, Dennis Developer of UNIX, with Ken Thompson, and the inventor of the C programming language, with Brian Kernighan.

rksh Command that runs a restricted version of the Korn shell.

rlogin Command used to establish a remote login session from your terminal to a remote.

rlogind Command used as a server that provides a remote login facility with authentication based on privileged port numbers.

rm Command used to remove the entries for one or more files from a directory.

rmail Command that only permits the sending of mail; UUCP uses rmail as a security precaution. Any application programs that generate mail messages should invoke rmail rather than mail for message transport and delivery.

rmail-delete-after-output Variable in the emacs text editor that controls whether rmail deletes electronic mail messages once they have been stored in a file.

rmail-dont-reply-to-names Variable in the emacs text editor that controls which names to omit when replying to mail.

rmail mode In the emacs text editor, a major mode for reading and sending electronic mail.

rmail-file-name Variable in the emacs text editor that contains the filename where rmail stores electronic mail messages.

rmail-primary-inbox-list Variable in the emacs text editor that contains a list of names of files that contain incoming electronic mail. This is usually nil, which causes the default mbox file to be read in the user's home directory.

rmalloc Device-driver library routine used to allocate space from the private space-management map.

rmallocmap Device-driver library routine used to allocate and initialize a pri-·vate map array that can be used for the allocation of space.

rmalloc_wait Device-driver library routine used to allocate space from a private map previously allocated using. rmallocmap.

rmdel Command used to remove the delta specified by the SID (SCCS identification string) from each named SCCS file.

rmdir
1. Command used to remove entries for the named directories, which must not be empty.
2. Library routine used to remove the directory named by the path-name. The directory must be empty, that is, must only contain dot (.) and double-dot (..) entries.

rmfree Device-driver library routine used to release space into the private space-management map and wake up any processes that are waiting for space.

rmfreemap Device-driver library routine used to free a private space-management map.

rmvb Device-driver library routine used to remove the specified message block from the specified message and return a pointer to the altered message.

rmvq Device-driver library routine used to remove the specified message from the queue specified.

rn Command used to read USENET news. The rn command provides a more sophisticated search and macro facilities.than does the readnews command.

roffbib Command used to print out all records in a bibliographic database, in bibliography format rather than as footnotes or endnotes.

ROFL "Rolling on Floor, Laughing," an abbreviation used in e-mail and newsgroups.

ROM Acronym for read-only memory) a computer chip memory from which instructions can be read, but not modified. It is used to contain such things as the first instructions needed to boot a computer.

root
1. Starting point in the UNIX direc-

tory tree, indicated by a slash (/). All files and directories (even if they are remotely mounted) branch off of the root.
2. Login name used to log in as the root user.

root user Special UNIX login, representing the user who has control of all administration of the UNIX system. The root user typically has permission to change any file or run any command. *See also* superuser.

rounding behavior When a floating-point value is converted to a smaller floating-point value.

route Command that manually manipulates the network routing tables normally maintained by the system routing daemon, routed, or through default routes and redirect messages from routers.

routed Command that is invoked at boot time to manage the network routing tables. The routed routing daemon uses a variant of the Xerox NS Routing Information Protocol in maintaining up-to-date kernel routing table entries.

router Communications device that routes information from one network to another network. The two networks are typically of the same type.

routines Another name for programming functions.

routing Refers to system support for packet network routing. The network facilities provide general packet routing. Routing table maintenance may be implemented in applications processes.

rows Command-line option used with the stty command for setting the window size.

RPC Remote procedure call, a high-level communications architecture for creating network applications. RPC hides many of the details of the underlying networking mechanism.

rpc
1. Group of library routines that allow C language programs to make procedure calls on other machines across a network. First, the client calls a procedure to send a data packet to the server. On receipt of the packet, the server calls a dispatch routine to perform the requested service, and then sends back a reply.
2. Refers to the rpc program-number database, which contains user-readable names that can be used in place of RPC program numbers.

rpcb_getaddr Library routine used to provide a user interface to the rpcbind service, which finds the address of the service on the host that is registered with the named program number and version, and that speaks the associated transport protocol.

rpcbind
1. Command that acts as a server to convert RPC program numbers into universal addresses. It must be running to make RPC calls.
2. Group of library routines used for RPC bind service. This group includes rpcb_getmaps,   rpcb_getaddr, rpcb_gettime,   rpcb_rmtcall,   and rpcb_set, rpcb_unset.

rpc_broadcast Library routine that works like rpc_call, except the call message is broadcast to the connectionless network specified.

rpcb_set Library routine that acts as a user interface to the rpcbind service, which establishes a mapping between the triple [prognum, versnum, netconf->nc netid] and svcaddr on the machine's rpcbind service.

rpcb_unset Library routine that acts as a user interface to the rpcbind service, which destroys all mapping between the triple [prognum, versnum, netconf->nc netid] and the address on the machine's rpcbind service.

rpc_call Library routine used to call the remote procedure associated with program number, version number, and process number on the specified machine.

rpc_clnt_auth Group of library routines for client-side remote procedure call authentication. This group includes auth_destroy, authnone_create, authsys_create, and authsys_create_default.

rpc_clnt_calls Group of library routines for client-side calls. This group includes clnt_call, clnt_freeres, clnt_geterr, clnt_perrno, clnt_perror, clnt_sperrno, clnt_sperror, rpc_broadcast, rpc_broadcast_exp, and rpc_call.

rpc_clnt_create Group of library routines for dealing with creation and manipulation of CLIENT handles. This group includes clnt_control, clnt_create, clnt_destroy, clnt_dg_create, clnt_pcreateerror, clnt_raw_create, clnt_spcreateerror, clnt_tli_create, clnt_tp_create, and clnt_vc_create.

rpcgen Command used to run the RPC protocol compiler. The compiler is a tool that generates C code to implement an RPC protocol. The input to rpcgen is a language similar to C known as RPC language (Remote Procedure Call language).

rpcinfo Command used to make an RPC call to an RPC server and report what it finds.

rpc_svc_calls Group of library routines for registering servers. This group includes rpc_reg, svc_reg, svc_unreg, xprt_register, and xprt_unregister.

rpc_svc_create Group of library routines

for dealing with the creation of server handles. This group includes svc_create, svc_destroy, svc_dg_create, svc_fd_create, svc_raw_create, svc_tli_create, and svc_tp_create, svc_vc_create.

rpc_svc_err Group of library routines for server side remote procedure call errors. This group includes svcerr_auth, svcerr_decode, svcerr_noproc, svcerr_noprog, svcerr_progvers, svcerr_systemerr, and svcerr_weakauth.

rpc_svc_reg Group of library routines for RPC servers. This group includes svc_auth_reg, svc_freeargs, svc_getargs, svc_getreqset, svc_getreq_common, svc_getreq_poll, svc_getreq_poll_parallel, svc_getrpccaller, svc_run, svc_run_parallel, and svc_sendreply.

RPC/XDR Programming library containing RCP and XDR function calls.

rpc_xdr Group of XDR library routines for remote procedure calls. This group includes xdr_accepted_reply, xdr_authsys_parms, xdr_callhdr, xdr_callmsg, xdr_opaque_auth, xdr_rejected_reply, and xdr_replymsg.

rpow Library routine used to calculate multiple-precision integer arithmetic. The rpow routine calculates a value raised to the power *b*.

rresvport Library routine used to return a descriptor to a socket with an address in the privileged port space.

rrouter Routine that rebuilds the IPX router table with route information from all known nearby routes.

RS-232 Standard for a type of interface between a computer and a peripheral device, such as a modem. Also know as a *serial port*. The connector can have either 25 or 9 pins.

RS/6000 IBM workstations that use RISC CPUs.

rsetcoff Command-line option used with the stty command for setting how the terminal's clock is set.

rsetcrbrg Command-line option used with the stty command for setting how the terminal's clock is set.

rsetcrset Command-line option used with the stty command for setting how the terminal's clock is set.

rsetctbrg Command-line option used with the stty command for setting how the terminal's clock is set.

rsetctset Command-line option used with the stty command for setting how the terminal's clock is set.

rsh Command used to connect to the specified hostname and execute the specified command.

rshd Command used as the server for the rsh program. The server provides remote execution facilities with authentication based on privileged port numbers.

rsoper Command used to service pending restore requests and media insertion prompts.

rtc Refers to the rtc driver, which supports the real time clock chip, allowing it to be set with the correct local time and allowing the time to be read from the chip.

RTFM Abbreviation for "read the fxxxxxx manual." This is a common response to questions in USENET newsgroups when the person asking the question has not checked the obvious places first.

rtpm Command used to monitor performance of a UNIX system in real time (as the system is running). Categories of information that are monitored in-

clude the CPU, system calls, memory, paging, file system, input/output, terminal processing, run and swap queues, lightweight processes, NetWare statistics, Ethernet statistics, and TCP/IP statistics.

rtsxoff Command-line option used with the stty command for setting the method of flow control.

run To execute an application or a computer.

runacct Command used as the main daily accounting shell procedure. It is normally initiated via cron. The runacct command processes connect, fee, disk, and process accounting files. It also prepares summary files for prdaily or billing purposes.

run level *See* system state.

run In FMLI, a command used to run an executable or a program. Once the program is completed, control is returned to FMLI.

run-lisp Command in the emacs text editor using the LISP mode to run a LISP interpreter as a subprocess of the editor.

runq Field in the real-time performance monitor (rtpm command) that shows the current number of processes waiting in the run queue for access to the CPU.

runtime.c Run-time trace package, typically located in /usr/ccs/lib/ctrace.

ruptime Command used to give a status line (similar to the one displayed by uptime) for each machine on the local network; these are formed from packets broadcast by each host on the network once a minute.

ruserok Library routine used by servers to authenticate clients requesting service with rcmd.

rusers Command used to produce output similar to who, but for remote machines. It broadcasts on the local network, and prints the responses it receives.

rusers Library routine used to return information about users on remote machines.

rusersd Command that acts as a server that returns a list of users on the host.

rwall Command used to read a message from standard input until EOF. It then sends this message, preceded by the line *Broadcast Message ...*

rwalld Command that acts as a server that handles rwall requests.

RW_ALLOC Device-driver library routine used to allocate and initialize a read/write lock.

RW_DEALLOC Device-driver library routine used to deallocate an instance of a read/write lock.

rwho Command used to tell who is logged in on local machines. It produces output similar to who, but for all machines on your network.

rwhod Command that acts as the server that maintains the database used by rwho and ruptime.

RW_RDLOCK Device-driver library routine used to acquire a read/write lock in read mode.

RW_TRYRDLOCK Device-driver library routine used to try to acquire a read/write lock in read mode.

RW_TRYWRLOCK Device-driver library routine used to try to acquire a read/write lock in write mode.

RW_UNLOCK Device-driver library routine used to release a read/write lock.

RW_WRLOCK Device-driver library routine used to acquire a read/write lock in write mode.

rx Command that lets users execute a command on a remote host.

rxlist Command that lists all remote execution services (REXEC) available. The command is located in the /usr/lib/rexec directory.

rxservice Command used to add or remove a remote execution service (REXEC).

rz Formatting option with the nl command that tells the formatter to right-justify the text with leading zeroes.

S

s5 File system type originally designed for standard UNIX System V systems.

sa1 Variant of sadc, a command that is used to collect and store system activity information in the binary file /var/adm/sa/sadd, where dd is the current day.

sa2 Variant of sar, a command used to write a daily report on system activity in the file /var/adm/sa/sardd, where dd is the current day.

sac Command used to invoke the Service Access Controller (SAC), which is the overseer of the server machine. The sac command is started with a sanity_interval of 300 seconds from /etc/inittab when the server machine enters multiuser mode.

sacadm Command used for port-monitor administration (for the upper level of the Service Access Facility hierarchy).

sact Command used to inform the user of any impending deltas to a named SCCS file.

_sactab (SAF) Configuration file containing information about port-monitor processes associated with the Service Access Facility.

sad Refers to the STREAMS administrative driver, which provides an interface for applications to perform administrative operations on STREAMS modules and drivers.

sadc Command used to run the data collector. It samples system activity data, with an interval of specified seconds between samples, and writes in binary format to a specified file or to standard output.

SAF Service Access Facility that manages access to the local system through devices. It can handle such things as login requests on serial ports or TCP/IP requests from the LAN.

SAMESTR Device-driver library routine used to check whether the next queue in a stream (if it exists) is of the same type as the current queue (that is, both are read queues or both are write queues).

Santa Cruz Operation Company that produces SCO UNIX, the most popular PC-based UNIX system.

sane Command-line option used with the stty command for resetting all terminal settings to reasonable values.

sar Command used to provide system activity information for individual processors, as well as summary information for average processor usage.

save-all-buffers Command in the Epsilon text editor that saves every buffer that is associated with a file.

save-buffer Command in the emacs text editor that saves the current buffer to its associated file. This command is usually bound to the keystroke Ctrl-X Ctrl-S. *See also* save-file.

save-buffers-kill-emacs Command in the emacs text editor that saves all buffer that are associated with files, then exits from the program. This command is usually bound to the keystroke Ctrl-X Ctrl-C.

saveconf Add-on package for the emacs text editor that implements functions for saving emacs configurations for future sessions.

save-context Command in the saveconf add-on package to the emacs text editor that enables the user to restart the program with the same buffers open and windows visible.

save-excursion Function in the emacs LISP programming language that saves the location of the cursor (point) and mark, executes a statement block, and restores the locations.

save-file Command in the Epsilon text editor that saves the current buffer into its associated file. *See also* save-buffer.

savehist In the C shell, a predefined shell variable that contains the number of commands that are saved in the .history file when the user logs off.

save-some-buffers Command in the emacs text editor that prompts the user for whether to save each buffer that is associated with a file. This command is usually bound to the keystroke Ctrl-X S.

savetty Library routine used to save the current state of the terminal modes in a buffer.

Save Workspace Program running under Open Windows that saves the appearance of the current workspace.

sb Structure defining the command block, which can be either an **scb** or an **sfb** structure. Use the **sb** structure when you call an SDI function that sends a request to a PDI device.

sbrk Library routine used to change dynamically the amount of space allocated for the calling process's data segment. The change is made by resetting the process's break value and allocating the appropriate amount of space.

scalar types Data types that include the pointer, arithmetic, and enumeration types of data. Arithmetic types include floating-point and integral types.

scalb Library routine used to manipulate parts of floating-point numbers. It returns the quantity value * 2 exp.

scalbn Library routine used to return x* 2**n, computed by exponent manipulation rather than by actually performing an exponentiation or a multiplication.

scale
1. Keyword used with the bc desk calculator program.
2. Specifies the number of decimal places to be used in computations.
3. Function used in bc to calculate the number of digits that are to the right of the decimal point.

scale_form Library routine used to return the smallest window size necessary for the subwindow of a form.

scancode Signal that is sent from a keyboard to a keyboard driver when a key is pressed. The scancode is interpreted by the keyboard driver, then delivered to the terminal.

scandir Library routine used to read the specified directory and build an array of pointers to directory entries using malloc.

scanf Library routine used to read from the standard input stream. It reads characters, interprets them, and stores the results through the specified argument pointers, under control of the character string format.

scanner Hardware device used to input printed images and text into a computer for processing.

scanw Library routine (curses) that corresponds to scanf. The effect of these routines is as though wgetstr were called on the window, and the resulting line used as input for the scan.

scb Refers to the command control block structure, scb, which is used to send a command to a PDI device. The scb contains a pointer to a command descriptor block (CDB) that describes the command to the target controller.

SCCS Abbreviation for Source Code Control System, a system for controlling the versions of software. SCCS is particularly suited for working on large-scale projects.

sccs Command used as a front end to the utility programs of the Source Code Control System (SCCS).

sccsdiff Command that compares two versions of an SCCS file and generates output showing the differences between the two versions.

sccsfile Refers to the format of an SCCS file. An SCCS (Source Code Control System) file is an ASCII file consisting of six logical parts: the checksum, the delta table (with information about each delta), user names (with login names and/or numerical group IDs of users who may add deltas), flags (with definitions of internal keywords), com-

ments (with arbitrary descriptive information about the file), and the body (with the actual text lines, intermixed with control lines). *See also* SCCS, sccs.

scheduler *See* process scheduler.

scheduler classes Definitions that define policies for scheduling processes.

Scheme mode In the emacs text editor, a major mode for editing programs in the Scheme programming language.

scheme-mode Command in the emacs text editor that enables Scheme mode, which is designed for editing programs in the Scheme programming language.

sci USENET newsgroup category that contains topics relating to science. Topics include aeronautics, archeology, biology (bio), chemistry (chem), math, medical (med), physics, and outer space (space).

.scm File extension for files containing Scheme source code.

scm Refers to Portable Device Interface (PDI) command structures. The scm structure is used by target drivers, and with the passthrough interface to send a command to a PDI device. It is a group 10 (ten-byte command length) CDB.

SCO *See* Santa Cruz Operation.

SCO ODT SCO Open Desktop, a version of UNIX sold by SCO that features UNIX System V Release 3.2 with some Release 4.0 features added. It also sports a GUI.

SCOMPAT Environment variable that allows SCO UNIX applications to run in a UNIX system V environment.

scompat Command used to set up XENIX system compatibility environment for console applications.

SCORLIM Tunable parameter that specifies the maximum-size core file that can be created. With a value of zero (0), no core files can be created.

SCPULIM Tunable parameter that specifies the maximum amount of user and CPU time combined that a process can consume. This value is set in seconds.

scratch
1. Temporary area for holding intermediate results and other information that will later be discarded.
2. Blank buffer created by the emacs text editor.

scr_dump Library routine (curses) used to write the current contents of the virtual screen to the specified file.

screen Generic term referring to the viewing portion of a video monitor.

screen descriptor In FMLI, defines the color of the screen background.

screen editor Any text editor that uses the full screen to display text and lets you freely move the cursor around the screen. *See also* vi.

screen real estate Available area on a screen. A larger monitor has more real estate than a smaller one and is therefore preferred for working at high resolution.

screen saver Software that blanks or displays a moving image around the screen. Older monochrome screens were prone to "burn-in," where the characters formed permanent etchings in the screen's phosphor. Screen savers prevent burn-in.

screen shot Image captured off a screen using appropriate software.

screen-shot utility Software for capturing a screen shot. *See also* screen shot.

Scribe Add-on package for the emacs text editor that implements a major

mode for editing Scribe text files.

scribe-begin Command in the emacs text editor used in Scribe mode to insert the Scribe command Begin into the text. This command is usually bound to the keystroke Ctrl-C [.

scribe-bold-word Command in the emacs text editor used in Scribe mode to insert the Scribe command to make the current word bold. This command is usually bound to the keystroke Ctrl-C B.

scribe-bracket-region-be Command in the emacs text editor used in Scribe mode to insert the Scribe command for a specified environment. This command is usually bound to the keystroke Ctrl-C Ctrl-E.

scribe-chapter Command in the emacs text editor used in Scribe mode to insert the Scribe command Chapter into the text. This command is usually bound to the keystroke Ctrl-C C.

scribe-electric-parenthesis Variable in the emacs text editor that controls parentheses in Scribe mode.

scribe-electric-quote Variable in the emacs text editor that controls double quotes in Scribe mode.

scribe-end Command in the emacs text editor used in Scribe mode to insert the Scribe command End into the text. This command is usually bound to the keystroke Ctrl-C].

scribe-insert-environment Command in the emacs text editor used in Scribe mode to insert the Scribe command for a specified environment. This command is usually bound to the keystroke Ctrl-C E.

scribe-italicize-word Command in the emacs text editor used in Scribe mode to insert the Scribe command to italicize the current word. This command is usually bound to the keystroke Ctrl-C I.

Scribe mode In the emacs text editor, a major mode designed for formatting text files for Scribe.

scribe-mode Command in the emacs text editor that enables Scribe mode, which is designed for editing Scribe text files.

scribe-section Command in the emacs text editor used in Scribe mode to insert the Scribe command Section into the text. This command is usually bound to the keystroke Ctrl-C Shift-S.

scribe-subsection Command in the emacs text editor used in Scribe mode to insert the Scribe command SubSection into the text. This command is usually bound to the keystroke Ctrl-C S.

scribe-tab Command in the emacs text editor used in Scribe mode to insert a Scribe tab. This command is usually bound to the keystroke Tab.

scribe-underline-word Command in the emacs text editor used in Scribe mode to insert the Scribe command to underline the current word. This command is usually bound to the keystroke Ctrl-C U.

script Command used to make a typescript of everything printed on your terminal, including prompts.

scripting language High-level language used for creating shell scripts.

scripts ASCII files containing shell commands. Scripts are often used to prototype software before a major programming effort is begun.

scroll Library routine (curses) used to scroll the window up one line. This involves moving the lines in the window data structure.

scrollable region Area of a window, typically a window pane, that contains text or images that can be scrolled.

scroll bar Horizontal or vertical bar with a slider that lets you move a window on a graphical screen either sideways or up and down.

scroll-down Command in the emacs text editor that scrolls the contents of the current buffer down one screen. (In Epsilon, it scrolls down one line.) This command is usually bound to the keystroke Meta-V.

scroll-left Command in the emacs text editor that scrolls the contents of the current buffer to the left. This command is usually bound to the keystroke Ctrl-X <.

scrollok Library routine (curses) used to control what happens when the cursor of a window is moved off the edge of the window or scrolling region, either as a result of a newline action on the bottom line or typing the last character of the last line.

scroll-other-window Command in the emacs text editor that scrolls the text in a window other than the current one. This command is usually bound to the keystroke Meta- Ctrl-V.

scroll-right Command in the emacs text editor that scrolls the contents of the current buffer to the right. This command is usually bound to the keystroke Ctrl-X >.

scroll-step Variable in the emacs text editor that controls how many lines of text emacs scrolls at once.

scroll-up Command in the emacs text editor that scrolls the contents of the current buffer up one screen. (In Epsilon, it scrolls up one line.) This command is usually bound to the keystroke Ctrl-V.

scs Refers to the Portable Device Interface (PDI) command structures. The scs structure is used by target drivers with the pass-through interface to send a command to a PDI device. It defines the layout for a group 6 (six-byte command length) command descriptor block (CDB).

SCSI *Small Computer System Interface*, pronounced "scuzzy," a high-speed interface for connecting peripherals to a computer. One SCSI adapter allows you to connect up to 7 SCSI devices.

scsi_ad Refers to the PDI device address structure, scsi ad, which is used by every scb or sfb structure with the appropriate PDI device. PDI interprets the external major and minor numbers, the logical unit number, and the extended logical unit number to send the scb or sfb to the correct device.

SCSI device Any peripheral device compatible with the SCSI standard. *See also* SCSI.

SDATLIM Tunable parameter that specifies the maximum size possible for a process's heap. The limit is expressed in bytes.

sdb Command used to invoke the symbolic debugger, used to debug C language code.

sdenter Library routine used to indicate that the current process is about to access the contents of a shared data segment.

sdevice.d Directory containing a separate system file for each driver installed on a UNIX system. The system file is named after the device. Each system file contains information that allows the kernel to interact with the driver's interrupt handler. The sdevice.d directory is in the /etc/conf directory.

sdget Library routine used to attach a shared data segment to the data space of the current process.

sdgetv Library routine used to synchronize cooperating processes that are using shared data segments.

SDI SCSI Device Interface, which connects the target hardware with the HBA drivers. This provides for a consistent interface for creating portable PDI drivers.

sdi_access Library routine used to claim or release ownership of a given device.

sdi_acfree Library routine used to free memory associated with the given idata structure array.

sdi_addevent Library routine that adds an event to an internal list of driver events, effectively registering the driver event handler, which may later be called by sdi_notifyevent.

sdi_aen Library routine that calls the target driver fault handling routine to signal an asynchronous event, such as bus error or device error.

sdi_blkio Library routine that blocks and issues non-block-aligned or non-block-sized requests.

sdi_callback Library routine used to call the target driver interrupt routine to signal completion of a request.

sdi_clrconfig Library routine that undoes what was done by a prior call to sdi_doconfig. When the value of flags is SDI DISCLAIM|SDI REMOVE, all devices claimed by the calling target driver are freed.

sdi_doconfig Library routine that searches the Equipped Device Table (EDT) looking for devices of the type controlled by the calling target driver.

sdi_errmsg Library routine that formats and prints cmn_err warning messages.

sdi_event_free Library routine that frees an sdi_event structure.

sdiff Command that uses the output of the diff command to produce a side-by-side listing of two files indicating lines that are different.

sdi_findspec Library routine that finds a matching device-specification routine.

sdi_free Library routine that returns the allocated area of memory back to the pool from which it was taken.

sdi_freebcb Library routine that frees the bcb structure, previously allocated by sdi_getbcb.

sdi_freeblk Device-driver library routine that returns a command block to the free block pool.

sdi_get Library routine that allocates a structure from the available pool of headp.

sdi_getbcb Library routine that allocates breakup-control block structures and calls the HBA getinfo routine, which initializes the breakup control blocks.

sdi_getblk Device-driver library routine used to allocate a command block structure.

sdi_getdev Device-driver library routine used to translate a device major/minor number pair into the pass-through interface major/minor number pair for that device.

sdi_gethbano Library routine used to get/validate a host bus adapter-controller number.

SDI_HAERR Error return that may be passed to the sc_comp_code field of the scb (command control block) structure, indicating a host adapter error. The sc_comp_code structure is used to send a command to a PDI device.

sdi_hba_autoconf Library routine used to allocate a new idata array for the calling HBA driver.

sdi_hba_getconf Library routine used to retrieve the idata structure corresponding to a resource manager key.

sdi_icmd Device-driver library routine used to send an immediate sb to a device. *Immediate* means that this function bypasses queued scb's and immediately accesses the device to perform the requested operation.

sdi_init Device-driver library routine used to initialize the SDI driver to accept SDI functions.

sdi_intr_attach Library routine that attaches the interrupt intr for each hardware instance whose idata structure is marked active (for example, the active field of the idata structure is nonzero).

sdi_mca_conf Library routine used by MCA HBA drivers to derive and store device parameters into the resource manager database.

sdi_name Device-driver library routine used to decode a device number into a character string so that the device number can be displayed (with cmn_err).

sdi_notifyevent Library routine that, together with sdi_addevent and sdi_rmevent, implements a driver-to-driver communication mechanism for PDI SCSI drivers based on event codes and SCSI device types.

sdi_poolinit Library routine used to initialize the head structure for the new pool of memory.

SDI_PROGRES Error return that may be passed to the sc_comp_code field of the scb (command control block) structure, indicating that a job is not complete. This is set by the PDI from the sdi_icmd and sdi_sent functions.

sdi_redt Library routine used to return a pointer to an Equipped Device Table (EDT) entry for the device specified.

SDI_RESET Error return that may be passed to the sc_comp_code field of the scb (command control block) structure, indicating that PDI has detected a reset on the HBA bus. Any outstanding jobs that are still queued at the target controller are sent back to the drivers with this code set.

sdi_rmevent Library routine that, together with sdi_addevent and sdi_notifyevent, implements a driver-to-driver communication mechanism for PDI SCSI drivers based on event codes and SCSI device types.

sdi_rxedt Library routine used in place of sdi_redt for HBAs that support multiple SCSI channels.

sdi_send Device-driver library routine that accepts a pointer to an sb command block structure, and sends the command to the controller for routing to a specific device.

sdi_swap16 Library routine that swaps the two bytes of the 16-bit argument and returns the swapped result.

sdi_swap24 Library routine that swaps the three bytes of the 24-bit argument and returns the swapped result.

sdi_swap32 Library routine that swaps the four bytes of the 32-bit argument and returns the swapped result.

sdi_target_hotregister Library routine used to register a target driver's support of hot insertion/removal.

sdi_timeout Library routine that calls the appropriate kernel DDI/DKI timeout routine for the selected HBA.

sdi_translate Device-driver library routine that allows PDI to perform machine-specific, base-level, virtual-to-physical address translation for the host adapter.

sdi_wedt Library routine that modifies the device type and inquiry string of an existing EDT entry pointed to.

sdiv Library routine that assigns the quotient and remainder, respectively, to its third and fourth arguments. The sdiv routine is like mdiv except that the divisor is an ordinary integer.

search-delete-char Variable in the emacs text editor that controls the keystroke that deletes a character from the search string. This keystroke is usually the Del key.

search-exit-char Variable in the emacs text editor that controls the keystroke that stops an incremental search. This keystroke is usually the Escape key.

search-exit-option Variable in the emacs text editor that controls the keystroke that stops an incremental search. If the variable's value is not nil, any control character exits from a search.

search path Group of directory paths that are used when searching for a file or other data.

search-quote-char Variable in the emacs text editor that controls the keystroke that quotes special characters in an incremental search. This keystroke is usually Ctrl-Q.

search-repeat-char Variable in the emacs text editor that controls the keystroke that repeats a forward incremental search.

search-reverse-char Variable in the emacs text editor that controls the keystroke that repeats a backward incremental search.

search-slow-speed Variable in the emacs text editor that controls how emacs displays the results of incremental searches.

search string Group of characters to be looked for. The search can take place within one or more files or within one or more directories.

search-yank-line-char Variable in the emacs text editor that controls the keystroke that, during a search, deletes the rest of the line following the cursor in the current buffer and inserts it into the search string. This keystroke is usually Ctrl-Y.

search-yank-word-char Variable in the emacs text editor that controls the keystroke that, during a search, deletes the word following the cursor in the current buffer and inserts it into the search string. This keystroke is usually Ctrl-W.

secondary prompt string Shell prompt used in multi-line commands (Bourne and Korn shells only).

SECONDS Built-in shell variable that contains the number of seconds since the shell was started (Bourne and Korn shells only).

seconvert Library routine that converts the value to a NULL-terminated string of ASCII digits in a buffer and returns a pointer to the buffer. The seconvert routine is a single-precision version of this function, and is more efficient than the corresponding double-precision version.

secret key Value that is passed during the process of exchanging encrypted messages during cr1 networking authentication. The secret key is a bit string that is only known by the client and the server.

section In the vi text editor, a group of characters ending with a section heading (defined by the vi sect= option).

section numbers In UNIX manual pages, numbers that are assigned to identify the type of component described in the manual page. Section 1 is commands, 2 is system calls, 3 is library functions, 4 is file formats, 5 is miscellaneous, and 7 is device-drivers. There is some variation of the number scheme for different versions of UNIX. Also, sometimes letters are used with the numbers to further define the type of manual page. For example, 1M is administrative commands.

secure Option added to NFS resources that are automatically mounted from the dfstab file.

Secure NFS Authentication mechanism used to ensure the security of shared NFS resources. Authentication is done at the RPC level. Those security features provided to NFS by Secure RPC make up Secure NFS.

Secure RPC General-purpose networking security features that can be used by networking client applications based on remote procedure calls (RPC). Secure RPC is managed by a network administrator who maintains a database of stored public keys.

security Practice of protecting computing resources (computers, networks, etc.) from being damaged or accessed by unwanted users. The primary protection method for securing UNIX systems is through assigned logins and passwords. Network security can be maintained by blocking unwanted requests, hosts, or remote users.

sed Command that copies the named file (standard input default) to the standard output, edited according to a script of commands.

seed48 Library routine used as an initialization entry point.

seek Hard disk operation where the heads move from one cylinder to another. Seeks are typically done by determining the number of cylinders between the current cylinder and the target.

seekdir Library routine that sets the position of the next read operation on the directory stream.

SEGMAPSZ Tunable parameter used to define the amount of virtual address space available to map kernel-to-user read/write requests. Up to 16 MB of kernel memory can be used for I/O requests.

segment Range of address space associated with a process that has consistent read, write, and execute attributes. The three normal segments are the *text segment*, the *data segment*, and the *bss segment*. The text segment has read-only data and instructions. The data segment has static data that is explicitly initialized. The bss segment has static data, initialized to zero.

SEGV Name of signal number 11, which can be sent to a running process (short for *segment violation*).

select Library routine that examines the I/O descriptor sets whose addresses are passed in the arguments readfds, writefds, and execptfds to see if any of their descriptors are ready for reading, are ready for writing, or have an exceptional condition pending, respectively.

select-buffer Command in the Epsilon text editor that selects the buffer to display in the current window. This command is usually bound to the keystroke Ctrl-X B. *See also* switch-to-buffer.

selected In a GUI, refers to a window, icon or other element that is currently active. Typically, items are selected by moving the mouse pointer to an item and clicking the left mouse button once.

selecting Choosing an object on which to act. With a GUI, the user can select an object by pointing to it with the mouse pointer and clicking the left mouse button. For example, in a window that displays a word processing document, some text might be selected,

while in a window that displays a spreadsheet, a cell might be selected.

selection Object that is currently selected. In a GUI, if several windows are displayed on the screen, there might be a selection in each window.

selective-display-ellipses Variable in the emacs text editor that controls whether hidden text is displayed as an ellipsis (...) in outline mode.

select-tag-file Command in the Epsilon text editor that changes to the specified tag file.

self-insert-command Command in the emacs text editor that is called whenever a printable key (keys that type letters, number, or punctuation) is pressed. The command inserts the character for the key that was just pressed into the buffer.

SEMAEM Tunable parameter used with semaphores. SEMAEM is used whenever a semaphore meets or exceeds the value of semop.

semaphore Non-negative integer count, normally used to coordinate access to resources such as files. There are *binary* and *counting* semaphores. A binary semaphore often is used to ensure that a critical portion of code is only executed by one process at a time. Counting semaphores usually are set up to protect a pool of resources.

semctl Library routine that provides a variety of semaphore control operations as specified by the arguments.

semget Library routine used to get a set of semaphores. It returns the semaphore identifier requested.

semicolon *See* ;.

SEMMAP Tunable parameter used to set the size of the semaphore map.

SEMMNI Tunable parameter that defines the number of semaphore identifiers in the kernel.

SEMMNS Tunable parameter used to specify the number of semaphores in the system.

SEMMNU Tunable parameter used to specify the number of undo structures in the system.

SEMMSL Tunable parameter that defines the maximum number of semaphores for each semaphore identifier.

semop Library routine used to automatically perform an array of semaphore operations on the set of semaphores associated with the semaphore identifier specified.

SEMOPM Tunable parameter that specifies the maximum number of semaphore operations that can be run for each semop system call.

SEMUME Tunable parameter that defines the maximum number of undo entries per process.

SEMVMX Tunable parameter that specifies the maximum value of a semaphore.

send
1. Library routine that queues requests for host bus adapter (HBA) drivers, and generally is used for every request.
2. Sockets library routine used to transmit a message to another socket. The send routine may be used only when the socket is in a connected state.

SENDFILES UUCP Permissions file option that defines when files can be sent to remote systems upon connection.

send files *See* rcp, uucp, uuto.

send mail *See* sendmail, mail, mailx.

sendmail Command that sends a message to one or more people, routing the message over whatever networks are necessary. The sendmail command does internetwork forwarding as necessary to deliver the message to the correct place.

sendmsg Library routine used to transmit a message to another socket.

sendto Library routine used to transmit a message to another socket.

sentence In the vi text editor, a group of characters ending with a period, exclamation point, or question mark, followed by two spaces.

sentence-end Variable in the emacs text editor that controls how emacs considers sentences to be delimited.

separator Character used to separate characters. For example, the space character is a valid separator between options and a UNIX command.

Sequent Manufacturer of large computers.

serial board Add-in computer board that provides one or more additional serial ports.

Serial Line Internet Protocol Protocol that allows computers to connect to the Internet using serial lines (abbreviated SLIP). This is a popular way for home personal computers to connect to Internet providers using standard telephone lines and modems.

serialize To convert a data representation from a particular machine to a standard format.

serial port Connector used to connect serial-type peripherals to a computer, such as a modem or mouse.

server Computer or process that offers computing services to a client. Servers can be defined by the types of services they offer. For example, there are file servers (for shared file systems), application servers (for shared programs), and name servers (for sharing lists of host computers and mapping them to network addresses).

service Computing entity that is offered for use to users or applications. Networking services include those things that allow users to log in, copy files, run commands, and send messages.

Service Access Facility *See* SAF.

service grade Code that defines the priority of data transfer between two computers using uux or uucp.

service primitive In networking, an item of information sent to a service provider that either requests a service or indicates a service.

services Refers to the services file that contains an entry for each service available through the DARPA Internet.

session Interaction time between two computing entities. For example, the action that occurs between the time the user logs in to when the interactions end can be referred to as a session.

set Library routine used to set local or global environment variables.

set-bell Command in the Epsilon text editor that enables or disables ringing the bell when there is an error.

setbuf Library routine used after a stream has been opened but before it is read or written.

setbuffer Library routine used to assign buffering to a stream.

set-case-fold Command in the Epsilon text editor that enables or disables case-folding in searches, that is, whether case is ignored when searching.

setclk Command used to set the internal system time from the hardware time-of-day clock. The command can be used only by a privileged user.

setcolor Command used to set the screen to a specific color.

set-comment-column Command in the emacs text editor that sets the value of the comment-column variable. This command is usually bound to the keystroke Ctrl-X; (that is, Ctrl-XSemicolon).

set_current_field Library routine that sets the current field of the specified form to the specified field.

set_current_item Library routine that sets the current item of the specified menu to the specified item.

set-debug Command in the Epsilon text editor that enables or disables single-stepping when executing a specified command or subroutine.

set-display-characters Command in the Epsilon text editor that selects screen characters.

setenv In the C shell, a command that displays or sets the value of a shell environment variable.

set_field_back Library routine that sets the background attribute of the specified field. The background attribute is the low-level curses display attribute used to display the extent of the field.

set_field_buffer Library routine (curses) used to set the buffer of the specified field to the named value.

set_field_fore Library routine (curses) that sets the foreground attribute of the specified field. The foreground attribute is the low-level curses display attribute used to display the field contents.

set_field_init Library routine that assigns an application-defined function
to be called when the form is posted
and just after the current field changes.

set_field_just Library routine that sets
the justification for the specified field.

set_field_opts Library routine that turns
on the named options of the specified
field and turns off all remaining options. Options are boolean values that
can be OR-ed together.

set_field_pad Library routine that sets
the pad character of the named field
to the specified pad. The pad character
is the character used to fill within the
field.

set_field_status Library routine that
sets the status flag of the named field
to the specified status.

set_field_term Library routine that assigns an application-defined function
to be called when the form is unposted
and before the current field changes.

set_field_type Library routine that associates the specified field type with the
named field.

set_fieldtype_arg Library routine that
connects to the field type additional
arguments necessary for a call to the
set_field_type routine.

set_fieldtype_choice Library routine that
allows the application programmer to
implement requests for the given field
type. It associates with the given field
type those application-defined functions that return pointers to the next
or previous choice for the field.

set_field_userptr Library routine that
sets the user pointer of the named
field.

set-fill-column Command in the Epsilon
text editor that sets the column at
which automatic line-filling occurs,

that is, the maximum number of characters to allow on a line.

set-fill-prefix Command in the emacs
text editor that specifies the characters to insert at the beginning of each
line in the current paragraph. This
command is usually bound to the keystroke Ctrl-X. (that is, Ctrl-X followed
by a period).

set_form_fields Library routine that
changes the fields connected to the
specified form to the specified fields.
The original fields are disconnected.

set_form_init Library routine that assigns an application-defined initialization function to be called when the
form is posted and just after a page
change.

set_form_opts Library routine that turns
on the named options for the specified
form and turns off all remaining options.

set_form_page Library routine that sets
the page number of the specified form
to the specified page.

set_form_sub Library routine that sets
the subwindow of the specified form to
the specified sub.

set_form_term Library routine that assigns an application-defined function
to be called when the form is unposted
and just before a page change.

set_form_userptr Library routine that
sets the user pointer of the specified
form.

set_form_win Library routine that sets
the window of the specified form to
the specified window.

set GID Means of setting the effective
group ID to a particular group. When
a set GID bit is turned on for an executable, any user who runs that application does so with the effective group
ID of the application's group.

setgid Library routine that sets the real group ID, effective group ID, and saved group ID of the calling process.

set-gosmacs-bindings Command in the gosmacs add-on package to the emacs text editor. The command enables emulation of the Gosling emacs editor.

setgrent Library routine used for rewinding the group file to allow repeated searches.

setgroups Library routine that sets the supplementary group access list of the calling process from the array of group IDs specified.

sethostent Library routine that opens and rewinds the file.

sethostname Library routine that sets the name of the host machine to be the specified name.

set_item_init Library routine that assigns the application-defined function to be called when the menu is posted and just after the current item changes.

set_item_opts Library routine that assigns an application-defined function to be called when the menu is unposted and just before the current item changes.

set_item_term Library routine that assigns an application-defined function to be called when the menu is unposted and just before the current item changes.

set_item_userptr Library routine that sets the user pointer of the named item.

set_item_value Library routine that sets the selected value of the named menu item.

setitimer Library routine that sets the value of the timer specified to the value specified in the named structure.

setjmp Library routine used to deal with errors and interrupts encountered in a low-level subroutine of a program.

setjmp.h Header file that defines values for nonlocal jumps.

setkey Command that assigns the given ASCII string to be the output of the specified computer function key.

set-kill-buffers Command in the Epsilon text editor that specifies how many kill buffers to use.

setlinebuf Library routine used to change the buffering on a stream from block buffered or unbuffered to line buffered.

set-line-translate Command in the Epsilon text editor that specifies whether return-newline sequences should be translated to newlines. This command is useful when reading files created in DOS or OS/2.

setlocale Library routine used to modify and query a program's locale.

setlogmask Library routine that sets the log priority mask and returns the previous mask.

set-mark Command in the Epsilon text editor that sets the position of the mark to the current cursor position.

set-mark-command Command in the emacs text editor that sets the position of the mark to the current cursor position. This command is usually bound to the keystroke Ctrl-Space or Ctrl-@.

set_max_field Library routine that sets a maximum growth on a dynamic field, or turns off any maximum growth.

set-mention-delay Command in the Epsilon text editor that sets the length of the pause before prompting for a key. This is useful when using a slow terminal.

set_menu_back Library routine that sets the background attribute of a menu. This is the display attribute for items that are unselected, yet are capable of being selected.

set_menu_fore Library routine that sets the foreground attribute of the named menu—the display attribute for the current item (if selectable) on single-valued menus and for selected items on multivalued menus.

set_menu_format Library routine that sets the maximum number of rows and columns of items that may be displayed at one time on a menu.

set_menu_grey Library routine that sets the grey attribute of a menu. This is the display attribute for items that are unselected, yet are capable of being selected.

set_menu_init Library routine that assigns an application-defined function to be called when the menu is posted and just after the top row changes on a posted menu.

set_menu_items Library routine that changes the item pointer array connected to the named menu to the item pointer array items.

set_menu_mark Library routine that sets the mark string of the named menu to a specified mark.

set_menu_opts Library routine that turns on the named options for the menu and turns off all other options.

set_menu_pad Library routine that sets the pad character for a menu to the specified pad.

set_menu_pattern Library routine that sets the pattern buffer and tries to find the first item that matches the pattern.

set_menu_sub Library routine that sets the subwindow of menu to the speci-

fied subwindow.

set_menu_term Library routine that assigns an application-defined function to be called when the menu is unposted and just before the top row changes on a posted menu.

set_menu_userptr Library routine that sets the user pointer of the named menu.

set_menu_win Library routine that sets the window of the menu to the named window.

setmnt Library routine that creates the /etc/mnttab table, which is needed for both the mount and umount commands.

setnetent Library routine that opens and rewinds the file.

setnetgrent Library routine used to set the network group entry.

set_new_page Library routine that marks a field as the beginning of a new page on the form.

setpgid Library routine that sets the process group ID of the named process to a specified ID.

setpgrp Library routine that sets the process group ID and session ID of the calling process to the process ID of the calling process, and releases the calling process's controlling terminal.

setpriority Library routine for setting the scheduling priority of a process. The default priority is set to zero. If lower values are set, scheduling is more favorable to the process.

setprocset macro Macro contained in the procset.h header file that initializes a procset structure. A procset structure specifies the set of processes whose scheduling properties are to be changed.

setprotoent Library routine that opens and rewinds the network database file.

setpwent Library routine that rewinds the password file to allow repeated searches.

setq Function in the emacs LISP programming language that assigns a value to a variable.

setq-default Function in the emacs LISP programming language that sets the default value of a variable.

setregid Library routine used to set the real and effective group IDs of the calling process.

setreuid Library routine used to set the real and effective user IDs of the calling process.

setrlimit Library routine used to set limits on the consumption of a variety of system resources by a process and each process it creates.

setrpcent Library routine that opens and rewinds the rpc program-number database file.

setscrreg Library routine used to set a software scrolling region in a window.

setservent Library routine that opens and rewinds the network services database file.

setsid Library routine that sets the process group ID and session ID of the calling process to the process ID of the calling process, and releases the process's controlling terminal.

setsockopt Library routine used to manipulate options associated with a socket.

setstate Library routine that returns a pointer to the previous state array; its argument state array is used for further random-number generation until the next call to initstate or setstate.

set-tab-size Command in the Epsilon text editor that sets the number of spaces between tab settings (the default is eight).

set term Library routine used to switch between different terminals. The screen reference new becomes the new current terminal.

setterm Library routine that defines the set of terminal-dependent variables.

settime Library routine that sets the access and modification dates for one or more files.

settimeofday Library routine that sets the system's notation of the current time. The current time is expressed in elapsed seconds and microseconds since 00:00 Universal Coordinated Time, January 1, 1970.

set top row Library routine that sets the top row of the specified menu to the named row.

set UID Means of setting the effective user ID to a particular user. When a set UID bit is turned on for an executable, any user who runs that application does so with the effective user ID of the application's user name.

setuid Library routine that sets the real user ID, effective user ID, and saved user ID of the calling process.

setuname
1. Command used to change the system name and the network node name.
2. Library routine that changes the parameter value for the system name and the network node name.

setupterm Library routine that reads in the terminfo database, initializing the terminfo structures, but does not set up the output virtualization structures used by curses.

setusershell Library routine that rewinds the file /etc/shells.

setutent Library routine that resets the input stream to the beginning of the utmp file.

set-variable Command in the emacs text editor that sets the value of a user-defined variable.

setvbuf Library routine used to assign buffering to a stream.

sfb Refers to the function block, sfb, which serves as a mechanism for sending control information from a target driver to the host adapter or to a PDI device.

sfconvert Library routine that converts a value to a NULL-terminated string of a specified number of ASCII digits (rounded as if for sprint(%w.nf) output) in the buffer and returns a pointer to buffer (single-precision version).

SFNOLIM Tunable parameter that defines the highest number of files a process can have open at a time.

sfsys Files that formerly contained device-driver information. The sfsys files have been replaced by System files, located in the /etc/conf.d/sdevice.d directory.

SFSZLIM Tunable parameter that defines the largest file size allowed on the UNIX system.

sgconvert Library routine that converts the value to a NULL-terminated ASCII string in a buffer and returns a pointer to the buffer (single-precision version).

sgetl Library routine that retrieves the four bytes in memory starting at the address pointed to by the buffer and returns the long integer value in the byte-ordering of the host machine.

sh Command that acts as a command programming language, executing commands read from a terminal or a file.

SHACCT Shell variable that contains a log of executed shell scripts (Bourne shell only).

shadow Refers to the file /etc/shadow, which is an access-restricted ASCII system file that contains an entry for each user on the system. The shadow file was created to remove encrypted passwords from the /etc/passwd file and keep them in a place that could not be viewed by average users

shadow passwords User passwords, stored in the /etc/shadow file in encrypted form, for each user on the system.

share Command that makes a resource available for mounting through a remote file system of type fstype.

shareall Command used to control sharing of distributed-file-system resources.

shared libraries Programming library that, when loaded into memory, can be used by multiple processes at the same time. *See also* shared objects.

shared memory identifier Unique integer identifying a segment of memory and a data structure.

shared objects Single object file containing code for every function in a library. If, at compile time, a programmer specifies that the shared object be dynamically linked, the entire shared object is brought into memory when the process is run. Then, if another program is run that requires that shared object, the program can share the object that is already in memory instead of loading its own copy.

sharetab Refers to the file, sharetab, which resides in directory /etc/dfs and contains a table of local resources shared by the share command.

shareware Type of software where the author gives permission for the user to try the software (usually for 30 days) at no charge. If after the trial period the user decides to keep using the software, the user is expected to register and pay the author's designated registration fee. If the user will no longer use the software after the trial period, he or she is expected to erase the software from the system. Shareware can be freely copied and passed along to other users, who must also follow the rules for the trial period.

shar message Electronic-mail message that contains a shell script, which, when run, re-creates one or more files. This method allows nontext files to be sent through electronic mail.

sharp sign *See* #.

SHELL Environment variable that defines the shell used during a terminal session.

shell
1. Command interpreter that handles the keyboard input. Various shells have different characteristics. *See also* csh, ksh, sh.
2. Command that concatenates its arguments, separating each by a space, and passing this string to the UNIX system shell.

shell archive Type of compressed file created using the shell.

shell-cd-regexp Variable used in the emacs text editor to contain a regular expression that matches the shell command used to change directories. This is usually set to cd.

Shell Command Output Buffer in the emacs text editor that displays the output of a shell command.

shell command output buffer Buffer in the emacs text editor that displays the output of a shell command.

shell enhancements Additions to an existing shell.

shell-file-name Variable in the emacs text editor that contains the filename of the shell program. This is usually set to $SHELL.

shell mode In the emacs text editor, a major mode for interacting with the shell.

shell-mode Command in the shell add-on package to the emacs text editor. The command enters shell mode, for interacting with a shell running under emacs.

shell-popd-regexp Variable used in the emacs text editor to contain a regular expression that matches the shell command used to change directories to the one on the top of the directory stack. This is usually set to popd.

shell-pushd-regexp Variable used in the emacs text editor to contain a regular expression that matches the shell command used to store the current working directory on the directory stack and change directories. This is usually set to pushd.

shell script *See* script.

shell-send-eof Command in the emacs text editor that types an EOF character in a process buffer. This command is usually bound to the keystroke Ctrl-C Ctrl-D.

shell-send-eof Command in the emacs text editor that types an EOF character in a process buffer. This command is usually bound to the keystroke Ctrl-C Ctrl-D.

Shell Tool Program running under Open Windows that opens a new UNIX command window.

shelltool Program running under Open Windows that opens a new UNIX command window.

shell variable Character strings that are assigned to values that can be used by the shell or by programs run from the shell. For example, the TERM variable defines the current terminal type and the HOME variable defines the home directory.

shift Command that shifts the positional arguments from the command line to the left one place. That is, $2 gets the value formerly assigned to $1, and so forth for the remaining positional arguments. This command is used in loops in shell scripts. Also, in the C shell, a command that shifts the values of words in a wordlist variable.

shl Command used to run shell layers. Shell layers let a user have several virtual terminals available on a single dumb terminal.

SHLBMAX Tunable parameter that specifies the total number of static shared libraries that can be attached to a process at a time. This parameter is only used with UNIX System V Release 3.2 applications.

SHMALL Tunable parameter that defines the maximum number of shared memory segments that can be used at one time. This parameter is only used with UNIX System V Release 3.2 applications.

shmat Library routine that attaches the shared memory segment associated with the shared memory identifier specified by shmid to the data segment of the calling process.

shmctl Library routine that provides a variety of shared memory-control operations as specified.

shmdt Library routine that detaches from the calling process's data segment (the shared memory segment located at the address specified by shmaddr).

shmget Library routine that returns the shared memory identifier associated with the specified key.

SHMMAX Tunable parameter that defines the maximum shared memory segment size allowed.

SHMMIN Tunable parameter that defines the minimum shared memory segment size.

SHMMNI Tunable parameter that defines the total number of shared memory identifiers allowed on the entire system.

shmop Group of library routines for performing shared memory operations. This group includes shmat and shmdt.

SHMSEG Tunable parameter that specifies the number of attached shared memory segments that are allowed for each process. This number can be further limited, however, to the available unused space the process has.

short int C programming qualifier that tells the compiler that the declared variable will be used to store fairly small integer values. This can be used when there is limited memory available to run the program.

show-all Command in the emacs text editor used in outline mode to display all hidden text.

show-branches Command in the emacs text editor used in outline mode to hide (not display) all body text lines while displaying all header lines.

show-children Command in the emacs text editor used in outline mode to display all the next-level headers under the header the cursor is on.

show descriptor FMLI descriptor that makes form fields appear or disappear. Field changes are based on values the user has entered in other fields.

show-entry Command in the emacs text editor used in outline mode to display all the body text under the header on which the cursor is located.

show-matching-delimiter Command in the Epsilon text editor that inserts the delimiter character typed, then moves the cursor briefly to the matching delimiter. For example, if this command is bound to the close-parenthesis key, pressing the key types a close parenthesis, then moves the cursor to the previous open-parenthesis character.

show-point Command in the Epsilon text editor that displays information about the current cursor position and the character following it.

showrgb Command in X Windows that displays the contents of the RGB database, which contains definitions of screen colors.

show-subtree Command in the emacs text editor used in outline mode to display all the subheaders and body text under the header on which the cursor is located.

show-variable Command in the Epsilon text editor that displays the current value of the specified variable.

shrink-window-horizontally Command in the emacs text editor that shrinks the current window horizontally by one column. This command is usually bound to the keystroke Ctrl-X-{.

shutacct Command run automatically at shutdown to stop process-accounting features. A reason for the shutdown is written into the /var/adm/wtmp file before the system is shut down.

shutdown
1. Command executed by a privileged user to change the state of the machine. In most cases, it is used to change from the multi-user state (state number 2) to a lower state.
2. Library routine that shuts down all or part of a full-duplex connection on the specified socket.
3. Process of turning off a computer by first closing all open applications, issuing the appropriate operating system command, and finally turning off the computer's power.

sig Parameter containing the number of a signal to be sent.

sigaction Library routine that allows the calling process to examine and/or specify the action to be taken on delivery of a specific signal.

sigaddset Library routine that adds the individual signal specified to the set pointed to.

SIGALRM alarm Signal sent to a process after a certain number of real seconds have elapsed.

sigaltstack Library routine used to define an alternate stack area on which signals are to be processed.

sigblock Library routine that adds the signals specified to the set of signals currently being blocked from delivery.

SIGCHLD Signal sent to inform a process that a child has exited.

sigdelset Library routine that deletes the individual signal specified from the set pointed to.

sigemptyset Library routine that initializes the specified set to exclude all signals defined by the system.

sigfillset Library routine that initializes the specified set to include all signals defined by the system.

sigfpe Library routine that allows signal handling to be specified for particular SIGFPE codes.

sighold Library routine that adds the specified signal to the calling process' signal mask.

sigignore Library routine that sets the disposition of the specified signal to SIG_IGN.

siginfo Refers to the siginfo.h header file, which provides information that tells why the system generated any signal caught by a process.

SIGINT Signal that sends an interrupt to a process.

siginterrupt Library routine used to change the system-call restart behavior when a system call is interrupted by the specified signal.

sigismember Library routine that checks whether the signal specified is a member of the set pointed to.

siglongjmp Library routine used for dealing with errors and interrupts encountered in a low-level subroutine of a program.

sigmask Library routine used to construct the mask for a given signal number.

signal
1. Electrical quantity transmitted over air or a wire.
2. Beep, flash of light, or other visual or aural way of getting the attention of a person.
3. Library routine that provides simplified signal management for application processes.
4. Refers to the signal.h header file.

signal name Name associated with a signal that is passed to a process.

signal number Number representing a signal that is passed to a process.

signals Refers to the signal numbers generated when sending a signal to a process.

sigpause Library routine used to automatically release blocked signals and wait for an interrupt.

sigpending Library routine that retrieves those signals that have been sent to the calling process but are being blocked from delivery by the calling process's signal mask.

sigprocmask Library routine used to examine and/or change the calling process's signal mask.

sigrelse Library routine that removes the specified signal from the calling process's signal mask.

sigsem Library routine that signals a process waiting on the semaphore sem_num that it may proceed and use the resource governed by the semaphore.

sigsend Library routine used to send a signal to a process.

sigset Library routine used to modify signal dispositions. When it is successful, sigset returns SIG_HOLD if the signal was blocked, or the signal's previous state if it was not blocked.

sigsetjmp Library routine used for dealing with errors and interrupts encountered in a low-level subroutine of a program.

sigsetmask Library routine that sets the current signal mask (those signals that are blocked from delivery).

sigsetops Group of library routines used to manipulate sets of signals. This group includes sigemptyset, sigfillset, sigaddset, sigdelset, and sigismemberm.

sigstack Library routine used to define an alternate stack, called the *signal stack*, on which signals are to be processed.

sigsuspend Library routine that replaces the process's signal mask with the set of signals pointed to by the argument set and then suspends the process until delivery of a signal whose action is either to execute a signal-catching function or to terminate the process.

SIGTTOU Signal sent to stop terminal (tty) output.

sigvec Library routine that provides a group of software signal facilities.

Simple Mail Transfer Protocol *See* SMTP.

Simple Network Management Protocol *See* SNMP.

simple redirection Input or output redirection that either takes input from a file, or sends output to a file. *Compare to* multiple redirection.

Simula mode In the emacs text editor, a major mode for editing programs in the Simula programming language.

Simula programming language Add-on package for the emacs text editor that implements a major mode for editing programs in the Simula programming language.

simula-mode Command in the emacs text editor that enables Simula mode, which is designed for editing programs in the Simula programming language.

sin Library routine that returns the sine of the specified argument, measured in radians.

single-precision Floating-point numbers that consist of three parts: a sign, an exponent, and a fraction. *Compare to* double-precision.

single quote *See* '.

single to decimal Library routine that converts a single-precision floating-point value to a decimal record.

single-user state Condition of the operating system when only one user is allowed to use the computer at a time. Also referred to as *maintenance mode*.

sinh Library routine that returns the hyperbolic sine of the specified argument.

sixth edition Early version of the UNIX system.

size
1. Library routine that produces segment or section size information in bytes for each loaded section in ELF or COFF object files.
2. Device-driver library routine used to return the size of a logical block device.

sizeof operator Operator that returns the size of an operand in bytes. When used with an array, sizeof returns the total number of bytes contained in the array.

skip Option used on the command line with the dd command. It specifies the number of input blocks to skip at the start of the input file. *See also* dd.

slash *See* /.

slattach Command used for assigning the tty line tty_name to a network interface, as well as for defining the network values for source_address and destination_address.

sleep
1. Command that suspends execution for an interval of time. The time interval can be as large as 2,147,483,647 seconds. The sleep command is used to execute a command after a certain waiting period.
2. Library routine that suspends the current process from execution for the specified number of seconds.

SLEEP ALLOC Device-driver library routine used to allocate and initialize a sleep lock.

SLEEP DEALLOC Device-driver library routine used to deallocate an instance of a sleep lock.

sleeping process Process that has been suspended by the sleep library routine or sleep command.

SLEEP LOCK Device-driver library routine used to acquire a sleep lock.

SLEEP LOCKAVAIL Device-driver library routine used to query whether a sleep lock is available.

SLEEP LOCKOWNED Device-driver library routine used to query whether a sleep lock is held by the caller.

SLEEP LOCK SIG Device-driver library routine used to acquire a sleep lock.

SLEEP TRYLOCK Device-driver library routine used to try to acquire a sleep lock.

SLEEP UNLOCK Device-driver library routine used to release a sleep lock.

slider Graphical element that can be moved along a bar with a mouse. Typically, the slider is used to change the value of a field within a specified range or to move text within a window.

slink Command that is a STREAMS configuration utility used to link together the various STREAMS modules and drivers required to use the STREAMS TCP/IP.

SLIP *See* Serial Line Internet Protocol.

slk bar descriptor In FMLI, a descriptor that defines the color of the function keys shown on the screen.

slk clear Library routine used to clear the soft labels from the screen.

slk init Library routine used to initialize soft function-key labels.

slk label Library routine used to return the current label for a label number with both leading and trailing blanks stripped.

slk layout descriptor In FMLI, a descriptor that sets the layout of the screen labels that represent function keys.

slk noutrefresh FMLI library function that copies the label information onto the internal screen image without causing the screen to redraw.

slk refresh FMLI library function that refreshes the screen-label function keys.

slk restore Library routine used to restore soft labels to the screen after they have been cleared.

SLKs *See* screen-labeled function keys.

slk set Library routine used to set soft function-key labels.

slk text descriptor FMIL descriptor that defines the text color on screen-label function keys.

sllogin Configuration file used for doing logins over SLIP protocols.

Small Computer System Interface *See* SCSI.

Smalltalk Object-oriented programming language created by Xerox. Although C++ is a more popular object-oriented language for UNIX systems, many concepts used in C++ can be traced back to Smalltalk.

SMTP Simple Mail Transfer Protocol, a facility for transferring mail messages using TCP/IP protocols. SMTP is defined in RFC 821 and RFC 974.

smtp Command used to send mail to a remote host using Simple Mail Transfer Protocol.

smtpd Command used to receive incoming mail using Simple Mail Transfer Protocol.

smtpqer Command that queues the mail message it reads from standard input for delivery by smtp to the host specified.

snail-mail Slang term for the ordinary postal system. Many UNIX users find electronic mail simpler, faster, and more convenient.

Snapshot Program running under Open Windows that allows the user to create raster-image files containing part or all of the current screen image.

SNMP Simple Network Management Protocol, a facility for managing a group of TCP/IP hosts over a network.

soc USENET newsgroup category that contains groups that discuss a variety of social issues. The soc category contains groups on cultures, history, politics, religion, and human rights.

socket
1. Communications endpoint that can be bound to a name. A socket is associated with a type and one or more processes.
2. Library routine that creates an endpoint for communication and returns a descriptor.

sockio Refers to the ioctls that operate directly on sockets.

socketpair Library routine that creates an unnamed pair of connected sockets in the specified address family.

Sockets Networking facility providing features to bind networking services to particular communication endpoints on a UNIX system.

soelim Command used to resolve and eliminate .so requests from nroff or troff input. It can be used as a preprocessor for nroff and troff files.

soft link See symbolic link.

soft mount Way of mounting a remote file system in NFS. If a remote file system is soft-mounted and a process

tries to access it, the operation will fail after a set number of retries. A hard mounted file system, on the other hand, will never return a failure, but will simply wait until the file system is remounted to complete the operation.

software Refers to computer instructions that are run as programs. Compare this to *hardware*, which makes up the physical components of a computer.

software applications packaging See package.

software testing tool Specialized software used to test other software.

Solaris 2.0 Version of UNIX distributed by SunSoft and based on SunOS and System V Release 4.0.

Solaris for Intel PC version of the UNIX system that is available from SunSoft, a division of Sun Microsystems.

sort Command that sorts lines of all the named files together and writes the result on the standard output.

sortbib Command used to sort a bibliographic database.

sort-buffer Command in the Epsilon text editor that copies the contents of the current buffer into the specified buffer, then sorts its lines into order.

sort-columns Command in the sort add-on package to the emacs text editor for sorting various types of text files.

sort-fields Command in the sort add-on package to the emacs text editor for sorting various types of text files.

sort-lines Command in the sort add-on package to the emacs text editor for sorting various types of text files.

source code Original programming code written by a programmer for a program. Source code is in human-readable form.

Source Code Control System *See* SCCS.

source file File containing source code. *See also* source code.

source-level debugger Program that debugs programming source code before it is compiled.

space
1. Refers to space, an ASCII file that gives information about disk space requirements for the target environment.
2. ASCII character represented by the number 32 decimal.

spacep Command-line option used with the stty command for controlling parity terminal settings.

Spafford, Gene Individual, currently a professor at Purdue, who has been active in organizing and moderating newsgroups on USENET.

SPARC Microprocessor created by Sun Microsystems based on RISC technology. (short for scalar processor architecture). The technology is used in many Sun workstations.

spawn To start up a child process from a parent process.

special character In the shell, a character that has a special meaning other than the meaning the letter, number, or grammatical marking has in normal text. For example, an arrow (>) is used to redirect output, and an ampersand (&) is used to run a command in the background.

special file File other than regular files, such as pipes, FIFOs, and special devices.

spell Command that collects words from the named files and looks them up in a spelling list to find spelling errors.

spell-buffer Command in the spell add-on package to the emacs text editor that checks the spelling of the current buffer.

spell-command Variable in the emacs text editor that contains the shell command that runs a spell-checker. The variable is usually set to spell.

spellin Command used to add words to an existing spelling list or create a new spelling list.

spell-region Command in the spell add-on package to the emacs text editor that checks the spelling of the currently-marked region.

spell-string Command in the spell add-on package to the emacs text editor that checks the spelling of a string typed into the minibuffer.

spell-word Command in the spell add-on package to the emacs text editor that checks the spelling of the word immediately following the cursor. This command is usually bound to the keystroke Meta-$ or Meta-Shift-4.

spike
1. Short, strong electrical burst that could cause a computer to become damaged or to simply reboot.
2. User name commonly used in examples in many books on the UNIX system. Some UNIX gurus believe "spike" to actually be a resident of Phoenix, Arizona.

spl Library routine used to block or allow servicing of interrupts on the processor on which the function is called.

split Command used to split a file into pieces.

split-line Command in the emacs text editor that splits the current line at the cursor position, inserting a newline character and enough spaces to indent the second line to the column containing the cursor. This command is usually bound to the keystroke Meta-Ctrl-O.

split-window-vertically Command in the emacs text editor that splits the current window into two windows vertically, with one beside the other. This command is usually bound to the keystroke Ctrl-X5.

spook
1. Add-on package for the emacs text editor that implements a function to add text to electronic-mail messages to make them interesting to the United States Central Intelligence Agency.
2. Command in the spook add-on package to the emacs text editor that adds CIA-oriented text to electronic-mail messages.

spool directory Place where files are put temporarily, waiting for a program to be ready to handle them. For example, files waiting to be printed or sent over the network may be copied into a spool directory until the printer or network is ready.

Spot Help Program running under Open Windows that displays information about the object pointed to by the mouse pointer.

spray
1. Command that sends a one-way stream of packets to the host using RPC, and reports how many were received, as well as the transfer rate.
2. Protocol used to send a lot of packets to a computer on a network to test how quickly and reliably the computer can receive them. The protocol counts the number of acknowledgments and returns that count.

sprayd Command that acts as a server to record the packets sent by spray.

spreadsheet Type of software used for modeling financial scenarios. For example, Lotus 1-2-3 is a very popular spreadsheet program.

sprintf Library routine used to perform formatted output conversion. It converts, formats, and prints its arguments under control of a specified format. It places its output in the specified storage.

SPTMAP Tunable parameter that sets the size of the map-entry array used to manage the kernel virtual-address space.

sputl Library routine that places long integer data in a machine-independent fashion.

sqrt Library routine that returns the square root of x, contained in the first or fourth quadrants of the complex plane.

square bracket *See* [and].

sr Option used on the command line with the dbx source-code debugger. It specifies that initialization commands should be read from a startup file, which should then be deleted.

srand Library routine used to reset the simple random-number generator to a random starting point.

srand48 Library routine used as an initialization entry point when generating uniformly distributed pseudorandom numbers.

srandom Library routine used to reset the random-number generator (random).

srchtxt
1. Command that searches message files for text strings. *See also* gettxt, grep, mkmsgs.
2. Command used to display the contents of, or search for a text string in, message databases.

srv Device-driver library routine used to provide greater control over the flow of messages in a stream by allowing the module or driver to reorder messages, defer the processing of some messages, or fragment and reassemble messages.

SS Abbreviation for spreadsheet. See also spreadsheet.

sscanf Library routine that reads characters, interprets them, and stores the results through the argument pointers, under control of the character string format.

ssignal Library routine used to implement a software facility similar to signal.

SSTKLIM Tunable parameter that sets the maximum size that a stack segment for a process can be. The value is set in bytes. If a process tries to create a stack that is greater than this limit, a SIGSEGV signal is sent to the process, possibly resulting in the termination of the process.

stack Ordered list of items from which the last item added is the first item removed. Adding an item to a stack is called *pushing* a item onto the stack. Reading and removing an item is called *popping* an item. The analogy is to a stack of dishes, where new dishes can be stacked on top (pushed) or removed from the top (popped).

Stallman, Richard Author of the emacs text editor and head of the Free Software Foundation. Also known as rms.

standalone Refers to hardware or software that is capable of working without the support of other hardware or software.

stand-alone program Program in the /stand directory (in UNIX System V) that is capable of booting the UNIX system. The file /stand/unix contains the default bootable standalone UNIX system program.

standard Set of detailed rules or guidelines that apply to a specific area. For example, in computing, there are standards for languages, such as C, as well as hardware standards, such as SCSI.

Standard C *See* ANSI C.

standard error By convention, where UNIX commands send their error messages. Typically, standard error is directed to the terminal, however, by placing a 2 and a redirect arrow on the command line, you can send error messages to another location. For example the command line nroff -man < cat.1 > cat.out 2> cat.err formats the man page cat.1, sends the formatted output to cat.out, and sends any error messages to cat.err.

standard input Standard means of directing input to a command. By default, standard input is taken from a terminal's keyboard. However, standard input can also be directed to the command using a pipe (¦) or an arrow (<).

standard I/O Umbrella term for standard input and standard output.

standard output Standard means of directing output from a command. By default, the standard output is sent to the terminal screen. However, standard output can also be directed to another command or file using a pipe (¦) or an arrow (>).

standardization Process of creating standards for an industry.

standend Library routine that turns off all attributes.

standout Library routine that turns on the named attributes without affecting any others.

stappl Command-line option used with the stty command for switching between line mode and application mode on a synchronous line. This option is used for terminals that connect to a computer via serial lines.

Starlan LAN type created by AT&T. Starlan uses both star and bus topology. Much of the early LAN integration of UNIX networking products, such as RFS and UUCP, were done with Starlan.

start
1. Command-line option used with the stty command for setting the start control character.
2. Device-driver library routine that is called at system boot time (after system services are available and interrupts have been enabled) to initialize drivers and the devices they control.
3. Option given to UNIX system startup scripts to start up UNIX services. Startup scripts are located in the rc.d, rc0.d, rc1.d, rc2.d, and rc3.d directories.

start color Library routine that must be called before using the curses routines that manipulate color on color alphanumeric terminals.

start-kbd-macro Command in the emacs text editor that defines a keyboard macro. In emacs, it executes the last macro defined, then adds keystrokes to it, as well as executing them. In Epsilon, it adds keystrokes to the accumulating keyboard macro as well as executing them normally. This command is usually bound to the keystrokes Ctrl-X(for starting a new macro, and Ctrl-U Ctrl-X(for adding to one. *See also* end-kbd-macro.

start-of-day counts Standard statistics an administrator or a large UNIX system should check at the beginning of each day. In particular, these statistics should include numbers on the amount of disk space being used.

start-process Command in the Epsilon text editor that runs a shell concurrently in a new buffer named Process.

START/STOP output control Type of communications flow control, also referred to as *XON/XOFF* and *DC1/DC3* flow control.

startup scripts UNIX shell scripts that are run each time the UNIX system starts up, shuts down, or otherwise changes state. *See also* system states.

stat
1. Library routine used to get information about a file.
2. Refers to the return data in a stat structure, which is defined in stat.h.

statd Command that starts a status monitor daemon. It interacts with lockd to provide the crash and recovery functions for the locking services on NFS.

state 2 UNIX system state that allows multi-user access to the computer. This is the standard state that most UNIX systems are booted to. Also called *multi-user state.*

statement In programming, a function or phrase that, when compiled, creates language instructions that can be used by the computer.

statement block In LISP, a group of statements. A statement block is defined by the let function.

statfs Library routine that gets file system information.

static In C programming, a way of declaring a global variable whose value doesn't need to be used by another program file. This prevents conflicts that might occur if two programming modules unintentionally use a global variable with the same name.

StaticColor Colormap used by X Windows to define the colors used on the screen.

StaticGray Colormap used by X Windows to define the colors used on the screen.

static linking When a C language program is compiled in a way that causes the programming library to be incorporated into the executable at link time. Compare this to dynamic linking, where the library is linked to the executable at the time the program is run, allowing many processes to share the same copy of the library.

statnps Library routine used to determine if the Internetwork Protocol Exchange (IPX) stack is loaded.

status In the C shell, a predefined shell variable that contains the exit status of the last command executed.

status code Eight-bit piece of information that is returned to indicate the success or failure of a process. The process passes the status code (also called the *exit status code*) to the parent process. Typically, the status code is set to 0 for success or any other number for failure.

statvfs Library routine that returns a "generic superblock" describing a file system; it can be used to acquire information about mounted file systems.

stdarg Refers to the set of macros that allow portable procedures, which accept variable numbers of arguments of variable types to be written.

stdio Refers to the standard buffered input/output package.

stdio.h Header file that contains the standard input/output library routines used in programming in the UNIX system.

stdipc Refers to the library routine ftok, which constitutes the standard interprocess communication package.

stflush Command-line option used with the stty command for enabling or disabling flush on a synchronous line. This option is used for terminals that

connect to a computer via serial lines.

sticky bit Bit that is set on a program so that, when the program is run, it goes into memory and stays there until the system is rebooted. The program is not removed from memory, even after the last user exits from the program. Sticky bits are used on applications that are used often on a system, so the system doesn't waste time loading and unloading the application. Commands like mailx and su typically have their sticky bits turned on. You can tell a sticky bit program because the execute bit is set to s rather than x when you do a long listing (ls -l).

stime Library routine that sets the system's idea of the time and date. It points to the value of time as measured in seconds from 00:00:00 UTC January 1, 1970.

stop Command in the Bourne or C shell that suspends a background job. Also, a command-line option used with the stty command for setting the stop control character.

stop bit Bit that is transmitted after each character in asynchronous communications.

stopped jobs Refers to running processes whose processing is temporarily suspended. From the shell, pressing Ctrl-Z stops a running process (job), and fg starts it running again in the foreground.

stop-process Command in the Epsilon text editor that aborts the concurrently executing process. *See also* start-process, stop-shell-subjob.

stop-shell-subjob Command in the emacs text editor that suspends the current job being run as a sub-job. This command is usually bound to the keystroke Ctrl-C Ctrl-Z. *See also* interrupt-shell-subjob, stop-process.

storage device *See* device.

storage medium Hard disk, tape, or other type of hardware that is used to store data from a computer.

store Library routine used to place data in a database under a specified key.

str Group of library routines used to manipulate strings. This group includes strfind, strrspn, and strtrns.

strace Command that, without arguments, writes all STREAMS event trace messages from all drivers and modules to its standard output.

straddr.so Programming library used with TCP/IP and other networking protocols. This library contains routines that do name-to-address mapping for any protocol that uses addresses in the form of character strings.

strapush Data structure used by the STREAMS facility when it is pushing modules and drivers onto a protocol stack. Information in the structure describes the type of configuration being done (sap_cmd), the major number of the device (sap_major), the minor device number (sap_minor), the range of device number if applicable (sap_lastminor), the number of modules to be automatically pushed (sap_npush), and an array of module names to be pushed in the order in which they are to be pushed (sap_list).

strategy Device-driver library routine called by the kernel to read and write blocks of data on the block device.

strbuf Data structure used by the STREAMS facility to describe the control and data parts of a message. Information in the structure includes the maximum length of the buffer, the length of data, and a pointer to a buffer.

strcasecmp Library routine used to compare strings and ignore differences in case.

strcat Library routine that appends a copy of a string, including the terminating null character, to the end of another string.

strccpy Library routine that copies the input string, up to a null byte, to the output string, compressing the C-language escape sequences (for example, \n, \001) to the equivalent character.

strcf File that contains the script that is executed by slink to perform the STREAMS configuration operations required for STREAMS TCP/IP.

strchg Command that pushes modules on or pops modules off the stream associated with the user's standard input.

strchr Library routine used in string operations. It returns a pointer to the first (or last) occurrence of the specified character in string.

strclean Command used to clean up the STREAMS error-logger directory on a regular basis (for example, by using cron).

strcmp Library routine used in string operations. It compares its arguments and returns an integer less than, equal to, or greater than zero, based upon whether the first string is lexicographically less than, equal to, or greater than the second string.

strcoll Library routine for string collation, used to provide for locale-specific string sorting. It is intended for applications in which the number of comparisons per string is small.

strconf Command that queries the configuration of the stream associated with the user's standard input.

strcpy Library routine used in string operations. It copies one string to another including the terminating null character, stopping after the null character has been copied.

strcspn Library routine used in string operations. It returns the length of the initial segment of the first string that consists entirely of characters from (or not from) the second string.

STRCTLSZ Tunable parameter that limits the maximum size of the control part of a STREAMS message.

strdup Library routine used in string operations. It returns a pointer to a new string that is a duplicate of the string pointed to.

Stream Stack of modules and drivers used to provide an interface between an application and a device. Modules and drivers can be pushed onto or popped off of a stream, to add or remove functionality of the stream.

stream head Part of a stream that is nearest the application. The stream head provides access from user space to the STREAMS device.

streamio Refers to the STREAMS ioctl commands, which are a subset of the ioctl system calls used to perform a variety of control functions on streams. These are strings that are passed to STREAMS devices by the ioctl system call. The commands do such things as push modules on to a stream, pop them off of a stream, retrieve module names, flush input/output queues, and compare the names of modules on the Stream to those on a list.

STREAMS UNIX system device-driver framework. STREAMS is particularly suitable for creating networking drivers and modules that can be mixed-and-matched to suit the particular communications needs.

STREAMS buffer Holding area for Streams data, consisting of two parts.

The first part is a memory array that holds the actual data, and the second part is the buffer header that identifies the buffer.

STREAMS driver Part of a stream that is nearest the physical hardware. Drivers and modules are similar in Streams, except that a driver is assigned a major and minor number, whereas a module is not. A stream does not require a module, but it does require a driver.

STREAMS message Unit of information that is passed between Streams modules and driver queues. Messages that are passed from the stream head toward the driver are traveling *downstream*. Those passed from the driver toward the stream head are traveling *upstream*.

STREAMS module Defined set of routines, operating at the kernel level, that process data, status, and control information. Using queues, the module passes information only between those modules and drivers that are directly upstream or downstream from the module. One or more modules may be pushed onto a stream between the Streams device and the stream head.

STREAMS queue Place where messages are passed between Streams modules and drivers. Between each set of modules and drivers there are two queues: a read queue and a write queue.

STREAMS tunable parameters Set of parameters that set a limit on how much resources Streams can consume on a system. Early release of Streams required that buffer pools be set to hold a variety of message sizes. Now, however, Streams buffers are allocated dynamically from a single buffer pool.

streamtab Refers to the STREAMS driver and module declaration structure.

strerr Command that receives error log messages from the STREAMS log driver and appends them to a log file.

strerror Library routine that maps the error number specified to an error message string, and returns a pointer to that string.

stress testing Type of testing that does high-volume and/or high-speed interactions to test the stability of software or hardware under difficult conditions.

strftime
1. Library routine used to convert the date and time to a string.
2. Refers to the file used to specify date and time formatting information. This file must be kept in the directory /usr/lib/locale/locale/LC_TIME.

string
1. Group of library routines used to perform string operations. This group includes strcat, strncat, strcmp, strncmp, strcpy, strncpy, strdup, strlen, strchr, strrchr, strpbrk, strspn, strcspn, strtok, strtok_r, and strstr.
2. Group of library routines (BSD) for performing string operations, including strcasecmp and strncasecmp.

string.h Header file that contains definitions for working with character strings.

string literal Series of characters that are interpreted literally, rather than being processed as special characters. For example, in a string literal, characters such as backslash (\) or asterisk (*) would be passed through literally and not interpreted by a shell.

string-match Command in the emacs text editor that determines whether a string matches a regular expression.

strings Command that looks for ASCII strings in a binary file. A string is any sequence of four or more printing characters ending with a newline or a null character.

string-search Command in the Epsilon text editor that searches forward from the cursor non-incrementally.

strioctl STREAMS data structure that defines the request being made to a module or driver. The structure contains the ioctl request, the timeout value, the length of the data argument, and a pointer to the data argument. *See also* streamio.

strip Command that strips the symbol table, debugging information, and line number information from ELF object files; COFF object files can no longer be stripped.

strlen Library routine that returns the number of characters in the specified string, not including the terminating null character.

STRLOFRAC Tunable parameter that reflects the percentage of data blocks in a particular class at which allocation of low-priority blocks automatically fails.

strlog Device-driver library routine used to submit formatted messages to the log driver.

STRMEDFRAC Tunable parameter that reflects the percentage at which medium-priority block allocation fails.

STRMSGSZ Tunable parameter that sets the largest possible data portion that can exist for a STREAMS message. This value is set to allow the largest packet size that may be used by all STREAMS modules configured on the system.

strncasecmp Library routine used to compare the strings and ignore differences in case. These routines assume the ASCII character set when equating lower- and uppercase characters.

strncat Library routine used in string operations. It appends a copy of a specified string to the end of a string, appending at most a specified number of characters.

strncmp Library routine used in string operations on a specified number of characters. It compares its arguments and returns an integer less than, equal to, or greater than zero, based upon whether the first string is lexicographically less than, equal to, or greater than the second string.

strncpy Library routine used for string operations. It copies a string to another string, including the terminating null character, stopping after the null character has been copied. It copies exactly a specified number of characters, truncating or adding null characters if necessary.

stroptions STREAMS data structure that is used to set options on a stream head. This structure is used in a STREAMS M_SETOPTS message. It contains the options to set, the read option, the write offset, the minimum read packet size, the maximum read packet size, the read queue high watermark, the read queue low watermark, and the band for watermarks. (High and low watermarks are checked to stop and restart the flow of message processing.)

Stroustrup, Bjarne Developer of C++ object-oriented programming language.

strpbrk Library routine used for string operations. It returns a pointer to the first occurrence in the string of any character from another specified string.

strptime Library routine used to convert the date and time.

strqget Device-driver library routine used to get information about a queue or a band of the queue.

strqset Device-driver library routine used to change information about a queue or a band of the queue.

strrchr Library routine used in string operations. It returns a pointer to the first (last) occurrence of the specified character in string.

strspn Library routine used in string operations. It returns the length of the initial segment of the first string that consists entirely of characters from (not from) the second string.

strstr Library routine that locates the first occurrence in a string of a specified sequence of characters (excluding the terminating null character) in another string.

STRTHRESH Tunable parameter that sets the maximum number of bytes that STREAMS can allocate. If that limit is passed, users without special privilege are not allowed to open or work with a stream.

strtod Library routine that returns a double-precision floating-point number for the value represented by the specified character string.

strtok Library routine that considers the string to consist of a sequence of zero or more text tokens separated by spans of one or more characters from the specified separator string.

strtol Library routine that returns as a long integer the value represented by the specified character string.

struct C object type that, when declared, reserves enough storage space so that all members of the struct can be stored at the same time. A member of the structure may consist of a set number of bits called a *bit field*.

struct.h Header file used for BSD compatibility.

structure *See* struct.

strxfrm Library routine that transforms the specified string and places the resulting string into the named array.

stty Command that sets certain terminal I/O options for the device that is the current standard input; without arguments, it reports the settings of certain options.

sttydefs Command that maintains the line settings and hunt sequences for the system's tty ports by making entries in and deleting entries from the /etc/ttydefs file.

studlify-region Command in the studly add-on package to the emacs text editor that capitalizes letters at random.

studly Add-on package for the emacs text editor that implements functions to capitalize letters at random.

stune Refers to one of the installable-driver/tunable-parameter kernel configuration files, the /etc/conf/cf.d/stune file. It contains tunable parameters for the kernel modules to be configured into the next system to be built.

stwrap Command-line option used with the stty command for enabling or disabling truncation on a synchronous line. This option is used for terminals that connect to a computer via serial lines.

style guide Document available with many computer systems or programming interfaces that defines a style for creating documents or programs that adhere to the interface.

su
1. Command that allows one user to become another user without logging off. The default user name is root.
2. Refers to the su options file, /etc/default/su. Options for the su command can be set or changed with keywords in /etc/default/su.

subdirectory Directory that is below the current directory on the file system tree. You can change to a subdirectory from the current directory using the cd command with the subdirectory name.

Subject Field in an electronic-mail message indicating the subject of the message.

subnet Method of dividing one network number so it can be used by several physical networks.

subnet mask Value used with TCP/IP to indicate what part of the local system's IP address represents the local network number. For example, if the local system's address were 123.45.67.89 and the subnet mask were 255.255.0.0, then 124.45 would identify the network and 67.89 would identify the local host on that network.

subnetwork mask *See* subnet mask.

subroutine Term synonymous with *library routine*, sometimes used to refer to routines that are shorter.

subscribing To sign on to receive articles for a particular USENET newsgroup.

substring Auxiliary data class in the C++ language for manipulating parts of strings.

subwin Library routine that creates and returns a pointer to a new window with the given number of lines and columns.

SULOG Environment variable that identifies the pathname to the file in which attempts to use the su command are logged. The su command is how a user changes from his or her current permissions to those of root (by default) or some other user.

sulogin Command that is automatically invoked by init when the system is first started. It prompts the user to type the root password to enter system-maintenance mode (single-user mode) or to type EOF (typically CTRL-D) for normal startup (multi-user mode).

sulog system log File that contains a history of su command usage. Typically, this file is located in /var/adm/sulog. Because this file can become quite large, it is typically cleaned up (copied somewhere else or deleted) using the cron command.

sum Command that calculates and prints a 16-bit checksum for the named file, and also prints the number of 512-byte blocks in the file.

Sun Microsystems Computer manufacturer of workstations based on UNIX. Through its SunSoft division, Sun Microsystems produces Solaris, a PC-based UNIX system.

SunOS Version of the UNIX operating system that runs on Sun Microsystems workstations. Originally, SunOS was based on Berkeley UNIX. However, SunOS was merged with AT&T's UNIX system to form UNIX System V Release 4.

SunView Windowing environment that ran on Sun Microsystems workstations. Because it was a proprietary system, it has since been replaced by the X Window System with associated look-and-feel interfaces on top.

supercomputer Expensive computers, designed for efficiently performing complex calculations. Typically, supercomputers have been used for sophisticated modeling techniques and forecasting.

supernet Method of using several Internet network numbers for one large network.

superuser Name for the user who has access to system files to which regular users do not have access. Also known as the *root user*.

surfing the net Phrase used to describe the act of browsing around the Internet for interesting sites and information.

susp Command-line option used with the stty command for setting the susp control character.

suspend To temporarily stop execution of a process, thread, or data transfer. When an item is suspended, it is expected to be started again in the future.

suspend-emacs Command in the emacs text editor that suspends the program. (It can be restarted using the shell fg command.) This command is usually bound to the keystroke Ctrl-Z.

SV_ALLOC Device-driver library routine used to dynamically allocate and initialize an instance of a synchronization variable.

SV_BROADCAST Device-driver library routine used to wake up all processes sleeping on a synchronization variable.

svc_create Library routine creates server handles for all the transports belonging to the class nettype.

svc_destroy Library routine that destroys the RPC service transport handle.

svc_dg_create Library routine that creates a connectionless RPC service handle, and returns a pointer to it.

svcerr_auth Library routine called by a service dispatch routine that refuses to perform a remote procedure call due to an authentication error.

svcerr_decode Library routine called by a service dispatch routine that cannot successfully decode the remote parameters.

svcerr_noproc Library routine called by a service dispatch routine that does not implement the procedure number that the caller requests.

svcerr_progvers Library routine called when the desired version of a program is not registered with the RPC package. Service implementors usually do not need this routine.

svcerr_systemerr Library routine called by a service dispatch routine when it detects a system error not covered by any particular protocol.

svcerr_weakauth Library routine called by a service dispatch routine that refuses to perform a remote procedure call due to insufficient (but correct) authentication parameters.

svc_fd_create Library routine that creates a service on top of any open and bound descriptor, and returns the handle to it.

svc_fds Global variable that is modified by the xprt library routine.

svc_freeargs Library routine that frees data allocated by the RPC/XDR system.

svc_getargs Library routine that decodes the arguments of an RPC request associated with the RPC service transport handle.

svc_getreq_common Library routine that processes incoming RPC requests on a file descriptor specified.

svc_getreqset Library routine called when poll has determined that an RPC request has arrived on some RPC file descriptors.

svc_raw_create Library routine that creates an RPC service transport, to which it returns a pointer.

svc_reg Library routine that associates a program number and version number with the service dispatch procedure.

svc_run Library routine that waits for

RPC requests to arrive, and calls the appropriate service procedure using svc_getreqset when one arrives.

svc_sendreply Library routine called by an RPC service's dispatch routine to send the results of a remote procedure call.

svc_tli_create Library routine that creates an RPC server handle, and returns a pointer to it.

svc_tp_create Library routine that creates a server handle for the network specified, and registers itself with the rpcbind service.

svc_unreg Library routine used to remove, from the rpcbind service, all mappings of the program number and version number to dispatch routines and network address.

svc_vc_create Library routine that creates a connection-oriented RPC service and returns a pointer to it.

SV_DEALLOC Device-driver library routine used to deallocate an instance of a synchronization variable.

SVGA Super VGA, a video standard that calls for higher resolution than standard VGA. SVGA resolution is 800x600 or higher.

SVMMLIM Tunable parameter that sets the maximum address space that can be mapped to a process.

SVR4 *See* UNIX System V Release 4.

SV_SIGNAL Device-driver library routine used to wake up one process sleeping on a synchronization variable.

SV_WAIT Device-driver library routine used to sleep on a synchronization variable.

SV_WAIT_SIG Device-driver library routine used to sleep on a synchronization variable.

swab Library routine used to swap bytes.

swap
1. Command that provides a method of adding, deleting, and monitoring the system swap areas used by the memory manager.
2. Act of moving data between RAM and the swap area, typically on a hard disk.

swapctl Library routine that adds, deletes, or returns information about swap resources.

swap space Area on the hard disk where information from RAM can be temporarily placed (or swapped) when RAM is full. The swap area is typically on the hard disk. If there is not enough RAM to meet the demands of the system, a lot of swapping might take place, which can severely hurt system performance.

switch statement C statement that lets the programmer test for different cases and act differently for each case.

switch-to-buffer-other-window Command in the emacs text editor that selects which buffer to display in another window. This command is usually bound to the keystroke Ctrl-X4B.

swtch Command-line option used with the stty command for setting the switch control character.

sxt Device file used by the shell layers command (shl) to allow several virtual terminals to be used from a character-based terminal.

symbolic Refers to the use of names or symbols to represent other information, such as numeric values.

symbolic debugger Programming tool used to debug a program using the symbolic names in a program. In UNIX, the debug command is the standard symbolic debugger. *See also* debug.

symbolic link Special file that is used to represent another file. The file contains information that points to the path of another file. A symbolic link is different from a *hard link* in that the link points to a file name rather than an inode. In this way, a symbolic link can point across file systems and to directories as well as regular files, where a hard link cannot. This allows links that identify a file that either doesn't exist or exists only if the file system containing the file is mounted. Symbolic links are created with the ln -s command.

symbol table In the C++ programming language, a table that contains the information for an object file. This information is required for finding the symbolic definitions and references for a program. A symbol table index can be used to access this array.

symlink Library routine that creates a symbolic link to the specified file.

syms Option used with the symbolic debugger to list the names of local variables within the current scope.

sync
1. Command that executes the sync system primitive. If the system is to be stopped, sync must be called to ensure file system integrity. It will flush all previously unwritten system buffers out to disk, thus assuring that all file modifications up to that point will be saved.
2. Library routine that causes all information in memory that should be on disk to be written out. This includes modified super blocks, modified inodes, and delayed block I/O.

synchronization constraints Rules to follow when creating multiprocessing drivers to ensure that multiple threads within the same application remain synchronized.

synchronous line Communications line that handles synchronous transmissions. *See also* synchronous transmission.

synchronous mode Mode of operation used in Transport Interface connection-oriented networking. In synchronous mode, the t_connect call will wait for a response to the connect request from the remote user before returning control to the local user.

synchronous protocol Rules that define how synchronous transmissions are done. Examples of synchronous protocols include High-level Data Link Control protocol (HDLC), Synchronous Data Link Control protocol (SDLC), and Binary Synchronous protocol (BISYNC).

synchronous transmission Mode of communication where blocks of information are sent without start or stop codes. For this to work, the transmitter and receiver must synchronize their clocks, so both sides know when bits will be sent and received. Also, each block of information must be preceded by a preamble and followed by a postamble bit pattern. This information, plus the data, make up the frame that is transmitted.

syntactic analyzer Programming tool that analyzes the grammatical form of the information given to it by the lexical analyzer. A syntactic analyzer is also sometimes called a *parser*.

syntactic expression *See* S-expression.

syntax
1. With commands, the order in which the command and its arguments must be given to work properly.
2. In programming, set of rules that defines how the different parts of a programming language can be used to-

gether to work properly.

SYS Name of signal number 12, which can be sent to a running process (short for *bad argument to system call*).

sysadm
1. Command that, when invoked without an argument, presents a set of menus that help you do administrative work.
2. Special administrative login that has permission to run the sysadm command to do system administration.

sysadm menus Menus, presented by the sysadm command, that allow administrators to configure different parts of the UNIX operating system.

syscall Category of events in the symbolic debugger (debug command) that tell the debugger what to do when a system call is encountered on a thread or a process.

sysconf Library routine that provides a method for the application to determine the current value of a configurable system limit or option (variable).

_sysconfig file Configuration file, located in the /etc/saf/pmtag directory, that is interpreted by the SAF service access controller when the SAF is started (usually at boot time). By default, this file is empty. It is up to the system administrator to add a script to this file to have SAF do any special processing required by the local system. The script is not a standard shell script, rather it is in a special form that can be interpreted by the doconfig library routine.

sysdef Command that analyzes the default bootable kernel and extracts configuration information.

sysexits.h Header file on UNIX System V systems that contain exit status return codes compatible with Berkeley

UNIX systems. This header file is located in the /usr/ucbinclude directory.

sysfs Library routine that returns information about the file system types configured in the system.

sys group Special administrative group that is the group assigned to many UNIX operating-system administrative commands and devices.

sysi86 Library routine that implements machine-specific functions.

sysinfo Library routine that copies information relating to the UNIX system on which the process is executing into the buffer pointed to.

sysinit entries Entries in the /etc/inittab file that are executed once when the system is first started up. These entries are used to start critical processes and initialize important devices. The sysinit entries are run and completed before the system can continue other startup procedures.

syslog Library routine that passes a message to syslogd, which logs it in an appropriate system log, writes it to the system console, forwards it to a list of users, or forwards it to the syslogd on another host over the network.

syslog.conf Refers to the /etc/syslog.conf file, which contains information used by the system log daemon, syslogd, to forward a system message to appropriate log files and/or users.

syslogd Command that reads and forwards system messages to the appropriate log files and users, depending upon the priority of a message and the system facility from which it originates.

sys login Special administrative login available on most UNIX systems. The sys login is the owner of such compo-

nents as devices that handle memory (/dev/kmem and /dev/mem).

SYSSEGSZ Tunable parameter that sets the amount of virtual address space that is available to be allocated. This amount can be set to a value of up to 16 MB (4,096 clicks).

sys_siglist Library routine used to simplify variant formatting of signal names by providing the vector of message strings. The signal number can be used as an index in this table to get the signal name without the newline.

system Library routine that causes a string to be given to the shell as input, as if it had been typed as a command at a terminal.

system administrator Person assigned to install software, configure, and maintain UNIX systems. Originally, UNIX system administration was done by UNIX specialists in computer centers. More and more today, however, individual users of UNIX desktop systems are doing some of their own system administration, such as configuring printers and adding users. On large systems, system administrators typically have root permissions to control all aspects of a system.

system buffers Memory storage areas that are used for storing information on inodes, indirect blocks and other information that is internal to the file system. System buffers do not hold data files.

system call Programming routine that requests an action from the operating system kernel.

system dictionary File containing the words used by the spell command for checking the spelling of text files.

system dump Memory image of the UNIX operating system, either while it is running or, more typically, after it has crashed. Using the crash command, you can interpret the system dump to determine what went wrong with the system.

system error Error that occurs within the operating system.

system files Configuration files used to set up the UNIX system. Typically, these files are only accessible by root or other administrative users.

system initialization Process of starting up the UNIX operating system. During system initialization, the file systems are checked and mounted, networking is started, and processes that allow multiple users to access the system are typically started up.

system logins Special user logins that have permission to do system administration tasks. System logins are assigned UIDs of number from 0 to 100.

system name String of characters that is used to identify the type of UNIX system currently in use. Sometimes, the system name is the same as the node name, which is the name given to identify a computer system to the network.

system owner Concept introduced in UNIX System V Release 4.2 to assign special permissions for a selected user to do basic system administration through a graphical user interface. The intent is to simplify administration for a user who has a desktop UNIX system that the user is responsible for maintaining.

system panics Fatal error conditions in the UNIX system from which the system cannot recover. A system panic is typically followed by a scary message on the system console and a total failure of the operating system.

system parameters Tunable parameters that set limits on basic system resources. These parameters prevent errant users or processes from consuming all the system resources by placing limits on what each user and process can consume.

Systems UUCP file that contains information about computer systems that can be reached over a UUCP network. Information in this file identifies the remote computer's name, an optional time when the computer can be reached, the type of device that can be used to reach it (such as a LAN or automatic call unit), transfer speed, telephone number or token, and an optional login sequence.

system security Refers to practices designed to prevent unwanted access and use of a computing system.

system software Refers to utilities that are used to support the operating system. *See also* operating system.

system state *See* initialization state.

System V *See* UNIX System V.

T

tab Command-line option used with the stty command, now outmoded. The option provides a way to slow down the output of tabs to slow terminals. The option tab3 converts tabs to spaces.

tabify Command in the emacs text editor that converts groups of spaces within the currently marked region to tabs.

tabify-region Command in the Epsilon text editor that converts the white space within the currently marked region to tabs.

tabs
1. Command to set the tab stops on the user's terminal according to the tab specification tabspec, after clearing any previous settings.
2. Modifiable hardware tabs on a terminal, serving the same function as those on a typewriter.

tab stops buffer Buffer displayed in the emacs text editor by the edit-tab-stops command. The buffer allows the user to set the locations of tab stops in the program.

tab-to-tab Command in the emacs text editor used in Scribe mode to insert a normal tab. This command is usually bound to the keystroke Meta-tab.

tab-width Variable in the emacs text editor that controls the position of tab stops in the current buffer. The default value is eight.

t_accept Library routine (Transport Interface) used to accept a connection request on a stream. It is called by a transport user after a t_listen call.

taddr2uaddr Library routine providing a generic interface for name-to-address mapping that will work with all transport protocols. The taddr2uaddr and uaddr2taddr routines support translation between universal addresses and TLI/XTI type netbufs. They take and return character-string pointers. The taddr2uaddr routine returns a pointer to a string that contains the universal address, and returns NULL if the conversion is not possible.

tag
1. Name of a source code file included in a tag table created by the etags facility of the emacs text editor.
2. The name of a C function definition in one of these files.
3. A string of characters used to identify an entry in a UNIX configuration file. For example, entries in the /etc/inittab file begin with a two-letter tag.

tag-files Command in the Epsilon text editor that locates all tags in the specified files.

tags-apropos Command in the emacs text editor, used with the etags facility to list the tags in the tag table that match the specified regular expression.

tags list buffer Buffer in the emacs text editor created by list-tags or tags-apropos. It is part of the etags facility of emacs.

tags-loop-continue Command in the emacs text editor, used with the etags facility to find all the definitions for the specified C function. This command is usually bound to the keystroke Meta-, (that is, Meta-comma).

tags-query-replace Command in the emacs text editor, used with the etags facility to do a regular expression query-replace on all the files listed in the tag table.

tags-search Command in the emacs text editor, used with the etags facility to search for any regular expression in all the source code files in the current directory.

tag table File used by the etags facility of the emacs text editor to keep track of the locations of C function definitions in source code files. The default tag table is named TAGS.

tail Command that displays the last part of a file, beginning at a designated place. If no file is named, the standard input is used. With the -f option, tail can display the output of a file as it is added to the file.

talk Command that allows you to talk to another user. It is a visual communication program that copies lines from your terminal to that of a user on the same host (or on another host).

talkd Command that notifies a user that somebody else wants to initiate a conversation. It acts as a repository of invitations, responding to requests by clients wishing a rendezvous to hold a conversation.

t_alloc Library routine used to allocate data structures associated with the specified endpoint. For struct_type T_INFO, fd is ignored, so that T_INFO structures may be allocated for use in calls to t_open.

tam Group of library routines (curses) used to port UNIX PC character-based TAM programs to any machine so that they will run using any terminal supported by curses, the low-level Extended Terminal Interface library.

TAM program Application written to run in character mode on the extinct UNIX PC.

tan Library routine that returns the tangent of its argument, x, measured in radians.

Tandy Corporation Manufacturer of personal computers, sold through Radio Shack stores.

tanh Library routine that returns the hyperbolic tangent of its argument.

tape Command used to maintain magnetic tapes. The tape command sends commands to and receives status from the tape subsystem and can communicate with QIC-24/QIC-02 cartridge tape drives and SCSI tape drives.

tapecntl Command that allows you to control tape devices. The tapecntl command sends the optional commands to the tape device-driver sub-device /dev/rmt/ntape*.

tape drive Hardware used to store information from computers to magnetic tape. The most popular tape drives with UNIX minicomputers has traditionally been quarter inch cartridge tape.

Tape Tool Program running under Open Windows that allows the user to copy files to or from a tape.

tapetool *See* Tape Tool.

tar Command that saves files on an archive medium (such as a floppy disk or a tape) and restores them from that medium. This is the most widely available archive command used with UNIX. Software installation is often done from tar archives. *See also* cpio.

task Part of a program or subroutine that can run independently.

t_bind Library routine (Transport Interface) used as a TLI/XTI local management routine that binds a protocol address to the specified transport endpoint and activates the endpoint.

tbl Command used as a preprocessor for formatting tables for nroff or troff. Often tbl is used on the same command line to pipe its output to nroff or troff.

tcdrain Library routine that describes a general terminal interface for controlling asynchronous communications ports. The tcdrain routine waits until all output written to the object referred to by fildes has been transmitted.

tcflow Library routine that describes a general terminal interface for controlling asynchronous communications ports. The tcflow routine suspends transmission or reception of data on the object referred to by fildes, depending on the value of action.

tcflush Library routine that describes a general terminal interface for controlling asynchronous communications ports. The tcflush routine discards data written to the object referred to by fildes but not transmitted, or data received but not read, depending on the value of queue_selector.

tcgetattr Library routine that describes a general terminal interface for controlling asynchronous communications ports. The tcgetattr routine gets the parameters associated with the object referred by fildes and stores them in the termios structure referenced by termios_p.

tcgetpgrp Library routine that describes a general terminal interface for controlling asynchronous communications ports. This routine returns the foreground process group ID of the terminal specified by fildes.

t_close Library routine (Transport Interface) used to close a transport endpoint.

t_connect Library routine (Transport Interface) used to request a connection to the specified destination transport user.

TCP Abbreviation for Transmission Control Protocol, a virtual circuit protocol of the Internet protocol family that provides reliable, flow-controlled, ordered, two-way transmission of data. It is a byte-stream protocol layered above the Internet Protocol (IP), the Internet protocol family's internetwork datagram delivery protocol.

TCP/IP Though TCP (Transmission Control Protocol) and IP (Internet Protocol) are two distinct networking protocols, the term is used to refer to a suite of protocols. Besides TCP and IP, those protocols include the actual services provided by TCP/IP, such as ftp, telnet, and SMTP. Every viable UNIX system can run TCP/IP protocols.

tcsendbreak Library routine that describes a general terminal interface for controlling asynchronous communications ports. If the terminal is using asynchronous serial data transmission, the tcsendbreak routine causes transmission of a continuous stream of zero-valued bits for a specific duration.

tcsetattr Library routine that describes a general terminal interface for controlling asynchronous communications ports. The tcsetattr routine sets the parameters associated with the terminal (unless support is required from the underlying hardware that is not available) from the termios structure referenced by termios_p.

tcsetpgrp Library routine that describes a general terminal interface for controlling asynchronous communications ports. The tcsetpgrp routine sets the foreground process group ID of the terminal specified by fildes to pgid.

technical writer Former English major who writes manuals for a computer company because the pay is better than he/she can get on a literary magazine.

tee Command that transcribes the standard input to the standard output and makes copies in the files. The sole purpose of tee is to serve, as its name implies, as a "T" in a pipe.

tek Type of terminal compatible with a Tektronics terminal. Also, the command-line option used with stty for selecting terminal settings appropriate for this type of terminal.

Tektronix Manufacturer of X Window System terminals (X-terminals) that are used with UNIX systems that support the X Window System.

telinit Command linked to /sbin/init, used to direct the actions of init. It takes a one-character argument and signals init to take the appropriate action. (This command was created to encourage administrators who were nervous about using the init command to simply use telinit -q to re-examine the /etc/inittab file.)

telldir Library routine that returns the current location associated with the named directory stream.

telnet Command used to communicate with another host using the telnet protocol. Essentially, telnet lets you log in to a remote TCP/IP site.

telnetd Command used as a server that supports the standard TELNET virtual terminal protocol. This process is started automatically when a remote client requests a telnet service. On some UNIX systems, this command is called in.telnetd.

telnet mode In the emacs text editor, a major mode for using telnet under emacs. Also, a command in the telnet add-on package to emacs, for running telnet under emacs.

tempnam Command that creates a name for a temporary file. The tempnam command allows the user to control the choice of a directory.

temporary data files Data files created by the UUCP facility to indicate that a file is being received from another computer. The file is in the form *TM.pid.ddd*, where *pid* is replaced by the process ID of the file transfer process and *ddd* is a three-digit number.

temporary directory Directory where applications can store files temporarily (usually work in progress). Standard temporary directories include /tmp and /var/tmp. These directories are emptied each time the system is rebooted.

terabyte One thousand gigabytes.

TERM Shell environment variable used to define the type of terminal currently being used. Setting the TERM variable is required to use screen-control applications such as the vi text editor.

term
1. Format of the compiled term file. Compiled terminfo descriptions are placed under the directory /usr/share/lib/terminfo. The compiled file is created from the source file descriptions of the terminals by using

the terminfo compiler, tic, and read by the routine **setupterm**. The file is divided into six parts in the following order: the header, terminal names, boolean flags, numbers, strings, and string table. The format has been chosen so that it is the same on all hardware. In BSD systems, term entries are stored in /etc/termcap.
2. Naming conventions for terminals. Terminal names are maintained as part of the shell environment in the variable TERM. These names are used by certain commands and functions. Files under /usr/share/lib/terminfo are used to name terminals and describe their capabilities.

TERMCAP Shell variable used to set the location of the termcap file. Usually, the file is located in /etc/termcap.

termcap file File that contains terminal definitions (BSD). It is usually located in /etc/termcap.

term.h Header file used with terminal control applications.

terminal Input/output device connected to a computer, which consists of a video display unit (VDU) and a keyboard.

Terminal Access Method *See* TAM.

terminal display attributes Characteristics that are set for a particular type of terminal. Attributes can include such things as underline, blink, and bold characters.

terminal emulator Software that lets a terminal emulate (act like) another type of terminal.

terminal information *See* terminfo.

terminal line settings Entries in terminal definition files that set characteristics of the connection. For example, line settings can include the line speed, parity checking, and duplex. In UNIX System V, terminal settings are chosen from entries in /etc/ttydefs and /etc/gettydefs.

terminal output stop mode Terminal setting in which a background job stops if it tries to send information to the screen.

terminal window Window in a UNIX GUI that provides access to a UNIX shell. In the X Window System, the xterm command starts up a terminal window.

terminate To stop and exit a process.

termination status *See* exit status.

terminator Hardware device (usually a resistor) used to terminate an electrical circuit. For example, Ethernet networks must have terminators at each end of a line.

TERMINFO Shell variable used to set the location of the terminfo database. Usually, the database is located in the file /usr/lib/terminfo or /usr/share/lib/terminfo.

terminfo database Database produced by tic that describes the capabilities of devices such as terminals and printers. Devices are described in terminfo source files by specifying a set of capabilities, quantifying certain aspects of the device, and specifying character sequences that affect particular results. This database is often used by screen-oriented applications such as vi and curses programs, as well as by some UNIX system commands such as ls and more. This usage allows them to work with a variety of devices without changes to the programs.

termio Refers to a general terminal interface for asynchronous communications ports that is hardware-independent. The user interface to this functionality is via function calls (the preferred interface) or ioctl commands.

termios Library routine that describes a general terminal interface for controlling asynchronous communications ports.

termiox Extended general terminal interface that supplements the termio general terminal interface by adding support for asynchronous hardware flow control, isochronous flow control and clock modes, and local implementations of additional asynchronous features.

t_error Library routine (Transport Interface) used to generate a message under error conditions. The t_error routine writes a message on the standard error file describing the last error encountered during a call to a TLI/XTI function.

test Command that evaluates an expression and, if its value is true, sets a zero (true) exit status; otherwise, a nonzero (false) exit status is set. The test command also sets a nonzero exit status if there are no arguments.

tex Command used to start the TeX formatter.

TeX Text formatting package that can be used with many UNIX systems.

TeX-buffer Command in the emacs text editor used in TeX mode to process the current buffer in TeX or LaTeX. This command is usually bound to the keystroke Ctrl-C Ctrl-B.

TeX-command Variable in the emacs text editor that contains the shell command that runs TeX.

TeX-dvi-print-command Variable in the emacs text editor that contains the shell command that prints a TeX-formatted file.

TeX-insert-braces Command in the emacs text editor using in TeX mode to insert a pair of braces. This command is usually bound to the keystroke Meta-{.

TeX-kill-job Command in the emacs text editor used in TeX mode to cancel TeX or LaTeX processing. This command is usually bound to the keystroke Ctrl-C Ctrl-K.

tex-mode Add-on package for the emacs text editor that implements a major mode for editing TeX and LaTeX files. Also, a command in the tex-mode add-on package to the emacs text editor that enables either TeX or LaTeX mode, modes designed for editing text files formatted for TeX or LaTeX.

TeX mode In the emacs text editor, major mode designed for formatting text files for TeX.

TeX-print Command in the emacs text editor used in TeX mode to print the buffer after processing with TeX or LaTeX. This command is usually bound to the keystroke Ctrl-C Ctrl-P.

TeX-recenter-output-buffer Command in the emacs text editor used in TeX mode to display the TeX shell buffer, showing TeX error messages. This command is usually bound to the keystroke Ctrl-C Ctrl-L.

TeX-region Command in the emacs text editor used in TeX mode to process the currently marked region in TeX or LaTeX. This command is usually bound to the keystroke Ctrl-C Ctrl-R.

TeX shell Buffer in the emacs text editor that displays the output of the TeX program.

TeX-show-print-queue Variable in the emacs text editor used in TeX mode to display the print queue. This command is usually bound to the keystroke Ctrl-C Ctrl-Q.

TeX-show-queue-command Variable in the emacs text editor that contains the shell command that displays the print queue.

text
1. Body of letters and numbers stored in a computer in human-readable form. Text files in UNIX are said to contain *ASCII characters* that can be viewed and manipulated with standard UNIX text commands (vi, cat, pg, etc.). 2. Area of a UNIX program that contains the machine instructions. Other parts of a program are stored in data and stack areas. *See also* text segment.

textedit Text editor running under Open Windows.

text editor Program designed for editing text files. It usually does not have all the functionality of a full-fledged word processor.

text file File that contains only printable ASCII characters.

text formatter Program, such as nroff, used for formatting text files. Formatting features include pagination, font changes, and justification, to name a few.

text mode In the emacs text editor, a major mode for editing text.

text pattern *See* regular expression.

text segment Part of a process in memory that contains the instructions the computer executes for the process.

TeX-terminate-paragraph Command in the emacs text editor using in TeX mode to insert two newline characters, indicating the end of a paragraph. This command is usually bound to the keystroke Ctrl-J.

text-mode Command in the emacs text editor that enters text mode.

tfind Library routine used for manipulating binary search trees. The tfind rou-

tine will search for data equal to *key in the tree, returning a pointer to the data if found. If it is not found, tfind will return a NULL pointer. *See also* tsearch.

t_free Library routine (Transport Interface) used to free memory previously allocated by t alloc. This routine will free memory for the specified structure, and will also free memory for buffers referenced by the structure.

tftp Command used as the user interface to the Internet TFTP (Trivial File Transfer Protocol), which allows users to transfer files to and from a remote machine.

tftpd Command that supports the DARPA Trivial File Transfer Protocol (TFTP). When a tftp request is received by UNIX, a tftpd process is automatically started to handle the request. (In some UNIX systems, the actual process is called *in.tftpd*.)

tgetent Library routine (curses) that describes curses interfaces (emulated) to the termcap library. These routines are included as a conversion aid for programs that use the termcap library. The tgetent routine looks up the termcap entry for name. The emulation ignores the buffer pointer bp. *See also* curs_termcap, terminfo, termcap.

tgetflag Library routine (curses) that describes interfaces (emulated) to the termcap library. These routines are included as a conversion aid for programs that use the termcap library. The tgetflag routine gets the boolean entry for id. *See also* curs_termcap, terminfo, termcap

t_getinfo Library routine (Transport Interface) used to return the current characteristics of the underlying transport protocol associated with the specified file descriptor.

tgetnum Library routine (curses) that describes curses interfaces (emulated) to the termcap library. These routines are included as a conversion aid for programs that use the termcap library. The tgetnum routine gets the numeric entry for id. *See also* curs_termcap, terminfo, termcap.

t_getstate Library routine used to return the current state of the provider associated with the specified transport endpoint.

tgetstr Library routine (curses) that describes curses interfaces (emulated) to the termcap library. These routines are included as a conversion aid for programs that use the termcap library. The tgetstr routine returns the string entry for id. Use tputs to produce output of the returned string. *See also* curs_termcap, terminfo, termcap.

tgoto Library routine (curses) that describes curses interfaces (emulated) to the termcap library. These routines are included as a conversion aid for programs that use the termcap library. The tgoto routine instantiates the parameters into the given capability. The output from this routine is to be passed to tputs. *See also* curs_termcap, terminfo, termcap.

third-party Company that produces hardware or software for another, existing product.

Thompson, Ken Inventor of UNIX, along with Dennis Ritchie.

thread Part of a program that can be processed as an independent entity.

ti700
1. Type of terminal compatible with a Texas Instruments 700.
2. Command-line option used with the stty command for selecting terminal settings appropriate for this type of terminal.

tic Command that translates a terminfo file from the source format into the compiled format. The compiled format is necessary for use with the library routines in curses.

ticks Items of time measured in one-millisecond units.

ticlts Datagram-mode transport provider offering service of type T_CLTS (connectionless). *See also* Transport Interface.

tiff Tag image file format, a standard graphical file format, used for storing and scanning images.

tilde Keyboard character (~) with many special uses in UNIX. In vi, a tilde changes a character from upper- to lowercase, and vice versa. In some networking commands, such as cu, a tilde is used to enter a conversation mode.

time
1. Command used to time the execution of a command. The time command prints the elapsed time during the command, the time spent in the system, and the time spent in execution of the command.
2. Library routine that returns the value of time in seconds since 00:00:00 UTC, January 1, 1970.

time and date formats Order and form in which time and dates are represented. Different locales (languages) use different formats.

times Library routine that returns time-accounting information for the current process and for the terminated child processes of the current process. All times are in 1/HZ seconds, where HZ is 60.

time-sharing System in which many jobs, or users, can share one computer. The UNIX operating system performs time-sharing.

timestamp Indication of the current date and time that is attached to a particular event. For example, an error logging program may attach a timestamp to each error event it logs.

timex Command that times the execution of a given command. The elapsed time, user time, and system time spent in execution are reported in seconds.

TIMEZONE Parameter that sets the local time zone.

timezone
1. Library routine that attempts to return the name of the time zone associated with its first argument, which is measured in minutes westward from Greenwich. If the second argument is zero, the standard name is used, otherwise the Daylight Savings Time version. If the required name does not appear in a table built into the routine, the difference from GMT is produced.
2. File used to set the default system time zone.

timod STREAMS module for use with the Transport Interface (TI) functions of the Network Services library. The timod module converts a set of ioctl calls into STREAMS messages that may be consumed by a transport protocol provider that supports the Transport Interface. This allows a user to initiate certain TI functions as atomic operations.

tip Telephone interface program, a command used to call up and log in to other UNIX systems, provided with BSD UNIX systems. Similar to the cu command.

tirdwr STREAMS module that provides an alternate interface to a transport provider that supports the Transport Interface (TI) functions of the Network Services library. This alternate interface allows a user to communicate with the transport protocol provider using the read and write system calls.

title Keyword used in a user's .Xdefaults file to configure the emacs text editor. It contains the text that appears in the title bar of the emacs window, and is equivalent to the emacs -wn command-line option.

title bar Top portion of a window in a graphical user interface. The title bar contains the title of the window.

TLI *See* Transport Interface.

t_listen Library routine (Transport Interface) used in establishing a transport connection. The t_listen routine listens for a connect indication from another transport user and is designed for use by server applications using connection-mode transport services.

TLI/XTI Library routine used to establish a transport connection. It is used by an active transport user to accept a connection request from the transport interface and provide the information needed to complete a virtual connection, following a call to t_listen.

t_look Library routine (Transport Interface) used to return the current asynchronous event on the transport endpoint specified. The event indicated reflects the service type of the transport provider. The t_look routine enables a transport provider to notify a transport user, when the user is issuing functions in synchronous mode, if an asynchronous event has occurred on the specified endpoint.

tmac Directory containing macro packages used with the troff text formatter. The directory's location is /usr/lib/tmac.

tmac.an Macro package (troff) used to format the manual pages displayed by the man command. *See also* man.

tmc8x0 Device used to support the Future Domain 8-bit SCSI host adapters. Supported controllers included TMC-850M, TMC-1680, and TMC-3260.

TMOUT Shell variable that contains the number of seconds the Korn shell waits after the last command is done executing, before exiting. For example, if TMOUT is set to 600, then if no command is entered within ten minutes of the last command finishing, the shell automatically exits (Korn shell only).

tmp Directory where a running process stores temporary files. *See also* temporary directory.

tmpfile Library routine that creates a temporary file using a name generated by the tmpnam routine and returns a corresponding FILE pointer.

tmpnam Library routine that generates filenames that can safely be used for a temporary file. The tmpnam routine always generates a filename using the path-prefix defined as P_tmpdir in the stdio.h header file.

tn300 Type of terminal compatible with a Terminet 300 terminal. Also, a command-line option used with stty for selecting terminal settings appropriate for this type of terminal.

tnamed Command that supports the DARPA Name Server Protocol.

To Field in an electronic-mail message indicating to whom the message is sent.

toascii Library routine used for converting characters. The toascii routine yields its argument with all bits turned off that are not part of a standard 7-bit ASCII character; it is intended for compatibility with other systems.

toggle To change states, as from on to off.

to-indentation Command in the Epsilon text editor that moves the cursor to the end of the indentation.

token Message that is passed between cooperating processes or computers to indicate that the owner of the token currently has the right to proceed. For example, in a Token Ring network, the computer with the token has the right to send its messages on the network. When it is done, it must relinquish the token.

Token Ring Network Type of local area network, created by IBM, that allows computers to communicate over twisted wire cable, using token-passing techniques to determine which computer is allowed to transmit data. The IEEE 802.5 standard defines Token Ring technology.

tolower Library routine used for converting characters. If the argument of tolower represents an uppercase letter, the result is the corresponding lowercase letter. All other arguments in the domain are returned unchanged.

toolkit Group of commands and applications that are used to perform helpful functions.

tools Term used to refer to a command, application, or utility that helps a user perform some function.

ToolTalk Service for application developers to exchange information.

t_open Library routine (Transport Interface) that must be called as the first step in the initialization of a transport endpoint. This routine opens a UNIX file that identifies a transport endpoint connected to a chosen transport provider (that is, transport protocol).

top-level Command in the emacs text editor that stops recursive editing and returns to the last previously interrupted global-search-and-replace operation.

top_row Library routine (curses) used to set and get current menu items. The top row routine returns the number of the menu row currently displayed at the top of menu.

t_optmgmt Library routine (Transport Interface) that enables a transport user to retrieve, verify, or negotiate protocol options with the transport provider associated with the bound transport endpoint specified.

tostop Command-line option used with the stty command for controlling whether to send a signal when background processes write to the terminal. This option is used for terminals that connect to a computer via serial lines.

touch Command that updates access and modification times of a specified file. If the named file doesn't exist, touch creates it.

touchwin Library routine (curses) that throws away all optimization information about which parts of the window have been touched, by pretending that the entire window has been drawn on. This is sometimes necessary when using overlapping windows, since a change to one window affects the other window, but the records of which lines have been changed in the other window do not reflect the change.

toupper Library routine for converting characters. If the argument of toupper represents a lowercase letter, the result is the corresponding uppercase letter. All other arguments in the domain are returned unchanged.

tput Command that initializes a terminal or queries the terminfo database.

This command uses the terminfo database to make the values of terminal-dependent capabilities and information available to the shell, to initialize or reset the terminal, or return the long name of the requested terminal type.

tputs Library routines (curses) that describes curses interfaces to the terminfo database. The tputs routine applies padding information to the specified string and outputs it.

tr Command that copies the standard input to the standard output with substitution or deletion of selected characters.

trace
1. To follow the processing of a program, possibly producing messages that track its progress. Tracing is used to check that the program is working properly and, if it's not, to highlight where the problems occur.
2. Option used with ftp to toggle the tracing of Ethernet packets.

traceoff Option with the m4 macro processor that turns off tracing globally or for macros that are specified individually.

traceon Option with the m4 macro processor that lets programmers turn on tracing either for all macros (including built-ins) or only for named macros.

track Circular area on a hard disk or floppy disk where data are stored. The number of tracks on a hard disk is important to know when you install the disk on your computer.

trackall Korn shell mode that automatically tracks aliases as they are defined. It is specified with the set command.

trackball Type of input device similar to a mouse but with a ball on the top side. When the ball is moved with the palm of the hand, the pointer on the screen moves accordingly.

track-eol Variable in the emacs text editor that controls how the cursor behaves at the end of the line.

transfer files To copy files from one computer to another over a network.

translation Act of changing information from one form to another, for example, translating a computer name to a network address.

Transmission Control Protocol *See* TCP.

transmit To send data.

transparent ioctl Special type of ioctl call, used with STREAMS, where the ioc_count is set to TRANSPARENT. Transparent ioctl means that STREAMS modules have to work with user data with M_COPYIN and M_COPYOUT messages.

transport endpoints Points at which two communicating applications communicate with the network (the transport provider). Transport endpoints exist on the computers that contain the two peer processes.

Transport Interface UNIX programming library (abbreviated TI) that provides an interface to OSI transport-level services. Also referred to as *TLI* (which stands for Transport Library Interface or Transport Level Interface, depending on who you are talking to). In theory, by writing programs that conform to TI specifications, the programs can be used to communicate with any networking software that conforms to the Transport Provider Interface (TPI). UNIX, TCP/IP, X.25, and other protocols have been implemented as transport providers.

transport layer Fourth layer of the OSI reference model. It provides reliable, end-to-end communications between transport users.

Transport Level Interface *See* Transport Interface.

transport provider Networking software that provides the services of the transport layer of the OSI reference model. In UNIX, most networking packages provide transport interfaces. These include TCP/IP, X.25, and IPX/SPX networking software packages. *See also* Transport Interface.

transport user Process that makes use of transport-level services. This is usually a program that sends requests to transfer information across the network.

transpose To switch the order of two adjacent items. For example, a text editor might have a command that transposes (swaps) two adjacent letters on a line.

transpose-characters Command in the emacs text editor that swaps the characters on either side of the cursor (also called transpose-chars). This command is usually bound to the keystroke Ctrl-T.

transpose-lines Command in the emacs text editor that swaps the current line with the line above it. This command is usually bound to the keystroke Ctrl-X Ctrl-T.

transpose-paragraphs
1. Command in the emacs text editor that swaps the current paragraph with the paragraph above it.
2. Command in the emacs text editor that swaps the current paragraph with the paragraph above it.

transpose-sentences Command in the emacs text editor that swaps the current sentence with the sentence before it.

transpose-sexp Command in the emacs text editor, used in LISP mode to transpose (switch) the two S-expressions before and after the cursor. This command is usually bound to the keystroke Meta- Ctrl-T.

transpose-words Command in the emacs text editor that swaps the current word with the word before it. This command is usually bound to the keystroke Meta-T.

trap Command in the Bourne and Korn shells that executes one or more commands if a specified signal is received.

TRAP Name of signal number 5, which can be sent to a running process (short for *trace trap*).

traps Feature used to catch information, such as a signal or an interrupt, and take some action to respond to it.

trash
1. To destroy, wreck, or otherwise mess up something on your computer. For example, if lightning hits your computer it will probably trash your hard disk.
2. Incomprehensible output from a command.

trchan Command used to translate character sets. The trchan command performs mapping as a filter. This allows a file consisting of one internal character set to be translated to another internal character set.

t_rcv Library routine (Transport Interface) that retrieves normal or expedited data received over a connection.

t_rcvconnect Library routine (Transport Interface) that enables a calling transport user to determine the status of a connect request that it issued to a responding transport endpoint. On successful completion of t_rcvconnect, the connection is initiated when an asynchronous t_connect is established.

t_rcvdis Library routine used to identify the cause of a disconnect and to re-

trieve any user data sent with the disconnect.

t_rcvrel Library routine used to acknowledge receipt of an orderly release indication. In t_rcvrel, the specified file descriptor identifies the local transport endpoint where the connection exists.

t_rcvudata Library routine used in connectionless mode to receive a data unit from another transport user. Data is received through the specified transport endpoint. On return, unitdata contains the information associated with the data unit, and flags points to a value that indicates whether the complete data unit was received.

t_rcvuderr Library routine used in connectionless mode to receive information concerning an error on a previously sent data unit.

tree Term used to describe the layout of the UNIX file system because files and directories branch outward from the root directory, forming a configuration that looks like a tree.

trig Group of library routines used for trigonometric functions, including sin, sinf, cos, cosf, tan, tanf, asin, asinf, acos, acosf, atan, atanf, atan2, and atan2f.

trim-versions-without-asking Variable in the emacs text editor that controls when emacs deletes backup versions of buffers.

trn Threaded news reader command used to read USENET news. Threading, in this case, means that articles branch off from the parent article and replies are connected together based on the order in which they were created.

troff Command that formats text in files. Input to troff is expected to consist of text interspersed with formatting requests and macros. While nroff output was intended to be read by any kind of output devices, troff output is intended for phototypesetters. *See also* nroff.

troff macro Special marking used in troff-formatted documents to indicate some kind of formatting. For example, macros can represent spacing, font changes, and page layout.

trojan horse Program that replaces a valid program in a computer system, but contains instructions that allow it to damage the system, allow its creator access, or do some other devious work.

trpt Command that transliterates a protocol trace. The trpt command interrogates the buffer of TCP trace records created when a socket is marked for debugging and prints a readable description of these records.

TruColor Colormap used by X Windows System to define the colors used on the screen.

true One of a pair of commands (the other is false) used to provide truth values. They are typically used in input to sh. true has exit status of zero, and false nonzero.

truncate One of a pair of commands (the other is ftruncate) used to set a file to a specified length. The file whose name is given has its size set to the specified length in bytes.

truncate-lines Variable in the emacs text editor that controls whether emacs wraps long lines when displaying them on the screen.

truncate-partial-width-windows Variable in the emacs text editor that controls whether emacs wraps lines that do not fit in windows that are not as wide as the screen.

truncation To shorten a string of charac-

ters at a particular length, usually dropping off the last part. For example, some UNIX-to-DOS interfaces will truncate any UNIX filenames that do not meet the DOS "8.3" naming convention. (It might also modify the name, if truncation doesn't make the name unique.)

Truscott, Tom One of the original developers of USENET software.

truss Command that executes another command while it traces its system calls, signals, and machine faults.

TRYLOCK Device-driver routine that tries to do a basic lock of a device-driver.

ts_dptbl Refers to the time-sharing dispatcher parameter table. The process scheduler (or dispatcher) is the portion of the kernel that controls allocation of the CPU to processes.

TSDU Abbreviation for transport service data unit, a unit of information that is passed between a transport service provider and a transport user. A TSDU contains information describing the type of message, as well as data. *See also* Transport Interface.

tsearch Library routine used to manage binary search trees. It is used to build and access the tree.

tset Command used to provide information to set terminal modes. The tset command allows the user to set a terminal's ERASE and KILL characters and define the terminal's type and capabilities by creating values for the TERM environment variable. The tset command initializes or resets the terminal with tput.

tsetcoff Command-line option used with the stty command to indicate that the transmitter-signal-element timing circuit is not set.

tsetcrbrg Command-line option used with the stty command to indicate that the transmitter-signal-element timing circuit (DTE source) is driven by the receive baud-rate generator.

tsetctset Command-line option used with the stty command to indicate that the transmitter-signal-element timing circuit (DTE source) is driven by the transmitter-signal-element timing circuit (DCE source).

TSMAXUPRI Tunable parameter that defines the range within which a user is allowed to adjust the priority of a time-sharing process. That range falls between the positive and negative values of TSMAXUPRI.

t_snd Library routine (Transport Interface) used to send either normal or expedited data over a connection.

t_snddis Library routine (Transport Interface) used to initiate a release on an already established connection with a responding transport endpoint. It may also be issued to reject a connect request.

t_sndrel Library routine (Transport Interface) used to initiate an orderly release of a transport connection associated with the transport endpoint. It indicates to the transport provider that the transport user has no more data to send.

t_sndudata Library routine (Transport Interface) used in connectionless mode to send a data unit to another transport user. Data is sent through the transport endpoint, which must be bound, and unitdata points to information associated with the data unit.

tsort Command used to do a topological sort. The tsort command produces on the standard output a totally ordered list of items consistent with a partial ordering of items mentioned in the input file.

t_sync Library routine (Transport Interface) used to synchronize TLI/XTI data structures and protocol-specific information.

ttcompat STREAMS module that translates the ioctl calls supported by the older Version 7, 4BSD, and XENIX terminal drivers into the ioctl calls supported by the termio interface.

tty
1. Command that prints the pathname of the user's terminal.
2. Refers to controlling the terminal interface. The file /dev/tty is, in each process, a synonym for the control terminal associated with the process group of that process, if any.

tty33
1. Terminal type compatible with the Model 33 Teletype (now outmoded).
2. Command-line option used with the stty command for selecting terminal settings appropriate for this type of terminal.

tty37
1. Terminal type compatible with the Model 37 Teletype (now outmoded).
2. Command-line option used with the stty command for selecting terminal settings appropriate for this type of terminal.

ttyadm Command used to format and output monitor-specific information. *See also* ttymon.

ttydefs File containing terminal line settings information for ttymon. An administrative file, /etc/ttydefs contains information used by ttymon to set up the speed and terminal settings for a tty port. *See also* ttymon.

ttymap Command that creates and updates /var/adm/ttymap.data with information from the /dev directory tree and the /etc/ttysrch file.

ttymon Command that is a STREAMS-based tty port monitor. Its functions are to monitor ports; to set terminal modes, baud rates, and line disciplines for the ports; to identify and authenticate users, if required; and to connect users or applications to services associated with the ports.

ttyname Library routine that returns a pointer to a string containing the null-terminated pathname of the terminal device associated with the specified file descriptor.

ttyslot Library routine that returns the index of the current user's entry in the /var/adm/utmp file.

ttysrch File that lists the names of directories in /dev that contain terminal and terminal-related device files, as well as the names of directories that contain no such files. The purpose of this file is to improve the performance of ttyname by identifying subdirectories in /dev to be searched first and subdirectories to be ignored.

tunable parameters Set of values that define the boundaries placed on various UNIX resources. These parameters can be changed (tuned) to suit the way a particular system is used. For example, a tunable parameter that limits the number of processes each user can run at a time can be changed if an administrator wants to let users run more processes.

tunable system parameters Tunable parameters that set boundaries on basic system resources. These include parameters for setting how memory is allocated or how the kernel is tuned.

t_unbind Library routine (Transport Interface) used to disable the transport endpoint specified, which was previously bound by t_bind. *See also* t_bind.

tunefs Command used to tune up an existing file system. The tunefs command is designed to change the dynamic parameters of a file system that affect the layout policies.

Tuxedo UNIX online transaction processing (OLTP) system originally developed by AT&T and currently owned by Novell. OLTP systems provide a "live" type of service to its users, as opposed to batch service which is processed at a later time.

twalk Library routine used to manage binary search trees.

twisted pair Pair of wires, usually twisted together, that were originally used to connect telephone jacks to the telephone system. Twisted pairs of wires are also used now for network connections.

twm Tab Window manager, available with the X Window System. Like most window managers, twm defines the look and feel of title bars, windows, and iconified windows. It also includes several windows for managing your system.

two's complement Unary operator used for representing negative numbers. The operation depends on the unit of storage (byte, 16-bit word, 32-bit word, etc.). The two's complement of a number is the number that when added to it, overflows the unit of storage and produces zero. For example, when working with bytes, the two's complement of 255 (or 11111111 binary) is 1 (or 00000001 binary) because 255 and 1 is 256 (100000000): the sum requires nine bits, the bottom eight of which are zeros.

two-way pipe Pipe (¦) with which information can flow in both directions, instead of the normal left-to-right flow.

type
1. To enter information using a keyboard.
2. Category of file (such as a plain file,

directory, symbolic link, named pipe, character special file, or block special file).

3. Command in the Bourne shell that displays the type of a specified command: built-in, defined shell function, or UNIX program.

4. Alias that is builtin to the Korn shell. It is equivalent to the command whence -v.

5. Command line option used with the find command that specifies files by type of file. *See also* find.

typeahead Library routine (curses) used for terminal input option control. curses does "line-breakout optimization" by looking for typeahead periodically while updating the screen. The type-ahead routine specifies that the file descriptor specified is to be used to check for typeahead.

typedef C programming facility used for creating new data type names.

typeover mode *See* overwrite mode.

types Refers to the types.h header file defining primitive system data types. The data types defined in types.h are used in UNIX system code.

typescript File containing the output of the script command.

typeset Command in the Korn shell that displays or sets the types of variables. Variables can be functions, integers, or strings, and can be read-only.

type specifiers Values used in C programs to note the kind of data being defined. Type specifiers include char, short, int, long, unsigned, float, and double.

TZ Environment Variable that contains time-zone information. This value is used by the ctime, localtime, strftime, and mktime functions to override the default time zone.

tzset Library routine used to converting the date and time to a string. It uses the contents of the environment variable TZ to override the value of the different external variables. It also sets the external variable daylight to zero if Daylight Savings Time conversions should never be applied for the time zone in use; otherwise, daylight is set to nonzero.

U

#undef C programming language control line that causes the identifier's preprocessor definition to be forgotten.

uaddr2taddr Library routine included in the group of netdir routines. The uaddr2taddr routine supports translation between universal addresses and TLI/XTI type netbufs. It takes and returns character string pointers.

uadmin
1. Command that provides control for basic administrative functions. It is tightly coupled to low-level system administration procedures and is not intended for general use.
2. Library routine that provides control for basic administrative functions. It is tightly coupled to the system administrative procedures and is not intended for general use.

ualarm Library routine that sends the SIGALRM signal to the invoking process in a number of microseconds given by the value argument.

ucase Option used on the command line with the dd command. Specifies that all text be converted to uppercase. *See also* dd.

ucontext Header file structure that defines the context of a thread of control within an executing process.

UDP Abbreviation for user datagram protocol, protocol, which can be used instead of TCP as the transport provider on top of IP in a TCP/IP protocol stack. Because UDP is a connectionless, non-acknowledged transport, it is often used for broadcast types of communications.

ufsdump Command that backs up all files in a specified file system or files changed after a certain date, to magnetic tape.

UFS file system Type of file system that is more complex than the standard UNIX System V file system. It is faster and more efficient for reading and writing large blocks of data than the standard file system.

ufsrestore Command that restores files from backup tapes created with the ufsdump command.

UID Abbreviation for user ID, a term used to describe the numeric value associated with a user name in UNIX. UID zero (0) is always assigned to the root user. UID numbers zero through 100 are reserved for special administrative users.

UID mapping Act of assigning one user the permissions to act as another user. For example, when using a distributed file system from another computer, the local user's permissions can be mapped into a remote user's permissions to provide access to otherwise restricted files.

UIL User Interface Language, a specification language that describes the initial state of a Motif window when the Motif application is started. The UIL also specifies the routines called when users change the state of the application.

uil Command that starts the UIL compiler to compile Motif applications. *See also* UIL.

UIMS User Interface Management System, a set of programs that allow a software developer to specify how an application program should work, and then create the application.

uio Device-driver data structure that describes an input/output request that can be broken up into different data storage areas.

uiomove Device-driver function that copies data using uio structures. It takes the data from a particular kernel address and copies it to the area defined by the uio structure. *See also* uio.

ul Command that reads the named files (or the standard input if none are given) and translates occurrences of underscores to the sequence that indicates underlining for the terminal in use, as specified by the environment variable TERM.

ULIMIT parameter Tunable parameter that sets a limit on the largest file that can be created on the system.

ulimit
1. Command that lets you view the *ulimit* of your system. If you're the root user, you can set the *ulimit* parameters to a new value with this command.
2. Library routine that provides for

control over process limits, getting and setting user limits.

umask
1. Command used to set the user file-creation mode mask. This mask affects the initial value of the file permission bits of subsequently created files.
2. Library routine that sets the process's file-creation mode mask and returns the previous value of the mask.

umount
1. Command used to unmount file systems and remote resources.
2. Library routine that requests that a previously mounted file system contained on the block special device or directory identified by file be unmounted.

umountall Command that causes all mounted file systems except root, /proc, /stand, and /dev/fd to be unmounted.

unalias Command in the Korn and C shells that deletes an alias from the current shell.

uname
1. Command used to print the current system name of the UNIX system to standard output. This command also can print the computer's node name, type of hardware it uses, operating system release, and operating system version. Using the -S option, uname can also change the system name and node name (although the setuname command is recommended).
2. Library routine that stores information identifying the current UNIX system in the structure pointed to by name.

unary operator Operator that accepts one input. For example, the NOT operator accepts one logical input, converting true values to false and false values to true.

unbalanced parentheses Open parenthesis with no matching close parenthesis or a close parenthesis with no matching open parenthesis. Unbalanced braces are similar.

unbind-key Command in the Epsilon text editor that removes the binding from the specified key.

unblock
1. Command used in the shl program that unblocks output for a layer.
2. Option used on the command line with the dd command. It specifies that fixed-length records in the input be converted to variable-length records. *See also* dd.

unbundle To remove a software item from a complete hardware and software package. Unbundling is done to allow a piece of software to be sold or installed separately.

uncompress Command to restore a previously compressed file to its uncompressed state and remove the compressed version. Compressed files are created by the compress command and have a .Z suffix.

uncompress-while-visiting Command in the uncompress add-on package to the emacs text editor that uncompresses a compressed file for viewing the file while visiting it.

unctrl Macro in the curs_util group of library routines that expands to a character string, which is a printable representation of the specified character.

undefined symbol In C programming, a symbol that is not defined within an application. During the linking process, the link editor searches every module of the program, plus any libraries used, for definitions of undefined symbols.

underline
1. To highlight text by printing under-
line (_) characters under the text. Also called underscoring.
2. Add-on package for the emacs text editor that implements a function for underlining text.

underline-region Command in the underline add-on package to the emacs text editor that underlines the currently marked region.

underscore *See* underline.

undo Command within an application that reverses the effects of the previous command. In many applications, such as the vi editor, undo is done by simply pressing the u key. In graphical applications, there is often an undo command under the Edit menu.

undo-changes Command in the Epsilon text editor that reverses the last change to the buffer.

unexpand Command that converts spaces to tabs in a document. This is a GNU command.

unexpand-abbrev Command in the emacs text editor that reverses the expansion of the last word abbreviation.

unfreezestr Device-driver routine that unfreezes the state of a stream. After a stream is unfrozen, activities on the stream can continue.

unget Command used to undo a previous get of an SCCS file.

ungetc Library routine used to push a character back onto the input stream.

unhash In the C shell, a command that deletes the hash table of commands and their locations.

unifdef Command used to resolve and remove lines marked with #ifdef from C program source.

Uniforum Professional association that helps create industry standards for open system computing. It also produces educational programs, trade shows and conferences, publications, on-line services, and peer-group interactions.

union C object that contains one of several possible types of members. Unlike a structure, a union only stores the value of one member at a time.

Unipress emacs Version of the emacs text editor distributed by Unipress, also called Gosling emacs after its author.

uniq Command that reads an input file and compares adjacent lines. By default, the second and succeeding copies of repeated lines are removed; the remainder is written to an output file.

unistd.h Header file that defines the symbolic constants and structures not already defined or declared in some other header file.

Unisys Large computer manufacturer, created when Sperry Univac and Burroughs merged in the 1980s.

units Command that converts quantities expressed in various standard scales to their equivalents in other scales.

universal address Network addressing scheme used by the UNIX system to map an address that is specific to a particular transport provider to a transport-independent address format.

universal-argument Command in the emacs text editor that repeats the following command the specified number of times. This command is usually bound to the keystroke Ctrl-U.

Universal Resource Locator *See* URL.

Universal Time Base time-zone that acts as a starting point from which all other time zones are measured. It is also referred to as *Greenwich Mean Time.*

unix Name of the file containing the bootable UNIX system kernel. This file is usually contained in the /stand directory.

UNIX International Consortium of vendors that advised UNIX System Laboratories on the development and marketing of UNIX System V. Both organizations are now defunct.

unixsyms Command that loads kernel debugger symbols into the UNIX kernel executable file after the kernel has been built and before it is run. In most cases, the symbols are loaded automatically when the kernel is rebuilt using the idbuild command. *See also* idbuild.

UNIX System Multi-user, multitasking operating system developed at Bell Labs in 1969 by Dennis Ritchie and Ken Thompson. Although many different versions of UNIX exist today, the two major variants are Berkeley Software Distribution (BSD) UNIX and UNIX System V. Various UNIX System look-alikes also exist today, such as the Linux operating system.

UNIX System V Version of UNIX being offered by Novell, current owner and key developer of UNIX, under the name UnixWare. UNIX System V is a direct descendent of the original UNIX operating system created at Bell Laboratories.

UNIX System V Release 4.2 Latest release of UNIX System V. Release 4.2 is the first standard UNIX system release to include a graphical user interface. This was also the last release put out by UNIX System Laboratories before it was purchased by Novell.

UNIX-to-UNIX copy *See* uucp.

UNIX-to-UNIX execution *See* uux.

UnixWare Version of UNIX System V Release 4.2 produced by Novell. Aside from standard UNIX System V features, UnixWare includes special software for connecting to NetWare servers. *See also* UNIX System V.

unlimit In the C shell, command that removes the limits on resources used by the current processes. These limits are set or displayed using the limit command.

Unlimited User License Package Software package that can be used with some UNIX Systems that are configured as single-user systems. This package allows an unlimited number of users to log in to the system at the same time.

unlink
1. Command used to remove linked files and directories.
2. Library routine that removes the directory entry named by the pathname pointed to by the argument path and decrements the link count of the file referenced by the directory entry.

unlinkb Device-driver function that removes a message block from a Streams message head. Once the message block is removed, unlinkb returns a pointer to the remainder of the message. Typically, this means removing the protocol information and returning a pointer to the data.

UNLOCK Device-driver function that releases a basic lock on a device.

unlockpt Library routine that clears a lock flag of a slave pseudo-terminal device associated with its master pseudo-terminal counterpart so that the slave pseudo-terminal device can be opened.

unmatched quotes Open quote with no matching close quote. The quote characters may be single (') or double (") quotes.

unmount Refers to disconnecting a file

system that has been connected (mounted) on the local UNIX file system. The unmounted file system can exist on the current disk partition, a separate partition, a different disk, a remote computer, or some removable media (such as a floppy disk or CD-ROM). Unmounting is done with the umount command. *See also* mount, umount.

unpack Command that expands files created by pack.

unpost_form Library routine in the curses library that erases a form from its associated subwindow.

unpost_menu Library routine in the curses library that erases a menu from its associated subwindow.

unset Command that deletes the definition of a shell variable or function.

unsetenv In the C shell, a command that deletes a shell environment variable.

unset variable Shell variable to which a value has not been assigned.

unshare Command used to make local resource unavailable for mounting by remote systems.

unshareall Command that unshares all currently shared resources.

unsigned In the original C programming language, unsigned values specified just one type. No unsigned chars, shorts, or longs existed. These additional unsigned values, however, were added to most compilers under a rule of unsigned preserving. So, to widen an unsigned type, it could be mixed with a signed type. ANSI C added the additional rule of unsigned preserving, where the relative sizes of the operand types affected the result type.

unsubscribing Refers to removing a newsgroup from the list of those to which you are subscribed. Once you unsubscribe, articles from that newsgroup no longer appear when you start your news reader.

untabify Command in the emacs text editor that converts all tabs to spaces within the currently marked region.

untabify-region Command in the Epsilon text editor that converts all tabs to spaces within the currently marked region.

until Command in the Bourne and Korn shells that begins a loop in a shell script. The loop is repeated until a condition is true.

untimeout Device-driver function that cancels the previous timeout request.

unzip To take a file comprised of one or more compressed files and expand it to recreate the original file or files.

upcase-region Command in the emacs text editor that capitalizes all of the letters in the currently marked region. This command is usually bound to the keystroke Ctrl-X Ctrl- U.

upcase-word Command in the emacs text editor that capitalizes all of the letters of the current word. This command is usually bound to the keystroke Meta-U. *See also* uppercase-word.

update
1. Daemon process called by the bdflush command to flush dirty buffers.
2. Software package containing enhancements and corrections to a base software release. An update usually has a release number associated with it. For example, the update to release 2.1 of a product might be called release 2.1.1.

updaters (/var/yp/updaters) Makefile used for updating Network Information Service (NIS) data bases.

up-line Command in the Epsilon text editor that moves the cursor to the previous line. *See also* previous-line.

up-list Command in the emacs text editor. In LISP mode it moves the cursor up one parenthesis level. In Scribe or TeX mode, it moves the cursor after the next closing bracket or brace. This command is usually bound to the keystroke Meta-.

upload Transfer a file from one computer to another, usually from a smaller (less powerful) computer to a larger (more powerful) one. Compare with download, file transfer.

uppercase To capitalize text.

uppercase-word Command in the Epsilon text editor that capitalizes all of the letters of the current word. *See also* upcase-word.

upper multiplexor Multiplexing Streams module that is pushed onto a protocol stack above a Streams device-driver. This multiplexor may provide access to the driver by many user processes at the same time.

upper stream In a STREAMS protocol stack, the part of the stream that is upstream of a multiplexing module or driver. Therefore, the upper stream is between the multiplexor and user space near the stream head, usually providing access by applications to the multiplexing driver.

UPS Uninterruptible Power Supply, an accessory used to ensure that a computer gets a continuous flow of power, regardless of line conditions. When the normal power for a computer is disrupted, the UPS activates and powers the computer via an internal battery or generator.

upstream In STREAMS, the part of a STREAMS protocol stack that is nearer the stream head. For example, in a TCP/IP protocol stack, the TCP protocol module is upstream from the IP protocol module.

uptime Command that displays the time, how long the user has been logged in, and other system statistics, including how long a computer system has been running since it was last turned on or rebooted.

upwardly compatible Refers to software or some other computer product that is designed to work with other products or future releases of the same product.

ureadc Device-driver function that copies a character to space pointed to by a uio structure. *See also* uio.

urestore Command that posts requests for files or directories to be restored from system-maintained archives.

URL Abbreviation for Universal Resource Locator, a name used to identify resources on the World Wide Web. A URL consists of two parts. The first part identifies the type of resource (http, gopher, ftp, archie, etc.) and the second part identifies the location. The location typically consists of the computer's host name and the location of the Web page.

usa Type of USENET newsgroup distribution in which articles are distributed within the United States (with exceptions).

usage message Message that appears when a command is entered with incorrect or incomplete syntax. These messages display the correct syntax for the command entered.

use_incorrect_pre4.0_behavior descriptor FMLI descriptor used to initialize FMLI applications that were written before FMLI Release 4 so they can run in Release 4 environments.

USENET Network facility that lets users share messages, called *news articles*, among other users with common interests. There are several thousand USENET newsgroups, with topics that range from computers, to music, business, and many social and alternative topics.

USENET site Computer that gathers USENET newsgroup articles so they can be disseminated to users on local or remote systems.

USENIX Professional organization of UNIX users that, among other things, helped to standardize the news reader software used with the USENET.

user Person who uses a computer.

useradd Command that adds a new user entry to the Identification and Authentication (I&A) data files. Options with useradd let you create a home directory and add setup files to that directory when you add a user.

User Datagram Protocol *See* UDP.

userdel Command that deletes a user's login definition from the system.

user environment variable Variables associated with a particular user's shell. These variables define such things as the terminal used, the location of the home directory, and the path to executable files.

user ID *See* UID.

user interface Refers to how a user interacts with a computer. Typical user interfaces include the command line, where users enter commands that instruct the computer what to do, and GUIs (graphical user interfaces) where a mouse is used to navigate inside and between windows. *See also* GUI.

usermod Command that modifies a user entry in the Identification and Authentication (I&A) data files.

user name Real name of a computer user. *See also* user ID.

user priority In printing, a value assigned to each user that determines the order in which queued print jobs will be completed.

user privileges Set of privileges assigned to a user. The privileges a user is assigned determines what a user can do on a system.

user2netname Library routine used to convert from a domain-specific username to an operating-system independent netname.

users Command that displays a list of the users who are logged in.

USL Abbreviation for UNIX System Laboratories, a subsidiary of AT&T that developed UNIX System V for several years. USL was purchased from AT&T by Novell, which no longer uses the name UNIX System Laboratories.

usleep Library routine used to suspend the current process for the number of microseconds specified by the argument.

/usr In UNIX System V, a directory located in the root directory. The /usr directory and its subdirectory typically contain user-accessible programs.

/usr/bin In UNIX System V, the directory that contains user-oriented commands.

/usr/sbin In UNIX System V, the directory that contains administrator-oriented commands.

/usr/spool In UNIX System V, the directory that contains files that are spooled, such as those waiting to be printed or sent across a network.

USR1 Name of user-defined signal number 1, which can be sent to a running process.

USR2 Name of user-defined signal number 2, which can be sent to a running process.

ustat Library routine used to get file system statistics.

utility Synonym for *command*.

utime Library routine that sets the access and modification times of the specified file.

utimes Library routine that sets the access and modification times of the file named.

utmp File that holds user and accounting information for such commands as who, write, and login.

utmpx File containing extended user and accounting information.

uucheck Command that checks for the presence of the UUCP system, required files and directories. It then alerts you if any are missing. With the -v option, uucheck reports the level of security that is set up for UUCP. This command is typically contained in the /usr/lib/uucp directory.

uucico Daemon process that runs the file-transport program for UUCP workfile transfers.

uucleanup Command that scans the spool directories for old files and takes appropriate action to remove them.

UUCP Name used to describe the set of networking commands that include uucp, uucico, uux, uutry, and uuto, as well as the protocols associated with them. Typically, UUCP networks communicate over serial lines, though there are implementations that allow connections over TCP/IP protocols.

uucp Command that copies files named by the source-file arguments to the destination-file argument.

uucp log file File that contains information about file transfers made using the uucp or uux commands.

uucppublic directory Directory in which file transfers are received from remote systems. Often this directory and its subdirectories have permissions open to allow remote systems to copy files there when other locations on the computer are not available. The uuto command automatically copies files to this directory, and the uupick command picks up the files from there.

uudecode Command that reads an encoded-file, strips off any leading and trailing lines added by mailer programs, and recreates the original binary data with the filename, mode, and owner specified in the header.

uudemon.admin Shell script that runs the uustat command to obtain status information on UUCP activities. It then mails those results to the UUCP administrator.

uudemon.cleanup Shell script that cleans out UUCP log directories, removes old work files, and returns mail that cannot be delivered. It then mails a summary of status information to the UUCP administrative user.

uudemon.hour Shell script that starts the UUCP scheduler, which examines work files created by uudemon.poll and polls the remote systems for file-transfer requests.

uudemon.poll Shell script that sets up work files used by UUCP for remote file transfer requests.

uuencode Command that converts a binary file into an ASCII-encoded representation that can be sent using mail.

uuencoded file Electronic-mail message that contains a shell script which, when run, re-creates one or more binary files. This method allows binary files to be sent through electronic mail. The uuencode program creates uuencoded files, and the uudecode program decodes them. *See also* shar file, uudecode.

uugetty Command used to listen for login requests on devices connected to serial ports. It also sets terminal type, mode, speed, and line discipline. Though this command is still available, its functionality has been replaced by the ttymon command in UNIX System V Release 4 and later releases.

uuglist Command that displays a list of all service grades available with uux and uucp.

uulog Command that queries a log file of uucp or uuxqt transactions in the file /var/uucp/.Log/uucico/system or the file /var/uucp/.Log/uuxqt/system.

uuname Command that lists the names of systems known to uucp.

uupick Command that accepts or rejects files transmitted to the user via public UNIX-to-UNIX system file copy.

uusched Command that runs the UUCP file transport scheduler.

uustat Command that displays the general status of, or cancels, previously specified UUCP commands, provides remote system performance information in terms of average transfer rates or average queue times, and provides the general, remote, system-specific, and user-specific status of UUCP connections to other systems.

uuto Command that sends source files to a destination via public UNIX-to-UNIX system file copy.

uutry Command that tries to set up a connection between a local and remote UNIX system via UUCP. If the connection is successful, any queued file transfers or remote execution requests between the two sites are done at that time.

uux Command that gathers files from various systems, executes a command on a named system, and then sends standard output to a file on another named system.

uuxqt Command that executes remote job requests from remote systems generated by the use of the uux command (mail sometimes uses uux for remote mail requests).

uuxqt log file File that contains information about file transfers made using the uucp or uux commands.

uwritec Device-driver routine that returns a character from space pointed to by a uio structure. *See also* uio.

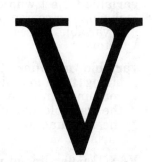

V.22 Modem protocol from CCITT that defines the 1200 bps standard outside the U.S.

V.22bis Modem protocol from CCITT that defines the 1200 bps international standard.

V.32 Modem protocol from CCITT that defines the 9600 and 4800 bps international standard.

V.32bis Modem protocol from CCITT that defines the 14.400 bps international standard.

V.42 Protocol from CCITT that defines modem error control.

V.42bis Protocol from CCITT that defines modem data compression.

vacation Command that automatically responds to electronic mail while the recipient is on vacation.

val Command that determines if the specified file is an SCCS file meeting the characteristics specified by the optional argument list.

VALIDATE option Option used in the UUCP Permissions file to add a level of validation to increase the security of some commands run remotely.

validate-TeX-buffer Command in the emacs text editor used in TeX mode to check the text in the current buffer for TeX formatting errors.

validation Process of determining that a user or host computer is who it says it is. Validation is typically done with passwords in UNIX.

valloc Library routine that allocates size bytes on a specified alignment boundary, and returns a pointer to the allocated block. The value of the returned address is guaranteed to be a multiple of alignment.

values File that contains a set of manifest constants, conditionally defined for particular processor architectures.

vaporware Tongue-in-cheek name given to software that is being marketed by a computer vendor, despite the fact the software doesn't yet exist, made popular by Microsoft.

VAR Acronym for value added reseller. VARs typically take a software product, add new features, and resell the product as their own.

/var Directory containing directories that hold UNIX administrative files, log files, lock files, and spool files.

varargs Set of macros allowing portable procedures that accept variable argument lists to be written.

variable Object whose value may change during the course of time. In the shell, a variable represents a string of characters.

variable modifier In the C shell, a string that modifies the information contained in a variable. For example, the variable modifier :e returns only the filename extension contained in a variable.

VAX Popular line of minicomputers from Digital Equipment Corp. that were among the first computers to run the UNIX operating system.

VC UNIX scheduling priority class, used only with DOS emulation.

vedit Command that invokes the vi editor in a form that is easy to use for beginning vi users. The difference between vedit and vi is that vedit has the showmode and novice flags set and magic enabled.

verbose
1. Mode of operation in which a program returns or displays descriptive messages instead of numeric codes.
2. Korn shell mode in which each shell command is displayed as it is read from a shell script. It is specified with the set command (Korn shell only).
3. In the C shell, a predefined shell variable that controls whether commands are echoed after history substitution.

verifiers In RPC, information that is used to verify that the credentials of a user who is requesting a service are valid.

ver_no Device-driver structure containing information about the driver interface version that the driver supports. This structure is defined in the /usr/include/sys/sdi.h header file.

Veronica Internet search tool available with some gopher sites. Veronica (also veronica) lets you use keywords to search databases of gopher documents.

version Particular release of a software product that is identified by a number.

version control Process of managing changes to a software development project. The UNIX source code control system (SCCS) lets you control software versions.

vertical bar See ¦.

vfork Library routine used to create new processes without fully copying the address space of the old process.

vfprintf Library routine used to place output on the specified output stream.

VFS *Virtual File System*, a UNIX file system structure that overlays specific file system types.

VFS architecture File system architecture that lets different file system types exist together in the same UNIX system kernel. VFS architecture is implemented in such a way that all file system types can be accessed using standard UNIX commands (mount, umount, df, fsck, and so on).

vfstab File containing a table of file system defaults.

VGA *Video graphics array*, a type of video board featuring higher resolution than older video standards, such as MGA, CGA, and EGA.

VGA monitor Monitor compatible with VGA video boards. *See also* VGA.

vhangup Library function that simulates a hangup on a terminal device.

vi Command that runs vi (visual), a display-oriented text editor based on an underlying line editor, ex.

video graphics adapter Computer hardware board that controls output on the video displays screen. The adapter controls such features as video resolution and colors.

vidi Command that loads or extracts a font or sets the video mode for the console.

vidmode Command used with Linux to specify the video mode. Values of -1 and -2 represent extended VGA and normal VGA, respectively.

view mode In the emacs text editor, a major mode for viewing files without changing them.

View Button on many graphical applications that controls your view of the application. Selections under View might let you zoom in or out or show draft or full-page views of documents.

viewdict Command used to read a dictionary database and print the contents.

view-emacs-news Command in the emacs text editor that displays information about updates to the program. This command is usually bound to the keystroke Ctrl-H N.

view-lossage Command in the emacs text editor that displays the last 100 characters typed. This command is usually bound to the keystroke Ctrl-H L.

vim Text editor specially designed for editing program code. The vim editor is compatible with the vi editor.

vi mode In the ed, ex, and edit text editors, a mode in which vi commands can be executed.

vi-mode
1. Command in the vi add-on package to the emacs text editor. The command enters vi mode, which emulates the vi text editor.
2. In the emacs text editor, a major mode in which vi commands are simulated as closely as possible. *See also*

ed, ex, edit.

vip-mode Command in the vip add-on package to the emacs text editor. The command enters vip mode, which emulates the vi text editor.

vip Add-on package for the emacs text editor which implements a major mode that emulates the vi text editor.

vip mode In the emacs text editor, a major mode that emulates the vi text editor.

viraw Korn shell mode that sets the command-line editor to be vi in raw mode. It is specified with the **set** command (Korn shell only).

virtual address Memory address that is stored in the UNIX kernel and mapped to physical memory. Using virtual addressing, UNIX shields machine-specific memory information from application programs.

virtual circuit Communication between two networking-transport entities that is established in connection-oriented mode.

virtual file system *See* VFS.

virtual memory *See* virtual address.

virtual terminal Scheme whereby one physical terminal provides access to multiple terminal interfaces. This can be done on a UNIX graphical user interface by opening xterm windows, each of which provides a standard shell command line interface.

virus Program that hides itself in computer systems, possibly to gain control of or do damage to the computer system.

visible-bell Variable in the emacs text editor that controls whether emacs flashes the screen off and on in place of ringing the bell.

visible transport type Type of networking transport provider available for use on the current UNIX system. A transport type is made visible by placing a *v* in the transport provider's entry in the /etc/netconfig file.

visit-file Command in the Epsilon text editor that reads the specified file into the current buffer.

visit-tags-table Command in the emacs text editor, used with the etags facility to specify the tag table file to be used.

VM *See* memory management.

VM parameters Set of tunable parameters that set limits on virtual memory resources. VM parameters include parameters for aging, kernel memory allocation, kernel virtual address space, page size extension, paging, segment drivers, and swapping.

VMSnet Type of USENET newsgroup that discusses topics of interest to VAX/VMS users. The names of newsgroups of this type begin with *vmsnet*. Most vmsnet groups are also available as mailing lists.

vnews USENET newsgroup article reader similar to rnews, except that it lets you read, save, move around in, and manage news articles from a screen-oriented interface, rather than simply a command line.

void
1. In C programming, the value that is returned when no return value is available.
2. Keyword used with programming functions to indicate that the function takes no arguments or returns no value.

volatile Keyword used with programming functions to indicate that the compiler should take no code generation shortcuts when accessing a particular object.

volcopy Command that makes a literal copy of the file system.

volume
1. In UNIX, a collection of data that is backed up on a particular medium.
2. In NetWare, a file system that can be made available from a NetWare server.
3. Term sometimes used to describe a hard disk or a section of a hard disk.

vpix DOS emulation system that is available on some UNIX systems.

vprintf Library routine that places output on the standard output stream.

vscanf Library routine used to read input from a stream pointer to a list of variables and scan that list for a particular string.

vsig Command that synchronizes a co-process with the controlling FMLI application.

vsprintf Library routine that converts, formats, and prints the specified output. The vsprintf routine is called with an argument list as defined by varargs.

vt *See* virtual terminal.

VT switching Changing from one virtual terminal to another. When you switch to another virtual terminal, the old virtual terminal disappears and the new one appears.

vt05
1. Type of terminal compatible with the DEC VT-05.
2. Command-line option used with the stty command for selecting terminal settings appropriate for this type of terminal.

VT100
1. Type of terminal compatible with the DEC VT-100.
2. Command-line option used with the stty command for selecting terminal

settings appropriate for this type of terminal.

vtgetty Command used to set terminal type, modes, speed, and line discipline. It is invoked by the init command.

VTIME Terminal device parameter used to set the value of TIME.

vtlmgr Command that monitors and opens virtual terminals.

vtop Device-driver function used to convert virtual addresses to physical addresses.

W

w Command that displays information about system usage, users currently logged in, and other system and user information.

WABI Acronym for *Windows Application Binary Interface*, a system developed by Sun Microsystems that allows UNIX systems to run MS-Windows applications. To use WABI, both WABI and MS-Windows must be installed on a Sun Solaris version of UNIX. The MS-Windows application then runs in a window on the Solaris GUI.

waddch Library routine (curses) used to put a character into a window at the current cursor position.

waddstr Library routine (curses) used to write all the characters of the null-terminated character string on the given window.

Waffle Shareware communications package used to communicate using UUCP features such as file transfer, e-mail, and USENET newsgroup distributions.

WAIS Acronym for *Wide Area Information Servers*, a service for searching the Internet. WAIS lets you search databases of information. Within the databases, you can do keyword searches to locate documents.

wait

1. Command used to wait for specified background processes and report termination status.
2. Library routine that suspends the calling process until one of its immediate children terminates or until a child that is being traced stops because it has received a signal.

waitid Library routine that suspends the calling process until one of its children changes state.

waitpid Library routine that suspends the calling process until one of its children changes state; if a child process changed state prior to the call to waitpid, return is immediate.

waitsem Library routine that gives the calling process access to the resource governed by a semaphore. If the resource is in use by another process, waitsem will put the process to sleep until the resource becomes available.

wait3 Library routine (BSD) used to wait for a process to terminate or stop. The wait3 library routine delays its caller until a signal is received or one of its child processes terminates or stops due to tracing.

wakeup Library routine (device-driver) that starts up processes that are sleeping on a particular address, and makes them eligible for scheduling.

wakeup call Call made to a process, requesting that it resume execution.

waking processes Process that was sleeping and is now being restarted.

wall Command used to write to all users. It reads the named file, or, if no filename appears, it reads the standard input until an end-of-file. The command is typically used to warn all users before shutting down the system.

wall buffer In the Epsilon text editor, buffer containing a chart of the current key bindings. The buffer is created automatically by the wall-chart command. *See also* wall chart.

wall-chart Command in the Epsilon text editor that creates a new buffer named *wall*, containing a chart of the current key bindings.

wall chart In the Epsilon text editor, chart of the current key bindings, that is, what command each key runs. The chart is created automatically by the wall-chart command.

wallpaper Refers to graphical images or patterns used as the background on a computer screen with a graphical user interface.

WAN *See* wide area network.

wastebasket An icon used on many graphical user interfaces to represent an area where you can discard documents. Typically, documents are discarded by dragging-and-dropping an icon representing the document onto the wastebasket icon. The document is then either immediately removed from the system or stored in the wastebasket for later removal.

wattroff Library routine (curses) used to manipulate the current attributes of the named window. Used to turn off attributes without turning other attributes on or off.

wattron Library routine (curses) used to manipulate the current attributes of the named window. It is used to turn on specified attributes without affecting others.

wattrset Library routine (curses) used to manipulate the current attributes of the named window. Used to set current attributes of the given window.

wc Command that counts the number of newline characters, words, and bytes in the named files, or in the standard input if no file is specified.

wclear Library routine (curses) that copies blanks to every position in the window. It also calls the clearok library routine, so that the screen is cleared completely on the next call to wrefresh for that window and repainted from scratch.

wclrtobot Library routine (curses) that erases all lines below the cursor in the window. Also, the current line to the right of the cursor, inclusive, is erased.

wclrtoeol Library routine (curses) that erases the current line to the right of the cursor, inclusive.

wcstombs Library routine that converts a sequence of wide character codes into a sequence of multibyte characters and stores these multibyte characters into another array, stopping if a multibyte character would exceed a specified limit of bytes or if a null character is stored.

wctomb Library routine used to determine the number of bytes needed to represent a multibyte character and store the multibyte character representation in an array.

wdelch Library routine (curses) used to delete the character under the cursor in the window. All characters to the right of the cursor on the same line are moved to the left one position.

wdeleteln Library routine (curses) used to delete the line under the cursor; all lines below the current line are moved up one line. The bottom line of the window is cleared. The cursor position does not change.

Web *See* World Wide Web.

Weinberger, Peter Coauthor of the awk utility.

werase Library routine (curses) used to copy blanks to every position in the window.

wgetch Library routine (curses) used to read a character from the terminal associated with the window.

wgetstr Library routine (curses) that acts as though a series of calls to getch were made, until a newline or carriage return is received.

what Command that searches the given files for the string of characters that causes the identification line from each file to print. This sequence of characters includes an at-sign, left parenthesis, number sign and right parenthesis: @(#). The what command is meant to be used with the get command to print information from an executable file. The information typically identifies the command, the release number, the date it was last modified, and the owner.

what-is Command in the Epsilon text editor that displays the command that is bound to the specified key.

whatis Command that displays a one-line descriptions of one or more commands. *See also* man, apropos.

whence Command in the Korn shell that displays the type of a specified command: built-in, defined shell function, alias, or UNIX program. It is similar to the type command. It only checks for commands in the current path.

where-is Command in the emacs text editor that displays the key that is bound to the specified command. This command is usually bound to the keystroke Ctrl-H.

Whetstone Type of benchmark program for testing the efficiency of floating-point operations. Any 32-bit and 64-bit operations are tested with Whetstone I and Whetstone II programs.

which Command that displays the name of the program file that would be executed if a command were given. If there are more than one program files with the same name on a system, the which command chooses the first one that is in the user's path.

while
1. Shell command that begins a loop in a shell script. The loop is repeated while a condition is true. This statement is used in C, the bc desk calculator, and other languages to specify repeated processing until a condition is no longer true.
2. Function in the emacs LISP programming language that executes a statement block repeatedly until a condition is false (or nil).

while statement *See* while.

whitespace Refers to characters that leave blank space in a text file, that is, spaces and tabs.

who Command used to list the user's name, terminal line, login time, elapsed time since activity occurred on the line, and the process ID of the command interpreter (shell) for each current UNIX system user. Other options let you display the run level and lines on which UNIX is waiting for login requests.

who am I Command that displays the name of the current user, as well at the controlling terminal and the current time and date.

whodo Command that produces formatted and dated output about who is doing what on the system. For each user logged in, a device name, user-ID, and login time is shown, followed by a list of active processes associated with the user-ID. The list includes the device name, process-ID, CPU minutes and seconds used, and process name.

whois Command used to search an Internet directory entry for an identifier that is either a name (such as Smith) or a handle (such as SRI-NIC).

wide area network Type of network used for long-haul communications. The X.25 network protocol is an example of a wide area network.

widen-buffer Command in the Epsilon text editor that restores normal access to the current buffer after it has been restricted by a narrow-to-region command.

widget
1. Object type in the Motif graphical user interface. A widget is usually connected with a window on the screen, displaying output, input areas, or both. 2. In the Windowing K shell (wksh), a section of program code that implements a discrete function on a window. A widget may represent a button, menu, text field, or other feature.

widget class Collection of code that generically implements a part of a graphical user interface look and feel. For example, a widget class might provide a standard structure for menus and buttons on an interface that information for a specific instance can be plugged into.

widget library Collection of widgets that can be included into an application.

width Command-line option used with the lp command that sets page width.

wildcard Refers to special characters used with the shell to provide shortcuts for matching one or more filenames. Wildcard characters include the asterisk (*), question mark (?), and brackets ([]).

wildcard expansion Action taken by the shell or an application to expand wildcards into the full names of the files that are matched.

winch Library routine (curses) used to return the character at the current position in the named window.

Winchester disk *See* hard disk.

window Rectangular area on a screen of a graphical user interface. A typical window includes a border, a title bar, and a pulldown menu of window functions. Particular windows might include buttons, input areas for text, icons representing files or devices, and scroll bars, to name a few items.

Window Controls Program running under Open Windows that allows the user to move or resize the current window.

windowing system Set of software programs that provides a framework for running graphical programs on your computer. A windowing system usually provides the interface between the mouse or keyboard and the operating system. Different "looks-and-feels" may be associated with a windowing system, to define how the icons, windows, menus, and buttons appear. The X Window System is a windowing system; OPEN LOOK and Motif provide different looks-and-feels.

window manager Program that controls the operation of the windows and icons in a graphical user interface. Popular window managers with UNIX are Motif and OPEN LOOK. Both provide the look-and-feel on top of the basic windowing features provided by the X Window System.

window-min-height Variable in the emacs text editor that controls the minimum height (in lines) of an emacs window.

window-min-width Variable in the emacs text editor that controls the minimum width (in characters) of an emacs window.

Windows NT Relatively new multitasking operating system by Microsoft. It is said to be an important component in the original Denver Airport baggage-handling system.

Windows Application Binary Interface *See* WABI.

winsch Library routine (curses) that inserts a character before the character under the cursor in a curses window.

winsertln Library routine (curses) with which a blank line is inserted above the current line and the bottom line is lost.

wizard UNIX techie who can do magical things with a UNIX system.

wksh Windowing Korn shell, a command-line interpreter that provides graphical extensions to the Korn shell (ksh). The windowing Korn shell lets you create and manage graphical user interface widgets. It supports OSF Motif widget sets.

WM_DELETE_WINDOW One of three X Window System WM_PROTOCOLS protocols, indicating a request from a user that a window be removed.

WM_PROTOCOLS Messages sent to an application from an X Window System window manager, alerting the application that immediate action must be taken. WM_PROTOCOLS includes the WM_DELETE_WINDOW, the WM_SAVE_YOURSELF, and the WM_TAKE_FOCUS protocols.

WM_SAVE_YOURSELF One of three X Window System WM_PROTOCOLS protocols, indicating a user request that an application be killed.

WM_TAKE_FOCUS One of three X Window System WM_PROTOCOLS protocols, indicating that keyboard focus has been given to the application.

wmove Library routine (curses) that moves the cursor associated with the window to a specified line and column.

wn Command-line option used with the emacs text editor to control the text that appears in the title

wnoutrefresh Library routine (curses) that copies the named window to the virtual screen. It must be called to get any output on the terminal, as other routines merely manipulate data structures.

word Basic unit of data. A word is made up of two bytes (16 bits).

word abbreviation In the emacs editor, a string that stands for a (longer) word or phrase. In word abbreviation mode, emacs automatically replaces each word abbreviation with the word or phrase for which it stands.

word abbreviation expansion In the emacs text editor, expanding a word abbreviation into the word or phrase for which it stands. *See also* word abbreviation mode.

word abbreviation file File that contains a list of word abbreviations for use by the emacs text editor. The file is usually named .abbrev_defs and is stored in the user's home directory.

word abbreviation mode Minor mode in the emacs text editor that allows the user to define abbreviations for frequently used words and phrases. Once the abbreviation is defined, whenever the user types it, emacs automatically expends it, that is, replaces it with the word or phrase it stands for. *See also* abbrev mode.

wordlist variable Space-separated word list that is enclosed in parentheses. It is used as a variable for the foreach and glob shell functions.

WordPerfect Word processing application from WordPerfect, now a subsidiary of Novell, Inc. Its word processing and office products run on a variety of computer platforms, including UNIX.

word processor Application program that provides features for creating, modifying, and formatting documents. Unlike plain text editors, word processors typically have integrated formatting and printing features.

word search Search that ignores spaces, newlines, and punctuation, used in the emacs text editor.

word-search-backward Command in the emacs text editor that searches backward through the buffer for a string, ignoring newlines, spaces, and punctuation (performing a word search). This command is usually bound to the keystroke Ctrl-S Meta-Ctrl-R.

word-search-forward Command in the emacs text editor that searches for a string, ignoring newlines, spaces, and punctuation (this is called a word search). This command is usually bound to the keystroke Ctrl-S Meta-Ctrl-W.

word substitution In the C shell, refers to using parts of previously typed commands when entering a new command. *See also* history.

working directory Directory currently in use. Each user has a working directory (also called the current directory). The pwd command returns the working directory. (pwd stands for present working directory.)

Workspace environment Graphical windowing environment provided by Open Windows. Properties of the Workspace can be set using the properties command from the Workspace menu.

Workspace menu Menu that is displayed by the Open Windows environment when the user clicks on the workspace. The menu contains ways of requesting basic workspace features.

workstation High-performance, single-user microcomputer that has traditionally been used for specialized scientific and business applications. Although UNIX workstations can operate as multi-user systems, they are typically configured and tuned for use by one user.

WORM Acronym for write once read many, a type of disk drive that can hold enormous amounts of information which cannot be modified. Instead, outdated information is marked as deleted, and the correct information is stored again.

worm Program that moves from one computer to another, typically over a network. A worm might damage systems or simply gather information used to gain access to other computer systems.

WP Abbreviation for Word Processor or Word Processing.

WR Library routine (device-driver) that is used to get a pointer to a write queue of a STREAMS driver or module.

wrap mode Text editor mode where the text at the end of a line is automatically wrapped to the beginning of the next line.

wrapper code Special code that lets a loadable module initialize itself dynamically.

wrefresh Library routine (curses) that copies the named window to the physical terminal screen, taking into account what is already there in order to do optimizations.

WRITE Option used in the file /etc/uucp/Permissions to allow users from remote systems to write to local file systems using uucp, uuto, and other basic networking commands.

write
1. Command that copies lines from your terminal to that of another user.
2. Library routine that writes to a file, writing from a specified buffer to a specified file.
3. A device-driver entry-point routine that writes data to a device. This routine is started by the driver to respond to a write system call.

write-abbrev-file Command in the emacs text editor that writes a word abbreviation file.

write enabled Term used to describe a floppy disk that can be written to.

write-file Command in the emacs text editor that saves the contents of the current buffer in the specified file and associates the buffer with the file. This command is usually bound to the keystroke Ctrl-X Ctrl-W.

write lock State of a file in which it cannot be written to until the process that created the lock on the file releases it.

write permission File or directory characteristic that allows a user to write to the file or create new files in a directory.

write-protect Term used to describe a floppy disk that cannot be written to.

write queue In STREAMS, a repository for storing write requests intended for a Streams module or driver until the requests are ready to be processed.

write-region Command in the Epsilon text editor that writes the currently marked region to the specified file.

write-state Command in the Epsilon text editor that saves all commands and variables in the specified file for later automatic loading.

writev Library routine that performs the same action as the write library routine (writing to a file), but gathers the output data from buffers specified by the members of a specified array.

wscanw Library routines (curses) that corresponds to the scanf routines. The effect of this routine is as though wgetstr were called on the window, and the resulting line used as input for the scan.

wsetscrreg Library routine (curses) that allows the application programmer to set a software scrolling region in a window.

wstandend Library routine (curses) that turns off all attributes.

wstandout Library routine (curses) that turns on the named attributes without affecting any others.

wstat Refers to the group of macros defined in sys/wait.h, for evaluating the status of a process waiting for its children via either the wait or the waitpid function.

wtimeout Library routine (curses) that sets blocking and nonblocking reads for a given window.

wtmp File used to store information about login and logoff activities. The file is read by different utilities, including those used for process accounting.

wtmpfix Command that examines the standard input or named files in utmp.h format, corrects the time/date stamps to make the entries consistent, and writes to the standard output. It is used to make the wtmp file human-readable.

wtmpx Extended version of the wtmp file, used for storing login and logoff activities.

wvline Library routine (curses) that draws a vertical line starting at the cursor position.

Wyse Company that makes a popular line of computer terminals.

WYSIWYG Acronym for what you see is what you get, pronounced *wisee wig*. This term is used to describe graphical software whose screen display exactly matches the printer's output.

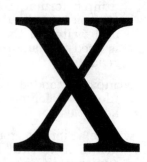

.Xdefaults File located in a user's home directory that contains configuration information for components and applications used on the graphical desktop.

.xsession File in the user's home directory that provides runtime clients during startup of the X Window System. If this file doesn't exist for the user, the file /usr/X/lib/xdm/Xsession executes the /usr/bin/shserv command to setup the environment.

X *See* X Window System.

X.25 CCITT standard that describes the protocols and message formats used in the interface between a terminal and a packet-switching network. This protocol is very popular in Europe, particularly for long-haul networks.

X.400 CCITT standard that describes an OSI-compliant mail and messaging protocol.

X.500 CCITT standard that describes an OSI compliant mail and messaging protocol that includes the ability to maintain user directories.

X11R4 Term used to refer to version 11, release 4 of the X Window System.

X11R5 Term used to refer to version 11, release 5 of the X Window System.

X11 Term used to refer to version 11 of the X Window System.

x286emul Command that provides Intel 80286 emulation, so a user can run applications intended for XENIX V/286 Release 2.3 or 2.3.2 systems. Most often, this command is run automatically when a user tries to run a XENIX 286 product.

x86 Family of CPU chips designed by Intel, including the 8088, 8086, 80286, 80386, 80486, and Pentium.

xalloc Algorithm used in the UNIX kernel to search a file's text region for a pointer to the inode of an executable file. If one is not found, it allocates and initializes a new text region.

xargs Command that constructs an argument list and executes a command. It is particularly useful for gathering long lists of files as input to other commands.

xauth Command used to edit and display information relating to connecting to the X server.

xbiff Utility that displays a mailbox image that indicates whether or not new mail has arrived. It is an X Window System client program.

x-buffer-menu Command in the emacs text editor, used with the X Window

System interface to display a pop-up menu of the open buffers. This is the mouse equivalent of the list-buffers command.

xcase Command-line option used with the stty command for selecting whether to convert between upper- and lower-case on local output. This option is used for terminals that connect to a computer via serial lines.

xcibrg Command-line option used with the stty command for setting how the terminal's clock is set.

xclipboard Utility distributed with the X Window System that stores the current selection on the clipboard. *See also* clipboard.

xclock Utility used with the X Window System to display a running clock.

Xcms Abbreviation for X color management system, a technology to provide the X Window System with device-independent color definitions.

xcmsdb Utility that sets screen color characterization data properties in an X Window System.

xconsole Utility used to display messages on an X Window System display that are intended for the console (/dev/console).

X Consortium Group of computer companies that provide input to X Window System standards.

xcrset Command-line option used with the stty command for defining how the terminal's clock is set.

xctset Command-line option used with the stty command for defining how the terminal's clock is set.

x-cut-and-wipe-text Command in the emacs text editor, used with the X Window System interface to copy the currently marked region to the kill buffer and delete it from the buffer being edited. This is the mouse equivalent of the kill-region command.

xcutsel Utility distributed with X Windows that displays the value of the primary selection.

x-cut-text Command in the emacs text editor, used with the X Window System interface to copy the currently marked region to the kill buffer. This is the mouse equivalent of the copy-region-as-kill command.

xditview Utility used to display ditroff output on an X Window System display.

xdm Command used to manage a collection of X displays. These displays may be located on the local computer or on a remote X server.

xdpyinfo Program used in X Windows to determine the number of color bits on a display.

xdr Group of library routines for external data representation. XDR routines allow C programmers to describe arbitrary data structures in a machine-independent fashion. Data for remote procedure calls (RPC) are transmitted using these routines.

xdr_accepted_reply Library routine used for encoding RPC reply messages.

xdr_admin Group of library routines that deal specifically with the management of the XDR stream (for external data representation).

xdr_array Library routine that translates between variable-length arrays and their corresponding external representations.

xdr_bool Library routine that translates between booleans (C integers) and their external representations.

xdr_bytes Library routine that translates between counted byte strings and their external representations.

xdr_callhdr Library routine used for describing RPC call headers. It encodes the static part of the call message header in the XDR language format. It includes information such as transaction ID, RPC version number, program and version number.

xdr_callmsg Library routine used for describing RPC call messages. It encodes the static part of the call message header in the XDR language format. It includes information such as transaction ID, RPC version number, program and version number.

xdr_char Library routine that translates between C characters and their external representations.

xdr_complex Group of XDR library routines for external data representation. They require the creation of XDR stream. The group includes xdr_array, xdr_bytes, xdr_opaque, xdr_pointer, xdr_reference, xdr_string, xdr_union, xdr_vector, and xdr_wrapstring.

xdr_create Group of XDR library routines for external data representation stream creation. The group includes the follow library routines: xdr_destroy, xdrmem_create, xdrrec_create, and xdrstdio_create.

xdr_destroy Library routine that invokes the destroy routine associated with the XDR stream, xdrs.

xdr_double Library routine that translates between C double-precision numbers and their external representations.

xdr_enum Library routine that translates between C enums (actually integers) and their external representations.

xdr_float Library routine that translates between C floats and their external representations.

xdr_free Library routine used as a generic freeing routine in the XDR library.

xdr_getpos Library routine that invokes the get-position routine associated with the XDR stream, xdrs. The routine returns an unsigned integer, which indicates the position of the XDR byte stream.

xdr_inline Library routine that invokes the in-line routine associated with the XDR stream. The routine returns a pointer to a contiguous piece of the stream's buffer.

xdr_int Library routine that translates between C integers and their external representations.

xdr_long Library routine that translates between C long integers and their external representations.

xdrmem_create Library routine that initializes the XDR stream object pointed to by xdrs. The stream's data is written to, or read from, a chunk of memory at a specified location of a specified length.

xdr_opaque Library routine that translates between fixed-size opaque data and its external representation.

xdr_pointer Library routine that provides pointer-chasing within structures, like xdr_reference, except that it serializes NULL pointers, whereas xdr_reference does not.

xdrrec_create Library routine that initializes the XDR stream object pointed to by xdrs. This XDR stream implements an intermediate record stream.

xdrrec_eof Library routine that can be invoked only on streams created by xdrrec_create. After consuming the rest of the current record in the stream, this routine returns one if the stream has no more input, and zero otherwise.

xdr_reference Library routine that provides pointer-chasing within structures.

xdr_rejected_reply Library routine that encodes the rejected RPC message in the XDR language format. The message could be rejected either because of version number mismatch or because of authentication errors.

xdr_replymsg Library routine that encodes the RPC reply message in the XDR language format. This reply could be either an acceptance, rejection, or NULL.

xdr_setpos Library routine that invokes the set position routine associated with the XDR stream.

xdr_short Library routine that translates between C short integers and their external representations.

xdr_simple Group of XDR library routines for external data representation of primitive types. The group includes: xdr_bool, xdr_char, xdr_double, xdr_enum, xdr_float, xdr_free, xdr_int, xdr_long, xdr_short, xdr_u_char, xdr_u_long, xdr_u_short, and xdr_void.

xdrstdio_create Library routine that initializes the XDR stream object pointed to by xdrs. The XDR stream data is written to, or read from, the standard I/O stream file.

xdr_string Library routine that translates between C strings and their corresponding external representations.

xdr_u_char Library routine that translates between unsigned C characters and their external representations.

xdr_u_long Library routine that translates between C unsigned long integers

and their external representations.

xdr_u_short Library routine that translates between C unsigned short integers and their external representations.

xdr_union Library routine that translates between a discriminated C union and its corresponding external representation.

xdr_vector Library routine that translates between fixed-length arrays and their corresponding external representations.

xdr_void Library routine that always returns one. It may be passed to RPC routines that require a function parameter, where nothing is to be done.

xdr_wrapstring Library routine that calls xdr_string with arguments xdrs, sp, and maxuint, where maxuint is the maximum value of an unsigned integer.

xedit Text editor available with the X Window System, providing simple text-editing features.

XENIX Version of UNIX, originally produced my Microsoft. Most XENIX features were folded into UNIX System V by release 4.

XENIX compatibility Ability of a UNIX system to run XENIX commands and applications.

xev Command that displays the contents of X events.

xfd Command that creates a window, displaying the characters for a particular font.

xfonsel Command that starts a graphical interface for selecting display font names in an X Window System screen.

x-get-cut-buffer Command in the emacs text editor, used with the X Window System interface to return the string in the X Windows cut buffer as a string.

xgrab Utility created by Bruce Schuchardt, that is used to capture X Window System screen images and store them in files. It outputs in Post-Script, xwd, and various bitmap formats.

XGUI Environment variable that identifies the type of graphical user interface being used with the X Window System. Typically, XGUI is set to MOTIF, to provide the Motif look-and-feel.

x-help Command in the emacs text editor, used with the X Window System interface to display a pop-up menu of online help topics.

xhost Command used to open or close access to an X Window System server display. When access is open, one or more remote systems can display applications on the local X server screen.

xinstall Command used to install XENIX system-distribution (or XENIX application program) floppies.

xkeymap Freeware X utility that displays keycode and keysym information.

xkill Command used to kill an X Window system client by killing the client's X resource.

XLFD Abbreviation for X logical font description, the conventions used with the X Window System to describe a standard syntax for font names.

Xlib *See* X library.

X library Programming library for creating X Window System applications. It is the lowest-level interface to the X Window System.

XListFonts Library routine provided in Xlib that generates a list of fonts available on an X server.

xload Command that displays the system load average on an X Window System display.

xloadimage Program used in X Windows to display images on the screen.

X Logical Font Description Format used to name fonts. It contains 14 fields of information about a font, including foundry, family, weight, slant, and point size.

xlogo Command that displays the X Window System logo on an X Window System display.

xlsclients Command that lists the client applications that are currently running on an X Window System display

xlwfonts Command that lists the available fonts on an X Window System display.

Xm Library Programming library that includes library routines and data structures for creating Motif applications in an X Window System environment. Elements in the Xm library begin with the letters Xm.

Xm Prefix used on library routines and data structures in the Xm library. *See also* Xm Library.

xmag Command that magnifies part of the screen on an X Window System display.

xman Command that displays the standard UNIX system manual pages on an X Window System display.

x-mouse-keep-one-window Command in the emacs text editor, used with the X Window System interface to display only one window in emacs, closing all but the current window. This is the mouse equivalent of the delete-other-windows command.

Xmodem Communications protocol, originally developed by Ward Christensen, used to transfer data between personal computers.

x-mouse-select-and-split Command in the emacs text editor, used with the X Window System interface to split the window vertically at the mouse pointer location. This is the mouse equivalent of the split-window-vertically command.

x-mouse-set-point Command in the emacs text editor, used with the X Window System interface to move the cursor to the location of the mouse pointer.

XON/XOF Asynchronous protocol used in communications that keeps the sending and receiving devices in synchronization.

X/OPEN Consortium of computer vendors dedicated to resolving standards issues related to the UNIX operating system.

XOR *Exclusive OR*, an operator that combines two logical values. The result is true if exactly one (not both) of the two input values is true.

x-paste-text Command in the emacs text editor, used with the X Window System interface to insert the contents of the kill buffer at the cursor location. This is the mouse equivalent to the yank command.

xpg Command-line option used with the cc C compiler. It specifies that the compiler generate benchmark code in a file named gmon.out.

xpixels Command-line option used with the stty command for setting the window size.

x-popup-menu Command in the emacs text editor, used with the X Window System interface to build menus.

xpr Command that takes an X window dump file and formats it for output on one of several printers.

xprop Utility distributed with X Windows that displays the contents of the cut buffers.

xrdb Command to load X Window System resources into the current display. Resources are typically loaded from the .Xdefaults file in the user's home directory.

xrefresh Command that refreshes either parts of or an entire X Window System display.

X resource file File containing entries that define the attributes of an X Window System session. *See also* .Xdefaults.

xrestore Command used to read archive media backed up with the XENIX backup command. Also spelled *xrestor*.

xsb Command line option used with the cc C compiler. It specifies that the compiler produce symbol-table data that is used by the Solaris 2.0 Source Code Browser.

xsbfast Command-line option used with the cc C compiler. It specifies that the compiler produce symbol-table data for use by the the Solaris 2.0 Source Code Browser, without actually compiling.

XSDSEGS Tunable parameter that specifies the number of shared data segments available to XENIX applications.

XSDSLOTS Tunable parameter that indicates the number of attached shared data segments available to XENIX applications.

XSEMMAX Tunable parameter that set the number of XENIX semaphores for the system.

X server Program that provides the basic framework for the X Window System interface. In UNIX, this program is often located in /usr/X/bin/X. Typically, additional processes, such as mwm (for the Motif GUI), are run to provide the full look-and-feel seen by the end user.

xset Command used to run a program that sets the various user preference and system options of an X display, including the X server's font path. It can also be used to show the current X server settings.

xsetroot Command used to set the appearance of the root window (the background) on an X Window System display.

xstdcmap Command that selectively defines standard colormap properties in an X Window System display.

x-store-cut-buffer Command in the emacs text editor, used with the X Window System interface to store a string in the X Windows cut buffer.

xstrconst Command-line option used with the cc C compiler. It specifies that the compiler add all string literals to the text segment, not to the data segment.

xterm Command used to start an xterm window.

X terminal Terminal that contains a small computer that runs the X server. An X terminal can be used to run Motif or OPEN LOOK GUIs.

xterm window Window in which a shell is running, created by the xterm command. An xterm provides an interface to the standard UNIX shell during an X Window System session.

xtetris Command that starts the game where you fit descending blocks together to make continuous.

XTI Standard for providing standard OSI transport services to UNIX applications, formerly called *AT&T Trans-*

port Interface or Transport Level Interface. This standard is currently maintained by X/Open.

Xt Library X Window System programming library that makes up part of the X Toolkit. The Xt library is the heart of the toolkit, providing library routines to create widgets.

xtom Library routine (BSD) used to initialize a MINT from a string of hexadecimal digits.

X Toolkit Collection of library routines and structures used to create X Window System applications. Included in the X Toolkit are C-language libraries Xt and Xaw. These libraries define widgets (representing scrollbars, menus, editing areas, and so on) that help simplify and standardize X Window System programming.

xtrace Korn shell mode that displays commands as they are read from a shell script, with debugging information. It is specified with the **set** command (Korn shell only).

xtract Command used to extract files from cpio archives.

xv Program that captures, saves, and alters screen images on an X Window System.

xwd Command used to produce a screen image from an X Window System X11 window.

XWD Graphical format for capturing X Window System X11 screen images.

X Window System Base windowing technology, designed at MIT, on which graphical user interfaces (GUIs) are built. Also called X. Two major GUIs, Motif and OPEN LOOK, are based on the X Window System. A primary attribute of X is its ability to work with applications started from other computers on the network.

XWINHOME Environment variable for identifying the location of the X Window System libraries and commands. Typically, XWINHOME is set to /usr/X.

xwininfo Command used to show window information relating to an X Window System display.

Y

y. Prefix used to identify yacc output files.

yank Action done in the vi editor with the y command to cut text from the file you are editing. Text can be returned to a different place in the file with the p (put) command.

y0 Library routine that returns a Bessel function of x of the second kind of order 0.

y1 Library function that returns a Bessel function of x of the second kind of order 1.

yacc Acronym for yet another compiler compiler, a command that reads a text file that contains a grammar and creates a file containing tables for parsing by a parser.

yank Command in the emacs text editor that inserts the contents of the kill buffer at the cursor position. This command is usually bound to the keystroke Ctrl-Y.

yank-pop Command in the Epsilon text editor that cycles through the kill buffers, inserting the contents at the cursor position and replacing the just-yanked kill buffer with the contents of the previous kill buffer.

yank-rectangle Command in the emacs text editor that inserts the contents of the kill buffer at the cursor position, as a rectangle. This command is usually bound to the keystroke Ctrl-Y.

Yellow Pages *See* YP.

Yellow Pages Service *See* YP.

yes Command that repeatedly outputs y or a single-string argument that it has been given, The yes command continues indefinitely unless aborted.

Ymodem Asynchronous protocol used in communications to transfer files between personal computers. It is similar to Xmodem-CRC, but also allows batch file transfers.

yn Library routine that returns the Bessel function of x of the second kind of order n. The value of x must be positive.

You Have Mail Standard message that is displayed on your screen after you log in if there is new mail awaiting you in your electronic mailbox.

yow Add-on package for the emacs text editor that implements a function to print quotations for the comic-strip character "Zippy the Pinhead." Also, the command in the yow add-on package to the emacs text editor that generates these quotations.

YP Abbreviation for yellow pages service, the previous name for the Network Information System (NIS). Because of this fact, many NIS commands and utilities still carry the *yp* suffix.

yp_all Library routine that provides a way to transfer an entire map from a server to a client in a single request using TCP (rather than UDP, as with other functions in this package).

yp_bind Library routine used to bind the client process to an NIS server that serves the appropriate domain.

ypbind Command for the Network Information System (NIS), used to store information that allows a computer to communicate with a ypserv process. The ypbind command must be running on every NIS client.

ypcat Command that prints out values in the Network Information Service (NIS) map specified by mname, which may be either a map name or alias.

ypclnt Group of functions providing an interface to the NIS network lookup service (yellow pages). Functions include ypclnt, yp_get_default_domain, yp_bind, yp_unbind, yp_match, yp_first, yp_next, yp_all, yp_order, yp_master, yperr_string, and ypprot_err.

yperr_string Library routine that returns a pointer to a read-only error message string that is NULL-terminated but contains no period or new-line.

ypfiles Database and directory structure of the Network Information Service (NIS), which uses a distributed, replicated database of dbm files contained in the /var/yp directory hierarchy on each NIS server.

yp_first Library routine that returns the first key-value pair from the named map in the named domain.

yp_get_default_domain Library routine used to fetch the node's default domain and use the returned outdomain as the indomain parameter to successive NIS name service calls.

ypinit Command that sets up the Network Information Service (NIS) on a server or a client.

yp_master Library routine that returns the machine name of the master NIS server for a map.

yp_match Library routine that returns the value associated with a passed key.

yp_next Library routine that returns the next key-value pair in a named map.

yp_order Library routine that returns the order number for a map.

ypixels Command-line option used with the stty command for setting the window size.

yppasswd Command that changes (or installs) the network password associated with a particular user in the Network Information Service (NIS) database.

yppoll Command that asks a ypserv process what the order number is, and which host is the master Network Information Service (NIS) server for the named map.

ypprot_err Library routine that takes an NIS name-service-protocol error-code as input, and returns a ypclnt layer error code, which may be used in turn as an input to yperr_string.

yppush Command that copies a new version of the named Network Information Service (NIS) map from the master NIS server to the slave NIS servers.

ypserv Network Information System (NIS) database lookup server.

ypset Command that tells ypbind to get Network Information Service (NIS) services for the specified ypdomain from the ypserv process running on server.

yp_unbind Library routine that makes the domain unbound, and frees all per-process and per-node resources used to bind it.

yp_update Library routine used to make changes in NIS databases. You can change existing entries, add entries, and delete entries.

ypupdated Command (daemon) that updates information in the Network Information Service (NIS) database.

ypwhich Command that tells which server supplies Network Information Service (NIS) services to the NIS client, or which is the master server for a NIS map.

ypxfr Command that moves a Network Information Service (NIS) map in the default domain for the local host to the local host, by making use of normal NIS services.

ytalk Command that allows multiple users "chat," letting them type messages to each other at the keyboard. It is similar to, and somewhat compatible with, the UNIX talk command, except that it allows more than two users to converse at a time.

Z

Z8000 16-bit microprocessor used in minicomputers in the 1980s for running UNIX systems. Z8000s were produced by Zilog, an affiliate of Exxon Corporation.

zcat Command that displays the uncompressed contents of a compressed file, without changing the file.

zcmp Command that runs the cmp command on compressed files. On the zcmp command line, you can hand off any options to cmp.

zdiff Command that runs the diff command on compressed files. On the zdiff command line, you can hand off any options to diff.

zdump Command that prints the current time in each zone name specified on the command line.

zero File that is a source of zeroed unnamed memory. Any reads from a zero special file always return a buffer full of zeroes. The file is of infinite length. Any writes to a zero special file are always successful, but the data written is ignored. The device file is located in /dev/zero.

zforce Command that forces a .gz suffix be placed on all gzip files. The .gz suffix prevents the file from being compressed twice.

zgrep Command that runs the grep command on compressed files. On the zgrep command line, you can hand off any options to grep.

zic Command that reads text from the file(s) named on the command line and creates the time-conversion information files specified in this input. If a filename is a dash (-), the standard input is read.

zip
1. Extension added to archives created with the DOS PKZIP command.
2. Command used to compress and combine one or more files into a single archive. It is compatible with the DOS PKZIP command.

zipinfo Command that provides detailed information about a zipped archive file, including permissions, encryption status, compression type, and version information. *See also* zip.

zipnote Command used to package and compress files. Using the -w option, you can append the version number to the resulting file name.

Zmodem Asynchronous protocol used in communications to transfer files between personal computers. It is capable of handling larger files than it predecessor, Xmodem-CRC.

zmore Command that runs the more command on compressed files. On the zmore command line, you can hand off any options to more. This command works on files compressed with compress, pack, or gzip.

znew Command that takes files that were compressed with the compress command (with a .Z suffix) and compresses them using the gzip format.

zombie Process that is no longer active, but, for some reason, remains in the process table and appears in the list of processes when you type the ps command.

zone Hierarchical group of hosts on the Internet. The purpose of a zone is to allow the central administration of a group of hosts by a single authority. Zones simplify the administration of the Internet by having a business, educational institution, or government branch administer its own computers, rather than have one organization administer every node on the network.

zoo Command used to create and manage collections of compressed files.

zoom To change the magnification of a window, or an area of a window, in a GUI-based application.

Zpixmap Format for storing bitmap images. A Zpixmap image is organized as a set of pixel values in scan line order.

zsh Command used to start the Z shell.

Data Warehousing

FOR

DUMMIES®

2ND EDITION

by Thomas C. Hammergren
and Alan R. Simon

WILEY

Wiley Publishing, Inc.

Data Warehousing For Dummies®, 2nd Edition

Published by
Wiley Publishing, Inc.
111 River Street
Hoboken, NJ 07030-5774

www.wiley.com

For general information on our other products and services, please contact our Customer Care Department within the U.S. at 877-762-2974, outside the U.S. at 317-572-3993, or fax 317-572-4002.

For technical support, please visit www.wiley.com/techsupport.

Wiley also publishes its books in a variety of electronic formats. Some content that appears in print may not be available in electronic books.

Library of Congress Control Number: 2009920908

ISBN: 978-0-470-40747-9

10 9 8 7 6 5 4 3 2

WILEY

About the Author

Tom Hammergren is known worldwide as an innovator, writer, educator, speaker, and consultant in the field of information management. Tom's information management and software career spans more than 20 years and includes key roles in successful business intelligence and information management solution companies such as Cognos, Cincom, and Sybase. Tom is the founder of Balanced Insight, Inc., a leading vendor of business intelligence lifecycle management software and services that also works on innovation in semantically driven business intelligence.

While working for Sybase, Hammergren helped design and develop WarehouseStudio, a comprehensive set of tools for delivering enterprise data warehousing solutions. At Cincom, Tom helped deliver the SupraServer product line to market, one of the first fully distributed data management solutions for highly survivable network implementations. During an earlier position at Cognos, he was one of the founding members of the PowerPlay and Impromptu product teams.

Tom has published numerous articles in industry journals and is the author of two widely read books, *Data Warehousing: Building the Corporate Knowledge Base* and *Official Sybase Data Warehousing on the Internet: Accessing the Corporate Knowledge Base* (both from International Thomson Computer Press).

Dedication

This book is dedicated to my mother and father. Thank you both for the foundation and direction growing up — and, most importantly, for always supporting me in my life endeavors, no matter how crazy they have been or are. You are the best — all my love!

Author's Acknowledgments

Writing a book is much harder than it sounds and involves extended support from a multitude of people. Though my name is on the cover, many people were ultimately involved in the production of this work. As I began to think of all the people to whom I would like to express my sincere gratitude for their support and general assistance in the creation of this book, the list grew enormous.

There are those that are most responsible for making this book a reality: Kyle Looper, Acquisitions Editor; Nicole Sholly, Project Editor; and Carole Jelen McClendon of Waterside Productions, my trusted agent for more than 10 years.

The most important thank-you is to my wife, Kim, and loving children, Brent and Kristen. They created an environment in which I could successfully complete this book — an accomplishment that I share with them and one that forced all of us to sacrifice a lot.

Publisher's Acknowledgments

We're proud of this book; please send us your comments through our online registration form located at http://dummies.custhelp.com. For other comments, please contact our Customer Care Department within the U.S. at 877-762-2974, outside the U.S. at 317-572-3993, or fax 317-572-4002.

Some of the people who helped bring this book to market include the following:

Acquisitions, Editorial

Project Editor: Nicole Sholly

Acquisitions Editor: Kyle Looper

Copy Editor: Laura K. Miller

Technical Editor: Russ Mullen

Editorial Managers: Kevin Kirschner, Jodi Jensen

Editorial Assistant: Amanda Foxworth

Sr. Editorial Assistant: Cherie Case

Cartoons: Rich Tennant (www.the5thwave.com)

Composition Services

Project Coordinator: Patrick Redmond

Layout and Graphics: Samantha K. Allen, Reuben W. Davis, Nikki Gately, Joyce Haughey, Melissa K. Jester, Sarah Philippart

Proofreaders: Dwight Ramsey, Nancy L. Reinhardt

Indexer: Sharon Shock

Publishing and Editorial for Technology Dummies

 Richard Swadley, Vice President and Executive Group Publisher

 Andy Cummings, Vice President and Publisher

 Mary Bednarek, Executive Acquisitions Director

 Mary C. Corder, Editorial Director

Publishing for Consumer Dummies

 Diane Graves Steele, Vice President and Publisher

Composition Services

 Gerry Fahey, Vice President of Production Services

 Debbie Stailey, Director of Composition Services

Contents at a Glance

Table of Contents

Introduction

The data warehousing revolution has been underway for over ten years within information technology (IT) departments around the world. If you're an IT professional, or you're fashionably referred to as a *knowledge worker* (someone who regularly uses computer technology in the course of your day-to-day business operations), data warehousing is for you! If you haven't heard of this phenomenon, you might be aware of the tools that access the data warehouse — business intelligence tools. *Data Warehousing For Dummies,* 2nd Edition, guides you through the overwhelming amount of hype about this subject to help you get the most from data warehousing.

If you're an IT professional (a software developer, database administrator, software development manager, or data-processing executive), this book provides you with a clear, no-hype description of data warehousing technology and methodology — what works, what doesn't work, and why.

If you regularly use computers in your job to find information and facts as a contracts analyst, researcher, district sales manager, or any one of thousands of other jobs in which data is a key asset to you and your organization, this book has in-depth information about the real business value (again, without the hype) that you can gain from data warehousing.

Why I Wrote This Book

Although data warehousing can be an incredibly powerful tool for you and others in your organization, pitfalls (a lot of them!) are scattered along your path, from thinking about data warehousing to implementing it. The path to data warehousing is similar to the yellow brick road in *The Wizard of Oz:* Even though the journey seems relatively straightforward, you have to watch out for certain obstacles along the way, such as which technology path to take when you have a choice and all kinds of things you don't expect. Although you don't have to figure out how to handle winged monkeys and apple-throwing trees, you do have to deal with products that don't work as advertised and unanticipated database performance problems.

I've been working with data warehousing since early in my career, in the late 1980s. Although the data warehousing revolution began in the early 1990s and you now can find a much broader array of technologies and tools, the principle of data warehousing isn't all that new (as mentioned in Chapter 1).

With the volume of information that companies produce internally and access externally, almost all organizations have a universal interest in data warehousing. You can't easily find an organization right now that doesn't have at least one data warehousing initiative under way, on the drawing board, or in production. Everyone wants to consume data — which leads directly to the need for a data warehouse!

This broad interest in data warehousing has, unfortunately, led to confusion about these issues:

- ✔ **Terminology:** For example, because no official definitions exist for the terms *data warehouse, data mart,* or *data mining,* product vendors declare definitions that best suit the products they sell.

- ✔ **How to successfully implement a large data warehousing system:** Should you build one large database of information and then parcel off smaller portions to different organizations, or should you build a bunch of smaller-scale databases and then integrate them later?

- ✔ **Advances in technology:** New facets of technology, such as the Internet, are having an effect on data warehousing.

This book is, in many ways, a consolidation of my down-to-earth, no-hype conversations with and presentations to clients, IT professionals, product engineers, architects, and many others in recent years about what data warehousing means to business organizations today and tomorrow.

How to Use This Book

You can read *Data Warehousing For Dummies,* 2nd Edition, in either of these ways:

- ✔ **Read each chapter in sequential order, from cover to cover.** If this book is your first real exposure to data warehousing terminology, concepts, and technology, you probably want to go with this method.

- ✔ **Read selected chapters that are of particular interest to you and in any order you want.** I wrote each chapter to stand on its own, with little dependency on any other chapter.

To give you a sense of what awaits you in *Data Warehousing For Dummies,* 2nd Edition, the following sections describe the contents of the book, which are divided into seven parts.

Part 1: The Data Warehouse: Home for Your Data Assets

Part I gets down to the basics of data warehousing: concepts, terminology, roots of the discipline, and what to do with a data warehouse after you build it.

Chapter 1 gets right to the point about a data warehouse: what you can expect to find there, how and where its content is formed, and some early cautions to help you avoid pitfalls that await you during your first data warehousing project.

Chapter 2 describes, in business-oriented terms, exactly what a data warehouse can do for you.

I describe the different types of data warehouses that you can build (small, medium, or way big!) and the circumstances in which each one is appropriate in Chapter 3.

Chapter 4 describes *data marts* (small-scale data warehouses), which have become the preferred method to deliver data to end users.

Part II: Data Warehousing Technology

In Part II, you go beyond basic concepts to find out about the technology behind data warehousing, particularly database technology.

Chapter 5 talks about relational databases (if you're an IT professional, you're probably familiar with them) and how you can use these products for data warehousing. Specialized databases, such as multidimensional and column-wise (or vertical) databases, as well as other types of databases used for data warehousing, are described in Chapter 6. In this chapter, you can figure out which type of database is a viable option for your data warehousing project.

You can read about data warehousing *middleware* — software products and tools used to extract or access data from source applications and do all the necessary functions to move that data into a data warehouse — in Chapter 7, along with the issues you have to watch out for in this area.

Part III: Business Intelligence and Data Warehousing

Part III discusses the concept of *business intelligence* — the different categories of processing that you can perform on the contents of a data warehouse. From "tell me what happened" processing to "tell me what might happen," it's all here!

See Chapter 8 for an overview of business intelligence and what it means to data warehousing.

Chapters 9 through 12 each describe, in detail, one major area of business intelligence (querying and reporting, analytical processing, data mining, and dashboard and scorecards, respectively). These chapters present you with ready-to-use advice about products in each of these areas.

Part IV: Data Warehousing Projects: How to Do Them Right

Knowing about data warehousing is one thing; being able to implement a data warehouse successfully is another. Part IV discusses project methodology, management techniques, the analysis of data sources, and how to work with users.

Chapter 13 describes data warehouse development (methodology) and the similarities to and differences from the methodologies you use for other types of applications.

Find out in Chapter 14 the right way to manage a data warehouse project to maximize your chances for success.

Chapters 15 through 18 each discuss an important part of a data warehouse project (compiling requirements, analyzing data sources, delivering the end solution, and working with users, respectively) and give you a lot of tips and tricks to use in each of these critical areas.

Part V: Data Warehousing: The Big Picture

This part of the book discusses the big picture: data warehousing in the context of all the other organizations and people in your IT organization (and even outside consultants) and your other information systems.

Find out in Chapter 19 how to establish an information value chain — from acquisition to internal data to the integration with external data (information about competing companies' sales of products, for example). You can also read about how to use that information in your data warehouse.

To understand how a data warehouse fits into your overall computing environment with the rest of your applications and information systems, see Chapter 20.

For an executive boardroom view of data warehousing, check out Chapter 21. Is this discipline as high a priority to the corporate bigwigs as you might imagine, considering its popularity?

For advice about what to do if you have systems already in place that are sort of (but not really) like a data warehouse, and which you use for simple querying and reporting, read Chapter 22. To replace those systems or upgrade them to a data warehouse — that is the question.

Chapter 23 describes how to deal with data warehousing product vendors and the best ways to acquire information at the numerous data warehousing trade shows.

You probably have to deal with data warehousing consultants (or maybe you are one). Chapter 24 fills you in on the tricks of the trade.

Part VI: Data Warehousing in the Not-Too-Distant Future

Every area of technology is constantly changing, and data warehousing is no exception. Because data warehousing is on the brink of a new generation of technologies, the chapters in this part of the book detail some of the most significant trends.

Data warehouses typically include only a few different types of data: numbers, dates, and character-based information (such as names, addresses, product descriptions, and codes). Chapter 25 fills you in on the next wave of data warehousing, in which unstructured data ripe with multimedia content (pictures, images, video, audio, and documents) are included as part of a data warehouse.

Chapter 26 uncovers the concepts around semantics. Semantics have begun to appear in Internet applications to enable programs and applications to surf the Web like humans do, and it's just a matter of time before this same technology invades the data warehousing and business intelligence environment.

Chapter 27 investigates collaborative technologies and the profound effect they'll have on making information ubiquitous and easily accessible in business.

Part VII: The Part of Tens

Last, but certainly not least, this part is the *For Dummies* institution: The Part of Tens. This part of the book has seven chapters chock-full of data warehousing hints and advice.

Icons Used in This Book

This icon denotes tips and tricks of the trade that make your projects go more smoothly and otherwise ease your foray into data warehousing.

Beware! This icon points out data warehousing traps, hype, and other potentially unpleasant experiences.

Data warehousing is all about computer technology. When you see this icon, the accompanying explanation digs into the underlying technology and processes, in case you want to get behind the scenes, under the hood, or beneath the covers.

The world is on the brink of a new generation of data warehousing! This icon tells you about a major trend in technology (or a way of implementing data warehousing) that you might find important soon.

Some things about data warehousing are just so darned important that they bear repeating. This icon lets you know that I'm repeating something on purpose, not because I was experiencing déjà vu.

About the Product References in This Book

(Consider this icon a test run.) In Parts II and III, I mention a number of products and list the Web sites where you can find information about them. I paraphrase the brief product descriptions from the respective vendors' Web sites, and those descriptions were up-to-date at the time this book was written. I've mentioned the products in those chapters simply as examples of products, rather than as recommendations. (How's that for a disclaimer?)

Part I
The Data Warehouse: Home for Your Data Assets

The 5th Wave   By Rich Tennant

In this part . . .

This part of the book explains, in absolutely no-hype terms, the basics of data warehousing: what a data warehouse is, where its contents come from and why, what you use it for after you build it, and options you have for choosing its level of complexity.

Chapter 1

What's in a Data Warehouse?

*I*f you gather 100 computer consultants experienced in data warehousing in a room and give them this single-question written quiz, "Define a data warehouse in 20 words or fewer," at least 95 of the consultants will turn in their paper with a one- or two-sentence definition that includes the terms *subject-oriented, time-variant,* and *read-only.* The other five consultants' replies will likely focus more on business than on technology and use a phrase such as "improve corporate decision-making through more timely access to information."

Forget all that. The following section gives you a no-nonsense definition guaranteed to be free of both technical and business-school jargon. Throughout the rest of the chapter, I assist you in better understanding data warehousing from its history and overall value to your business.

The Data Warehouse: A Place for Your Data Assets

A *data warehouse* is a home for your high-value data, or *data assets,* that originates in other corporate applications, such as the one your company uses to fill customer orders for its products, or some data source external to your company, such as a public database that contains sales information gathered from all your competitors.

If your company's data warehouse were advertised as a product for sale, it might be described this way: "Contains high-quality, refined and purified information, all of which has undergone a 25-point quality check and is offered to you with a warranty to guarantee hassle-free ownership so that you can better monitor the performance of your business."

Classifying data: What is a data asset?

Okay, I promised a definition free of technical and business-school jargon — but in the preceding section, I introduced a term (data asset) that might be considered jargon. So, I'll clarify what the term data asset means.

You can classify data that's managed within an enterprise in three groupings:

- ✔ **Run-the-business data:** Produced by corporate applications, such as the one your company uses to fill customer orders for its products or the one your company uses to manage financial transactions. The raw materials for a data warehouse.

- ✔ **Integrate-the-business data:** Built to improve the quality of and synchronize two or more corporate applications, such as a master list of customers. Data leveraged to integrate applications that weren't designed to work with each other.

- ✔ **Monitor-the-business data:** Presented to end users for reporting and decision support, such as your financial dashboard. The data is cleansed to enable users to better understand progress and evaluate cause-and-effect relationships in the data.

A *data asset* is the result of taking the raw material from the run-the-business data and producing higher-quality-data end products to integrate the business and monitor the business. Your data warehouse team should have the mission of providing high-quality data assets for enterprise use.

Manufacturing data assets

Most organizations build a data warehouse for manufactured data assets in a relatively straightforward manner, following these steps:

1. The data warehousing team (usually computer analysts and programmers) selects a *focus area,* such as tracking and reporting the company's product sales activity against that of its competitors.

2. The team in charge of building the data warehouse assigns a group of business users and other key individuals within the company to play the role of subject-matter experts.

   Together, the data warehousing team and subject-matter experts compile a list of different types of information that can enable them to use the data warehouse to help track sales activity (or whatever the focus is for the project).

3. The group then goes through the list of information (data assets), item by item, and figures out where the data warehouse can obtain that particular piece of data (raw material).

   In most cases, the group can get the data from at least one internal (within the company) database or file, such as the one that the application uses to process orders over the Internet or the master database of all customers and their current addresses. In other cases, a piece of information isn't available from within the company's computer applications, but you could obtain it by purchasing it from some other company. Although a bank doesn't have the credit ratings and total outstanding debt for all its customers internally, for example, it can purchase that information from a third party — a credit bureau.

4. After completing the details of where the business can get each piece of information, the data warehousing team creates extraction programs.

   Extraction programs collect data from various internal databases and files, copy certain data to a *staging area* (a work area outside the data warehouse), cleanse the data to ensure that the data has no errors, and then copy the higher-quality data (data assets) into the data warehouse. Extraction programs are created either by hand (custom-coded) or by using specialized data warehousing products — ETL (extract, transform, and load) tools.

You can build a successful data warehouse by spending adequate time on the first two steps in the preceding list (analyzing the need for a data warehouse and how you should use it), which makes the next two steps (designing and implementing the data warehouse to make it ready to use) much easier to perform.

Interestingly, the analysis steps (determining the focus of the data warehouse and working closely with business users to figure out what information is important) are nearly identical to the steps for any other type of computer application. Most computer applications create data as a result of a transaction or set of transactions while a particular application is being used to run the business, such as filling a customer's order. The primary difference between run-the-business applications and a data warehouse is that a data warehouse relies exclusively on data obtained from other applications and sources. Figure 1-1 shows the difference between these two types of environments.

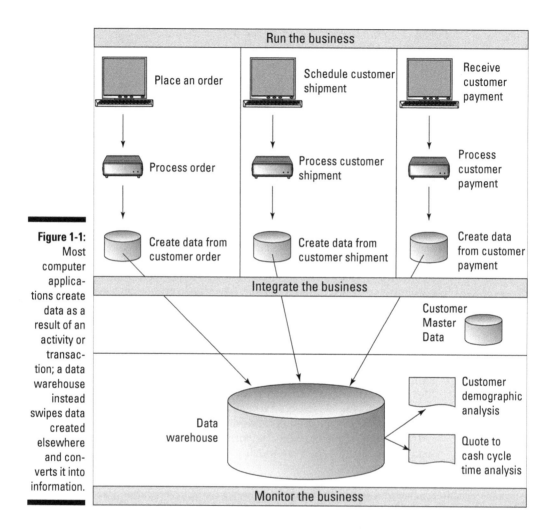

Figure 1-1: Most computer applications create data as a result of an activity or transaction; a data warehouse instead swipes data created elsewhere and converts it into information.

Data Warehousing: A Working Definition

If you cringe at the thought of defining the concept of a data warehouse and the associated project to your executive sponsors, the following sections provide a more detailed and hype-free definition and explanation that you can use to wow them.

So, what's a data warehouse? In a literal sense, it is properly described through the specific definitions of the two words that make up the term:

✔ **Data:** Facts and information about something

✔ **Warehouse:** A location or facility for storing goods and merchandise

Today's data warehousing defined

Data warehousing is the coordinated, architected, and periodic copying of data from various sources, both inside and outside the enterprise, into an environment optimized for analytical and informational processing.

The keys to this definition for computer professionals are that the data is copied *(duplicated)* in a controlled manner, and data that is copied periodically *(batch-oriented processing)*.

A broader, forward looking definition

A data warehouse system has the following characteristics:

✔ It provides centralization of corporate data assets.

✔ It's contained in a well-managed environment.

✔ It has consistent and repeatable processes defined for loading data from corporate applications.

✔ It's built on an open and scalable architecture that can handle future expansion of data.

✔ It provides tools that allow its users to effectively process the data into information without a high degree of technical support.

The information that you use to formulate decisions typically is based on data gathered from previous experiences — what works and what doesn't. Data warehouses capture similar data, allowing business leaders to make informed decisions based on previous business data — what's working in the business and what's doesn't work in the business. Executives are realizing that the only way to sustain and gain an advantage in today's economy is to better leverage information. The data warehouse provides the platform to implement, manage, and deliver these key data assets.

Data warehousing is therefore the process of creating an architected information-management solution to enable analytical and informational processing despite platform, application, organizational, and other barriers.

The key concept in this definition is that a data warehouse breaks down the barriers created by non-enterprise, process-focused applications and consolidates information into a single view for users to access.

A Brief History of Data Warehousing

Many people, when they first hear the basic principles of data warehousing — particularly copying data from one place to another — think (or even say), "That doesn't make any sense! Why waste time copying and moving data, and storing it in a different database? Why not just get it directly from its original location when someone needs it?"

To better understand the "why we do what we do" aspect of data warehousing, I outline its historical roots — how data warehousing became what it is today — in the following sections.

Before our time — the foundation

The evolution of data warehousing can trace its roots to work done prior to computers being widely available, including

- **The continuous marketing research conducted by Charles Coolidge Parlin (1872–1942).** Parlin is now recognized as the Father of Marketing Research. He did marketing research for the Curtis Publishing Company to gather information about customers and markets to help Curtis sell more advertising in their magazine, *The Saturday Evening Post.*

- **In 1923, Arthur C. Nielsen, Sr., established ACNielsen in the United States.** Arthur C. Nielsen was one of the founders of the modern marketing research industry. Among many innovations in consumer-focused marketing and media research, Mr. Nielsen created a unique retail-measurement technique that gave clients the first reliable, objective information about competitive performance and the impact of their marketing and sales programs on revenues and profits. Nielsen information gave practical meaning to the concept of market share and made it one of the critical measures of corporate performance.

These two events in history led to what we now know as data warehousing because each of them required high-quality data to formulate trends and enable business users to make decisions.

The 1970s — the preparation

The 1970s: Disco and leisure suits were in. And the computing world was dominated by the mainframe. Real data-processing applications, the ones run on the corporate mainframe, almost always had a complicated set of files or early-generation databases (not the table-oriented relational databases most applications use today) in which they stored data.

Although the applications did a fairly good job of performing routine data-processing functions, data created as a result of these functions (such as information about customers, the products they ordered, and how much money they spent) was locked away in the depths of the files and databases. It was almost impossible, for example, to see how retail stores in the eastern region were doing against stores in the western region, against their competitors, or even against their own performance in some earlier period. At best, you could have written up a report request and sent it to the data-processing department, where it was put on a waiting list with a couple thousand other report requests, and you might have had an answer in a few months — or not.

Some enterprising, forward-thinking people decided to take another approach to the data access problem. During the 1970s, while minicomputers were becoming popular, the thinking went like this: Rather than make requests to the data-processing department every time you need data from an application's files or databases, why not identify a few key data elements (for example, a customer's ID number, total units purchased in the most recent month, and total dollars spent) and have the data-processing folks copy this data to a tape each month during a slow period, such as over a weekend or during the midnight shift? You could then load the data from the tape into another file on the minicomputer, and the business users could use decision-support tools and *report writers* (products that allowed access to data without having to write separate programs) to get answers to their business questions and avoid continually bothering the data-processing department.

Although this approach worked (sort of) in helping to reduce the backlog of requests that the data-processing department had to deal with, the usefulness of the extracted and copied data usually didn't live up to the vision of the people who put the systems in place. Suppose that a company had three separate systems to handle customer sales: one for the eastern U.S. region, one for the western U.S. region, and one for all stores in Europe. Also, each of these three systems was independent from the others. Although data copied from the system that processed sales for the western U.S. region was helpful in analyzing western region activity for each month and maybe on a historical basis (if you retained previous batches of data), you couldn't easily answer questions about trends across the entire United States or the world without copying more data from each of the systems. People typically gave up because answering their questions just took too much time.

Additionally, commercial and hardware/software companies began to emerge with solutions to this problem. Between 1976 and 1979, the concept for a new company, Teradata, grew out of research at the California Institute of Technology (Caltech), driven from discussions with Citibank's advanced technology group. Founders worked to design a database management system for parallel processing with multiple microprocessors, specifically for decision support. Teradata was incorporated on July 13, 1979 and started in a garage in Brentwood, California. The name Teradata was chosen to symbolize the ability to manage *terabytes* (trillions of bytes) of data.

The 1980s — the birth

The 1980s: the era of yuppies. PCs, PCs, and more PCs suddenly appeared everywhere you looked — as well as more and more minicomputers (and even a few Macintoshes). Before anyone knew it, "real computer applications" were no longer only on mainframes; they were all over the place — everywhere you looked in an organization. The problem called *islands of data* was beginning to look ominous: How could an organization hope to compete if its data was scattered all over the place on different computer systems that weren't even all under the control of the centralized data-processing department? (Never mind that even when the data was all stored on mainframes, it was still isolated in different files and databases, so it was just as inaccessible.)

A group of enterprising, forward-thinking people came up with a new idea: Because data is located all over the place, why not create special software to enable people to make a request at a PC or terminal, such as "Show per-store sales in all worldwide regions, ranked in descending order by improvement over sales in the same period a year earlier"? This new type of software, called a *distributed database management system* (distributed DBMS, or DDBMS), would magically pull the requested data from databases across the organization, bring all the data back to the same place, and then consolidate it, sort it, and do whatever else was necessary to answer the user's question. (This process was supposed to happen pretty darned quickly.)

To make a long story short, although the concept of DDBMSs was a good one and early results from research were promising, the results were plain and simple: They just didn't work in the real world. Also, the islands-of-data problem still existed.

Meanwhile, Teradata began shipping commercial products to solve this problem. Wells Fargo Bank received the first Teradata test system in 1983, a parallel RDBMS (relational database management system) for decision support — the world's first. By 1984, Teradata released a production version of their product, and in 1986, *Fortune* magazine named Teradata Product of the Year. Teradata, still in existence today, built the first data warehousing appliance — a combination of hardware and software to solve the data warehousing needs of many. Other companies began to formulate their strategies, as well.

In 1988, Barry Devlin and Paul Murphy of IBM Ireland introduced the term *business data warehouse* as a key component of the EBIS (Europe/Middle East/Africa Business Information System). *EBIS* was defined as a comprehensive architecture aimed at providing a cross-functional business information system that's easy to use and has the flexibility to change while the business environment develops, even at a rapid rate. The flexibility and cross-functional support are a result of the relational database technology on which the EBIS system is based. When describing the business data warehouse, they articulated the need to "ease access to the data and to achieve a coherent framework for such access, it is vital that all the data reside in a single logical repository."

Additionally, Ralph Kimball founded Red Brick Systems in 1986. Red Brick began to emerge as a visionary software company by discussing how to improve data access. They were promoting a specialized relational database platform which enabled large performance gains for complex ad-hoc queries. Often, they could prove performance over ten times that of other vendor databases of the time. The key to Red Brick's technology was indexes — a software answer to Teradata's hardware-based solution. These indexes where technical solutions to the key manners in which users described the data within a data warehouse — customers, products, demographics, and so on.

In short, the 1980s were the birth place of data warehousing innovation.

The 1990s — the adolescent

During the 1990s, disco made a comeback. At the beginning of the decade, some 20 years after computing went mainstream, business computer users were still no closer to being able to use the trillions of bytes of data locked away in databases all over the place to make better business decisions.

The original group of enterprising, forward-thinking people had retired (or perhaps switched to doing Web site development). Using the time-honored concept of "something old, something new" (the "something borrowed, something blue" part doesn't quite fit), a new approach to solving the islands-of-data problem surfaced. If the 1980s approach of reaching out and accessing data directly from the files and databases didn't work, the 1990s philosophy involved going back to the 1970s method, in which data from those places was copied to another location — only doing it right this time.

And data warehousing was born.

In 1993, Bill Inmon wrote *Building the Data Warehouse* (Wiley). Many people recognize Bill as the Father of Data Warehousing. Additional publications emerged, including the 1996 book by Ralph Kimball, *The Data Warehouse Toolkit* (Wiley), which discussed general-purpose dimensional design techniques to improve the data architecture for query-centered decision support systems.

With hardware and software for data warehousing becoming common place, writings began to emerge complementing those of Inmon and Kimball. Specifically, techniques appeared that enabled those employed by Information Systems departments to better understand the trend that involved not going after data from just one place, such as a single application, but rather going after all the data you need, regardless of how many different applications and computers are used in the organization. Client/ server technology can be used to put the data on servers and give users new and improved analysis tools on their PCs.

The 2000s — the adult

In the more modern era (the 2000s, the era of reality television shows and mobile communication devices), people are more connected than ever before. Information is everywhere. New languages are being created because of texting and instant messaging. Acronyms such as TTYL (talk to you later), LOL (laughing out loud), and BRB (be right back) are commonplace. And a huge number of people provide feedback to vote people off of competitions on shows such as *American Idol* — bringing new meaning to market research and understanding what will sell. For example, in 2006, viewers cast 63 million votes for the contestants in the *American Idol* finale — which exceeded the most votes obtained by a United States president (Ronald Reagan, with 54.5 million votes). So, the world is definitely now connected!

In the world of data warehousing, the amount of data continues to grow. But, while it does, the vendor community and options have begun to consolidate. The selection pool is rapidly diminishing. In 2006, Microsoft acquired ProClarity, jumping into the data warehousing market. In 2007, Oracle purchased Hyperion, SAP acquired Business Objects, and IBM merged with Cognos. The data warehousing leaders of the 1990s have been gobbled up by some of the largest providers of information system solutions in the world.

Although the vendor community has consolidated, innovation hasn't ceased. More cost-effective solutions have emerged, led by Microsoft enabling small and mid-sized businesses to implement data warehousing solutions. Additionally, less expensive alternatives are emerging from a new set of vendors, those within the open source community, including vendors such as Pentaho and Jaspersoft. Open source business intelligence tools enable corporate application vendors to embed data warehousing solutions into their software suites. And other innovations have emerged, including data warehouse appliances from vendors such as Netezza and DATAllegro (acquired by Microsoft), and performance management appliances that enable real-time performance monitoring. These innovative solutions can also provide cost savings because they're often plug-compatible to legacy data warehouse solutions.

While time ticks by, you need to have a plan in place before you begin your data warehousing process. Know the focus of what you're trying to do and the questions you're likely to be asking. Will you be asking mostly about sales activity? If so, put plans in place for regular monthly (or weekly or even daily) extractions of data about customers, the products they buy, and the amounts of money they spend. If you work at a bank and your business focus is managing the risk across loan portfolios, for example, get information from the bank's applications that handle loan payments, delinquencies, and other data you need; then, add in data from the credit bureau about your customers' respective overall financial profiles.

Is a Bigger Data Warehouse a Better Data Warehouse?

A common misconception that many data warehouse aficionados hold is that the only good data warehouse is a big data warehouse — an enormously big data warehouse. Many people even take the stance that unless they have some astronomically large number of bytes stored, it isn't truly a data warehouse. "Five hundred gigabytes? Okay, that's a *real* data warehouse; it would be a better data warehouse, however, if it had at least a terabyte (1 trillion bytes) of data. Twenty-five gigabytes? Sorry, that's a data mart, not a data warehouse." (See Chapter 4 for a discussion of the differences between data marts and data warehouses.)

The size of a data warehouse is a characteristic — almost a by-product — of a data warehouse; it's not an objective. No one should ever set out with a mission to "build a 500-gigabyte data warehouse that contains (whatever)."

To determine the size you need for your data warehouse, follow these steps:

1. **Determine the mission, or the business objectives, of the data warehouse.**

   Ask the question, "Why bother creating this warehouse?"

2. **Determine the functionality that you want the data warehouse to have.**

   Figure out what types of questions users will ask.

3. **Determine what *contents* (types of data) the data warehouse needs to support its functionality.**

   Understand what types of answers your users will seek.

4. **Determine, based on the content volume (which is based on the functionality, which in turn is based on the mission), how big you need to make your data warehouse.**

Realizing That a Data Warehouse (Usually) Has a Historical Perspective

In almost all situations, a data warehouse has a historical perspective. Some amount of time lag occurs between the time something happens in one of the data sources (a new record is added or an existing one is modified in a corporate application, for example) and the time that the event's results are available in the data warehouse.

The reason for the time lag is that you usually bulk-load data into a data warehouse in large batches. Figure 1-2 illustrates a model of bulk-loading data.

Bulk-loading is giving way to *messaging,* the process of sending a small number of updates (perhaps only one at a time) much more frequently from the data source to a target — in this case, the data warehouse. With messaging, you have a much more up-to-date picture of your data warehouse's subject areas than you do with bulk-loading because you're putting information into an operational data store (as discussed in Chapter 20), rather than into a traditional data warehouse. Additionally, the world of service-oriented architectures (SOAs) and Web 2.0 are driving the messaging and presentation of data to near real-time in some industries. The combination of the data warehouse's historic perspective with this near-real-time sourcing of information enables business leaders to monitor the situation and make decisions at the speed of the business.

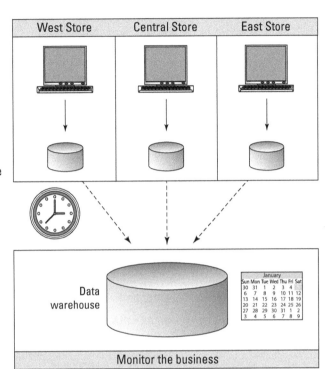

1 Orders placed during store hours (9-5)

2 Data for each transaction (order) is stored in the application database

3 All transactions (orders) for the data are sent to the data warehouse at midnight; and purges transactions older than 30 days

4 The data warehouse retains historical data (it doesn't delete it)

Figure 1-2: Because you bulk-load data into a data warehouse, the time delay gives you a historical perspective.

It's Data Warehouse, Not Data Dump

An often-heard argument about what should be stored in a data warehouse goes something like this: "If I have to take the trouble to pull out data from all these different applications, why not just get as much as I possibly can? If I don't get everything, or as much as possible, I won't be able to ask all the business questions I might want to."

In a commonly related story about knowledge gained from a successful data warehouse implementation, a grocery-store chain discovered an unusually high correlation of disposable baby diapers and beer sales during a two- or three-hour period early every Friday evening and found out that a significant number of people on their way home from work were buying both these items. The store then began stocking display shelves with beer and disposable diapers next to one another, and sales increased significantly.

Although I don't know whether this story is true (it certainly has been told often enough), I believe that it confuses the issue when you have to figure out what should — and should not — be in your data warehouse. The moral of this story is usually mistaken as, "Put as much data as possible in the warehouse." In reality, the data warehouse just described was probably one that focused exclusively on sales activity. Remember that although disposable diapers and beer are dramatically different products, they're both members of the same *type* of data (retail products).

The following example emphasizes why you should be selective about what goes in your data warehouse and not just assume that you have to get every possible type of data from all the sources, just in case you want to ask your data warehouse any question.

Suppose that you're creating a data warehouse for a cruise ship company. As shown in Figure 1-3, the Tucson Desert Cruise Ship Company (its motto is "Who needs an ocean?") uses four applications that handle different tasks:

✔ Reservations and cancellations

✔ Food-and-beverage service for all cruises

✔ All trip itineraries and after-the-fact information about the weather, unusual events, and all onboard entertainment scheduling

✔ All crew assignments

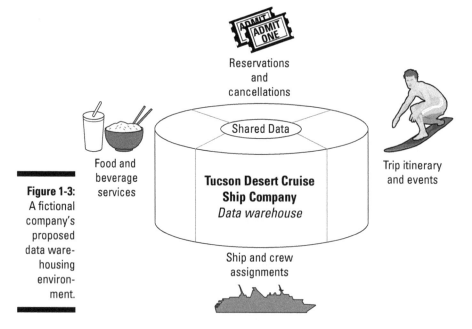

Figure 1-3: A fictional company's proposed data warehousing environment.

Reservations and cancellations

Shared Data

Food and beverage services

Tucson Desert Cruise Ship Company *Data warehouse*

Trip itinerary and events

Ship and crew assignments

Figure 1-4 shows one possible environment for your data warehouse if you pursue the philosophy of "Go get everything you possibly can," or what I call the *data dump* approach.

By having the information shown in Figure 1-4 in your data warehouse, you — and every other person who uses the warehouse — can ask questions and make report requests, such as "What's the average number of room-service vegetarian meals ordered by passengers who were on their third cruise with Captain Grumby in command and in which a half-day stop was made in Grand Cayman when its temperature was between 75 and 80 degrees?"

Asking this type of question doesn't have any real business value, however. Assuming that you receive an answer to the question, what can you do with that information to have a positive business effect?

For some types of data, you can analyze, analyze, and analyze some more — and still find out little of value that could positively affect your business. Although you can put this data in your warehouse, you probably won't get much for your trouble. Other types of data, though, have significant value unavailable until placed in the data warehouse. Concentrate on the latter, and ignore the former!

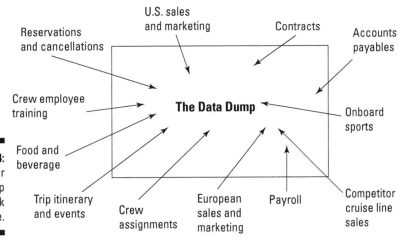

Figure 1-4: What your data dump can look like.

Chapter 2

What Should You Expect from Your Data Warehouse?

In This Chapter

▶ Making business decisions based on facts, not intuition

▶ Realizing the value of "data at your fingertips"

▶ Looking at cross-organization communications and your data warehouse

▶ Changing your business because of insights from data warehouse information

*A*ll too often, the members of a data warehouse development team proudly unveil their creation, get a few "oohs" and "aahs" from their user community, and then find out that "if you build it, they won't necessarily come." The data warehouse just sits there, quietly being restocked every week or every month, and supporting only a few random user information requests until plans eventually are drafted for its replacement.

You can avoid many, or perhaps most, of these unfortunate situations if everyone, from the executive sponsors to the technicians and developers, focuses their efforts on a single question: "What do you do with a data warehouse?"

The contents of the warehouse (the data) aren't important; rather, how the data is used in everyday business life is what makes the warehouse really useful.

Using the Data Warehouse to Make Better Business Decisions

Suppose that John is a district manager at MegaRetroMania, Ltd., a national chain of video-rental stores that specializes in movies from the 1950s and earlier. Mary is John's counterpart in another district. Both excitedly awaited the rollout of MegaRetroMania's brand-new data warehouse, an event that finally occurred a month ago. John and Mary both attended the data warehousing orientation class in which they figured out how to run reports and make information requests by using the contents of the warehouse. Each person received a handsome, ready-for-framing certificate indicating successful completion of the course.

On July 20, the day after June's results had been finalized and loaded into the data warehouse, John sits down at his PC, clicks the icon that enables him to access the data warehouse, and makes this request:

> Show me, for all my stores, a breakdown of second-quarter sales compared to first-quarter sales, each store's second-quarter sales from a year earlier, and the sales of all competitors within two square miles of each store's location.

While John watches the little "Working, please wait" hourglass icon twirl for a few seconds on-screen, he thinks, "It's fascinating how they can make it seem like the sand is really sifting from top to bottom like that." After the results of his request are displayed on-screen, he prints the report, walks over to the printer to retrieve the five printed pages, flips through them for a few moments, and then thinks, "That's really neat!"

Then he slips the report into the middle drawer on the left side of his desk before leaving for lunch.

And he never looks at it again.

Mary runs the same identical report for her district; after printing the report and flipping through the pages, however, she (unlike John) has a pen in hand and circles one number, underlines another, and writes "Uh-oh!" next to the line containing information for a store that she knows is having problems.

Then, Mary returns to her desk, report in hand, and picks up the telephone. First, she calls her problem-child store and, after the manager comes to the phone, spends the next half hour making follow-on information requests from the data warehouse, discussing the result of each request with the store manager, and considering various options, such as sales promotions.

After Mary takes her regular two-mile lunchtime walk, she calls the manager of another store in Madison County, Iowa, whose second-quarter sales were relatively flat after experiencing at least 15-percent growth every quarter for the past three years (a fact she obtained from the data warehouse when she noted the lack of growth in the second quarter). While the store manager is on the phone, Mary gets a week-by-week sales breakdown from the warehouse, which shows that the first three weeks of the quarter had been fairly good, with sales during each week slightly ahead of the preceding one. During the fourth week of April, however, a large dip occurred, followed by an even larger dip the following week and yet another drop the week after that (the worst week any store had ever had, it turns out, in the long, distinguished history of MegaRetroMania) before sales began picking up in mid-May.

Suddenly, the store manager has an idea — maybe the Olympic Games were causing the problem! The Olympics had been held in Madison County for the first time ever, and *everyone* had attended. Even that store's primary customer base, the legions of photographers who usually come to Madison County to take pictures of covered bridges during a four-day period and rent movies to watch in their motel rooms at night, were preoccupied for those three weeks by the Olympics.

Satisfied that no burgeoning problem is waiting in the Madison County store — just a once-in-a-lifetime anomaly, most likely — Mary turns her attention to the other annotations on her printout. By the end of the day, five stores have action plans in place for special promotional campaigns to combat competition that's opened in the past few months near those MegaRetroMania locations.

Here's a quiz. True or false: Mary and John both used the data warehouse today.

The answer: False.

You might be thinking, "What? Of course John used the data warehouse today. He ran a report and looked it over."

Although John accessed the data warehouse, he didn't use it. He looked over a printout and stuffed it away forever, and then returned to business as usual. When you compare his action to Mary's, the differences are obvious. No matter what else appears on a data warehousing project's mission statement, and no matter what the project's sponsors say to convey the project's merits to the people who control funding, the primary purpose of a data warehouse is to help people make better business decisions. Data warehousing isn't about simply accessing data and then doing nothing with it; it's about *really using* data.

Here's one way to make sure that data warehouse users act more like Mary than John: When you conduct training sessions before you turn users loose on the new data warehouse, explain to them not only how to access data (which types of queries and reports they can run or which types of data are available, for example), but also include real-world examples of how to use the results of their warehouse access.

The training session for MegaRetroMania district managers (and other warehouse users), for example, might feature end-to-end hands-on training that explains how to get sales reports and what the reports look like. To make sure that users understand the usefulness of the data warehouse, the instruction could also feature role-playing or some other type of training in what to do with those reports to improve the stores' performances.

Finding Data at Your Fingertips

Everyone has heard the phrase "information (or knowledge) is power," and the more skillfully people use information in the course of their jobs, the greater their chances for success.

The process of gathering data from many different sources (if you can even get the data at all) has traditionally been tedious, particularly before computers became commonplace — and it has remained that way during the information age. Some novels and movies would have you believe that after you press just a few keys, you can automatically access vast amounts of data from anywhere in the world, regardless of the platform you're using, the structure of the data (how it's organized), or how the data is encoded or keyed.

The real world isn't quite that orderly, and anyone who has struggled to perform what should be simple tasks (merging Pacific Rim sales data from one system with North American sales data from another, for example) is probably aware of the difficulties.

Suppose that Steve is a district sales manager at BlackAndWhiteVideos, Inc., MegaRetroMania's upstart archrival. Unlike John and Mary, though, Steve has no data warehouse from which to make requests, such as "Show me the top 20 BlackAndWhiteVideo stores across the district in which monthly total comedy video rentals are at least double those of action videos so that I can adjust the inventory accordingly." Instead, Steve has to get the answer to this question the old-fashioned way, as shown in Figure 2-1, by following these steps:

1. He writes and distributes to all store managers in the district an e-mail stating that he wants a report sent to him no later than the fifth day of each month of rental dollars by category (such as comedy, action, and romances), based on transaction records from each store's point-of-sale (POS) computer system.

2. On the fifth day of each month, he looks through the reports received and notes each store from which he hasn't received a report.

3. He spends most of the next two days calling store managers who haven't sent reports and hearing something like, "Oh, wow, I totally forgot all about that; what do you want me to send you again?"

4. While waiting for each of the missing reports, he begins entering into a spreadsheet the numbers from the reports received so far.

   Each month, it occurs to Steve that he should send a new e-mail asking managers to e-mail him a disk with each store's data on it (already in spreadsheet format) so that he doesn't have to reenter the information. He never quite gets around to that request because he assumes that it takes several months to train someone in each store to be able to extract data from the POS application into a spreadsheet.

5. By the 12th of each month, he makes another round of phone calls to the stores that still haven't submitted their reports, and this time threatens to — well, you get the idea.

6. Finally, by the 20th of each month, after the spreadsheet program has all the necessary information, he runs a few simple sorting routines to get the necessary reports.

7. And he prepares to start all over for the next month's data.

Figure 2-1:
Without a data warehouse, data isn't at a user's fingertips — it's usually out of reach!

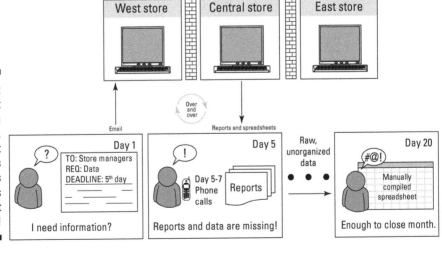

I have four questions about Mary at MegaRetroMania and Steve at BlackAndWhiteVideos (forget about John at MegaRetroMania — he's a loser):

✔ Who's making more effective use of technology?

✔ Who's likely to be more productive in a district manager's role?

✔ Who'll likely make more timely business decisions with (using business-school talk) a more positive impact on short-term and long-term revenues (top line) and profit (bottom line)?

✔ Who's more likely to be frustrated and look for another job that involves much less wasted time?

(Answers: Mary, Mary, Mary, Steve)

Both Mary and Steve *could* have access to the same information and in the same way because both MegaRetroMania and BlackAndWhiteVideos have similar computer systems with similar data. The difference is that because MegaRetroMania has invested in data warehousing technology, Mary and her counterparts (even that loser John, if he would only get with the program) can make information-based and timely business decisions.

Here are two more questions to consider:

✔ Does your current job more closely resemble Steve's or Mary's in how you're able to get access to information you need?

✔ Based on how you answered the first question, would you rather have a job more like the other's?

Facilitating Communications with Data Warehousing

A benefit of data warehousing that's much less tangible than having information for better business decisions is that data warehousing often facilitates better communications across a company than what existed before the warehouse project began:

✔ The information technology (IT) organization — the organization that handles infrastructure (hardware and software platforms, networking, and communications, for example) — begins working more cooperatively with its customers in the business organizations.

✔ Business organizations that are drawn together as part of a data warehousing project often gain more appreciation for each other's missions and challenges.

Part of the better communications picture occurs (usually) between applications development and customers in the organization's business units.

Data warehousing can promote increased levels of communication across different business units.

IT-to-business organization communications

If you're a veteran of an IT-organization-versus-business-organization war in your company, you might have won some battles and lost others. Make no mistake about it, though: The other side is the enemy!

If you're on the IT side, you might grumble about these issues:

✔ Business users make unrealistic requests for new applications and enhancements to existing applications.

✔ Users don't participate during application development and testing.

✔ Users are so technology-challenged that they require hand-holding for the simplest application functions.

On the other side, business users commonly make these types of complaints:

✔ IT application developers have no idea about how the company's business is run and usually don't even bother to ask.

✔ Developers just put whatever features they want into the applications, regardless of whether those features are applicable to the business processes.

✔ IT is too slow in responding to requests for support.

Since the early 1980s, when the then-new personal computer and local-area network permitted business organizations to take direct responsibility for part of their information management and application capabilities, many companies have experienced an era of mistrust and lack of communications between IT and business. This level of mistrust has continued to grow with the proliferation of business productivity tools such as Microsoft Excel — enabling users to formulate their own solutions without IT. And the war within IT has also grown with the concept of Central IT, which manages the shared services within IT, and Line of Business (LOB) IT, which is closer to the business customer and manages his or her specific applications. Often, the data warehouse is managed by Central IT, which *isn't allowed to talk with the business* — people from Central IT can talk only to the LOB IT personnel. Talk about dysfunctional!

Data warehousing projects often give organizations a chance to mend the rift between IT and business users, as well as LOB IT and Central IT. The nature of data warehousing (for example, the focus on business questions and the data necessary to answer those questions) gives people from both sides an opportunity to better understand the other group's roles and concerns.

Increased IT-business organization communications often leads to more effective and efficient working relationships because everyone develops a degree of trust. A successful project or two usually can do wonders in achieving increased cooperation.

You don't necessarily get better communications between IT and business organizations just because they jointly embark on a data warehousing effort. For example, if you use the word "dysfunctional" to describe the relationship between IT and the business community in your company, you might want to look at some team-building workshops or other remedial training before proceeding with a data warehousing project.

Communications across business organizations

Data warehousing involves, in many ways, the use of technology to break down barriers that are inherent in large companies, such as different computer systems performing similar functions for different groups of users, or different databases with information that would be better kept in a single database. A sales-and-marketing organization responsible for one of its company's products naturally wants to help integrate its data (performance results) with that of another sales-and-marketing organization, responsible for a different product, that uses a different computer system (maybe because of a corporate acquisition), right?

Corporate intrigue and turf wars are the hallmark of business. Business executives and their staff members usually think of information not as a *corporate* strategic asset, but rather as a *personal* one.

TIP

The breaking-through-barriers nature of data warehousing usually takes a top-level mandate from a chief executive officer (CEO) or chief operating officer (COO): "Thou shalt all cooperate, or thou shalt look for another job." That type of mandate is probably a corporation's best chance for overcoming detrimental corporate politics.

Suppose that you're a senior company executive at a consumer products company, and that company has an environment that looks like the one shown in Figure 2-2. You decide that you want to dedicate a large part of your capital budget to enable your managers and analysts to get timely access to data so that they can make better business decisions. Implementing a data warehouse would move the data from the separate division's product sales applications into one central location for the users to access.

Using the cooperate-or-else mandate, you can ask — and receive answers to — the barrier-busting questions that present you with a consolidated picture of your sales, regardless of how many source systems the data come from. In addition, after the first successful collaborative, cross-organization data warehousing effort, people probably feel less territorial and work more closely together for the common good of the company.

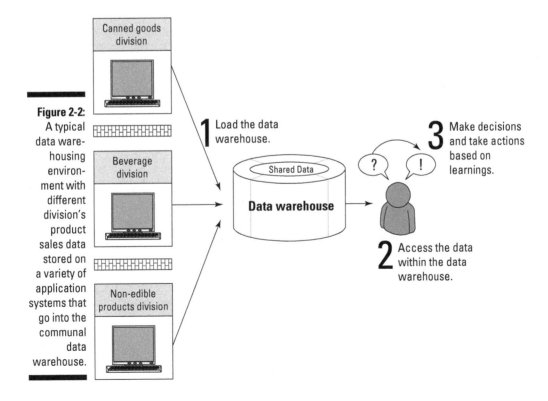

Figure 2-2: A typical data warehousing environment with different division's product sales data stored on a variety of application systems that go into the communal data warehouse.

Canned goods division

Beverage division

Non-edible products division

1 Load the data warehouse.

Shared Data

Data warehouse

2 Access the data within the data warehouse.

3 Make decisions and take actions based on learnings.

Or they might not. Any lack of cooperation on the part of the leaders and members of a particular business organization, however, becomes extremely apparent because their data either aren't in the warehouse (often called a *data gap*) or, worse, the data warehouse project fails — and you can easily tell who's at fault, the data gap owner.

I don't mean to imply that you need to make finger-pointing and blame-casting a part of your data warehousing project; rather, you should implement, from the beginning, a clear directive for cooperating with peers that everyone has to follow.

Facilitating Business Change with Data Warehousing

Data warehousing involves facilitating change in business processes. In addition to being able to make better, information-driven operational and tactical decisions, you gain insight into key areas that can help you make strategic decisions about the fundamental aspects of your business.

Your data warehouse can act as an early-warning system to let you know that you might need to make some major business changes. Imagine that it's 2000 and you just got into the video-rental business. You're the part owner and purchasing manager for a regional chain of retail stores that rents digital video discs (DVDs) and video games, and sells compact discs (CDs). If you had a data warehouse that gathered information from the point-of-sale computers in all your stores and external data about your competitors' sales activity (purchased from an external source), you probably would have noticed a couple of interesting trends when you looked at product revenues over time:

- Sales of music in their historically popular CD format have dropped off remarkably. Because your competitors' sales for those items are also way off, you might decide that you don't need to devote the shelf space to stock these types of items anymore.

- Video games for Playstation 2 (PS2) are rented much more frequently than the same games in Dreamcast format. Because the video game business is rapidly evolving (remember, it's 2000), your rental numbers might be declaring PS2 the winner of the next-generation gaming consoles and that the Dreamcast games are another item probably not worth ordering and putting on the shelves.

Both these decisions are, for the most part, tactical because they involve product-stocking decisions. Neither decision fundamentally changes the way your company does business, but rather helps you decide which products you want to keep in stock.

But suppose that trend-line information coming back from the data warehouse shows relatively flat sales of all types of music and dramatically increasing revenues from DVD and video game rentals. The future of your chain might lie not in sales of music at all, but rather in DVD and video game rentals. Rather than have to rely on a gut feeling, you can make data-driven strategic decisions about how your business should change.

Imagine having to make the same type of decision in 2008 if you're in the automotive business. Gas guzzler sales are plummeting as fast as the price of gas is increasing. While worldwide demand for oil grows, the supply and demand curve isn't friendly to traditional car sales. The highly positive growth curve that sport utility vehicles (SUVs) had a few years ago is giving way to the hybrid and green products. Again, your data warehouse gives you the information to make data-based decisions, rather than have to rely on hunches or, at best, bits and pieces of data gathered from various computer systems.

Chapter 3

Have It Your Way: The Structure of a Data Warehouse

In This Chapter

▶ Constructing your data warehouse to fit your business needs

▶ Understanding the different data warehouse architectures

▶ Deciding whether to make your data warehouse centralized or distributed

*A*lthough I generally dislike trite sayings, I have to make an exception: "No two data warehouse implementations are exactly alike."

One of the worst data warehousing mistakes you can make is to try to force your business analysis and reporting needs to fit into an environment that you copied from somewhere else. Although a certain amount of analysis is standard across companies, the interpretation and actions you formulate from your data assets can give you a competitive edge in the global marketplace.

Leverage the knowledge and experience of other people by studying their experiences with data warehousing products; asking questions about the most difficult problems they encountered during product development and after they put their data warehouse into use; and determining how effective their users have been in making better, information-based business decisions.

Don't automatically assume, however, that every aspect of someone else's data warehousing environment is exactly right for you.

Ensuring That Your Implementations Are Unique

A data warehouse is composed of many different components, each of which can be implemented in several (perhaps many) ways. These components include

✔ The breadth; the number of different subjects and focus points, for example, or the number of different functional or regional organizations that will use it

✔ The number of sources that will provide raw data

✔ The means by which data is moved from source applications and loaded into the data warehouse

✔ The business rules applied to the raw source data to produce high quality data assets

✔ The target databases in which data assets are stored

✔ The data assets; the elements, the level of detail in each element, and how much history is being maintained, for example

✔ The business intelligence, front-end tool used to access the data assets

✔ The overall architectural complexity of the environment

No two data warehouse implementations (neither the implementations now in existence nor all those to be completed in the future) will be identical in all the preceding eight categories.

Two companies in the same industry, for example, each might have a sales-and-marketing data warehouse that supports 300 users across four different business organizations, allows access by using the same business intelligence tool set, and uses the same database management system in which to store approximately 50 gigabytes of data.

The two companies probably have these differences, however:

✔ Different data sources, unique to each company

✔ Different data, as a result of the different sources; for example, reference data that defines stages in the sales and qualification process

✔ The use of different source-to-warehouse movement techniques — for example, business rules for forecasting future revenue

Because of these differences, trying to adapt another company's data warehousing solution in its entirety would be a big mistake. (Or, like your schoolteachers used to tell you, "Do your own work — no copying!")

Classifying the Data Warehouse

Although you must ensure that your data warehouse fits your own unique needs, some guidelines can help you determine the probable complexity of its environment and structure. I use a three-tier classification for planning a data warehouse. By determining a likely category for an implementation, I have — early in the project — some specific guidelines for the project's complexity, development schedule, and cost.

Here are my classifications:

- ✔ **Data warehouse lite:** A relatively straightforward implementation of a modest scope (often, for a small user group or team) in which you don't go out on any technological limbs; almost a low-tech implementation

- ✔ **Data warehouse deluxe:** A standard data warehouse implementation that uses advanced technologies to solve complex business information and analytical needs across a broader user population

- ✔ **Data warehouse supreme:** A data warehouse that has large-scale data distribution and advanced technologies that can integrate various "run the business" systems, improving the overall quality of the data assets across business information analytical needs and transactional needs

Each of these classifications of data warehouses implements various aspects of an overall data warehousing architecture, as shown in Figure 3-1.

This architecture assures that your data warehouse meets your user's information requirements and focuses on the following business organization and technical-architecture presentation components:

- ✔ **Subject area and data content:** The content of a data warehouse is grouped by subject areas. A *subject area* is a high-level grouping of data content that relates to a major area of business interests, such as customers, products, sales orders, and contracts. Subject area and data content will drive your user access to this data and the associated presentation through business intelligence tools.

- ✔ **Data source:** Data sources are very similar to raw materials that support the creation of finished goods in manufacturing. Your data sources are the raw materials that are refined and manufactured into the subject area's data content. Depending on the class of data warehouse you're building, you might have more comprehensive data sources — all dependent on the business user's requirements.

- ✔ **Business intelligence tools:** The user's requirements for information access dictate the type of business intelligence tool deployed for your data warehouse. Some users require only simple querying or reporting on the data content within a subject area; others might require sophisticated analytics. These data access requirements assist in classifying your data warehouse.

Data Warehouse

	Lite	Deluxe	Supreme
Scope	Personal departmental scope with minimal investment for specific purpose and smaller segment of the business	Line of Business through enterprise scope with mid-sized investment to assist in integrating the business	Enterprise scope with large multi-year investment to drive strategy and integrate various aspects of the business incorporating internal and external user populations

Technology

	Lite	Deluxe	Supreme
Visualization	Managed reporting and business analysis	Business Intelligence suite (query, reporting, business analysis, dashboards, scorecards)	Business Intelligence suite + (query, reporting, business analysis, dashboards, scorecards) along with intelligent agents
User Access	1 to 2 subject areas	1 to 25 subject areas	Unlimited access to internal and external data
Target Data Structures	Small OLAP cubes (MDB) and/or relational database	Multi-tiered data layer including operational data store, data warehouse supreme feeding data warehouse deluxe and lite	Federated Query layer along with traditional data stores including structured and unstructured data
Data Quality & Movement	File transfer with simple business rules to extract, transformation, and load (ETL) tools	Extract, transform, and load (ETL) tool with data quality tools for complex rules like house holding	Extract, transform, and load (ETL) tools along with federated query middleware
Sources	1 to 25 sources	25 to 100 sources	Unlimited sources

Figure 3-1: You can classify a data warehouse by these features.

✔ **Database:** The database refers to the technology of choice leveraged to manage the data content within a set of target data structures. Depending on the class of data warehouse, a personal, departmental, or enterprise database management system may be required.

✔ **Data integration:** *Data integration* is a broad classification for the extraction, movement, transformation, and loading of data from the data's source into the target database. This is where the business rules are put to action to assure that the data content is of the highest possible quality for broad user adoption.

The data warehouse lite

A data warehouse lite is a no-frills, bare-bones, low-tech approach to providing data that can help with some of your business decision-making. No-frills means that you put together, wherever possible, proven capabilities and tools already within your organization to build your system.

The term *data mart* is commonly used to refer to what I call the data warehouse lite. A data mart (as described in Chapter 4) should be, in its purest sense, an environment that receives a portion of a data warehouse's content, providing easier access to this information subset for a select group of users. As often happens in information technology (IT) areas in which vendors jockey for market share, however, many people now think of a data mart as little more than a small-scale data warehousing environment.

Don't be confused by the terminology! I prefer my lite-deluxe-supreme classification because it's easy to remember and helps me visualize the complexity of the environment I'm setting out to build. When I discuss project opportunities with clients, however, and they mention that they want to build a data mart, they're usually referring to what I call a data warehouse lite. The wording doesn't really matter because all these definitions are continually being revised anyway. If you concentrate on the aspects of the environment that drive the overall complexity of the implementation — breadth, database, data content, tools, extraction and movement, and architecture — you can avoid getting confused.

Subject areas and data content

A data warehouse lite is focused on the reporting or analysis of only one or possibly two subject areas. Suppose that in your job at a wireless division of a telephone company, you analyze the sales of services such as in-network minutes, out-of-network minutes, text messaging, Internet access, and other mobile usage to consumer households. If you build a data warehouse lite exclusively for this purpose, you have all the necessary information to support your analysis and reporting for the consumer market. You don't have any information about business users' and payment history, however, because that information is part of a different subject area, as shown in Figure 3-2.

Based on the subject area limitation, a data warehouse lite has just enough data content to satisfy the primary purpose of the environment, but not enough for many unstructured what-if scenarios its users might create. You must choose carefully, therefore, from among the set of all possible data elements and select a manageable subset — elements that, without a doubt, are important to have. This process is the same for any data warehouse implementation, except that you must be extremely disciplined when you're making decisions about what content to include.

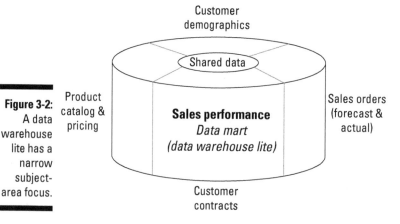

Figure 3-2:
A data
warehouse
lite has a
narrow
subject-
area focus.

Use standard reports, particularly those that currently require a great deal of manual preparation, as one of your primary guides to determine data content in a data warehouse lite.

Data sources

A data warehouse lite has a limited set of data sources — typically, one to a handful. As part of an overall single-application environment, for example, the data warehouse lite acts as the restructuring agent for the application's data to make it more query- and report-friendly.

The most common means of restructuring a single application's data is to denormalize the contents of the application's relational database tables to eliminate as many *relational join operations* (the process of bringing together data from more than one database table) as possible when users run reports or do simple querying. Denormalization is the opposite of the relational database concept of normalization, a somewhat complex set of guidelines that tells you which data elements should be in which tables in a database (see Chapter 5). For purposes of data warehousing, denormalization is the important concept to understand, and, fortunately, it's a simple one. When you *denormalize* a database, you don't worry about duplicated data; you try to create rows of data in a single table that most likely mirrors the reports and queries that users run. Figure 3-3 shows an example of a single-source data warehouse lite built on denormalization.

Although you can use externally provided data (see Chapter 19) in a data warehouse lite implementation, the data you use is rarely newly acquired. You're more likely to incorporate data that you already use for analysis (perhaps in a stand-alone manner).

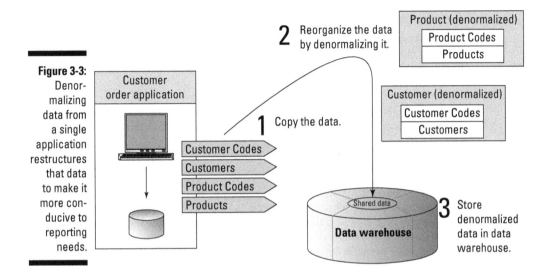

Figure 3-3: Denormalizing data from a single application restructures that data to make it more conducive to reporting needs.

Business intelligence tools

The users of a data warehouse lite usually ask questions and create reports that reflect a "Tell me what happened" perspective, as described in Chapter 9. Because those users don't do much heavy-duty analytical processing, the products they use to access the data warehouse should be easy for them to use. Although some power users might use more advanced tools to access the data warehouse for more complicated processing, they're a minority of the user community.

Database

Data warehouse lite solutions are limited by users, data content, and the type of business intelligence tools utilized. These limitations are the primary reason that a data warehouse lite is usually built on a standard, general-purpose relational database management system (you can find out about RDBMSs in Chapter 5). Your organization's general familiarity with RDBMSs, particularly the easy-to-use structure built around tables and columns, can help users easily access the managed data content. In some situations, though, a multidimensional database (MDB) is used, as described in Chapter 6, because of your users' knowledge of the data content and their need or desire to analyze more than to report.

For a data warehouse lite implementation, you can use either a general-purpose RDBMS or MDB product. Because of relatively modest data volumes and the narrow subject-area focus, you probably don't have to worry about technical barriers that might drive your database platform decision one way or the other.

Data extraction, movement, and loading

Simplicity is the name of the game in a data warehouse lite. Therefore, make the process of extracting data from sources and performing all the functions necessary to prepare that data for loading as straightforward as possible by using these two elements:

✔ Simple file extracts from the run-the-business systems and file transfers that allow you to move data from its sources to the data warehouse lite

✔ Straightforward custom code (or perhaps an easy-to-use tool) that can extract and move the data

If the data source for your data warehouse lite is built on a relational database and you're planning to use the same database product for your data warehouse, use SQL to easily handle data extraction and movement. These steps — as shown in Figure 3-4 (they're easier to understand than SQL code!) — provide a standard procedure for this process (you'll want to tailor these steps to your particular environment, of course):

1. **On the system that houses your warehouse, use the SQL CREATE TABLE statement to create the definition for each table in your data warehouse lite.**

2. **Create a database backup that contains copies of all tables from the source that provide data to the warehouse, and then reload those tables into a staging area on the system where you plan to locate your data warehouse.**

   You should ensure that the network bandwidth and time window are adequate to copy all the source tables to the system by using a file-transfer program.

3. **Use the SQL INSERT statement, with a nested SELECT statement specifying the source tables and their respective columns that will populate the data warehouse table (and how the tables will be joined), to load the data into your data warehouse lite.**

4. **Run a series of quality assurance (QA) routines to verify that all data has been loaded properly.**

   Check row counts, numeric totals, and whatever else you can.

Architecture

The architecture of a data warehouse lite is composed of the database used to store the data, the front-end business intelligence tools used to access the data, the way the data is moved, and the number of subject areas. The watchword of this environment is minimalist: no bells, no whistles, nothing fancy — just enough technology applied to the environment to give users access to data they need.

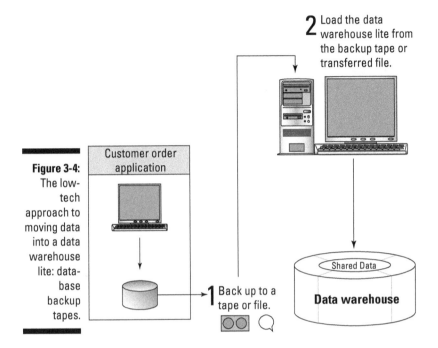

2 Load the data warehouse lite from the backup tape or transferred file.

Customer order application

1 Back up to a tape or file.

Shared Data

Data warehouse

Figure 3-4: The low-tech approach to moving data into a data warehouse lite: database backup tapes.

The architecture of a data warehouse lite, as shown in Figure 3-5, contains these major component types:

- A single database contains the warehouse's data.
- That database is fed directly from each of the sources providing data to the warehouse.
- Users access data directly from the warehouse.

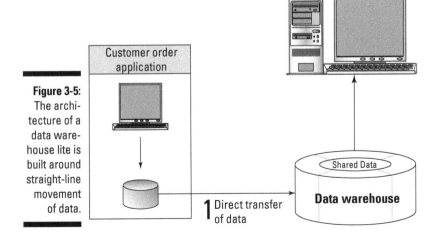

Customer order application

Shared Data

Data warehouse

1 Direct transfer of data

Figure 3-5: The architecture of a data warehouse lite is built around straight-line movement of data.

The data warehouse deluxe

You'll most likely focus most of your data warehousing-related activities on the data warehouse deluxe environment, as shown in Figure 3-6. Data from many different sources converge in these "real" data warehouses, which make available a wealth of architectural options that you can tailor to meet your specific needs.

Data warehouse deluxe:
Broadening the horizon

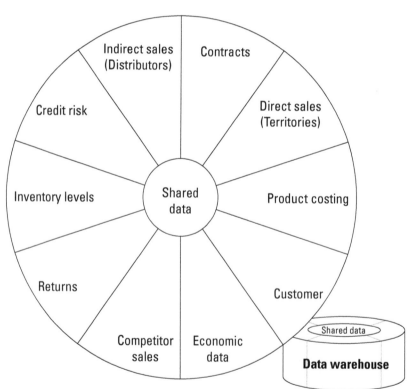

Figure 3-6:
A data warehouse deluxe has a broader subject-area focus than a data warehouse lite.

Subject areas and data content

A data warehouse deluxe contains a broad range of related subject areas — everything (or most things) that would follow a natural way of thinking about and analyzing information.

In a data-warehouse-deluxe version of the telephone-company example I give in the "Subject areas and data content" section of the data warehouse lite description, earlier in this chapter, you likely find not only the subject area of consumer wireless services (among other items), but also these elements:

- Consumer basic calling revenues and volumes
- Consumer long-distance calling revenues and volumes
- Consumer wireless calling revenues and volumes
- Business wireless services
- Business basic calling revenues and volumes
- Business long-distance calling revenues and volumes
- Business wireless calling revenues and volumes
- Internet access (DSL) services
- Internet revenues and volumes

The subject range is broader than a data warehouse lite for a data warehouse deluxe because

- The user base is broader (more organizations have their people use the data warehouse).
- The scope of any given user's queries and reports is broader than just one or two subject areas. For example, a user might run reports comparing trends in add-on services for businesses and consumers to see where to concentrate future sales-and-marketing efforts.

When you implement a data warehouse deluxe, you almost always need access capabilities (unlike with a data warehouse lite), in addition to simple results reporting. Therefore, although you might be able to use standard reports as a starting point when you're deciding what should be in your warehouse, that's rarely enough. Follow these steps to thoroughly understand your source systems:

1. **Take a complete inventory of available information.**

   This inventory is called a *source systems analysis,* as discussed in Chapter 16.

2. **Review each candidate source element and answer these questions:**

   - What data do you need to include in the data warehouse and what should you leave out?

- What information should be summarized and what should be left at the detailed level?

- What data should remain in the data warehouse forever, and what data should you purge from the data warehouse after it has aged?

- What else do you need to know about the data before you put it in your data warehouse?

This step is one of the most severe tests of how well the IT people and business users get along throughout the data warehousing project.

Data sources

You won't be lucky enough to find any single-source environments when you're building a data warehouse deluxe.

Now, you have a whole new set of — I have to use the word — problems that you must deal with, including the ones in this list:

- ✔ **Different encodings for similar information:** Different sets of customer numbers come from different sources, for example.

- ✔ **Data integrity problems across multiple sources:** The information in one source is different from the information in another when they should be the same.

- ✔ **Different source platforms:** As an example, an IBM mainframe that has DB2/MVS databases might contain the data in one of the sources, another IBM mainframe that has VSAM files might have another set of source data, a set of servers might contain data within Oracle databases, and the rest of the source data might all be stored in SQL Server databases on Windows servers.

Although the exact number of data sources depends on the specifics of your implementation, data warehouse deluxes tend to have an average of eight to ten applications and external databases that provide data to the warehouse.

Business intelligence tools

The broad range of subject areas and the wealth of data in a data warehouse deluxe means that you usually have several different ways of looking at that warehouse's contents. This list shows the different ways that you can use a data warehouse (Part III discusses them in-depth):

✔ **Simple reporting and querying:** Like with data warehouse lite, the purpose of the warehouse deluxe is to "Tell me what happened."

✔ **Business analysis:** You use the warehouse to "Tell me what happened — and why."

✔ **Dashboards and scorecards:** In this model, a variety of information is gathered from the data warehouse and that information is made available to users who don't want to mess around with the data warehouse — they want to see snapshots of many different things. Its purpose is to "Tell me a lot of things, but don't make me work too hard to get the answers I want."

✔ **Data mining or statistical analysis:** In this area, statistical, artificial intelligence, and related techniques are used to mine through large volumes of data and provide knowledge without users even having to ask specific questions. Its purpose is to "Tell me something interesting, even though I don't know what questions to ask, and also tell me what might happen."

You're likely to employ at least three — and perhaps all four — of these types of data warehouse user-access techniques when you use a data warehouse deluxe. Although tool vendors increasingly try to provide suites of products to handle as many of these different functions as possible, you do have to deal with different products — and so does your user community.

Don't assume that you can simply select a single vendor whose products satisfy all the business intelligence capabilities your users need. Make sure that you carefully check out the vendors' products — all of them — because you have no guarantee that a top-notch OLAP vendor's data mining tool is equally as good, for example. Don't be afraid to mix and match; you have no reason to shortchange your data warehouse's users simply to avoid having to deal with one more vendor.

When evaluating your user access needs, ask yourself the following questions:

✔ Do my users want the best-of-breed tools, which might not necessarily be integrated, requiring professional developers to build visualization solutions?

✔ Do my users want a well-integrated platform that enables integration between user-access strategies so that they can develop all visualization solutions themselves?

Answers to these questions (and if you answer "Yes" to one of them, you answer "No" to the other) can help you evaluate the business intelligence tools.

Database

Data warehouse deluxe implementations are big — and getting bigger all the time. Implementations that use hundreds of gigabytes (a gigabyte equals 1 billion bytes) and even terabytes (1 trillion bytes) are increasingly more common. To manage this volume of data and user access, you need a very robust server and database.

Data extraction, movement, and loading

Prepare for the challenge! With a data warehouse lite, you can usually handle source-to-warehouse movement of data in a straightforward, low-tech manner — but with the data warehouse deluxe, you're now entering the Difficulty Zone, where many data warehousing projects meet their Waterloo.

You're likely to experience difficulty in this domain for several reasons:

✔ **You're dealing with many different data sources, some of which might contain overlapping data.**

For example, suppliers' information might come from two different purchasing systems, and some of your suppliers have entries in both systems. You'll probably run into different sets of identifiers that you have to converge (for example, six alphanumeric characters that are identified as the SUPPLIER_ID in one of the systems and a unique integer known as SUP_NUM in the other).

✔ **If your data warehouse is large (measuring more than about 250 gigabytes), you're likely to experience difficulties in extracting, moving, and loading your batch windows.**

Batch windows, the time frames in which updates are made to the warehouse, are complicated by the number of data sources you have to handle.

✔ **The chances of having a messed-up extraction, movement, transformation, and loading process is exponentially related to the number of data elements to be loaded into the data warehouse.**

If you could assign some difficulty factor (an integer, for example) to the process of getting data into the warehouse, the following measures would hold true: You have n data elements that you want to include in the data warehouse with a difficulty factor of x. If you now have $2n$ data elements, your difficulty factor isn't $2x$; rather, it's x squared.

To make this difficulty factor easier to understand, assign some numbers to n and x. Say that your data warehouse has 100 elements *(n)* and the difficulty factor *(x)* is 5. If you double the number of elements *(n = 200)*, your difficulty factor is 25 (5 squared), not 10 (5×2).

✔ **The process of dealing with so many data sources, all headed toward one place (your data warehouse deluxe), has all the elements of too many cooks in the kitchen, or whatever that saying is.**

To make the extraction, movement, transformation, and loading process go smoothly, you probably have to deal with many different application owners, official keepers of the database, and other people from a variety of different organizations, all of whom have to cooperate like they're part of a professional symphony orchestra. The reality, though, is that they perform more like a group of kindergarten students who each pick a musical instrument from the toy bin and are told, "Now play something!" Although the process isn't necessarily doomed to failure, expect a number of iterations until you can get the data warehouse deluxe loaded just right.

Architecture

A data warehouse deluxe can have three tiers (like a data warehouse lite), and it has architecture similar to what's shown in Figure 3-5, except with more data sources and perhaps more than one type of user tool accessing the warehouse. But the architecture for a data warehouse deluxe probably looks more like what's shown in Figure 3-7. In addition to other necessary "way stations" for your particular environment, your environment might have these elements:

✔ **Data mart:** Receives subsets of information from the data warehouse deluxe and serves as the primary access point for users. (Data marts are discussed in depth in Chapter 4.)

✔ **Interim transformation station:** An area in which sets of data extracted from some of the sources undergo some type of transformation process before moving down the pipeline toward the warehouse's database.

✔ **Quality assurance station:** An area in which groups of data undergo intensive quality assurance checks before you let them move into the data warehouse.

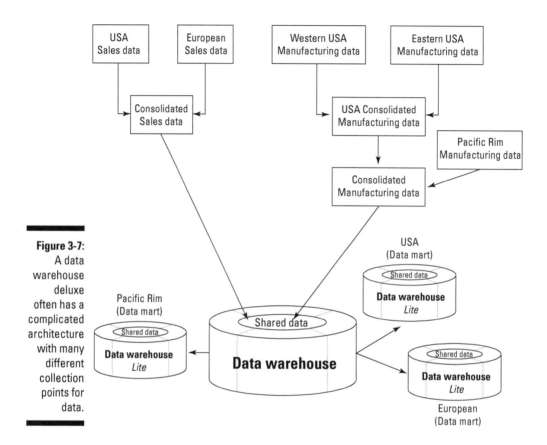

Figure 3-7:
A data
warehouse
deluxe
often has a
complicated
architecture
with many
different
collection
points for
data.

The data warehouse supreme

Although today's state-of-the-art data warehouse typically looks like a complicated data warehouse deluxe, if you read the following sections, you can
know what the data warehouse of tomorrow will look like. There are few
enterprises that have ventured in this direction, though due to overall cost
and capabilities, it is still rare to find many data warehouse supremes.

Subject areas and data content

The number of subject areas in a data warehouse supreme is unlimited
because the data warehouse is virtual; it isn't all contained in a single
database or even within multiple databases that you personally load and
maintain. Instead, only part of your warehouse (probably a small part) is

physically located on some data warehouse server; the rest is out there in cyberspace somewhere, accessible through networking capabilities as though it were all part of some physically centralized data warehouse. With a data warehouse supreme, your warehouse users have an infinite number of subject-area possibilities — anything that could possibly be of interest to them.

Think of how you use the Internet today to access Web sites all over the world — sites that someone else creates and maintains. Now, imagine that each of those sites contains information about some specific area of interest to you — rather than advertising, job ads, electronic storefronts, and whatever else you spend your time surfing the Internet trying to find. Also imagine that you can query and run reports by using the contents of one or more of these sites as your input. That's the model of the data warehouse supreme: opening up an unlimited number of possibilities to users.

The leading-edge corporations are beginning to pursue and deliver seamless convergence of different types of data: narrative documents, video, image, and ordinary data (such as numbers and character information). A data warehouse supreme has all this — all the different types of data that you need to support better business decision-making.

In terms of total capacity, a data warehouse supreme is huge; it surpasses today's limits. The distribution of the information across many different platforms, much faster and higher-performance networking infrastructure, and increasingly "smarter" database management systems — in addition to, of course, steadily increasing disk storage capacities — create this capacity expansion.

Data sources

Because of the wide breadth of subject areas in a data warehouse supreme, it has numerous data sources. The good news: Because many of the sources are external to your own warehousing environment, you aren't personally responsible for all the extraction, transformation, and loading to get them into your warehouse. The bad news: Someone has to perform those tasks, and you have little or no control over elements such as quality assurance processes or how frequently the data is refreshed.

I have more good news, though: Because the most critical part of a data warehouse supreme is still *internally acquired data* (the data coming from your internal applications), from that aspect, the things you do today to make the data warehouse-ready will still be done in the future.

Because you populate your data warehouse supreme with multimedia information — in addition to traditional data, such as numeric, alphabetic, and dates — the types of data sources broaden from traditional applications to video servers, Web sites, and databases that store documents and text.

Business intelligence tools

As far as I can tell, the Big Four types of business intelligence discussed in the section "Business intelligence tools" in the discussion of the data warehouse deluxe, earlier in this chapter — basic reporting and querying, business analysis, dashboards and scorecards, and data mining — are all part of the data warehouse supreme environment. Of the four, the most significant advances and improvements during the next few years probably will occur with data mining while vendors push enhancements into their products. However, these user-access methods will be relegated to providing information that will be visualized in other forms. The business intelligence tools will enable users to pull information from the data warehouse supreme and integrate it with a better visualization — for instance, Google Earth or Microsoft Virtual Earth. Such combinations, known as *mash-ups,* are becoming more prevalent and enable users to see the data from the data warehouse supreme in more realistic forms — not columns on a report, but dots or shadings on a map.

The biggest difference between today's state-of-the-art data warehouses and the data warehouse supreme, however, is the dramatically increased use of push technology. By using intelligent agents ("assistants" you program to perform certain functions for you), you can have information fed back to you from the far ends of the Internet-based universe, not to mention your own large data warehouse servers within your own company. Figure 3-8 illustrates some of the ways in which intelligent agents can help you make very efficient use of data warehousing.

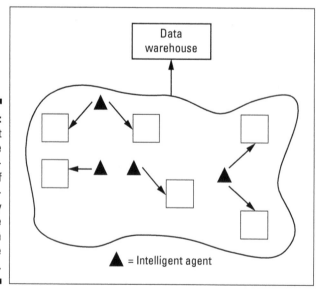

Figure 3-8: Intelligent agents are an important part of the push-technology architecture of a data warehouse supreme.

Database

A data warehouse supreme most likely consists of a database environment that meets these requirements:

- ✓ It's distributed across many different platforms.

- ✓ It operates in a location-transparent manner: Users make queries that access data from the appropriate platform without the users having to know the physical location (in much the same way that you access Internet Web sites by name, rather than by network address).

- ✓ It has object-oriented capabilities to store images, videos, and text in addition to the traditional data, such as numeric and date information.

- ✓ Because of dramatically faster performance than current data warehouses, it increasingly permits you to access data directly from transactional databases without having to copy the information to a separate data warehouse database.

Data extraction, movement, and loading

Here's how the extraction, movement, and loading of data occurs in a data warehouse supreme:

- ✓ Data that's moved (copied) from a source application's database or file system into a separate database in the data warehouse is handled almost identically to how you perform those tasks in a data warehouse deluxe.

- ✓ The increasing use of *operational data stores,* or ODSs (real-time availability of analytical data so that you don't have to deal with delayed access) means that more messaging occurs between your data sources and your warehouse database. The data source determines when data should be moved into the warehouse environment, so the warehouse doesn't have the responsibility to request updates and additions. When new data is inserted into the source database (or existing data is modified or deleted), the appropriate instructions and accompanying data are sent to the warehouse.

Architecture

Figure 3-9 shows an example of what the architecture of a data warehouse supreme might look like. But with all the upcoming technology trends and improvements discussed in the preceding sections, your data warehouse supreme can look like (almost) anything you want.

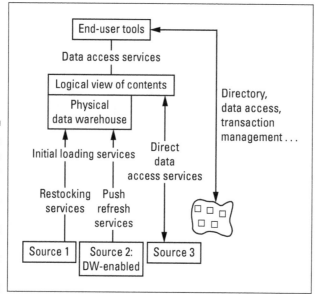

Figure 3-9:
Sample
architecture
from a data
warehouse
supreme
(although it
can look like
just about
anything).

To Centralize or Distribute, That Is the Question

Traditional data warehousing — creating a data warehouse lite or data warehouse deluxe — usually involves copying data from one or more different source databases and files into a single warehouse-owned database. Whether that database is relational or multidimensional is irrelevant. The main point is that it's centralized: Only one database is on one platform that all users access.

Even when you take part of your data warehouse's content and copy that information into one or more data marts for users, as shown in Figure 3-7, you still have a single, centralized collection point into which all the source data converges.

While data warehouse environments become larger and more complex, though, you should consider not funneling all your data into a single database; rather, you could make your data warehouse a collection of databases that make up your overall information delivery and analytical environment. Figure 3-10 shows what a brokerage firm's distributed, non-centralized data warehousing environment might look like.

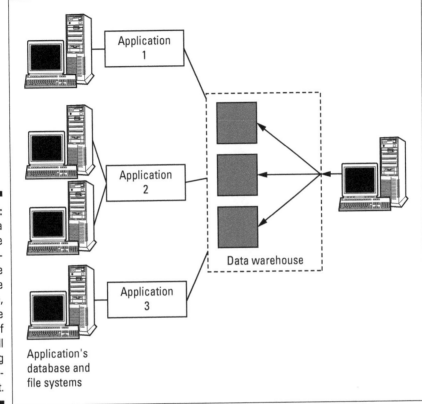

Figure 3-10:
A data warehouse might consist of more than one database, under the control of the overall warehousing environment.

Application 1

Application 2

Application 3

Data warehouse

Application's database and file systems

Chapter 4

Data Marts: Your Retail Data Outlet

. . . .

. . . .

Several years ago, a regional (I think) hardware chain in southern California ran a radio ad based on this premise: "Shop at our stores because we have fewer products than the big warehouse-like competition. You can much more easily get in and out here quickly with what you need." Interestingly, another hardware chain (on the east coast) had run ads a few years earlier with almost the identical theme. This chain used to make fun of the warehouse-size competition by featuring radio ads that had helicopter search parties looking for shoppers lost in a distant department and references to shuttle buses having to take shoppers between departments in the warehouse-size stores. The premise was the same: "We have less merchandise than the other guy, so shop with us because it's easier."

And that's the idea of the data mart.

Don't get caught up in the hype. The idea of a data mart is hardly revolutionary, despite what you might read on blogs and in the computer trade press, and what you might hear at conferences or seminars. A data mart is simply a scaled-down data warehouse — that's all.

Vendors do their best to define data marts in the context of their products; consultants and analysts usually define data marts in a way that's advantageous to their particular offerings and specialties. That's the way this business goes; be prepared to ask the tough questions.

Architectural Approaches to Data Marts

You can take one of three main approaches to creating a data mart:

✔ Sourced by a data warehouse (most or all of the data mart's contents come from a data warehouse)

✔ Quickly developed and created from scratch

✔ Developed from scratch with an eye toward eventual integration

In the following sections, I examine each approach separately.

Data marts sourced by a data warehouse

Many data warehousing experts would argue (and I'm one of them, in this case) that a true data mart is a "retail outlet," and a data warehouse provides its contents, as shown in Figure 4-1.

In an environment like the one shown in Figure 4-1, the data sources, data warehouse, data mart, and user interact in this way:

1. The data sources, acting as suppliers of raw materials, send data into the data warehouse.

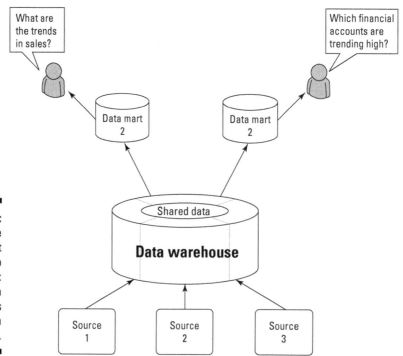

Figure 4-1: The retail-outlet approach to data marts: All the data comes from a data warehouse.

2. The data warehouse serves as a consolidation and distribution center, collecting the raw materials in much the same way that any data warehouse does.

3. Instead of the user (the consumer) going straight to the data warehouse, though, the data warehouse serves as a wholesaler with the premise of "we sell only to retailers, not directly to the public." In this case, the retailers are the data marts.

4. The data marts order data from the warehouse and, after stocking the newly acquired information, make it available to consumers (users).

In a variation of the sourced-from-the-warehouse model, the data warehouse that serves as the source for the data mart doesn't have all the information the data mart's users need. You can solve this problem in one of two ways:

✔ Supplement the missing information directly into the data warehouse before sending the selected contents to the data mart, as shown in Figure 4-2.

✔ Don't touch the data warehouse; instead, add the supplemental information to the data mart in addition to what it receives from the data warehouse, as shown in Figure 4-3.

 If your data mart is the only one within your company that needs additional data (be sure to ask around), leave the warehouse alone and bring the supplemental data directly into your data mart. If other data marts or other projects served by the data warehouse can use the additional information, add that information to the data warehouse first and then send it, along with the other contents you need, to the appropriate data marts.

Figure 4-2:
Sprucing up the data ware-house's contents as part of a data mart project.

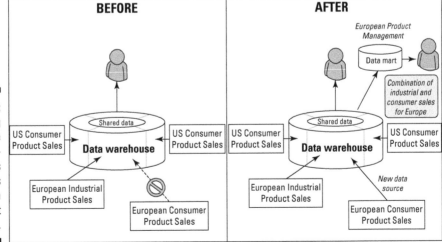

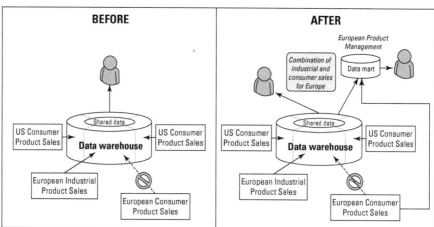

Figure 4-3: Supplement the data mart's contents with additional information acquired directly from the missing sources.

Top-down, quick-strike data marts

Sometimes, you just don't have a data warehouse from which to get data for your data mart, so you have to source the data from applications yourself. In many (probably most) of these situations, you create a *quick-strike data mart* — in effect, a miniature data warehouse but built to meet the demands of a set of users who need the data content now. You follow the same methodology and complete the same processes of data extraction, transformation, quality assurance, and loading as described in Chapter 3. The difference is that you use this methodology on a smaller scale than you do with a full-blown data warehouse.

As shown in Figure 4-4, you often need to bring data into a top-down, quick-strike data mart to answer a specific set of business questions within relatively narrow confines. For example, you can add data about a specific region or territory within a company, a subset of a company's overall product line, or some other subsetting model.

So, if you need to start from scratch and don't have a data warehouse to provide data to your data mart, why not build a full-scale data warehouse instead? Here are three reasons to go the data-mart route:

- **Speed:** A quick-strike data mart is typically completed in 90 to 120 days, rather than the much longer time required for a full-scale data warehouse.

- **Cost:** Doing the job faster means that you spend less money; it's that simple.

- **Complexity and risk:** When you work with less data and fewer sources over a shorter period, you're likely to create a significantly less complex environment — and have fewer associated risks.

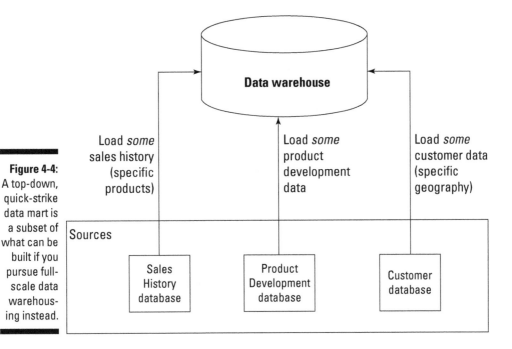

Figure 4-4:
A top-down, quick-strike data mart is a subset of what can be built if you pursue full-scale data warehousing instead.

Bottom-up, integration-oriented data marts

If pressing business needs steer you toward a quick-strike data mart but you have a longer-term vision of integrating its contents with other data, what can you do? Have you created an architectural dead end in your data mart? Will you have to throw away your data mart at some point and start over with a "real" data warehousing effort? Will Harry Potter save his mates from Lord Voldemort? (Sorry about that — the numerous releases are getting to me.)

Theoretically, you can design data marts so that they're eventually integrated in a bottom-up manner by building a data warehousing environment (in contrast to a single, monolithic data warehouse).

Bottom-up integration of data marts isn't for the fainthearted. You can do it, but it's more difficult than creating a top-down, quick-strike data mart that will always remain stand-alone. You might be able to successfully use this approach . . . but you might not.

What to Put in a Data Mart

If a data mart is a smaller-scale version of a data warehouse, this question comes up: What does "smaller scale" mean in reference to the contents of a data mart? The answer to this question is typically that the data will be a subset of the overall *enterprise data*.

The following sections describe some ways that you can select subsets of information for a data mart and the circumstances under which you might want to try each approach.

Geography-bounded data

A data mart might contain only the information relevant to a certain geographical area, such as a region or territory within your company. Figure 4-5 illustrates an example of geography-bounded data.

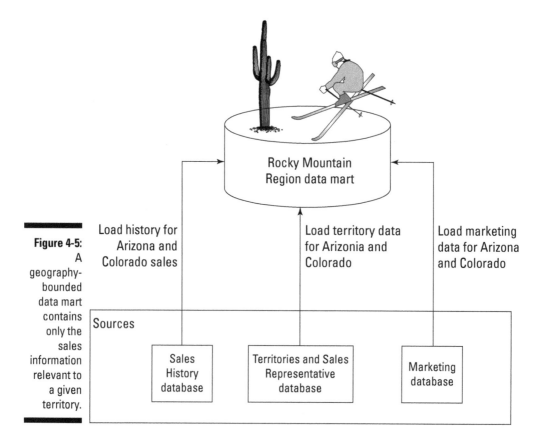

Figure 4-5: A geography-bounded data mart contains only the sales information relevant to a given territory.

Rocky Mountain Region data mart

Load history for Arizona and Colorado sales

Load territory data for Arizonia and Colorado

Load marketing data for Arizona and Colorado

Sources

Sales History database

Territories and Sales Representative database

Marketing database

Although you technically can use a geography-bounded data mart in a relatively straightforward way, you probably don't want to subset your data in this manner. Users often want to see a cross-geography comparison (for example, "How are our Arizona stores doing versus our Pennsylvania stores?") in their data warehouse environment. When you create separate data marts for various geographical reasons, these types of comparisons become much more difficult to make.

Organization-bounded data

When deciding what you want to put in your data mart, you can base decisions on what information a specific organization needs when it's the sole (or, at least, primary) user of the data mart. As shown in Figure 4-6, a bank might create one data mart for consumer checking-account analysis and another data mart for commercial checking accounts.

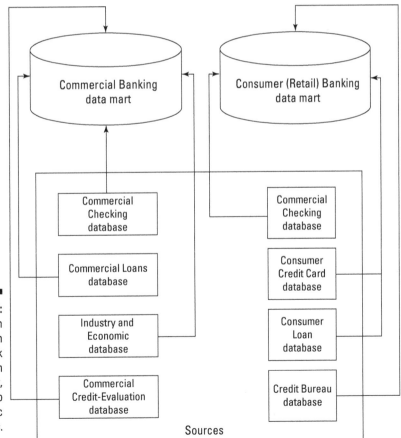

Figure 4-6:
Each organization in this bank gets its own data mart, tuned to its specific needs.

This approach works well when the overwhelming majority of inquiries and reports are organization-oriented. For example, the commercial checking group has no need whatsoever to analyze consumer checking accounts and vice versa. It pays to dig into the business needs during the scope phase of a data warehousing or data mart project. Outsiders, for example, might think, "Okay, put all checking-account information, both consumer and commercial, into the same environment so that Marketing or Risk Management Analysts can run reports comparing average balances and other information for the entire checking-account portfolio at the bank." After additional analysis, though, you might notice that the bank doesn't do this type of comparison, so why not keep the two areas separate and avoid unnecessary complexity?

Function-bounded data

Using an approach that crosses organizational boundaries, you can establish a data mart's contents based on a specific function (or set of related functions) within the company. A multinational chemical company, for example, might create a data mart exclusively for the sales and marketing functions across all organizations and across all product lines, as shown in Figure 4-7.

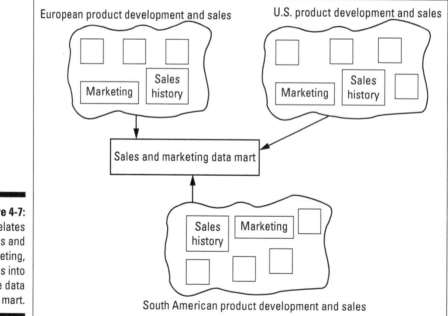

Figure 4-7:
If it relates to sales and marketing, it goes into the data mart.

Chapter 4: Data Marts: Your Retail Data Outlet

Market-bounded data

A company might occasionally be so focused on a specific market and the associated competitors that it makes sense to create a data mart oriented with that particular focus. As shown in Figure 4-8, this type of environment might include competitive sales, all available public information about the market and competitors (particularly if you can find this information on the Internet), and industry analysts' reports, for example.

To truly provide the business intelligence that a company needs in a competitor-driven situation, construct the data mart to include multimedia information, in addition to the traditional data types typically found in a data warehouse. (Chapter 25 describes multimedia data and data warehousing.)

Figure 4-8:
The data mart as a weapon of war: Collect information about your market and competitors, and see how you stack up.

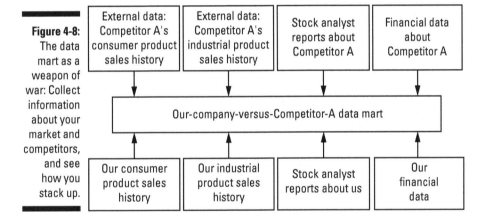

Answers to specific business questions

The answers to a select number (often a handful) of business questions occasionally drive an organization's operations. Based on the answers, a company might speed up or slow down production lines, start up extra shifts to increase production or initiate layoffs, or decide whether to acquire other companies.

Business questions that have this degree of weighty importance traditionally cause nightmares for the in-house employees chartered with digging out data and reports, consolidating and checking the information, and reporting the results to executive management. Sounds like a job for a data warehouse, you say? Unfortunately business analysts have often used spreadsheets, such as

Microsoft Excel. These types of "spread marts" often lack the repeatability and data quality required to leverage the data for more than one moment in time. So, I'll say it again — sounds like a job for a data warehouse!

Before constructing a full-scale data warehouse that can answer these (and many other) business questions, however, you probably want to consider whether a small-scale data mart designed specifically to answer those high-impact, high-value "How are we doing?" type of questions can get the job done.

Later, this type of environment might grow into a larger-scale data warehouse. It often makes more sense, however, to concentrate your efforts on supporting a data mart that has known business value, instead of on supplementing it with volumes of additional data that might provide business value (but can also slow response time or significantly complicate the end-to-end architecture). Again, the job you do in the early phases of your project makes a big difference in the direction you take and your level of success.

Anything!

Any set of criteria that you can dream up can determine a data mart's contents. Some make sense; others don't. Some take you into an architectural dead end because you get only limited value and have to start all over to expand your capabilities.

Data mart or data warehouse?

If you start a project from the outset with either of the following premises, you already have two strikes against you:

- ✔ "We're building a real data warehouse, not a puny little data mart."
- ✔ "We're building a data mart, not a data warehouse."

By labeling your project as one or the other of these terms, you already have some preconceived notions about the work you'll do, before you even begin to dig into the business problem. Until you understand the following three issues, you have no foundation on which to classify your impending project as either a data mart or a data warehouse:

- ✔ The volumes and characteristics of data you need
- ✔ The business problems you're trying to solve and the questions you're trying to answer
- ✔ The business value you expect to gain when your system is successfully built

If you're extracting and re-hosting a subset of data from an existing application into another environment, you can accurately call what you're building a data mart.

But if you're starting from scratch, extracting data from one or more source systems, handling the quality assurance and transformation, and copying that data into a separate environment, what determines whether you're building a data warehouse or a data mart? Although some guidelines exist, such as number of subject areas and volumes of data, it all comes down to this statement: As soon as you start labeling your environment as one or the other, you're adding preconceived notions and beliefs about its characteristics that might not fit your business needs.

Here's the answer: Forget about the terms data warehouse and data mart. Concentrate instead on your business problem and its possible solution. What data do you need in order to perform certain informational and analytical functions; where is that data now and in what form; and what do you have to do to make it available to your users?

Leave the terminology wars to the vendors and analysts. Don't get caught up in the hype.

Implementing a Data Mart — Quickly

No matter how you decide to divide the universe of possible contents into some subset for your data mart, remember that in order to obtain maximum business value from your data mart, you must implement it quickly.

Here are the three keys to speedy implementation:

- ✔ **Follow an iterative, phased methodology.** As described in Chapter 13, you spend the majority of your upfront time on the project focusing on the specific business value the end user wants and over several iterations build the solution into their vision.

- ✔ **Hold to a fixed time for each phase.** If you set aside two weeks for your scope, for example, stick to that window. Don't extend any phase (especially the early ones) unless the project is doomed to failure if you don't.

- ✔ **Avoid scope creep at all costs.** Although costly and dangerous in any project (data warehousing or otherwise), *scope creep* (when additional feature requests keep creeping in long past the cutoff point) can devastate a data mart effort. By adding these last-minute features, you probably add complexity to your data mart with only marginal incremental business value (if any), so you do little other than put your project at risk.

Part II
Data Warehousing Technology

The 5th Wave — By Rich Tennant

"Yes, I know how to query information from the program, but what if I just want to leak it instead?"

In this part . . .

A data warehouse without a database is like a day without sunshine. But what kind of database do you need for your data warehouse?

Whether you're inclined toward making a traditional relational database, a multidimensional database, or a somewhat newfangled column-wise (vertical) database as the home for your warehouse's data, you have to understand the basics of all the options and when each one is appropriate. It's all here!

Chapter 5

Relational Databases and Data Warehousing

*Y*ou don't, strictly speaking, have to store the contents of a data warehouse in a relational database. However, in nearly all situations, your project benefits significantly from the use of a relational database management system (RDBMS).

This chapter explains the use of relational database technology (today's overwhelmingly dominant database technology) for your data warehouse, including its benefits and challenges. Chapter 6 discusses alternative technologies that you can use to store and manage your data warehouse.

The 1990s generation of data warehousing implementations grew up on multidimensional databases, but the current marketplace is experiencing a clear-cut trend toward using relational databases, particularly for large-volume data warehouses (more than about 250 gigabytes of data). Multidimensional databases aren't dead — they can still provide value to smaller-scale environments (data warehouse lite systems or data marts, as discussed in Chapters 3 and 4, respectively).

The Old Way of Thinking

Jump back to 1995. The data warehousing revolution was picking up steam, and companies all over the U.S. (yours was probably one of them) and around the world were captivated by not only the concept of data warehousing, but also the principles of online analytical processing (OLAP — discussed in more detail in Chapters 6 and 10).

In 1995, the world of data warehousing and OLAP widely held the belief that you absolutely couldn't successfully build a data warehouse by storing data in a relational database; you could use only a multidimensional database.

This relational-versus-multidimensional war ranked up there with the all-time champion of polarized technology proponents: the Ethernet-versus-token-ring-LAN (local area network) wars of the mid-1980s. (Proponents of either LAN technology fervently — and sometimes savagely — argued that their approach was far superior to the other and that only fools would attempt to implement a LAN by using the other technology. If you were involved with client/server computing or networking back then, you probably remember the argument well. Relational-versus-multidimensional was a 1990s version of this memorable classic!)

The following section describes how this can't-do-it-with-relational belief got started.

A technology-based discussion: The roots of relational database technology

Relational database management systems (RDBMSs) have their roots in the relational data model developed by Dr. E.F. Codd, then with IBM, back in 1970. (He first described it in his landmark paper "A Relational Model of Data for Large Shared Data Banks," published in *Communications of the ACM, Vol. 13, No. 6,* June 1970, pp. 377–387. You can check out the paper on the Web, at www.sigmod.org/codd-tribute.html). Throughout the 1970s, in an attempt to commercialize relational technology, IBM and a few other organizations worked on prototypes, proof-of-concept systems, and early starts at product development.

When you join tables in a relational database, problems start occurring. Back in the early, pre-relational days of databases, data usually was linked together by using pointers, which told the DBMS software the location of the next logical piece of data or the previous piece of data, or some other path that made sense. Because it's somewhat complicated, don't worry about the details — you just need to know that old-style databases usually had pointers intermixed among the data.

Relational databases *don't* have pointers in them because one of the fundamental principles of this relational approach is that you can join together any pieces of information in the database, so pointers don't make sense. (Again, although the principle is somewhat more complicated than that and has to do with set-based operations on the data, just remember that relational databases, unlike their predecessors, don't use pointers.)

What's a relational database management system?

Forget all about the mathematical foundations of the relational model, the principles of normalization, and other highly technical aspects of RDBMSs. If you're interested, consult any one of the many available textbooks that discuss RDBMS principles and technology in detail.

For purposes of this book, an *RDBMS* is a software system that manages relational databases. So, what's a relational database?

In a typical spreadsheet program, columns and rows form a series of cells. If each column is headed by the name of a data attribute (CUSTOMER_NUMBER, PRODUCT, and QUANTITY_PURCHASED, for example) and each row has a single value for each attribute, you have the basics of a relational database table, as shown in this example:

```
CUSTOMER_NUMBER     PRODUCT              QUANTITY_PURCHASED
12345               Vegetable soup       5
45678               Cooking oil          3
42973               Lawn fertilizer      2
81115               Blankets             88
81115               Vegetable soup       33
```

A relational database typically has many different tables — a CUSTOMER_MASTER table and a PRODUCT_MASTER table, for example, in addition to the preceding table, which you could call ORDER_DETAIL or WHO_ORDERED_WHAT. You can combine information from across the various tables by *joining* those tables (making a match between tables, usually by looking for columns in two or more tables that are the same). For example, CUSTOMER_MASTER might contain the following rows of data:

```
CUSTOMER_NUMBER     CUSTOMER_NAME
12345               Mark Jones
45678               Daniel Michaels
42973               Karen Warner
81115               Susan Robinson
```

Joining these two tables, using CUSTOMER_NUMBER as the common attribute, might tell you that customer number 81115, named Susan Robinson, ordered 88 blankets and 33 cans of vegetable soup. (She must be going on a camp-out!) From either of the individual tables, you have only bits and pieces of this information: You don't know the customer's name from looking only at the first table, for example, and you don't know what products Susan Robinson ordered from looking only at the second table. The power of the relational database becomes evident when you join tables together.

Back when databases used pointers, accessing logical sequences of data was fairly quick, even on older hardware. Data access went something like this:

1. Go directly to the first record you want (usually from some type of index).

2. After reading the record, read the pointer attached to it that indicates where to go next.

3. Go directly to the record indicated by that pointer.

4. Read that second record, and then read its pointer.

5. Repeat this process until you reach the end of the list or until some other criteria tells your program to stop.

In a relational database, without pointers, the RDBMS (remember, the RDBMS is a software program that manages the relational database) has to figure out how to *most efficiently* access data and provide the answer you're looking for. Using the example in the sidebar "What's a relational database management system?" in this chapter, you might want to know how many products Susan Robinson ordered, as well as how many of each.

The RDBMS could find this information by scanning the CUSTOMER_MASTER table from top to bottom until it finds the customer named Susan Robinson. (To keep this example simple, assume that no two customers have the same name.) After the RDBMS finds that row of data, it gets the customer number and goes to the WHO_ORDERED_WHAT table. The RDBMS then scans that table, from top to bottom, looking for any row of data where CUSTOMER_NUMBER is equal to 81115 (Susan Robinson's customer number). Unlike in the first table, though, the RDBMS doesn't stop when it finds the first row of data that meets these criteria because the table might have 1, 100, 1,000, or any number of rows indicating what Susan Robinson ordered.

A relational database doesn't store data in any kind of sorted order, though you could use an index to help locate data. In an official sense, the exact physical order in which data is stored is *implementation-defined:* The DBMS product decides how the product works (and it's none of your business), as long as the product does work.

Back to the history of relational databases (this discussion is leading somewhere, I swear!). Vendors spent most of the 1970s (the research era of relational databases) and the 1990s trying to solve a nasty problem: If a relational database doesn't have pointers to efficiently tell the software how to return data to users, could they build dynamic logic to speed the retrieval of data? An RDBMS product has a subsystem, usually known as a *query optimizer* (or a similar term), that determines the best method to retrieve stored data by evaluating many aspects of how the data is organized, such as the ones in this list:

- The number of tables from which you're asking for information as part of the join process

- The size (if it's known) of each of those tables

- Any indices that are available to prevent having to scan each table from end to end

- System characteristics (for example, what type of CPU processors are configured, how much memory is available, and how the data is stored and physically on the disks)

Here's the punch line: RDBMS vendors spent about two decades working on their query optimizers to make relational database technology suitable for online transaction processing (OLTP) applications, such as customer-order processing, checking-account systems, and zillions of other types of applications that companies use to run their businesses. Finally, near the end of the 1980s, the corporate IT world (most of it, anyway) became convinced that you could use RDBMS products for more than just play. Real-world OLTP applications began to use RDBMSs, replacing the old-style databases (the ones with the pointers) or file systems.

And along comes data warehousing. So what's the significance? Here it is, summed up in a few sentences: OLTP applications typically access a small number of tables (preferably one, but usually only two or three) during a given *transaction,* a series of steps that either access data from a database or put data into it. That 20 years' worth of optimization, therefore, was oriented toward making these OLTP-style transactions, which included a small number of tables, as efficient as possible.

Data warehousing applications — the business analytics, or online analytical processing (OLAP) ones, as described in the following section — rarely access one, two, or three tables at a time. Rather, the nature of data warehousing (bringing together a lot of information that, when the pieces of data are related to one another, provides business intelligence capabilities) usually means that a single query must access a large number of tables.

The way you design your relational database plays a large part in the number-of-tables situation you have to deal with.

When RDBMS products that had evolved over two decades to support OLTP-type database access with reasonable performance were suddenly put to work in OLAP environments, they began performing in a somewhat less-than-desirable manner. It wasn't anyone's fault: The products just couldn't do what they hadn't been developed to do — analyze and aggregate large volumes of data distributed across various database tables. So, the philosophy of not using RDBMSs for data warehousing was developed.

To use an analogy, a four-wheel-drive, off-road vehicle and a sports car both have similar characteristics: an engine, four wheels with tires, and a steering wheel, for example. A sports car, however, has been developed to use the basic common framework of an automobile to go fast; in off-road situations out in the wilderness, the driver of a sports car is probably in trouble.

The OLAP-only fallacy

Because the preceding section says that performance in the 1990s was subpar when RDBMSs were used for OLAP purposes, you might think that RDBMSs were therefore deemed unsuitable for data warehousing.

Wrong!

Without going off on a tangent of blaming vendors and their marketing pitches (I do that in Chapter 23), you absolutely can't make an indelible link between OLAP functionality and a data warehouse. Consider the following points:

- ✔ OLAP and data warehousing hit the big leagues at the same time.
- ✔ You almost always perform OLAP business analysis functionality by using data that you've loaded into a data warehouse.
- ✔ You can do much more than business analysis functionality, or OLAP, with a data warehouse.

Part III of this book discusses the area of business intelligence, which is the reason you build a data warehouse. Go ahead — take a peek at the Table of Contents or jump ahead to those chapters. OLAP business analysis capabilities are only one of four different classes of business intelligence.

To make a blanket statement that RDBMS technology is unsuitable for data warehousing means unequivocally that the only thing you want to do with a data warehouse is OLAP processing. Again, that is incorrect. You will find the data warehouse valuable for data quality purpose necessary to integrate your run-the-business applications as well as other business intelligence capabilities, such as data mining and historical consolidated reporting.

The New Way of Thinking

So, now it's the 21st century; relational database vendors have updated their products so they are now optimized for data warehousing.

Fine-tuning databases for data warehousing

Smart people run RDBMS vendors — at least, the vendors still in business after surviving the Great Database Wars of the 1980s and 1990s. These smart people saw what was going on — the growth of data warehousing and the problems the vendors' respective products were having in supporting the type of processing most commonly done after the data warehouse was built — and they figured, "Hey! We have to do something about this situation."

The major problem vendors faced was that, unlike OLTP applications, many data warehousing queries against a database involved database join operations with four to ten tables, and sometimes even more tables. The typical relational query optimizer, when faced with a join operation that involved a large number of tables, would do the programming equivalent of throwing its hands in the air, shaking its head in confusion, and saying, "I dunno — you tell me!" (I'm oversimplifying a little, but it gets the point across.) The query optimizer would give up and do one large "join the tables in all possible ways and then figure it all out afterward" response (known as a *Cartesian product*). This inefficient means of joining tables caused these types of queries to run slowly.

So, for the first couple decades in the history of RDMSs, the vendors focused on optimizing their products for run-the-business capabilities. Then, the vendors focused for a couple of decades on how to enhance their RDBMS' query optimizers for monitor-the-business capabilities.

Optimizing data access

As described in the preceding section, the challenges that the RDMS vendors had to address involved the method in which users accessed data. Business analysis queries tend to pull two forms of data — descriptive data, often called dimensions; and measurement data, often called facts. The optimization techniques that many RDBMS vendors provide recognized this design technique — which became known as a *star schema* (discussed in the section "Exploring new ways to design a relational-based data warehouse," later in this chapter).

When a database was designed according to the principles of a star schema, the problems that occurred because of the large number of tables involved in a single query were dramatically reduced by using new data access optimizations, such as a *star join* — a different, more efficient way of doing joins when you have a large number of tables involved in a query.

Avoiding scanning unnecessary data

When users performed their business analysis, they commonly ran into problems when they needed to scan large volumes of data. This type of activity occurs when someone asks a question of the data, such as, "How many customers have orders with more than 50 items?" In the run-the-business database design, this information appears in a column on the WHO_ORDERED_WHAT table. However, this type of question forces every row in the table to be read.

Yikes! Just think of a user asking this question of Wal-Mart, whose staff would have to read all the cash register receipts from all their stores worldwide. In general terms, the old way of thinking forced the database to

1. Read a row in the WHO_ORDERED_WHAT table.

2. Ask itself whether the value in QUANTITY_PURCHASED is greater than 50.

3. If the QUANTITY_PURCHASED is greater than 50, return it to the user and move on; if the QUANTITY_PURCHASED isn't greater than 50, skip that row and move on to the next.

4. Repeat this process until it reaches the end of the WHO_ORDERED_WHAT table.

Once again, envision this happening at Wal-Mart! You don't have enough time in the year or processing power to make this data come back to you. So, RDBMS vendors came up with creative indexing schemes to assist in directly finding data that have high *cardinality* — basically, the number of unique values in a database column. Traditional indexing technology supported only low-cardinality indexing. The new way of thinking introduced the concept of high-cardinality indexing.

Handling large data volume

In the early days of data warehousing, most data warehouses were rather small when compared to the current data warehouses, measuring about 50 gigabytes of data or smaller. While technologies mature and IT professionals become more comfortable with data warehousing (and when they become more daring after getting a few successful projects behind them), those IT folks commonly need or want increasingly larger amounts of data in a warehouse. They want not only larger amounts of data, but also increasing levels of detail (not just summarized information).

For years, the DBMS world has had a term that applies to very large databases. The term is *very large database,* or VLDB. How's that for descriptive?

 VLDB has become increasingly synonymous with data warehousing. And, almost without fail, VLDB data warehouses have been implemented by using RDBMS technologies. The combination of warehouse-sensitive query optimization (the star joins mentioned in the section "Optimizing data access," earlier in this chapter), new types of indices, and parallel processing capabilities have permitted RDBMS products to deal with VLDB situations much more effectively than they could in the 1990s.

 Parallel processing in the RDBMS world is a relatively complex proposition and a vendor-versus-vendor battlefield because of different ways of doing it. The mechanics of parallel processing (not to mention the arguments used by both sides) don't matter much here. It's important, though, to understand that in parallel database processing, a single database table is divided into multiple *partitions* (different segments of the same table, each containing different rows of data). Furthermore, queries against the database table run in parallel against each of the partitions, effectively reducing the time it takes to get an answer to a query because each parallel query is operating against a smaller amount of data than in the non-partitioned entire table.

Designing Your Relational Database for Data Warehouse Usage

The traditional usage of relational databases, to support the run-the-business transaction-processing applications, has meant that you had to follow certain design principles. If you deliberately violated one of those principles, you had to handle your own work-arounds.

The following sections give you the story behind relational database design and data warehousing.

Looking at why traditional relational design techniques don't work well

In their purest sense, relational databases are designed according to the principles of normalization. Without getting into all the mathematical formalities, the following sections explain what normalization means.

Explaining normalization in plain language (or trying to)

Because a relational database is laid out like a table, it can't have any repeating groups of data (more than one telephone number for a customer, for example) within that row. Although you could have columns called PHONE_NUMBER_1 and PHONE_NUMBER_2, those columns are technically different pieces of data, even though they relate to the same concept (a telephone number). The official way to handle repeating groups, known in the world of conceptual data modeling as *multivalued attributes,* is to create a separate table that has a primary-key join column. (In this example, you put the CUSTOMER_ID column in both the master customer table and in the table that has the phone numbers so that you can reconstruct a customer's complete record.)

You go through this seemingly ridiculous, overly complex set of steps to ensure that a relational database is in *first normal form* (meaning it has no repeating groups of data).

You can also design a relational database to include other normal forms. *Second normal form* (which has no partial-key dependencies) and *third normal form* (which has no non-key dependencies) are the mostly commonly used forms in relational database design, though the seldom-used fourth normal form, fifth normal form, and Boyce-Codd normal form are also options. (A database modeling book can give you more information about these terms.)

To get to the point: A relational database is *normalized* (when the rules of normalization are followed or mostly followed) because of the way it is designed for and accessed during typical OLTP functions.

One of the primary purposes of normalization is to prevent *update anomalies,* which occur when you update a column in a given row but don't update the other rows in that column that have the same value. Update anomalies are a little complicated, and you don't really need to understand them unless your focus is on OLTP database modeling. Just remember that normalization is important for update operations — more specifically, for optimizing the run-the-business database design.

A data warehouse almost never permits update operations because data is modified by bulk reloading operations, rather than single in-place updates as part of a transaction. One of the main benefits of normalization-based relational design, therefore, doesn't really apply to a data warehouse.

The side effect of normalization

What if update operations don't really apply to a relational database? One of the side effects (results) of a highly normalized database is that it has many tables in it; to create data warehousing facts of information (sales by quarter by territory, for example), many multi-table join operations must occur.

If a highly normalized database has a number of tables because facts are broken down into multiple tables (primarily to prevent update anomalies), and if a data warehouse doesn't support update operations (in the OLTP sense), why normalize?

Exploring new ways to design a relational-based data warehouse

Over the last ten years or so, the design techniques for data warehousing by using RDBMSs have largely boiled down to three options:

- ✔ **Corporate Information Factory (CIF):** A comprehensive architectural framework that houses various data architectures leveraged to support the three styles of applications within most enterprises (run-the-business, integrate-the-business, and monitor-the-business). These data architectures include the operational data store (ODS), data warehouse, and data marts, along with various interfaces for applications and the operational environment. Bill Inmon, Claudia Imhoff, and Ryan Sousa developed the CIF.

- ✔ **Star schema:** This method mimics the multidimensional structures of facts and dimensions, discussed in Chapter 6, but it uses RDBMS tables — specifically, fact tables and dimension tables. The star schema design techniques leverage highly denormalized structures. You gleefully throw away the rules of normalization and put data where it makes the most sense, not based on update-oriented restrictions but based on query patterns. Ralph Kimball developed the star schema design technique.

✔ **Data vault (Common Foundational Integration Modeling Architecture):**
This is a data integration architecture that contains a detail-oriented database containing a uniquely linked set of normalized tables that support one or more functional areas of business tables with satellite tables to track historical changes. This hybrid approach encompasses the best of breed between third normal form (3NF) and star schema. The design is flexible, scalable, consistent, and adaptable to the needs of the enterprise. This data model is architected specifically to meet the needs of enterprise data warehouses.

Inside the data vault model, you can find familiar structures that match traditional definitions of star schema and 3NF that include dimensions, many-to-many linkages, and standard table structures. The differences lie in relationship representations, field structuring, and granular time-based data storage. The modeling techniques built into the data vault have undergone years of design and testing across many different scenarios, giving them a solid foundational approach to data warehousing. Dan Linstedt is the data vault method author, creator, and inventor.

Choose your relational design approach carefully. Although people have a tendency to choose one method over another, the technology and tools that you leverage impact your design approach. In other words, you can't find one "silver bullet" method. Based on your needs and tool selection, one technique might work better than the others. Check out all these approaches: Run benchmarks, but don't just assume that one or the other design approach can efficiently support your enterprise's data warehousing requirements.

Relational Products and Data Warehousing

The following sections discuss some leading relational database products that you might want to use for your data warehouse. Almost all these vendors have, during the past few years, acquired additional products, including OLAP or multidimensional-oriented technology and other RDBMSs to support very diversified platforms and integrate into their product lines and architectures. You might want to keep an eye on the whole picture because a data warehousing environment might well have both relational and multidimensional servers. In such an environment, you need integration that's as seamless as possible.

IBM Data Management family

www.ibm.com/software/data/management

The IBM Data Management family is an outgrowth of the IBM flagship DB2 relational DBMS product for MVS/ESA mainframes, as well as a number of acquisitions, including Informix. Many organizations that have corporate standards and mandates, such as "Thou shalt do all large database processing on the mainframe," deploy data warehousing by using a version of DB2 for this platform.

Microsoft SQL Server

`www.microsoft.com/sqlserver`

Microsoft initially targeted SQL Server technology for many departmental applications in which Microsoft products are dominant. Over the years, Microsoft has added features to enable organizations to expand capacity for data warehousing, changes which have made SQL Server the preferred platform for data marts.

Oracle

`www.oracle.com`

Oracle, a leading RDBMS vendor, has been a mainstay in the areas of data warehousing and data marts since mid-1990s. In the early years, Oracle was the alternative to IBM, and it was a dominate factor in the non-mainframe data warehousing and data mart environments. Oracle has continued to innovate its database platform to address needs for data warehousing.

Chapter 6

Specialty Databases and Data Warehousing

Relational databases have become the steady, general-purpose champion of the data-management world. The straightforward table-row-column structure, not all that different (at least, conceptually) from a basic spreadsheet, is a flexible method by which you can organize data for many different purposes.

That's the good news.

The not-so-good news is that the flexibility comes with a price. Specifically, in some areas of data management (not many, but some), the table-row-column structure, also known as a *horizontal storage manager,* is inefficient and performs poorly — at least, until you enhance (or, in some cases, overhaul) the relational database management system (RDBMS) to handle these out-of-the-ordinary missions.

One of these areas is *multidimensional analysis,* a way of looking at data as facts organized by dimensions. (I cover all this stuff in the section "The idea behind multidimensional databases," later in this chapter.) As Chapter 5 points out, RDBMS products have been augmented with specialized, enhanced multi-table query optimization so that they can handle data more efficiently in a multidimensional manner.

Multidimensional Databases

This isn't the first time in recent history that new types of database products have emerged and overcome RDBMS inefficiencies. Back in the 1980s, a class of applications was identified in which RDBMS products ill-handled the data-management needs (especially the generation of RDBMSs available at that time). These applications all needed user-specified data types that varied among different implementations. For example, computer-aided design/computer-aided manufacturing (CAD/CAM) applications had to be capable of specifying data types that related to product drawings, blueprints, and other related factors. Computer-aided software engineering (CASE) needed data types to represent applications and systems, databases, graphical representations of entities and attributes, process and data flows, and other parts of the application-development process.

What resulted was *object-oriented database management systems (ODBMSs)*, which eliminated the table-row-column structures of relational databases and instead introduced the concepts of classes and subclasses (or types and subtypes), objects, properties, methods, and the other parts of object-oriented technology directly into the database engine.

Because RDBMS technology wasn't well-suited to multidimensional analysis, particularly in terms of performance, vendors set out to develop their own structures tuned and optimized for improved performance.

If you track happenings in the database management world, you're probably familiar with the convergence of relational and object-oriented database technology, as mentioned in Chapter 5. RDBMS products are being equipped with object-oriented extensions. Arguably, this approach to handling complex data types (objects) has won out over non-relational products ("pure" ODBMSs), primarily because of the large installed base of relational products and applications running on top of them. Will the same thing happen in the data warehousing world — relational technology overtaking and then overwhelming specialized multidimensional products? Only time will tell.

The idea behind multidimensional databases

Multidimensional databases (MDDBs) throw out the conventions of their relational ancestors and organize data in a manner that's highly conducive to multidimensional analysis. To understand multidimensional databases, therefore, you must first understand the basics of the analytical functions performed with the data stored in them.

Multidimensional analysis is built around a few simple data organization concepts — specifically, facts and dimensions:

- **Facts:** A *fact* is an instance of some particular occurrence or event and the properties of the event all stored in a database. Did you sell a watch to a customer last Friday afternoon? That's a fact. Did your store receive a shipment of 76 class rings yesterday from a particular supplier? That's another fact.

- **Dimensions:** A *dimension* is a key descriptor, an index, by which you can access facts according to the value (or values) you want. For example, you might organize your sales data according to these dimensions: time, customer, and product.

The basics

In these simple examples, you can organize and view your sales data as a three-dimensional array, indexed by the time, customer, and product dimensions:

- In October 2008 (the time dimension), Customer A (the customer dimension) bought class rings (the product dimension) — 79 of them for $8,833.

- In 2007 (the time dimension), Customer A (the customer dimension) bought many different products (the product dimension) — a total of 3,333 units for $55,905 (the facts).

Notice the subtle different between the way the dimensions are used in these two examples. In the first one, the time dimension relates to a month; the customer dimension relates to a specific customer; and the product dimension is for a specific product.

In the second example, however, time is for a year, not a month; customer is still the same (an individual customer); and product is for the entire product line.

Multidimensional analysis supports the notion of *hierarchies* in dimensions. For example, you can organize time in a hierarchy of year⇨quarter⇨month. You can view facts (or the consolidation of facts) in the database at any one of these levels: by year, quarter, or month.

Similarly, you can organize products in a hierarchy of product family⇨ product type⇨specific products. Class rings might be a product type; "class ring, modern style, onyx stone" might be a specific product. Furthermore, class rings, watches, other rings, and other items all would roll up into the jewelry product family.

Is there a limit to the number of dimensions?

Theoretically (and I do mean theoretically), you can have as many dimensions in your multidimensional model as necessary. The question always exists, however, of whether your multidimensional database product can support them. But here's a more important question — even if a product allows for a certain number of dimensions (15, for example), does it make sense to create a model of that size? You should work closely with your users to determine whether the number of dimensions makes your solution too complex — and therefore limiting the population of users — or improves the ease of use — and therefore expanding the user population.

You can, for example, add geography to the dimension list that contains time, customer, and product so that you can see and organize facts according to sales territories, states, cities, and specific stores.

How should I choose the levels in a hierarchy?

The levels in a hierarchy enable you to perform *drill-down* functionality, as discussed in Chapter 10. And by having multiple levels within a hierarchy, you can quickly get answers to your questions because of the information that has been set up at each of those specified levels, so that information is just waiting for your queries.

Unfortunately, unless you explicitly determine that you want to include a level in a hierarchy, you can't see your facts at that particular level by using a multidimensional database. (You might see them at a higher, more summarized level of detail or at a lower level of detail, but not at *that* level).

Before you create a bunch of levels in each of your dimension hierarchies (just in case you need them), first consider that every one of these pre-defined levels affects storage requirements for your multidimensional model.

Because multidimensional databases have fairly rigid structures built around the *pre-calculation* of facts (creating and storing aggregates in the database, rather than performing report-time aggregation and calculation), the more dimensions you have and the more levels in each dimension you have, the greater your storage requirements and the longer your build or load times.

Physical database structures in an MDDB

Although nearly all MDDB products are built around the concept of facts, dimensions, and hierarchies, no one has come up with an MDDB standard definition. In the relational world, non-standardization has also been somewhat of a problem, particularly in relation to value-added features, such as constraints and stored procedures. The basic relational table-row-column structure, however, has been fairly easy to export or unload into a flat file of some type and then reload it into another RDBMS product.

Don't forget your spreadsheet!

Though MDDB products typically provide data to an OLAP tool, many users happily use a plain old spreadsheet program as their primary analytical tool. For example, Essbase (an Oracle-Hyperion product), SQL Server Analysis Server (a Microsoft product), and PowerCubes (a Cognos product) all have an add-in interface to Microsoft Excel. You use the interface to make your data requests and then, after receiving data back into your spreadsheet, manipulate it like you manipulate any other data in a spreadsheet.

When you put together a multidimensional-analysis component for your business development environment, don't forget about your spreadsheet users: They might happily receive dimensionally stored data through their spreadsheet product, rather than through the interface that the underlying MDDB product provides.

In the MDDB world, vendors have taken a variety of different approaches to their respective products' physical representations of data. They're all seeking ways to overcome storage and complexity problems caused by large numbers of dimensions (for example, more than 15) and deep levels of hierarchies (for example, 20 levels deep).

MDDB vendors have tried to use, wherever possible, "sparse array-management techniques" to reduce the amount of wasted space in any data model. (If you're a computer science or MIS major, you might recall this subject from a class in data structures. A *sparse array* is an array in which most of the elements have the same value known as the default value — usually 0 or null. A naive implementation of an array might allocate space for the entire array, but in the case where there are few non-default values, this implementation is inefficient. MDDB vendors have leveraged algorithms that determine the sparcity of the array in advance and arrange the data according in blocks.) The vendors have all taken different paths, and portability from one MDDB product to another hasn't exactly been a high priority for these companies.

When you're evaluating products, don't get caught up in worrying about physical storage techniques: Just make sure the logical representations that come with the products (such as the hierarchies, levels, and facts) can meet your business needs. Eliminate products that seem clunky or that have, for example, a hierarchy model that doesn't seem quite right for your data. Then, after you find products that seem to fit your business, kick the tires a little (so to speak) to see how they work inside.

Are multidimensional databases still worth looking at?

If relational technology is absorbing the multidimensional world and quickly becoming capable of handling this area of data management, are MDDBs now a dead-end technology? Not necessarily. This question is much the same as the continuing ROLAP-versus-MOLAP debate. (Check out Chapter 10 for guidelines on the style of OLAPs you should consider under various circumstances.) You might well have specific needs that make MDDBs the sensible answer for your environment.

Horizontal versus Vertical Data Storage Management

Most relational database managers have been built on a *horizontal storage manager,* which places all data in a database by row (or record) when a transaction occurs. A database table is represented as a chain of database pages that contain one or more data rows. A horizontal storage manager provides fast online transaction processing (OLTP) support because most transactions occur in a record format — for example, inserting a general ledger entry or writing a check. However, when a user requests a record, the database page that contains the data is often moved into memory, which for business intelligence applications is highly inefficient.

Several specialty database products have emerged over the years designed to assist and optimize query-centered applications, such as business intelligence. Such products enable you to more readily develop interactive data warehouses. The goal of these column-wise databases is to increase the speed of decision support queries performed against large amounts of data.

When speaking to audiences around the globe, I often asked database administrators in the audience if they would ever place an index on a column that contains a person's area code, a student's grade point average, or a customer's total transactions. The response is a resounding, "No!" They usually give this adamant response for reasons based on technology, such as:

- We index based only on standard, well-known paths (such as name) because of the overhead of indexes.

- The *cardinality,* or unique occurrence of data, would force the database to perform a table scan anyway.

Yet, when you ask users what information they need to fulfill their job responsibilities, they respond with these kinds of requirements:

✔ See the number of people by area code in my territory so that I can more effectively manage my promotions.

✔ Identify the top-ranked students in the graduating class so I can arrange the proper interviews.

✔ Figure out which customers do business with my company and spend between $100,000 and $500,000 annually.

Each of these three requirements characterizes a different user request, yet they all perform similar functions: They're decision support-oriented queries. A need to access data drives user information requirements, but the users' access patterns aren't compatible with most RDBMS indexing strategies. In short, the RDBMS technology gets in the way of the applications' success.

A database table is represented as a chain of database pages that contain one or more data rows, as shown in Figure 6-1. A horizontal storage manager provides fast online transaction processing (OLTP) support because most transactions occur in a record format.

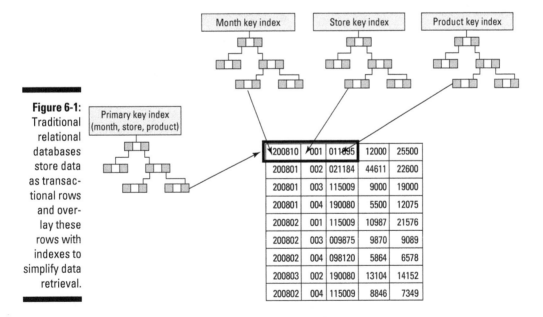

Figure 6-1: Traditional relational databases store data as transactional rows and overlay these rows with indexes to simplify data retrieval.

These relational databases assist query activity by using indexes. Indexes are built on top of the rows to simplify and accelerate data retrieval on common paths, as show in Figure 6-1. Data warehousing solutions, such as business intelligence, don't use many of these indexing techniques because they have been crafted to assist OLTP applications in the frequent need to find and update individual rows within database tables.

To properly support typical user queries found in business intelligence, other storage and indexing techniques are required. Vendors such as Sybase and Vertica have built vertical storage managers. Instead of storing data by row, these products store the data by columns — hence the name *vertical storage manager* or column-wise storage. This method of storage effectively solves the problem of user queries against large sets of data because a user often seeks only a few columns, versus the large number of columns managed in a row by a horizontal storage manager. With the data stored as a series of page changes, with each page containing column data, query processing time is reduced by a factor of 500 or more to 1. Additionally, these products support other optimizations that assist in the speed of query processing, including data compression, parallel query operations, and multiple indexing techniques per column. The challenge in implementing such technologies involves standardization. Therefore, many data management departments refuse to implement such technologies because those technologies require additional support labor.

Data Warehouse Appliances

Like with bell-bottom jeans, hardware-assisted databases are on the come-back trail. (Actually, my daughter tells me that bell-bottoms are out of style again, but hardware-assisted databases aren't.) Microsoft, Oracle, and Netezza are all the rage at database seminars around the globe. In the mid- to late 1980s, vendors Britton Lee and Teradata (which eventually merged) were all the rage. They provided dedicated machines that optimized database processing — the first machines used by heavy data consumers, including many of the consumer-packaged goods companies. The objective of these boxes was to dedicate all aspects of a computer to getting data to the users faster. This dedicated machine included a query-centered database, memory, CPU, and disk operations. Eventually, such products moved out of vogue, and the database management systems were migrated to a more open, run-on-any-box architecture.

Now, they're back!

A *data warehouse appliance* is an integrated set of servers, storage, operating system, DBMS, and software specifically pre-installed and pre-optimized for data warehousing. Data warehouse appliances provide solutions for the mid- to large-volume data warehouse market, offering low-cost performance on data volumes in the terabyte to petabyte range (that's a lot of data!).

Most data warehouse appliance vendors use massively parallel processing (MPP) architectures to provide high query performance and platform scalability. MPP architectures consist of independent processors or servers executing in parallel. Most MPP architectures implement a *shared nothing architecture,* in which each server is self-sufficient and controls its own memory and disk. Shared nothing architectures have a proven record for high scalability and little contention. Most data warehouse appliances distribute data onto dedicated disk storage units connected to each server in the appliance. This distribution allows the appliances to resolve a relational query by scanning data on each server in parallel. The divide-and-conquer approach delivers high performance and scales linearly when you add new servers into the architecture.

And, from a price perspective, most of the vendors in this arena are attempting a strategy of plug-and-play. For instance, Netezza typically sells a new user their product as plug-compatible with Teradata for less than the Teradata maintenance cost. This price point makes the products very attractive, giving them a growing adoption rate.

Data Warehousing Specialty Database Products

The following sections discuss vendors that have data warehousing specialty database products that you might want to check out.

Cognos (An IBM company)

www.cognos.com

Cognos was one of the early vendors to offer a multidimensional database that had PowerPlay. The product has a modeling environment (Transformer) that produces physical MDDBs known as PowerCubes. Additionally, Cognos acquired TM1 in the mid-2000s. TM1 is one of the innovation leaders in the area of in-memory MDDBs.

Microsoft

www.microsoft.com

Microsoft introduced its first MDDB, SQL Server Analysis Services, with SQL2000. The product has gone through a number of innovations, and its scale and capabilities have expanded in the latest release, SQL2008. Additionally, Microsoft recently acquired DATallegro, a database appliance, and will begin providing customers and partners early access to the combined solution through community technology previews in 2009. Full product availability is scheduled for the first half of calendar year 2010.

Oracle

www.oracle.com

Oracle offers a plethora of specialty database stores, including a new database appliance introduced in 2008 — multidimensional databases Express and Essbase. Oracle also has other index-based innovations within their traditional relational database platform.

Sybase IQ

www.sybase.com

Sybase introduced IQ in the mid-1990s, a product built on bit-mapped indexing technology. Sybase IQ is a column-wise, vertical storage manager that supports bit-mapped indexing for both low-cardinality and high-cardinality data. For example, a particular attribute that has a small range of values (the colors of an automobile, for example) is low-cardinality data; high-cardinality data consists of range-oriented values (for example, sales volumes and unit sales).

Vertica

www.vertica.com

Vertica is the commercial release of a Michael Stonebraker database product which grew in the university research environment known as C-Store. (Stonebreaker was the father of Ingres, PostgreSQL, and other successful database products.) Vertica is relatively new to the market, founded in 2005, and consists of a scalable, vertical storage manager focused on analytical applications such as data warehouses.

Chapter 7

Stuck in the Middle with You: Data Warehousing Middleware

*I*n the world of *distributed computing* — basically, any environment in which data has to move from one system to another — middleware is a key component in making it all work. This chapter discusses data warehousing middleware in detail, from the basics to the specific services that apply to your data warehousing environment. At the end of the chapter, you can find a list of vendors that have middleware products you might want to use in your data warehousing project.

What Is Middleware?

Loosely defined, *middleware* is a set of services that perform various functions in a distributed computing environment, across a wide set of server and client systems. In essence, middleware is computer software that connects software components. Here are some types of middleware services:

- ✓ **Security:** Authenticates a particular client program to some system component to verify, for example, that the client program and its user are really who they say they are.

- ✓ **Transaction management:** Ensures *transactional integrity* — that a system or database doesn't get corrupted if problems occur.

- ✓ **Message queues:** Enables loosely coupled systems to pass messages back and forth to each other, and those messages trigger actions and/ or transactions to occur. Messages sent from one application to another are collected and stored until they're acted on, while the application continues with other processing.

✔ **Application server:** A server that hosts an application programming interface (API), which exposes business logic and business processes so that other applications, either on the same or different servers, can use the shared logic and processes.

✔ **Web server:** A computer program that's responsible for accepting requests from Web browsers, as well as sending responses and content to those browsers — usually Web pages, such as HTML documents, and linked objects, such as images.

✔ **Directory:** Enables a client program to find other services or servers located in a distributed enterprise.

These types of services are typically part of a distributed transaction-processing environment. I don't mean that a data warehousing environment can't also include these services; it's just that other middleware services are more important to a data warehousing environment, as described in the following section.

Middleware for Data Warehousing

In a data warehousing environment, the middleware services are the set of programs and routines that do the following:

✔ Pull data from the source (or sources).

✔ Make sure that the data's correct.

✔ Move the data around the environment from platform to platform, as necessary.

✔ Handle any necessary data transformations.

✔ Load the data into the data warehouse's database (or databases).

The services

In a more formal sense, the items in the preceding list are handled by these middleware services (described in more depth later in this chapter):

✔ Data selection and extraction

✔ Data quality assurance, part I (at the component level)

✔ Data movement, part I (also at the component level)

✔ Data mapping and transformation

✔ Data quality assurance, part II (after transformation has occurred)

  ✔ Data movement, part II (into the data warehouse's platform environment)

  ✔ Data loading (into the data warehouse)

Figure 7-1 illustrates how these middleware services flow together in a moderately sized data warehousing environment.

But your data warehousing environment might differ from Figure 7-1, particularly in the area of the data-movement services. A data-movement service is necessary every time data crosses system boundaries. Your conceptual picture differs, depending on the details of your particular end-to-end environment.

You absolutely, positively need to plan, design, and otherwise think about data warehouse middleware in terms of the individual services in the preceding list (and described in the section "What Each Middleware Service Does for You," later in this chapter), rather than in generic terms, such as "extraction tools." Many different vendors provide some, many, or all these services as part of a single product or a suite of products. But a tool that has strong mapping and transformation services, for example, might be weak in data-loading services, or a tool that provides a rich set of extraction services might be less effective in the mapping and transformation space, in addition to data quality assurance.

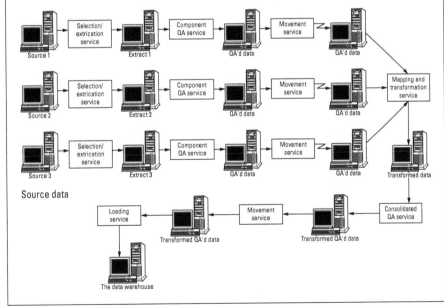

Figure 7-1: The data warehousing middleware services flow together, from end to end, from data sources to the data warehouse.

Before selecting a tool for your data warehousing project (if that's the route you take, rather than custom coding, which I discuss in the following section), make sure that you have a good idea about the particular challenges in your environment. If you have relatively straightforward data-extraction needs, for example, but challenging data-quality problems, concentrate on finding the best quality-assurance tool available, even if it has only so-so extraction capabilities. (This advice applies even if the tool has no extraction capabilities, in which case, you have to combine it with another tool.)

Should you use tools or custom code?

In the early days of data warehousing, most organizations handled middleware services through custom coding, rather than with the few tools available at the time, as shown in this example:

1. An organization writes a program in a programming language such as COBOL, or perhaps in an environment such as SAS, to handle the data extracts from a mainframe data source and then do the quality assurance checking and the transformation.

2. A file-transfer service, such as standard FTP (File Transfer Protocol), is used to copy the transformed and "cleansed" data to the machine on which the data warehouse will reside.

3. Plain old SQL, or a bulk loading utility, is used to load a relational database with the new (or updated) contents of the data warehouse.

Nothing's wrong with this programmatic approach. Always determine for your specific environment whether custom coding or tools are the "right" way to go. Don't automatically assume that you should implement your data warehouse by using middleware tools. But your team might find replicating the reusable logic built into most middleware tools very expensive. And, furthermore, you can find open-source (free) middleware tools available, making the argument of "we'll save money by using internal resources" a difficult one to justify. Therefore, most implementations today are done using *Extract, Transform,* and *Load* (ETL) tools.

What Each Middleware Service Does for You

The following sections describe each of the data warehousing middleware services and what they mean to your data warehousing environment.

Data selection and extractions

The primary purpose of the data-selection and -extraction service is to *select* from (find in) a data source the data that you want to move into the data warehouse and then *extract* (pull out) that data into a form that can be readied for quality assurance services.

You can use one of two different types of selection and extraction services for your data warehousing environment:

- ✔ **Get 'em all and sort 'em out later:** Find and extract all the data elements in a source that you want to load into your data warehouse, regardless of whether a specific element has been previously extracted.

- ✔ **Change-oriented:** Find and extract only the data elements that have been either newly added to the data source or updated since the last extraction.

The first type of service requires less complex logic in order to perform the extraction. But you have to deal with larger volumes (sometimes, much larger volumes) of data than with the second type, the change-oriented service.

The change-oriented method of selection and extraction is fairly straightforward when your source is a relational database that has a time stamp you can use to detect when a row of data was added or last updated. You can compare a row of data against the date and time of the last extraction process to determine whether data needs to be selected and extracted. But when the data is stored in a file that doesn't have a time stamp (a VSAM file, for example), this process can be significantly more difficult.

You might also face a challenge when source data has been deleted from either a file or a database. If the business rules for your data warehousing environment call for the deletion of corresponding data from the warehouse, you must have a way to detect deletions that were made since the last extraction process to ensure that appropriate deletions are made in your warehouse.

The result of the selection and extraction is, well, an extract of data that's ready to undergo additional processing: checking out the data quality (covered in the following section).

Data quality assurance, part 1

You should establish two different quality assurance (QA) services in the flow of middleware services. You have to perform the first QA tasks against the extract from the data source before you perform any more middleware services. Try to catch (and correct) errors and problems as early in the process as possible. Moving data down the pipeline toward the data warehouse is pointless if problems are so significant that they either require significantly more effort to correct later in the process or simply can't be corrected.

So, what types of problems should you look for? Here are a few:

- **Values in data elements that exceed a reasonable range:** A customer has submitted 150 million purchase orders in the past month, for example, or an employee has worked with the company for 4,297 years, according to the employee database and the stored hiring date.

- **Values in data elements that don't fit the official and complete list of permissible values:** A value might have an A code, for example, when the only permissible values for that field are M and F. (If that field were labeled GENDER, A might stand for androgynous!)

- **Cross-table inconsistencies:** For entries in the CUSTOMER_ORDER table, no corresponding entries (as identified by CUSTOMER_ID) exist in the CUSTOMER_MASTER_TABLE.

- **Cross-field inconsistencies:** Records that have an incorrect state or zip code for the city indicated.

- **Missing values:** Records that have missing values in certain fields where they should have contents.

- **Data gaps:** For example, a source table should contain one row of data that includes total units sold and sales dollars for each month over the past two years. For a large number of customers, however, no rows exist for at least one of those months.

- **Incomplete data:** If information about every product the company sells is supposed to be available, for example, are all products included in the extract?

- **Violations of business rules:** If a business rule states that only one wholesaler can sell products to any one of the company's customers, you should check to see whether any customer records indicate sales made through more than one wholesaler, which could indicate incorrect data in the source.

- **Data corruption since the last extract:** If extraction occurs monthly, for example, you should keep track of data values or sums that should be constant, such as SALES PER CUSTOMER PER MONTH. If, in a subsequent month, the value of SALES PER CUSTOMER PER MONTH changes for a given customer for a previous month, the underlying data might have been corrupted.

- **Spelling inconsistencies:** A customer's name is spelled several different ways, for example.

What do you do when you find problems? You can try one of the following techniques:

- ✔ **Apply an automatic-correction rule.** When you find an inconsistent spelling, for example, do a lookup in a master table of previous spelling corrections and automatically make the change in the data.

- ✔ **Set aside the record for a team member to analyze and correct later.** In this case, you might do the human part of the QA in conjunction with automatic correction. For example, automatic corrections are made, if possible, and a report about other problems are put into a separate file and sent to the QA person. When the QA person makes all the manual corrections, you merge the corrections back into the data that has gone through the automatic QA process.

- ✔ **Cool your jets.** If you discover enough problems that are serious or require an indeterminate amount of research, consider halting the entire process until after you find and fix the problem.

You can make the QA process much more efficient, and much less problematic, if you perform a thorough source systems analysis, as described in Chapter 16. If you have a fairly good idea about what types of data problems you might find in each data source, you can reprogram your QA process to detect and (hopefully) correct those problems before continuing.

Historically, organizations treated the data warehouse QA process as a one-directional flow. Problems are corrected before the data is moved further into the flow of middleware processes but is never corrected in the data sources. Most new data warehouses have a built-in feedback loop from the QA process that corrects data quality issues in the source data.

Data movement, part 1

In most situations, the two services I describe in the preceding sections (selection and extraction, and quality assurance) take place on the same *platform* (system) on which the data source resides. If your data warehouse will be hosted on a different platform than the data source, though, you have to use a data-movement service to effect the system-to-system transfer of the data.

You can likely use a relatively simple service (handled by a simple file-transfer program, for example). The movement service, if you need it at this point, simply moves the QA'd data into the environment in which you plan to make additional transformations.

Data mapping and transformation

Figure 7-1 shows an environment in which data is being extracted from three different data sources for inclusion in a data warehouse, and each of the three sources is on a different platform. At some point in the middleware process, these QA'd extracts must be brought together for a combined mapping and transformation process.

The mapping and transformation service handles classical data warehousing problems. Suppose that one data source stores customers by using a five-character customer ID, and another source uses a six-digit numeric customer identifier. To enable comparisons and other data warehouse processing, you need a common method of customer identification: One of the identification schemes must be converted to the other, or perhaps a third, neutral identification system, depending on the environment's characteristics.

In addition to handling cross-system incompatibilities, additional transformations might include

- **Data summary:** A summary can be performed earlier in the process, before cross-system movement, depending on the peculiarities of your specific data warehousing environment.

- **Selective inclusion of data:** You might include records from only one data source, for example, if you get a comparable record from another extract. You don't know, until you converge all the data source's contributions, how selective inclusion rules are applied.

- **Data convergence:** Certain elements from one data source are combined with elements from another source to create one unified record for each customer, product, contract, or whatever type of data you're dealing with.

The main point to remember about the mapping and transformation service is that you should have, at its conclusion, a unified set of data that's ready to load into the data warehouse — as soon as you complete a few more steps.

In complex data warehousing environments, you might want to consider multiple transformation processes. As shown in Figure 7-2, for example, data extracts converge at several different levels of transformation before moving farther down the middleware pipeline, enabling you to apply more horsepower to the transformation process by using multiple servers early in the flow.

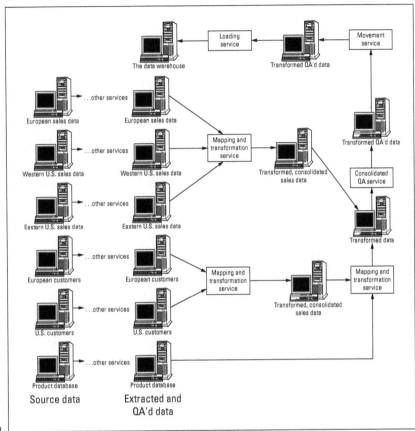

Figure 7-2:
Complex
data ware-
housing
environ-
ments
might have
several
different
mapping
and trans-
formation
points.

Data quality assurance, part II

Following completion of the transformation processes, data must be QA'd — again. You never know what type of errors or discrepancies the transformation process might have introduced into the data. After changes have occurred, any previous QA processes are no longer valid.

Run the consolidated, transformed data through the same type of QA steps discussed in the section "Data quality assurance, part I," earlier in this chapter. Although you probably don't find as many rudimentary errors (such as spelling mistakes or values that are out of range) if you did a thorough job on your first-level QA, you still want to make sure. Furthermore, ensure that the code or scripts used for data transformation didn't accidentally cause new errors to creep in.

The goal of this second-level QA is to make sure that your consolidated and transformed data is ready to load into the data warehouse — as soon as one more step occurs, if necessary.

Data movement, part 11

If you're doing your transformation and QA processing on a platform that's different from the platform on which you run your production data warehouse (on a development server, for example, rather than on the operational server), you must execute one more data-movement service to get the data to the place where you want it to eventually reside. This process usually involves only a relatively simple file transfer.

Data loading

The data-loading service loads the extracted, QA'd, transformed, and re-QA'd data into your warehouse. You might load data via a customized program, SQL (an INSERT statement, for example), or a utility.

If you need to load a large volume of data, try to use a fast-loading utility, which usually involves much less time than a programmatic or SQL-based approach.

If you use SQL to load your data into a relational database, try to make the loading as efficient as possible by turning off logging (if your DBMS product permits it). If the loading job is abnormally terminated, you just have to use the DROP or TRUNCATE statement to get rid of your partially loaded table, fix the problem that caused the termination, and restart the job. This process usually is much faster than if you turn on the facilities needed for OLTP-style data and transaction integrity (with accompanying overhead).

Specialty Middleware Services

For more sophisticated and/or simplified data warehousing needs, you can deploy a set of specialty middleware services. These services include

- ✔ Replication and change data capture
- ✔ Virtual, or federated, data access (also known as Enterprise Information Integration, or EII)

The following sections describe each of these specialty middleware services and what they mean to your data warehousing environment.

Replication services for data warehousing

Replication middleware services combine selection and extraction, movement, and loading from one database to one or more others, usually managed by a single DBMS product. (The source database and all the targets are all Oracle, all Sybase, or all Microsoft SQL Server, for example.)

Although replication service capabilities vary among DBMS products, traditionally, they've been snapshot-oriented: A snapshot of either an entire database or the changes since the last replication occurred are extracted, at a predetermined time, from the source and copied over a networked environment to the intended targets. The data is then transmitted and loaded as-is (no transformation occurs). Many database vendors have implemented their replication by reading the log files for changes. This style of replication is very efficient because it doesn't increase the overhead of your transactional systems to replicate the data.

But replication doesn't replace the long list of data warehousing middleware services discussed in this chapter. You want to use replication in a data warehousing environment primarily when capturing changes in the source database, often called *change data capture* (CDC), or after you load the data into your data warehouse and then extract data and send it to data marts, as shown in Figure 7-3.

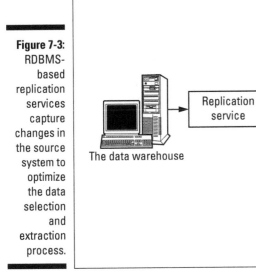

Figure 7-3:
RDBMS-based replication services capture changes in the source system to optimize the data selection and extraction process.

Data mart 1

Replication service

The data warehouse

Data mart 2

Data mart 3

Enterprise Information Integration services

Around 1995, vendors began positioning their software as virtual data warehousing tools. The fundamental premise was that sometimes it just doesn't make sense to copy and manipulate a bunch of data, just in case someone needs it. Why not access data directly from the source on an as-needed basis?

Alas, accessing data over a network at its source has proved to be the least challenging of the problems in trying to provide a kind of in-place data warehousing. The same challenges faced in any data warehousing environment (such as dealing with data quality, deciding what types of transformations must occur, and choosing how to handle those transformations when different sources are inconsistent) are still present. Just because you can get to data at its source (in almost any database or file structure) doesn't mean that data provides the necessary business intelligence when it's in your hands.

To solve these data quality issues, many data architects have begun to perform bottom-up data mart construction to develop a component-based data warehouse. Rather than have a single database into which you feed all data (creating your data warehouse), a series of components each handles a particular set of functions (such as answering specific business questions) or certain subjects. Together, these data marts (or components) comprise a data warehousing environment.

This component-based, dynamic access data architecture is the basis for virtual data warehousing and, more specifically, what *Enterprise Information Integration* (EII) servers are offering to the market.

EII architecture

Figure 7-4 shows an environment in which individual components are created within the data warehousing environment in a bottom-up manner. Instead of combining the components into one large database (and copying all the data again), EII creates a data warehousing environment in which users can access each component's contents from a business intelligence tool like they were all stored together, even though they're not.

Think about how you use a Web browser on your desktop. You either click a link or type a specific URL, and the environment, working behind the scenes, takes you to the right place for the content you asked for. Now, imagine the Internet running much faster. When you go to various sites, you're not accessing ads for the latest four-wheel drive you've been coveting, sports scores, Dilbert cartoons, or whatever else it is you do on the Internet. You're bringing back pieces of data that are then combined and sent back to your browser. That's virtual data warehousing — it's just like the Internet!

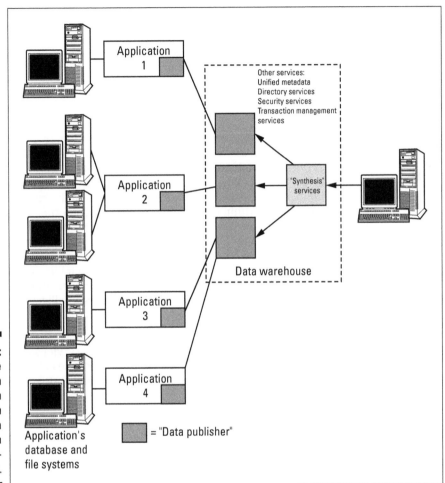

Figure 7-4:
Enterprise
Information
Integration
(EII) can
provide a
virtual data
warehous-
ing service.

I highly recommended that you don't build a virtual data warehousing environment to access source data directly, in its native format. As mentioned earlier in this chapter, your challenge isn't figuring out how to join cross-platform
databases (combining IMS data with DB2 data, for example) and handling
those types of system-level transformation, it's ensuring that the quality of the
data is high and doesn't require the user to manually cleanse the data.

Each application should therefore be warehouse-enabled (refer to Chapter
25) and contain a data publisher that's responsible for all the middleware
services (such as extraction and quality assurance), as specified in the
environment's business rules. The data publisher could conceivably operate
almost in real-time mode, like it would have to do in an operational data store

(again, refer to Chapter 25), or it could function in a periodic (batch-oriented) mode if instantaneous updates aren't required. In this situation, the data publisher is a mini-middleware product embedded in the application (or a service accessed by the application).

When you think of virtual data warehousing, replace the question "Can I get to the data?" with the question "Can I get to usable data?" The data publisher plays an important role, and should not be neglected.

You also can't neglect data architecture. Just because you're developing components in a bottom-up manner and they're being accessed in place, rather than being copied into a larger data warehouse database, doesn't mean that you can neglect this function. Say that one component stores customer IDs as five-digit numbers after transformation occurs and contains only customers who made purchases within the past six months. And another component, which contains all customers who have ever bought your company's products, uses seven-character alphanumeric identifiers. In this situation, you might have the same type of data mismatch problems you would if you were accessing data directly from the sources. Although EII allows for differences between component contents, you must understand and manage the differences so that you don't impede the business intelligence mission.

Additional EII services

Your virtual data warehousing environment includes services that a single database would handle in a centralized environment. These true middleware services complement the traditional data warehousing middleware, such as extraction and transformation:

- ✔ **A unified metadata service:** Users see a single logical view of the environment's contents without having to know the location and particulars of each component.

- ✔ **A directory service:** Individual components within the environment, even if they're relocated or otherwise modified.

- ✔ **Security services:** These services handle permissions, authentication, and other security needs in a distributed environment.

- ✔ **Synthesis services:** Unlike traditional Internet usage, for example, where each hit returns information that probably won't have to be correlated with information from other hits, a virtual data warehouse might have to combine facts from one component with facts from another. (Figure 7-4 shows a synthesis service component within the virtual data warehouse.)

    If the data warehousing environment, which "knows" that it's *virtually* (remotely) accessing data from multiple sources, has a component that handles the synthesis of results from the other components, the responsibility for consolidating these independent results sets can be offloaded from the requesting business intelligence tool.

✔ **Transaction-management services:** In addition to the synthesis service, which is a type of transaction-management function, these services provide routing, load balancing, conflict resolution, and other functions necessary to ensure data integrity. (Yes, you need these services, even in a supposedly read-only environment.)

Facing the EII infrastructure challenge

Wow! Virtual data warehousing sounds like a fairly neat, state-of-the-art idea. Why isn't it more widespread?

The answer, in a word, is infrastructure. Although you can talk all you want about emerging networking and communications technologies, and the tremendous throughput we'll all have someday, most corporations are still several generations behind the state of the art in their networking infrastructure. They're struggling to deal with the major investment required for what's essentially the Internet and Distributed Computing Age.

Delivering virtual data warehousing that includes EII services requires significant throughput of data in what's often an unpredictable manner. The irony is that a virtual data warehousing environment almost assuredly requires, over time, significantly less data movement across the enterprise than traditional data warehousing, which has a philosophy of copying millions (perhaps billions) of bytes, just in case someone wants to ask a question possibly requiring that data.

Traditional data warehousing has the advantage, however, of working the clock (as they say in football) by scheduling large-scale batch loads for either system downtimes or relatively light operational loads, using offline data-transfer means (tape, for example), rather than network file transfers and other tricks of the trade.

Until an organization's communications infrastructure can pump the data through, EII services and concepts (such as virtual data warehousing) probably will remain on the fringes, just out of reach.

If you're interested in virtual data warehousing as an architecture that uses EII services, here's a list of what you have to do:

✔ **Supercharge your networking infrastructure.** Yes, it's expensive, but you gotta do what you gotta do.

✔ **Stop thinking about data warehousing in centralized terms.** Think distributed but interconnected subject areas of data. Free your mind!

✔ **Insist that any new application developed for your organization, no matter who does it, be warehouse-enabled.** (See Chapter 20.)

✔ **Supercharge your EII servers with memory and processors.** Reading data from memory is far faster than across the network or off a disk. Most EII servers enable you to cache the results of a query in memory and share them across users. By providing the proper memory and processor configuration, the EII server gets faster with each user request through reuse.

✔ **Think enterprise!** Just because you're dealing with bottom-up component development doesn't mean that you're developing a stand-alone piece of data. The last thing you want to wind up with is an islands-of-data-mart problem to replace the islands-of-data situation you've been dealing with your entire career. (I know that you have because we all have.) In a traditional data warehousing environment, you're forced to deal with these enterprise-scale data architecture issues. Don't let your foray into virtual data warehousing undermine all the good that you've done in your organization when it comes to dealing with enterprise data architecture.

Vendors with Middleware Products for Data Warehousing

The following sections list the names of vendors that offer data warehousing middleware products you might want to take a look at.

Composite Software

www.compositesw.com

Composite provides Enterprise Information Integration (EII) products and technology. By using Composite, you can access and combine data from disparate data sources, including packaged applications such as SAP, custom applications, data warehouses, and XML data stores, as well as other data sources.

IBM

www.ibm.com

IBM Information Integration provides a data integration platform that incorporates EII; Extract, Transform, and Load (ETL); change data capture; replication; and other data warehousing middleware functionality.

Informatica

www.informatica.com

Informatica provides a platform for data integration. The specific offerings from Informatica include the PowerCenter, On Demand data loader, B2B Data Exchange, and Data Quality.

Ipedo

www.ipedo.com

Ipedo XIP is a data virtualization platform that allows organizations to aggregate and present information from disparate sources into their business intelligence, enterprise reporting, corporate portal, or service-oriented architecture (SOA) applications. Ipedo XIP's Virtual Views allow applications to provide users with the information they want on-demand in real-time.

Microsoft

www.microsoft.com

Within the Microsoft SQL Server product offering, you can find an ETL component known as SQL Server Integration Services (SSIS). This ETL technology leverages Microsoft's .NET and SQL Server platforms for execution and deployment.

Oracle

www.oracle.com

Oracle Warehouse Builder (OWB) enables you to design ETL processes and implement data integration solutions for your data movement requirements. Using a common metadata repository, OWB combines data integration capabilities with enterprise data quality tools to deliver end-to-end data integration optimized for Oracle databases. Additionally, the Oracle Business Intelligence (BI) foundation component provides a unified business model, along with an enterprise information model that unifies metadata across the Oracle BI tools and analytical applications. This BI infrastructure integrates with a majority of the popular data sources, major business applications, and databases, including IBM DB/2, Teradata, Microsoft SQL Server; SAP Business Information Warehouse (BW), Microsoft Analysis Services; flat files; XML data; and unstructured data.

Sybase (Avaki)

www.sybase.com

Sybase Avaki is an enterprise application integration software product designed for EII systems. Avaki uses a federated approach, delivering data from original sources.

Part III
Business Intelligence and Data Warehousing

The 5th Wave
By Rich Tennant

"I started running 'what if' scenarios on my spreadsheet, like, 'What if I were sick of this dirtwad job and funneled some of the company's money into an off-shore account?'"

Part III

Business
Intelligence and
Data Warehousing

In this part . . .

*N*o, the phrase business intelligence isn't an oxymoron. You have no reason to build a data warehouse, in fact, if you don't have the objective to provide business intelligence to members of your organization.

But what is business intelligence? The chapters in this part of the book explain different aspects of business intelligence — from the simplest to the most complex — in down-to-earth, hype-free language, complete with examples and a description of products that might interest you.

Chapter 8

An Intelligent Look at Business Intelligence

*I*n Chapters 5 and 6, I discuss the various types of database management systems (DBMSs) that are suitable for data warehousing. In the early days of data warehousing, controversy swirled around what type of DBMS to use — the focus was very technical, not solution-oriented. At times, the controversy stemmed from the lack of understanding of a new technology form and the immaturity of data warehousing architectures.

It is now understood that you can make the generalization that you create a data warehouse for the purposes of business intelligence. One variety of business intelligence includes query, reporting, and OLAP functionality.

If you build a data warehouse without clearly understanding what types of business intelligence your organization needs, you're almost certain to build and put into use something that doesn't even come close to providing the business value you're seeking, regardless of how error-free your data, how sophisticated your user tools, and how wonderful your environment's performance.

This chapter helps you make sense of the business intelligence quandary. (*Note:* Much of the information in this chapter is explored in-depth in the other chapters in this part of the book. This chapter, however, provides a place where you can skim through the descriptions of each of these categories to see how they relate to each other.)

The Main Categories of Business Intelligence

At the outset of your data warehousing project, don't focus on the type of tools you need — yet. Instead, concentrate on figuring out the types of questions users will ask against the data warehouse's contents, the types of reports that will be run and for what purposes, and the general models of processing that will occur.

To help you get past hype, buzzwords, and techno-jargon, use the model shown in Table 8-1, which describes the four categories of business intelligence functionality.

Table 8-1	Business Intelligence Categories	
Type	*Information You Want*	*See This Chapter*
Basic querying and reporting	"Tell me what happened."	9
Business analysis (OLAP)	"Tell me what happened and why."	10
Data mining	"Tell me what might happen" or "Tell me something interesting."	11
Dashboards and scorecards	"Tell me a lot of things, but don't make me work too hard."	12

Each of the four categories in Table 8-1 describes a way of accessing data, doing something with the information that's retrieved, and providing information to whomever requested it. Each category, however, has different attributes.

Querying and reporting

Basic querying and reporting largely represents the traditional uses of data for analytical purposes. The data is retrieved in accordance with either regular standard reports or in response to a particular question (an ad hoc query, for example); and then it's formatted and presented to the user in a specific format, either on-screen or in a printout. The interaction model is usually a set of regular, predictable steps:

1. **Make a data request.**

2. **Retrieve the data.**

3. **Manipulate the data slightly.**

   Summarize or reorganize, for example, if necessary.

4. **Format the data.**

5. **Present the data.**

Business analysis (OLAP)

Business analysis is the term used to describe visualizing data in a multidimensional manner. Query and report data typically is presented in row after row of two-dimensional data. The first dimension is the headings for the data columns; the second dimension is the actual data listed below those column headings.

Business analysis allows the user to plot data in row and column coordinates to further understand the intersecting points. In essence, this visualization of OLAP is most often utilized with an OLAP specialty database, although the business analysis can be done without such a database. The most common form of this business analysis involves using Microsoft Excel PivotTables, in which a user can plot data as rows, columns, or intersecting cells.

Business analysis introduces analytical processes and a degree of variability into the user interaction model. Conceptually, the first steps are pretty much the same as the steps in the preceding section for querying and reporting, but then the user takes over:

6. **Manipulate the data.**

   Look at it in a different way. Place some data on the rows, place other data on the columns, place the interested measurement at the intersecting cell.

7. **View the new results.**

   Change the presentation style of the data into a bar graph or line chart. Add in another column of data to refine the points on the graph. In addition, the user can request the data beneath the data, such as the details underneath a summary.

From that point, the variability of the process might iteratively cycle through the preceding steps (continually manipulating and reviewing the new results, for example) or even add new data for more analysis.

Data mining

At times, data mining isn't comingled with the other forms of business intelligence. This lack of integration occurs for two reasons:

- ✔ Business users don't have the required knowledge in data mining's statistical foundations.

- ✔ The mainstream business intelligence vendors don't provide the robust data mining tools, and data mining vendors don't provide robust business intelligence tools.

Data mining tools provide a degree of technical analysis that requires a base understanding in statistical algorithms to be successful in their use.

Data mining is often presented as a magical technique that you can use to uncover the secrets of the universe from your organization's data. In reality, data mining is an umbrella term for a series of advanced statistical techniques and models born in the 1980s as part of artificial intelligence research (neural networks, for example). I don't focus on individual technologies in this chapter (you can read about those in Chapter 11), but data mining as a technique has one or both of these aspects:

- ✔ **Predictive:** Data mining tools and capabilities search through large volumes of data, look for patterns and other aspects of the data in accordance with the techniques being used, and try to tell you what *might* happen based on the information that the data analysis found. Notice the emphasis on the word *might:* Data mining is a technique of probability, not a fortune-telling service.

- ✔ **Discovery-oriented:** Both the basic querying-and-reporting and business analysis/OLAP categories of business intelligence tools provide business intelligence based on either questions users explicitly ask (sort of the question of the moment) or "institutionalized" questions that members of the organization regularly ask in the form of regular reports (or both). The key word is *question:* If no questions are asked, no answers are forthcoming.

Data mining's discovery-oriented nature is intended to provide answers, even if you don't ask any questions. (I always refer to this model as "tell me something interesting, even if I don't know what questions to ask.") The data mining system typically provides these answers by building complex models that are used to analyze data, looking for some trend or tendency within the data that might be appropriate, and then telling you what it found.

Dashboards and scorecards

The early and mid-1980s experienced a frenzy in executive information systems (EIS) technology, a sort of predecessor to the 1990s data warehousing boom. Early EIS technology received a mixed welcome and sort of faded away near the end of the decade. Some people therefore consider EIS to be a predecessor to, but not a relative of, data warehousing. When you consider the aspect of entire systems, this view seems accurate because many EISs were built on top of relatively simple data extracts (see Chapter 22) with a narrow range of content.

In this new era of data warehousing, though, EIS systems are characterized by portals that contain dashboards and scorecards. Therefore, EIS is alive and well — just more mature and informative. Dashboards and scorecard environments best serve the broad category of users who want to receive key business information and indicators that can help them understand how the users are performing.

The analogy of your car's dashboard is very useful here. You can look at your tachometer to find out that your idle speed is somewhere near 1200 RPM. You also realize that the red line on the tachometer signifies danger — and therefore, you avoid revving the engine to that level. This is your dashboard. If, for some reason, you notice that the engine is idling faster — say, 3000 RPM — you might take your car to the mechanic for further analysis. The mechanic wants to investigate the details, making him or her similar to users of query and reporting technology. These individuals are very interested in the detailed information that can assist in fixing a "red line" problem. There are subtle differences between dashboards and scorecards that are covered in Chapter 12. In general, a dashboard presents current information on your operational performance while a scorecard shows your performance against a plan or set of objectives.

Dashboard and scorecard users certainly don't want to sift through reams of data from dozens or hundreds of reports. The philosophy of the dashboard and scorecard user is, "Tell me what I need to know — just a little information so that I know I'm on the right course — and please don't make me work too hard to get to it!"

Results either from querying and reporting tools, or from business analysis tools, typically feed dashboards and scorecards. A tool in one of those categories does the work, and a dashboard or scorecard makes the result available to the user.

Dashboards and scorecards aren't only for executives! And executives don't use only dashboards and scorecards to the exclusion of other categories of tools, either. Every person driving a car has a dashboard, and in business, all employees can have their own personal dashboards or scorecards to align their activities across the enterprise.

Dashboard and scorecard technology involves two major types of environments (both discussed in Chapter 12):

- **Briefing books:** A *briefing book* is an electronic (though it can be printed) sequence of key information and indicators that someone regularly uses for decision-making or performance monitoring. Users typically don't "wander" through information; rather, they take a relatively particular path.

- **Command centers:** The *command center* might be a console of on-screen push-buttons (perhaps a lot of them), each of which shows the user a different kind of information — a report, document, image, or indicator.

Command center interfaces are tailor-made for multimedia integration environments, such as Web pages presented on your company's intranet. From such an environment, you can integrate key components, such as the enterprise strategy, high-level plan focal areas, and performance across the organization. Incorporating the dashboard and scorecard information into such a Web page, along with nontraditional data, makes for a very robust business intelligence environment.

Other Types of Business Intelligence

Alas, the neat, organized model that has four different types of business intelligence categories can be expanded for more complex applications. For example, an OLAP or dashboard tool might have geographical information system (GIS) capabilities — or it might not. As shown in Figure 8-1, several other horizontal categories of business intelligence can apply to some or all of the categories discussed in the preceding sections.

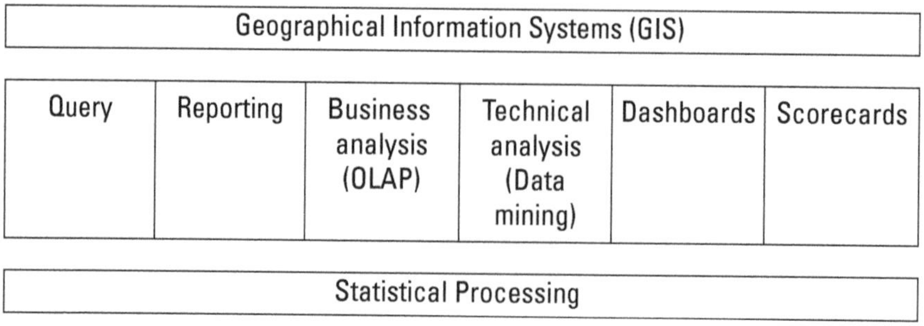

Figure 8-1:
Business intelligence includes horizontal categories that span some or all of the vertical types.

Geographical Information Systems (GIS)					
Query	Reporting	Business analysis (OLAP)	Technical analysis (Data mining)	Dashboards	Scorecards
Statistical Processing					

Statistical processing

Most business intelligence tools do rudimentary statistical processing, such as averages, summaries, maximum values, minimum values, and standard deviations.

Think back, though, to that statistics class you endured in college. (If statistics class was easy for you, more power to you.) Remember z-scores? Chi-square tests? Poisson distributions? Some folks in the real world really use those concepts (and many other related concepts that most of us left way behind) as part of their jobs.

These people always want statistical functionality integrated into a business intelligence tool so that they don't have to save results from one tool into an intermediate storage facility (such as a Microsoft Excel spreadsheet) and import that data into a statistical tool for processing. Tool integration is a good thing!

Additionally, a large part of some data mining processing is based on *heavy stats* (advanced statistics, such as probabilities). Some environments include simulation and gaming capabilities that can identify and test various outcomes, and try to handle sophisticated what-if processing based on real data, rather than on assumptions and hypotheses.

Geographical information systems

Geographical information systems (GISs) make up a category of business intelligence functionality that spans multiple categories. The simplest way to understand GIS technology is to consider the concept of maps. You could, for example, do querying in a tabular manner and show product sales by country. Those sales are divided into product sales by territory and then broken down into product sales by increasingly smaller groupings, down to product sales by department in each store, for example.

I have a customer who made the profound statement, "Our business is geographically based — why can't I see our key information on a map?" GISs do just that: They provide a way of viewing information based on presenting that information by using maps. Suppose that all countries colored in red indicate that sales revenue is lower in the most recent quarter than it was in the preceding quarter. If you click your mouse on any of those countries, another map appears, which is divided into sales territories and again color-coded. Clicking on a red-colored territory displays another map (a U.S. map by state, for example) with additional levels of detail.

When you use GIS technology, data isn't just managed in a hierarchy such as this:

Departments⇨stores⇨states⇨territories⇨countries

The data is also managed *spatially* — in a manner that's sensitive to on-screen layout. For example, when you click a map of Pennsylvania, the GIS would "know" that you want to see sales in Pittsburgh, without you having to type or otherwise select that city from a drop-down list or other on-screen control.

Mash-ups

The capability to mix and match information and presentation services, such as those found on the Web, is a simple example of a mash-up. Companies such as Google, Yahoo!, and Microsoft are driving much of the technology platforms for future applications and provide key technologies in the area of mash-ups. Therefore, the example for GIS (in the preceding section) could actually take your standard database query and present that data by using Microsoft's Virtual Earth technology. Furthermore, you might want to combine that information with external benchmark information to give you greater insight. For example, if your marketing team felt that a new product would sell well to those individuals who have a median income of $50,000, you could plot census data with your sales performance data on a map provided by Google, Yahoo!, or Microsoft. How cool is that?

Although few companies are using mash-ups today, mash-ups will likely emerge as the future presentation vehicle. Current mash-ups combine external data, such as information that you can find on Craigslist or Amazon, with external visualization tools, such as Google documents or maps.

Business intelligence applications

While the business intelligence and data warehousing markets mature, large vendors of commercial off-the-shelf software, as well as specialty boutique firms, have started offering out-of-the-box business intelligence applications. These solutions typically are targeted at a functional area of a business, such as finance, supply chain, or customer relationships. The solutions combine all aspects of what I discuss in Chapter 3: subject area data content that has an associated database and set of business intelligence tools. These business intelligence applications can help solve 60 to 70 percent of issues you might commonly find in a functional area of your business. The application comes with a set of predefined content, views, or reports that enable you to simply hook up the application to your current systems and go. Vendors such as SAP and Oracle dominate this area because they also control much of the "run the business" components required as data sources for the "monitor the business" applications that they provide.

Business Intelligence Architecture and Data Warehousing

The early days of business intelligence processing (any variety except data mining) had a strong, two-tier, first-generation client/server flavor. (Some business intelligence environments that were hosted on a mainframe and did querying and reporting were built with a centralized architecture.)

Conceptually, early business intelligence architectures made sense, considering the state of the art for distributed computing technology (what really worked, rather than today's Internet, share-everything-on-a-Web-page generation).

Many of these early environments had a number of deficiencies, however, because tools worked only on a client desktop, such as Microsoft Windows, and therefore didn't allow for easy deployment of solutions across a broad range of users. Additionally, long-running reports and complex queries often bottlenecked regular work processes because they gobbled up your personal computer's memory or disk space.

Most, if not all, tools were designed and built as *fat clients* — meaning most of their functionality was stored in and processed on the PC. In addition to the bottleneck problem, all users' PCs had to be updated because software changes and upgrades were often complex and problematic, especially in large user bases.

The beginning of a new era of business intelligence architecture has arrived, regardless of whether your tool of choice is a basic querying and reporting product, a business analysis/OLAP product, a dashboard or scorecard system, or a data mining capability. Although product architecture varies between products, keep an eye on some major trends when you evaluate products that might provide business intelligence functionality for your data warehouse:

- ✔ **Server-based functionality:** Rather than have most or all of the data manipulation performed on users' desktops, server-based software (known as a *report server*) handles most of these tasks after receiving a request from a user's desktop tool. After the task is completed, the result is made available to the user, either directly (a report is passed back to the client, for example) or by posting the result on the company intranet.

- ✔ **Web-enabled functionality:** Almost every leading tool manufacturer has delivered Web-enabled functionality in its products. Although product capabilities vary, most products post widely used reports on a company intranet, rather than send e-mail copies to everyone on a distribution list.

✔ **Support for mobile users:** Many users who are relatively mobile (users who spend most of their time out of the office and use laptops or mobile devices, such as a Blackberry, to access office-based computing resources) have to perform business intelligence functions when they're out of the office. In one model, mobile users can dial in or otherwise connect to a report server or an OLAP server, receive a download of the most recent data, and then (after detaching and working elsewhere) work with and manipulate that data in a standalone, disconnected manner. In another model, mobile users can leverage Wi-Fi network connectivity or data networks, such as the Blackberry network, to run business intelligence reports and analytics that they have on the company intranet on their mobile device.

✔ **Agent technology:** In a growing trend, intelligent agents are used as part of a business intelligence environment. An intelligent agent might detect a major change in a key indicator, for example, or detect the presence of new data and then alert the user that he or she should check out the new information.

✔ **Real-time intelligence:** Accessing real-time, or almost real-time, information for business intelligence (rather than having to wait for traditional batch processes) is becoming more commonplace. In these situations, an application must be capable of "pushing" information, as opposed to the traditional method of "pulling" the data through a report or query. Like with traditional data-extraction services (described in Chapter 7), business intelligence tools must detect when new data is pushed into its environment and, if necessary, update measures and indicators that are already on a user's screen. (In most of today's business intelligence tools, on-screen results are "frozen" until the user requests new data by issuing a new query or otherwise explicitly changing what appears on the screen.)

Chapter 9

Simple Database Querying and Reporting

. . . .

. . . .

*Q*uerying and reporting is the low end of the spectrum of business intelligence functionality that applies to your data warehouse. (Chapter 8 provides an overview of business intelligence functionality.) Querying and reporting handles "tell me what happened" processing that's relatively static and predictable, for the most part. The data is retrieved in accordance with either regular standard reports or in response to a particular question (an ad hoc query, for example). Then, that data is formatted and presented to the user either on-screen or on a printout.

The interaction model for querying and reporting business intelligence typically follows a pattern of regular, predictable steps (these steps are also in Chapter 8, so you can skip ahead if you've already read that chapter):

1. **Make a data request.**

2. **Retrieve the data.**

3. **Manipulate the data slightly.**

   Summarize or reorganize, for example, if necessary.

4. **Format the data.**

5. **Present the data.**

These steps don't vary much between tools, scenarios, or users. If a user decides that the presented result looks odd or otherwise needs to be augmented, the process usually just begins again with a new request.

What Functionality Does a Querying and Reporting Tool Provide?

To help you understand the functionality that a querying and reporting tool offers, this list describes some of the tasks they can help you perform:

- ✔ **Run regular reports.** Your organization might regularly produce standard reports that come from an operational system or from data extracted from one or more of those systems.

- ✔ **Create organized listings.** You might produce a list of all the salespeople in your company or those who meet a specific criteria (they cover more than two territories, for example), and their sales in the most recent month. Organized means that you can list your report or query alphabetically by salesperson's last name; alphabetically by customer name and the salesperson who covers that customer; by rank, from highest sales revenue generated to the least; or any other way you want to look at the data. Figure 9-1 shows an example, using fictional company names.

- ✔ **Perform cross-tabular reporting and querying.** Cross-tabular reports, sometimes called cross-tabs, are slightly more complex than a basic organized listing of data. In addition to the sequential, ordered vertical listing (the company's salespeople), you see across the top (the other axis) of the report a decomposition of various categories and values associated with each category. In the example shown in Figure 9-2, sales revenues are broken down by product.

Figure 9-1: You can use a querying and reporting tool to produce a comprehensive, organized listing of monthly sales revenue by company salesperson.

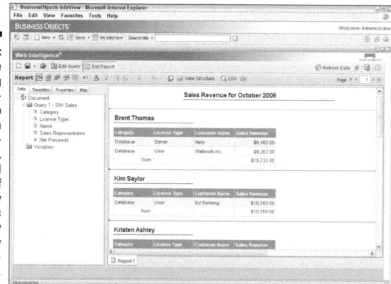

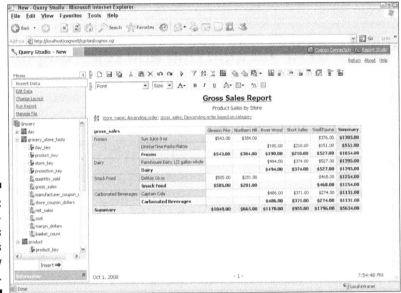

Figure 9-2:
This cross-tab breaks down sales revenue by product.

The barriers between business analysis/OLAP tools and products that have historically been oriented toward querying and reporting are getting somewhat grayer. Query tools, for example, commonly also permit some level of *drill-down,* an OLAP function that enables you to see underlying, more detailed data, as explained in Chapter 10.

The role of SQL

SQL is the official database language of the National Football League; any use of an SQL tool without the express written consent of the National Football League is strictly prohibited. (Sorry about that — a little too much football fever.)

SQL is the official database query language used to access and update the data contained within a relational database management system, or RDBMS.

The roots of SQL go back to IBM and its research labs during the early days of relational database technology. IBM and Oracle were among the first to adopt SQL as the language used to access their relational products (other RDBMSs used different languages that their respective vendors invented). In the mid-1980s, SQL was submitted for approval to both the American National Standards Institute (ANSI) and the International Organization for Standardization (ISO), and during the next few years, other database access languages faded away. Later versions of the SQL standard were published every few years.

Doesn't OLAP do querying and reporting also?

Without jumping ahead to Chapter 10, let me answer a question you might be wondering about if you have business analysis, OLAP experience: Wouldn't an OLAP tool have the capabilities listed in the section "What Functionality Does a Querying and Reporting Tool Provide?" in this chapter, plus many more?

Absolutely! Querying and reporting is, at least conceptually, a subset of OLAP functionality. OLAP architectures and capabilities are more complex than those oriented toward reporting and querying, though. I split the functionality of OLAP between the visualization (business analysis) and storage (OLAP specialty database) for

this reason. More business intelligence tool vendors are enabling the use of their query and reporting tools against relational and OLAP databases. However, business analysis tools don't always support visualizing relational databases.

If all you need is basic querying and reporting capabilities — and you're absolutely sure that's all you need! — you might not want to deal with the overhead of setting up and maintaining an OLAP environment if you don't anticipate gaining much business benefit from those capabilities (if you just don't plan to use them, for example).

The significance of SQL for querying and reporting (and for data ware-housing) is that the language has represented a *mostly* standard way to access multiple RDBMS products.

Each RDBMS product has a slightly different SQL dialect. Although the basic syntax is the same, especially for the most commonly used commands, all SQL dialects are slightly different. In the early 1990s, despite these syntactical differences, several different efforts provided a common gateway to SQL RDBMS products. The most successful was Microsoft Open Database Connectivity (ODBC). The phrase *ODBC-compliant* became important to RDBMS applications in the early and mid-1990s. A similar standard for the Java community also emerged in the late-1990s — Java Database Connectivity (JDBC). Virtually all major database manufacturers today have accessibility through both of these standard connectivity interfaces.

Technical query tools

The use of SQL as the basis for most querying and reporting tools was both good and bad for data warehousing. On the positive side, many more product-to-product matchups are possible in data warehousing environments, enabling tools to be provided both by RDBMS vendors and other third-party vendors.

On the negative side, though, SQL is a relatively complex language after you get past the basics. A series of query tools primarily allow users to type in and edit SQL queries. I don't see these tools as designed for end users and therefore refer to them as technical query tools, though I'm amazed how often I find these tools deployed in end-user organizations.

User query tools

Most end-user querying and reporting tools provide visually oriented, painting, environments that enable users to design screens for report layouts, the data columns desired for the report, or the rows of data that they want to select (only salespeople who have met their quota, for example).

Using all this "painted" information, most tools have increasingly taken a smart query generation approach. Instead of generating a single, overly complex SQL statement that could get you an A in database class but draw a disgusted shake of the head from someone who has done this stuff in the real world, a sequence of SQL statements (usually taking advantage of temporary tables for intermediate results) is generated. This sequence, in effect, decomposes the query into a more efficient series of steps.

Reporting tools

When end users want more complex user interaction or sophisticated formats, a tool with more reporting features is leveraged. You can find a separation between pure query tools and pure reporting tools. The query tool provides data access, filtering, and simple formatting. If you're distributing reports across your enterprise or need to generate form-safe presentation, you use a reporting tool.

Like with query tools, reporting tools provide an environment that enables you to create sophisticated layouts that focus on formatting the data retrieved by the database query.

The idea of managed queries and reports

Turning the average group of users loose with a querying and reporting tool and directing them to "go forth and ask all kinds of questions against the data warehouse" is a dangerous idea. Even with visual tools to aid in generating queries and reports — and even with wizards to help — at least some of these people will undoubtedly issue all kinds of overly complex queries that do little more than bring your data warehouse to its knees.

Although you certainly want to enable *power users* (technically sophisticated users) to do whatever they need to do, you should handle average users differently.

In a *managed querying and reporting environment,* users get templates of queries or reports that they can use to ask questions and perform business intelligence functions in the data warehousing environment. Each template is set up so that it's not too rigid and not too flexible — it's just right.

Suppose that a user must run a report periodically (daily, weekly, monthly, or quarterly) and needs different data, depending on which period is indicated. For example, the user might need to run a weekly report for all product sales to wholesalers, a monthly report for all product sales directly to retailers, and a quarterly report for wholesaler, retailer, and cross-company product sales. Also, one variation of the report must show sales for the entire United States, and the user needs to distribute another report for each sales territory to the appropriate sales manager.

To complicate matters, sales managers sometimes request a weekly preview run of what would ordinarily be a quarterly or monthly report. The reports can't be totally *canned* (set up once and never modified), and each run requires a little (although not much) human input.

The managed environment might have a preset format and links to the tables that are needed. Before running the report, however, the user is prompted for which type of customer he or she wants to include in the report; whether the report covers the entire United States or a specific territory (or perhaps more than one); and any other parameters (for a previous month's sales if someone requests a rerun of a previous report, for example).

Other than these types of guided inputs, the queries and reports are managed and controlled to reduce the chance of runaway queries that use an enormous amount of system resources and probably never run to completion.

Is This All You Need?

Suppose that querying and reporting sounds like a good idea, but you really want to check out that OLAP stuff, too.

You can give some users basic tools and still let others use OLAP tools (and, for that matter, let your statistician use a data mining product). One of the benefits of designing and developing your data warehouse in this flexible, component-oriented manner is that you can equip users with the tools that are most applicable to their respective missions and the business value they're expected to provide from using the data warehouse.

Designing a Relational Database for Querying and Reporting Support

Your data warehousing environment or a specific data mart that your main data warehouse will feed might have the mission of generating a finite and predictable set of reports. This section gives you one approach to designing a relational database to support that mission, built around the principle of *database denormalization,* or deliberately violating good relational database design principles in the interest of performance efficiency. (Chapter 5 discusses normalization, if you're interested in the background to this approach.)

Denormalization is best suited for *quick-hit solutions,* in which you must get a small-scale relational data warehouse or a data mart up and running quickly. For example, you might create a denormalized relational database for a *specific* charter to produce a certain set of reports that will no longer be available as a result of a legacy system migration effort. Although denormalization isn't quite a dead end, it does create a great deal of duplicate data, and the database structures you create don't have much flexibility. Additionally, you probably have limited querying capabilities (in addition to your standard reports) because those capabilities are closely tied to the reporting structures formalized in the table design. Still, you might want to check out this approach.

A simple example of denormalization in Figure 9-3 shows what the source database tables look like in an application that tracks sales performance, with those tables structured primarily according to standard relational database design principles (they're normalized). To support the report format shown at the bottom of the figure, the source structures are mapped into a denormalized table from which the report can be generated without having to join any tables. (To put it more simply, your report runs very quickly.)

Note: A real-world example would involve many more tables (from 10 to 50 or more) and many more reports than Figure 9-3. This figure should get the idea across, however.

Alternatively, you might want to follow the principles and techniques of dimensional design. Because RDBMSs now have much less trouble dealing with dimensionally oriented structures than in the past, you're likely to get adequate performance for your reporting needs and still have the flexibility to support a large variety of ad hoc, multidimensional queries.

For rapid deployment that's reporting-oriented, though, at least consider denormalization-based design for relational data.

CUSTOMERS

CUST_ID	CUST_LAST_NAME	CUST_FIRST_NAME	CUST_TYPE	GROUP_ID
12345	Ashley	Kristen	W	1
23456	Thomas	Brent	W	2
34567	Saylor	Kimberly	R	2

GROUP_TYPES

GROUP_ID	GROUP_DESCRIPTION
1	Exporter only
2	Importer only
3	Importer/exporter

PRODUCT_MAIN

PRODUCT_ID	PRODUCT_DESCRIPTION	CATEGORY_CODE
1000	Glasses	1
2000	Coffee Cups	1
3000	Ski Poles	2

CUST_TYPES

CUST_TYPE	TYPE_DESCRIPTION
W	Wholesaler
R	Retailer
O	Other

SALES

DATE	CUST_ID	PRODUCT_ID	QUANTITY	DOLLARS
3/10/2007	12345	1000	3	$ 4.50
7/6/2007	23456	2000	15	$ 22.50
3/19/2008	34567	1000	55	$ 82.50
3/20/2008	12345	3000	1	$ 25.00
7/27/2008	23456	1000	1	$ 1.50
9/5/2008	34567	2000	30	$ 35.00

PRODUCT_CATEGORIES

CATEGORY_CODE	CATEGORY_DESCRIPTION
1	Drinking containers, household
2	Athletic gear

— Required sales report format —

PRODUCT_CATEGORY	SALES_DATE	GROUP_TYPE	TOTAL_QTY	TOTAL_$	WH_QTY	RET_QTY	OTHER_QTY	WH_$	RET_$	OTHER_$
Drinking containers, households	yyyy/mm/dd	Exporters only	#,###.##	$##,###.##	#,###.##	#,###.##	#,###.##	$##,###.##	$##,###.##	$##,###.##
	yyyy/mm/dd	Importers only	#,###.##	$##,###.##	#,###.##	#,###.##	#,###.##	$##,###.##	$##,###.##	$##,###.##
	yyyy/mm/dd	Importer/exporter	#,###.##	$##,###.##	#,###.##	#,###.##	#,###.##	$##,###.##	$##,###.##	$##,###.##
Athletic gear	yyyy/mm/dd	Exporters only	#,###.##	$##,###.##	#,###.##	#,###.##	#,###.##	$##,###.##	$##,###.##	$##,###.##
	yyyy/mm/dd	Importers only	#,###.##	$##,###.##	#,###.##	#,###.##	#,###.##	$##,###.##	$##,###.##	$##,###.##
	yyyy/mm/dd	Importer/Exporter	#,###.##	$##,###.##	#,###.##	#,###.##	#,###.##	$##,###.##	$##,###.##	$##,###.##

Figure 9-3: Normalized database tables in a source application.

Vendors with Querying and Reporting Products for Data Warehousing

The following sections list some vendors that provide querying and reporting tools you might want to consider using with your data warehouse.

Business Objects (SAP)

www.businessobjects.com

Business Objects, now an SAP company, provides a suite of products for query and reporting. Specifically, they provide

- ✔ **WebIntelligence:** Also known as WebI; a Web-based solution for ad-hoc querying, reporting, and analysis
- ✔ **Crystal Reports:** Formerly from Seagate Software, a tool for report creation and distribution

Both of these tools operate against the Business Objects semantic layer, known as a Universe, which maps business terms to their technical match within the data warehouse. Allowing for broader user adoption by minimizing the need for technical knowledge of how things are stored and organized within the data warehouse.

Cognos (IBM)

www.cognos.com

Cognos, now an IBM company, provides a suite of products for querying and reporting:

- ✔ **Query Studio:** A Web-based solution for ad-hoc querying
- ✔ **Report Studio:** A Web-based tool for report creation, query aggregation, and distribution

Both of these tools operate against the Cognos semantic layer defined within the design tool, known as Framework Manager, that maps business terms to their technical match within the data warehouse. Cognos's semantic layer allows for broader user adoption by minimizing the need for technical knowledge of how things are stored and organized within the data warehouse. The older Cognos technology also includes Impromptu, which was a Microsoft Windows–based tool that Query Studio and Report Studio have replaced.

Information Builders

www.informationbuilders.com

Information Builders produces the Focus family of reporting and querying products, which has its roots in the mainframe Focus system. WebFOCUS enables you to produce an ad-hoc query or managed reporting environment on a broad range of database management systems.

Microsoft

www.microsoft.com/bi

Microsoft provides a suite of data warehousing products, including products for reporting, although they don't currently provide a competitive query tool. The SQL Server product line incorporates SQL Server Reporting Services (SSRS), which provides a sophisticated server-side reporting tool. Because SSRS is a server-side technology, companies can deploy these reports for visualization purposes within Microsoft Excel and Microsoft SharePoint, as well as other integrated productivity tools.

Oracle

www.oracle.com/solutions/business_intelligence/index.html

Oracle has not only built its own tools over the years, but also acquired Hyperion (which had acquired Brio). Therefore, Oracle has a number of query and reporting tools to assist people in the area of data warehousing:

✔ **Oracle Business Intelligence Publisher:** A reporting solution for authoring, managing, and delivering highly formatted documents, such as operational reports, electronic funds transfer documents, government PDF forms, shipping labels, checks, and sales and marketing letters

✔ **Oracle Business Intelligence Suite, Enterprise Edition Plus:** A comprehensive business intelligence platform, formerly Siebel Analytics, which provides querying and reporting functionality across distributed data sources, including data warehouses

Chapter 10

Business Analysis (OLAP)

. . . .

. . . .

A man walks down the street in Manhattan carrying a data warehouse under his arm. From the other direction, a woman approaches, carrying an OLAP. (Bear with me — this stuff will make sense in a second.)

The man sees a billboard advertising a watch he's had his eye on, and now it's on sale. To catch the ending date for the sale, he keeps his eyes on the billboard while he walks.

The woman notices a crowd of people gathered outside a theater and looks in that direction to see what the commotion is. She too continues walking.

Suddenly, the man and woman collide. Stunned for a moment, the man looks down and then says to the woman, "Hey, you got OLAP in my data warehouse!" The woman recovers from her surprise, looks down, and says to the man, "Hey, you got a data warehouse on my OLAP!"

Together, they both say, "Mmmmm . . ."

If you're at least as old as I am, this scenario should bring back memories of a mid-1980s series of commercials for a certain chocolate-covered peanut-butter-cup candy. If it doesn't sound familiar, check out the retromercials (old, original television commercials) on YouTube. You might see this one.

Step over from TV Land to Data Warehousing Land. Without OLAP, data warehousing would hardly be what it is today. At the same time, the roots of OLAP — or, more precisely, multidimensional business analysis — go back to the 1960s.

The Origins of OLAP

You can find an interesting history of OLAP, written by Nigel Pendse, on the Internet. It traces multidimensional analysis back to the APL programming language, developed at IBM in the late 1960s based on work done a few years earlier. Products were introduced throughout successive decades, including a convergence with spreadsheet technology in the 1980s. But not until the early 1990s, when data warehousing became popular, did the two disciplines click and make history.

OLAP-based business analysis and data warehousing made each other what they are today: an intensely popular mode of data analysis that almost every organization has either implemented or is considering.

Despite the natural synergy between data warehousing and OLAP, you can, and likely will, do more with a data warehouse than with OLAP. For that matter, OLAP isn't performed exclusively against a data warehousing environment. (If you want, you can use an OLAP tool against multidimensionally oriented tables in a low-volume production database.)

What Is Business Analysis?

Business analysis is the visualization capabilities provided by OLAP platforms. The business analysis style of accessing data relates to "tell me what happened and why" processing that you do after you build your data warehouse. Unlike querying and reporting tools, business analysis leverages OLAP functionality, enabling you to dig deeper, poke around a little, and (hopefully) come up with the "why" aspect of what's happening in your business.

The distinguishing characteristic of business analysis is that it enables you to perform multidimensional analysis. As discussed in Chapter 6, users have a natural tendency to view business results in different ways, organized by various dimensions. By using the dimension of time, for example, you can perform trend analysis. By using other dimensions particular to a given fact (products, business units, and geography, for example), you can get down to the nitty-gritty of finding problem areas, pinpointing your company's strengths, and generally getting a clear picture of what's going on and why it's happening.

The OLAP Acronym Parade

In the data warehousing world, business analysis hit the big time by operating against multidimensional databases specially structured to support this type of processing. These environments have come to be known as multidimensional OLAP (MOLAP) systems.

A corresponding approach (the archenemy of MOLAP) is relational OLAP, or ROLAP. ROLAP uses plain old relational databases, rather than specialized multidimensional structures. As discussed in Chapter 6, however, ROLAP requires that the DBMS products perform cross-table joining of data somewhat more efficiently than they traditionally have done.

Ah, but I'm not done yet. Hybrid OLAP, or HOLAP, is an attempt by vendors to call a truce in the ROLAP-versus-MOLAP war and bridge the gap. Different vendors are taking different approaches. Some vendors link a MOLAP front end to a ROLAP back end and route user requests to the engine that can serve the answer most efficiently. Other vendors cache multidimensional aggregated results for subsequent use, instead of re-creating those aggregates. Others cache the dimension data, such as product and customer, to optimize navigation while dynamically retrieving the fact data, such as sales amounts and costs.

Want more? How about desktop OLAP (DOLAP) environments, in which a client system (rather than an OLAP server) is the primary storage repository for a specialized multidimensional structure. DOLAP is particularly useful for laptop users who want to perform business analysis when they're not hooked up to the company network — while on the road or at a client site, for example.

To help explain the OLAP architecture, I've broken the OLAP world up into three architectural layers: business analysis (visualization), OLAP middleware, and OLAP databases. I discuss all three in the following sections.

Business analysis (Visualization)

Business analysis, or the visualization capabilities of OLAP, is the focal point of most end users. Probably the most familiar visualization tool that enables business analysis is Microsoft Excel's PivotTable. Within the visualization tool, OLAP features (discussed in the section "Business Analysis (OLAP) Features: An Overview," later in this chapter) are available. These features allow users to slice and dice, nest, pivot, trend, and change displays — all with the click of a mouse. (It sounds like I'm selling the ginsu knife collection, doesn't it?)

All these capabilities enable users to discover trends within the information presented without needing support from technical personnel. These trends might be good or bad — either way, the user has the ability to get to the root cause within the analysis.

OLAP middleware

OLAP middleware emerged in the late 1990s and early 2000s. In essence, standards have been driven to allow the world of OLAP to split between vendors that are good at business analysis (visualization) and those that are good at physical storage and access optimization. The OLAP middleware market is between standards, such as multidimensional expressions (MDX) and XML for Analysis (XMLA), and the ROLAP vendor community.

MDX was initially introduced by a consortium of vendors led by Microsoft as part of the OLE DB for OLAP specification. MDX provided a query language for OLAP data stores in a fashion very similar to SQL for relational databases.

XMLA is the most recent attempt at a standardized application programming interface (API) for OLAP products. What differentiates XMLA from previous attempts at a standard is that it offers broader solution provider support with companies such as Oracle (Hyperion), Microsoft, SAP, and SAS. XMLA allows client applications to talk to multidimensional or OLAP data sources through the exchange of messages back and forth by using Web standards — HTTP, SOAP, and XML. The query language used is MDX. Oracle (Hyperion) Essbase, Microsoft Analysis Services, and SAP Business Warehouse all support the MDX language and the XMLA specification.

ROLAP providers include vendor offerings from MicroStrategy, IBM/Cognos TM1, and Pentaho Analysis (Mondrian). You need a strong understanding of data access and modeling to properly implement these offerings because they most often work against a relational data store — simulating the OLAP database in memory on a server, called *building a cube on the fly*.

OLAP databases

OLAP databases are the physical storage locations for multidimensional databases. While middleware standards and processing capabilities of middleware solutions have evolved, this community of products has shrunk to a handful. The most popular include Oracle (Hyperion) Essbase, Microsoft Analysis Services, SAP Business Warehouse, and Cognos PowerPlay (PowerCubes).

First, an Editorial

This section provides you with some valuable context to the OLAP hype you might face, if you haven't already. Just browse the Internet and check out vendor's white papers about OLAP. Vendors make a serious amount of definitive statements about why whatever approach they *don't* sell won't work for you.

Here's my opinion: No OLAP silver bullet exists — at least, not of this writing. Here are some guidelines and trade-offs for OLAP architectures:

✔ Strongly consider a MOLAP solution (and check out ROLAP alternatives) if response time is a key factor; if summarized data, rather than detail-level data, can address your business intelligence mission; and if your data volumes won't grow to more than 50 gigabytes.

✔ Some financial-analysis and budgeting packages are tied to a particular multidimensional database product. In these cases, you might want to set up a financial-analysis data mart that uses MOLAP technology, regardless of the other data marts and data warehouse databases in your environment.

✔ If detail-level data is important to your business intelligence processing and you're likely to have a very large database (VLDB) environment, consider ROLAP solutions. You might also want to consider a HOLAP environment, however, if your descriptive, dimensional data is relatively static as described in the section "The OLAP Acronym Parade," earlier in this chapter.

✔ Regardless of the approach you take, check out products carefully. Look for hidden performance "gotchas," recalculation times for multidimensional structures, inefficient relational processing in ROLAP environments, scalability problems (after you reach a certain number of users or a certain database size, problems occur), and other events that can cause your data warehousing environment to be less than satisfactory.

Business Analysis (OLAP) Features: An Overview

The following sections present a brief list of some business analysis (OLAP) features so that you can get an idea of what to expect from products. Because it's impossible to discuss this subject in detail in a few pages, I hit just the strategic highlights to show you what this area means to you and your data warehouse.

TIP

For more details about these and other features, check out vendors' Web sites (see the section "Data Warehousing Business Analysis Products," later in this chapter), product brochures, and demos; textbooks and tutorials; magazine articles; and other sources.

Drill-down

Drill-down analysis is probably the feature that average users use most frequently. The concept is fairly simple: A user can see selective increasing levels of detail as required.

Figure 10-1 shows a report of Zip's Video and Games third-quarter sales, broken down by region on one axis and by product on the other.

Suppose that you want to see the next level of detail for sales in the northeast region. You can double-click that row to display an additional level of detail for sales by product in Pennsylvania and New Jersey (as shown in Figure 10-2).

Say that you're curious about the additional level of detail for sales in cities in Pennsylvania. Double-click Pennsylvania, and — presto! — you have the results shown in Figure 10-3: sales for each city.

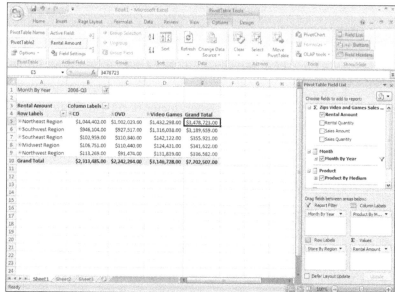

Figure 10-1:
A basic
level of
detail on a
quarterly
sales report.

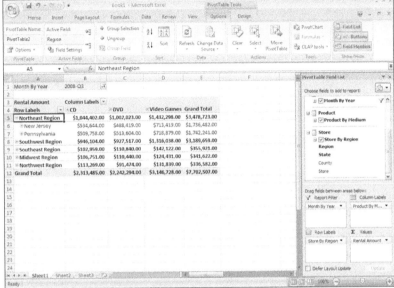

Figure 10-2: Drilling down to the next level of detail for the northeast region doesn't affect other summary levels.

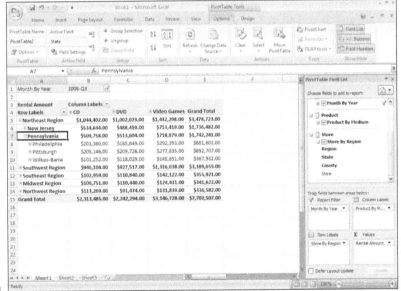

Figure 10-3: Drilling down even further, you can see sales by city in Pennsylvania.

Now, you want to see the sales amount for each store. After you double-click each city's name, you see the lowest level of detail — quarterly sales by product and by store — as shown in Figure 10-4.

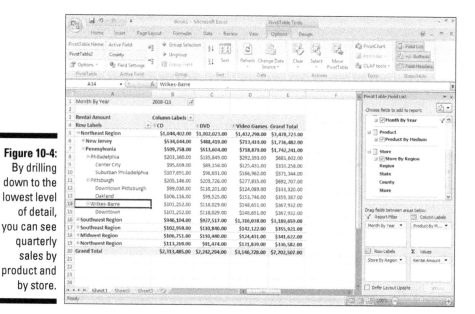

Figure 10-4:
By drilling
down to the
lowest level
of detail,
you can see
quarterly
sales by
product and
by store.

Drill-down analysis can be selective. Suppose that your particular area of interest is the northeast region, but you're filling in for the analyst who usually handles Arizona because that person's on vacation. You can use drill-down on only the portions of the total result set, as shown in Figure 10-5.

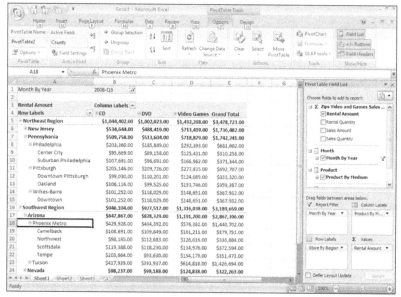

Figure 10-5:
You can
pick and
choose
the level of
detail you
want to
see in mix-
and-match
mode.

What's so great about this drilling stuff?

"Big deal," you might be thinking. "I can run reports with varying levels of detail in the query tool I've been using for years. What's so wonderful about this drill-down and drill-across business?"

The major advantage of business analysis (OLAP) drilling capability, as compared to traditional methods of getting this information, is that basic querying and reporting tools usually have had to run separate database access queries for each level of detail (often by using the SQL GROUP BY clause and along with an associated SQL WHERE clause). Each run is a separate SQL statement issued to the database, a separate pass through the database, a separate return of all the requested data, and a separate formatting of the results.

Multidimensional analysis and its drilling capability, on the other hand, are instantaneous because the information you need is staged for

you. By clicking the mouse or selecting a command, you see less detail, more detail, or whatever you want. The tool and the database don't have to collaborate for successive data access requests — it's all there for you.

Hint: If you haven't used a drill-down feature and want to get a feel for it, try using the HIDE/UNHIDE features for rows and columns in your spreadsheet program. Set up a set of detailed rows of data, total them into another row, and then do the same thing again. When you HIDE the detail rows, you're performing a drill-up function; when you UNHIDE them, you're drilling down.

As mentioned in Chapter 9, some reporting tools now have business analysis (OLAP) drill-down capabilities, which blurs the distinction between members of these two classes of business intelligence tools.

Drill-up

Drill-up analysis is, not surprisingly, the exact opposite of drill-down analysis. Using a detailed report, such as the one shown earlier in Figure 10-5, you can drill up to group the results from all the stores in the northeast region to the city level, and then all the cities to the state level, and eventually all the states to the regional level.

Drill-across

Drill-across analysis takes some value on a horizontal axis (in the example in Figures 10-1 through 10-5, the type of product) and receives an additional level of detail. Suppose that you want to see why Nintendo Wii sales are so high in your New Jersey stores (not that you're complaining). Figure 10-6 shows how to get this increased level of detail by doing a drill-across function.

Figure 10-6: Drill-across analysis, combined with drill-down, can give you a fix on problem areas.

Drill-through

When you use drill-through analysis (sometimes referred to as reach-through analysis), you get as much detail as possible from your data. You set up the data warehousing environment (ideally, in a behind-the-scenes manner) so that users can access additional levels of detail from a supplemental data-base. In a typical scenario, you get the types of reports shown in the figures in this chapter from a data mart and then request to see daily sales by store, perhaps further divided by hour. For example, your environment drills through to a main relationally based data warehouse that has a large store of detailed data, pulls out the information that applies to your request, and sends it back to you.

It's still early in the game for drill-through technology. Check out capabilities such as drill-through carefully, especially if you're looking at multivendor, multiproduct solutions. Because users frequently request this feature, expect to see increased capabilities in this area leveraging Web services that support multivendor, multiproduct drill-through.

Pivoting

Another business analysis (OLAP) capability is pivoting. You can rearrange the look of an on-screen report (drag spreadsheet columns over to become rows, for example) by using a few drag-and-drop mouse operations.

Trending

One of the strengths of multidimensional business analysis is that you can perform trending of key information relatively easily when time is one of the dimensions (which it usually is). You can see, for example, how sales data, market share, units sold, or any other measurement changes over time without having to go through a number of gyrations in your database model to support this capability.

Nesting

The ability to present more than one dimension on either a row or column is often described as *nesting*. If you want to see the trend in product sales across regions, you can place product on the rows, nesting the region within the product rows, as shown in Figure 10-7.

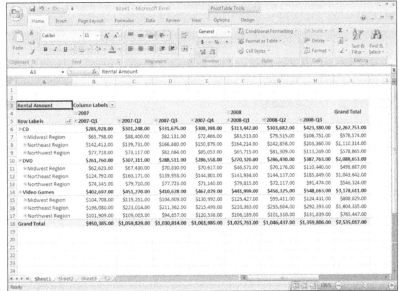

Figure 10-7: Nesting enables you to present more than one dimensional descriptor on a row or column of a report.

Visualizing

Today's business analysis (OLAP) tools offer a robust set of visualization capabilities. These capabilities include cross-tabs, as shown in Figures 10-1 through 10-7, as well a graphics, such as the line graph shown in Figure 10-8. Data and trends often jump out when you change the style of visualization. And you can perform most of the features described in the preceding sections, regardless of the visualization style you choose.

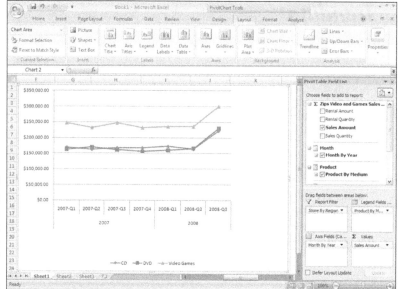

Figure 10-8:
Leverage
in-line chart
visualization
to better
spot trends.

Data Warehousing Business Analysis Vendors

The following sections describe some vendors that provide business analysis (OLAP) products and where you can find them on the Web. Check out these vendors' products (and those from other companies).

IBM

```
www.ibm.com
www.cognos.com
```

In January 2008, IBM acquired Cognos Corporation, increasing IBM's capabilities in the area of business analysis (OLAP). Cognos brought several business analysis (OLAP) products to IBM, including PowerPlay, Cognos8 Analysis Studio, and TM1. The PowerPlay engine is predominately leveraged for its DOLAP and MOLAP storage. The TM1 engine is predominately leveraged for high-volume solutions or dynamic ROLAP capabilities. And Cognos8 Analysis Studio is emerging as their business analysis visualization tool.

MicroStrategy

www.strategy.com

MicroStrategy produces a suite of ROLAP products that are part of its business intelligence platform. MicroStrategy OLAP Services is an extension of the MicroStrategy Intelligence Server that allows MicroStrategy Desktop, Office, and Web users to manipulate Intelligent Cubes™, a finite set of report objects that are automatically or dynamically populated by MicroStrategy's multi-pass SQL generation engine. Users can analyze the full depth and breadth of their data warehouse by using OLAP Services.

Oracle

www.oracle.com

Oracle, like many other enterprise vendors, has acquired a number of products in the area of business analysis. These products include Express from IRI, which has been embedded into the Oracle database platform, and (most recently) Hyperion Essbase, a MOLAP/MDDB environment which evolved from Arbor in the 1990s. Oracle is integrating these products into Oracle Business Intelligence (OBI), a middleware offering rebranded from the acquired Seibel Analytics Platform. Additionally, Oracle inherited Hyperion Intelligence, the Brio tools of which were integrated into the Hyperion suite.

Pentaho

www.pentaho.org

Pentaho is the commercial open source business intelligence (BI) solution. Pentaho Analysis combines the Mondrian OLAP server with JPivot visualization to enable users to perform business analysis (OLAP). Users who want powerful capabilities that they can embed into applications seamlessly, or who aren't focused on all the bells and whistles of the more mature business intelligence providers, might find Pentaho (or other open source BI solutions) a viable alternative.

SAP

www.sap.com
www.businessobjects.com

SAP, though initially focused on "run the business" applications, has grown over the years to offer more capabilities in the area of business intelligence. In 2008, SAP acquired Business Objects, which had previously acquired Crystal Decisions. With these acquisitions, SAP now possesses several business analysis products, including Business Objects XI, Crystal Analysis, SAP/BW, and Business Explorer (BEx). The strength of SAP's legacy offerings include the ability to activate the solution orientation, or content, with the "flip of a switch." With Business Objects in the fold, SAP also now has a general-purpose tool that can enable business analysis.

SAS

www.sas.com

SAS provides a multidimensional data store, known as the SAS OLAP Server, that's designed to provide quick access to pre-summarized data. Although SAS is often known for its roots in more technical, statistical analysis, it has grown its BI offerings so that it can move more into the business analysis arena with such products.

Chapter 11

Data Mining: Hi-Ho, Hi-Ho, It's Off to Mine We Go

The distinguishing characteristic about data mining, as compared with querying, reporting, or even OLAP, is that you can get information without having to ask specific questions.

Data mining serves two primary roles in your business intelligence mission:

✔ **The "Tell me what might happen" role:** The first role of data mining is predictive, in which you basically say, "Tell me what might happen." Using hidden knowledge locked away in your data warehouse, probabilities and the likelihood of future trends and occurrences are ferreted out and presented to you.

✔ **The "Tell me something interesting" role:** In addition to possible future events and occurrences, data mining also tries to pull out interesting information that you probably should know about, such as a particularly unusual relationship between sales of two different products and how that relationship varies according to placement in your retail stores. Although many of these interesting tidbits are likely to exist, what questions would you ask if you were using a querying or OLAP tool, and how would you interpret the results? Data mining assists you in this arduous task of figuring out what questions to ask by doing much of the grunt work for you.

Data Mining in Specific Business Missions

Data mining is particularly suited for these specific types of business missions:

- ✔ Detecting fraud

- ✔ Determining marketing program effectiveness

- ✔ Selecting whom, from a large customer base or the general population, you should target as part of a marketing program

- ✔ Managing customer life cycle, including the customer retention mission

- ✔ Performing advanced business process modeling and what-if scenarios

Think about what's behind each of the business missions in the preceding list:

- ✔ A large amount of data

- ✔ An even larger number of combinations of various pieces of data

- ✔ Intensive results set analysis, usually involving complex algorithms and advanced statistical techniques

Now, think about what you would have to do if you were using a reporting or OLAP tool to accomplish these missions. You'd find it virtually impossible to thoroughly perform any of the preceding missions if you had to ask a question and get a result, ask another question and get another result, and then keep repeating those steps.

Data Mining and Artificial Intelligence

If you've been in the information technology (IT) field for at least a decade, some of the preceding terms might sound vaguely familiar. Unlocking hidden knowledge? Predictive functionality? Wait a minute — that's artificial intelligence!

From the earliest days of commercial computing, there has been a tremendous interest in developing "thinking machines" that can process large amounts of data and make decisions based on that analysis. Interest in artificial intelligence (AI) hit its zenith in the mid-1980s. At that time, database vendors worked on producing knowledge base management systems (KBMSs); other vendors came out with *expert system shells,* or AI-based application development frameworks that used techniques such as forward-chaining and backward-chaining to advise users about decisions; and neural networks were positioned as the next big AI development. Interest in AI waned in the early 1990s, when expectations exceeded available capabilities and other frenzies, such as client/server migration and (of course) data warehousing, took center stage.

Now, AI is back!

The highest-profile AI technique used in data mining is neural networks. Neural nets were originally envisioned as a processing model that would mimic the way the human brain solves problems, using neurons and highly parallel processing to do pattern solving.

Applying neural network algorithms to the areas of business intelligence that data mining handles (again, predictive and "tell me something interesting" missions) seems to be a natural match.

Although the data mining/neural network game is definitely worth checking into, you should do it carefully. You can find a lot of interesting and exciting technologies that, in the hands of those who don't understand the algorithms, will likely fail. However, with proper knowledge and education, you can make a full-scale commitment to bringing this type of processing into your business intelligence framework as the technical-analysis pairing for the OLAP-focused business analysis.

Data Mining and Statistics

The more mature area of data mining is the application of advanced statistical techniques against the large volumes of data in your data warehouse. Different tools use different types of statistical techniques, tailored to the particular areas they're trying to address.

Without a statistical background, you might find much of data mining confusing. You need to do a lot of work to train the algorithms and build the rules to assure proper results with larger datasets. However, assuming that you're comfortable with this concept, or have a colleague who can assist, here are some of the more widely leveraged algorithms:

✔ **Classification algorithms:** Predict one or more discrete variables, based on the other attributes in the dataset. By using classification algorithms, the data mining tool can look at large amounts of data and then inform you that, for example, "Customers who are retained through at least two generations of product purchases tend to have these characteristics: They have an income of at least $75,000, and they own their own homes."

✔ **Regression algorithms:** Predict one or more continuous variables, such as profit or loss, based on other attributes in the dataset. Regression algorithms are driven through historical information presented to the data mining tool "over time," better known as *time series* information.

✔ **Segmentation algorithms:** Divide data into groups, or clusters, of items that have similar properties.

✔ **Association algorithms:** Find correlations between different attributes in a dataset. The most common application of this kind of algorithm creates association rules, which you can use in a market basket analysis. Note that, for example, if a customer purchases a particular software package, he or she has a 65-percent chance of purchasing at least two product-specific add-on packs within two weeks.

✔ **Sequence analysis algorithms:** Summarize frequent sequences or episodes in data, such as a Web-path flow.

Many more methods exist. Dust off that old statistics book and start reading.

Some Vendors with Data Mining Products

The following sections detail vendors that sell data mining products.

Microsoft

www.microsoft.com

Microsoft introduced server-side data mining with Microsoft SQL Server 2005. Although it's not as mature and sophisticated as SAS and SPSS, Microsoft has proven over time their ability to simplify and generalize technology offerings. Their integration of common data mining routines into SQL Server Analysis services provides an interesting, cost-effective solution. In addition, you can use several algorithms within Microsoft Excel when you access your data warehouse or data mart.

SAS

www.sas.com

SAS, one of the two industry leaders in analytics, provides an integrated environment for predictive analytics and descriptive modeling, data mining, text mining, forecasting, optimization, simulation, experimental design, and more. Their analytic solutions provide a range of techniques and processes for the collection, classification, analysis and interpretation of data to reveal patterns, anomalies, key variables, and relationships — leading ultimately to new insights for guided decision making. SAS is one of the more mature vendors and a leader in this market segment.

SPSS

www.spss.com

SPSS is one of the two industry leaders that have focused heavily in the area of statistics and data mining. Through acquisitions and internal development, SPSS has built out a comprehensive set of tools to help you with predictive modeling through Clementine and various statistical algorithms through SPSS Statistics.

Chapter 12

Dashboards and Scorecards

. . . .

In This Chapter

▶ Getting a quick look at important data with dashboards and scorecards

▶ Understanding the relationship between dashboards, scorecards, and business intelligence

▶ Keeping tabs on key indicators for executives

▶ Using briefing books and portal command centers to summarize reports and data

▶ Finding quality dashboard and scorecard products

. . . .

*T*hink about how a child learns to read. You begin by reading a picture-oriented book to the child, one with a short sentence at the bottom of each page ("See the bunny eat lettuce!"). Pretty soon, the child figures out how to read the book without your help. The child turns the pages, occasionally squealing in delight because of that favorite picture coming up on the next page.

Now, think about how behavioral researchers work with dolphins or chimpanzees to better understand how they think. When the chimp pushes a button, a banana drops down; when the dolphin presses a lever with a flipper, it's rewarded with a dolphin treat (whatever that is).

These are the principles behind dashboards and scorecards. Wait a minute! Stop that booing and hissing, and put down those rotten vegetables! I'm not trying to insult anyone! I'm very serious. Dashboards and scorecards are intended to be a ridiculously easy way to provide online business intelligence to people who are, uh, "too busy" to figure out how to use the full complement of business intelligence tools.

Dashboard and Scorecard Principles

The fundamental principle behind dashboard and scorecards is, "Tell me a lot of things, but don't make me work too hard." Despite the best efforts of vendors, despite all the human factors and usability research that's gone into business intelligence products, and no matter how much training you provide to your data warehousing users, you always have someone who doesn't grasp the concept of painting a report screen, doing a drill-down analysis, or taking full advantage of the power available from today's tools.

Or these folks might think they're too busy to figure it all out. Believe it or not, the mentality that computers are for "clerical types" still pervades many of corporate America's executive suites. Most of these folks grudgingly accept delivery of that brand-new, supercharged laptop (although they still refuse to type their own letters) and want to do only "a couple of things" with the computer.

Should those people be shut out of the world of business intelligence in your data warehousing environment? No!

In most cases, you need to create an environment that has a set of dashboards and scorecards. Dashboards and scorecards, like other areas of business intelligence, predate the data warehousing era — evolving from the executive information systems (EIS) of the 1980s and 1990s. Alas, like early multidimensional analysis (pre-OLAP OLAP), no one realized the full power of an EIS at the time, and the EIS faded to the background while full-scale business intelligence solutions took hold along with data warehousing.

Dashboards

A *dashboard* is a collection of graphs, reports, and KPIs that can help monitor such business activities as progress on a specific initiative. Everyone who's driven a car has seen a dashboard. A dashboard (whether in your car or on your computer) provides a lot of information in a summary form to show you how you're currently performing in an operational manner. Your car dashboard shows you how fast you're currently going, and you have to evaluate whether this value falls within the target speed limit. Alongside this information, you can find out what your fuel level is, how many miles you've traveled, what the temperature of the engine is, and . . . well, whatever that tachometer thing is supposed to tell you.

A business intelligence dashboard is the equivalent of your car's dashboard. In your data warehousing environment, this business intelligence dashboard shows users the effectiveness of operations. You can build a dashboard that supports a wide variety of users, from individuals to the company as a whole. As shown in Figure 12-1, when built correctly, dashboards can give you quick insight into company performance.

Figure 12-1:
Dashboards
monitor
the perfor-
mance of
operational
processes.

Scorecards

A *scorecard* is a visual representation of your company's strategy. A scorecard helps make it easy to take critical metrics and map them to your
strategic goals throughout the organization. Scorecards offer a rich, visual
gauge that everyone in your organization can reference in order to see

 ✔ The performance of specific initiatives, business units, or the company
   as a whole

 ✔ Individual goals in the context of larger corporate strategy

Scorecards, as shown in Figure 12-2, distill information into a small number of
metrics and targets. With a scorecard, your users get an at-a-glance perspective of information. Scorecards are designed to increase productivity by
allowing users to stop sifting through stacks of reports to find what's right or
wrong with the business in relationship to the corporate strategy. Scorecards
show users immediately how the company, a division, their team, or they
themselves are performing against targets that were set within the overall
strategy or plan.

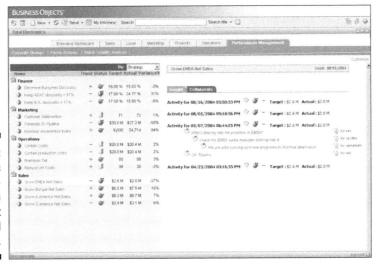

Figure 12-2:
Scorecards
show per-
formance
against
goals and
strategies.

The Relationship between Dashboards, Scorecards, and the Other Parts of Business Intelligence

Dashboards and scorecards are often linked to results from other business intelligence tools, representing a presentation mechanism, rather than an analytical mechanism. For example, you might create the "pages" of a briefing book (discussed in the section "The Briefing Book," later in this chapter) from the results of various standardized reports (run from the reporting tool) in addition to a rudimentary multidimensional analysis from the organization's OLAP tool that's ready for inclusion in the briefing book.

Often, geographical information system (GIS) capabilities, as described in Chapter 8, are included with dashboards and scorecards. A dashboard that has GIS integration, for example, might present a series of standardized views of important information to a user by using maps or other geographical tools as the primary interface. The user then can take a cursory look through each screen of information; if everything looks okay, the user can continue to the next page, or if something looks askew, he or she can perform GIS operations, such as double-clicking a map to access the underlying data.

Dashboards and scorecards aren't just for executives. Almost any user in an organization can have a dashboard or scorecard. You might find presenting everyone in your organization dashboards and scorecards preferable to giving everyone the "official" business intelligence tool and having three-quarters of the group never use it.

Don't assume that you automatically need to give anyone classified as an executive (above a certain level) in your organization a dashboard or scorecard to the exclusion of other tools. Many a computer-savvy executive can wind up as the primary user of OLAP or a reporting tool. In addition, don't assume that users access their dashboards and scorecards only from a Web browser. Blackberries, iPhones, and other smart phone devices are quickly becoming the preferred delivery platform for the busy executive.

EIS and Key Indicators

In keeping with the philosophy of "Don't make me work too hard to get my information," many dashboards and scorecards are built around the concept of key indicators. An executive might have, for example, a handful of (seven or eight) items that are monitored on a weekly basis and that represent the pulse of the organization. If all these items fall into the expected range (whatever that means for each measure), he or she doesn't have to worry about the business and can go off for a quick nine holes of golf during a long lunch break.

On the other hand, an indicator that's out of whack likely means that the user should do a little digging — or maybe a great deal of digging — in that particular area.

A quick snapshot of key indicators (ideally, all on a dashboard or scorecard) can therefore be a valuable part of a well-organized enterprise portal environment.

Customize your dashboard and scorecard implementations! One executive's key indicators aren't likely to be the same as another's. Make dashboards and scorecards personal, an environment for communication — not an unvarying, rigid set of screens installed on several users' respective browsers.

During the scope phase of your project, spend enough time working with likely users to determine each person's key indicators. Explore other possibilities and show examples; in the end, however, let users decide which indicators they want to see and how they want those indicators to look.

The Briefing Book

If you've ever used a presentation program (such as Microsoft PowerPoint) that contains a slide show feature, you have a basic understanding of the briefing book concept. A briefing book is usually constructed to flow from one screen to another, covering key information, indicators, and other pertinent data in a relatively predictable manner.

You can design a briefing book to have an up-front screen or indicator that provides an overall assessment: "All is well" or "Update your résumé," for example. Then, each successive screen displays the items important to that user.

One interesting aspect of a well-architected briefing book is that you must strike a balance between not enough detail and too much detail in the information presented to a user. For example, include a browser link or button labeled More Information that the reader can click to access additional detail. A large part of the simplicity of the briefing book, however, is that the flow from scorecard to dashboard to analytical view is predictable and not too complex, as described in the section "The Relationship between Dashboards,

Scorecards, and the Other Parts of Business Intelligence," earlier in this chapter. Therefore, make users' More Information navigation paths access only one more visualization, perhaps two. If the user needs additional information, he or she might need assistance getting it. Don't lose the flow of the briefing book by trying to make the environment overly elegant and flexible.

The Portal Command Center

The portal command center is a type of dashboard and scorecard that, in one way, is less predictable than a briefing book environment but, in another way, is just as predictable.

Huh?

The less predictable aspect is that, unlike the sequentially oriented nature of a briefing book, a command center user can choose whether to check out a particular set of information. If the user's in-browser scan of visual indicators shows that all is well, no more information access occurs.

In the just as predictable part, though, each portal command center user has an environment tailored to a set of reports or sets of data that are important to that particular user. A sales executive, for example, might have on his or her portal command center one link for each region the person is responsible for, including a visual indicator that provides a quick look at the state of that region. The visual indicator might be a stoplight, for example: green for "Everything's okay," yellow for "Better check this out before things get worse," and red for "Uh-oh."

Collaborative portal products that are leveraged to build a portal command center interface are tailor-made for multimedia business intelligence environments (see Chapter 25). For example, certain links on a portal command center can lead to posted results from standard OLAP-generated reports on the company's intranet. Other links can lead to the company's latest ads, product diagrams, training videos, or other elements. You can make your presentation of key business intelligence perspectives by using dashboards and scorecards just like a spiffy Web site home page with both structured and unstructured data underneath.

You can also use command centers operationally, rather than analytically. Sometimes, the distinctions between the two are subtle. In an operational command center, an executive usually monitors the environment regularly (daily or perhaps more frequently) as an active part of operational decision-making; analytical command centers usually are usually accessed less frequently (weekly or monthly, for example), with the purpose of determining "How did we do?" rather than "What do I have to do?"

Who Produces EIS Products

Because most business intelligence suites now have dashboard, scorecard, and portal components to them, I recommend checking out these components when you research business intelligence tools in these other areas.

 Alternatively, you can use Internet technology to develop your own presentation and visualization environment as part of a Web-enabled business intelligence framework for your users. You can develop a home page, for example, that uses hyperlinks to guide users through briefing books or to enable them to navigate among command-center-driven capabilities.

Part IV
Data Warehousing Projects: How to Do Them Right

The 5th Wave   By Rich Tennant

"Look you've got Project Manager, Acct. Manager, and Opportunity Manager, but Sucking Up to the Manager just isn't a field the program comes with."

In this part . . .

A data warehousing project is just like any other application development project. Or, to be more blunt, you can mess up a perfectly good data warehouse effort in a lot of ways: poor project management, putting the wrong people on the development team — you get the idea.

If you want to find out how to do a data warehouse project the right way, this part of the book is for you! I uncover what aspects of developing data warehouses are the same as traditional applications and what few subtleties can alter your approach to building a data warehouse from traditional applications.

Chapter 13

Data Warehousing and Other IT Projects: The Same but Different

*P*sst! Yes, you. Do you want to know a secret? No, this isn't the Beatles song; this secret is about data warehousing projects and how you can almost guarantee success.

I thought that would get your attention! Listen closely because I sum up this secret in three sentences:

✔ Data warehousing projects are remarkably (about 95 percent) similar to any other application development project.

✔ The 5 percent that's different is because of two key items: an unclear method for identifying requirements and scope, and the reliance on data from other applications' databases and files (as discussed in Chapter 1).

✔ By applying your organization's application development "best practices" to the 95-percent similar portion (as though this project is just like any other) and by following a few guidelines to handle the other 5 percent, you can almost certainly develop your data warehouse successfully.

Why a Data Warehousing Project Is (Almost) Like Any Other Development Project

Way back in the mid- and late 1970s, when disco reigned supreme, IT professionals realized that certain things made sense and other things didn't in developing computer applications and systems. One of the things that made sense was that before choosing hardware, off-the-shelf products (such as DBMSs), and even programming languages, you first had to determine the business requirements you were trying to satisfy and then take a number of steps to specify and design the programs you plan to develop. Then, after gaining a good understanding of these details, you could make an informed decision about your hardware and development software.

Then, in the early 1990s, a tremendous, growing interest in data warehousing emerged. I can't tell you how many times I sat in a room with clients, discussing their data warehousing projects, when someone (not me!) said, "I think that we want to use Brand X business intelligence tool and the Brand Z extraction, transformation, and load (ETL) product." They made this choice before they'd even begun to analyze their business requirements, let alone specify their architecture or do any design work.

The lessons from the 1970s seemed to have disappeared. You don't even have to look at IT projects to see these lessons. I recently asked a customer of mine in the energy and utilities business whether his company would build a nuclear power plant by using a technique that involved picking the technology first and then determining the requirements — of course, he almost shouted, "No!" When I asked him why, he explained that you must understand the requirements, properly design the architecture, and then — only then — begin selecting the technologies and building the finished product, or solution, to the specifications you established.

Some of the application development revelations made in the '70s (and remade in the '90s) about choosing hardware and software that are appropriate for the business problem at hand still make a great deal of sense for any type of project — even a data warehousing project.

Maybe premature software purchases were made because of the data warehousing vendors and their product hype: The phrase, "It slices! It dices!" is appropriate for business analysis software found in OLAP (refer to Chapter 10). Rather than try to find someone to blame, however, how about if everyone agrees to make a fresh start? No premature selection of hardware, database software, business intelligence tools, middleware products, or any other products without first concentrating on business requirements and then doing appropriate analysis and design work.

How to Apply Your Company's Best Development Practices to Your Project

I hope that your company has jumped on the application development methodology bandwagon and has published a set of guidelines that you're supposed to use in developing applications. The Sarbanes-Oxley (SOX) Act of 2002 essentially mandated that large companies publish guidelines. If you happen to be with an enterprise that hasn't clearly defined a development method, read this section anyway because it describes how your company is supposed to develop applications.

The current conventional wisdom says that no matter how large or complex the business problem for which you're developing an application, you should, if at all possible, divide that problem into chunks, each of which you can deliver in a manageable, relatively short time (typically, three to nine months). By using *agile* methods of delivery, you often can deliver solutions to these problems in closer to three months.

A number of methodologies exist based on this philosophy of manageable chunks. Methods that are well documented by industry thought leaders such as Ralph Kimball, Larissa Moss, Dan Linstedt, and others fall in line with such a philosophy.

My company, Balanced Insight Incorporated, uses an approach that's oriented toward extremely fast delivery of results (the Information Packaging Method), with each project (and each project chunk) divided into several iterations that cross very traditional phases:

✔ **Requirements:** Capture the business needs for information including how the user community desires to navigate the information in the final solution. This is done by clearly defining the scope through a series of rapid solution workshops:

- *Scope:* All relevant people reach consensus about what you're going to build, why you should build it, and other factors.

- *Rapid solutions workshop (RSW):* Visible results are delivered in a few days to a few weeks, leveraging tools such as Balanced Insight Consensus.

✔ **Design:** All the technical details are decided to make sure that development (the next phase) goes smoothly and delivers an application that meets the business requirements.

✔ **Development and testing:** Databases are created, logic is developed to move data from the various sources to the new destination, the user access semantic layer is built out, and maybe pre-built views of the data are developed in the business intelligence platform if the user population is inexperienced.

✔ **Deployment:** The customer delivers the application to the users, and they begin using it.

For my company's data warehousing projects, we follow the same methodology that we use for building our product set — Balanced Insight Consensus, which is an Agile development method.

Agile methodologies generally promote

✔ A project management process that encourages frequent inspection and adaptation

✔ A leadership philosophy that encourages team work, self-organization, and accountability

✔ A set of engineering best practices that allow for rapid delivery of high-quality software

✔ A business approach that aligns development with customer needs and company goals

Although the data warehousing version of the methodology is tailored to handle the transfer of data from the source systems into the data warehouse, Balanced Insight's employees engage the end user in frequent inspection of the target solution. They begin, for example, by working with clients on the project scope that is leveraged to build the business case for the data warehouse. They collect requirements and help the client determine what business value to expect from the data warehouse by simulating what the final target application will deliver. We don't sit down with a client in the first meeting and, after hearing that they're interested in developing a data warehouse, tell them, "Okay, you should use Brand X OLAP tool and the Brand Z extraction-and-transformation product. Now, what do you want this data warehouse to do?" As shown in Figure 13-1, we clearly gain an understanding of what data the client needs so that they can understand their business better, and we also figure out how the user wants to navigate, traverse, and integrate the data.

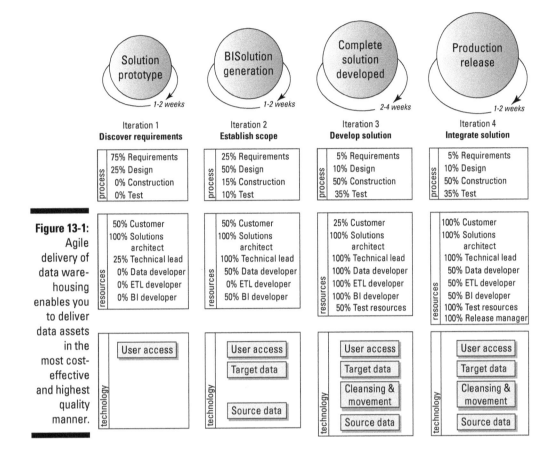

Figure 13-1:
Agile
delivery of
data ware-
housing
enables you
to deliver
data assets
in the
most cost-
effective
and highest
quality
manner.

Properly defining scope within the boundaries of the business's need is the ultimate key to success. Data warehousing teams often overlook this step, leading to numerous failures. Performing a *Field of Dreams*–oriented project — the "If you build it, they will come" method — fails more often than it succeeds.

If your company's application development methodology works (if you usually deliver projects on time and on budget), use that methodology as the foundation for your data warehousing project and make adjustments (such as the ones described in the following section) to handle the unique properties of data warehousing.

How to Handle the Uniqueness of Data Warehousing

Your company's standard application development methodology probably doesn't cover how to handle all the issues that come with integrating data from a plethora of applications that were never intended to integrate. Most run-the-business applications create data in their databases as a result of transactions (a customer making a savings account deposit, for example, or someone placing an order for season tickets to Pittsburgh Steelers games). As long as the application's internal processes that are responsible for creating, storing, modifying, and retrieving the data are correct, you most likely don't have to worry about data problems or data integration problems within your application.

The following steps, which are for your warehouse's data environment, differ from the steps in a traditional application development project. The project phase is listed in bold, followed by a brief explanation of how the task is different from a traditional application.

Requirements

1. **Identify the key questions.**

   Working with the business users, identify key business questions and declarative statements that require information to assist the business in making decisions.

2. **Define the focused answers.**

   Within a workshop, analyze the questions and statements that have been defined to determine the measurement answer sought by the business.

3. **Define the key business objects.**

   Within a workshop, pull the key words out of the business questions and declarative statements that appear to be the descriptors of the business — called *business objects* (not to be confused with the vendor product!).

4. **Determine usability requirements.**

   Working with the business users, determine how they want to navigate the data — including how they want to drill into details, what they need from an aggregation perspective, and other key reporting requirements.

5. **Prototype the solution.**

   Using a tool such as Balanced Insight Consensus, prototype the requirements so that the users can see what they asked for early and clarify their requirements before you get the expensive team working on the effort.

Design

6. Identify all candidate data sources.

Have the users identify the system that they typically use to get this information or where they enter that information. It's remarkable how good they are at this type of thing — and how challenged IT people are in this area.

7. Prioritize data sources.

Most applications don't use external data. Because some applications do need the data for processing, no one does prioritization: The application won't work without the data.

8. Obtain several data extract samples.

This step is more important than in a traditional application, even if you use external data.

9. Quickly create a database design.

You must orient the design toward the type of business intelligence the warehouse will support (reporting and querying, and OLAP, for example) rather than make it a general purpose design.

10. Populate the database design with extracted data.

You usually don't do this step in a traditional application.

11. Get feedback from users about whether they like the views of the data you created.

This step usually isn't important in a traditional application. In addition to giving you feedback on the user access strategy, users will also explain data quality issues that might not be obvious by merely looking at the raw data, including items such as data that has embedded meaning or missing values.

Development and testing

12. Create a complete database design.

Depending on the complexity of your environment, you might orient the design of the data warehouse toward business intelligence, rather than toward transactions. Make your decision based on whether you're implementing a monitor-the-business solution only or also including integrate-the-business solutions (transactional integration). If you're merely doing a monitor-the-business solution, look into methods such as Ralph Kimball's. If you're performing a more robust and comprehensive solution to both integrate and monitor the business, investigate Dan Linstedt's Data Vaulting Method.

13. Do a complete inventory of target data elements and match them to the proper source data elements.

This step is much more extensive than when you're developing and documenting a traditional application that has external data needs, and you need business assistance to define the key business rules necessary to transform the data from the source systems to the target data warehouse consistently across the enterprise to improve the quality and confidence in the data for future use.

14. **Spend time meeting with owners of source data.**

Although you perform this step in a traditional application that has external data needs, you have to understand the details of the data quality, availability, and dependencies much more extensively when building a data warehouse.

15. **Dig into source data.**

Analyzing data integrity and other issues is an important part of the process (see Chapter 16).

16. **Create transformation algorithms.**

This step is much more extensive than for a traditional application that has external data needs. Translating the business rules that have been identified within your specifications into properly coded transformation logic is complex, often involving data from more than one application.

17. **Dig into old versions of the data that might be needed in the data warehouse.**

Look for different versions of the data and different codes, for example. This step is rarely done in a traditional application because old data isn't applicable.

18. **Select tools or design code to handle middleware tasks.**

You usually don't have to do this step for a traditional application; for a data warehouse, do it once and reevaluate periodically to assure a consistent architecture across the enterprise.

19. **Make sure that middleware functions exist for initial warehouse loading and updates.**

You don't usually have to worry about this step for a traditional application.

20. **Define quality assurance (QA) procedures for all source data.**

This step is much more extensive than even a traditional application with external data needs. Data warehousing leverages much more reference data than traditional applications, where the reference data might be optional or user entered. You will need to make sure you understand how data will be investigated and tried out by the user community.

21. **Spend extensive time coding, or using tools, to extract, transform, move, and load data.**

This step is much more extensive than even a traditional application with external data needs. The need to sequence data loading is key to properly deliver high quality data. Building "one version of the truth" from numerous systems can be tricky. The logic that you build should be standard and reusable across applications that are sources for the data warehouse.

22. **Conduct preliminary tests for all the source-to-warehouse data extraction, transformation, movement, and loading.**

This step is much more extensive than even a traditional application with external data needs. The interdependencies between applications and their associated data, as well as volume and sequencing of your data loads, can make the extraction, transformation, movement, and loading processes tricky.

23. **Conduct end-to-end performance tests.**

You conduct a step similar to this one when performance testing in a traditional application, but this step is more complex because of the unpredictability of how users will access data.

24. **Conduct performance tests for user access to data.**

This step involves different measurement techniques than you need for a transaction-processing application. You want to assure that the data warehouse can be loaded within a defined time period, often during off-business hours. Additionally, you want to assure that users' queries will return in the proper amount of time, defined as *response time*.

25. **Do preliminary determinations of data summary levels.**

You usually don't have to do this step for a traditional application; only rarely do you do any kind of intra-database summarization in a traditional application. However in a data warehouse, based on performance testing, you might want to create pre-stored aggregations of the data to optimize user access and scalability.

Deployment

26. **Perform initial population of the warehouse's database.**

This step is much more extensive than the initial population of a traditional application's database.

27. **Monitor the data warehouse reloading process.**

This step is much more extensive than the equivalent in a traditional application. Your testing of performance during the development and testing often does not clearly reflect your production environment. Therefore, once you deploy your data warehouse, you might need to further tune the loading process to fit within defined time boundaries, such as a late-night batch window.

28. **Determine purge and archive strategies.**

   Because data warehouses have historic content, you need different strategies from those you use for traditional applications. A larger volume of data will be kept online, and users might need access to archives in quicker recovery periods than typical applications.

29. **Put plans in place to keep track of source data changes.**

   Again, this step is much more extensive than that of a traditional application. Change management routines should be altered to assure that application changes are not implemented without determining their impact to the data warehouse.

Why Your Data Warehousing Project Must Have Top-Level Buy-In

Although your data warehousing project might be the most important part of your job, you must keep in mind that others within your company probably don't share your perspective. For example

- ✔ Most of the people who operate the applications from which you acquire data probably see your project as one large nuisance that does little more than cause them to work a number of overtime hours.

- ✔ Some users who already perform rudimentary analytical tasks by using extracts from an application's database (quasi-warehouses, as discussed in Chapter 22) likely don't want to change the way they operate, even though the data warehouse can provide them with a much richer set of data.

- ✔ When you try to divide a large data warehouse project into the chunks mentioned in the section "How to Apply Your Company's Best Development Practices to Your Project," earlier in this chapter, each business organization sees its piece as the most important, and you have a battle over whose chunk is most important on your hands.

Many other issues might arise that are a result of organizational politics and have nothing to do with data warehousing technology.

This situation calls for a hero — a courageous person willing to take a stand and look at the big picture. This person has to make and enforce statements such as, "You will support this data warehousing project. Put some people on it; if you don't have any, go hire some consultants." Or the person might say, "Hold on, this data warehouse will certainly support your group, but you'll be in the second phase of development. In the meantime, I need you to participate in evaluating business intelligence tools and put a couple of people on source data analysis." (We data warehousing consultants love people who say things like that.)

In case you haven't guessed, this job calls for an executive, someone as high up as possible in the organizational chart, such as the company's chief financial officer (CFO) or the chief marketing officer (CMO) or whatever title the director of operations has. Better yet, try to get a joint directive from the chief executive officer (CEO), the chief operating officer (COO), and the chief information officer (CIO) that will get everyone on the same page of the playbook, indicating that both the business and technology organizations are behind the data warehousing project.

So what's the big deal? This prospect seems straightforward, right? Unfortunately, the complications usually occur in large (Fortune 500–size) companies that have a number of different business divisions, each with its own organizational structure, from a president on down. Each division also often has its own CIO and COO, as well as its own data center. To put it bluntly, you can have problems determining who in the overall picture reports to whom. As soon as a data warehousing project crosses these divisional boundaries, the turf wars spring to life. Unless you're one of these high-powered individuals, the best you can hope for is that whoever sponsors your data warehouse project has enough clout and interpersonal skills to get everyone to support it. If not, be prepared.

How Do I Conduct a Large, Enterprise-Scale Data Warehousing Initiative?

For large, complex data warehousing projects that cross a large number of organizational boundaries (the upper bounds of the data warehouse deluxe group, discussed in Chapter 3), choose one of following approaches:

- ✔ Top-down
- ✔ Bottom-up
- ✔ Mixed-mode (combining the best aspects of the other two methods)

Top-down

To develop a large data warehouse in a top-down manner, follow these steps:

1. **Proceed with scope and design phase activities from the perspective of the entire data warehousing environment, no matter how large.**

   I discuss scope and design phase activities in the section " How to Apply Your Company's Best Development Practices to Your Project," earlier in this chapter.

2. **Create an all-inclusive data model of your data warehouse (called an *enterprise data warehouse model*).**

   For your blueprint, use all the data elements that you plan to store anywhere in the data warehouse and the source for each element.

3. **Decompose the enterprise data warehouse model into as many *component models* (smaller models) as appropriate for your environment.**

   Group data elements and subject areas according to the primary function of each sub-model area, with little or no data overlap between models. (Your goal is to have one official storage place for each data element.)

4. **Develop each part of your data warehouse, with each part containing one of the component models.**

This approach is similar to the way most people have been taught to handle any type of large problems, not just those in the information technology business: Get an idea of the "big picture," decompose the problem into manageable chunks, and then work on each chunk. The problem is that although this approach makes sense conceptually, carrying it out successfully in the real world is difficult. The major stumbling block is the creation of the enterprise data warehouse model because of the large number of source applications you need for an enterprise-scale data warehousing project. Even if you're successful, you can have even more trouble keeping a model that large up-to-date, especially with all the data sources you have to consider. More often than not, the enterprise view of data turns out to be of little value.

Use the business users as the sounding board — if they need the data, they should say so in the requirements; if they don't, it will come in a secondary iteration. Get the business objects clearly defined — not that all data elements that exist in your enterprise for the business object are defined in the first iteration. If you want to follow a top-down method, use the business requirements as your guide rather than what you know exists in the various databases.

Bottom-up

You can develop a large data warehouse environment from the bottom up. After you identify a number of different subject areas, or groups of subject areas, that are within the scope of your project, you treat each one as a separate project with little overlap between them. When you finish these different projects, you have your data warehouse — sort of.

The major risk of this approach is that even if each of the smaller projects is successful, the components of the data warehouse probably won't fit together neatly forever, and the environment will eventually fall into disuse. Additionally, without the level-headed influence of the business user, you might spend an enormous amount of time reconciling, transforming, and moving data that's germane to only the source application and therefore has no use in the data warehouse.

Mixed-mode

In mixed mode (my preferred approach), you combine the best parts of the top-down and bottom-up methods by following these steps:

1. **Start with a project scope phase.**

   As discussed earlier in this chapter, explore the business mission, vision, and other defining constraints for the overall data warehouse environment that you want to build.

2. **Initiate a separate data warehouse architecture phase.**

   Concentrate on the overall architecture for the enterprise. For example, catalog all the data sources and the platforms on which they run, identify the entire user community and who will perform which functions, and identify which external data sources are likely to be necessary. The goal of this phase is to create a complete conceptual picture of your corporate data environment (from the data sources to the data warehouse, and all points in between) so that you can identify the pieces that overlap and the pieces that are stand-alone.

3. **Create a data warehouse architecture pilot program.**

   All the overlapping pieces of your environment (the pieces that must communicate with one another) undergo an evaluation, both in concept (checking out vendor literature, for example) and in implementation (seeing whether vendor products do what they're supposed to do and whether they're suitable for your environment, for example).

4. **Revise the data warehousing architecture, based on the results of your pilot program.**

5. **Create two separate design and development paths: one for infrastructure capabilities (the shared pieces used across much or all of your data warehouse) and another path for the functionality of each component of the data warehouse.**

Assign "systems people" (IT staff members) to the design and development tasks for the infrastructure capabilities. Assign a mix of business and IT people to the tasks associated with developing the component data warehousing features.

6. **Decompose the component data warehousing functionality into a series of projects.**

Each series lasts from three to nine months and has few dependencies on any other project piece.

7. **Continue with the other project phases.**

I describe these phases in the section "How to Apply Your Company's Best Development Practices to Your Project," earlier in this chapter: requirements, design, development and testing, and deployment.

Each project piece, as well as your infrastructure, incorporates all these phases.

Create a data warehousing project office that includes representatives from each thread of development activity, including the infrastructure development. Even though each thread of development activity should proceed as independently as possible, to make your overall effort proceed smoothly, ensure that information such as business intelligence product evaluation, issues, and risks can be shared. Data warehousing project offices have recently begun to fall under titles of Business Intelligence Competency Centers or Business Intelligence Centers of Excellence, and key resources from the business and IT departments staff them. Creating such an organization can provide great value to your enterprise because the program will continually improve the manufacturing and maintenance of your key data assets.

Chapter 14

Building a Winning Data Warehousing Project Team

. . . .

In This Chapter

▶ Avoiding assumptions when creating your data warehousing team

▶ Understanding the roles that you need in your team

▶ Putting the right people in the right roles

▶ Organizing how your team members will work together

. . . .

*Y*our attention, please. Here's the starting lineup for your data warehousing project.

Batting first, and playing data architect, with four years of data warehousing experience, Vicki. (Applause from the crowd.)

Batting second, your project manager, with seven years of project-management experience and three of those years spent in the data warehousing area, Paul. (More applause.)

Batting third, last year's most valuable player for her key role on a 90-day data mart development project that was delivered two weeks ahead of schedule, and serving as the senior developer, Amanda. (Still more applause.)

Okay, being part of a data warehousing team isn't exactly like being a member of a major-league baseball team. In reality, it's nothing like being a member of a major-league baseball team, except for one thing: teamwork.

Your best chances of data warehousing project success lie with building a winning team. Like in baseball, your team must have a balance of skills across a variety of roles. If your baseball team has ten excellent pitchers bound for the Hall of Fame, but all the infielders play baseball like I did in Little League, you probably won't win many games.

Don't Make This Mistake!

A development team that does a top-notch, bang-up job of developing or deploying an application (an SAP deployment or your online commerce site designed to handle large volumes of product orders over the Web) might also do a great job if it's assigned to a data warehousing project.

Then again, it might not. Don't make these assumptions:

- A person who can code in Visual Basic, Java, or C#, for example, can handle data warehousing and/or business intelligence tools.

- A project manager, comfortable with and successful in transactional, production-oriented application development, can deal with the twists and turns of informational, analytical data warehousing projects.

- A database administrator who can tune a database for transaction-processing performance has the knowledge and skills to do the same for data warehousing performance, which has different access patterns.

In short, don't make decisions about building your data warehousing project team without performing some research, including the role of each team member and the qualifications of the people who will fill those roles.

The Roles You Have to Fill on Your Project

The following statement might seem obvious: The size of your data warehousing project dictates the number of team members you need.

Wow! And you're reading this chapter for that piece of wisdom? Wait! Don't skip ahead, thinking that the rest of this chapter is a waste of your time.

The reason I made that statement is that although the number of people on your project might vary, the roles they fill almost always remain constant from one data warehousing project to another. Depending on the size and complexity of your project, it might have

- One person filling each role
- One person filling more than one role
- More than one person filling a single role

In the section "And Now, the People," later in this chapter, I discuss how to determine the matchup of people and roles. The following sections focus on the roles you must assign, before you begin to choose people to fill them.

The following roles almost always have to be filled in a data warehousing project:

- ✔ Project manager
- ✔ Technical leader
- ✔ Chief data-warehousing architect
- ✔ Business requirements analyst
- ✔ Data modeler and conceptual/logical database designer
- ✔ Database administrator and physical database designer
- ✔ Data movement and middleware specialist
- ✔ Front-end tools specialist and developer
- ✔ Quality assurance specialist
- ✔ Source data analyst
- ✔ User-community interaction manager
- ✔ Technical executive sponsor
- ✔ User-community executive sponsor

If you don't assign one or more of these roles, either explicitly or because of an oversight, you put your data warehousing project at risk. In all except the rarest circumstances, each of these roles is critical to the success of your project.

Project manager

Here's Rule Number One about your data warehousing project manager: The manager must be a full-time, dedicated resource. Dedicated means, in this case, 100-percent assigned to the data warehousing project, not dedicated as in "very interested in and passionate about" (although also fulfilling the latter definition doesn't hurt).

I mention this rule because I've seen a lot of data warehousing projects get totally messed up because someone wanted to scrimp on the resources or budget assigned to the project, and the temptation is often to say, "Well, maybe we need a project manager assigned to this job on only a half-time basis." Before you know it, someone has been assigned as your project's manager on an additional-duty basis, schedule conflicts pull this person all over the place, and the project goes to pieces.

This situation seems to happen more often on data warehousing projects (particularly smaller-scale projects that can be classified as data warehouse lite) because of the tendency to think, "We're not developing a real application; it's only copying data from a bunch of different places and putting that data in one place. How difficult can that be?" This type of tremendously shortsighted thinking often occurs in one of these situations:

- ✔ An organization, already short on resources, has so many projects taking place that an internal full-time project manager "just doesn't make sense."

- ✔ Because of budget pressures, the people responsible for a data warehousing project that's contracted out to one or more consulting firms have this attitude: "We can save thousands of dollars over the life of the project by paying for only a half-time project manager."

Forget the shortsighted thinking. Assign, pay for, or find a full-time project manager for your data warehousing project.

Your data warehousing project manager should be able to do the following:

- ✔ Create, manage, and adjust to project plans.

- ✔ Communicate effectively, both verbally and in writing, to people in both the technical and user communities.

- ✔ Weather project storms without falling to pieces.

- ✔ Stick to the project plan and, at the same time, be flexible. That's not a contradiction: When a project is going well, the project manager must ensure that it continues to go well; when a problem surfaces, however, the project manager must be able to steer team members around the obstacle without losing sight of the objective.

- ✔ Be both responsive to team members' needs and dedicated to the successful completion of all project tasks.

- ✔ Be organized.

- ✔ Be diplomatic without being wishy-washy.

- ✔ Know enough about data warehousing to be effective in the project manager role.

- ✔ Make timely decisions.

Does the same person have to manage all phases of the data warehousing project?

Although some project managers are skilled in managing all phases of a project (scope, rapid development workshop, design, development, and deployment, as described in Chapter 13), others might be more adept at one or two of the phases than at others. An individual might be a top-notch project manager for the construction activities of development (visualization development in OLAP tools and database creation, population, and testing, for example) and struggle during the early phases of a project (such as scoping the project and working closely with the end users to determine their requirements). Other people might have a knack for early-phase activities and have problems with all the nitty-gritty details of development and deployment.

An organization that has a number of data warehousing initiatives might reasonably have a pool of project managers, some of whom concentrate on the earlier phases (scope and design) of a data warehousing project and others who concentrate on development and deployment. Early-phase project managers can hand off projects to managers skilled in the latter phases, in much the same way that a starting pitcher in baseball might regularly leave the game after the seventh or eighth inning (no matter how well he had been pitching) and yield the pitching mound to the ace reliever to close out the game. (Sorry, I couldn't resist a baseball analogy.)

Even if this type of setup makes sense for your organization, however, the key is to make sure that the project manager (whoever is filling that role) is still, at any phase, 100-percent dedicated to the project.

Technical leader

From the first stages of design activity through the successful deployment of the data warehousing environment, the technical leader is the person whom other team members look to for, well, technical leadership. All the details, all the issues, all the product problems, and all the interface issues eventually fall under the realm of the person in this role. The project manager might make assignments and ensure that they're successfully completed, but while team members accomplish these assignments, the technical leader has to make sure that all the assignments fit together and lead toward a successful data warehousing implementation. The pairing of a technical leader with one or more project managers is often good because the chemistry of the leadership team and the relationship between them can help you achieve success in your implementation. Much like Robin had Batman covered, Tonto had the Lone Ranger covered, Patrick had SpongeBob covered — oops, sorry about that one!

Chief architect

The role of chief architect isn't the same as the role of technical leader. (But, as I discuss in the section "And Now, the People," later in this chapter, one individual sometimes fills both roles.) Although the technical leader has to make sure that all aspects of the data warehousing technology (front-end tools, networking, databases, and middleware tools, for example) are successfully implemented and deployed, these activities occur according to the initial architecture created primarily by the project's chief architect.

The architect performs architectural functions, based on the convergence of business needs, the current data warehousing and computing technology, and an organization's internal standards and guidelines. When the chief architect completes that work, though, the implementation becomes the responsibility of the technical leader and the team members involved in the development process.

When only one person serves as both chief data warehouse architect (in the early phases of the project) and, later, as the technical leader, he or she must "change hats" at the appropriate time. Specifically, the role of data warehousing architect has an element of creativity to it: The architect has to take a fresh look at how your company can use technology and products to meet business objectives or to solve business problems. An architect should look at a number of different approaches and architectures, and then choose (or recommend) one that's most sensible for that specific environment. When the architect changes roles and becomes the technical leader, though, he or she must restrain creativity. For example, a technical leader can reasonably look at different ways that a selected OLAP tool might perform some task and then implement a better method. It's risky, however, for that person to begin adjusting the data warehousing architecture several weeks into development.

Business requirements analyst

During the data warehousing project's scope phase, the business requirements analyst collects, consolidates, organizes, and prioritizes business needs and problems that the user community presents. He or she eventually wants to create a set of requirements that ensure the data warehouse accomplishes its original intent when it's deployed.

The business requirements analyst is therefore important to defining the business scope of the data warehousing project. Unless the analyst correctly notes and subsequently validates business needs and problems, and all their characteristics, you run a substantial risk of creating a data warehouse that's successful in a technological sense (users can make requests and receive data back) but a failure in a business sense. If the data warehouse is not tied to business requirements, users won't obtain any business value from making requests and getting responses, no matter how quickly or how elegantly the results are formatted.

The business requirements analyst must

- ✔ Be a good listener.
- ✔ Ask insightful questions.
- ✔ Be able to create a consolidated set of requirements from bits and pieces of information that surface throughout the early days of a data warehousing project.
- ✔ Understand the basics of data warehousing (that most of or all the data exists somewhere and that it's important to find out what pieces are really necessary and determine how to prioritize those needs).
- ✔ Be a diplomat, especially in dealing with user groups created from different organizations that probably have conflicting objectives and priorities.

Data modeler and conceptual/logical database designer

After the business requirements analyst collects and validates business needs, someone needs to organize the resulting bucketful of data elements in a manner that can be implemented in whatever database management system the warehousing environment features. The person who does this organizing is the data modeler (sometimes known as the conceptual/logical database designer).

The person in this role concentrates on the conceptual side of the data requirements, a business- and application-specific focus, rather than physical and implementation-specific issues (such as tuning the database for performance and the various nuances of a particular database management system). (The fine-tuning tasks are performed by the person filling the role of the database administrator and physical database designer, as described in the following section. Although one person can fill both these roles, the roles themselves are distinct.)

The data modeler creates data structures that are in tune with the way users will access data and the types of reports and queries they'll run, as determined during the scope phase and the early design stages. If the implementation database has a dimensional nature (refer to Chapter 5), the data modeler identifies facts and dimensions; if the database features relationally oriented structures that have some degree of denormalization (refer to Chapter 5), data modeler structures the data model in that way.

Does a business requirements analyst have to be an industry specialist?

A school of thought in not only the data warehousing realm, but also general applications development, says that unless the people filling the business requirements analyst role are industry specialists (sometimes referred to as *vertical-market specialists*), accurately specifying business requirements that the analyst hands off to people in the design phase becomes difficult (if not impossible).

In my opinion, not only is this school of thought wrong, the exact opposite is true.

During the first days (the scope phase) of a data warehousing project, the business requirements analyst must ask users many questions. One of the dangers of vertical-market specialists serving as data warehousing requirements analysts is that they tend to do two things:

✔ Enter into a project with solutions already in mind, based on previous successes.

✔ Close their minds to new, innovative possibilities for how they can transform data into business intelligence (the "Aha!" factor) because they feel that they already have

the answers (and the data required to support those answers).

In the worst extremes, an industry specialist can seem arrogant when interacting with a group of users, particularly when an outside vertical-market consultant fills the business requirements analyst role (see Chapter 24).

Whoever leads the scope phase must ask a lot of questions; users, in turn, must provide a lot of explanation. A business requirements analyst should continually ask users questions such as, "Can you explain why you use (some group of data elements) in this way?" and "So, what would the business impact be if it weren't available until the second phase of the project, rather than at the initial delivery?" A data warehousing project is much more likely to deliver a high degree of business value when the business requirements analyst provokes users into thinking about and justifying their data needs and the expected usefulness of the data warehouse, instead of some expert leading users into a solution that might or might not be suitable for their business requirements.

 In a data warehousing environment, unlike a traditional application environment, the conceptual data modeling process is complicated by source-to-target data mappings. The conceptual data modeling function concentrates on the target side (the data warehouse), rather than on the source side and various transformations. The data warehousing middleware specialist (discussed in the section "Middleware specialist," later in this chapter) is responsible for mapping and transforming source data into the target environment that the data modeler specifies. One person can fill both these roles, or a team of individuals (each with his or her own assignments and responsibilities) can fill them on a larger project. Regardless of how you establish the team and their assignments, the data modeler must concentrate on data delivery needs and avoid getting bogged down in the difficulties and problems of data transformation and quality assurance.

Database administrator and physical database designer

A conceptual data model makes an environment understandable by grouping data elements into structures such as dimensions or facts. The relationships among different data objects present a fairly clear picture of which data relate to certain other data.

Until you implement a conceptual data model, however (which is the physical database designer's job), the conceptual data model is useful only in a descriptive manner.

The physical database design role is extremely important. The person in this role takes a set of concepts created by the conceptual data modeler and adjusts them for the constraints of the real world. Whoever fills this role typically also serves as an ongoing database administrator during development by performing these tasks:

- Create the initial database *schema* (the physical structure).
- Modify the database schema, as required, throughout development.
- Run load scripts to handle initial population of the database with either test data or real data, and run scripts to reload the database with new data (the data warehouse restocking processes).
- Tune the database for performance by analyzing where response-time problems occur and how you can tweak the database structure to make it run faster.
- Perform backup and restore operations, as necessary.

Front-end tools specialist and developer

The conceptual data modeler and database administrator deal with the database environment. The developers evaluate, select, and build programs in the front-end visualizations that users have access to through the enterprise portal or business intelligence environment: Tools used for simple reporting and querying, online analytical processing, data mining, dashboards, or scorecards. (Part III of this book describes these various types of business intelligence tools.)

The role of front-end tools specialist is much the same as any developer's role: That person creates specifications and designs based on user requirements. Many of a traditional (C or Visual Basic) programmer's characteristics and skills apply to a data warehousing tools specialist. In addition to being creative, a tools specialist must be able to

✓ Debug logic.

✓ Determine which of several different implementation strategies makes the most sense in a specific environment — and why.

✓ Define strategies for verifying the data, building a testing environment to certify the results through the front-end tool.

✓ Follow design and specification guidelines to ensure that whatever is implemented is correct — such as rules that transform the data and presentation logic that evaluates the data. This requirement is probably the most important.

Middleware specialist

The unique nature of data warehousing (specifically, the reliance on extracting, transforming, and moving data across environments) requires that the middleware functions of extraction, selection, transformation, and other tasks (as described in Chapter 7) be performed to change source data into warehouse-ready data.

The middleware specialist makes sure that data is moved efficiently and accurately into the data warehousing environment, whether by tools or custom code.

Quality assurance (QA) specialist

When I was starting out in the world of computers, people fashionably referred to the "garbage in, garbage out" metaphor in discussing the process of edit-checking input data before writing it to a file or database. That metaphor is just as valid today, especially in data warehousing environments.

The source data isn't the only thing that that has to undergo rigorous quality checking. Someone (the QA specialist) must determine whether variables and parameters in the tools are used correctly; whether all the transformation algorithms and code are done correctly; how exception handling works when data errors occur; and all the other QA tasks necessary for any application development.

You might be tempted to let quality assurance be done "after the fact" — after you develop a system and prepare to deploy it. Don't make this mistake. You need to perform quality assurance from day one in any data warehousing project. Don't think about saving money in your budget by ensuring quality only near the end of a project, and don't think about how much faster you can meet scheduled deadlines if QA doesn't "interrupt" design and development. Pay attention to quality from the first day of a project and assign someone full-time to this role (on a large project, assign more than one person). The data warehouse is only as good as the data it stores. Therefore, you should architect quality into the flow of the system.

Source data analyst

Source data analysis plays a key role in a data warehousing project because all the subsequent extraction and transformation processes depend on what information the data sources contain. Chapter 16 describes source data analysis — how to do it and why. After reading that chapter, you can't possibly question why you need a source data analyst on a data warehousing project. The success or failure of a data warehousing project often depends on whether a source data analyst has done a thorough job.

User community interaction manager

Chapter 18 discusses the importance of actively involving users in all aspects of a data warehousing project. User involvement is so important that you need to establish a definitive, formal role so that someone can manage interaction with the user community: their requests, issues, and concerns — everything.

Technical executive sponsor

Even though the project manager serves as day-to-day Project King or Queen, you need to officially recognize someone (usually a "high-placed muckity-muck") in the information technology (IT) organization as the project's executive sponsor. When issues and conflicts surface during the project (and they will), resolution and getting back on track often depends on the executive sponsor taking a stand, such as saying in a more formal way, "This is my project. Stop acting like children, solve your problems, and get this thing going again."

The technical executive sponsor does more than just step in when a situation starts getting bad. This person also usually deals with the project's budget, sticking up for the data warehousing project during budgeting time (especially during potential cutbacks), and convincing even higher levels of management that the data warehouse is important.

The technical executive sponsor, though not officially a day-to-day team member, should be more than just a figurehead or a name that shows up on a project's organizational chart. The more involved this person is (by attending regular status meetings and briefings, for example), the more likely the hands-on team members will take the technical executive sponsor role seriously and make use of it for guidance or clarifications, as necessary.

User community executive sponsor

The counterpart to the technical executive sponsor from the user community side is, of course, the user community executive sponsor. Everything about the technical executive sponsor (as mentioned in the preceding section) applies also to this person: Don't be a figurehead, be involved on a regular basis, sell the project's importance — the whole bit.

And Now, the People

You fill the roles in your data warehousing project differently, depending on the size of the project:

- ✓ **Large data warehousing project:** A bunch of hands-on people should fill all the different database, middleware, and front-end development roles.

- ✓ **Small data warehousing project:** Some individuals might be able to fill more than one role (one person can be both the business requirements analyst and the data modeler, for example, or both the data modeler and the physical database administrator).

How's that for stating the obvious? You were expecting something of substance in this section, weren't you?

Try this suggestion: Don't make assumptions about or definite assignments for the composition of your team until you know what you're dealing with. Because you know that Brandon is both a top-notch data modeler and a pretty darned good database administrator, you probably can have him handle both tasks if the workload and the project schedule allow for it. Or you might realize that Amanda is a first-rate data warehousing project manager and that her diplomatic manner makes her the perfect person to be the primary interface with the user community. Because the project management will mostly involve managing by exception after things get going, she should be able to fit both roles into her schedule.

You might want me to make more definitive statements in this section, such as "You need one source data analyst if you have three or fewer data sources, two analysts for four to six sources, and three analysts if you have seven to nine sources." Because every data warehousing project (or every project, in general) is unique, however, generalizations about exact staffing levels and who should fill which role don't provide anything of value and can even cause harm to your project.

After you've been creating data warehouses for a while, you begin to get a sense that "this one feels like a five-person project," for example. You might think, "This one's so big that we need a project control person to do nothing other than manage the project plan so that the project manager can be free to handle all the issues that are likely to surface." You begin to recognize the people who can handle a variety of tasks, such as analyzing source data, modeling the data warehouse's database, and serving as the project's database administrator. You also get to know the specialists who might be good in one particular role but who really don't have the background and experience to perform other roles. This insight helps you figure out your team's composition a little faster than if you have no knowledge of people and their capabilities and no sense of a project's complexity.

 Don't, however, let this data warehousing "sense" strictly govern the way you assign people to project roles. Plan your data warehousing project and its roles, and decide carefully who will fill those roles.

Organizational Operating Model

You need to consider how the project team members will organize and operate with each other. In recent years, the concept of a Business Intelligence Competency Center (BICC) or a Business Intelligence Center of Excellence (BICOE) has begun to emerge. This structure enables the roles and people described in this chapter to operate with one focus — building one thing; the enterprise data warehouse that manages all the information assets of your company.

I like to frame things this way — you're architecting and building one thing, a data warehouse. Users think they should go one place to securely get access to the information assets they need to do their job, and that's what you need to provide. By establishing this vision of building one data warehouse, you can begin to create an operating model. While your efforts mature, you can shift the roles and people defined in this chapter into three main areas:

✔ **Solution management:** These roles interact mostly with the end-user business customers. The people filling these roles can define the features that end users want in the data warehouse.

✔ **Information factory:** Your flex staff, including your key technical resources, such as architects and developers. Their jobs are to build, in an integrated manner, the new features that the solution management team defines. Most importantly, this staff packages the features into well-integrated releases of the one product — without breaking previous releases.

✔ **Operations:** Manage key functions, such as quality assurance, configuration management, release management, infrastructure liaison work, and production support. In essence, this team acts as the door to production and those who keep the lights on for the one system that everyone uses to monitor the business.

You can see this organizational operating model in Figure 14-1.

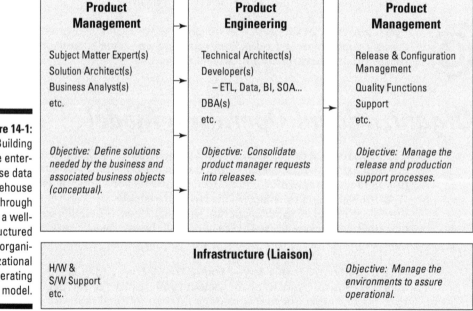

Figure 14-1: Building one enterprise data warehouse through a well-structured organizational operating model.

Product Management	Product Engineering	Product Management
Subject Matter Expert(s)	Technical Architect(s)	Release & Configuration Management
Solution Architect(s)	Developer(s)	
Business Analyst(s)	– ETL, Data, BI, SOA...	Quality Functions
etc.	DBA(s)	Support
	etc.	etc.
Objective: Define solutions needed by the business and associated business objects (conceptual).	*Objective: Consolidate product manager requests into releases.*	*Objective: Manage the release and production support processes.*

Infrastructure (Liaison)

H/W & S/W Support etc.

Objective: Manage the environments to assure operational.

Chapter 15

You Need What? When? — Capturing Requirements

*E*very time I think of those who don't listen to user's requirements, I think about that famous *Saturday Night Live* skit depicting a busy diner owned and run by the blustering, mustachioed Pete Dionasopolis. Pete doesn't let a customer order what she really wants to eat (a club sandwich and tea), instead giving her a cheeseburger and soda. In the end, he relents and gives her tea, but not without first frustrating her and probably making her wish she had gone somewhere else.

When it comes to finding out users' needs, you don't want to be like Pete. Instead, listen to and hear what users say they need. Then, you can build an effective data warehouse that users love to use.

Choosing between Being Business or Technically Driven

Hopefully, you decide that if the user wants a tea, you give him or her a tea! Many IT people find focusing on what innovations and implementations will drive the greatest value for the investment a challenge. So, should the business drive IT, or should IT drive the business? A long time ago, when I was consulting with key IT personnel at Procter and Gamble, a leader by the name of Bob Herbold declared, "We are not a software company, we are a consumer goods company." This quote really set my perspective. Such declarations by business leaders should lead us all to focus on understanding what the business will benefit from the most in our deliverables.

Which brings us to the question of being technically driven or business driven with your data warehouse initiatives. This is a trick question — because the answer should always be business driven! However, at times, you need a technical solution. For example, two companies merge, and you need to integrate the data to improve the quality of both systems. This integration creates more of an operational data store than a data warehouse — but it could lead to a business intelligence implementation.

Seriously question an initiative that doesn't define business involvement or inherent business value. Although the ball players finally arrived in Kevin Costner's baseball field in the film *Field of Dreams,* don't risk taking such an approach with your data warehouse — if you build it, they might not come, especially if the data warehouse underserves the users' information needs.

Technically-Driven Data Warehousing

If you proceed down the path of a technically-driven data warehousing initiative, base that decision on the key business principle of finding data that's widely dispersed across a differing set of systems that the business will benefit from. An example of data that is widely dispersed across multiple systems is customer data!

I once worked on a project for the State of Indiana. The premise behind the data warehouse initiative was defined as a business need for understanding the number of customers — a business need that all businesses seem to have a problems with. Specifically, the governor wanted to know how many citizens of Indiana, their customers, were receiving government services. IT came back with a number of people larger than the population of Indiana. Guess it was all those Ohioans or Illinois citizens sneaking across the border.

A technically-driven data warehousing solution doesn't have a true business requirement defined, and the business itself isn't involved in creating the data warehouse. Often, these kinds of projects fail because the business doesn't get involved with and commit to it. For this reason alone, I often recommend that technically driven data warehousing projects not be initiated.

Subject area

When doing a technically-driven project, pick off subject areas. Master data management (MDM) initiatives have driven many of the technically driven data warehousing initiatives of late. Although these technically driven projects do have business value, they're often low-level system integration initiatives to improve data quality. The benefit to the business is clear, so having the business involved can be a good thing — but, at times, IT just wants to go it alone. Key subject areas that are ripe for the picking in most companies include

- ✔ **Customer:** Businesses today need to know who their customers are — and identifying customers can be challenging (see Chapter 26). After you establish a good working definition of your customer, you can begin integrating the customer data. The customer data integration MDM initiative that you undertake works on integrating all systems that own, create, update, delete, or read customer data. The key here is to unify around one customer identifier and then uniquely mark each customer with this *gold key* — one unique identifier of the customer across all applications.

- ✔ **Product:** The product master-data initiative cleans up all the data associated with products and the raw materials that make up products. All too often, the manufacturing facilities — which are out of central control — implement the systems that manage products. Therefore, your company manages unnecessarily high volumes of inventory or produces too many finished goods. If you can create a baseline definition for what constitutes a product, you have the basis for integrating the disparate systems and coming up with one uniform product (or item) master.

Enterprise data modeling

To technically build an enterprise data model, begin working on one uniform model that has a centralized meaning for the enterprise data entities. This model assists the technical team in harnessing rogue data throughout the enterprise. Although enterprise data modeling has gotten a bad name over the years, you still need to do it to successfully answer your information management question — and, more specifically, to build out an enterprise data warehouse. The key is to build the enterprise data model one project at a time; *don't* model the whole enterprise and then begin building what you modeled! Attempting to build an enterprise model, and then build it, will take too long before business value is seen — and your project will likely be canceled.

Business-Driven Business Intelligence

The best method for gaining the most momentum and impact on the business is to drive your data warehousing needs from business requirements. You can find those business requirements for business intelligence everywhere, and you don't even have to be a detective — you just need to listen!

Business-driven business intelligence always gets you kudos. It provides users with answers to the business questions they're constantly asking:

- ✔ How many profitable customers do we have?
- ✔ Which profitable products are being cannibalized by new products?
- ✔ How does the employee attrition impact the business most?
- ✔ What market scenarios pose the greatest risk to our success?
- ✔ Which customers pose the greatest risk to us because of credit concerns?

I'm sure you've heard questions like the ones in the preceding list in the halls of your enterprise. Answering questions such as these provide the basis for your requirements.

When looking at your requirements, consider several key principles for successfully capturing the essence of the business needs:

- ✔ You need a consistent methodology to deliver a uniform architecture for strategic applications such as a data warehouse.

- ✔ Any business that has a planning process has articulated key performance metrics, so you can often start your initiative by focusing on the business strategy and delivering information to demonstrate progress (or lack of progress) against the corporate goals.

- ✔ The human view of data is, by its very nature, multidimensional, so model and deliver information to your users in a dimensional manner so that they can more easily consume and understand the data.

- ✔ No one person needs to see it all. Users ask for all the data so that they can do what the data warehouse should do. In other words, they think, "If you can't do it, either I will or I'll find someone who will." Information overload happens often when users are given *all* the data — most people live their lives on six to eight key metrics.

- ✔ All data is interconnected and therefore needs an infrastructure to support these connections. It sounds like six degrees of Kevin Bacon! In the end, a set of interconnected processes within your enterprise produce the data. So, build your data warehousing efforts understanding this concept — working to share and reuse data as frequently as possible, as well as enable the user to surf the data from subject area to subject area over connections between that data.

Starting with business questions

When you begin your quest to build a business-impacting data warehousing solution, search for high-impact, highly feasible solutions. To make this a successful search, you first need to understand the business. Gain a strong understanding of the business value chain. Recently, I worked with an energy and utilities company — I had no experience in this industry, but I did with manufacturing. So, I first focused on the value chain. As it turns out, the energy and utilities industry is very similar to manufacturing, with one exception — the product of this industry, energy, has no shelf life. So, here's the energy and utilities value chain that I created:

- ✔ **Fuels:** The raw material — in this instance, coal — purchased to produce the end product.

- ✔ **Generation:** The manufacturing process in which coal is burned to generate power, the end product.

- ✔ **Trading:** Because energy must be consumed as soon as it's produced, enterprises must determine whether they need to purchase generated power from another enterprise in the situation that they underproduce or sell off excess production.

- ✔ **Transmission:** Distributing the product in a non-consumable form, over those big towers that span the highways and countryside.

- ✔ **Delivery:** The final mile to your house. From the high wires of transmission, down to various stations, to the transformer outside your house, and finally to the outlet in your wall.

You must understand how the business executes its value chain (expense to revenue/profit) before you can determine where key data assets are produced and consumed. From this perspective, you can begin to understand the consumption of data across the value chain. Ask the target business user several key questions:

- ✔ What information do you need to do your job?

- ✔ From whom do you receive this information?

- ✔ In what form do you receive the information?

- ✔ How often do you receive the information?

Of course, information also formulates its own value chain. Some data serve as raw materials to drive decisions or actions (the final product). Therefore, when asking the questions in the preceding list, also finish the flow of information by asking the following questions of the target business user:

✔ What information do you owe others?

✔ To whom do you send this information?

✔ In what form do you send this information?

✔ How often do you send the information?

If you perform enough of these interviews, you can connect the information flow throughout the enterprise and determine where you need to fill missing information gaps to optimize decision making and drive fact-based decision making — a quantum leap from most intuition-based decision making that occurs in the old-boy network!

Accessing the value of the information

After you understand what information the business requires, perform a bit of an assessment to understand that information's overall value and cost. To gain insight to these two important factors, assess

✔ Which questions, answers, and decisions do you need to manage and which are optional and therefore nothing needs to be done about them? What information do these questions demand?

✔ How do the users receive this information? Do they get it with

- **No pain:** They get the information in a report or spreadsheet, so they can consume it without having to modify it.

- **Moderate pain:** The end user merges various sources into spreadsheets, manually integrating the data in a non-automated fashion, probably riddled with quality problems.

- **High pain:** The user doesn't receive any information and therefore has to make assumptions.

✔ What's the value (in dollars) of the decisions that users make by using the required information?

✔ What's the feasibility of delivering the required information? Is the information readily accessible, or do users find it very difficult or impossible to obtain?

Using a scale from 1 (low) to 7 (high), formulate your assessment of the business questions and plot them in a two-by-two matrix, as shown in Figure 15-1. Documenting and classifying key business questions allows you to assess which business intelligence and data warehousing solutions can have the greatest return on investment.

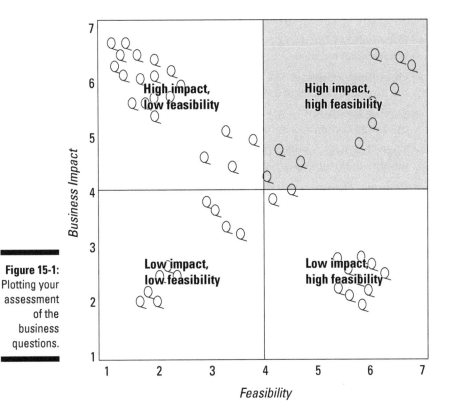

Figure 15-1:
Plotting your
assessment
of the
business
questions.

Defining key business objects

After you determine the questions that will be included in your project scope, you need to extract key terminology and assure that these words are properly defined. For example, say that you assess the following business requirement:

We have a receivables problem approaching $50M. Do we know whether it's isolated to an operating company or a service area? Is it getting worse over time? Why aren't customers paying?

Key terms for the preceding requirement include answers or focal points of the questions, as well as key descriptors. Performing this analysis would lead you to pull out the following terms:

- **Receivables:** The users clarify that this term might be best described as outstanding balances.

- **Operating company:** The users state that this is a legal entity performing business and recording independent financial statements.

- **Service location:** The users define as a geographical location where an operating company's services are offered to a customer.

- **Time:** The users explain that this term really refers to time periods of months, quarters, and years, enabling trending.

- **Reasons:** The users say this term might be best defined as non-payment reasons (or the non-political word — excuses!).

- **Customers:** The users explain that this term refers to a person, or company — also known as a legal entity — who pays for services from an operating company.

You really need to capture the business objects and their associated definition in business terms. You need a technology solution that enables access to such information for users and other project members if you want to drive consistency and reuse, as shown in Figure 15-2.

Figure 15-2:
Capture vocabulary to enable better understanding and reuse to optimize your data warehousing efforts.

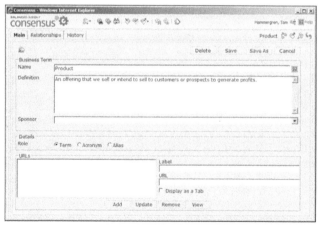

Building a business model

After defining key business objects (as I talk about in the preceding section), work with key users so that you can understand the usability requirements that they have for surfing the data, including key navigational hierarchies and reporting attributes required by your solution. Through your work with the users, you begin to develop a business data model.

The *business data model* provides a visual representation of the desired solution required by the users, consolidating their business questions. The model you produce enables analytical reporting and includes data hierarchies and measures for use by every stakeholder in the data warehouse team. Ultimately, this business data model formulates focused documentation of reference, defining the way the business wants to use the information and capturing the analytical business requirements for reporting and data. You must leverage a tool to formulate linkage between the business questions and their use of key terminology, business objects, and finally formulated into solution-oriented business models, as shown in Figure 15-3.

Figure 15-3: Present the key relationships between business objects and measures to document and solidify your project's scope.

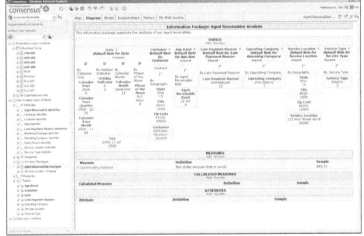

Prototyping and iterating with the users

Documenting the requirements helps to a certain degree, but the business users don't necessarily believe that you've captured their needs and will ultimately deliver. Therefore, you need to build out, using the business terminology you've captured, a simulated version of the target application, including the target database environment, possibly OLAP cubes, and the business intelligence semantic layer.

Power users can best understand the ad-hoc environment by using this simulation, and they usually get verbal diarrhea (as a friend of mine charmingly calls it). When a user sees a real, working version of the solution, he or she begins blurting out impressions, such as

- ✓ That's not right. Can you add another level to group that information?
- ✓ I don't want that at all. Can you change the presentation to include these additional measures?
- ✓ Oh, that's what you were trying to tell me — now I see! This is great!

Signing off on scope

After you go through a set of iterations with the users and have their confidence that you've captured the business metadata (semantics) and usability requirements, it's time to go in for the kill: time to get them to sign off on the business requirements and associated business models and then move to the next phase of your development efforts. The technical aspects of the project (design, construction, and testing) typically require less user time than gathering the requirements does. Proceed with users' blessing — not with their concern. Be certain that they're confident you captured their needs. After that happens, get sign-off in some recordable form, whether that's an e-mail or through an electronic approval system.

Obtaining this official sign-off on the business requirements allows you to successfully manage scope, changes, and delivery for the remaining phases of your data warehousing project.

Chapter 16

Analyzing Data Sources

. . . .

In This Chapter

▶ Digging into source data

▶ Putting together an action plan for analyzing source data

▶ Ensuring that you assign the right people to the job

▶ Employing different techniques to analyze source data

▶ Analyzing what's not there

▶ Introducing mapping and transformation logic

. . . .

Although the process of extracting, transforming, and moving data from its sources to the data warehouse is complicated, some people would have you believe that it's still a relatively straightforward mapping exercise that you do at the *structural* (database definition) level.

I would (and do) argue that the structural transformation is the least complicated part of the process of determining what you want to include in the data warehouse and then populating that warehouse. The most complicated part of the process involves digging through the source data (the files, databases, and various archives formats) and finding whatever quirks, oddities, omissions, and outright errors are waiting to bite you directly in the — you get the idea.

Source data analysis plays a key role in a data warehousing project because all the subsequent extraction and transformation processes depend on what data the data sources really contain.

A couple of years ago, I was working on a data warehouse lite project (see Chapter 3) that was being done in conjunction with an application migration project. One team (another consulting company) was working on the application migration, and my team was developing a reporting and querying environment to replace the current one.

The other team was responsible for converting the source data files into the new application's database environment (SQL 2005 running on a Windows Server). While the other team completed phases of the database migration, they made the converted data available to my team so that we could check out our scripts and screens against real data. Until that point, we had been working to build our reporting environment from a long list of database table definitions, as well as their accompanying data element descriptions and database-enforced business rules (lists of permissible values and rules for cross-table data relationships, for example).

After we began receiving the post-conversion data, though, I decided to dig into the data to see what was there. Using plain old SQL SELECT statements through Microsoft SQL Server Management Studio, I poked around, looking for nothing in particular — just checking out the interesting little tidbits of information.

While browsing through a list of the company's customers, I saw the name of an Ohio supermarket chain where I had held a summer job in college. Because I couldn't remember, 20-plus years later, the specific store number and address, I issued an SQL SELECT statement to return all the store numbers so that I could see whether an address would jog my memory.

(Because the client organized and grouped its customers according to how the client issued their contracts, a master customer record was linked to all the members — in many cases, individual store locations belonging to that customer. The use of SQL to get my "show me all their stores" query answered was, therefore, relatively easy.)

Much to my surprise, I found the address of the store where I had worked and others where I had occasionally shopped. (I even found the location of a store in another part of Cincinnati where my college girlfriend had worked.) I also found records, however, for individual stores from several different national drugstore chains, linked back to the master record for this regional grocery chain. Puzzled at first and then suspicious, I dug a little more into the database and found a number of similar discrepancies (or so I assumed) in which the associations between customer master records and individual stores seemed to make no sense.

The strange records had shown up because problems with the data-conversion routines had messed up the associations between a large number of customer data records. After fixing the problem, the application-migration team had to redo most of its data conversion.

You should remember two things from this story:

✔ Unless someone (perhaps more than one person) is filling the role of source data analyst, by digging into files and databases to see what's there and trying all sorts of different hands-on inquiries to find problems, you might be populating your data warehouse with all kinds of erroneous information, which puts the success of your entire project at risk.

✔ Because I had once worked at this supermarket chain — computer jobs were hard to come by in the early 1980s, before personal computers became popular — I was able to use my old summer job in my data warehousing career, even if it was only the store's address and location. (It probably wouldn't have worked the other way around: putting data warehouse knowledge and experience to use in a career at a supermarket chain.)

Begin with Source Data Structures, but Don't Stop There

Before you begin digging into the data, spend some time looking at the structural definitions of your warehouse's various data sources:

✔ Database table and column definitions, constraints, and other Data Definition Language (DDL) statements

✔ The structures of source data files (VSAM or ISAM files on an IBM mainframe, or Relational Tables on a DB2 or Oracle Database, for example), as described in source program listings

✔ COBOL "copy book" definitions (if they're used — and yes, for all you young ones out there, COBOL still exists in the modern world)

✔ Definitions that might be stored in a centralized data dictionary or repository

Begin with program listings and other such material and then gain access through various tools to look at the content of the files and databases as soon as possible. You must ensure that your analysis is based on the most recent information available.

Your goal is simple: Begin building up your knowledge about the data that's likely to find its way into your data warehousing environment.

You might have to study more than just the current versions of database and file structures. If your data warehouse contains historical information — which it probably does, especially if you perform any type of trend analysis — you're likely to use archived data from one, two, three, or more years ago that has been dumped from the active production systems onto various storage formats (online and offline), including tape, optical disk, or some other medium (even regular files just sitting around on your disk drive). Over time, application changes almost certainly required data structure modifications. For each iteration of archived data, you must determine the structure that was in use at that time in order to understand what data elements and their respective characteristics (data types and size, for example) you have to bring into the data warehouse.

Identify What Data You Need to Analyze

Suppose that you face the following situation:

- ✔ The data warehouse obtains data from five different source systems.

- ✔ Two of the source systems have more than 200 database tables apiece, and each source system has more than 3,000 data elements (the two systems have more than 6,000 data elements between them).

- ✔ Two other source systems have approximately 100 database tables apiece and collectively another 3,000 data elements (a total of 9,000 data elements, if you're counting).

- ✔ A fifth data source has 50 database tables and 1,000 data elements, for a grand total of 10,000 data elements across the five data sources.

To do the source system analysis in this scenario, therefore, you must know the structural definitions for approximately 650 database tables and 10,000 data elements, right?

Wrong! (Fortunately.)

Under the guiding principles of the good data warehousing seal of approval, you want to bring into your warehouse only the data that's part of your business intelligence picture. Therefore, you have to study only the data that's aligned with the set of business needs for which you're building the data warehouse.

As I mention elsewhere in this book (and specifically in Chapter 15), you don't do data warehousing for the sake of doing data warehousing. After you have a specific business mission in mind, align everything you do in designing and building the data warehouse to meet that mission. This point might seem repetitive, but I can't stress it enough.

To put an action plan in place that can help you sift through the numerous volumes of data elements in a reasonable, timely manner, follow these steps (Chapter 13 has more details about the recommended data warehousing project phases):

1. **During the scope phase, identify a number of facts as they relate to possible data warehousing functionality.**

   During this phase, you're trying to figure out what you need to do with a general business objective that best works in a data warehouse format. To analyze each store by department sales against how the same store did in the preceding month, for example, your data warehouse must have sales data. Digging a little more into the project's specific needs during the scope, you (or users taking part in the scope work) might determine that the sales data must have dollar and unit amounts by product and department, and be cross-referenced with the staff member responsible for the sale.

2. **Based on the consolidated set of facts (and the data it represents), identify the data sources necessary to provide the elements to build those facts within the data warehouse.**

   For example, two different applications might have sales information recorded as part of the production environment: one that handles the eastern half of the United States and another that handles the western half. These systems are different from one another: The western stores are part of the overall environment from a corporate merger, and the systems conversion (to get everyone on the same sales-tracking application) hasn't occurred yet. You also need to incorporate order completion and bill collection information housed in the enterprise's financial system.

3. **Begin the data warehouse design phase.**

   While your data modeler begins designing the warehouse's database environment (refer to Chapter 5), the source systems analyst begins figuring out what data you need from the various sources and what you need to do to the data to bring it into the data warehouse.

   The source systems analyst studies each data source and its tables or files to match them against the facts and data sources identified during the scope phase. If he or she doesn't identify a need for data in a source, you don't have to analyze it any further (for now, anyway). It's that simple.

In addition to continually checking the guidelines developed in the scope phase, you can use a couple of tricks to make the source systems analysis go even faster by eliminating data you almost certainly don't need for your data warehouse. Here are the guidelines you should follow:

- ✔ You can usually eliminate any source database table that's used for systems management purposes, such as storing the physical addresses of nodes on a network, from additional analysis because that data is of no value for the business intelligence mission of the data warehouse in most (if not all) situations.

- ✔ Any source database table that contains only a single column that has a nondescript name, VARCHAR2(255) data type (or some other large number of characters), and a description that indicates it's an "interface table" for electronic data interchange (EDI) or some other type of inter-environment data exchange is usually not useful to your data warehouse, so you don't have to look at it.

✔ Any source database table that includes the comment "reserved for future use," despite having what seems to be a complete list of database columns, is likely to be empty. No data, no analysis.

When you find a table with this kind of comment, you must ensure that the table is empty and that you're not just looking at an old comment. The best way to do that quickly is to issue the SQL statement SELECT COUNT(*) FROM *table-name*. If a value of zero is returned, the table is empty, so just move on.

Line Up the Help You'll Need

Never, never, never call up a person responsible for maintaining an application and its database (or files) and say something like this: "Hey, Ellen, can you do me a favor? I need to analyze that inventory application you maintain to see what the data looks like. If you have some time later in the week, could you let me know whether the data has any problems I should know about? Thanks. I'll talk with you Friday."

Don't make the person (or people, if you're working on a larger project that has multiple data sources) assigned to perform source systems analysis for your data warehousing project the same staff member responsible for maintaining the applications and their data. Get a fresh set of eyes and a curious mind looking at every data source — someone who wants to hunt out little oddities and tidbits of information. If you assign the source systems analyst role to someone who struggles to keep the application running day after day, it doesn't matter how conscientious the person is: You're unlikely to get the same level of data analysis that you would with someone from the "outside."

That outside person can be an external consultant or even a person working on the data warehousing project who works mainly with another organization. If you rationalize that the source systems analysis can go faster if someone familiar with the application and the data it manages, you're probably right. I can almost guarantee, however, that the quality of the analysis work won't be as good as when someone else has to dig around a little to get the answers — and find all kinds of interesting items in the process.

Techniques for Analyzing Data Sources and Their Content

You have to consider both the structures of the data sources and each source's contents (the data). Here are some techniques you can use to accomplish these tasks:

- ✔ If your source data is stored in a relational database management system (Oracle, SQL Server, DB/2, or Sybase Adaptive Server, for example), SQL is your best friend. The more skilled you are with variations of the SQL SELECT statement, particularly nested sub-queries for cross-table data relationships, the more productive and efficient your source data analysis. You probably won't use many INSERT, UPDATE, or DELETE statements as part of your source data analysis, unless you're using temporary tables for interim results storage and subsequent comparison.

- ✔ Use the SQL SELECT COUNT(*) FROM table-name statement frequently to obtain quick counts of the rows in a table so that you can quickly determine whether one table has missing data based on relationships with the content of another.

- ✔ Use the DISTINCT phrase in SQL to quickly identify duplicate key values.

- ✔ Use a data profiling tool or statistical tool, such as SAS, to execute functions so that you can determine statistical frequencies of source data. Additionally, these tools can assist in finding values that shouldn't be there, either through patterns or rules (for example, dates that have months greater than 12 or less than 1).

- ✔ Look at all coded data fields (A = ACTIVE or I = INACTIVE, for example) that are candidates for inclusion in your data warehouse so that you can see whether any data rows or records have invalid values, as shown in this example:

```
SELECT * FROM CUSTOMERS
WHERE STATUS <> A AND STATUS <> I
```

Be careful to use AND, not OR; otherwise, every row is returned to you.

- ✔ Check out the summary tables that some application databases contain. A point-of-sale application, for example, might contain, in addition to the details of every time-stamped sales transaction, a by-day and by-product summary (how many of each product were sold that day) and a monthly summary, also organized by product.

See whether the sales dollars and units recorded for a specific product on a specific day match the sum of all the detailed transactions for that day. See whether the daily dollars and units roll up correctly into the monthly table. By performing such verifications, when you choose the level of data warehouse detail, you know that you can extract the appropriate information from your data source (at the right level of detail) and that it's correct.

Analyze What's Not There: Data Gap Analysis

As challenging as it is to analyze what's in a source system's data, it's even more of a challenge to determine what should be there — and isn't. This data gap analysis is an important piece of your source systems analysis. Here's what you should look for:

- **"Holes" in otherwise complete data, such as no sales data for February 2007:** These holes might exist because, for example, a systems migration occurred that month and data was lost during the cut-over, a monthly archive is missing, or for a similar reason.

- **An inadequate level of detail to support the business needs of the data warehouse being built:** Here's a real-life example: A client purchased external data about its competitors' product sales activity. (Chapter 19 describes external data in a warehousing environment.) In concert with a systems migration, the client was changing its data-purchasing policies and would still be acquiring competitive sales data from the same source, except that its data would be summarized at a higher level of detail. The problem: To do the business analysis functions that were a key part of the reason it was building the data warehouse, it needed the lower level of detail it had previously been receiving. The result is a (subtle) data gap. Competitive sales data was still there; it just wasn't adequately detailed for the client's needs.

- **Changes over time in the structure and contents of a data source:** For example, you might have made programming changes a year earlier that resulted in the database tables no longer storing some not-so-important data values after you used those values during transaction processing (a purchase order, for example). For trend analysis, however, you find those data values important — or you would, if you had them.

When you're using SQL or some other language to analyze data contents, make sure that you issue a number of queries to find and list spaces, zeroes, or null values in place of data. For example, suppose that a mail-order processing application has a MAIL_ORDERS table and a NUM_PRODUCTS_NOT_IN_ STOCK column originally used to record how many products on the order weren't available and had to be back-ordered. Because no one used this column, the code was changed during a maintenance update so that it no longer calculates and writes a value into this column when a new database row is written. From a business analysis perspective, however, this information is extremely valuable. You have identified a data gap. At a certain point, you can no longer get information on an order-by-order basis about the number of products that were ordered but are no longer available.

You might find handling data gaps either easy or difficult, depending on the ability to recover or re-create the missing data. In some cases, you can re-create history by doing the following:

✔ Run old programs to re-create missing files (if you know the starting data values or saved them in some type of transaction log).

✔ Repurchase missing externally provided data from the original source.

✔ Dig through old transaction logs and, by writing specialized programs, create the missing data elements.

In other situations, you just can't fill data gaps, and you must make decisions about how you want the data warehousing environment to handle these issues.

Determine Mapping and Transformation Logic

You perform source systems analysis as part of a data warehousing project for one important reason: When you write code or use a tool to extract and transform source data, you must ensure that the data warehouse can handle any types of conditions or oddities in the source data that you find. Newcomers to data warehousing often think of the transformation process as being fairly straightforward: "If Source A has a five-character alphabetic customer identifier and Source B uses a four-digit numeric customer identifier, just select one. For the other source, have a conversion table on hand to unify the customer data from the two sources."

But what about inactive customers? If the data warehousing functionality is intended for only active customers, why should data about inactive customers (perhaps a large volume of data) be brought into the data warehouse?

Or how about the SUPPLIER_TYPE column in the SUPPLIERS table in Source C, the one that's supposed to have a value of either W for Wholesaler or F for Factory, but actually has a large number of rows in which SUPPLIER_TYPE is equal to B? (Originally, the source analyst thought that the B stood for Bob, a guy on the street corner who used to occasionally provide parts that were in high demand, but no one ever asked any questions about "the Bob connection.") Should you bring those rows into the data warehouse? If so, should you leave the code as the unknown B or change it to U for Unknown?

Without doing the source data analysis and knowing the real contents of the data, the mapping and transformation portion of your data warehousing project is, at best, a hit-or-miss proposition. You might have to slow development, therefore, to handle these problems that you didn't identify earlier. Or someone (not you, of course) might say, "Oh, to heck with it. Just load the data anyway, and we'll deal with it in the warehousing environment." In either of these options, the overall quality of the data warehouse and ability to support the loading process in production might be compromised.

Doing a thorough source systems analysis goes a long way toward preventing unpleasant surprises during a data warehousing project. When the source data analyst completes this source systems analysis, a source-to-target specification (as shown in Figure 16-1) can aid developers so that they can create high-quality extract, transform, and load logic in their preferred tool.

Source to Target Data Map

Target table	Target column	Data type	Len	Target column description	Source system	Source table / file	Source col / field	Data txform notes
Inventory facts	PERIOD_KEY	Date	--	See primary key table.	POS	TRANS	TXN_DTE	Direct
Inventory facts	PROD_KEY	Num	8	See primary key table.	POS	TRANS	X_CAT_ID, X_P_ID	Concatenate X_CAT_ID + X_P_ID
Inventory facts	units_sold	Num	9	The number of units sold.	POS	TRANS	REG_UNITS	Direct
Inventory facts	dollars_sold	Num	9.2	The dollar amount for the purchase.	POS	TRANS	REG_AMT	Direct
Inventory facts	Inventory	Num	9	The number of consumer units in stock.	POS	TRANS	UNITS_R MN	Direct

Figure 16-1: This source-to-target specification uses the Kimball Method template.

And, with regard to source system analysis naysayers, I go with the theme of a certain shoe company's motto — "Just do it."

Chapter 17

Delivering the Goods

. . . .

. . . .

Remember the old Abbott and Costello routine in which they went back and forth about who was on first? Confusion ran rampant throughout that conversation — just like confusion reigns (unfortunately) in many data warehousing delivery efforts. In this chapter, I attempt to provide you with a common-sense framework to bring order to the chaos found in many enterprise data-management organizations attempting to deliver a data warehouse.

Exploring Architecture Principles

Have you ever been envious of other companies and their ability to deliver information to their users in a rapid, well-organized manner? You've purchased all the best-of-breed products. You have your first data mart up and running — well, you originally called it a data warehouse, but it serves only a small section of the enterprise, so you reclassified it as a data mart. You've found a receptive and excited user base just waiting for you to pick their business area for your next project. But while you begin to expand your data mart, you quickly begin to realize the products, platforms, and tools you previously implemented can't handle the voluminous data and users that you need to support in the new business area.

So, what do you do? Do you reevaluate the products? Purchase similar products from different vendors? No! These actions often just make the problem of nonintegrated data worse, project by project.

The answer to the question of how you can best deliver a data warehouse is easily stated — you need to build an adaptable architecture.

What's an architecture?

Architecture has many meanings among people who develop and use computer systems. The literal definition of architecture is "a style and method of design and construction with an orderly arrangement of parts." But when you ask someone about their data warehouse architecture, they usually say, "Oracle" or "DB2" — the name of a product.

When looking at your data warehouse architecture, make sure that it can facilitate and create a resource that's accurate, shareable, and easily accessible throughout the enterprise. An architecture provides a blueprint that explains how you plan to deliver the enterprise's vision, goals, and objectives for the data warehouse. The components of your architecture include shared data, technical infrastructure, and reusable program logic.

To build a data warehouse, you must establish the proper architecture before you start development, not after development has begun. The enterprise needs to accept, in principle, your established data warehouse architecture before you proceed with development. Without acceptance and support, development efforts that target an integrated enterprise data warehouse will inevitably fail. Widely accepted architecture, along with its associated components, can help ensure that everyone is aware of factors such as what business functions your data warehouse will support and which decision-making functions your data warehouse will enable.

What's an adaptable architecture?

If companies want to build a sustainable competitive advantage, they must deliver an architecture that changes faster than the business does. The goal is *faster cycle time* — the ability to complete a task faster and faster over time. Just like in a manufacturing company, your data warehouse development function needs faster cycle time. You can deliver on this requirement by using an adaptable architecture.

Adaptable means capable of being made suitable to a specific use or situation. Historically, information systems departments have utilized methodologies that produce rigid and inflexible architectures. These methodologies used the same system development life cycle: Analysts and designers defined a black box; got users of the system to sign off on a specification; and, in 12 to 18 months, delivered a system. These development cycles never took into account that in their time period, the business might change. Therefore, more times than not, the final system was out of synchronization with the business.

One of the most important aspects of a data warehouse is its ability to assist the enterprise in managing shrinking business cycles. Top management doesn't tell current information systems departments to show payback in 12- to 18-month intervals if those departments want funding for their projects.

Users want the business to drive the implementation of a key system such as a data warehouse — not for the data warehouse to drive the business process. Because of this desire — or, probably better stated, this goal — you must realize that your project isn't data driven, it's process driven.

Data is the artifact of a process. Any change to the business is in the process, but the data will reflect such a change. An adaptive architecture allows you to facilitate changes in your business processes — almost at the speed of the business. Taking an adaptive approach to architecture fundamentally changes how a system behaves. Specifically for a data warehouse, an adaptive architecture provides users with the ability to take the data that they've always used and dynamically view and navigate through it. This process provides a new, dynamic behavior that's characteristic of interactive data warehousing. Everyone on the development team must understand this concept. Those data warehouse designers who understand adaptive architectures will succeed, those who don't understand these architectures will build systems that are beautiful to look at but don't fundamentally allow the type of leverage that they could.

Understanding Data Warehousing Architectural Keys

Based on the concepts that I describe in the preceding sections, focus on several areas when defining a consistent method of delivery within your data warehouse:

- ✔ People and their roles
- ✔ A repeatable process
- ✔ A standard delivery platform

In the following sections, I describe in detail what each area entails.

People and their roles

As discussed in Chapter 14, one of the most difficult concepts for management to recognize is that the course of developing software in new areas is a human-intensive process. While the development process evolves, people acquire new skills and find different ways to solve problems.

When you begin the process of developing data warehouse solutions, you have an immature development process — and so too do the people associated with the effort. So, start your first project with a foundation team who will become the experience base for future projects. You'll split and clone this team over time to expand the knowledge of how to build, in rapid progression, your data warehouse — and how to groom the development process to your enterprise.

Although the need for dedicated resources to improve the development process might seem obvious, organizations often avoid allocating such resources. A matrix-style organization in which managers rely on borrowing or reassigning their people as needed has become commonplace. But you really need to build and clone a strong knowledge base throughout an organization when you enter into a data warehousing effort to improve the delivery process in areas such as planning, automating, testing, training, and quality.

Consistent delivery process

Like with consistency in people, you need to establish a consistent process (as discussed in Chapter 13). A data warehouse provides a single source for key performance measurement and historically significant information assets. All the entities contained in the data warehouse are interconnected — therefore, the processes that comprise the delivery of a data warehouse should also be interconnected. Decisions that are required within the project management space of development rely on these interconnections. These stated items lead to an iterative development methodology — similar to the agile methods leveraged within the application development space. Such a process can quickly deliver, in an iterative fashion, new subject areas within the data warehouse that target audiences require.

Have a consistent delivery process in place to overcome potential weaknesses in the development staff. These potential weaknesses don't disappear when you use a consistent delivery process, but the methodology compensates and allows the implementation team to counter the inevitable problems that arise in development situations. Thinking about your own development projects, does anyone really understand the complete system requirements until you have some part of the system implemented, prototyped, or clearly modeled? An iterative approach assists you in more rapid discovery and delivery cycles — allowing your development staff to avoid lengthy development cycles that miss the requirements.

Standard delivery platform

Make certain that the people involved all realize that you're building one data warehouse. Even if your data warehouse architecture has a number of servers and databases — making it appear, technically, as multiple data warehouses — you're building one. You don't want your users thinking something like this:

```
CASE what system am I using?
  If SAP then information is accessed by Bex
  If not SAP then
     Do I want to perform a query?
        Then I use Business Objects WebIntelligence
     Do I want to write a report?
        Then I use Cognos ReportStudio
           Etc.
```

If your users have to think this way, you've failed as a data warehouse designer. If you do fail, a user organization will evolve that builds a series of queries to extract data from the data warehouse and do what you should have done in the first place — except the users don't really know how to build such a system, and it will be a labor-intensive system (meaning users assemble data rather than analyze it). Consequently, your business suffers and you get a key indicator that you need to make your data warehouse adaptable.

Think about all projects for data warehousing as merely releases for one product — which means you're thinking like a software engineer, but this perspective enables you to build a highly integrated solution. Therefore, the delivery platform should provide key components in the various software areas that I discuss in Parts II and III of this book.

Assessing Your Data Warehouse Architecture

So how do you know if you are in good shape with all that I discuss in the preceding sections? I guide people down a very simple path to perform an assessment. And in the section "Is the delivery automated?" later in this chapter, I ask you to assess yourself, which can help you correct any and all evil ways that you might currently possess in your data warehousing efforts. Start with these key questions:

 ✔ What are you building?

 ✔ How are you building it?

 ✔ Have you made the delivery process as automated as it can be?

The answers to these key questions can provide you with a method of assessing your current data warehousing status.

What are you building?

Knowing the answer to this question enables you to understand a lot about your enterprise's maturity as it relates to integrated and adaptable architectures. The key to understanding this question lies in a four-layer reference architecture, as shown in Figure 17-1.

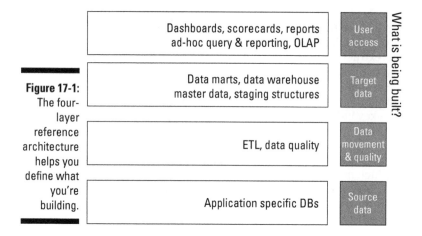

Figure 17-1: The four-layer reference architecture helps you define what you're building.

The answer to this question doesn't contribute to what the users understand — it helps inform you, the designer.

What one platform is being used to delivery user access? User access comprises a set of tools or a platform, as described in Part III. This platform constitutes your business intelligence suite of products. Each time you extend your data warehouse, more queries, reports, dashboards, scorecards, and OLAP views will be added to your data warehouse. Do you want to incorporate these changes in a uniform technology, or do you want to require the user to determine what system and data he or she needs to choose a technology? I hope by now you understand that, to access the data, the user should have to go only to one place to request the data!

The end user really cares about only this layer — but for your own optimization of costs and delivery cycle time, you need to focus on two other key architectural layers, including the target data structures and the data movement and quality layers.

You can make your target data structures very sophisticated and robust — supporting all layers of the monitor-your-business and integrate-your-business components that I discuss in Chapter 1. Additionally, you might incorporate various specialty database technologies, as discussed in Chapter 6. However when you set up your data structures and layers, every delivery person needs to understand why he or she uses the specific technology and how the data warehousing architecture plans to extend that technology for project deliverables.

Lastly, you need to assure that the data movement and quality layer is consistent. Give the platform that you use a consistent set of standards and peer code reviews — whether it be an extract, transform, and load (ETL) tool or a scripting engine. Similarly, data quality modules or products should be integrated and leveraged for their specific purpose across project boundaries — not specifically for one project.

The source data layer is comprised of the various *run-the-business* applications and external data sources that provide the raw materials to build the data assets in the data warehouse. For more information on sources and analyzing source data, see Chapter 16.

Build one technical architecture stack to deliver your data warehousing solutions and stick with that stack through thick and thin!

How are you building it?

After you determine the technical architecture being leveraged as the delivery platform for your data warehouse, you need to assess the process you're using to deliver your data warehouse. The key here is to maintain consistency and establish enterprise understanding of the process. Although I profess that iterative, agile techniques are the best for delivering a data warehouse, I believe that a consistent and repeatable method is the true requirement (even if you use a waterfall method).

Because I'm attempting to make your assessment an easy one, draw the columns to intersect with the delivery platform rows. In this effort, you want to answer questions like those in Figure 17-2.

Around the country and the world, people often have great difficulty clearly articulating their data warehousing delivery process. But they can usually describe their delivery process for many traditional applications. I'm not certain how the business world got to this point, but you need to fix it, and quickly!

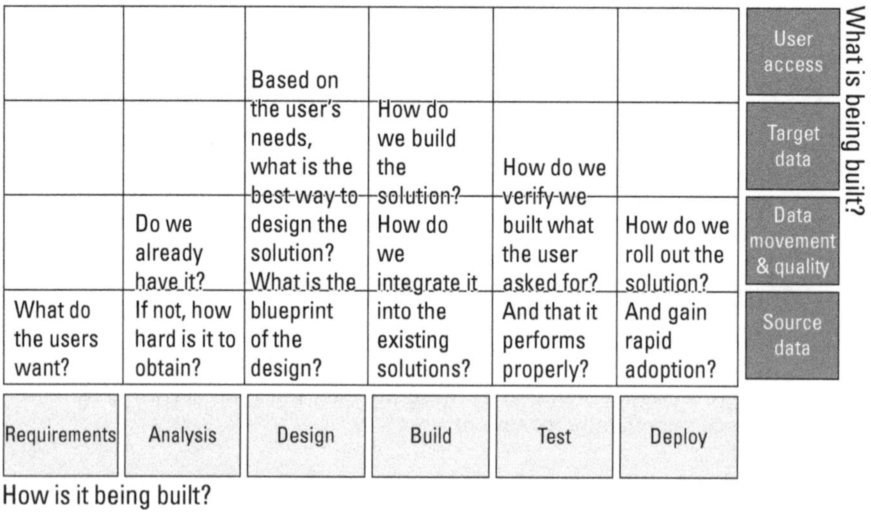

							What is being built?
						User access	
		Based on the user's needs, what is the best way to design the solution? What is the	How do we build the solution? How do we integrate it into the	How do we verify we built what the user asked for? And that it		Target data	
	Do we already have it?					Data movement & quality	
What do the users want?	If not, how hard is it to obtain?	blueprint of the design?	existing solutions?	performs properly?	How do we roll out the solution? And gain rapid adoption?	Source data	
Requirements	Analysis	Design	Build	Test	Deploy		

Figure 17-2: Defining a consistent and repeatable delivery method for all data warehousing projects to follow.

How is it being built?

The key parts of your data warehousing delivery process should include

- ✔ **Requirements:** A standard method of defining what information users need.

- ✔ **Analysis:** A technique that your data warehousing team leverages to see whether the required data already exists in the data warehouse. If it doesn't exist, how can you properly source it and determine what you need to do to transform it into useful information?

- ✔ **Design:** Based on the user needs and sourcing. What's the best way to design the solution, and how do you present that to the developers in a manner similar to a blueprint being presented to a construction crew building a house?

- ✔ **Build:** How can your team build the solution and integrate it with other solutions that other delivery teams have built or are building?

- ✔ **Test:** How can the delivery organization and user organization verify the correctness and quality of the information prior to releasing the solution? Also, how can you assure that user access times are reasonable for the user and technical load times can occur within the allotted schedule?

- ✔ **Deploy:** How can you successfully train users to accept and utilize the solutions and therefore drive the adoption rate for consuming the information in the user community?

Is the delivery automated?

After you answer the questions "What are we building?" and "How are we building it?" you're ready to do an assessment of your environment. Simply answer these questions in each cell of the matrix in Figure 17-3:

✔ Who does this function?

✔ What tool does he or she use to capture and automate the delivery of the key deliverables?

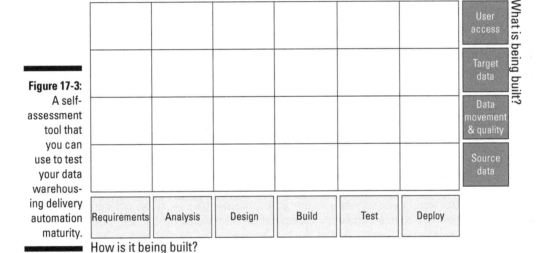

Figure 17-3:
A self-assessment tool that you can use to test your data warehousing delivery automation maturity.

Over my years of assisting companies in strategically delivering data warehouses, I've discovered that completing this simple picture is very difficult and implementing it can get convoluted. I implore you — make your environment simple to deliver by putting productivity tools in place that enable faster delivery cycle time. Meaning the process of moving from one cell to the next is automated, which drives reuse and consistency throughout your delivery. The last thing you want is manual rekeying, as shown in Figure 17-4.

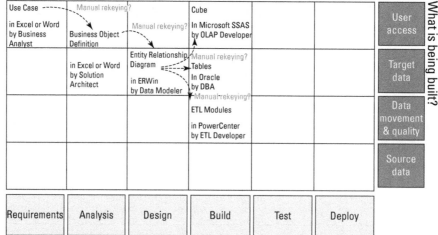

Figure 17-4:
Avoid
manual,
error-prone
delivery
processes
at all cost!

Architecting through Abstraction

One thing's certain in the technology field — things change rapidly. I've seen some very significant shifts during my career. Those shift might not be obvious to people who have only just entered the information technology field in the last couple of years — but you can now store more on a thumb drive than you could on a mid-range computer drive in the early 1980s!

Along the way, various technologies have evolved, assisting the information technology department in building things better but not offering similar value to the end user. For instance, is Java better than COBOL? The technical audience gives a resounding, "Yes!" But if you simply implement the same accounting system in Java that you had in COBOL without adding distributed computing, Web interfaces, and other nice new features that you can more easily do in Java, the users tell you the rewrite was a waste of money.

Technical people can very easily fall in love with technology and attempt to use every bell and whistle provided, regardless of the ultimate value to the business. If you want to be successful in your efforts to migrate through the continuing progress of platform technologies, work to abstract the keys to your solution away from proprietary technologies, including items such as

✔ **Business intelligence tool modeling and semantics:** Where possible, generalize the platform but standardize business metadata and access standards. If you work for a company that currently uses Cognos and you acquire a company that uses Business Objects, an abstracted semantic layer that has simplified presentation can enable you to bring the new employees from the other company on board more rapidly without swapping out the business intelligence tool.

✔ **ETL tool logic:** Where possible, build externalized routines for classes of data, such as dates, that can enable you to go to one place for the specific logic. Most people code such logic in each transformation, which is not advisable. Modular programming principles enable you to swap out ETL platforms or upgrade in a much more cost-effective manner.

After you perform your self-assessment by leveraging the matrix in Figure 17-3, verify that there is a standard guide for each cell of the matrix that tells people how to perform their functions rapidly in a standard method across projects. Having such a repeatable process allows you and your team to decrease cycle time for delivering new information to your users.

Chapter 18

User Testing, Feedback, and Acceptance

▶ Making users an important part of your data warehousing project

▶ Letting real business situations determine how you design your data warehouse

▶ Defining user acceptance

*A*nd now, presenting The Data Warehousing User's Anthem, as sung by a misinformed, snooty data warehousing specialist (with apologies to James Taylor):

> *Don't know much about the OLAP tool*
>
> *I think data mining is for fools*
>
> *Don't know what a database is for*
>
> *Just give me a bunch of data to the core.*
>
> *Now, I don't claim to be a technologist*
>
> *But I'll pretend to be*
>
> *Cause then I can sit in meetings all day long*
>
> *Rather than become just another worker bee.*

This song summarizes the most contemptible attitude I've seen (occasionally) on the part of those who deem themselves data warehousing professionals.

To be perfectly clear, this song doesn't reflect my view of users in a data warehousing project (or any project, for that matter). Increasingly, however, I've noticed a changing perception among some data warehousing specialists. They seem to be saying, "We know what's best for your data warehouse — not just the tools, but also how you should use the data, what levels of detail you should have — all that. Step aside, step aside: professionals at work."

Without user involvement during all stages of a data warehousing project (from the first moments of the project's scope, not just during after-the-fact testing of what has been developed "for them"), you can't have a successful project.

Getting Users Involved Early in Data Warehousing

Don't build a data warehouse unless you can directly relate the project to a specific set of business needs. Furthermore, the purpose of the data warehouse is to make selected data available to business users (maybe just a handful and maybe a number of them) to help them perform informational and analytical functions, such as "Tell me what happened and why" or "Tell me what might happen."

I hope that you consider it difficult (or impossible) to argue with this premise of data warehousing tied to business value. When you consider the business-value premise, no one but the organization members who do the business work should establish and prioritize the data warehouse's functionality, right?

You need to ask questions of users, such as, "Why do you do a particular task this way?" or "What would the effect be if you couldn't perform this task the same way you do it now?" You must handle a likely overflow of requests for features in some sort of order. Users need some help with prioritization and figuring out which features they want delivered first and which ones can wait.

A skilled data warehousing technologist must work with users while he or she evaluates tools in order to point out various products' advantages and disadvantages (by using real-world examples) and to help users choose products to fit their needs.

When a data warehousing initiative crosses organizational boundaries (and corporate politics inevitably become part of the picture), someone who has no vested interest in those politics must be able to steer or cajole people from various organizations toward a potential win-win solution.

Every data warehousing professional, every executive sponsor (on either the IT or business side), and everyone else involved in a data warehousing initiative must keep the following statement in mind: Unless a data warehouse is used regularly (over a period of at least six months) and real business decisions and actions are based on information from the data warehouse, the project is a failure. Lack of use indicates that your data warehouse either doesn't do what users need it to do or that it contains poor quality data. You might want to review Chapter 2 where I cover successful data warehouse implementations. Even if you build a database, deploy tools, reengage outside consultants for a follow-on phase or for another project, and throw a congratulatory party (with cake and ice cream), your project might still have failed.

So, unless you want your data warehousing project to be one that "grasps defeat from the jaws of victory" (I've always loved that little saying), make sure that your business users will use what you're building after you implement and deploy it.

If you complete the scope phase of your data warehousing project without establishing user consensus about the warehouse's functionality and purpose, you're in trouble. Unless the collective frame of mind of the user community is in general consensus, you should seriously think about delaying the start of the design phase until such consensus is achieved.

Using Real Business Situations

One frustration that both users and data warehousing professionals experience during the early stages of a project is that discussions are often too conceptual and too imprecise for many people to relate to. From the outset of the project, you need to tie together all discussions about warehouse functionality, the data necessary to support that functionality, and the effect of not having these capabilities available to real business situations.

Regarding real-world business situations, make sure that you discuss and analyze both *business problems* (situations that could benefit from more accurate, timely information) and *business opportunities* (situations that aren't now part of the business environment but which, with appropriate information available, could soon become important).

Like in golf, be sure to follow through. Don't just touch on real business situations and then say, "Okay, put that one on the functionality list. What's next?" Dig into each item. Explore the end-to-end impact, all the way through the system (the customer life cycle) to figure out what might happen if a data warehouse that has the features and capabilities you're discussing is successfully implemented. Then, discuss what might happen if the project fails.

At some point, you have to brief the executive sponsors or possibly even people higher up in the organization. And you shouldn't get people interested in the data warehousing project only based on how cool the idea of data warehousing is. Frankly, no one on the business side of your organization whom you have to ask for project funding or continued support should care about issues such as ROLAP versus MOLAP or Cognos versus Microsoft. These folks want to know what this expensive funding request can buy them in business value — either a hard return on investment (ROI) or at least "softer" returns, such as improved customer service or better supply chain management. Using real-life examples from the proposed data warehousing functionality, you should be able to walk decision-makers through the end-to-end processes of how that data can help people in your organization do whatever must be done.

Ensuring That Users Provide Necessary Feedback

Behold, the reluctant user — drafted into the data warehousing scope phase, ticked off because he or she has "real work" to do, and resistant to any project that takes away those comfy little extract files that he or she has used for the past five years (and work just fine, thank you).

You must do whatever it takes to break through this reluctance, determine why a user is skeptical about or resistant to the project, and ensure that each individual contributes to the data warehousing project. If you don't, that person might become a one-person threat to your project's success.

I'm a firm believer in facilitated work sessions as the primary vehicle for involving users as efficiently as possible when you're trying to determine and prioritize data warehousing functionality. With reluctant users, however, you can often get the most valuable insights from one-on-one discussions (perhaps in an informal setting, such as over lunch) to try to draw out the true reasons for their reticence or resistance.

Whoever's running the data warehousing work sessions during the scope phase has the responsibility of keeping a checklist of each user's level of interaction and involvement. Like in most group settings, a small number of (perhaps only one to three) strong personalities emerge who dominate conversation, perhaps intimidating others into silence. The *facilitator* (the person standing up in front of the room and leading the discussion about functionality and data needs) must call on others as necessary to achieve a more balanced view. That person can use techniques such as voting or requesting that everyone in the room state an opinion or make a contribution.

For larger user groups, don't overlook the value of *breakout sessions:* dividing the overall group into a number of smaller groups and sending them to separate rooms for discussion. Cluster stronger personalities together where they can counteract each other so that you can draw out the opinions and specific business needs of people in other groups.

After the Scope: Involving Users during Design and Development

This chapter talks mostly about the importance of user involvement in the scope phase — the point at which you make critical discoveries and decisions about the business mission of the data warehouse, its specific functionality, and the data necessary to support that functionality.

User involvement doesn't end when the scope phase moves into the design and development phases. For more on the data warehousing delivery process and phases, see Chapter 13. Rather, involve users throughout all phases, performing roles such as the ones in this list:

- ✔ Provide feedback about different user interaction options, screen layouts, and other features of front-end tools.

- ✔ Help with the source-data analysis process (refer to Chapter 16) to decipher often cryptic codes and assist in analyzing potential source-data problems and data gaps.

- ✔ Work with the quality assurance (QA) team members as early as possible to ensure that requirements are being implemented correctly.

- ✔ Participate in regular status meetings to discuss issues such as training, deployment, desktop integration issues, and the next phase of development.

Understanding What Determines User Acceptance

Some folks might define user acceptance as the point at which users stop making last-minute requests for changes in functionality or database contents, and actually begin using the data warehouse.

I don't like this definition. It's too haphazard and depends too much on imprecise criteria. Set the exact criteria to determine user acceptance early in the project — ideally, during the scope phase. Although the exact nature of the acceptance criteria varies from one project to another, all parties should agree to these types of statements:

- ✔ **What constitutes preliminary user acceptance:** Usually, you've completed development, the development team has run the final QA processes, a user QA team has verified that the system is performing correctly, and a user QA team has verified all numbers tie out with the source systems.

✔ **What constitutes final user acceptance:** You've completed training and deployed tools to all appropriate desktops, and all users have performed a series of "check it out" steps to ensure that they can correctly access data with acceptable performance and data quality.

Remember, user acceptance doesn't occur when everyone gathers in the company cafeteria for the congratulatory party. Users truly need to use the data warehouse.

Part V
Data Warehousing: The Big Picture

The 5th Wave   By Rich Tennant

"Okay, well, I think we all get the gist of where Jerry was going with the site map."

In this part . . .

No data warehouse is an island. And it definitely isn't the island on *Lost*!

This part of the book describes a data warehouse in the context of many other parts of your professional life: how the folks in the executive boardroom look at data warehousing, how to acquire external data about your customers or your competitors (and what to do with it after you get it), and how to avoid letting changes in other applications affect your data warehouse in, I'll just say, unpleasant and unfortunate ways.

Chapter 19

The Information Value Chain: Connecting Internal and External Data

*Y*our data warehouse is most likely incomplete until it includes data that comes from sources outside your company. You might want to build a picture of sales activity across all your divisions for the past three years; but wouldn't you also like to include competitors' sales results so that your data warehouse users can see how your company is doing in comparison?

If you call a competitor's chief information officer to ask whether someone could send you a regular stream of data pulled from the company's sales applications or reports from the consolidated sales analysis data warehouse that the company has already built, you probably get a response similar to, "Are you crazy?" Fortunately, you can obtain much of this type of information from publicly available sources.

Identifying Data You Need from Other People

Simply ask yourself this question: Looking at the complete list from within your company of all data sources that will provide data to the warehouse, what else do you need that you don't already have on the list — and what can you not get somewhere else within the company to help make business decisions?

Here's a list you can use as a starting point:

- ✔ Your competitors' unit and revenue sales results from the regions in which you both compete (or will compete)

- ✔ Historical demographic data, such as population trends, per-household and per-capita income, and local and regional unemployment data

- ✔ Economic forecasts

- ✔ Information about your customers' activities and behavior with companies other than your own

In addition to comparative data, be certain to look into partnerships. You might want to determine whether an *information value chain* has emerged because of key relationships with suppliers and vendors within your companies supply chain. I describe an information value chain as a set of interconnected data that relates to your business's value chain, hopefully including the extended value chain data from your suppliers and buyers. For example, Wal-Mart provides stocking and sales information to Procter and Gamble — enabling proper store inventory levels and shipments to avoid overstocking, as well as making certain that stores always have stock available. Similarly, a raw-materials provider needs to gain insight into a finished-goods manufacturer's plans for production. And to connect all the components of this information value chain, the raw materials provider sees the finished goods manufacturer's plans, which the manufacturer formulates by using the distribution partner's sales figures. If your company currently hasn't opened up or gained access to your key partners' data, try to pursue this style of information value chain.

Recognizing Why External Data Is Important

External data is important for one simple reason: To ensure that you make the right business decisions, you need to see the big picture, which usually means you can't find all the answers stored in your company's various computer applications and databases. Here are some examples:

- ✔ Your data warehouse might be able to tell you that a customer's bill-paying record throughout all her accounts with you has been satisfactory, with only an occasional brief blip. Before you offer a dramatically increased credit limit, however, you might want to know that this same customer has been continually late with payments almost everywhere else and has a poor credit rating.

✔ According to the consolidated results in your data warehouse, pulled in from 20 different sales applications across the world, the trend is "up, up, up!" no matter how you slice and dice the data. Your archenemy competitor, however, is doing much better than you and, worse, is getting 75 percent of all new business in key geographic regions, leaving you only the crumbs.

✔ Your unit sales across your entire product line have been increasing steadily in all stores nationwide except for every store in Colorado. Is the problem an economic slowdown there? New competitors moving into the area? A steady, dramatic population decrease during the past 12 months?

Viewing External Data from a User's Perspective

This section outlines how a data warehouse user sees external data and its importance. Consider these two tables. Table 19-1 shows the sales performance for Good Guys, Inc., and Table 19-2 shows the sales performance Bad Guys, Inc.

Table 19-1	Good Guys, Inc. Sales Performance		
Region	*2007 Q1 Results*	*2008 Q1 Results*	*Change*
Northeast	$2,000,000	$2,500,000	+25 percent
Southeast	$1,500,000	$2,000,000	+33 percent
Midwest	$2,000,000	$2,200,000	+10 percent
Southwest	$1,000,000	$1,200,000	+20 percent
Pacific	$3,000,000	$3,300,000	+10 percent

Table 19-2	Bad Guys, Ltd. Sales Performance		
Region	*2007 Q1 Results*	*2008 Q1 Results*	*Change*
Northeast	$1,500,000	$2,000,000	+33 percent
Southeast	$0	$0	N/A
Midwest	$0	$0	N/A
Southwest	$1,000,000	$2,000,000	+100 percent
Pacific	$0	$2,000,000	+100 percent

The first table doesn't lie: It shows analysts and executives at Good Guys, Inc., that its sales in every region have increased in the first quarter of 2008, as compared with the first quarter of 2007. Based solely on year-to-year sales increases, they might easily assess the sales performance and growth in each region as good.

The big picture (as shown in Table 19-3), though, should tell even the most out-of-touch executive that if someone doesn't do something soon, all those stock options will be about as valuable as a flowery Hawaiian shirt, baggy shorts, and sandals at the North Pole. The Northeast, Southwest, and Pacific regions of Good Guys, Inc are all being outperformed by their competitors — Bad Guys, Ltd.

Table 19-3	Year-to-Year Competitive Assessment		
Region	*Good Guys, Inc (Us) Change*	*Bad Guys Ltd (Them) Change*	*Competitive Assessment*
Northeast	+25 percent	+33 percent	Problem
Southeast	+33 percent	N/A	Good
Midwest	+10 percent	N/A	Good
Southwest	+20 percent	+100 percent	Big Problem
Pacific	+10 percent	+100 percent	Uh-Oh!

Determining What External Data You Really Need

Don't overdo it. The same rule that applies to internal data in your warehouse is just as applicable to externally sourced data: Make sure that your analysis and decision making will have *true* business value before you go through the trouble of analyzing, transforming, storing, and making available all this data. If your competitors' sales data helps you get a clear picture of how you're doing, go get it. If the knowledge that certain city populations are dramatically increasing or decreasing has no bearing on your company's decision making, why bother acquiring and storing that data?

Suppose that the database service bureau from which you decide to purchase sales data has an extensive catalog of companies, time periods, and types of data elements, with a variety of package prices available. When you're considering raw data for your data warehouse, you might be tempted to think more is obviously better. Just like with internally provided data, however, you have to apply your business needs analysis before you begin to consider what data to acquire.

Some, perhaps many, of the data warehouse users will probably apply the simple "tell me what happened" style of querying and reporting, not OLAP "help me understand why something happened" or data mining "tell me what might happen" styles. (Part III describes the different types of business intelligence.) Because simple querying and reporting almost always has an internal focus, you don't need to consult those types of users about external data needs.

By process of elimination, therefore, you must make the remainder of the user community part of the external data business-needs analysis. Figure out who falls into this group as soon as possible so that you can focus your analysis and design efforts toward externally focused users. Follow these steps:

1. **Revalidate your list of total users.**

   This list includes everyone in the company who's a potential data warehouse user, as described in Chapter 14. Is everyone on the list still a candidate to use the data warehouse? (Or, if you've already deployed the data warehouse, does everyone on the list actually use it?) Do you need to add anyone to the list? If you're satisfied with the accuracy of your data warehouse user list, continue to Step 2. If not, make sure that you adjust the list until it's correct.

2. **For each person on the list, answer this question: To perform most effectively his or her assigned business functions, does this person need any data that's not available from the company's internal computer systems?**

3. **Using the results from your interviewing, create a consolidated list of external data needs, the sources from which you can obtain the data, prices and fees, restrictions, and contact information.**

4. **Talk to your project sponsor about budget approval.**

   Make the request and do whatever else your company requires.

Often, in dealing with large user populations (100 or more people), data warehousing developers have a tendency to take a shortcut and apply the preceding question to groups of users, not to individual people, in the interest of meeting deliverable schedules. If a bank's credit-analysis organization, for example, has five people (Martha, Robin, Karen, Robert, and Sidney), all who have the same title of credit risk analyst, report to Suellen as peers on the organizational chart, and use the data warehouse, the same data needs apply across the entire group, right?

Don't make this mistake. In more cases than not, a group of this size has at least two distinct business roles, each of which requires different external data (not to mention internal data). Robin and Robert might focus, for example, on credit card risk, so they need credit scores and market data only for bank cards; others in the group might concentrate on installment loan risk and therefore need external credit-risk data and other market data for different types of installment loans, such as auto, small business, and signature. If you work with Robin and find out that she needs credit-card-oriented external data but wouldn't use externally provided installment-loan data even if she had access to it, you absolutely don't want to assume that no one else in Robin's organization needs installment-loan data and that you don't need to pursue that information.

Talk to everyone, even if it takes a little extra time.

Ensuring the Quality of Incoming External Data

After you determine what external data you need, place an order (similar to ordering clothes or a fruit basket from an online site). After you begin receiving data via a stream, file transfer, or some other means, it's smooth sailing — or is it?

What about the quality of the incoming data? You absolutely must apply the same set of quality assurance (QA) procedures to externally provided data that you do to data coming from your own internal systems. Just because you purchase the information on the open market doesn't guarantee that the data is flawless.

Apply QA procedures to every incoming batch of data by following these steps:

1. **Find out whether the incoming data has check values appended to the files.**

   Some examples of check values are the number of records in each file, the total value of each numeric column (total sales dollars for all records and total units sold for all records, for example), and subsets of the total column values (total amounts of sales and units by state, for example). If check values are provided, they must be stored and used as part of the end-to-end loading procedures. No one should officially update the warehouse's contents until the check totals agree with the calculations that you made when you prepared the data for loading.

2. **If no check values are provided, request them.**

   Although the request might take a few cycles (a few weeks or months, for example) to fill, any data provider interested in providing a high level of customer service takes this type of request seriously and strives to make the requested control information available.

3. **During your loading procedures, filter each row.**

   Make sure that the following conditions are true:

   - *Keys* (unique identifiers for each record) are correct across all the information. For example, if each record in the SalesMasterRecord group of data must have exactly 12 related records in SalesDetail Record (one for each month), make sure that all the detail records are present by comparing record key values.

   - Ranges of values are correct. Product sales per month, for example, must be within reasonable bounds for that type of product (airplanes are different from bolts, for example).

   - Missing fields of information (a likely — almost inevitable — occurrence with externally provided data) don't distort the meaning of the incoming data. For example, although the absence of supplemental pieces of data (defined according to the business rules for your specific industry or organization) might not be too serious a problem, if half the incoming records have an empty space where UnitsSold, TotalSalesPrice, or some other critical type of information should be, the value of the data is questionable at best.

   - Especially in the early stages of acquiring external data (the first three or four months, for example), use your analytical tools, as described in Chapter 10, to perform data quality analysis before your users use the same tools to perform business analysis.

   Search for oddities, anomalies, puzzling results, inconsistencies, apparent paradoxes, and anything else that just looks weird. Then, drill down to the roots of the data to check for the source of the weirdness. Remember that you're probably dealing with many millions of rows of incoming data: In addition to not being able to personally check out every single row, you might have difficulty setting up your filtering and QA checking criteria for every possible condition. Anyone who has ever done anything with externally provided source data has come across all kinds of strange inconsistencies and missing data in the incoming information. By putting yourself in the place of users and using the same tools they use, you can probably discover a thing or two that you can correct, making your data warehouse a much better store of valuable business information.

Filtering and Reorganizing Data after It Arrives

The same rules regarding levels of detail and the organization of data-warehouse-resident information (which I talk about in Chapter 1) apply to externally provided data. If your provider sends you a tape that has detailed transaction-level information on it, you have no reason not to summarize and regroup that data into a more manageable format that takes up less disk space.

If you choose to summarize incoming information before it's loaded into your warehouse, do you lose the detailed data? Not necessarily. Even though your main data warehouse might have sales for all your competitors summarized by state and by week, you can keep the raw data that comprises those summarizations in a *data warehouse auxiliary* — some storage mechanism that you don't routinely use but that you can access on a just-in-case basis. Your data warehouse auxiliary might include parts of your data warehouse for staging information, your operational data store, or a stand-alone database that looks like a source.

To help train and educate all your data warehouse users about these supplemental places to seek business intelligence data, give them a guidebook that has a section titled something like "All the places other than the main data warehouse where you can possibly find additional detailed information in case you need it."

Restocking Your External Data

You have to determine, based on your data warehouse business requirements and source analysis (refer to Chapter 16), which of the following four models apply to each externally provided source when you receive a new batch of data and update (restock) your data warehouse.

Model	*What Happens*	*Why*
Complete replacement	Incoming data over-writes older, now obsolete data in the warehouse.	Because the information provider is continually updating all data, even historical information might be different from the last time you received data.
Example: Although the information provider collects sales data from many different chemical companies, the chemical companies provide not only new sales (those in the past month, for example), but also old sales that they hadn't previously provided. Historical sales are then constantly changing; to make sure that your data warehouse has the most accurate information, you have to do a complete replacement.		

Model	What Happens	Why
Append	You append incoming data to existing data in the warehouse.	History never changes; the information provider gives you only new information.

Example: Each monthly incoming file from the credit bureau contains activity and credit-score changes since the bureau sent you the last file, in addition to the most recent balances. To perform trend analysis over multiple time periods, your data warehouse should always retain the old credit information and add the new information when it acquires that information.

Model	What Happens	Why
Rolling append	Although you append incoming data to existing data in the warehouse, you delete the oldest data to make room for new data.	Users perform analysis on a 24-month rolling basis, for example; in this situation, any data older than 24 months is useless, so you no longer have to keep it in the data warehouse (although you can, and should, retain it in the archives.

Example: You receive a monthly file that contains econometric and demographic data, and your statistical models are all built for at most 48 months of data. The oldest month's data in the data warehouse can therefore be deleted and replaced by the incoming data.

Model	What Happens	Why
In-place update	You apply each record of incoming data to some record (or records) in the data warehouse, doing the same SQL UPDATE statement.	Although you probably don't use this scenario for externally provided data (it's more common with internal sources), in some circumstances, such a small percentage of the group of data needs to change that you can more efficiently send along only change information.

Example: You receive not only full information provided monthly by a credit bureau, but also daily file-transfer critical-information reports about any of your customers whose credit rating has changed dramatically. You don't get a complete list each day — only a list of customers who meet some "I want to know about this!" criteria (typically about 2 percent of your total customer list). You can apply this update information directly to those records in your data warehouse.

Acquiring External Data

Up to this point in the chapter, I do my best to convince you that you usually need externally provided data to get maximum value from your data warehouse. Now, what can you do about it? In the following sections, I show you ways to go about acquiring that external data.

Finding external information

If you're looking for industry-specific data, your industry probably has some type of clearinghouse or online exchange from which you can purchase data consolidated from many different sources — a kind of mega-warehouse that provides data to your own data warehouse.

These industry clearinghouse companies get the data they sell directly from you — and your competitors. If you ask around in your information systems organization, you probably can find a person or small department responsible for sending a regular feed of results data to one or more of these clearinghouses. A weekly, monthly, or quarterly transmission is typically done in the form of a direct file transfer that contains information such as sales by product or by geographic region. Standards often dictate the format and content of these transmissions; if you're curious about the details, find out who in your company is responsible for sending data to the clearinghouse company and ask him or her for the scoop.

Why in the world would someone in your company make this information available so that your competitors can get their hands on it? The answer is simple: so that you can have access to your competitors' detailed results. One of the first rules of most private providers of industry sales data is that if you don't participate and send your information, you're not allowed to buy information from them.

In some cases, the process of acquiring external data isn't as simple as the old song: "If you want it, here it is; come and get it." Some companies that collect industry-specific sales results from you and your competitors attach restrictions to what information you can access. You might be able to obtain only certain types of credit information and ratings for your customers and anyone who wants to be your customer. Before performing any detailed analysis and design on the external data that you want to put in your data warehouse and how the information will be used, make sure that you understand all the rules and restrictions that apply.

Gathering general information

You can get a lot of information that cuts across most, if not all, industries. *Econometric data* (a lot of statistical stuff), as well as demographic and population data, are some examples. You can obtain this type of information from a variety of private and public governmental sources.

Cruising the Internet

The Internet is changing the relationship between data warehousing and external data. With increasing frequency, you can find the data you need somewhere on the Internet. Look for financial information at Yahoo! Finance (`http://finance.yahoo.com`) or Google Finance (`http://finance.google.com`).

Data that you can find at these kinds of sites used to be available only if you purchased contracts with clearinghouses. You can readily access some of this data by using tools to pull information from Web pages — but read the fine print to determine whether you're *legally* allowed to tap into such a source.

Maintaining Control over External Data

Imagine ordering online a couple of expensive, white, cotton, button-down dress shirts from one of those catalog places in New England. After you receive the package, you eagerly open it and say, "Hey — this isn't what I ordered!" while you stare at two chocolate brown, polyester, no-top-button shirts that would have gone great with your lime green leisure suit and platform shoes in the mid-1970s. The same sort of thing (but less startling) happens occasionally when you acquire externally supplied data for use in your data warehouse.

Last month, perhaps PRODUCT-FAMILY was a three-character field that, within each record structure, came right after MARKET-CODE. On this month's data feed, PRODUCT-FAMILY has four characters, and a new field called MARKET-SUBTYPE-CODE appears before it. Keeping track of changes in your external data isn't an easy job, but someone has to do it. That someone is likely you. Lucky for you, in the following sections, I detail how you can wrangle unforeseen changes and prevent new ones from catching you unaware.

Staying on top of changes

Sometimes, the changes aren't as obvious as new or missing data fields, or easy-to-spot modifications to the data types or formats. Have regions been shuffled and rearranged? Has the provider's database dropped certain products for some reason? Has one of your competitors stopped providing information to a certain clearinghouse because that competitor now uses a different clearinghouse? You have a right to know whether situations change from one month (or quarter or whatever your acquisition timetable is) to the next because you're paying for this data.

At any company that provides you with external data for your warehouse, demand that your customer liaison tell you of upcoming changes before those changes show up on your doorstep. You don't want surprises when they affect your data warehouse. Play the customer-service card as much as necessary. You're paying for information that you can easily integrate with your internal data, not a surprise package that you have to continually adjust every time a new version appears.

Depending on the volume of data you're receiving, you might need to build an XML-style parser. XML stands for *extensible markup language,* which leverages tagging mechanisms to define not only the data (its type and value) but what the data is and represents (its true business definition). This standard enables applications to communicate more effectively without the need for heavy change management. However, even with descriptive tags embedded in your files via XML, you want to know whether new information is available or old information has been deleted.

Knowing what to do with historical external data

If your company has been acquiring external data for a while for specialized analysis outside a data warehouse (building statistical datasets, for example), when you begin building a data warehouse, you probably have to use as a data source a couple years' worth of backups that are sitting in some archived, offline form such as tapes, CDs, or DVDs, collecting dust.

Be prepared to analyze each archived media for its structure and content before loading the data into the warehouse. You can't stop your data analysis after you study only the current format and content guidelines because at least a few things probably have changed over the period of time that those tapes, CDs, or DVDs represent.

Determining when new external data sources are available

Suppose that you finally get everything situated in the external-source corner of your data warehouse. What about six months from now? Or next year? One phenomenon of the Internet era has been the proliferation of homegrown service providers, with small companies encroaching on larger ones by being able to quickly and cost-effectively deliver information to you. How do you know when new, potentially valuable sources of data appear?

Pay close attention to your industry's trade periodicals. These periodicals almost always announce new providers, mergers of existing information bureaus, and similar events, and they analyze the impact of those occurrences.

Switching from one external data provider to another

Knowing what you need to do to switch to another data provider depends on these considerations:

- ✔ **The format and structure in which data is provided:** If your current data source complies with some type of industry standard and your potential new provider supports that standard, *in theory,* you should have no changes. That's the theory, of course. Although most standards have options associated with them (ever wonder, then, why they're called standards?), you hope that changes are minimal.

- ✔ **The means of transportation:** No, you don't make a choice about whether Federal Express or the U.S. Postal Service ships the data to you. In this context, transportation refers to whether the data is shipped by CD/DVD (which format? which density?), by file transfer (which protocol? between which operating system platforms?), or over the Internet.

- ✔ **Data gaps:** Does your new source provide all the data you get — every single element? Are range constraints (which time periods are included, for example) the same?

- ✔ **New data:** Perhaps the reason you're considering switching is that the new external source can provide more data — perhaps much more — than your current source. Would this new data be of value to users of your warehouse, and if so, how would they use it? How will this data affect the size and performance of your data warehouse?

Don't underestimate the complexity of switching from an existing provider of external data to another. Like with anything else in computing (your applications, your hardware — you name it), you can benefit from change, but surprises are almost always waiting for you. Carefully plan any changes to external data like they're development projects in their own right. Overplan so that you don't have to be stuck in a situation in which you've canceled a contract with an existing provider, no more data is forthcoming, and your switch to the new provider is running months behind schedule.

Chapter 20

Data Warehousing Driving Quality and Integration

In This Chapter

▶ Working a data warehouse into your information systems infrastructure

▶ Understanding data warehouse data stores

▶ Dealing with inter-organizational conflict

*T*he nature of a data warehouse (that it's composed primarily, or exclusively, of data that comes from elsewhere, other application databases, and is converted into a data asset) means that it can't stand alone as an independent entity within your organization. Here are some examples of the relationships between your data sources and data warehouse:

✔ Users have requested new data for evolving business needs, which require adding functionality to the data warehouse. In turn, you must review and modify all transformation, movement, quality assurance, and extraction procedures back to the data sources that are impacted by this new functionality and data.

✔ Changes to an application that provides data to a warehouse likely affect the contents of the data warehouse and how data moves along the path to the warehouse.

✔ Acquiring another firm drives you to integrate their systems, which are different from yours, with the data warehouse.

✔ Application developers might undertake an initiative to validate data from your run-the-business operational systems against the data warehouse master data to improve the overall quality of customer data — which can help reduce customer complaints.

In short, a data warehouse is part of a system (probably fairly complex, rather than relatively simple) of interacting components that you must review from end to end every time change occurs anywhere in the system.

The Infrastructure Challenge

The phenomenal growth of distributed computing (Internet and intranet, as well as data warehousing internal and external data) has resulted in a fundamental shift in the way applications are constructed. In the old days of mainframes and minicomputers, a single physical system largely contained the infrastructure (operating systems, databases and file systems, and communications and transaction managers). With distributed computing now the dominant model (even mainframes and minicomputers are usually part of a larger distributed environment), the infrastructure is spread over many different platforms across your enterprise and possibly outside of your enterprise.

I sum up the significance of distributed infrastructures in this way: When you develop any application or system, either data warehousing or a more traditional transaction-processing application, you have significant dependencies on pieces of the overall environment over which you have no direct control. Here are some examples specific to data warehousing:

- You design a data warehouse that, based on business requirements and applications' data availability policies, must have approximately 25 gigabytes of new and updated data extracted from various sources each evening and sent over the network to the hardware platform on which the data warehouse is running.

  Your corporate networking infrastructure is still undersized. After additional analysis, the network can't come close to supporting the throughput necessary to move the data into your warehouse in the available time window.

- During the data warehousing project's scope phase, you determine that a push strategy to update the data warehouse is the most appropriate model to follow. To implement a push strategy, though, you must modify each source application to include code that detects when that application must *push* (send) data to the data warehouse.

  The legacy applications that provide data to the warehouse are, unfortunately, so difficult to understand that a policy of making no changes unless absolutely necessary is in effect for each application.

- You decide to pursue a relational OLAP (or ROLAP, as described in Chapter 10) solution and run a series of benchmarks against three relational DBMS (RDBMS) products to see which one best supports informational and decision-support processing (rather than transaction processing).

  The product that performed most poorly in your benchmarks is, unfortunately, also your corporate standard, and any relational database installed anywhere in your company must be of this variety, no matter how you plan to use it.

Think conceptually (not worrying about implementation details) in the early stages of a data warehousing project, or any other application development effort — it's not only acceptable, it's also good systems development practice. At some point, however, you must consider hardware, software, costs, budget, and other types of real-world constraints. Before you begin construction, be sure to consider everything that can affect your designs and plans for your data warehouse. This project is very similar to building a house. You follow a process whereby you determine your needs, and then the architect draws up blueprints. The blueprints highlight the materials that you need to support your requirements — assuring that the finished product fulfills the vision established in the beginning.

Data Warehouse Data Stores

A data warehouse is, by its very nature, a distributed physical data store. Distribution of your information assets assists in the performance and usability across systems and across the enterprise. Make this level of usability the cornerstone of your data warehousing mission and objective.

Figure 20-1 shows how the important data stores of a data warehousing architecture incorporate sources of data, the data warehouse, an operational data store, data marts, and master data.

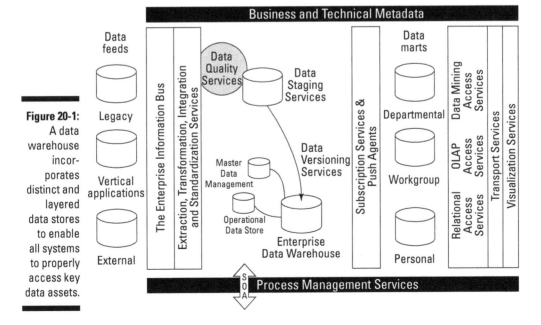

Figure 20-1: A data warehouse incorporates distinct and layered data stores to enable all systems to properly access key data assets.

Source data feeds

Source data feeds are the inputs that feed the data warehouse — typically, your run-the-business application databases, as well as external data sources, such as credit rating data or market segment information. Although the data warehousing team doesn't manage the data and architecture associated with these data stores, the team needs to understand the data feeds. Just like a horse without hooves can't function properly, a data warehouse without sources can't get the job done. The most difficult task you face in data warehousing is choosing the right source, or system of record, for data that moves into the data warehouse. If the data is of low quality or isn't readily available, you have a hard time supporting a high-quality data warehouse.

Operational data store (ODS)

One of the more confusing concepts in the world of data warehousing is the operational data store. No one really agrees on what an ODS actually is.

Some definitions of an ODS make it sound like a classical data warehouse, with periodic *(batch)* inputs from various operational sources into the ODS, except that the new inputs overwrite existing data. In a bank, for example, an ODS (by this definition) has, at any given time, one account balance for each checking account, courtesy of the checking account system, and one balance for each savings account, as provided by the savings account system. The various systems send the account balances periodically (such as at the end of each day), and an ODS user can then look in one place to see each bank customer's complete profile (such as the customer's basic information and balance information for each type of account).

If you want to call an environment such as this one an ODS, by all means, go right ahead. (Oooh — sarcasm.) Terminology aside, this example is just a batch-oriented data warehousing environment doing an update-and-replace operation on each piece of data that resides there (and, of course, adding new data as applicable), rather than keeping a running history of whatever measures are stored there. You can implement this so-called ODS pretty easily, and you can apply almost everything discussed in the earlier chapters of this book to this ODS (for example, you can use the batch-oriented middleware tools and services described in Chapter 7, and the reporting and OLAP tools described in Chapter 10).

My version of an ODS is a little more architecturally challenging. It uses an end-to-end approach that requires warehouse-enabled applications (because you know that they'll provide data to a data warehouse). Warehouse-enabled applications support a push or pull architecture and enable an informational database to be refreshed in real-time (or near to real-time).

Although the premise of breaking down application and system barriers is very much in concert with what you do with a data warehouse, you have one major problem: The pace of updates into your informational and analytical environment is much too slow if you use classical data warehousing and its batch-oriented processes for extracting and moving data.

Forget about terminology and buzzwords. Focus instead on the architectural and time-oriented differences between the ODS that I describe in this chapter and the information I provide about data warehousing earlier in this book.

The ODS defined

Here's my definition of an ODS (it's a long one): an informational and analytical environment that reflects at any point the current operational state of its subject matter, even though data that makes up that operational state is managed in different applications elsewhere in the enterprise. This list explains each part of the preceding definition:

- **Informational and analytical environment:** The user interface and behavior of an ODS look and feel like a data warehouse. So, an ODS user has a querying and reporting tool, an OLAP tool, or possibly other business intelligence tools through which he or she can request and receive information and analysis.

- **Reflects at any time the current operational state:** Okay, sit down at your query tool and ask the ODS a question. The answer you get back must reflect data as it's currently stored in whatever operational system it came from. If an update occurs in an operational system to a customer's checking account balance, the ODS must make that same change in real-time or almost real-time (meaning very quickly). In almost all situations, therefore, extracting batch-oriented data for inclusion in an ODS doesn't work.

- **Subject matter:** Like with a data warehouse, create an ODS with a specific business mission in mind for a manageable set of subject areas.

- **Data managed in different applications elsewhere in the enterprise:** An ODS isn't a single unified database that a number of applications use. Rather, it's a separate database that receives information from various sources through the appropriate transformations, quality assurance, and other processes.

An ODS example

Suppose that you work in a large financial company that provides a variety of services to elite companies and individuals across the world. Your company has grown to its current form as a result of a series of mergers and acquisitions throughout the last 25 years. The trend in recent years toward a convergence of banking and securities services has given your company an opportunity to become a full-service provider to your customers.

Your company's average customer is likely to participate in many (perhaps all) of these types of activities:

- Traditional stock brokering (buying and selling shares of stocks, including margin-account activity)
- Fixed-income investments (corporate and governmental bonds)
- Options trading accounts, including risk arbitrage
- Cash asset management
- Short-term loans and other debt instruments
- Intermediate- and long-term loans and other debt instruments
- Venture capital investments

You want your customers to use your company as one-stop shopping for anything involving large sums of money. Your company's situation is a little complicated, however — particularly in these two areas:

- The mergers and acquisitions have left your IT infrastructure with a large number of solo applications (applications that aren't integrated with one another, even though they probably should be). One system handles stock trading for U.S. stocks, for example, and another system handles stock market activity from non-U.S. global exchanges. In addition, separate systems handle fixed-income activity, all debt activity in the U.S., all short-term debt in Europe, and all intermediate-, and long-term European debt. And the list goes on.
- The definition of a customer is somewhat hazy. Individuals set up corporations and partnerships through which they make investments or secure loans for business deals. Your corporate customers might be subsidiaries of other corporations, which might also be your customers.

Your business practices call for all credit activity with every customer to pass through a series of quality assurance checks before being approved:

- Every customer of yours, whether an individual or a company, has several ceilings on debt activity. One ceiling is an amount of total outstanding debt at any given time. Until a customer reaches this first-level ceiling, he or she can, without human intervention, automatically take out a new loan or act against a credit line, buy stocks on margin, or perform any other type of activity that increases debt.
- Every customer can exceed the first-level ceiling to a second ceiling amount after receiving approval from one of your company's executives.

✔ For an executive to approve credit activity past the first ceiling to the second, he or she must check a series of measures. For example, the customer must have a certain asset balance in place; the customer might not have reduced total assets on hand in all accounts of all types (such as cash, stocks, and bonds) by more than 15 percent in the preceding 30 days; and the bank has maximum amounts for total debt in each country, adjusted by assets held in each country.

✔ To help control risk, your company tracks the relationships between all your customers to get a real picture of a customer's financial state. For example, an individual might control a series of corporations, each of which you treat as an individual customer with its own asset and debt activity, in addition to that of the individual's own accounts. When your company's executives approve any additional beyond-the-first-ceiling debt, however (for a real estate partnership that involves that individual, for example), the executives must assess an overall picture of what's going on with that individual's activity to avoid too much risk exposure in case of financial problems.

Although the quality assurance checks described in the preceding list are conceptually straightforward, they're extremely complex to implement, for one simple reason: Those checks need data from systems all over your enterprise, from many different systems. This data includes information such as all the asset activity, all the debt activity and current loans outstanding, and information about which loans were just paid down earlier in the day.

BEHIND THE SCENES

Can an ODS contain historical data?

Some folks declare that an ODS can't contain historical data — only the current values for all its data elements. They say that if the environment has historical data, it's a data warehouse, not an ODS.

I disagree. I worked not long ago on a banking client's ODS that fit all the real-time update requirements from various data sources, pushed out via messaging, as described in the sections "Master Data Management and Service-oriented architecture," in this chapter. The client requested that the ODS have some summarization tables because its customers

occasionally ask for historical information, such as, "What was the total interest paid on all loans of all types in the preceding three quarters?" The client's objective was to have a single place for its users to access not only all the various operational data points, such as the current outstanding balance on various credit instruments, but also the answers to these historically oriented questions.

So, what's wrong with a little history stored in some summarization tables in the ODS? I say, "Nothing."

One approach you can try is to provide your company's executives (the ones who have to make the loan-approval decisions) with interfaces into every system in which they might find necessary data. These executives then can run a long series of queries (if they can even be supported), pull out the appropriate values, paste them into a spreadsheet program, and make the decision.

This approach has two problems, however: The chance for human error is high, and the pace at which this type of activity must occur is okay only during "ordinary" times. During a time of financial crisis, when many or most of your firm's customers are buying and selling stocks, covering margins, buying and selling options, trying to handle their hedge accounts, executing against credit lines, and doing all kinds of other activities very quickly, your company's employees just can't keep up.

In this situation, the ODS comes to the rescue. Figure 20-2 illustrates a conceptual architecture that you can use to implement an ODS that meets your business missions. First, the ODS provides a consolidated picture of a client's balances for automatic loan processing under the first ceiling. Next, the ODS enables executives to make yes-or-no decisions about loan requests up to the second ceiling.

Figure 20-2:
The ODS
provides
users with
a con-
solidated,
almost
instan-
taneous
picture of
different
data in
support of
a specific
business
mission.

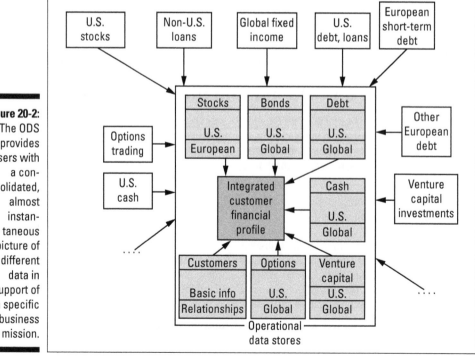

To get a better look at the data flows within the ODS environment, see Figure 20-3, in which updates to one of the data sources (the system that handles U.S. debt) propagate into the ODS environment.

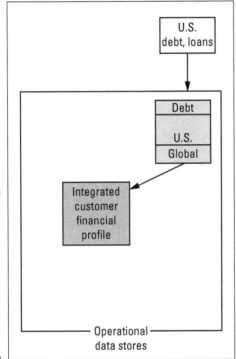

Figure 20-3:
The ODS has to reflect the state of data throughout the enterprise as quickly as possible.

The following steps indicate what occurs in the ODS environment:

1. A customer makes a regularly scheduled loan payment, and the system that handles payments on U.S. loans and lines of credit processes the payment.

2. The loan payment application updates its database to reflect the payment.

3. The loan payment application then immediately pushes the updated data to the ODS.

4. The ODS receives the update and processes it, updating its database contents (in this example, reducing the customer's total outstanding debt amount).

5. The ODS performs any internal processing, consolidation, alerts, or other necessary functions.

An environment like the one in the preceding list can — if everything is architected properly — provide a picture of all relevant data from all over the place — now — in support of the firm's risk-management mission.

You must validate the need for real-time updates into your ODS because these updates are complex to create, as described in the following section. Constantly challenge assumptions and ask questions: "What happens if you have to wait until the end of the day? What if updates were twice a day? Every hour?" Be absolutely certain that the mission dictates real-time updates because creating an ODS takes longer (and is more expensive) than a data warehouse.

ODS feedback loops

One of the main challenges you face in an ODS environment isn't in the technical arena (which is challenging enough!) — it's in business processes and how you might have to change them.

Consider the example from Figures 20-2 and 20-3. Suppose that you've traditionally used the two different source applications that handle customer credit-line payments to also approve new loans or permit a customer to act on an established line of credit.

According to the guidelines and business rules (the reason for the ODS in the first place), loan approval can't happen in those applications. The loan system doesn't have access to all the necessary information (such as cash and other asset balances, loan activity handled by other systems, and the relationship among various customer partnerships and corporations) to make the decision according to the business rules.

You can handle this type of problem in one of two ways. The first approach is to remove that type of functionality from the source application — or, at least, block it from being able to be used. After you put the ODS in place, users of the ODS make all the yes-or-no loan decisions according to the business rules.

I generally recommend this approach: Make business decisions by using environment support wherever it exists (in this case, in the ODS).

If organizational politics and other considerations come into play, however, you might have to take the second approach. Assume that your firm's chief credit officer insists that all U.S. and global loan decisions remain with credit officers who continue to use the respective systems they've been using for the past five years.

In this situation, you can enhance the enterprise with feedback loops from the ODS to one or more of the data sources, as shown in Figure 20-4. This scenario operates as follows:

1. As described earlier in this chapter, all data sources propagate all relevant updates into the ODS environment from their respective databases and files as soon as those updates occur.

2. The ODS still provides a consolidated picture of the state of each customer, and other nonloan decisions and information are handled through the ODS.

3. A request to act on a line of credit or take out a new loan, however, is entered into one of the three systems that handle loan processing.

4. Each of those systems makes a request to the ODS for advice for that customer, and the ODS provides a yes-or-no answer about the loan in a message (as indicated by the heavier arrows in the figure), based on its internal business rules.

5. The credit officer, using the regular system, either books a loan or declines it.

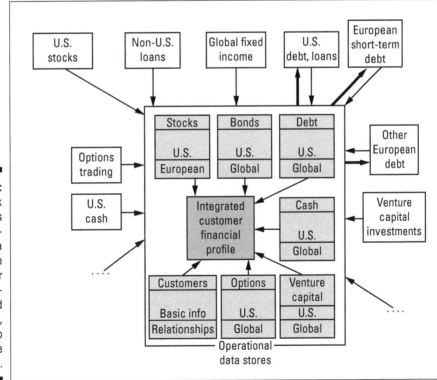

Figure 20-4: A feedback loop sends consolidated data from the ODS, or an ODS-produced decision, back to a source application.

Feedback loops are complicated! They cause increased network traffic, and they introduce another set of cross-application, cross-system dependencies.

Master data management (MDM)

In recent years, ODS-style feedback systems defined for a specific purpose — reference data — have emerged. All systems are packed with reference data. This data can include the set of data you use to describe the stage of a sale opportunity (for example, a lead, a qualified lead, an opportunity, a forecasted opportunity, and so on). Additionally, this reference data can be far more complex. In the financial services example from the preceding section, the integrated customer profile can also be considered reference data.

At a basic level, MDM seeks to ensure that an organization doesn't use multiple (potentially inconsistent) versions of the same reference (or *master*) data in different application systems or parts of its operations. Here's a common example of poor MDM: A bank at which a customer has taken out a mortgage begins to send credit-card solicitations to that customer, ignoring the fact that the person already has an account relationship with the bank. The customer information used by the mortgage-lending section within the bank lacks integration with the customer information used by the credit card organization of the bank. Often, this problem exists because the applications were written to optimize internal processes — not to unify customer information. Similar situations exist for products, locations, employees, and vendors — all considered reference data.

Processes commonly seen in MDM solutions include source identification, data collection, data transformation, normalization, rule administration, error detection and correction, data consolidation, data storage, data distribution, and data governance. These processes are also used in the logical evolution of the ODS feedback loop. A set of tools that have been put together to enable the efficient interchange of reference data between various systems — including run-the-business and monitor-the-business solutions.

What entities you consider for MDM depends somewhat on the nature of your organization. In the common case of commercial enterprises, MDM might apply to such entities as customer (Customer Data Integration), product (Product Information Management), employee, and vendor. MDM processes identify the sources from which to collect descriptions of these entities. In the course of transformation and normalization, administrators adapt descriptions to conform to standard formats and data domains, making it possible to remove duplicate instances of any entity. Such processes generally result in an organizational MDM repository, from which all requests for a certain entity instance produce the same description, irrespective of the originating sources and the requesting destinations.

With the emergence of MDM, data warehousing teams can resolve problems such as issues with the quality of data, consistent classification and identification of data, and data reconciliation.

Service-oriented architecture (SOA)

If you establish more data integration by using ODS and MDM data stores, you also need a messaging, or communication, architecture to enable systems that weren't built to communicate with each other to do so. Enter the concept of service-oriented architectures, or SOAs.

SOA is a method for systems development and integration in which functionality is grouped around business processes and packaged as interoperable services. SOA also describes IT infrastructure that allows different applications to exchange data with one another while they participate in business processes. An SOA aims to loosely couple services with operating systems, programming languages, and other technologies that underlie applications. This process is very similar to what happened with audio visual equipment while it evolved. You can buy the best speakers for your surround-sound system, hook them up to your audio-visual receiver, hook the receiver up to a high-definition projector, and operate it all with a universal remote. The interfaces between these components has been standardized so that different manufacturers can interoperate with each other's "best of breed" components.

SOA separates functions into distinct units, or services, which are made accessible over a network so that the run-the-business and monitor-the-business applications can combine and reuse those functions. Ultimately, these services reside in the integrate-the-business layer that I discuss in Chapter 1. These services communicate with each other by passing data from one service to another, or by coordinating an activity between two or more services. SOA concepts are built upon older concepts of distributed computing and modular programming that advancement in various technical infrastructure components and general software engineering have made possible.

SOA provides messaging as a mechanism for moving data (in this case, master data) from one environment to another. Regardless of the products and technologies you use, take a look at cross-system messaging architectures.

Messaging is typically an asynchronous means of communications from one environment to another. The source of the message (in this case, the application in which someone makes an update) can continue with its own work without having to hook up with the recipient of the message (in this case, the MDM system). The messaging system and its associated protocols handle verification and validation services. Messaging and asynchronous communications give you a great deal of flexibility in architecting distributed environments in which you must send data back and forth across systems quickly and can't afford to tie up any one system while it waits for another to do whatever it needs to with the message.

MDM, along with SOA, provides you the technology platform to deliver a number of feedback loops between several different operational data stores and your run-the-business application portfolio. MDM helps resolve the problem of point-to-point data integration between systems. Before MDM implementations, point-to-point solutions typically resulted in a spider's web of communication lines that were complex to manage and maintain. MDM and SOA provide a robust alternative approach that implements a data message hub architecture which serves as a collection and distribution point for messages across your enterprise. Each application then *publishes* (makes available) a certain set of messages and also *subscribes to* (accesses) other messages that might come from other applications. Each hub keeps a list of which applications are subscribing to which messages and, after receiving any message, distributes that message to the appropriate destinations.

Dealing with Conflict: Special Challenges to Your Data Warehousing Environment

One thing's for certain — data warehousing isn't like most IT projects that have a beginning and an end. The data warehouse, if done properly, becomes the heart of your systems — managing the data assets and assuring their quality and accessibility. You absolutely need a knowledgeable team to properly invest in and manage these data assets if you want your data warehouse to succeed.

Not everyone you come in contact with, or depend on, will agree with you about the importance of your data warehousing project. Many of them, in fact, might think that it's little more than a downright nuisance. Some might take it a step further and think that you came up with this little data warehousing scheme solely to make their professional lives miserable. Others will minimize the importance of the data warehousing — defining it merely as a "dumb reporting solution."

Why would someone define it this way? Consider these factors:

- ✔ Because your data warehousing project affects every application from which you plan to extract data, no matter how un-intrusively, the project also affects the staff members who support those applications and their databases (or files).

- ✔ The network administration staff, already struggling with major company-wide networking initiatives, now must help you figure out whether the network has enough bandwidth available to support your regular data extraction, movement, and loading procedures — and, furthermore, whether you can secure the data from outside intrusion.

- ✔ The *database administration group,* the people who handle all database structure creation and modification, are appalled that you want to frequently make changes to your data warehouse's database definitions — by yourself, without their involvement.

- ✔ The program management office (PMO) is wondering why you haven't filled out their mandatory set of templates to be Sarbanes-Oxley (SOX) compliant because the PMO doesn't realize that you're not using their long, drawn-out waterfall technique for delivery (instead going with a more apt agile-delivery technique).

- ✔ The business organization whose members today use data extracts along the lines of "they aren't perfect, but they give us mostly what we need" (as discussed in Chapter 22) suddenly find out that they're losing their report-writing tools. To get their regular reports, they must figure out how to use the new business intelligence suite of tools that you're deploying with the data warehouse.

To say it in plain language, more than a few people might be less than enthusiastic about your data warehousing project (and they won't be disappointed if your project is a miserable failure).

You need these people — make no mistake about it. Here's how to handle these situations:

- ✔ **Take the "I feel your pain" approach.** Never treat these people like they're members of your personal support staff for your project. And don't treat users like you're doing them a great favor by developing a data warehouse for their use. Talk to these folks, take the time to understand their concerns, and work with someone to find an amicable solution when the concerns are valid (for example, when a database administrator's workday gets extended by 50 percent for the next three months because of the effect of your new data mart project).

- ✔ **Address problems and conflicts as soon as you're aware of them.** Don't let situations fester — that's just asking for trouble. Talk to someone, call a group meeting, elevate an issue that you just can't resolve — just do something!

✔ **Don't make unreasonable requests.** If the normal turnaround time for putting in a database structure change request is two hours in a development environment, don't pout or cause problems because you can't get changes done in a half-hour. Although the situation might not be perfect, it could be worse.

✔ **Explain yourself.** Don't assume that everyone understands data warehousing concepts, let alone the myriad of technology and implementation options.

✔ **Never be arrogant.** Don't have the attitude that "data warehousing is where it's at today," especially with the people responsible for supporting the production applications. They hate that attitude, and you'll feel the effects of their wrath. Instead, communicate to others your belief that data warehousing is one part of an effective, state-of-the-art information management solution.

Chapter 21

The View from the Executive Boardroom

In This Chapter

▶ Telling top management what they need to hear

▶ Analyzing data warehousing business trends

▶ Deciding whether data warehousing in a cross-company setting can work

▶ Getting your organization connected from executive to front line worker

1'll try to say this gently and not upset you too much (it has to be said): Executive management doesn't care one iota about data warehousing.

You might think, "This guy doesn't know what he's talking about. Why, just last week, both our chief operating officer and chief financial officer said that the two data warehousing projects that are under way are two of the most important IT initiatives in the corporation. How could anyone have the audacity to say that executive management doesn't care about data warehousing?"

They don't. It's that simple. They do care about the business value a successful data warehousing project delivers. To be blunt, if your company had done a better job in the past of implementing and managing its information systems and applications, it wouldn't need data warehousing projects, at least the way you're probably doing them or are about to do them (such as copying massive amounts of — mostly — poor-quality data into another database, trying your best to clean up that data, or handling ridiculous situations such as product codes sorted alphabetically in one application and numerically in another).

Just try to pontificate to executive management about the wonders of data warehousing. As soon as you explain what you need to do, you already have two strikes against you.

Although this description is somewhat harsh, the plain truth is that the folks at the top don't care about the mechanics of data warehousing, the methodology you follow, or even the principles of OLAP and data mining.

What *do* they care about? The principle of return on investment, or ROI. *ROI* includes both tangible benefits (expenses avoided or additional revenue generated as a result of the investment made in data warehousing, for example) and intangible benefits, which are more difficult to quantify because they might not have a near-term monetary result.

What Does Top Management Need to Know?

Somewhere in your organizational hierarchy, somebody has control over budgeted funds that he or she can allocate to your data warehousing project or to another project elsewhere in the organization, to purchase capital equipment (more computers, for example), or to pay for some other purpose.

You have to sell that person on the business value of a successful data warehousing implementation and deployment.

And you also have to convince that person's boss. And that next person's boss, and the next person's boss, and all the way up the hierarchy until you present your argument on the business value of data warehousing to someone whose job title has the words *chief* and *officer* in it. Whether that person is the chief operating officer, the chief financial officer, or even the chief executive officer, someone at or near the top must believe that a substantial return on investment will come from successful data warehousing in your company.

All the job titles in the preceding paragraph are from the business side of your organization. Although you do need the chief information officer or the chief technology officer from the IT side of the business to be 100-percent behind both the principles of data warehousing and the investment in your organization's data warehousing projects, IT support isn't enough.

Executives up the organizational hierarchy on the business side don't have to know about the mechanics behind data warehousing. Some of them might have attended conferences where data warehousing was discussed, or they might have read about the subject. (Subliminal suggestion: Every executive should read *Data Warehousing For Dummies*.) They might even be grounded in its fundamentals.

Tell them this

When you're pitching a data warehousing project, work the following two statements into your presentation:

- ✔ "We have data all over the place on a bunch of different machines, and frankly, we can't get at any of it. Oh, yeah, much of it's inconsistent, too."

- ✔ "You know those reports you and your staff are always complaining about — the ones that always show up too late every quarter to be of any value? And the ones that have incorrect data, and no one uses them anyway? Do you want to fix that problem once and for all, using technology that really works?"

In these two statements, you have addressed both the technology side and the business-value side of data warehousing. The first statement, the data warehousing side, addresses the reality that the company doesn't have one big data bank in which every piece of information is carefully catalogued, organized, and available to everyone in your company who needs it.

Don't laugh. You might be surprised at how many people without an IT background think that corporate systems are much better than they really are. These folks probably get this idea from movies and novels in which you can use a few keystrokes to access, in just seconds, every piece of information about an individual — for evil purposes, of course — or change it, or even delete it, all in a flawlessly seamless way. Hah!

A good dose of reality about the state of corporate data assets is usually a good topic to mention to justify why a project will take more than a weekend to complete.

The second statement addresses the question, "Why bother to do anything with that dispersed, inconsistent data? Why not just ignore it?"

You can talk all you want about scorecards, dashboards, and data mining in your pitch. You can show slides and demos that depict drill-down and other OLAP principles. You can go on and on about being predictive, not reactive. I've never seen anything work better, however, to explain what a data warehouse can do than to put the business-value discussion in the context of what's almost always a point of pain in an organization: dealing with those convoluted reports that are always late, inaccurate, and worthless.

I strongly believe in the hypothesis that every business manager has between four and seven attention points that he or she uses to help run an organization's operations and make decisions. In business life, the traditional way many managers address these points has involved reports (usually one or two for each attention point) that they use to analyze information and make decisions.

In many settings, any information-driven analysis and decision making (rather than seat-of-the-pants decision making) boils down to the use of reports. That's right — reports. Reports are a concept that most managers and executives can understand, so talk about the benefits in terms of reports when you're trying to sell data warehousing.

So, what's a recommended way to sell the concept of data warehousing and your project, in particular, to executive management? As a much better, much more timely way to generate reports. (I figured the point in the preceding paragraph came across — I wanted to make sure.)

Keep selling the data warehousing project

Anyone who has been involved in any type of application development effort, whether from the corporate, consulting, or vendor side, knows that continued funding is almost always in question. No matter how enthusiastic the support is at the beginning of the project, no matter how many statements they make that "this project is the most important one in the corporation today," and no matter what they budget for your project, budget cuts or shifting priorities can always disrupt a project.

Therefore, from the earliest possible opportunity in the project (90 days at most — 60 days is even better), you need to establish a tangible business benefit for real-life use by the highest-ranking business executive who holds the funding strings for your project. Be sure to

- ✔ Provide a set of interconnected reports, dashboards, and OLAP views that you know can help this person perform analysis and make decisions. (***Hint:*** Just ask.)

- ✔ Use real, not fake, data (even a small amount).

- ✔ Solicit feedback about usability, later steps, and everything else you can think of to ensure that the executive fully believes in your project and (unless something out-of-the-ordinary happens) will continue the funding until you complete the project.

Data Warehousing and the Business-Trends Bandwagon

Business process engineering, six sigma, balanced scorecard, the loyalty effect, and managing in one-minute increments.

I entered the business world in the mid 1980s; in the 20-plus years since then, a number of trends and fads have come and gone. First, the book arrives, then the seminars and consulting engagements that have extremely high daily fees, and then more books by others trying to jump on the bandwagon. In some cases, these events are even followed by the "Uh-oh, I guess we were wrong" books, seminars, and damage-control consulting engagements that have extremely high daily fees.

Okay, maybe that description is a little cynical. Or maybe I'm just envious and bitter because none of my books has ever started a major business or management fad.

Now that the data warehousing era is here, the next generation of business and management trends (you had better believe that a next generation will come along) might have a little more substance — a little more information — that you can use to determine whether a trend is a step in the positive direction or just another fad that will eventually be as useful as a snowmobile in Phoenix.

If you've done your data warehousing correctly and have access to a large amount of corporate business intelligence, you can get the numbers to see whether your company has a problem in whatever area a trendy business approach might address. You can also perform a what-if analysis *before* you spend a gazillion dollars on consulting fees (and disrupt your business processes and organization) to implement whatever's being sold as the answer.

Suppose that data warehousing were as mature in the 1990s as it is today and your organization had successfully implemented a data warehousing environment. Your profits are down, sales are flat, and the boom days your company experienced in the 1990s are gone. Along comes a consulting firm pushing this new idea of lean six sigma and business-process management as the answer to all your corporate woes. You engage a team of consultants to study your business processes and to make recommendations for improvement. If your team of consultants is anything like many others, it spends a large amount of your money and then makes a standard recommendation: Fire many of your employees and let the consulting company employees outsource the work they leave behind.

(Oops, cynicism creeps in again.)

Before taking such a drastic step, like many organizations did, you could use information from your data warehouse to perform extensive analysis on the effect of such a drastic measure. Using what-if analysis with data pulled from the data warehouse, you might determine that the purported benefits and cost savings from the move just don't exist.

Before following any business trends, try to figure out whether they have any substance. In most situations, it's nearly impossible to determine that information without looking into real corporate data, such as current sales and how they're likely to be affected by a recommended set of actions, current expenses across departments, how proposed budget cuts and staff recommendations would affect those expenses, and how those cuts might affect sales and marketing.

Data Warehousing in a Cross-Company Setting

Data warehousing is usually a private affair. Even when external data about your competitors is part of your environment, as described in Chapter 19, it's still your company's data warehouse, built for your company's benefit and use.

An interesting trend — one that's surely noticeable at the executive boardroom level, primarily because those folks are steering corporations in this direction — is to have multi-company cooperation. Two or three pharmaceutical companies might share the research-and-development expenses on a new generation of drug products, or two manufacturing companies might work together in a partnership to develop a product. A commercial bank and a brokerage institution might work together to offer jointly a series of financial products to the mass market, with the bank administering some products and the brokerage administering others.

Whatever the specifics of the industry and the situation, your company has a good chance of being involved in a multi-company partnership in which cross-company cooperation and sharing of information is a key part of success.

To that end, an interesting spin on the theme of data warehousing as a breaker of barriers is to have a multi-company data warehouse dedicated to more efficient analytical and information-delivery capabilities in support of a joint effort between your two companies.

As you might guess, a multi-company data warehouse is a slightly more complex creature than one dedicated to the support of a single company. Although you experience all the wonderful challenges of data extraction and transformation, tool selection, performance support, and other aspects of data warehousing, you also have to consider these issues:

- **Corporate standards:** Two (or more) sets of corporate standards can affect how you deploy your data warehouse and its tools. For example, one company might be a Business Objects environment, and another might be a Cognos environment. Whose standards will you use, and what's the effect on the other company's users?

- **Proprietary and sensitive data:** The business case for the multi-company data warehouse, and the accompanying functionality and data necessary to support the data warehouse's business mission, might require that sales history information is made available for predictive sales forecasting. Sales history information involves a breakdown by region, territory, and possibly even customer. What are the effects of revealing customer lists, and strengths and weaknesses in various regions, to a partner that's also a competitor?

- **Security concerns:** In addition to data security issues, any linkage between two environments can open up one environment to any security weaknesses in the other, such as unauthorized outside access and hacking.

- **Support costs:** Which organization has primary support responsibility for the data warehouse? Does it bear the full burden of support costs, or will the two organizations share those costs? If the organizations share the costs, how do they calculate support costs, and how do they bill and pay those costs?

- **Development methodology:** One organization might develop its data warehousing applications and environments by using Kimball techniques, but the other organization uses Inmon techniques. Who controls the development processes? Do individuals from one organization have to figure out and use the other's methods and techniques?

- **Dispute resolution:** Resolving any type of dispute in which parties are from different companies always proves an interesting challenge.

- **Ongoing enhancements:** What cross-company management structure must you put in place to prioritize and approve enhancements to the environment?

Connecting the Enterprise

Regardless of whether you create a single- or multiple-company integration, one thing is certain — if you can get the executives the timely information they need in an accurate form, the herds of analysts they employ can now focus on analyzing the data, rather than assembling it. And, furthermore, the executives can begin connecting the strategy of the enterprise with key metrics by using the organizational layer. Each person up and down the food chain can have the four to six metrics that he or she focuses on — and possibly are compensated on. With this level of connectivity and focus, the company can much more easily deliver upon a strategy.

But you must take that first step — convince your executive sponsor or team that the enterprise from an intuition-based decision-making model to a fact-based one. In that simple statement, you go from the decisions being made "because my gut tells me that is the right decision" to "based on the trends we should be investing in . . . or change our direction."

Which type of organization would you rather oversee? I'm sure you're no different than many executives or shareholders: The proof is in the execution, and to execute a data warehouse, you need executive leadership.

Chapter 22

Existing Sort-of Data Warehouses: Upgrade or Replace?

*Y*our organization has overwhelmingly favorable odds of having at least one *sort-of data warehouse* — a reporting system that provides informational capabilities and, sometimes, analytical capabilities to one or more groups of users. Your users probably use the term *extract file* to describe this type of environment because it's populated by extracts of data from production systems, rather than by users being forced to execute their queries or receive their reports from the operational production databases or files. Still interested in playing the odds? Here are a few more examples of types of data environments that might be described as sort-of data warehouses:

 ✔ Although the extracted data is almost always housed in a single file or database, a merge process probably combines extracted data from more than one application source.

 ✔ Only selected elements, not all elements from all tables or files, from each data source are usually extracted and copied to the extract file.

 ✔ Some sort of data quality assurance process is usually going on each step of the way, from the initial extract to loading the data into the extract file.

 ✔ Some power users probably can execute queries or create statistical programs (in SAS or SPSS, for example) against the data, but many users aren't likely to touch the data directly. Instead, they probably regularly receive reports generated either automatically or in response to their requests.

Sure sounds like a data warehouse, doesn't it? The reality is that these sort-of data warehouses are typically serving a very small population and are not done in a standard manner to support the broader needs of the enterprise. You might also call them *wanna-be data warehouses.*

The Data Haves and Have-Nots

About two years ago, I began working on a data warehousing project with a fairly large bank. I was working with the retail part of the bank, in which individual consumer (credit card, lease, and mortgage) loans were handled. (The wholesale side handled large commercial loans and other financial transactions with companies.)

I set up a kickoff meeting with the project's sponsor, who outlined all the (numerous) initiatives the project encompassed. We put together a time line of which areas to tackle first and which ones would follow, and we then set up a series of meetings with different managers and technologists in the various business groups in the bank's retail organization.

The first meeting was held with a group responsible for analyzing how the bank's customers handled their payments for consumer loans: how many paid on time, paid only the minimum amount due each month, and defaulted on or missed payments, for example. This group's goal was to manage the bank's risk against its entire portfolio of loans and to perform statistical analysis in an attempt to predict where problems might occur. To accomplish this goal, the group would look at historical payment patterns and perform trend analysis and other statistical functions.

The meeting began with the project sponsor explaining what the group was planning for the bank: Build a data warehouse to support risk management for consumer loans in addition to other functions handled by other departments. We spent the rest of the meeting with the loan payment analysts describing how they did their analysis, what data they used and where it came from, and other pertinent information.

A few days later, I was speaking with the manager of the group who had been in the meeting. He said, "You know, I don't understand this data warehousing thing. We already pull key data elements from our production systems into an Excel spreadsheet — I personally hand-picked which elements we need — and we've been doing this type of analysis for about two years. Tell me again, what additional benefit will I get from a data warehouse?"

To complicate matters, the second group meeting was with another organization responsible for analyzing credit bureau scores for the bank's customers. This group would periodically receive, from a provider of external data (refer to Chapter 19), credit bureau data about anyone who had any type of line of credit (including a bank card) or loan.

This meeting began much like the first one, except that the project's sponsor wasn't there and I was facing the group alone. At their request, I explained the principles of data warehousing and how data would be pulled from various sources and made available for analysis. Next, they took turns explaining to me how they performed statistical analysis with their own data extracts that merged data from different sources and analyzed bankruptcies, delinquencies, and a lot of other measures in concert with the credit bureau data.

Again, the request was made: "Explain again what new functionality a data warehouse will give me."

Why aren't extract files considered to be data warehouses?

They are, sort of. Chapter 1 describes the historical roots of data warehousing in the 1970s. Extract files, whether in the 1970s, 1980s, 1990s, or still in use today, exist for the same basic reasons that a full-fledged data warehouse or a data mart does: to provide information delivery despite a variety of barriers, such as hard-to-understand data structures, "don't touch the production system" rules, and the lack of multi-file or multi-database cross-reference.

Some data warehousing proponents argue that combining and reconfiguring data simply for the purpose of generating reports or to perform statistical analysis is hardly a data warehouse in the modern sense of the term. Extract files aren't equipped with multidimensional or business-analysis capabilities, such as drill-down and data pivoting.

I argue that if you separate the data-warehouse side (what it takes to gather, move, and reconfigure data from one or more sources) from the business-intelligence side (what you do with the data after you have it available), the picture becomes much clearer. Extract files, or whatever you want to call them, are very much part of the barrier-breaking philosophy of a data warehouse. Many of what users refer to as "extract files" are file-based systems (rather than built on databases), and they probably aren't flexible enough to support ad hoc querying and dimensional analysis. In a real sense, however, these environments serve the purpose of warehousing data for subsequent use.

To many users, business-analysis capabilities, such as drill-down and data pivoting, have little or no use — at least, not in the context of their current job definitions. The users' jobs call for functionality that these extract files can deliver, as well as the static reports and statistical analysis accomplished with that data.

I'm not saying that everyone should scrap their data warehousing initiatives and continue to run on top of existing extract files. But, for as much interest as data warehousing has generated since the early 1990s, the premise of "getting the job done" is the same old story for a large segment of the business community.

The moral of the story: Don't go into an organization that effectively uses data through extract files and expound on the wonders of data warehousing. Instead, as discussed in the section "Choice 3: Retain It," in this chapter, be cautious about proposing any data warehousing solution that can be viewed as a step backward. If you do make this kind of proposition, you're in for a long, bumpy ride.

The real answer to this request, made by both groups, was, "In your particular situation, not much." Doing the tap dance of a good data warehousing consultant, I explained the big picture: It wasn't just their own respective groups, but also many other groups on the retail side of the bank, who needed that same information. The data in its current form just wasn't available or wasn't in a flexible enough form to be used in other ways (business analysis, for example) than the statistical processes that were being used.

Honestly, each individual had the right to ask, "What do I gain from this data warehousing project?" Neither organization had its own data warehouse or was doing its processing against a data mart extracted from some larger organizational data warehouse. What they were doing, however small-time it was, was well suited to their respective needs. Their business needs didn't call for business analysis, OLAP-style functionality, and other advanced business intelligence capabilities. Summarized data? "Sorry, no can do." These folks needed detail-level data for their statistical analysis. Drill-down? "Not interested, thanks for asking." They needed only statistical processing to do their jobs, and mainframe SAS did that just fine, thank you.

Note: Other groups on the retail side of the bank did need to do drill-down analysis by region against summarized data. To their managers and analysts, the idea of a data warehouse supported by business analysis tools was an enticing, high-value proposition because they didn't have anything similar at the time.

Here's the dichotomy of most organizations access to data:

- **Data analysis "have-nots":** Organizations and individuals who have few (and more likely no) capabilities to do the type of analysis that can bring about information-driven decision-making

- **Data analysis "haves":** Organizations and individuals who might not have a data warehouse up and running, but are doing something with data that they're getting from somewhere. In many cases, it's suiting their business needs just fine.

The first step: Cataloguing the extract files, who uses them, and why

Before you even begin to consider what to do about the extract files and other types of sort-of data warehouse environments that exist, you must find them — which you might find difficult, considering the homegrown nature of these environments.

Here's a hint: Follow the reports. Through group work sessions and individual meetings, determine and catalog the reports that employees use throughout the organization that you're working with to build a data warehouse. Some of those reports probably come directly from the production applications, and their respective databases and files. For now, don't worry about these production application reports. (Keep track of them, though, because you can use them as an excellent starting point for the "what data do we need?" analysis, which determines what you want to put in the data warehouse.) Other reports come from data extracted from one or more applications and stored somewhere. Those reports are the ones to concentrate on now.

Using the set of reports as your starting point, first determine who's using them and who's responsible for generating them. You need to know who is using the generated reports because you might find that nobody uses them anymore. Just by assessing the inventory of reports and their current utilization, you're halfway finished with eliminating this don't-really-use-it functionality from your data warehousing environment (and managing its complexity).

Once you understand the report usage patterns, get to know the people responsible for generating the reports. They're the ones who probably can tell you where they get the data, what processes they use to prepare and load that data before running the reports, and what issues and problems they have with data availability and integrity.

Sometimes, no single individual knows the entire end-to-end sequence of steps used to extract data, prepare and organize that data, and run the reports — especially when these processes cross organizational boundaries. (For example, the IT organization handles the initial extraction of the data and some rudimentary quality assurance, and the business organization handles the merge processes and runs the reports.) In these situations, get all these people in the same room to discuss and agree on how things work. You can avoid spending a great deal of time playing "he said, she said" with people who, frankly, you're probably aggravating with your constant questions and requests for meetings.

Eventually, through diligence, you get a complete picture of who's using which data, who's responsible for making that data available, and what's going on behind the scenes to make it all happen.

Don't forget the why part of the picture — for what business purposes extract files are being used. You have to find out this information anyway, as part of your requirements analysis. While you're checking out what's going on today, ask questions while you have the users' attention, such as:

- ✔ Why do you need the information in the report?
- ✔ What decisions does this report assist you in making?
- ✔ When you analyze the data on the report, who do you communicate your findings to?

Your line of questioning should follow a traditional understanding of what the report's requirements are as discussed in Chapter 15. Getting a firm understanding of these questions at this analysis point will save you time in the long run.

And then, the review

Don't skip this section. If you do, serious problems lie ahead.

After you create your catalog of information, you must embark on a candid, no-holds-barred review process with each organization that uses extract files. Although you'd ideally make this process part of the data warehousing project's scope (Chapter 13 discusses how to choose a methodology), schedule conflicts and timing constraints might require additional meetings to complete the review process. To help you establish the proper project scope, conduct these meetings — to gain a firm understanding of the extract files' use and purpose — as early in the process as possible.

You want to determine the true business value that the organization obtains from using these extract files and what additional business value that organization might obtain. You have to take this approach with the extract file users: "Forget this data warehousing stuff — tell me about your extracts." They're already likely to feel that the evil data warehousing empire is about to take away their capabilities (as discussed in the section "Beware: Don't Take Away Valued Functionality," later in this chapter).

While the data warehousing project moves forward, figure out what part of the existing environment is worth salvaging (not only functionality, but also steps and processes).

Decisions, Decisions

If you have been diligent, you've now ferreted out a complete inventory of extract files that fill the role of prehistoric data warehouse, each one most likely serving a single organization's needs. Next, you and the business users have reached consensus about what's good about each file, what needs to be improved, and other aspects of the data use throughout the organization.

Now, it's decision time.

Although it might come as a surprise to you, you have no reason not to build a data warehousing environment to contain one or more existing extract files. Although a single, monolithic data warehouse probably would have difficulty interacting with these extract files, an environment constructed in a mixed-mode, component-oriented manner (refer to Chapter 13) can encompass a long-in-the-tooth component or two.

You must test each extract file (as I describe in the following sections), and then you will be left with one of three answers regarding what to do with that extract file:

✔ Discard it.

✔ Replace it.

✔ Retain it, possibly with some upgrades or enhancements.

Choice 1: Get rid of it

If, and only if, you have universal agreement from every corner of the organization that an extract file has absolutely no use (for example, no one looks anymore at the reports it generates, and no one has updated the data-extraction and data-input processes, so the system is generally doing little, other than wasting disk space and processing time), you can probably just dump the file without any type of replacement or upgrade.

Although some individual data elements might eventually find their way into the data warehouse, they have no business value in how the data is currently organized (data organized in a specific way).

Be brave: Throw it out.

Choice 2: Replace it

Suppose that an organization does actually use an extract file, but, honestly, that file is somewhat cumbersome and difficult to use. It doesn't include all the necessary information, users struggle to change the extraction processes to extend the list of attributes, and it meets only about 50 percent (or less) of the users' needs.

In this situation, replace the file by following these steps:

1. **Retain the extract file's functionality that users want as part of your data warehousing environment.**

2. **Create designs and plans for the functionality that users need but don't have in the extract files.**

3. **Replace the extract file by folding the existing functionality into the data warehouse, along with the newly designed features.**

   Just get rid of the old, antiquated environment.

Choice 3: Retain it

If these conditions exist with the current extract-file setup, strongly consider retaining this type of environment:

- ✔ The extract file is a relatively recent addition to the organization's capabilities (within the past one to three years, for example).
- ✔ The data is stored not in a flat file, but rather in a relational database.
- ✔ The data quality is excellent.
- ✔ Users have access to basic reporting tools and are doing some degree of ad hoc querying on their own.
- ✔ The environment generally doesn't look too bad. (A grandmotherly saying is appropriate here: "Your data warehouse should look and feel so good when it's that age.")

Although you might want to consider upgrading the extract file a little (you can read more about upgrading in the following section), definitely don't throw it out and try to replace it.

These kinds of upgrades might be appropriate:

- ✔ Add data elements closely related to ones that already exist (their point of origin is the same application file or database, for example), which people in other organizations might use.
- ✔ Do a little performance tuning to increase response time if a larger group of users will access the database.
- ✔ Increase the frequency of updates, and improve the freshness of the data if business needs dictate doing so.
- ✔ Equip users with new tools, in addition to their existing ones, to expand their horizons in business analysis and use.
- ✔ Add — only if you're daring — a new subject area or two to this environment to provide an even richer set of data for business analysis purposes. Be careful to avoid disrupting existing functionality.

If you're considering adding new subject areas to your extract, look at an extract file that's worth salvaging as a '67 Corvette that needs a little work and has been garaged for a while. Although you can always sell the car and buy a new one, when you step back and consider all your options, it's probably less expensive to invest in the required maintenance. Besides, you're already familiar with the car. It might not be new, and it doesn't have all kinds of advanced computer controls, GPS, and antilock braking; it might not have a back seat or a rear window; but it still gets you where you want to go. ("Yeah, we're going to Surf City, gonna have some fun. . . ."

Caution: Migration Isn't Development — It's Much More Difficult

When you decide to replace an extract file (discussed in the section "Choice 2: Replace it," earlier in this chapter), you face a migration situation: moving functionality and data from an existing environment to a new environment.

Because I can't possibly describe in just a few short paragraphs all the complexities of migration and how to deal with them, I hit just the highlights in this section.

Unlike a development project, in which no functionality exists, a migration project requires that you not only develop and deploy capabilities in a new environment, but also retire that same functionality from the system you're replacing. You have to consider these issues:

- **Cut-over requirements:** For example, what functionality moves, in how many phases, and when?

- **Your fall-back plans:** For example, what happens if the new system doesn't work?

- **Additional staff requirements:** Potentially, you need additional staff to support two environments simultaneously, if you have a multiphase migration plan. And you might need special staff to train employees in new technologies and products, for example.

- **User training in the new tools and contents:** What new data is available and how can (and should) it be used?

The process of migrating an informational and analytical environment, such as an extract file and the processes used to populate it, is often significantly less complex than migrating a transaction-processing system that's mission-critical to your organization, such as the customer order-entry system or the payroll system.

Don't overlook the complexities of migration, however, even when a data warehouse is a target.

Beware: Don't Take Away Valued Functionality

If you decide to pursue a replacement-migration strategy for your existing extracts, please pay careful attention to this section. (Don't say that I didn't warn you.)

One of the worst things you can do (something that causes users to snarl every time your name is mentioned) is implement a newfangled, much-improved, all-kinds-of-gadgets data warehouse and, at the same time, take away functionality and capabilities from the users of existing extract files.

Oh, sure, you might have a certain feature on your Phase II list and another one on the maybe-next-year-if-we-get-funding list. But average business users don't care whether answers are provided by a data warehouse that has all the bells and whistles or a plain-vanilla extract file. They care only about reports, business analysis, statistical analysis, or whatever else they need to do.

Keep in mind that functionality in this context might equate to certain data, such as the facts used to support decision-making or provide analytical capabilities. Your new data warehousing environment might have several reporting and OLAP tools that support querying, generate reports, or perform statistical analysis, just like the old environment did. But if users can no longer access data that was in the old extract files because that data isn't in the data warehouse, you've done it — you've taken away functionality.

You don't need to propagate every data element into the data warehouse or automatically generate every report by using the new tools. Getting down and dirty with users about what business value truly exists (like I talk about in the section "The first step: Cataloguing the extract files, who uses them, and why," earlier in this chapter) can help you deliver a high value data warehousing solution. Don't spend time and effort moving data and functionality that no one uses; at the same time, don't take away necessary capabilities. If you do remove functionality, the users will hunt you down in a manner similar to the villagers going after Frankenstein's monster — with pitchforks and torches — to burn you in the public square.

Chapter 23

Surviving in the Computer Industry (and Handling Vendors)

- -

In This Chapter

▷ Shopping the smart way at conferences and trade shows

▷ Dealing effectively with data warehousing vendors

▷ Looking at the future of data warehousing and mainstream information technologies

- -

*T*he name of the game in data warehousing since the early 1990s has been hype. A lot of hype. Massive amounts of hype. Hype. Hype! HYPE! Whew — I had to get that out of my system. I'm serious, though. Whether you're talking about business intelligence suites (the best-of-breed versus highly integrated), OLAP tools (ROLAP versus MOLAP), middleware tools (data-movement-ETL versus federated-EII), or any other aspect of data warehousing, you may have a lot of trouble separating merit from empty promise, fact from fiction, in the wonderful world of data warehousing.

Although data warehousing has more substance and provides more value than many of its predecessors on the hype hit parade, the discipline has, in my opinion, been somewhat compromised by the usual bag of tricks that the shiftier side of some product and service providers (vendors and consultants) like to pull out.

Although I'm not one to point fingers, anyone who has been to a data warehousing trade show or sat through a couple of product demonstrations (and then tried to implement a real-world data warehousing environment with products that just didn't work as promised) knows what I'm talking about. A world of difference exists between looking at a few glossy brochures before watching an oversimplified drill-down demonstration and facing real-world problems while you try to implement a data warehouse (for example, struggling with performance and response-time problems, or integrating fact data that has mixed levels of detail).

Hype: Is it all part of the game?

Back in the early 1980s, the new Ada programming language was the answer to everyone's software development woes, especially for military and government systems. Ada was supposed to solve everything. It was the language of the future, built especially to overcome all the shortcomings of every other programming language in existence at that time.

In the mid-1980s, computer-aided software engineering (CASE) tools were touted as the answer to software-development woes. You drew your data models and process flows by using the tools, and — presto! — out came a complete application, ready to go. This was productivity, brought to you by the wonderful world of CASE.

Back in the late 1980s and early 1990s, enterprise computing architectures, such as the IBM SAA, the Digital Equipment NAS, and nearly a dozen others from different hardware vendors, were the answer to the problems and challenges of distributed heterogeneous (multivendor) computing. You just wrote all your applications to use the application programming tap-dance interfaces (APIs) for this set of standards, and before you knew it, you had a seamlessly integrated enterprise across multiple platforms.

The mid- to late 1980s held the promise of artificial intelligence (AI) and expert systems shells. A little forward chaining here, a little backward chaining there, throw in a neural network, and — poof! — you created a "thinking" application that could aid your decision making.

The list goes on, including first-generation client/server computing (remember the promise that you could save millions of dollars in maintenance costs as compared to your mainframe?) and specific change-the-industry standards efforts that no longer exist, such as Unix International and the Distributed Management Environment (DME) standard from the Open Software Foundation.

More recently, the claims of service-oriented architecture (SOA), software as a service (SAAS), and Web 2.0 bring the same vendor promises of the past.

The common theme was highly touted silver-bullet solutions from vendors (sometimes one and sometimes a pack of them operating in a consortium) that provided significantly less benefit to you (and often no benefit), despite the thousands — sometimes tens or hundreds of thousands — of dollars you spent on their products and services.

Here are some data warehousing facts of life:

- Vendors are in the business of making money by selling products.
- Vendors' sales representatives make money if they sell products to you and others. If they don't sell those products, they don't make money and can even lose their jobs.

✔ Data warehousing consultants would love to tell you everything you have to know to successfully develop a data warehouse in your organization and maybe would even want to help you develop it. But they have to regale you with the wonders of data warehousing and the fabulous benefits you can gain and — oh, yeah — give you the reasons why you should listen to and employ them on your project.

✔ Within every IT discipline (data warehousing is no exception), stories get old, and you're bombarded with products with this theme: "Okay, maybe the old version didn't work quite the way you wanted it to, or maybe it wasn't as scalable as you needed it to be, but guess what? Our new version has all these new features."

The challenge you face involves dealing with these issues in a productive, non-confrontational manner without being steered down a path that doesn't make sense for you. In this chapter, I tell you how.

How to Be a Smart Shopper at Data Warehousing Conferences and Trade Shows

Make no mistake about it: You can gain tremendous value from attending any type of conference or trade show, including those oriented toward data warehousing. Vendors tout and demonstrate their latest products, you get to hear real-life case studies and stories about successful data warehousing implementations, and you can gain unique insight into up-and-coming problems you're likely to face from consultants and others.

When you attend a data warehousing event, behave like you're shopping for a car or other expensive personal item:

✔ Do your homework before you attend.

✔ Ask a lot of questions.

✔ Be skeptical.

✔ Don't get rushed into a purchase.

The short version: Be a smart shopper.

Do your homework first

When you register for a data warehousing trade show or conference, you typically do so from a schedule on the Internet that gives you a complete list of vendors who'll attend, consultants and other speakers who'll give presentations, their respective topics, special sessions and seminars, and hospitality suites and other services you can use to spend more time researching your specific data warehousing needs.

Plan your entire agenda well in advance of the event. Most conferences have a number of parallel session tracks, with anywhere from two to five simultaneous lectures and presentations. After reviewing the entire agenda for each day, mark for each time block the topic that's most interesting or pertinent to you. In addition, mark a secondary topic, just in case the presentation you had as your primary is cancelled or you lose interest in the first five minutes — always have a back-up. Don't be distracted by the headings given to tracks, such as systems track or OLAP track. Plan your schedule by topic.

If you're attending an event with other people from your organization, split up whenever possible and cover as many sessions as you can.

Ask a lot of questions

Asking questions at presentations and during demonstrations at vendor booths is not only permissible, it's also encouraged. After all, you're there to find out as much as possible about specific techniques, experiences, and products. Don't use your question-asking time, however, to do any of the following:

 ✔ Show off how much you know (or think you know) about a particular subject.

 ✔ Pointedly contradict or embarrass a speaker, especially on matters of philosophy that have no right or wrong answers and are just different ways of doing things.

 ✔ Do or say anything that reflects negatively on your company (which probably appears prominently on your name badge).

Although these statements may seem somewhat silly, most of us have had the experience of attending a session that's continually disrupted by an audience member who argues with the presenter and who seems to be doing little other than trying to draw attention to him- or herself. Don't be one of those people.

Be skeptical

Wait a minute. In the previous section, I say that contradicting a speaker or presenter is considered to be in poor taste. How, then, could I now advise you to be skeptical? Simple. First and foremost, be skeptical. When you hear about "revolutionary new features," "order-of-magnitude increases in performance over our previous product version," or anything else that sounds a little too hype-tinged, say to yourself: "What has changed so dramatically in the past few months that suddenly the product offers all these wonderful new capabilities?"

Next, ask questions privately or in small groups, not in a large forum in which a speaker may feel defensive. If you see something that seems too good to be true during a demonstration, ask the presenter after the session is over. If the waiting line is too long, go back later; that person, or someone else who works for that vendor, will still be there. An even better idea is to ask several people at a vendor's booth the same question on different days and see whether you get consistent responses.

Although your questions may be somewhat general at first, try to present a specific, real-life example from your environment as the context for digging into whether a feature or capability would truly benefit your data warehousing project. You may say something like this, for example: "We looked at Version 3.1 of your product six months ago and ran some tests against a demo copy to check on performance. Although we were okay with 250 gigabytes of data, as soon as we went above that number, volume performance was terrible, even though we had only two fact tables and four dimensions. You mentioned that response time with 500 gigabytes in the new version is as good as we used to get with 250 gigabytes. Please tell me what has changed in the new version to make performance so much better."

Don't get rushed into a purchase

You may be faced occasionally with a limited-time-only offer of a steep discount on a product, but only if you order before the end of the trade show.

Never buy a data warehousing product at a trade show. Okay, maybe a book (such as this one, if you're thumbing through it while standing in a trade show booth) or another low-priced item, but never buy a business intelligence tool, middleware product, data quality assurance tool, or an entire database management system at a trade show.

Use a conference or trade show as a fact-finding mission. Collect the glossy brochures and white papers. Take home the conference proceedings with the presentation slides, but don't buy on impulse.

Dealing with Data Warehousing Product Vendors

The same basic smart-shopper guidelines that you use at trade shows apply when you deal with data warehousing product vendors:

- ✔ Do your homework.
- ✔ Ask a lot of questions.
- ✔ Be skeptical.
- ✔ Take your time before committing to purchasing products.

The one-on-one nature of the vendor-customer relationship is somewhat different from the contact interaction that occurs at a conference or trade show. On the positive side, you (and your data warehousing needs) can get much more attention from a vendor when you're meeting in your office to discuss your data warehousing project and that vendor's sales representative is trying to make a sale to you, compared to the trade show cast-the-net approach, when a vendor tries to reach as many new prospects as possible.

On the negative side, though, the vendor's sales rep can focus tactics specifically on you and others in your organization, and you must be particularly cautious regarding the sales techniques that the rep uses.

A product sales representative isn't in the business of solving your business problem through a cost-effective, timely data warehousing solution. Although that person (and, in a larger sense, the product company as a whole) wants very much for you to be successful in your data warehousing endeavors (particularly so that your success story becomes a reference for them), never forget that their product sales and revenue take precedence over your budget and schedule.

Check out the product and the company before you begin discussions

Any category of data warehousing product (such as OLAP tools, data mining tools, basic reporting and querying tools, database engines, extraction products, data quality tools, and data warehouse administration and management tools) has a lot of different products. Each vendor that makes one or more of those data warehousing products wants to involve you in a one-on-one discussion with a sales representative.

But your time is a valuable commodity. Even if you weren't dealing with project schedule pressures, you and others in your organization should give only a finite amount of time to vendor meetings.

Do your research at trade shows and conferences (and, as noted in the section "Do your homework first," earlier in this chapter, even before you go to the trade shows). See which user interfaces look most appealing, and study performance and response-time statistics (as many as are available) for database volumes similar to what your environment will have. Don't just lug around those glossy brochures you pick up at the trade show booths — read them.

Next, get on the Internet and check out vendors' Web sites. Use an Internet search engine to retrieve product reviews, analysts' comments, news releases, and anything else you can find about the vendor's company (history, financial strength, and what others say about them, for example) and the products in which you're interested.

Request or download a demonstration copy of the product, if one is available.

Then, you're ready to talk to a sales representative in person or over the Web, assuming that the vendor and their wares seem to fit your needs.

Take the lead during the meeting

Before a vendor sales representative sets foot inside your office or initiates a Web conference with you, make absolutely clear what you expect to cover during that one- or two-hour initial meeting. You should do at least the following:

- ✔ Hear a presentation of no more than ten minutes about the company's history and background, as well as the background of the products you're discussing.

- ✔ See an initial, end-to-end (or as close as possible) demonstration of a product's capabilities. The demonstration should last no more than a half-hour.

- ✔ Have a list of specific questions that cover features and capabilities, product installation base (how many copies have been sold and used and at how many companies), new version enhancements and features, and product architecture (interfaces, different platforms supported and differences across platforms, and scalability). Again, make these questions specific to your environment and data warehousing project.

During discussions before the vendor meeting, give some, but not all, of the questions to the vendor representative. State that those items are important to you and that you want to discuss them during your meeting. You can gauge vendor responsiveness by how well the representative answers your prepared questions and also compare those answers to the responses that he or she gives to your impromptu questions. With the latter, you can gauge how well vendors know their own products and how well they react to unanticipated questions and challenges (rather than just hear scripted responses).

Be skeptical — again

You need to have down-to-earth, open discussions with your product vendors (not chats held in a crowded booth at a trade show). If you've heard certain things about a product that concern you (product scalability above a certain number of users, for example), ask! Demand proof (reference sites, discussions with a development manager, and hands-on testing in your organization, for example) of anything and everything that concerns you.

Be a cautious buyer

No matter how attractive a product looks, take your time in committing to a purchase. It's software, not a one-of-a-kind work of art. You have no reason to hurry, even if your data warehousing project has an aggressive schedule.

Always test-drive software under your environment's conditions:

- ✔ Use your data.
- ✔ See how many attempts it takes to install the software correctly.
- ✔ Determine the responsiveness of the vendor's support staff.
- ✔ See what works as advertised — and what doesn't.
- ✔ Ask what your users think about the product's usability.
- ✔ Find out how stable the software is. Does it cause your client and/or server systems to crash or lock up? If so, how frequently?
- ✔ Find out what performance is like in your environment.

Sometimes, a desktop product (a business-rule design tool, for example) is suitable for only a certain portion of your user base. Perhaps only a small number of power users would use that tool, and the rest of the user community would use a basic reporting tool or, for the first iteration of the data warehouse, no tool. Perhaps casual users would use a standard browser to access standard reports posted on the company intranet. In these situations, never let a vendor pressure you into purchasing more copies of a product than you need. You can always buy more later, if necessary. The last thing you want is a bunch of shelf-ware sitting around and taking valuable funds out of your budget.

A Look Ahead: Data Warehousing, Mainstream Technologies, and Vendors

While data warehousing and traditional computing technologies converge, you're looking at a whole new ball game when you try to sift through vendors' claims and promises. Traditional data warehousing vendors are already trying to make their products' respective capabilities *go enterprise* (be able to work in large, enterprise-wide global settings), and others vendors see the lucrative data warehousing market as an area into which they can expand.

Beware! I've already seen more than a few 1980s-era marketing messages from the distributed database world make a comeback:

- ✔ "This product provides transparent access to any data in any database anywhere."

- ✔ "Put one subject area into this data mart and another subject into a second data mart, and — presto! — you can join them whenever you need to and treat the two data marts as one logical data warehouse."

Although I'm not one to scoff automatically at everything I hear about new and improved product capabilities, much of what's showing up to address shortcomings in first-generation data warehousing has a feel (to me, anyway) of "been there, done that." I don't mean to imply that they don't work; it's just that many of the capabilities from "best of breed" products are now appearing in the "mainstream" products.

The proof is in the pudding. (I have no idea what that saying means, and I don't think that it applies to data warehousing. It just seemed like the right thing to say.) Dealing with vendor promises and claims (and the consequences of product characteristics that you wish you knew about before you bought those products) will become even more of a burden when the extract-and-copy-and-copy-again first-generation data warehousing morphs into a more advanced data warehousing solution including features discussed in Part VI of this book, which describes topics such as near-real-time updates to the data warehouse, the access of data at its point of origin (rather than from the database into which you copy it), and the inclusion of multimedia in your data warehouse.

Chapter 24

Working with Data Warehousing Consultants

▶ Deciding whether you need data warehousing consultants for your project

▶ Being careful when choosing a consultant

▶ Considering all your consultant options

*L*et me begin this chapter with a disclaimer: I'm a data warehousing consultant and a data warehousing product vendor — a double whammy!

I try to treat the subject of whether you need data warehousing consultants fairly in this chapter. You won't see any subliminal advertising (call Tom . . . blink, blink . . . call Tom) anywhere in this (use Tom for your data warehouse needs) chapter.

The reason I discuss data warehousing consultants is simple: You'll most likely need consultants for your data warehousing project, and I give you as unbiased a perspective on this subject as I can, like I did in Chapter 23, which deals with the product vendors.

Do You Really Need Consultants to Help Build a Data Warehouse?

You probably need data warehousing consultants, not because people from within your organization aren't capable of working with data warehousing technology or completing a project without outside help. A simple fact of current corporate IT life overwhelms factors such as capabilities and knowledge: We're in a consulting-driven era, plain and simple.

I've been in the software and consulting industry since the early 1980s, and the demand year after year for outside consulting expertise in nearly every medium- to large-size organization has skyrocketed remarkably. The increased demand for consulting services partly stems from the convergence of two major factors:

✔ **The increasing pace of technological change:** Client/server computing, the Internet, and improvements in relational database capabilities, for example.

✔ **The aftereffects of the U.S. economic recessions and downturns in the early 1990s, 2000s, and the current market:** Although some areas were hit harder than others, companies across the board were hit hard by downsizing, reengineering, and the rest of the slow-economy stuff that we all know so well. Corporate IT organizations continue operating under the "stay lean and mean" philosophy.

The combination of these two factors means that outside consulting organizations are doing (at least, in part) an overwhelming majority of new systems development, including data warehousing.

You can always fight the trend and try to do in-house data warehouse development, and you can easily be successful. Your internal IT staff is probably spread fairly thinly across a multitude of initiatives, however, and applying for personnel requisitions for a major hiring plan is just plain out of style in most corporations. (Can you say outsourcing? Off shoring?)

I wholeheartedly encourage you to try to accomplish your data warehousing initiatives through the use of in-house staff, either exclusively or with the majority of your team members, at least, being employees of your organization. If your organization is like most others, though, your data warehousing fate rests solely on how well you identify and use outside data warehousing consulting expertise.

Watch Out, Though!

If you've ever worked with IT consultants (data warehousing specialists), you realize that not all consultants are equally skilled, equally dedicated, or equipped with the same, shall we say, degree of ethics.

Before getting into the aspects of individual consultants and the roles they can play on your data warehousing team, let me distinguish between different types of consultants and their relevance to your project.

A large part of the growth in consulting services in the 1990s and into the 2000s has been in the area of consulting formally known as *staff augmentation,* and less formally known as body shopping. A number of consulting companies have been successful in creating a collection of individuals (sometimes employees of the company, sometimes independent consultants, and sometimes both) and placing these individuals, one or two at a time, in organizations looking to fill a personnel gap here and there.

To be fair, many consulting companies that perform primarily staff augmentation work put together small-scale project teams of four or five people (rather than provide a person here and there) when they have an opportunity to do an entire client project. These firms typically steer away from project-oriented work, however, because placing individuals in staffing augmentation positions is, to be blunt, a relatively low-risk way to build a company.

If your organization has an ongoing data warehousing initiative staffed primarily by internal IT members, but your team has a few open slots, you might best be served by working with a staff-augmentation-oriented consulting company to find the one or two missing links on your project team.

If you're a data warehousing consultant

This chapter is oriented primarily toward the user community and how the people in it might find and retain you (or your consulting brethren) for their data warehousing projects. If you're a data warehousing consultant, though, here are some tidbits of advice:

✔ **Stay on top of all the changes taking place in the field of data warehousing.** Have you heard of hybrid OLAP? Vertical databases? What are your thoughts about data mining? Is it for real? What are the new products in the middleware game for federating data? Although you never know everything that goes on in this or any other technology area, you have to avoid getting caught by surprise during an interview or business development session if you're asked your opinion about a new product or architectural trend.

✔ **Remember that it's not only technology skills that make a successful data warehousing consultant, but also business skills.**

Although I don't believe in the industry-expert approach to data warehousing implementation, you must have a core knowledge about business to be able to ask the right questions during the scope process or to create, for example, a definition for a sales-and-marketing fact table.

✔ **Be flexible.** Be able to work as a hands-on technologist (performing source systems analysis or data modeling, for example), a data warehousing architect or advice-oriented consultant, a project manager, or other types of roles. This flexibility helps you stay billable (whether you're independent or working for a consulting company) and generally helps make you a better consultant by giving you a broader perspective of both data warehousing and the consulting profession than if you continually play the same role in one engagement after another.

Be careful, though: If you're paying good money (and you will, believe me) for the services of these individuals, be prepared to complete a thorough interview process to ensure that they're not only technically qualified but also a good cultural fit for working on-site, or increasingly remote, within your organization. When a consulting company uses subcontractors, they're likely to have little or no history. They might have been chosen for your project based solely on a few keywords that showed up on a résumé database search. Make sure that you carefully determine whether these people are the right fit for your data warehousing project.

The other side of consulting, the part dominated by large systems integrators, is oriented primarily toward project work, rather than staffing services. Many of these firms eschew staffing work and engage a client only (or primarily) if the client gives the firm control over a project's methodology, the resources assigned to the project (even those from your own company), and the format of deliverables.

Although this rigid stance might sound harsh at first ("Do it my way or else, even though you're paying me"), a sound theory is behind it. Some firms are so experienced at putting together successful project teams and performing in a certain, methodology-driven manner that to do otherwise can lead a client's project to fail — so, they continually adapt their processes and techniques for each client.

In the area of data warehousing consulting, it's almost comforting to work with a firm that has these qualities:

- ✔ A successful track record of data warehouse implementations, using a variety of technologies (for example, not just data warehouses or data marts, but both)

- ✔ Insight into the direction of data warehousing technology and architecture as they apply to your business problem, rather than a canned solution ("We've always done it this way") that might not be a good fit for you

- ✔ A commitment to the success of your project by taking on full responsibility for all aspects of implementation, rather than offering a supply of technologists who don't assume responsibility for project management and direction

In many situations, the lines between consulting companies — the different types of firms, and even firms within the same category (staffing-oriented or project-oriented, for example) — are somewhat blurry. In this section, I don't want to steer you in one direction, but rather point out that a data warehousing consultant from one type of environment might be a good fit for your particular needs — but he or she might not. Similarly, a particular consulting firm might best serve your needs, depending on how you want to proceed with your data warehousing project (for example, how many — if any — people internal to your organization will work on the project). Or perhaps that consulting organization, regardless of its data warehousing expertise, isn't a good fit for the particular implementation model you're pursuing.

 Here's the key to avoiding mistakes: Before you talk with any consulting firms or individuals about your data warehousing needs, have a good idea first about what type of model you're most likely to pursue (internal management of the project, rather than management by the consulting organization). With this information, you can better determine not only the technical capabilities, but also the cultural fit, that best meets your needs, deliverable dates, and budget.

A Final Word about Data Warehousing Consultants

Although it's important for both individual consultants and consulting companies to check references and technical and business qualifications (such as product and industry experience), follow your instincts. Information is growing and data warehousing technology is changing so rapidly that you might do more harm than good if you insist on using a consultant (or a company) who has experience with specific products, who has previously implemented a data warehouse in your industry, or who otherwise fits a checklist of qualifications.

Certainly consider someone who lacks experience in a particular industry or in the use of a certain product, but who otherwise impresses you as an insightful, hard worker who can get the job done. For example, you might want to see the person in action for perhaps a week or two, as part of a team doing the data warehousing scope. Don't get caught up in the laundry-list mode of finding and retaining consulting assistance.

Part VI

Data Warehousing in the Not-Too-Distant Future

The 5th Wave   By Rich Tennant

"We've got a machine over there that monitors our quality control. If it's not working, just give it a couple of kicks."

In this part . . .

You may think of data warehousing as old technology. However, data warehousing is changing — right before your eyes.

Five to ten years from now, you're likely to implement a data warehouse in a way that's much different from how you do it today. You'll have to make the leap from today's generation of data warehousing to a new generation of technologies and architectures.

Be prepared: Read this part of the book to see what's coming soon and what these new data warehousing models mean to you.

Oh, yeah — you might also want to visit some of the Internet sites mentioned in this part to get a very real sense of what's coming.

Chapter 25

Expanding Your Data Warehouse with Unstructured Data

*T*oday's data landscape now encompasses a dizzying array of new information channels, new sources of data, and new analysis and reporting imperatives. According to analyst groups, nearly 80 to 85 percent of today's data is unstructured, and new information channels such as Web, e-mail, voice over IP, instant messaging (IM), text messaging, and podcasts are rapidly creating huge stores of nontraditional data. Data from any of these sources will be requested from your users to be integrated into your data warehouse.

Traditional Data Warehousing Means Analyzing Traditional Data Types

Unless you've used an extraordinary, state-of-the-art data warehouse, your business intelligence functionality has probably been limited to these types of data:

✔ **Numbers:** Numeric data in the technical form of integers and decimal numbers

✔ **Text:** Character data, typically fixed-length alphanumeric information that's rarely more than about 255 characters per occurrence, although (very rarely) it might go up to 4,000 characters

✔ **Dates and times:** Either actual dates and times or, more likely, ranges of dates (such as a month and year for which product sales are grouped and stored)

That's about it.

To be fair, data warehousing in its original incarnation, as a storage place for information drawn from legacy applications to support reporting and analysis, hasn't needed anything other than these traditional data types. These traditional data types form the basis of structured data managed by databases, the most popular being relational databases or multidimensional databases.

You know what Bob Dylan said about the times and how they change.

It's a Multimedia World, After All. . . .

Fire up your Web browser. Spend a few hours poking around the Internet, checking out all kinds of cool sites. (If you're at work and your boss walks in, point to this chapter and say that you're doing data warehousing research — honest!) You can find images, video and audio clips, entry forms for filling out information to submit to a site's database, tabular results based on requests you might make — almost anything.

Today, an organization typically stores a large proportion of its data in documents created by using productivity tools such as Microsoft Excel and Word. Additionally, digitization advances in photography, document scanning, video production, and audio formats have further extended the range of unstructured data formats that you can use for business data.

The lines between structured data (traditional data types that computer applications have been using for years) and unstructured data (such as multimedia documents) have blurred. Not that long ago, if you wanted to create a multimedia environment that included both structured and unstructured data, you loosely followed these steps:

1. Build a relational database for your structured data.

2. Use a document-management system or an image-management system for your unstructured data.

3. To handle logical links across environments, set aside in each relational database row one or more columns that point to related documents or images, as appropriate.

These environments were relatively awkward and prone to problems. For example, software upgrades to one system had an adverse effect on the other (links that break, for example).

The emergence of a new generation of business applications that merges traditional relational data structures with unstructured digital content has already begun. This profusion of digital content means that organizations are now seeking to manage both relational (structured) data and unstructured data at the enterprise level.

For example, consider a medical records application. Fifteen years ago, the application would most likely have maintained a list of medical records that were stored as simple rows and columns. Today, and in the near future, a medical records application is more likely to manage a set of visit records that have reference images, x-rays, CAT scans, prescriptions, and other reference documents — and those records might also include higher-level capabilities such as spatial visualization, reporting, and analysis.

Many businesses will be (or currently are) eager to turn this unstructured data into useful information, but they'll find (or they found) that their current data warehousing and business intelligence technology can't deliver thorough analysis of this data. Traditional data warehousing and business intelligence technologies and infrastructure have inherent technological constraints that limit their ability to address this data.

How Does Business Intelligence Work with Unstructured Data?

Suppose that you're using an unstructured, multimedia-enabled data warehousing environment to do comparative analysis between services offered by your company (a bank) and your competitors' corresponding offerings.

You run some basic reports and a few queries (as I talk about in Chapter 9) to check out market share, portfolio performance, and other measures. Or, for more advanced analysis, you use a business analysis OLAP tool (refer to Chapter 10) to perform all kinds of drill-down analysis on the data in an attempt to fully understand the intricacies of your company's performance with respect to your competitors.

Sometimes, though, you can't find the answers in the numbers. Suppose that you notice a sudden increase in account closures at your bank during the past two months. What's going on?

You can understand the premise of business intelligence in the term itself: Get as much intelligence as possible — as fast as possible — from as many sources as possible, to help you understand what's going on and take informed action. Under this broad definition, intelligence can easily include the following types of information that you can't find in (or access through) a traditional data warehouse:

- ✔ A competitor's local newspaper advertisement offering no-fee checking for one year and an extra 1.5 percent earned on money-market deposits if a potential customer shows a bank statement indicating that he or she has closed an account at your bank

- ✔ An advertising banner on Google that features your competitor's same offer

- ✔ A link to each of your competitors' Web sites, where you can analyze the types of electronic banking services they offer

- ✔ A transcript of an interview with a regional economic expert stating that your bank is a prime takeover target and probably won't be in business under its current name at the same time next year

In this simple example, because the items occur locally or regionally, you might believe that you can access all this information from a multimedia-enabled data warehouse. ("A good banking analyst probably knows all this stuff anyway," right?)

Think about this example on a global scale, however. Are you wondering why your company's sales are slipping in Sweden? You might need to have these types of real-time, intelligence-gathering capabilities for a globally competitive situation.

I once created for a client in the chemical industry the architecture for a quasi-data warehouse environment (*quasi* because it had only a single source of data but a huge amount of historical information that I had to bring into the new system).

About 80 percent of the historical information was on paper, and the client was considering eventually entering that information into a document-management system. For budgetary reasons, I dealt only with the conversion of traditional historical data (character, numeric, and date information), and mapping and transforming the new incoming data. The documents would be handled later.

Imagine an environment in which you can treat all this data, which deals with the same subject matter, equally. If the data is on paper, you can scan it in as an image, index it by keyword, and make it accessible through the same environment as the traditional data. You tremendously increase the client's business intelligence by giving them access to this information.

An Alternative Path: From Unstructured Information to Structured Data

The example in the preceding section demonstrates an approach of putting structured data first, in which a business analyst uses data warehousing as a gateway into appropriate unstructured supporting information.

You can just as easily take the opposite path toward a unified approach to business intelligence. Suppose that you're browsing the Internet or the company intranet, and a product diagram, blueprint, or some other type of image or document catches your attention. Each piece of unstructured information can just as easily provide a path for you to access an OLAP-generated report posted on the company intranet (which can, in turn, have links that point you toward other structured or unstructured information) or can involve a mash-up with your information projected on a Google Map (as discussed in Chapter 26).

The structured and unstructured data barriers are breaking down quickly, just like the pathways across those softened barriers. Increasingly, businesses are amassing large volumes of non-relational, unstructured data in the form of digital images, documents, videos, and other multimedia formats — and these new data formats are quickly becoming a key component in formal and informal business processes that integrate with existing business applications, comply with regulatory requirements, or simply provide a richer user experience. Consider the following business scenarios:

- A pharmaceutical company needs to access lab documentation compiled over years and generations of clinical trials to gain FDA approval for a new medicine.

- An insurance company needs to store policy documents and retrieve them for claims processing.

- A call center company needs to store agent-recorded sessions as audio streams so that they can be retrieved remotely for quality assurance and contract compliance.

- An industry analyst firm needs to make a searchable library of podcasts available for download from its Web site.

- A legal practice needs to store electronic copies of documents as images and easily retrieve the documents relating to an individual client or case.

- An architect partnership needs to store and retrieve digital plans with the associated client data.

- A library needs to convert and archive large volumes of existing paper and analog content for indexing and use in a digital research tool (remember microfiche?).

The preceding list gives you a few examples of the ways in which businesses throughout the world can and do use unstructured digital data. You can analyze such information as easily as you can create digital content. Organizations are finding new, innovative ways to use this digital content to improve or extend their business capabilities, and many of those organizations need data warehousing and business intelligence solutions to leverage this information.

If you use traditionally collaborative work processes, performing tasks such as workflow or image management, you can easily augment those processes to point you toward data warehousing capabilities that provide you with additional value. In addition, the reports and query results you get and use as part of traditional analytical processing can serve as a pathway into a world of multimedia information that can supplement the data you typically handle.

Chapter 26

Agreeing to Disagree about Semantics

. . . .

In This Chapter

▶ Defining semantics in computer science

▶ Anticipating the Semantic Web

▶ Using semantics in data warehousing

▶ Preparing for the semantic wave

. . . .

*I*n researching how best to present the topic of semantics, I searched many areas on the Web, including sites such as Wikipedia (www.wikipedia. org) and the World Wide Web Consortium (www.w3.org). The concept of the *Semantic Web* is one with deep technical roots, but in its simplest sense, it's making the Web as easy to navigate for applications as it is for you and me (humans). You know to go to Google and search for *the Finnish word for "monkey"* — a computer cannot accomplish the same task without direction from you or me.

Defining Semantics

Semantics is the study of meaning in communication, including the meaning (or an interpretation of the meaning) of a word, sign, or sentence. How many times in the middle of an argument have you heard the phrase, "Let's not argue about semantics"? Linguists and semanticists have been dealing with semantics for a long time. However, in the world of computer science, semantics are relatively new.

In May 2001, Tim Berners-Lee, James Hendler, and Ora Lassila authored an article in the magazine *Scientific American* titled "The Semantic Web." You can find the article here:

```
www.sciam.com/article.cfm?id=the-semantic-web
```

In the final line of this article, the authors state that the Semantic Web will open up the knowledge and workings of mankind to software agents — productivity applications that will perform analysis on our behalf.

With this article, The Semantic Web era began. The Semantic Web is about two specific technical standards:

- ✔ **Common integration formats:** The Semantic Web uses common formats to integrate and combine data drawn from diverse sources. The original Web mainly concentrated on the interchange of documents.

- ✔ **Language for relationship mapping:** The Semantic Web uses language to record how the data relates to real-world objects. These records allow a person, or a machine, to start off in one database, and then move through an unending set of databases connected by a common subject.

These two concepts can be applied to data warehousing and business intelligence efforts. In the reference architecture I present in Chapter 17, a user access layer maps to a target data layer; additionally, a target data layer maps through data movement rules to the source data layer. In this context, business intelligence and data warehousing architectures are no different than Web architectures — they all need common integration formats and a language for relationship mapping.

Emergence of the Semantic Web?

Between the Semantic Web article being published in 2001 (which I describe in the preceding section) and now, what technical innovation has emerged? The answer is Web 3.0, although I'm not too certain many of you have heard of this version of the Web. The Semantic Web is really no different than the current Web, aside from *agents,* or programs that do work on your behalf (and which can now surf the Web, too). Just what you wanted, your programs wasting time trying to find something out there!

Web 3.0 will most likely not be up and running until sometime after 2010. This third generation of the World Wide Web will be filled with Internet-based services that collectively comprise what you might call The Intelligent Web. Technologies and techniques, such as the Semantic Web, natural language search, data-mining, machine learning, recommendation agents, and artificial intelligence technologies will formulate the foundation of Web 3.0 and emphasize machine-facilitated understanding of information in order to provide a more productive and intuitive user experience.

You can already see small samples of what will come with Web 3.0 in the form of mash-ups. In Web development, a *mash-up* is an application that combines data from more than one source into a single integrated tool; for example, Google Maps uses geospatial map data to add location information to real-estate data, thereby creating a new and distinct Web service that neither source originally provided. Many people are experimenting with mash-ups by using Amazon, eBay, Facebook, Flickr, Google, Microsoft, Yahoo!, and YouTube APIs. Examples of mash-ups include

✔ **The Chicago Police Department CLEARMAP Crime Summary:** This mash-up application summarizes crime data by using mapping software to help warn citizens of high crime areas within the city:

```
http://gis.chicagopolice.org/CLEARMap_crime_sums/
        startPage.htm
```

✔ **Flickrvision:** This mash-up application combines the power of mapping software with a popular photo sharing site. The applications are separate and distinct, but by using APIs and semantics, they integrate to provide you with a very unique experience that neither of the application originators intended:

```
http://flickrvision.com/maps/show_3d
```

This level of innovation demonstrates what's possible with technology, and both data warehousing and business intelligence platforms can really benefit from enhancement through semantics. The biggest challenge involves the need for openness among the community of vendors.

Think of a world in which you can use Cognos query and reporting tools against a Business Objects Universe running on a Composite Software federated data access layer, which accesses data from your data warehouse and various streams of information from the World Wide Web — presenting the final results on a Google Map. The world is headed in this widely distributed, yet easily integrated direction in the not too distant future!

Preparing for Semantic Data Warehousing

If you evaluate how the technologies associated with data warehousing work, a lot of metadata is managed in a proprietary manner within the tool. Some have attempted in the past to solve the integration problem by creating yet another technology, known as *technical metadata repositories,* to integrate all this metadata from the various tools. Such technologies generally have failed to provide overall business value because they're point-to-point solutions, and a data warehouse must have support and funds to stay alive.

You must begin separating the language for relationship mapping and integration formats from a proprietary base into one that's abstracted away from the tools. Several technologies are emerging to assist in this area:

- **Balanced Insight Consensus (`www.balancedinsight.com`):** Defines key business terminology and, through a set of relationships, the inherent business models that exist within data. From there the business terms and models are mapped to data structures, thus producing business intelligence and data warehousing solutions in specific technologies. With a press of a button, you can see the exact same model generated in Microsoft, Cognos, Business Objects, Pentaho, and other business intelligence platforms. Balanced Insight Consensus is the first open business modeling tool on the market that has significant promise to drive the semantic layer, regardless of which tool or database you use.

- **Composite Software (`www.compositesw.com`):** Provides a layer of software that you can use for data services such as virtualization, integration, and federation. Composite Software's platform has key technology in the areas of optimization, caching, and integration that enables you to take one query and execute it against data sources that are structured and/or unstructured; internal and/or external — proving that there can be very separated sources of information integrated that originally were not intended to be in an optimized fashion.

- **Expressor Software (`www.expressor-software.com`):** Redefines data integration by employing a fundamentally new design concept around semantics, allowing organizations to rationalize physical metadata constructs around common business terms and write target-specific data transformation and business rules that are highly reusable. Expressor Software tackles the complexity and cost of enterprise IT projects, and it delivers much higher productivity and data processing performance based on its semantic metadata foundation.

These products are just three of the growing list of companies you'll see emerging in the area of semantics.

All these tools don't try to reinvent technologies such as relational databases, business intelligence tools, or data movement platforms — however, they do all optimize the business-to-technology interfaces so that the existing technologies you are using for your data warehousing and business intelligence products can work more efficiently together to solve business problems.

Starting Out on Your Semantic Journey

Ask yourself and your data warehousing project teams this question: How will you prepare for these technologies? Focus on three areas that you're probably already working in — your business intelligence semantic layer, business rules management, and possibly federated query definition.

Business intelligence semantic layer management

If you dig deep enough into your process and tools (as discussed in Chapter 17), you can find someone in the business or delivery team who maps key business terminology to technology requirements or implementations. People who use Business Objects Designer or Cognos Framework Manager should map key business terminology (or business metadata) to technical database tables and columns. If your process is mature, you might even find that business analysts capture the business metadata in Microsoft Word templates, which your business intelligence tool administrators leverage. If this is the case, raise the bar on these efforts. Begin to define the *semantics* (another word for the business metadata) and initiate an alignment process across the silos of your business. By performing such a process, you can begin to determine key terminology conflicts across lines of business or functional areas of your business. The sales department might refer to the dollar amount on a contract as Revenue, but the finance department refers to it as Bookings. If finance and sales worked together to resolve this term, they might agree to use the term Booked Revenue, defined as *money committed by a customer legally for the delivery of products and/or services within a given specification laid out in a contract.* Additionally, the finance and sales team might conclude that the business needs to monitor a revenue life cycle that spans sales (Booked Revenue), field operations (Deferred Revenue), and accounting (Recognized Revenue). If you want to bring the semantic world to your data warehousing environment, you start by understanding key terms, as well as their associations and rules.

Business rules management

Additionally, investigate the process around business rules — both how you define those rules and how you generate them. The process of defining business rules is very similar to the business intelligence semantic definition process. Users define key concepts; for example, Customer means *a legal entity which has conducted business by purchasing goods or services from one of our companies in the current 12-month period.* Such a definition evolves into a database query or data movement routine that flags a legal entity as a customer or not. You can move your enterprise toward the world of semantics by creating an alignment process that gathers a cross section of the business community together to agree on such terminology and rules.

Chapter 27

Collaborative Business Intelligence

According to Wikipedia, *collaboration* is a recursive process where two or more people or organizations work together toward an intersection of common goals — for example, an intellectual endeavor that's creative in nature — by sharing knowledge and building consensus. Collaboration doesn't require leadership and can sometimes bring better results through decentralization and egalitarianism. In particular, teams that work collaboratively can obtain greater resources, recognition, and reward when facing competition for finite resources.

Collaboration technology has an enormous role in driving user interactions in the areas of entertainment and problem-solving. Collaboration in the technology sector refers to a wide variety of tools that enable groups of people to work together through asynchronous and synchronous methods of communication. Examples of collaboration technology include synchronous Web conferencing, using tools such as Microsoft Live Meeting or Cisco Webex, and asynchronous collaboration by using software such as Microsoft SharePoint. Additionally, Instant Messaging platforms such as those from Yahoo!, AOL, ICQ, and Microsoft enable peer-to-peer and group forum collaboration.

If properly implemented, a collaborative work environment can assist companies in making work dramatically easier. Not only can a group cheaply communicate and test, but the wide reach of the Internet allows such groups to easily form in the first place, even among niche interests, creating virtual

communities online. The Internet has enabled low-cost and nearly instantaneous sharing of ideas, knowledge, and skills by leveraging collaborative
technologies such as wikis and blogs.

Future Business Intelligence Support Model

Currently, business intelligence support is often relegated to is-it-working
support — if the system is down, the support personnel get it running again.
This support model (along with vendor pricing schemes) has prevented
broad adoption of business intelligence. This support model is like a sit-down
restaurant that has a limited menu.

For broad adoption of business intelligence to occur, you need a support
model that enables collaboration. The necessary technology does exist —
but no one is really combining data warehousing, business intelligence, and
collaboration software. Some early adopters are venturing down this path,
and some vendors are beginning to introduce limited collaboration functionality into their products.

In the future, you'll see concepts that are currently emerging from leading
Internet sites such as Amazon, Facebook, YouTube, Google, and Wikipedia
become commonplace for business intelligence solutions. It has to happen, it's
such a natural support model. And collaboration is all about sharing knowledge
and building consensus: Business intelligence is about gaining knowledge —
the missing link is sharing and building consensus.

As we move to the next phase of business intelligence, in which everyone can
have access to the data that's important to them, the need for collaboration
is growing. Users will need to support users, both internal and external to an
enterprise.

Internal support could come from regional managers trying to isolate shared
costs and quickly collaborating with a functional analyst in finance to determine the correct slice or drill to perform on their data (see Chapter 10 for
business analysis functionality). External support could come from a customer whom you've enabled to surf through his or her orders, who needs
some quick assistance on how to combine your enterprise's data with other
data that he or she has — say, from his or her bank — and merge that data
within a GoogleDoc. Such support isn't way out in the future.

Knowledge retention

Every day, no one captures the millions of items of intellectual property (conversations, e-mails, and telephone calls) in organizations all over the world. Using collaborative software to institutionalize *quantitative* (structured) and *qualitative* (unstructured) information — which would otherwise be lost — can enable the sharing of information, thoughts, insights, and best practices.

How we have progressed this far without leveraging collaboration within business intelligence solutions is beyond me. The use of collaboration software can enable your users to capture intelligence from outside the data warehouse and operational systems and use this captured intelligence as part of the business intelligence solution.

Knowledge discovery

Collaborative business intelligence is an environment within which users can easily collaborate and communicate with each other, sharing ideas, information, and decision making within their community. Through such collaboration, users can begin reusing existing ideas and/or capabilities, removing the need to reinvent the wheel — which happens quite often when information technology departments isolate a user's experience to reports. Using collaboration software side by side with business intelligence software can enhance information presented to users, enabling everyone to share insights they gain with other users in their community.

Knowledge proliferation

Collaboration allows participants to share knowledge, observations, and analytics in a community of interest with the goal of producing an action response to a situation. This sharing can become infectious. Remember your first experience with eBay or YouTube? You probably arrived at these very popular sites after one of your friends or colleagues directed you there. This guidance is viral in nature. If users find software sites and solutions easy to use, discuss, and gain support for, they pass the word on to others.

Such activities resulting from user-to-user collaboration will drive the sharing of knowledge across organizational boundaries — including observations, insights, and data from customers; economic and industry information; and psychographic information (interests, attitudes, and opinions). In other words, your data warehouse will grow and become more virtual in nature because the conversations that occur will require much information from both inside and outside the boundaries of a single organization's data warehouse.

Leveraging Examples from Highly Successful Collaboration Solutions

Collaborative business intelligence might look like today's Internet-based collaborative experience in several ways. The following sections discuss features that are most likely to become commonplace within a collaborative business intelligence solution.

Rate a report

If you look up a book on Amazon, you find a rating and customer feedback. This rating and associated feedback might be the information that drives you to purchase that book — or go for a different book. In the world of business intelligence, users could leverage report rating features to locate the most valuable information for their needs and provide descriptive feedback, which allows users to understand how the report serves the user population best.

Report relationships

When you access a particular book's page on Amazon, you can scroll down a little on the page to see a section that highlights books that other shoppers purchased at the same time they bought the one you're evaluating. This feature in your data warehouse could assist users in understanding interrelated reports and views provided within the business intelligence environment. For example, you might be looking at the top ten sales report and see that users who viewed this report also reviewed the active promotions report, the commission schedule report, and the products by territory analytical view. The relationship of data across reports (which you might not see within individual reports) can become obvious if you see the patterns of users' report access.

Find a report

You're probably comfortable with searching technologies, such as the ones that Google offers, and taxonomies, such as those you can find through Yahoo!. Search-engine technology has evolved over the years to incorporate relationships, ranking, popularity, and user weighting, along with various linguistic capabilities needed to search.

Most business-intelligence vendors have begun offering search capabilities, often from vendors such as Google, within their platforms. In the future, you'll use the search engine inside your firewall, out on the Internet, in your data warehouse, and in public data sources — in essence, securely searching all over the place for the information you need.

Find the meaning

Wikis, such as Wikipedia, enable users to capture content (edit and publish) and shape it to become key intellectual property that you can think of as corporate knowledge. How many times have users come to you with that question mark look on their face, trying to decipher the meaning of a report or the data presented in a column or graph? Leveraging and integrating this technology enables a growing knowledge base to form around each view or perspective presented out of the data warehouse and business intelligence solution, which can establish the corporate knowledge on the user of your data assets.

Shared interests — shared information

Social networking brings people together through shared interests — for example, your sales teams with marketing promotions personnel or inventory control personnel. YouTube, Facebook, MySpace, and Flickr are all examples of social network environments that consumers are now swarming. Are bored people at home the only people going to these sites? Definitely not! Large advertisers, such as Procter and Gamble, have spotted this trend and are spending large sums of their advertising budgets on these sites because they see a huge transfer of consumers from the old technology (television) to the new technology (social networking on the Internet).

Imagine being able to post a view of information that you don't quite understand so that your peer group can try to figure out a reasonable explanation for the changes that have you confused — especially before the boss comes asking for an answer.

Visualization

Gaming software of today provides stimulating entertainment and intriguing lessons in interface design. These interfaces provide a strong attraction for users, which is very different from the anxiety and resistance that users display when they utilize the tools you provide them for accessing their data warehouse. Advances in visual technology have been in place for some time, and with Nintendo's Wii, even the hardware devices are simplified! And now that you can access gaming online, you can play some death-and-destruction game with your long-lost college roommate who now lives in Thailand.

Well, why not get together with your sales counterpart in the Far East to determine how to better sell your products to a specific ethnic community? You can make this connection by collaborating on utilizing all the technologies described within this chapter and both of you surfing the data with more natural techniques. If you don't think this kind of collaboration will happen, just watch some movies. The creative minds are working on these kinds of technological collaborations, and they'll expand on the concepts that I talk about in Chapter 26, giving the world mash-ups of data access technologies with visualization and manipulation technologies soon enough.

The Vision of Collaborative Business Intelligence

Collaborative business intelligence is real in many consumer situations. eBay, Amazon, and Google all leverage key data to present information to you, the consumer. Companies such as eBay are even contemplating products in the area of data warehousing and business intelligence to assist vendors in better moving products through their platform.

But these technologies need a more open vendor community than currently exists. At this point, Microsoft has all the tools — you just have to find a really good consultant to put it all together because Microsoft is so subdivided that one person employed by Microsoft could never help (you'd need three to five people). Business Objects, now an SAP company, has introduced collaboration for their data integrator product, enabling project teams to communicate. Because Business Objects is now part of SAP, various collaboration features of NetWeaver will eventually sneak into the solution — of course, you'll have to sole source it initially. Cognos, now part of IBM, has the same story as Business Objects. And Oracle — yes, they have all the tools.

I'm guessing that each vendor will sneak in and try to provide you with the "complete solution," but the open vendors of the Internet will win out. Current trends, with companies such as Google, which has GoogleDocs working with Panorama Software, against Microsoft's Analysis Services or SAP's BW InfoCubes, suggest that multi-vendor solutions will begin to emerge. This will be far more appealing to users than a single proprietary vendor solution that requires heavy migration of solutions that are already in place.

Part VII
The Part of Tens

The 5th Wave   By Rich Tennant

In this part . . .

*1*f you want easy-to-access, succinct advice about many different data warehousing topics, this part of the book is for you.

Chapter 28

Ten Questions to Consider When You're Selecting User Tools

In This Chapter

▶ Asking questions about using tools

▶ Getting the scoop on how a tool might work in your organization

▶ Finding out about the quality of online help

▶ Figuring out how a tool deals with the computer-crash test

*F*ew things are more frustrating than successfully building a data warehouse and then having it rendered unusable by less-than-satisfactory user tools. This chapter presents some questions to consider when you're evaluating tools that you might want to purchase.

Do I Want a Smorgasbord or a Sit-Down Restaurant?

Bet you weren't expecting a question like this to pop up, were you? I use this analogy often because it helps frame the discussion of what you're looking at in a tool. When business intelligence was initially created, there was a broad vision that users could serve themselves. The user would go to one environment, insulated by all the underpinnings of the data, and merely ask a question and get an answer, ask the next question, and so on. But IT has often restricted the tool so that end user can't access it, so they can't self-serve — like in a sit-down restaurant. Let me explain:

✔ The diner must wait to be seated at the restaurant, which is equivalent to the user trying to find someone in IT to listen to him or her.

✔ When a waiter is assigned to a section of the restaurant that the diner is seated in, that waiter must serve the other customers while the diner sits and waits, much like someone in IT supporting multiple departments in your enterprise (and we all know some people seem to find all kinds of ways to pull attention away from your needs).

✔ When the waiter does finally come and take your order, he delivers this order to a cook — who, by the way, is supporting all the waiters in the restaurant. This relationship is equivalent to IT's way of prioritizing who's request gets a project assigned — yet another period of waiting.

✔ And, of course, the cook can't serve you until she has plates from the dishwasher, who can't provide the plates until the busboy finishes clearing tables — much like the user waiting for the current projects that are over budget and off schedule to complete.

You have to determine whether you want the users to take on the burden of writing a majority of their own reports — or whether you want to make IT a report-manufacturing shop. If you want the sit-down restaurant, you need to find the best query tool, best reporting tool, best OLAP tool, and so on. If you want the smorgasbord, you want to get the most integrated product that allows the user to move easily from tool module to tool module.

In most data warehousing environments, a significant portion of the user community has a substantial number of report and query screens and templates, and the development team builds these capabilities for the users. At the same time, to avoid creating a backlog of requests that the support staff can't easily handle, users must be able to create and use their own queries and reports.

 While you're evaluating a tool, find two users who have no experience in user reporting and querying products, and a third user who has used another product but not the one you're considering. A few days before you run your usability test, give the tutorial documentation (the written version) to only one of the users who has no experience. Then, have all three people try to solve two or three business problems of varying difficulty by creating a query or report with the tool. See how they do! If the users can perform query, reporting, and analysis tasks, you might avoid requiring the technical support staff to build all reports for the users.

Can a User Stop a Runaway Query or Report?

Almost every tool user occasionally submits a query (or performs some other type of operation, such as running a report) that keeps going and going and going. . . .

A user tool must give users a way to stop this type of query or report gracefully, without doing any of the following:

- ✔ Locking up the user's desktop PC and forcing him or her to turn it off or reboot

- ✔ Interfering with other users' work (by requiring that you halt the database server and restart it, for example)

- ✔ Otherwise causing a disruption in business as usual

Check out each product, and make sure that any user can stop a runaway query or report from his or her browser or desktop PC.

How Does Performance Differ with Varying Amounts of Data?

You may have determined during the project scope that your data warehouse will start with 500 gigabytes of data, for example, and grow to 1 terabyte during the next two years. It pays to know, however, how each tool will perform with not only the initial 500 gigabytes and the eventual target, but also with 2 or even 3 terabytes, just in case.

In case of what? Here are just a few possibilities:

- ✔ New data sources that no one could foresee during the project scope.

- ✔ A decision to add an increased level of detail to the data.

- ✔ A decision not to delete old data, but rather to keep it in the data warehouse.

- ✔ An unforeseen merger occurs, and you must incorporate the new entities' information into your data warehouse.

If your data warehouse will never approach terabyte-size (a trillion bytes of data), don't worry about how a tool performs with that much data — it's irrelevant. What's more significant is whether the tool can perform as well (or nearly as well) with 100 gigabytes of data as it does with 500 gigabytes. This information will allow you to sleep at night knowing that the tool will scale to perform beyond the defined requirements.

Performance isn't a tool-only situation; it also depends on the DBMS you use, how you design your database, and many other factors. Ask your questions in an environment as close as possible to what will be available during production.

Can Users Access Different Databases?

I'm talking about different databases of information from the same tool, not necessarily different DBMS products. For example, a user may access the regular data mart stored on a local Windows NT server for most queries and reports and, by using the same tool, have access to this information:

- Another department's data mart, for occasional queries
- The organization's main data warehouse
- An external data provider over the Internet

Users shouldn't have to switch tools to perform similar functions (basic querying and reporting, or OLAP, for example) against different data sources.

And, furthermore, the extra credit question would be: Can the user access the different databases within one query or report? Although you may not require this ability currently, it may become something you want to incorporate in the future. For example, you may want to tie your historic data warehouse data with the transactional data in real time or with external data in near real time.

Can Data Definitions Be Easily Changed?

Although the process of getting the first set of data definitions up and running is fairly easy in most user tools, you need to ask yourself these questions about when you need to make modifications:

- How easily can you update your entire user community's data definitions, and how long does it take? (Do you have 100 users? 1,000? 5,000?)
- How do you modify queries and reports that use data that no longer exists or data with a modified structure (its data type and size, for example)?
- What happens to scripts and programs that are part of the tool?

How Does the Tool Deploy?

Does the tool require desktop deployment, or can you deploy it within your organization's standard browser configuration? If you're looking at a tool that's not available for deployment in a browser, you may want to reevaluate your criteria. Server-side deployment lowers a lot of costs that exist when you have to deploy tools on the PC.

However, most business intelligence suites haven't advanced in one area — their modeling and administration tools. There still is a heavy leaning towards desktop tools in this area. Considering that most organizations have internal standards for their client PCs, the process of figuring out how well a tool fits into your standard configuration should be straightforward. Assuming that the product runs on your desktop operating system (always a showstopper if it doesn't), you should consider these issues:

✔ How well the connectivity and interoperability software you need works, such as drivers for database connectivity and repository connectivity.

✔ Whether you should load the software in any special order. Yes, vendors still provide software that conflicts if you don't load it in the proper sequence.

✔ When you have choices about where certain components of a tool can reside (on each client, for example, or located once on each server), determine the recommended configuration and whether any problems exist in your environment.

As far as the end-user interface, these components should run in the browser without the need for any special downloads — do yourself a favor and get an Internet-architected tool. You have plenty to choose from!

How Does Performance Change If You Have a Large Number of Users?

You have to know how performance changes when the number of users increases. You should see little or no performance effect if a tool's environment is designed correctly and efficiently — make sure the tool you're considering falls in this category.

What Online Help and Assistance Is Available, and How Good Is It?

Any tool worth its salt should include pretty extensive online help. Features to look for include wizards, tutorials, context-sensitive help, and templates for queries and reports.

Does the Tool Support Interfaces to Other Products?

The desktop analysis tool of choice is the handy-dandy, trusted spreadsheet program (and this preference probably isn't going to change for many years). Although some OLAP products feature direct interfaces from their database into a spreadsheet (typically Microsoft Excel), even if you use a product's reporting and querying capabilities, users should always be able to bring data back from the business intelligence tool and pop it into Excel for more analysis, manipulation, or whatever they want to do.

You generally should be able to include reports in word-processing documents (such as a Microsoft Word file), graphics and presentation programs (for example, Microsoft PowerPoint), a personal database (such as Microsoft Access), and (of course) a spreadsheet (such as Excel).

What Happens When You Pull the Plug?

Go ahead — try it. In the middle of a query or report, turn off your PC and see what happens. You want to ensure not only that users can restart a desktop PC without any leftover configuration problems (for example, temporary files and workspace errors that prevent the user from doing additional work until the errors are fixed), but also that the interruption doesn't affect your warehouse's database (and any intermediate servers). Or better yet, find out whether the product is smart enough to welcome the user back through his or her browser, reconnecting that user to his or her query.

Chapter 29

Ten Secrets to Managing Your Project Successfully

In This Chapter

▷ Dealing effectively with everyone involved in your project

▷ Keeping an eye on the project plan

▷ Connecting your project team members and supporters

▷ Taking a break from project work every now and then

*B*eing a successful data warehouse project manager means that you have to do more — much more — than simply create project plans and ask team members to turn in weekly status reports. This chapter presents the secrets to success.

Tell It Like It Is

It doesn't matter whether you're working with users, executive sponsors, consultants, vendors, team members, or anyone else. The most important thing you can do to set the groundwork for successfully managing a data warehousing project is to speak your mind in a completely honest manner.

You don't have to be abrupt or rude, or have the attitude "It's my way or no way." Follow these guidelines to keep communication open and to solve problems sooner rather than later:

✔ When problems occur, don't bury them or pretend that they don't exist. Other people know about the problems, so deal with them aggressively.

✔ Don't be afraid to tell an executive sponsor that those out-of-the-blue budget cuts or the absence of those three team members who have been reassigned "for just a little while" will adversely affect your project.

✔ Don't hesitate to tell a vendor when a product isn't performing as promised and demand that they do something about it.

The key: Communicate quickly, openly, and with integrity. You won't be sorry.

Put the Right People in the Right Roles

The right person in the right role is an important key to project success.

You have to recognize that the best database designer might be somewhat challenged when it comes to working with front-end OLAP or data mining tools. The person who can do whiz-bang tasks with a particular OLAP tool might be a lousy facilitator and should, during the scope phase of a project (refer to Chapter 13), either sit silently in the back of the room or just not even be there.

Be a Tough but Fair Negotiator

Budget cuts, pressures to compress the development schedule, vendor support, working with the corporate infrastructure group to line up installation and rollout support — the project manager usually has responsibility for all these issues, and many more. The manager must ensure that these tasks, which all involve negotiation, take place. After you speak your mind, as discussed in the section "Tell It Like It Is," earlier in this chapter, you establish the groundwork for tough, fair negotiations that are grounded in reality, not in emotion or speculation. Don't be afraid to negotiate from this basis: "If X happens, Y will be the result."

Deal Carefully with Product Vendors

Be careful when you gather information from vendors and other sources (as described in Chapter 23) and when you question a vendor about a product (as explained in Chapter 34). Recognize that vendors want to sell you products, not solve your business problems. Although it's great when they can do both, you don't share the same priorities as the vendors.

It's *your* project. Don't be pushed into making product decisions that aren't in your best interest.

Watch the Project Plan

Although I firmly believe that being a good project manager means more than just tracking how the project schedule is going, you can't ignore the project plan.

If you're not interested in gathering team members' regular submissions to help keep your project plan up-to-date, add to your team a project-control staff member who has the specific task of managing the project plan. Work with a local college or university to get a work-study or cooperative education (co-op) student; it's a cost-effective way to handle this important task.

Don't Micromanage

Everyone has a particular management style. Some people focus on delegating tasks, and others are more hands-on. If you're the type who likes to handle most things yourself, the advice in this section is for you.

Don't *micromanage,* or insist on knowing every little detail about every task that everyone is doing. (That panicky, out-of-control feeling will go away.) Even on smaller projects, trust your developers and analysts to know their jobs. Check in on them to see how they're doing, and make sure that they're progressing on schedule. Let them do their jobs, though — especially on larger projects. You have enough to worry about as a project manager; don't take on additional worries that team members usually can resolve for you.

Use a Project Wiki

Start off every project with a comprehensive project wiki to which you provide access to every member of your extended team (not only the developers and key users, but also the executive sponsors).

For those of you not familiar with wikis, a *wiki* is a page or collection of Web pages designed to enable anyone who accesses it to contribute or modify content, using a simplified markup language. Wikis are often used to create collaborative Web sites and to power community Web sites. Wikis are used in business to provide intranets and knowledge-management systems.

The wiki should have these items:

- Copies of key memos
- A description of earlier work done on the data warehousing project (prototypes, for example)
- A summary of discussions you've already had with vendors
- High-level statements of requirements
- Whatever else you need to ensure that the wiki represents the complete picture of what you're trying to accomplish

Even if your organization has a fantastic *intranet* (an Internet environment inside the company) or a widely used Lotus Notes (or other type of groupware) environment, build out a wiki — which you can find out how to do in *Wikis For Dummies,* by Dan Woods and Peter Thoeny (Wiley). Because you can't assume that everything you need is available in electronic form (it usually isn't), be sure to have access to a scanner to pull in those items that aren't currently electronic. Additionally, you might want to provide secure access for consultants and others who might be working remotely. Be sure to have your wiki available and operational at your kickoff meeting so that no one gets left out.

Don't Overlook the Effect of Organizational Culture

Suppose that you work for a consulting firm whose employees typically work 50 or 60 hours each week on projects. You're assigned to be the project manager for a client's data warehousing effort and will manage a team composed of four members from your company and four from the client's. You develop an aggressive (but realistic) project plan, based on the client's budget and time constraints, that will likely involve some late-night and weekend work. (That concept is nothing new to your company's employees.)

Suppose, however, that your client's employees won't even consider working more than 40 hours a week. Now what?

Although you can factor this attitude into the workload of the client's team members as best you can, you have to consider other factors, too:

- ✔ If your client insists on having responsibility for database builds and rebuilds, who will handle those tasks if they have to be done over the weekend or late at night during a critical stage of development?

- ✔ When the unavoidable project hiccups occur (and you had better believe that they will), will your client's team members be as likely as your firm's team members to give a little more effort?

Don't overlook the impact of organizational culture on the project you're managing, especially if you're an outsider (a consultant, for example, or someone from another company who's working on a joint cross-company data warehousing project).

Don't Forget about Deployment and Operations

Design and development are difficult enough for a data warehouse (or any environment, for that matter). Don't overlook how the results of your work will function in the real world, with real users. Make sure that your project plan allows time for lining up support after the data warehouse goes live.

Take a Breather Occasionally

Insist that everyone leave early on Friday after a particularly hard week. Don't sneer and scowl when team members tell you that they want to go to the company picnic when you're a day or two behind schedule with three weeks to go.

It's only work. By taking an occasional breather, you (and your team members) become reinvigorated, and productivity increases. It's well worth your while to take off a weekend here and there, or to spend slightly fewer hours working overtime.

Chapter 30

Ten Sources of Up-to-Date Information about Data Warehousing

In This Chapter

▶ Checking out specialized data warehousing Web sites

▶ Turning to industry analysts' Web sites for information

▶ Getting product details by going to vendors' Web sites

*Y*ou probably won't be surprised to hear that the term *up-to-date* means "go look on the Internet." It's worth your time to check out the Web sites in this chapter.

The Data Warehousing Institute

www.tdwi.org

At the Data Warehousing Institute's comprehensive site, you can find these items:

✔ Education information

✔ Upcoming events

✔ White papers, including links to white papers at other sites

✔ Case studies

✔ A directory of vendors

✔ Best practices (so that you can find out how others have succeeded in various data warehousing categories)

The Data Warehousing Information Center

www.dwinfocenter.org

At the Data Warehousing Information Center, you can find out about data warehousing technology, find links to a variety of other sites, and provide the site's operator (Larry Greenfield, of LGI Systems, Incorporated) a place for "rants and raves" (his words) about data warehousing.

The site has tables of various tool categories and products in those categories, along with links to the vendors' respective sites. It also has links to white papers, articles, periodicals, conferences, and many other services.

The OLAP Report

www.olapreport.com

The OLAP Report is published by Business Application Research Center, a subscription service. This Web site has information available for nonsubscribers, including

- ✔ Documentation on the origins of OLAP
- ✔ Product reviews
- ✔ Benchmarks
- ✔ Market analysis, including market share information
- ✔ Case studies

Intelligent Enterprise

www.intelligententerprise.com

Intelligent Enterprise has articles, interviews, white papers, and resources about the various technologies leveraged for data warehousing. It's focused on how technologies can work together to form the strategic applications vital to businesses. This Web site offers both the context and the technical detail needed to go from concept to purchase to deployment.

b-eye Business Intelligence Network

www.b-eye-network.com

The Business Intelligence Network focuses on business intelligence, performance management, data warehousing, data integration, and data quality, serving these communities with industry coverage and resources. The site has a plethora of industry expert blogs, product spotlights, white papers, and podcasts to help you through your data warehousing journey.

Wikipedia

www.wikipedia.org

This Web site might seem misplaced, but Wikipedia is a growing source for key information — it's nearly the new Encyclopedia Britannica! Though, at times, the articles and information might be self-serving for vendors or consultants, in general, this site is a wealth of information.

DMReview.com

www.dmreview.com

DMReview.com delivers market insight through interviews with, as well as articles and columns written by industry consultants, hands-on practitioners, and technology solution leaders. Editorial focus is on business intelligence, performance management, analytics, integration, and enterprise data warehousing, as well as emerging areas that include business process management and technology architectures.

BusinessIntelligence.com

www.businessintelligence.com

BusinessIntelligence.com provides articles, white papers, research, and news for the business intelligence marketplace.

Industry Analysts' Web Sites

You can get information about data warehousing, and the IT industry in general, from sites run by some of the leading industry analysts:

- ✔ Gartner: www.gartner.com
- ✔ International Data Corporation (IDC): www.idcresearch.com
- ✔ Forrester Research: www.forrester.com
- ✔ Ventana Research: www.ventanaresearch.com

Product Vendors' Web Sites

Hundreds, if not thousands, of sites exist for product vendors. Although the vendors are dedicated to selling their respective products, a lot of their sites have white papers, late-breaking news about their products and features, and other worthwhile material.

In addition to using a search engine to find these sites, you can find links to vendor sites from many of the Web sites listed in this chapter.

Chapter 31

Ten Mandatory Skills for a Data Warehousing Consultant

In This Chapter

▶ Knowing a little about a lot of data warehousing topics

▶ Knowing a lot about a few data warehousing topics

▶ Working well and effectively with the people in your organization

▶ Having access to up-to-date information

▶ Using a hype-free vocabulary

A good data warehousing consultant has certain abilities in dealing with people and a knowledge of various aspects of data warehousing. This chapter lets you in on a few required skills that all data warehousing consultants should possess.

Broad Vision

Even a data warehousing consultant who's an expert in a particular area (star schema design in a relational database in support of OLAP functionality, for example) should have a broad vision in at least these areas:

✔ Overall end-to-end data warehousing architecture, from tools to middleware to data quality to orchestration software

✔ An understanding of client/server, Web-based, and server-side computing architectures

✔ A firm understanding of database optimization concepts for tuning data access queries

✔ Skills in digging through data sources to see what's really there

Because the components of a data warehousing environment are interrelated, a consultant must be able to not only provide technical expertise in one or two areas of a project (as discussed in the following section), but also see the big picture.

Deep Technical Expertise in One or Two Areas

If you're going to pay the big bucks for a consultant who claims to be a data warehousing expert, that person must be a true expert. More specifically, a consultant should be able to claim, proudly and *accurately,* to be the best in one or two areas (database design and front-end tools, for example).

Communications Skills

"Um, well, you know, I think that, uh, that requirement the guy in back mentioned, like, last week, right? You know, like, what were we talking about?"

Although a consultant's written and verbal grammar doesn't have to be perfect (an occasional dangling modifier is okay), even the most technically astute consultant must be able to convey ideas and understand what others are communicating. It's critical!

The Ability to Analyze Data Sources

A consultant should never design the necessary transformations for a data warehouse (refer to Chapter 7) solely by using listings of data structures and definitions provided by the keepers of an application or the IT department. A consultant must be able to dig into source databases, even if this source analysis is only a secondary role for the consultant. For example, even a consultant who isn't the primary source-data analyst might have to figure out why the business intelligence tool returns strange results.

The Ability to Distinguish between Requirements and Wishes

A consultant's ability to distinguish between user requirements and wishes is important primarily in working on the scope (the first phase) of a data warehousing project. A disparate group of users probably bombard you with cries of, "I need this!" and "I want that!" During crunch time, good facilitation and negotiation skills are essential when functionality has to be cut from the list — or, at least, deferred until the next version of the data warehouse.

Conflict-Resolution Skills

No matter what role a consultant plays, from project manager to data analyst to quality assurance (QA) specialist, that person is an outsider to the members of an organization — and someone from the client company is almost always resentful of the outsider's "intrusion." A consultant on a data warehousing project (or any other project, for that matter) must identify these situations early and do the best possible job of diffusing any conflict that threatens to destroy a project.

An Early-Warning System

A consultant should act as an early-warning system to identify and report problems to you, the client, so that you can deal with them. The consultant shouldn't be a snitch, but he or she should be more than just a nose-to-the-grindstone technician. Because this person is an outsider and not involved (you hope!) in your internal organizational politics, he or she should have some freedom to notify you of problems.

A consultant whose organization has problems (another consultant who isn't performing up to par, for example) might not feel free to let you know about those problems. That's where your company's people should also act as an early-warning sign for the consulting organization's staff members. (That's why conflict-resolution skills, discussed in the preceding section, are so important!)

General Systems and Application Development Knowledge

While data warehousing and mainstream computing continue to converge, an increasing number of warehouses will be built using distributed objects; the use of messaging and other data-movement technologies for near-real-time business intelligence will increase; and a lot of other capabilities that weren't part of a typical first-generation data warehousing environment will develop. A consultant who has strong skills should have at least a working knowledge of these areas, in addition to basic programming skills and other abilities.

The Know-How to Find Up-to-Date Information

From data warehousing product bug fixes to information about the latest architectural trends, a good consultant knows how to find up-to-date information quickly — in time to be put to good use on your data warehousing project.

A Hype-Free Vocabulary

Because it's almost impossible to avoid catchy buzzwords (can you say "data mart"?) in the data warehousing world, don't hold it against a consultant (or anyone else) who uses these phrases. But I'm generally wary of consultants who sound like they went to a trade show and met up with the data warehousing pod people: "Don't be afraid. Join us for some neural network data mining that uses subject-oriented data to give you predictive pattern recognition built by using data vaulting techniques in SSAS (Microsoft SQL Server Analysis Services) and SSIS (Microsoft SQL Server Integration Services) — we are your friends!"

Chapter 32

Ten Signs of a Data Warehousing Project in Trouble

In This Chapter

▶ Failing to agree on your project during various phases

▶ Making bad project decisions

▶ Losing team members

▶ Dealing with poor communication

▶ Discovering problems with your data warehousing products

*Y*ou can most easily tell that your data warehousing project is in trouble when you don't have anything to show for your efforts when you thought you would. Try to get some indication that trouble's brewing, however, *before* you reach that point. This chapter presents ten early warning signs.

The Project's Scope Phase Ends with No General Consensus

The allotted time for the scope phase of your data warehousing project ends (usually two or three weeks — a little longer for large projects), and the members of your constituency are unhappy. They're still grumbling and disagreeing about the project's direction and its potential business value (or lack thereof), the relative priorities of capabilities and how they map to various project phases, and other points of contention.

You're in trouble.

The Mission Statement Gets Questioned after the Scope Phase Ends

You're three weeks into the design phase, following a four-week scope. You're in an all-morning status meeting with the IT and business organization executive sponsors, as well as four key managers from the business groups who plan to use the data warehouse the most.

Just before a coffee break, one of the managers says, "You know that mission statement we talked about on the second day of the project? I want to talk about that some more because I have some problems with it."

You're in trouble.

Tools Are Selected without Adequate Research

A project decision-maker looks around the room in disgust, sighs deeply, and says, "Look, we just don't have time to check out these tools because the schedule is too tight. That vendor who was in here yesterday — what was that company's name again? You know, the ones with the product that — I can't remember all the details. Anyway, I liked their demo. We'll buy that tool."

You're *probably* in trouble.

People Get Pulled from Your Team for "Just a Few Days"

"I'm going to borrow Mary, John, and Sue Ellen for a couple of days because we have something important over in the shoelace plastic-tips division that must get done as soon as possible. Anyway, I think that it'll be for only a few days. Try to stay on schedule."

You're in trouble.

You're Overruled When You Attempt to Handle Scope Creep

You're in the last week of the design phase, and a business unit manager sits down across from you in the cafeteria. Between mouthfuls of Chef's Daily Surprise, he tells you about "these one or two things I just thought of that would make this data warehouse thing work much better." You politely explain the concept of scope creep in the context of "Wait until the %$#^@ next phase of the data warehouse!" (except that you're more diplomatic about it). Then, two days later, the manager's boss (who also happens to be your boss) sends an e-mail message directing you to "add those one or two things to the features list, but don't let them affect the schedule."

You're in trouble.

Your Executive Sponsor Leaves the Company

You've done a fantastic job of selling the business value of your data warehousing project to executive management, and everything is rolling along nicely. Suddenly, two days after a stunning announcement of disappointing quarterly sales and earnings, the executive sponsor from the business side of the organization resigns. Now, your project doesn't have an executive sponsor.

You *might* be in trouble: Work fast and don't look back.

You Overhear, "This Will Never Work, but I'm Not Saying Anything"

Everyone in the company is supportive of your data warehousing project. You're pushing the cutting edge of technology, and everyone on your team is enthused. Their weekly status reports even reflect the progress they're making. The project's chief architect assures you that the more you get into the project, the more everyone is convinced that you've made sound technical decisions.

Then, in the cafeteria, you overhear two of the more senior developers discussing the project. One says, "There's no way that this thing can work. Performance is terrible, and half the time the same query against the same data returns different results! But I'm not going to be the one to bring it up!"

You're in trouble.

You Find a Major "Uh-Oh" in One of the Products You're Using

Despite your best efforts at product evaluation, something has slipped through the cracks, and a major feature simply doesn't work. Although you can use one work-around, that work-around really negatively affects performance. The vendor's representatives slyly say, "Well, we had heard that it might be a problem. Our development organization is looking into it and will probably make a patch available in the next month or so."

You're in trouble.

The IT Organization Responsible for Supporting the Project Pulls Its Support

Your development group is in charge of most of the data warehousing development, including the business intelligence tools and the database definitions. The IT organization, though, is responsible for creating the databases and performing the loading routines, performing the backup and restore procedures, and taking care of many of the project's other infrastructure elements.

Because of higher priorities, the IT organization pulls the people responsible for supporting your project, and their manager promises to "look into another answer." She says, "Maybe we'll hire a couple of contractors, but I won't be able to look into that until next week."

You're in trouble.

Resignations Begin

Resignations are a sure sign that major problems lie ahead. Even people who are unhappy with a company often give in to loyalty or a sense of duty, and they stick around until the completion of a project. (Or maybe they just want the résumé fodder.)

When a number of people resign in the middle of a project, however, you're in trouble.

Chapter 33

Ten Signs of a Successful Data Warehousing Project

. . . .

In This Chapter

▷ Getting praise from executives and coworkers

▷ Seeing people actually use and discuss the data warehouse

▷ Gaining your CEO's confidence

▷ Climbing the corporate ladder

. . . .

As mentioned elsewhere in this book, just because everyone gathers in the company cafeteria for cake and plasters the walls with congratulatory banners doesn't mean that your data warehousing project was a success. This chapter gives you some ways to tell that you were really successful.

The Executive Sponsor Says, "This Thing Works — It Really Works!"

Suppose that a senior executive at your company makes it a point to find you so that he or she can tell you that you did a great job *and* that you're a nice person *and* that the data warehouse you built and delivered really works — and everyone is using it. The executive even points out that the warehouse is delivering information that is being factored into boardroom-level decisions.

You succeeded!

You Receive a Flood of Suggested Enhancements and Additional Capabilities

Sometimes, after the celebratory party in the cafeteria, a data warehouse slowly fades away like an old soldier. (Quiz: Who used a similar phrase, to what audience, and in what year?)

Users and their managers might bang on your office door (or, more likely, invade your cubicle) to show you memo pads that contain sketches of additional reports and queries that they want, asking questions such as, "How hard would it be to add this feature?"

You succeeded!

User Group Meetings Are Almost Full

Your company should always organize a data warehouse user group in which you can discuss and handle issues such as training, enhancement requests, and tips and tricks for how to use query tools in a coordinated manner.

User group meetings that often get canceled because no one has issues to discuss gives you a good indication that few people are using the data warehouse. In contrast, regular user group meetings that are packed give you a strong indication that . . . you succeeded!

The User Base Keeps Growing and Growing and Growing

You start off with an initial user community of 50 business-area analysts. Two months later, you add another 50. During the next six months, an additional 150 users, including several in executive management, join the "family."

You succeeded!

The Executive Sponsor Cheerfully Volunteers Your Company as a Reference Site

Your executive sponsor is so enamored with the data warehouse that management wants your company to serve as a reference for product vendors and for the outside consulting company that worked with you to build it.

You succeeded!

The Company CEO Asks, "How Can I Get One of Those Things?"

The big cheese wants his or her own executive dashboard system (and all his or her direct reports) to have access and monitor it daily. To that end, you are summoned to the CEO's office for a weekly hour-long private session to answer specific questions on further uses for data warehousing within the company.

You've succeeded!

The Response to Your Next Funding Request Is, "Whatever You Need — It's Yours."

Corporations are notorious for this type of funding policy: "Don't tell us what you did yesterday. Tell us what you'll do tomorrow *if* we deem you worthy to send funding your way, and don't you dare fail to deliver because you and your résumé will be on the street faster than. . . ."

But if your data warehouse is popular and held in high esteem, your organization might give you a blank check for your next project.

You've succeeded!

You Get Promoted — and So Do Some of Your Team Members

Nothing says lovin' in the corporate world like a promotion. Suppose that the job you did on your data warehouse leads directly to a promotion for you *and* for other members of your team.

You've succeeded!

And although it might not feel as good, if your team is suddenly raided and all your direct reports get promotions, you've also succeeded!

You Achieve Celebrity Status in the Company

Company employees stop you in the hallway or invite you to lunch to ask your opinion about technology, development methods, and all sorts of other subjects. Although you're not quite at the level of rock star or professional athlete, diners in the cafeteria point toward your table and whisper, "That's the one!"

You've succeeded!

You Get Your Picture on the Cover of the Rolling Stone

Okay, your data warehousing project won't get your picture on *Rolling Stone* magazine — but if it did, you'd know that you truly succeeded!

Chapter 34

Ten Subject Areas to Cover with Product Vendors

In This Chapter

▶ Finding out who works for a vendor (and whether they stay)

▶ Asking about the vendor's customers

▶ Figuring out the vendor's role in the marketplace

▶ Looking at the vendor's future plans

▶ Determining the vendor's integrity

*T*his chapter presents ten subject areas that you should discuss with any data warehousing product vendor, no matter which product category (business intelligence tool, middleware tool, or RDBMS, for example) you're considering buying. I've also listed the specific question you might want to ask. All these questions are somewhat odd because they have little to do with product features and how they work; if you do a good job of hands-on evaluation of the products, you can figure out how the features work by yourself. The questions in this chapter are more along the lines of "I want to know your company's character." In my opinion, these questions are *extremely* important because it will provide an understanding of the vendor's openness with its customers as well as its position in the market at large.

Product's Chief Architect

Who's your product's chief architect, and what background does this person have?

Most companies have a single individual who's primarily responsible for crafting and setting a product's technical direction. This person isn't often the same as the "company visionary," who might be the CEO who has seen a market need and is now trying to fill it.

You're asking about the person whose imprint is all over the product. Find out as much as you can about this person's background and experience.

If the current chief architect isn't the original chief architect, ask what happened to that person. It's not a good sign when a person who probably had a decent compensation package and attractive stock options is no longer with a company, especially if it's a relatively new company.

Development Team

How big is your development team, and how does it compare with last year's?

Here are some guidelines to consider when you ask this question:

- ✔ A relatively small development staff (for example, five or six people for a commercial product) might indicate skimpy quality assurance (QA) and product testing. It might also indicate that the vendor (or their financial backers) is taking a wait-and-see attitude toward the product before pumping in more funds. You might also see other signs that the company is making a less-than-full-scale commitment to the product.

- ✔ A development team that's the same size as or — worse — smaller than it was a year earlier most likely indicates internal concern about the product's market viability.

- ✔ A development team that's significantly larger than it was a year earlier indicates the vendor's enthusiasm for the product's chances and viability in the marketplace.

Customer Feedback

How have you addressed the top three customer complaints about the preceding version of this product?

Vendors have customer-support service organizations and call centers, so they should know the answer to this question. (If they don't, consider it a bad sign.)

You should determine whether customer complaints occur in clusters according to specific features, performance, connectivity, or whatever — and then determine the company's reaction and responsiveness.

Employee Retention

How high was employee turnover in the past year?

Pay attention to this indicator of a company's internal mood, especially if it's a relatively young company that hasn't gone public yet. Few people leave a growing company in which a big payoff waits around the corner.

Marketplace

Which company do you see as your chief competitor?

A vendor usually targets one company as their chief competitor and strives to overtake it. Or, if a vendor is the industry leader, they might just try to stay ahead of the latest up-and-comer.

You can find out a great deal about the product direction and use from the way the vendor answers this question.

If a vendor responds, "We really don't have any competitors," they're either blissfully ignorant or arrogant. Either way, watch out!

Product Uniqueness

What are the three most significant innovations in your product?

In what's often described as a *commodity product marketplace*, vendors' products are pretty much the same in terms of features and capabilities. Vendors usually base competition on price and other basic attributes, or they can try to position their product as truly innovative and worthy of market leadership — as well as a hefty price tag and significant support costs.

If the vendor claims their product is innovative, ask this question to see what makes the vendor tick.

Clients

How many clients have bought this product, and how many can serve as references?

What kind of market share does this product have?

Of the companies who bought it, how many are happy enough to tell others about their wonderful decision?

Watch out for vendors who claim that their customers are happy but don't want the vendor to identify them because they're doing top-secret, strategic work. How could the world knowing that a company purchased and is using a product be damaging to that company if it doesn't have to reveal application and business use? If a product vendor avoids providing references, start asking questions!

The Future

What significant advances do you expect in this market segment this year, and what are you doing in each area?

Here's what you want to find out (but without asking the question this way): "Are you guys just standing still, milking money off this product, or are you continuing to improve it?"

Internet and Internet Integration Approach

What's your strategy for Internet technologies and how are you opening your product up to enable integration with other Internet technologies?

Almost everyone has a Web-enablement story. Ask the vendor for their version. With the Internet moving into semantic connectivity, often called *mash-ups,* how is the vendor assuring that their technology can be leveraged in ways they never expected?

Integrity

Do you guarantee that your product will work as advertised?

Ah, a truly inspirational question. Gauging a vendor's response to this question tells you a great deal about the character of both the company and its sales representatives. It also generally indicates whether you're in for a bumpy ride if you do business with these folks.

Index

• Q •

CPSIA information can be obtained
at www.ICGtesting.com
Printed in the USA
BVHW02s0528231217
503462BV00003B/5/P